# *the* Gate Lodges *of* Ulster

*A GAZETTEER*

J.A.K. Dean

Ulster Architectural Heritage Society
1994

Published by the Ulster Architectural Heritage Society
185 Stranmillis Road
Belfast BT9 5DU

Printing - W. & G. Baird Ltd.
ISBN 0-900457-46-5

Front cover:
*South Lodge, Drumcairne, Stewartstown, Co. Tyrone.*

Frontispiece and title page:
*Belfast Castle Lodge, Antrim Road, Belfast. (U.M.)*

Back cover:
*Summer Island, Loughgall, Co. Armagh.*
*Drenagh, Limavady, Co. Londonderry.*

# Contents

*To*
*Lynne*

# ACKNOWLEDGMENTS

The Ulster Architectural Heritage Society gratefully acknowledges the generous financial assistance towards the publication of this book of the following:

ULSTER LOCAL HISTORY TRUST
G.P. BELL FUND
NORTHERN IRELAND TOURIST BOARD

The Society also gratefully acknowledges a bequest from the late Mr David Alexander Boyd which assisted with the funding of the publication.

The Society is very grateful to the many anonymous subscribers who assisted with the publication of this book and to the following:

David H. Anderson
Peter Anderson
Mr & Mrs T.W. Atkinson
Nelson & Clover Bell
Douglas Black
Sir Charles Brett
Richard Bryson
R. & G. A. Campbell
Lady Carswell
Don Cheyne
Julian & Anne Clarke
Misses A. & B. Clyde
Eve S. Corken
Clive & Gillian Corry
John R. Cowdy
G.R.A. Darling RD QC DL MA & Mrs Darling
Stephen Dornan
Dr Eull & Mrs Dorothy Dunlop
David A. Eakin
Miss E. Eccles
Mr Berkley Farr
Dr M. Dorothy Faulkner
Ferguson & McIlveen
Lyn Gallagher
Rosemary & Keith Gilmour
W. D. Girvan
Angus Gordon
Frances W. Green
Richard Gregg
Hon. Desmond Guinness
John P Hagan
Colin Hatrick
Mrs M.E. Hawthorne
David Hogg
James Howley
Mr H.S. Irvine
Brian & Ann Irwin
Colin Kerr
Mr James Kingan
Mr & Mrs T.J.A. Kingan
Dr Paul Larmour
Dr & Mrs C.J. Latimer
Shaun Leavey
Stephen Leighton
Mr J. F. Leslie
Warren Loane
McCusker Power Leeson Mackel
Mrs R. E. McDowell
Professor Mary G. McGeown
Mrs & Mrs B. McGlaughlin
Mr B. T. McKee
Mr Ciaran Mackel
Mr Sean Mackel
Mr & Mrs D. McKelvey
Robin McKelvey
W. Denis G. Mackie
Robert McKinstry
Daniel MacLaughlin
Paul McMaster
Ian B. McQuiston
Daniel J. MacRandal
Graham Mawhinney
A.C.W. Merrick
Dr Haldan & Margaret Mitchell
Mr Paul Monaghan
Miss Mildred Moore
W. D. Mullan
Gordon Nabney
John Watson Neill
The Lord O'Neill
R.W. Oram
Mr & Mrs I.O.G. Perrott
Denis Piggot
Mrs J.D. Pollock
Mr & Mrs A.J. Rankin
Mr P. J. Rankin
Jeanne Sheehy
Mrs R. M. Starrett
Victoria & Albert Museum
Martin & Valerie Wallace
Ellis A. Wasson Ph.D
Dr & Mrs John A. Weaver
Henry A. Wheeler
W.G. Wheeler
Mr Hugh & the Hon. Mrs W.L. Weir
Demelza Wilson
Edward & Primrose Wilson
Jeremy Wilson
Lydia Wilson
S. H. Wilson
W. Woolhouse

This work owes much to the help and support of many people. I wish especially to acknowledge the contribution of Hugh Dixon who encouraged me to continue the research I first undertook as a university student and then to publish my findings. His distinctive style is evident in the preface, introduction and evolution sections which, perhaps to ease a guilty conscience for having driven me into print, he co-authored.

In any work of this kind a major source of information is, of course, the buildings themselves. I am particularly grateful to the numerous landowners and gate lodge dwellers for their courtesy and understanding and I hope that not too many of them suffer disillusionment on discovering that their lodge is not "at least 300 years old".

Invaluable specialist knowledge was generously provided by many experts and my thanks go to Jennifer Cunningham (North-east Londonderry), Robert Foye (Antrim), Ian Gow of the National Monuments Record, Scotland (W. H. Playfair), B. J. Gunn-King (Mid-Antrim), Jack Johnston (Clogher Valley), Alison Kelly (Coade Stone), Eilish McGuinness (S. P. Close), Tony Merrick (North Down), Paul Millar (Blackwood and Jury), the late T. G. F. Patterson (Counties Armagh and Tyrone), Peter Rankin (The Earl Bishop) and David M. Walker of the Historic Buildings and Monuments of Scotland (William Burn and William Spence). Mr and Mrs I. O. G. Perrott contributed mightily to the information gathered on County Fermanagh and Paul Larmour unstintingly shared his unrivalled knowledge of Ulster architecture which was of particular assistance in attribution of architects. Nigel Temple made available his remarkable collection of architectural pattern books and provided much information on the Reptons' and John Nash's smaller buildings. To him for his moral support, and to his wife Judith for her hospitality, my gratitude.

Academic research has been greatly assisted by facilities and staff in the following organisations and institutions: Armagh County Museum, the Lisburn Museum, Sir John Soane's Museum, Stranmillis Training College Library, Belfast Central Library, the cartographic section of the Northern Ireland Housing Executive, officers and members of numerous historical societies, but especially to the accommodation afforded by the Linenhall Library and the Ordnance Survey Office of Northern Ireland. I am particularly indebted for their assistance to Gayle Pollock, Terence Reeves-Smyth and Peter Turner of the Historic Monuments and Buildings Branch of the D.O.E., Elizabeth Kirwan, Keeper of Prints and Drawings at the National Library of Ireland, Peter Marlow of the National Trust, Ann

Martha Rowan and Ann Simmons of the Irish Architectural Archive, Karen Latimer of the Architectural Library, QUB, Aiden Walsh, late of the Monaghan Museum, Helen Lanigan Wood of Fermanagh County Museum and Noel Nesbitt, late of the Ulster Museum.

The Duke of Abercorn, the Earl of Belmore, the Marchioness of Dufferin and Ava, Mr Patrick Forde, Dermot P. Johnston and Sir John Leslie all generously allowed me access to their private architectural records and gave me permission to photograph and reproduce them.

I would like to express my profound obligation to all of the following who have contributed in no small way with information and illustrations:

Alan W. Anderson, Thomas J. Barron, Evelyn Beattie, Scott Beattie, Pauline Beaumont, Florence Bell, Eileen Black, Rosemary Boreland, Kenneth Boyd, Liam Bradley, Mr & Mrs J. Brankin, Jennifer Brennan, Sir Charles Brett, Evelyn Brown, Kevin Brown, Evelyn Cardwell, Norman Cardwell, Kieran Clendenning, Christina Colvin, Howard Colvin, S. Clive Corry, Margaret Cowan, The Custodians of Stokesay Castle, Beryl Dean, Edith Dempsey, Tom Douglas, Eileen Drayne, Joy Duncan, The late Lord Dunleath, Pat Dunlop, Frances Elliott, Helen Elliott, Richard Elliott, Kathleen Emerson, David Evans, Dermot Faloon, Paul Fitzsimons, Lt.-Col & Mrs H. Garner, D. J. T. Gilliland, Donald Girvan, Richard Graham, David Haddow, Roger Hall, Margaret Hamilton, Maude Harbinson, Capt. O. W. J. Henderson, Helen Hossack, Robert Huffam, Belinda Jupp, Rosalind Kerr, Joan Kinch, Larry Kinkade, J. F. Leslie, Stella Little, Ronald Loe, Jean McConnell, Mr & Mrs Campbell McCormack, Patricia McCullough, Hugh McDermott, Patricia McElhinney, Billy McGivern, Robert McKinstry, John McRobert, Adeline Mefford, Sean Minshull, Timothy Mowl, Peadar Murnane, Mrs T. Newell, Sean O'Hare, James P. O'Kane, Lord O'Neill, Richard Oram, Mary Peters, Louanne Pickles, Richard Pierce, Moyne Ramsey, Alan Rankin, Tony Rolston, Peter Rowan, Peter Scott, Robert Scott, Zillah Scott, Jim Shaw, Major John Shirley, David Sinnamon, Jack Stevenson, David L. Stewart, Mrs M. K. Summerville, Richard Todd, I. V. W. Watson, Ian Wilson, Philip Wilson, John Witchell, and Tony Wright.

Numerous other people including Richard Bryson, B. R. Cobain, Ruth Hamilton, Paul Larmour, Peter Leonard, Tony Merrick, Peter Rankin, Alistair Rowan and Barry Watson permitted me to peruse their collections of photographs and postcards many of which are reproduced in the gazetteer and are credited as they occur. I am also grateful for kind permission to reproduce their illustrations to the British Architectural Library: Drawings Collection (R.I.B.A.), the Public Record Office of Northern Ireland (P.R.O.N.I.), the Irish Architectural Archive, Dublin (I.A.A.), the Historic Monuments and Buildings Branch of the Department of the Environment for Northern Ireland (H.M.B.B.), and the National Library of Ireland (N.L.I.) for use of the Lawrence Collection. The Hogg and Welch photographs are reproduced by kind permission of the Trustees of the Ulster Museum (U.M.) and views from the Green Collection are by courtesy of the Ulster Folk and Transport Museum (U.F.T.M.). The Crawfordsburn, Co Down painting from George Stanley Repton's Pavilion Notebook has been reproduced by generous permission of the Royal Pavilion Arts Gallery and Museum, Brighton. Otherwise all illustrations are by the author and my sincere thanks go to Brendan O'Connor for printing and enhancing many of my substandard photographs with such skill and patience.

My thanks also go to Christina Simpson and Roisin McShannock who were unfailingly patient and generous in typing a manuscript which necessarily came to them in dribs and drabs.

I am particularly indebted to the UAHS, under the chairmanship of Primrose Wilson, for the opportunity to publish this text in such a comprehensive form and to Karen Latimer, the Society's Editor, for her constructive guidance and editorial advice.

Above all there are no words to fully express my thanks to my wife Lynne who has driven most of the highways, byways and potholes of Ulster to facilitate my pursuit of the oft-time elusive gate lodges recorded in this book.

# Preface

The gate lodges of Ulster have an enduring fascination. The research on which this book is based began as a university thesis thirty years ago. It seemed then that gate lodges had much to teach, albeit on a small scale, about the developing awareness and ambitions of patrons, and the changing skills of builders and architects. Lodges provided a succinct reflection of the Province's grander building ventures. Their variety ranged from vernacular tradition to architectural sophistication. Yet the need they were created to meet, that of housing a gate-keeper and his family, was simple. Many according to the varied standards of the time, were inhabited. And, while there had been some noted demolitions, lodges seemed in 1964 still to be plentiful and occupied.

Much has changed in the ensuing thirty years. The accelerating tide of demolition and decay was the main spur to renewing the study of lodges in a more comprehensive way some ten years ago - while, indeed, there were still lodges to study. For, by 1984, Ulster's lodges were a diminishing asset, almost a threatened species and certainly one which demanded understanding and protection. The reasons for this are not hard to find, and the county-by-county gazetteer shows repeatedly where the main dangers lie. Gate lodges are, almost by definition, roadside buildings. Though often very small, their building details are sometimes extensive. Frequently they are remotely situated. It is little wonder that owners of estates, faced with rising taxes and repair costs, should find resources exhausted by the demands of the bigger and more useful buildings, especially the 'big house'. Inevitably, the smaller buildings suffered. But the fragmentation of estates was by no means the only reason for the difficulties lodges faced and still face.

Often it is the uncomfortable location of lodges and the meanness of their accommodation which counts against them. Even the most elastic and sympathetic of housing officials, ignoring for a moment the fistfuls of building regulations, must have despaired at lodges placed a few feet from busy trunkroads with thundering traffic; or with rooms so small that there is not even space to swing a mouse. Moreover, their prominent siting in public view, though frequently constrained by carriageways, gate screens and mature planting, makes lodges difficult to extend sympathetically.

There are other considerations, too, which add to the economic difficulties. Some lodges have elaborate architectural details which may make repairs expensive. Some are protected by 'listing', though this in itself does not guarantee survival and can add to costs in professional fees and official modifications (without any guarantee of grant-aid for repairs). Equally, remote locations can make the provision of services prohibitively expensive.

Not least important is the process of decline. The longer these vulnerable little buildings remain untended, the greater is the likelihood that they will decline to a point where restoration cannot be justified. Worse still, they can descend into the spiral of neglect becoming prey successively to boys-being-boys, more serious vandalism, theft, and lastly, demands for demolition ostensibly on health and safety grounds.

Curiously, however, it is some of the very same characteristics which provide this bleak horizon which also offer lodges glimpses of new-dawn light. Some people wish to live in small and elaborate buildings and can afford to do so. Others do not mind remote settings or proximity to traffic (provided they are behind double-glazing). Others, again, have found ways of extending lodges (not always sympathetically) to provide better accommodation and a new lease of life. And, in a world where criminal activity is ever increasing, some owners have realized again the advantages of having a keeper at the gate. Lodges may be on the brink of a revival!

It is logical, therefore, that this book should have several distinct purposes. The first is to acknowledge the gate lodge as an outstanding building type, rich in history and variety, which has enlivened Ulster's architectural heritage and well repays study.

Secondly, it is vital to underline a reality, which must be obvious even to those with only a passing interest, that lodges are disappearing at an accelerating rate, and not always for the best reasons.

By analysing the reason for disappearances and identifying those factors primarily responsible, it is hoped to encourage owners of gate houses to accord them more sympathetic management. Equally it is possible to identify those agencies whose handling of gate lodges could be improved.

Finally, it is intended to acknowledge instances where gate lodges have been handled with sympathy and imagination. Such cases are of more than individual or local importance. In brief, it is argued that the gate lodges of Ulster have a distinguished past and ought to be allowed a proper role in the Province's architectural future.

# INTRODUCTION

The gate lodges of Ulster have received too little attention. Ancient structures and medieval remains have been subject to detailed examination since the mid-19th century. Larger Georgian and Victorian buildings, and smaller houses built within local vernacular traditions, have all gained from scholarly recording and popular publication in recent decades. Architectural and local historians have busied themselves with a multitude of building types ranging from market houses and mausoleums to poor houses and pubs. Gate lodges have been noticed, however, only (and sometimes literally) in passing, or as an insignificant part of a group. But to find a building type with such a wide distribution as gate lodges, and so ignored, it seems necessary to turn to such recent arrivals as filling stations and supermarkets (both, no doubt, ripening for doctoral attention).

Yet only in one obvious sense, that of size, can gate lodges be regarded as among the least of the Province's buildings. They have an uninterrupted lineage which stretches back through the gate houses of great medieval castles to simple shelters for those who guarded access into prehistoric structures. They have their own architectural history which includes some of the greatest Georgian and Victorian designers who worked in Ulster; and, indeed, through the medium of their pattern books, several that did not. Their social history, poised on the economic and physical divisions of Ulster society is fascinating and revealing. In their size, style, placing, and relation to other buildings, they have much to tell about their owners and about those who were expected to occupy them. Sometimes they herald the style of the big house they shield. Often, nowadays, they represent the last stylistic vestige of a house that has gone (Moneyglass, Antrim; Drumbanagher, Armagh; Erne Hill, Cavan; Lanesborough Lodge, Monaghan). Occasionally they were themselves an architectural experiment, a test of style which, when fashionable, could not be afforded for the big house. Or that process may have been reversed, with the big house being remodelled while the lodges remain as witness to its former character.

Moreover, while the gate lodges' relation with the big houses can not be ignored, their importance was arguably greater in that they brought the notion of domestic architectural style to the greater majority of the Province's population. For the greater part of the 18th and 19th centuries most of Ulster's big houses were distant from the public thoroughfare, and increasingly screened expressly to be invisible from it. Not so the gate lodges which would have been familiar to ordinary people passing, and, of course, also particularly to those ordinary people who occupied them. Thus, during their heyday, gate lodges were built to mark and maintain divisions in society; but in doing this they provided through their building, and rebuilding, a barometer of architectural fashions which could be seen and eventually imitated for the houses of an emerging middle class. No doubt there were other important influences, especially in an urban context, but the influence of gate lodges deserves closer study. And, just as they provided ready examples on a manageable scale to their contemporaries, so, given the chance, they can still offer a roadside history of Ulster building over three centuries.

That history would have been richer but for the loss of so many gate lodges; once there were very many more. Timothy Mowl and Brian Earnshaw in their inspirational study of English and Welsh gate lodges *Trumpet at a Distant Gate* [1984] recognize the pre-eminence of Britain in a European context for the number of its gate lodges. They estimated that well over ten thousand lodges have survived in England and Wales. Even if this is an underestimate, Ireland seems to have been at least as well endowed. In Ulster alone two thousand lodges have been identified since the First Ordnance Survey (1930s). The social situation in Ireland must have contributed to the wealth of lodges. The largely Anglo-Irish landowning class preserved a yawning gulf between their station in life and that of the vast majority of the population. It is not surprising that many proprietors found it comfortable and occasionally necessary to have enclosed demesnes and all routes to their homes gated with attendant lodges. When in the late 19th century Mrs Alexander, wife of the Bishop of Derry wrote her celebrated children's hymn 'All things bright and beautiful' she included the now unsung verse:-

*The rich man in his castle,*
*The poor man at his gate,*
*God made them, high or lowly,*
*And ordered their estate.*

To those who sang it originally this was a simple statement of how society was divided; and on the division stood the gate lodge. As resentment of inequalities has grown this century, so, it appears, have gate lodges - the evident embodiment of earlier privilege - found few to champion their intrinsic worth. Although many have not been outstanding buildings, all have had the disadvantage of association with past unfairness. While there are many more obvious and practical reasons for the loss of so many gate lodges, it is clear that underlying these is an acceptance, doubtless unstated or unconscious, that lodges are only a peripheral part of an extensive holding which can be trimmed without loss. Nor is it unimportant to notice that such an acceptance can be exhibited by owner or outsider alike.

The rate of losses is staggering. Of the two thousand lodges identified more than half have vanished completely or are in a very advanced state of decay. Many more have been effectively lost through unsympathetic repairs or remodellings (Shane's Castle, Antrim), or their setting has been destroyed by inappropriate development or suburban encroachment (Cornacassa, Monaghan). Understandably, the most recent lodges, often built in connection with Victorian parks, cemeteries and schools, being relatively commodious and well built and still having a clear purpose, have faired best. Conversely smaller, earlier lodges, and most notably those built in groups for now-vanished houses, show the most casualties.

Of the four lodges built for Cecil Manor, Tyrone, only one, and that 'improved', survives intact. At Churchill, Armagh, all six lodges have vanished. Among the losses have been many of stylistic importance, sometimes displaying the latest building flourishes in miniature, others expensive in their ostentatious decoration (Lismara, Antrim; Knappagh, Armagh; Huntly and Stormont Castle, Down; Drumcairne and Roxborough, Tyrone and many more).

Frequently it is the division of demesnes or estates which placed lodges in jeopardy. The Thomastown lodge, now sundered from the core of the Castlecoole estate, Fermanagh, provides a striking though not untypical example of what can happen.

Nor does the continued integrity of estate lands guarantee the safety of its buildings. Some owners can not afford to maintain their lodges. There is some evidence elsewhere to suggest that neglect may be more wilful. This is difficult to prove, but there is a temptation to allow an inconveniently small gate lodge to decay in order to secure planning approval for demolition or a replacement dwelling. Unfortunately the lack of appreciation of the lost lodge's qualities is too often underlined by the replacement being mundane in detail and inappropriate to its setting.

No doubt firmer application of planning controls, more comprehensive 'listing' (allowing for the particular difficulties which gate lodges pose) and more generous grant-aid could do much to avoid such tragedies as that at Sion, Tyrone; but it has to be acknowledged that governments on both sides of the border are hampered to some extent by the records of their own departments. Road widenings and realignments have caused destruction and blight (Stradone and Tullyvin, both Cavan; Lismara and Macedon, both Antrim) and it is fair to say that some of this is unavoidable if roads are to be improved. Certainly things have improved since the 1960s when, for example, a minor adjustment to a new road could and should, but did not, save the fine 'tea-caddy' pair of lodges at Belvoir Park, Down.

The prize for wholesale removal of lodges, however, undoubtedly belongs elsewhere. Pomeroy and Seskinore in Tyrone, and Learmount, Somerset and Derrynoyd all in Londonderry, have barely a lodge between them. All are in the care of the Forestry Service, which also looks after Tollymore Park, Down, that treasure of estates where the loss of the Barbican Lodge was one of the country's architectural tragedies. Happily the building-removal policy has itself been removed, as is shown by the excellent treatment of the lodges at Drum Manor, Tyrone. The situation at Dartrey in Monaghan shows that forestry problems have not been confined to the north.

Private institutions can be equally culpable, of course, and golf clubs seen to have a particular proximity to the decline of lodges designed by prominent architects: Ballydrain (Blore), Antrim; Tandragee (Farrell), Armagh; Killymoon (Nash), Tyrone. Even the National Trust has not been entirely blameless. For a while it seemed that its big houses were receiving all the attention; now it remains to be seen whether the good work on lodges at Castle Ward and Mountstewart, both Down, can be continued.

It must be admitted that, in whatever hands, gate lodges can present particular conservation challenges. Often they are very small and low (though the recent relaxation in Building Control legislation to permit lower ceilings is an important relief); sometimes a well-meaning restorer is faced with the impracticality of twin lodges, both small, and fifteen feet or so apart with a drive between (Pellipar, Londonderry; Hollymount, Down; Castledillon, Armagh). Frequently they stand close to carriageways, where noise, smell and vibration cause discomfort.

The siting of lodges, together with their compact style, can make extension difficult. The essential features need to be understood and respected (Longwood, Antrim; Craigavad, Down; Ely Lodge, Fermanagh) if fundamental mistakes are to be avoided. Yet examples of good extensions are to be found and deserve better publicity: Lismoyne and Ahoghill, both Antrim; and Lisgoole, Fermanagh. Similarly, total ruins have been successfully restored (Narrow Water, Down; Carrick Lodge, Donegal); and others could be consolidated as attractive landscape features (Elmfield, Down).

The surviving gate lodges of Ulster, however varied their condition, represent together an important aspect of the Province's building past, and a resource for architectural history. They offer picturesque variety, skilled craftsmanship, scholarly design, and simple delight to Ulster townscape and countryside. Deserving study, they have had little since James Boyle and Thomas Fagan first referred to them seriously for the Ordnance Survey Memoirs in the 1830s (when many of the most interesting were not yet built). In recent years they have received better attention in U.A.H.S. Lists, and it is good to see a chapter devoted to them in James Howley's *The Follies and Garden Buildings of Ireland* [1993].

This catalogue and study is offered to all who own and care for gate lodges, and to those who would like to know more about them, in the belief that the better these little buildings are noticed and understood, the greater will be their contribution to Ulster's architectural heritage.

# EVOLUTION OF THE GATE LODGE IN ULSTER

The earliest relatives of the gate lodge were shelters provided for those charged with the particular responsibility of securing access to an enclosure. They varied in sophistication from piles of stones acting as windbreakers for prehistoric watchmen at the mouth of caves, to well furnished rooms providing comfortable accommodation in the *atriensis* for the doorkeeper of a Roman villa. In Ulster, however, the direct antecedents of gate lodges were the gatehouses of medieval castles. As Anglo-Norman castles were extended away from the defensive strength of the central keep, so wards were enclosed with curtain walls through which gateways were provided. It soon became apparent that these gates could be best defended if they were set within strong houses providing shelter for the guard, and with their own defensive features. Thus, in the 13th century at Dundrum, Down, and Carrickfergus, Antrim, gatehouses were built with their own architectural identity, distinct in style, and strong in their own right though not yet rivalling the strength of the keep. The Maguires' Castle at Enniskillen, Fermanagh, vividly portrayed during an attack in 1594 in a painting by John Thomas, shows this combination.

As the middle ages progressed, castle designers increasingly concentrated defences on the curtain wall with towers set at intervals. The defended area became larger until small towns or ports were enclosed, as at Ardglass, Down in the 15th century. During the process the gatehouse became increasingly important and the point of most strength, either usurping the keep's role, or often continuing both functions. Curiously, in County Down there was developed in the 15th century a type of tower house which, though not a gatehouse, used a prominent gatehouse feature, the arched machicolation (or drop hole), a feature which was to reappear in decorative form two centuries later, to defend the door. These towers, including Kilclief, Audley's and Jordan's, have become known as the 'gatehouse type'. Secure walls allowed, too, the building of more comfortable, better ventilated, and lighter houses within the defended area. Thus was a pattern established which was to last with many variations until our own times of a well-defended perimeter enclosing an area of privilege, safety and comfort - with access controlled from a gate building.

In England the pattern was established with Tudor manor houses set in moated or walled gardens and approached through gatehouses. In Ulster the disrupted state of the country, caused by successive Tudor attempts to subdue the Irish, resulted in little undefended building until after the Flight of the Earls in 1607; and even then the dominant feature of plantation settlements were defensive bawns and castles. Gateways into the bawns, or walled enclosures, might be defended by crossfire from a flanked, projecting corner tower; but occasionally, as at Castlecaulfield, Tyrone, and Joymount, Carrickfergus, Antrim, an undefended house with wide, mullioned windows regularly arranged in the modern fashion, was set within a walled enclosure with a gatehouse.

The difference between the gatehouses at Castlecaulfield (c1615) and Joymount is striking. The former, as it survived, was unadorned and functionally defensive with access between a pair of guardrooms. Joymount built about the same time was, as befitted the house of Sir Arthur Chichester the Lord Deputy, much more ambitious. The walled forecourt to the great house was fronted on its main axis with a handsome gatehouse with circular towers at its four corners each topped with an onion-shaped cupola. This is the first documented example in the Province of an entrance conceptually more decorative than defensive. It was intended, no doubt, to express architecturally the qualities of the new order - strength with style, Renaissance balance, regularity and organization. The building marks at once the moment when sheltering of gatekeepers ceases to be a matter of convenience and function, and the beginning of a tradition which combines the defence of a perimeter with a self-conscious show of building style. The tradition continues to our own times.

The display of architecture at Joymount was possible within the safety of the town walls of Carrickfergus. A similar, though less ostentatious arrangement, was made at Chichester's other house, Belfast Castle, with a forecourt gateway flanked by a pair of lodges with pyramidal roofs. These appear in a view of 1685 and may date from not long before. The troubled years of the mid-century left little opportunity for ostentatious building, especially away from the safety of the eastern ports, but after the Restoration there were significant stirrings. The royal fort at Charlemont, Armagh, was repaired in 1673 and enhanced with a pedimented gate building probably designed by Sir William Robinson, Engineer and Surveyor General. Such classical sophistication, though isolated in Ulster at this time, sowed a seed which would eventually bear fruit. Similarly, there is the remarkable and unique survival at Cloncarney Castle, Armagh (now the Gosford Estate) of a pair of lodges linked by a tall plain archway. The date is not known but the curved gables in the Dutch taste suggest that they may have been an improvement by Sir Nicholas Acheson, 4th Baronet, who succeeded in 1685. This bold reworking of the twin arrangement at Belfast was to have many important descendants in the twin lodges of the following two centuries.

Meanwhile the development that was most important was not of the lodges themselves but of their setting. The comparative tranquillity of the country following the Battle of the Boyne allowed owners to think more expansively about improving their surroundings. Small, compartmental gardens of Jacobean character were extended into formal Baroque landscapes with regular water features, tree-lined vistas and long, straight drives. As these privileged areas were increased, so the fencing which enclosed them became more remote from the houses; and at the main points of access secure gates were needed. While some of these gates could be locked and left, others needed more constant attention. So the lodge which had started as an integral part of the castle, continued the journey which took it from the front of the house's courtyard, first to the barely visible ends of straight drives; and finally out of sight altogether along winding drives into the shelter-belt woods at the edges of informal landscapes. There, often with elaborate gatescreens, they established their own identity, visible from the public highway, combining a curious mixture of warning and welcome with as much architectural swank as the proprietor thought appropriate and could afford.

Walled demesnes with grand gateways set against mature planting have become so much an image of rural Ulster that it is difficult to imagine the 'big houses' without them. Yet this combination does not make its first appearance until the middle of the 18th century, with the beginnings of informal landscaping, and was still being created over a century later.

Iron gates, worthy of study in their own right, will be mentioned here only in the direct relationship with lodges. Their long history is not to be ignored and indeed, it has much in common with that of the gate lodges. They appear as functional items at castles, reinforcing wooden gates and then on their own, securing doorways and gateways. As their use is extended to gardens and courtyards, so are the opportunities for elaboration and display exploited. Surviving early examples are rare in Ulster but two sets of gates serve to show advances in the 18th century. A drawing of 1716-26 of old Crom House, Fermanagh shows a relatively plain spread of gates and railings to the forecourt. A generation later the forecourt gates of Richhill Castle, Armagh (now at Hillsborough) of about 1748, are one of the Province's most sophisticated works in wrought iron - a magnificent set of gates and flanking screens with leaf and spiral decorations and an overthrow embellished with the Richardson crest. Later gates and screens were larger, and, after the arrival of cast-iron in the mid-19th century more sculptural, but rarely if ever was the quality of the Richhill gates challenged.

The earliest extended gardens and landscapes were enclosed, if at all, by fences or hedges. Demesne walls only seem to have become an economic possibility in the 1740s. Even then, and for long after, walling involved major expenditure which many proprietors could not afford. Only rarely were full walled circuits completed. Many were limited to those boundaries visible from the public roads.

Walls provided not only defence against intruders. Lord Orrery of Caledon, Tyrone, explained in a letter of 1747 that his were built "*at once to give us fruit and security*". But, while the south side of a wall might help the crops on espaliered apple trees, security against theft was the main concern. Although the situation varied from estate to estate, according to convenience of access and popularity of the proprietor, in some places in Ulster the tenantry may have been as avaricious and resourceful as that described by Arthur Young in the 1780s at Pakenham Hall, Longford:

"*they steal everything ... all sorts of iron hinges, chains, locks, keys ... Gates will be cut to pieces and conveyed away ... as fast as built. Trees big as a man's body ... that would require ten men to move, gone in a night*".

Even the wall itself was at risk:

"*Good stone out of a wall will be taken for a firehearth, etc., though a breatch is made to get at them, nor is it easy to catch them for they never carry their stolen goods home, but to some boghole*".

Wall building was a major undertaking which could take many years. Lord Macartney began his improvements at Lissanoure, Antrim, in 1770 but it was not until almost twenty years later that his agent could report the wall to be almost complete and "*exceedingly well built*". Frequently, according to tradition, walling was only carried out in the 1840s as famine relief work. As the 19th century progressed, and demesnes were developed on a comparatively small scale and often near growing towns, so privacy joined security as a prime reason for wall building.

Had proprietors instructed gatekeepers to build their own houses, the gate lodges of Ulster would have followed local vernacular traditions - largely thatched roofs, whitewashed walls, doors and windows placed for convenience rather than in subjection to whole design. A very few lodges with strong vernacular features have survived as for example at Dresternan, Fermanagh. More often, however, owners wanted something different, and in the 18th century the way to make a small house different was to give it symmetry and regularity - in effect to apply to it principles of formal design as at Donagh just across Upper Lough Erne. In achieving this the owner's taste was displayed and his home signposted. Even by contemporary standards the size of lodges was often small. The early aim was to provide the minimum of accommodation to give the maximum visual effect in public views. Rear elevations remained unadorned, and symmetry was the main concern.

Vernacular tradition was not set aside completely. The asymmetrical traditional house of the hearth-lobby type

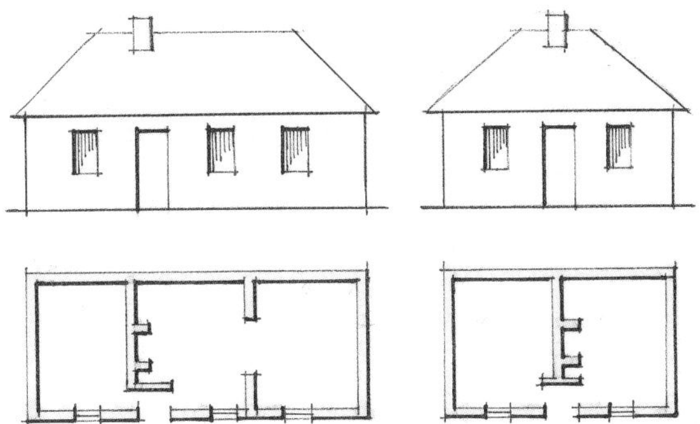

*Figure I* *Figure II*

[Fig. I] seems to have provided one origin for the most recognisable type of Irish gate lodge [Fig. II]. External symmetry demands a balanced interior and a central chimney; and the jamb wall opposite the front door now straddles the chimney wall rather than being set to one side of it allowing a spy hole from the main hearth. The accommodation may be smaller, and is less flexible, but enough for an elderly or childless couple with gatekeeping duties. The features of the roof were often exaggerated - tall chimneys, on either very steep pitches or on very shallow ones with deep eaves, - all devices to give a small building more consequence. Very shallow-pitched slate roofs were particularly popular just after 1800; very steep pitches, almost pyramidal sometimes, suggest original thatching. That the simple box-like appearance was universally recognized is shown by Maria Edgeworth's comment in 1806 on a visit to her aunt at Fort Hamilton (now Ballyedmond), Down, that a pavilion there was like *"any square porter's lodge"*.

While lodges were usually small, there are exceptions such as the remarkable pair at Castledillon, Armagh, which suggest that larger families had to be housed. If so, this was again unusual. In his *Designs for Lodge and Entrances* [1823] T.D.W. Dearn comments, as if merely repeating what was generally understood, that:

*"an entrance lodge is usually intended either for an old man, an old woman, or both, or for a mother and daughter; in short for anything but a family"*.

Maria Edgeworth on a visit in Denbigh in 1813 also mentions encountering a "porter-ess". Dearn again as early as 1807 comments on gate lodge occupants when in *Sketches in Architecture*, in a text accompanying a plate showing a pair of classical temple lodges, he warns of the depravity of the labouring classes:

*"these men cannot be too much exposed ... there are none more liberally imbued with low cunning ... none possessing a more predatory disposition than farmer's servants; it is therefore of the utmost importance to place them where their conduct will be most liable to observation"*.

One of the problems of being a gatekeeper was boredom which could lead to drunkenness. Writing of English gatekeepers, also in 1807, in his *Architectural Designs*, W.F. Pocock recommended gardens for gatekeepers:

*"in cultivating which they may occupy their leisure hours, it may prevent their spending their time and money in scenes of intemperance, whereby their habits of industry are relaxed, and their morals corrupted"*.

It is one thing to drink oneself but another to encourage it in others, and the consequences could be serious. In 1779 Lord Abercorn's agent had to report a sad situation which, however, may not be untypical:

*"Arthur, I understand has taken up the selling of spirituous liquors. In short for this and other reasons, he must be discharged. The time when I submit entirely to you. A decent person will be wanted to take care of the gate"*.

The appearance of gatekeepers also became important. At Baronscourt in 1783 a request was made for the successor to the unfortunate Arthur as follows:

*"be pleased to allow Semple the gatekeeper, a livery ... same as the park keeper"*.

The provision of such uniform became usual at grander establishments and survived, with top hats and tailcoats, well into the photographic age at Tollymore and Belvoir, both in Down. More colourful, but also disconcerting, was the experience of the Rev. Daniel A. Beaufort who was initially refused entry to Downhill by an officious porter in full tartan plaid.

After 1800 owners became weary of the simple cubic 'tea-caddy' lodge, and designs became more complex. Variation was achieved through novel decorative details or by altering overall shape. Most fundamental were changes in plan. Both octagonal and circular lodges became popular and, although John Plaw in *Sketches for Country Houses, Villas and Rural Dwellings* [1800] argued that such shapes were *"calculated to give the least resistance to the wind"* (!) the main purpose was decorative. Perhaps because of its impracticality, and the difficulty of positioning furniture, few such lodges have survived. There were good octagonal examples at Maryfield, Down and Castleroe, Londonderry, and one remains with its umbrello roof at Drumraymond, Antrim. Round lodges have disappeared at Richmond Lodge, Down and Cremore, Londonderry, but a charming two-story version survives at Ballylough, Antrim. At Ashfield Park, Tyrone, there was a rather more practical ovoid lodge of cut stone with a thatched roof. The two ovoid lodges at Ballymenoch, Down, because of their conical roofs and central chimneys became known as the 'Ink pots', an affectionate appellation which was also applied to the round lodge at Baronscourt, Tyrone.

From the late 18th century, too, lodges become associated with grand gateways, elaborate railings, and sweeping gatescreens which the owners and their architects used as an opportunity for architectural show. The employment of architects from across the Irish Sea and experience of the Grand Tour becomes increasingly apparent in the complication of designs and the sophistication of classical details. Rusticated or vermiculated stone piers topped with ball finials, vases, or pine cones occurred frequently. The zenith of these developments was reached at Downhill, Londonderry, for the most prominent of Grand Tourists, the Earl Bishop; in the Lion Gate two great cats (Hervey ounces rather than lions) raised on twin piers with attached columns and full entablatures, faced each other above the gateway; and at the Bishop's Gate, really a triumphal arch, the gateway is arched beneath a full pediment. James Wyatt had become acquainted with the Earl Bishop and was probably responsible for both entrances which display much classical vocabulary gathered from travels in France and Italy.

What is striking about these entrances as built, however, is the lack of reconciliation between the entrance and the gate lodge to which, in each case, it is attached by a screen wall. Neither scale nor style accord, and, as at Cloverhill, Cavan, the lodge appears to be (and probably was) an afterthought, charming but not a wholly appropriate adjunct. Although there were other attempts to incorporate the lodge into the screen wall, this does not seem to have been a favoured solution. Almost identical designs for Castlecoole, Fermanagh, and Baronscourt, Tyrone by Sir Richard Morrison attempting to balance gateway and lodge remained unexecuted. Similarly, attempts to incorporate accommodation within and over an archway at Montalto, and Portavo, both Down, remained on paper, though a castle-style version was built at Carrowdore, Down. Also at Carrowdore, and also in Gothick style, another option for lodge accommodation was tried with two pavilions immediately to each side of, and connected to, the central archway. A similar classical design for Caledon, Tyrone, was not built.

Ultimately far more enduring was the treatment of the gatescreen and lodge as separate entities, often in matching style, with the lodge set at a respectful distance behind the gate. Seaforde, Down, and Colebrooke, Fermanagh, are good early examples of an arrangement which achieved wide acceptance. The lodges were not diminished in their decoration because of this subordinate positioning. On the contrary, wherever placed, lodges normally received some embellishment. Sculpted family armorial bearings were frequently placed in gables and pediments. Niches were used to enliven plain walls, though the provision of two demure goddesses to inhabit them at Ely Lodge, Fermanagh, is rare.

Around 1800 Coade stone casts provided a wide choice of fine decorative motifs at relatively low cost. At Caledon twin lodges received arms and sphinxes, as specified by John Nash; and at Dawson's Grove, Monaghan the lodge had a Coade keystone and an improbable chimney pot in the form of a funerary urn. A much more elaborate scheme of such pieces by Samuel Woolley was rejected for Seaforde but was actually built at Glenanea outside Ulster in Co. Westmeath. After the screen was re-erected nearby, the two statues of *Flora and Pomona* did come to the north - but, alas, not to a gate lodge.

Gothick, eventually the architectural expression of the Romantic movement, made its appearance in Ulster in the 1760s. The style, with lancet arches, quatrefoils, and cruciform arrowslits, provided a pretty and light-hearted alternative to scholarly classicism. It also had suitable rustic associations, and was readily adapted for gate lodges. Indeed, whether in regular symmetrical lodges or asymmetrical romantic ones, the pointed window is a very common feature in Ulster gate lodges. Size could vary enormously. The pace was set at Hillsbough Fort in 1758 in the Gothick remodelling, apparently influenced by Sanderson Miller, of the fort gatehouse. The gazebo gate close by has ogee arches, a feature which appears again on the pair of lodges at Seaport Lodge, Antrim. An even earlier influence was Thomas Wright 'the Wizard of Durham', a great designer of follies who visited Tollymore in 1746. The demesne is now one of the wonders of Gothick design, though the Gothick Bryansford Gate, and the castle-style Barbican Gate, both clearly influenced by Wright, were not built until forty years after his visit; and the gate lodges now accompanying them did not appear until the 1820s.

With such a long period of popularity - which extended well into the Victorian period - it is not surprising to find Gothick used in many shapes and sizes, and being used by some notable architects. At Castle Leslie, Monaghan, John Nash used his 'Abbey' Gothick for a pinnacled screen and a distinctive traceried gable to the lodge. The one lancet window at the lodge to the Observatory, Armagh, appears to be the only use of Gothick in Ulster by Francis Johnston. Spikey finials and pointed windows appear in such varied situations as Friar's Bush graveyard, where the lodge is divided by the entrance arch, and at Greyabbey, Down, where the lodge has pointed windows in a canted front, a feature repeated in County Down lodges at Mountstewart, Montalto, Florida Manor and Saintfield, and also at Mount Irwin, Armagh; Drumcarban, Cavan; Ards, Donegal; and by variation to a pair of octagonal lodges at Milltown, Antrim. Elsewhere Gothick appears in gate pillars, like early English cluster columns, as at Elm Park, Armagh and Derrybard, Tyrone.

The Georgian preference for symmetry made the placing of single lodges at entrances a particular challenge. Balance could be achieved in three ways:-

i. Positioning the lodge between two carriage entrances. This had obvious difficulties for the keeper and never became popular though the system was used at Glenalla Glebe, Londonderry, and later at Glenmore, Antrim, and Northland, Tyrone.

ii. Placing the lodge across the public road opposite the gates. Rare outside Ireland, the system found wide favour; by 1850 about 10% of lodges were so placed. The ratio became smaller later when fewer people owned land on both sides of the public road, and as the increase in traffic made the arrangement inconvenient.

iii. By having two lodges. This was the earliest and most enduring solution.

The 1830s Ordnance Survey map shows that at least 5% of lodges were by then in pairs. The earliest were little more than single space sentry boxes often nicknamed 'Salt and Pepper' lodges. Usually both parts were occupied by a single gatekeeper or a couple, and were often dubbed 'Day and Night'. Occasionally the second lodge was occupied by another servant such as the gamekeeper.

Early pairs have not done well; those at Greenmount, Leslie Hill and Oldpark, Antrim, and Eglantine and Edgecumbe, Down have been demolished. At Beardiville, Antrim, two different pairs survive: the first are perfect cubes with pyramidal roofs set at the outer ends of concave quadrant walls; the second set are a classical version of Friar's Bush, with naive outsized Diocletian windows, and the central archway providing a sheltered link.

Most late 18th century lodges were spartan in accommodation and architecturally unassumming, but one of the delights of lodges is that there are usually exceptions to every pattern. Quite exceptional are the pair of lodges built in 1760 for Sir Capel Molyneux, reportedly to designs by Sir William Chambers, for Castledillon, Armagh which were described in *Playfair's Baronetage* as *"the most costly park gates, perhaps at that time in the three kingdoms"*. Two very large cubes in muscular Roman Palladian manner flank gargantuan gate pillars, all constructed in huge rugged limestone blocks. Although each lodge provided a single large room, it is difficult to escape the conclusion that external effect rather than domestic convenience was the primary concern. No one built lodges on such a grand scale again.

Movement towards picturesque planning, and particularly away from slavish symmetry, in the early 19th century was bound to result in attacks on twin lodges. Humphry Repton, the greatest designer of English picturesque parks set the trend in his revolutionary *Landscape Gardening* [1803]:

*"The custom of placing a gate between two square boxes, or, as it is called, a "pair of lodges", has always appeared to me absurd, because it is an attempt to give consequence to that which in itself is mean; the habitation of a single labourer, or, perhaps of a solitary old woman, to open the gate, is split into two houses for the sake of childish symmetry; and very often the most squalid misery is found in the person thus banished from society who inhabits a dirty room of a few feet square".*

The advice was not taken very quickly in Ireland. Twenty years later T.D.W. Dearn in his *Designs for Lodges and Entrances* [1823] was still commenting:

*"... a building whether of a single room or more, stuck at each end of a gate, has something in it too trite, stiff and formal to be pleasing".*

A further fifteen years pass and J.C. Loudon in *The Suburban Gardener* [1838] was still attacking the paucity of accommodation such a box lodge provided:

*"...few things connected with an elegant country residence are more offensive to a humane mind than to see boxes set down as lodges, not more perhaps than 10ft. or 12ft. square with rooms not above 7ft. high in the clear when this is the case, and the occupant has children, he is sometimes obliged to live with half his family in a box on one side of the gate, and to send the other half to sleep on the other side".*

Although all three authors were making a plea for the Picturesque, it was Repton's influence in particular which is seen in Nash's irregular castellated Tudor gate house at Killymoon, Tyrone. The *"trite, stiff and formal"* persisted though with an increase in the accommodation. In the Regency period independent two-roomed lodges were provided on each side of the entrance drive and Nash was again responsible for the twin classical pair of 1812 at Caledon, Tyrone. Other examples in similar style are to be found at Pellipar, Londonderry and Hollymount, Down. Gothick versions were the umbrello pair to Millbrook, Antrim and the two exceedingly pretty lodges at Summer Island, Armagh. The extraordinary Jacobethan pair at nearby Loughgall Manor House are exceptionally late in date as the twin lodge tradition went out of favour after the first quarter of the 19th century.

The single sentry box lodge on a square plan was not able to provide two well-proportioned rooms, so the plan was developed into a rectangle with the consequent elongation of the main elevation. The resulting building form is that which survives in hundreds of examples today. The two-roomed plans with three-bay leading facades offer more opportunites for architectural embellishment. Many remained unadorned but the early 19th century saw the real birth of the Neo-Classical era. Little Greek or Roman porticos began to appear. The porch behind the columns might be square or even circular as at Greenvale, Tyrone, Ely Lodge, Fermanagh and Derramore, Down where the hapless occupant depended upon it for shelter to move between the two rooms.

There are many examples of pedimented, two-column (distyle) porticos such as at Camla Vale, Monaghan and the Lodge, Donegal. Even more sophisticated four-column (tetrastyle) examples are found at Clogher Palace, Tyrone, Dalriada, Antrim and Drenagh, Londonderry where Charles Lanyon borrowed details from Stuart and Revett's *Antiquities of Athens* [1841]. At Gwynn's Institute, Londonderry is a forerunner of numerous lodges designed by Thomas Jackson for conservative clients who preferred classical symmetry to the Picturesque.

Sadly the true classical temple, which should have been an ideal gate lodge design, never became popular in Ulster. It has been shown that Sir Richard Morrison failed to sell his temple designs at Castlecoole and Baronscourt. He had devised a variation of the standard lodge simply turning the structure through 90° to present itself gable-on to the visitor; this provided a full width portico across the leading elevation. Examples are to be found at Fota, Cork and Ballyfin, Leix. Morrison did succeed, however, in designing a Greek rustic cottage version for the Thomastown gate at Castlecoole. His erstwhile assistant J.B. Keane designed the Grecian lodge at Stradone, Cavan in the same style. There was a neat little in antis variant at Knappagh, Armagh by Alexander McLeish; finest of all is the Doric school lodge at Caledon now in disgraceful condition.

Few architects or patrons gave more than a passing thought to the gate lodge dweller. None of the graceful Georgian lodges had more than two small rooms. The privy was often hidden away in the garden behind the lodge so that it could not be seen from the road or avenue even though this might make it uncomfortably remote. Witness the amusing little Gothick example to a classical lodge at Inishmore, Fermanagh.

As the 19th century progressed, there was mounting pressure for housing reform. The gate lodge with its meagre accommodation and dingy interiors, however elegant or charmingly situated, required improvements which landowners increasingly could not ignore. While taste dictated a balanced front elevation, additional rooms could only be provided by extending to the rear producing an L, or less conspicuously a T, plan. It was also common for very restricted bedspace to be provided by means of a loft lit by skylights and reached by a ladder. The solution for new buildings was to raise the eaves line giving two up, two down accommodation. The resultant "high-brow" effect can be seen at Conlon's Lodge, the Argory, Armagh, the Bawn, Tyrone, the Gothick lodges to Florida Manor, Down and the Castlecoole pair probably rebuilt about 1840.

In the wake of squabbles about the essence of the Picturesque, improved, pretty tenants' houses had been designed by Repton's partner John Nash at Blaise Hamlet in 1811. In Ulster Nash had proved completely flexible in designing to his clients varying needs. He designed formal classical lodges to Crawfordsburn, Down and Caledon, Tyrone; in the Gothick idiom at Castle Leslie, Monaghan, and pioneered the Picturesque with his romantic castellated lodge at Tynan Abbey, Armagh and Tudor Revival effort at Killymoon, Tyrone. His influence is also seen in the Cottage Orné at Fenaghy, Antrim.

There was, however, another more direct and even greater influence upon the radical change to improved architecture in the Province. This was the effect of the pattern book. Until about 1800 the simple Georgian lodge held sway, Castledillon apart, in Ulster. The architectural profession was in its infancy and the lesser landowner often could not afford the luxury of a professional designer. Pattern books provided an alternative source of design ideas. They were produced mainly by architects to show off their wares but in remoter areas, where an architect might not be available, proprietors found that pattern books offered a range of designs for a variety of buildings. Pattern books though mostly produced outside Ulster were to have a profound effect on the Province's buildings.

The first illustration of a porter's lodge occurred in 1740 in Batty Langley's *The City and Country Builder's, and Workman's Treasury of Designs* but it seems not to have had any impact. John Miller's *The Country Gentleman's Architect* [1787], with six elegant Palladian twin lodge designs, was the first book to offer *"lodges for park or garden entrances and ornamental wooden gates"*. The first example of gate lodges in Ulster to have been inspired by a pattern book may be the pair at Florencecourt with their projecting canted fronts which are closely parallel to the one shown on Plate 28. The early pattern books had little influence in the Province although Charles Lilly in an unexecuted proposal for a gate screen at Seaforde House, Down [1805], may have been influenced by Robert Adam's design for Syon House, Middlesex, which was published in his *Plans, Elevations and Sections of Buildings* [1778].

Pattern books came into their own with the advent of the Picturesque movement. As a means of self promotion many architects published collections of designs for cottages in various styles. As many as forty such publications were produced between 1790 and 1840. Many pattern books included outrageously revolutionary designs. Joseph Michael Gandy, for example, portrayed a pair of pyramid lodges in his *Rural Architect* of 1805. These would have provided only a few square feet in which to stand upright. Unrepentant he published, in the same year, *Designs for Cottages, Cottage Farms and Other Rural Buildings* in which he shows a pair of cones thatched to the ground and supported on metal frames. It was this sort of nonsense which Humphry Repton considered to be a social scandal. Not surprisingly, none seem to have been built.

Gandy's considerably more practical master John Soane, had, in 1793, produced *Sketches in Architecture* which included an innovative rustic Greek cottage design. It was this design that Sir Richard Morrison used for the Thomastown lodge at Castlecoole, also in an unexecuted proposal for Baronscourt and at Kilruddery, Wicklow (recently demolished). Morrison unashamedly complemented many of his lodges with a gate screen taken from an illustration in J.B. Papworth's *Rural Residences* [1818]. These sturdy stone pillars, in the form of Greek stellae, were hung on secondary iron piers because, as the author explains *"... the rusting and expanding of the metal damaged the stonework..."*. Morrison proposed this design for Baronscourt and actually used it at Langford Lodge, Antrim. Papworth's influence can also be seen in the entrances to J.B. Keane's Stradone, Cavan, Necarne, Fermanagh and in the gates to Ely Lodge also in Fermanagh designed by William Farrell.

Edward Gyfford's *Designs for Small Picturesque Cottages* [1807] seems to have been the source for the lodge at Glenalla Glebe, Londonderry, albeit a basic version of the original, *"a park entrance intended as an entrance to two paddocks"* as the central lodge is flanked by two carriage openings. T.D.W. Dearn's pattern book *Designs for Lodges and Entrances* in two editions of 1811 and 1823 was the first to be devoted entirely to gate lodges. As in many other contemporary publications, they contained plans showing indifference to the needs of the gatekeeper and concentrating instead on the external effect. Only after the Regency did a number of books expounding the delights of the picturesque cottage show more generously scaled accommodation.

There were two leading pioneers of "chocolate box" architecture, T.F. Hunt and P.F.Robinson. Hunt in his *Half a Dozen Hints* of 1825 announced *"in these designs the Old English Domestic style has been preferred to every other as admitting of greater variety of form and outline, and as being more suited to the scenery of this country, than the Greek temple or Italian villa"*. Nevertheless in 1827 he published *Architettura Campestre* with a selection of Italianate designs because of alleged public demand. Hunt attempts to justify his ornate designs in the earlier book by claiming *"economy has never the less been kept in view and all unnecessary ornament avoided"*! He also mentioned *"... that pictorial effect which they could only acquire by time and the growth of roses or other embellishing plants"*. No exact replicas of his designs are known to survive in Ulster but a typically decorative and irregular English gabled cottage beside a buttressed Tudor entrance archway was illustrated in his *Exemplars of Tudor Architecture* [1830]. This was then reproduced in J.C. Loudon's *Encyclopaedia of Gardening* [1834 ed.] where it is stated to have been *"erected in the north of Ireland"*. If it was indeed built, it has not yet been located. Hunt's influence is to be found, however, in such lodges as that of Lanyon, Lynn and Lanyon's at Stranmillis and at Murlough in Down.

Peter Frederick Robinson's amazing number of books with many varying designs made the greatest impact in Ulster. Though mainly in the Old English Cottage style, they also include Tudor Revival and Romantic Castellated designs. His first book *Rural Architecture* [1822] was followed by many others extolling the virtues of elaborate bargeboards and curly chimneys. The Newry architect, Thomas J. Duff, collected pattern books and Robinson's influence is evident at, for example, Aberdelghy, Antrim and Tamnaharny and Narrowwater, Down, all of which have intricately carved ornamental bargeboards, picturesque chimney stacks and label-moulded small-paned windows.

Robinson's *Designs for Lodges and Park Entrances* [1833] concentrated on the Picturesque with a selection of Castellated, Norman, Swiss Chalet and Tudor Revival designs as well as, most significantly, his beloved Old English Cottage style. Three lodges derived from this source can be found in Ulster. There are two at Baronscourt: the beautiful and unique Rock Cottage (Design No.3) and the Newtownstewart Lodge (Design No.4) both of which copy the elevations but with adapted plans. Also in Tyrone at Parkanaur is a handed version of another illustration (Design No.1); an old photograph of the lodge even shows creeper around the entrance porch just as Robinson envisaged. It seems likely that for once the architect was directly involved in these buildings because Rock Cottage predates the book and also Robinson was working at Seaforde between 1825 and 1833.

Another essential reference book for designers was *Ornamental Gables* [1831] produced by Augustus Charles Pugin, a French emigré who was John Nash's draughtsman. This book contains many examples of decorative English and French bargeboards. Three of these were used for lodges at Shane's Castle and Brecart Lodge both in Antrim. Gables from Coventry and Warwick can be seen here copied down to hipknobs, finials and pendants and apparently executed by James Sands.

James Sands seems to have relied particularly heavily on pattern books especially those of John Claudius Loudon. Although originally a professional gardener, Loudon's most important contribution ,was the collection and reissue of others' work. He reproduced designs from the books of T.F. Hunt and P.F. Robinson and others. His works became an accepted resource in Victorian architects' offices. Loudon produced plans in many styles: Gothic, Old English, Grecian, Italian, Castellated and even Swiss

Chalet. He is recorded as being particularly gratified that his work *The Suburban and Villa Companion* [1838] sold well in Ireland.

Sands applied a Pugin bargeboard to Antrim Lodge at Shane's Castle. The design was adapted from Loudon's *Designs for Ornamental Cottages* [1846], the original being by the Northumbrian architect , John Dobson. It is more closely copied at Carncastle Lodge, Antrim, complete with skewtable gables and barley twist chimney pots. There is reason to believe that even Charles Lanyon was inspired by this work because his favourite , frequently repeated, Italianate lodge with porte-cochère seems to owe its origin to a perspective of a design by a mysterious "F.H." reproduced in Loudon's book.

That Loudon's books continued to be used as works of reference by Ulster architects is clear from two Castellated Tudor entrances in the Province, both dating from about 1870. A superb informal composition at Red Hall, Antrim is almost as illustrated in *Cottage, Farm and Villa Architecture* [1833]. The architect was probably Alexander McAlister whose copy of Loudon survives signed and dated 1858; the original was a design by Thomas Allason, a regular Loudon contributor. In 1840 Loudon edited a reprint of *Landscape Gardening* [1803] written by his idol, Humphry Repton and a remote result is a rather poor reproduction of the lodge and archway of Blaise Castle, Somerset at the entrance to the great gaunt ruin of Altinaghres Castle, Tyrone. Loudon's influence is also seen in the work of his friends and pupils. One of these, Ninian Niven, was particularly active in transforming northern demesnes. He had a hand in an unexecuted castellated fantasy entrance to Castle Leslie, Monaghan. Another, Alexander McLeish, designed the chaste little temple lodge at Knappagh, Armagh and perhaps also worked at Cranaghan, Cavan.

There were few Irish pattern books. Lady Helen Domville, from an aristocratic Dublin family, published some pretty domestic pictures in her *Eighteen Designs for Glebe Houses and Rural Cottages* [c1840] some of which were borrowed from P.F. Robinson including a variation of his Rock Cottage, Baronscourt.

In 1841 Arthur Creagh Taylor published *Designs for Agricultural Buildings Suited to Irish Estates* which includes eight illustations of cottages or lodges. Given the competence of the designs and the wide cross section of subscribers from the local aristocracy and gentry it is peculiar that none can be identified as having been built. He deserved better and not least for very helpfully including:-

*"Rules for Estimating the Cost of Building the Annexed Designs.*
*Any of the designs built in accordance with the specification appended and in a locality where materials are at hand, labour and workmanship low, and the proprietor is himself the builder, the calculation has been made, that where it does not exceed one story high, $1^1/2$ d. per cubic foot of its contents will be the cost of building such. When it exceeds one storey, 2d. per cubic foot; and where the advantages alluded to above are only in part obtained, $^1/2$d. additional per cubic foot in such case be added.*
*N.B. In ascertaining the cubic contents of any building, in order to arrive at the amount of the estimate, the height of the house is to be taken as only up to half the height of roof and beginning one foot lower than surface".*

Many pattern books gave guidance on the cost of building gate lodges. T.F. Hunt's *Half a Dozen Hints* [1841 reprint] gives prices for picturesque cottages ranging from £255 to £490 *"depending upon embellishment"*. Francis Goodwin in his *Rural Architecture* [3rd. ed. 1850] estimates the cost of a lodge in the Grecian style would vary depending upon the finish chosen;

| | |
|---|---|
| *Brick and Stucco* | *£380* |
| *Brick and Stone Dressing* | *£420* |
| *Stone* | *£560* |

At the upper end of the market, his vast Markree Castle, Sligo entrance extravaganza at £1,000 would be a fair indication of the O'Neills' outlay on the Randalstown gate to Shane's Castle. Closer to home, where labour was cheaper, Sir Richard Morrison offered striking entrance gateways priced between £150 and £350 according to materials used. A Morrison handbill of c1823 advises his fees for professional services to be charged as a percentage of the work value; the design and superintendence of a building including working drawings, etc. - 5%. The same, less superintendence - $2^1/2$%. Travelling charges were rated at one shilling per mile. Alternatively John Nash in 1804 quoted lump sums for cottages at 3 guineas, presumably for designs only!

Around the middle of the 19th century architectural pattern books were gradually displaced by periodicals such as the *Dublin Builder* and its successor the *Irish Builder*, in which architects' work was featured. William Batt's Bladon Park lodge in Antrim appeared in the *Irish Builder* 1st April 1877 and 15th September 1880 and an unexecuted proposal for a lodge to Antrim Castle by William J. Fennell was illustrated in the issue for 1st October 1885. On the 25th July 1884 *Building News* highlighted William J. Unsworth's singular neo-medieval gate lodge to Sion, Tyrone; the *Architect's Journal* as late as 1925 contained an article on the pair of Arts-and-Crafts lodges to Greenmount Agricultural College by Roland Ingelby-Smith. Architects in the late Victorian period also issued compendia of their work as publicity material rather than as source books. John

Birch's *Picturesque Lodges* [1879] was such a book and it included two of his Irish commissions, the lodge to Glenart Castle, Wicklow and White Lodge, Tollymore Park, Down.

The Georgian tradition which had dominated architecture in Ulster in the 18th century was replaced by the 'Revivalism' of the 19th century. The Picturesque lodge was a challenge to the safe style of Georgian symmetry. In architecture the Picturesque almost entirely rejected the classical Georgian past. No more did designers have to distort and twist the internal plans of their lodges to ensure that the facades were evenly balanced around a central axis.

While different styles were considered especially appropriate for certain building types - Gothic for churches, Tudor for schools, Italian Renaissance for civic buildings - for the country house and its gate lodge anything became permissable.

Picturesque comes from "pitteresco" meaning "in the manner of the painters" and it was a concept of 18th century origin which defined a building in a landscape resembling a composition by the painters, Claude or Poussin. Asymmetrical composition was approved of and features suggesting natural growth. The incorporation of sham ruins and Gothick architecture into compositions was encouraged as was eclecticism or borrowing from many styles. It is the antithesis of Classicism and became associated with the rediscovery of medieval styles.

Architectural writers embraced the new style with enthusiasm. James Malton in his pioneering *British Cottage Architecture* [1798] argues that the cottage exterior:

*"... should follow the most convenient internal arrangement of rooms - on a judicious contrast of light and shade does the picturesque in a great measure depend". He goes on to recommend: "A porch at the entrance, irregular breaks in the direction of the walls; one part higher than another; various roofing of different materials thatch particularly, boldly projecting ...".*

Similarly, Robert Lugar in *Sketches for Cottages, Rural Dwellings, Etc.* [1805] advises:

*"The architect, not less than the painter, should feel the true value of varied lines in the contour of buildings and he should frequently compose with the painter's eye .... A lean-to closet, a bow-window, a pent-house, chimneys carried high and in masses, or gable-ends .... suitable Picturesque objects .... will generally produce the wished for effect".*

These utilitarian additions and irregularities in building were the meat of the Picturesque. No longer would the privy be detached, deliberately concealed at an inconvenient distance, now it was to become an attractive lean-to, an important part in the composition.

This period not only coincided with the emergence of the middle classes but also with the growth of a new architectural profession. There had been architects before but architecture had not been a calling with professional and corporate identity.

What a relief it must have been for these early 19th century architects to be released from the strictures of Classicism and given an opportunity to explore the scope afforded by the Picturesque with its variety of plan and elevation. Not all were initially equipped to cope with it. Edward Blore, for all his prowess, got into a tangle in his lodge at Crom Castle, Fermanagh, the interplay of roof pitches failing to give first floor landing headroom. Perhaps the design was entrusted to an office junior and the problem had to be overcome on site with an awkward dormer. He was to employ the same relatively complicated plan soon after at Ballydrain, Antrim, with better results.

One of the virtues of the irregularity of Picturesque design was that it gave small dwellings the appearance of being larger than they were, particularly if a porch or verandah was attached. No longer was a rambling plan form essential to achieve an informal outline. Rockcorry Lodge on the Dartrey demesne is a simple two up, two down design on a rectangular layout with a simple lean-to at the back; but it is given its interesting form by the application of a gable to a front bay, and by means of an eccentrically located porch;a canted bay window is added here and a gablet there, with a pair of diagonally set chimney stacks, all giving the desired effect. Home Lodge at Lough Fea, in the same county is equally successful with another asymmetrically placed entrance porch and the simple device of repositioning the stairs in an octagonal turret expressed on one corner.

There are features which render this style of ornamental cottage instantly recognisable. Foremost is the steeply pitched roof which replaced the shallow-hipped Georgain one and contained the attic rooms in comfort. The gables could have skewtables to portray the Tudor Revival Cottage or alternatively the verges could project to display the most decoratively carved bargeboards in the Old English Domestic manner. Common to both types were label mouldings to the opening and, most revolutionary of all, tiny paned windows invariably fixed in latticed cast iron.

If the pattern book was the most influential factor in the popularity of the Picturesque styles then the impact made by the advent of cast iron was also crucial. Until the 1820s wrought iron had been hammered out by hand in a smithy; it was purpose-made and expensive. By the 1830s cast iron was being mass-produced cheaply and it became possible to simulate the Tudor leaded light, previously only affordable to the rich.

J.C. Loudon in his *Encyclopaedia of Cottage, Farm and Villa Architecture* [1833] advises on availability:

*"windows of cast iron, very fit for cottages, are now made of different forms, and very cheap. (One), which is one foot two inches and a half wide, and two foot four inches high, and weighs 8lbs; cost in London, in 1832, by retail, only 3s.6d. (Another), in the Gothic form, which is one foot four inches wide, and three feet seven inches high, weighs 23 lbs., and costs 6s. ...".*

Arthur Creagh Taylor in his 1841 Irish source book advises *"metal sashes and diamond panes are recommended"*. No reference was made to the appalling lack of natural lighting, although there was some compensation in an increase in size and number of window openings.

Variations on the simple squared or diamond patterns began to appear in the 1840s in oblong, hexagonal and octagonal shapes produced in central Ulster and seen at Corcreevy, Tyrone, Colebrooke and Crocknacrieve, Fermanagh, and Scarvy, Monaghan. There are even more intricate examples at Hawthorn Hill, Armagh and Clifton Lodge, Fermanagh. Not all designs were simply geometrical and many exuberant curvilinear patterns were manufactured in the south of the Province. Elaborate designs appear in Cavan at Stradone and Tullyvin, on the adjacent Leslie properties of Annaghroe, Tyrone and Castle Leslie, Monaghan and also at Annaghmakerrig in the same county. The material continued in use in a type of margined ecclesiastical manner at Clonleigh, Donegal, Tyrella, Down and Drumard, Fermanagh, all dating from the 1860s.

The adaptability, availability and economy of cast iron also brought about a revolution in the variety of railings to be seen substituting for the old quadrant walls which had flanked Georgian entrance gate openings. Designs seemed infinitely varied culminating in the richest and most intricate of patterns especially after the Great Exhibition of 1851.

The early Victorian architect was, therefore, encouraged to embrace the Picturesque and this along with the arrival of cast iron meant that the landowner was able to choose from an assortment of Romantic styles. The main categories of lodge design, although there were many hybrids, can be summarised as Cottage Orné, Old English Cottage, Tudor Revival Cottage, Romantic Castellated, Vernacular Italianate and Swiss Chalet . Each deserves attention.

It is not always easy to differentiate between the Cottage Orné and the Old English Cottage since they are closely related. In Ireland it is particularly confusing. In simple terms Old English lodges can be identified as having roofs sufficiently steeply pitched to contain gable attic windows and fancy bargeboards whereas Cottages Ornés tended to have thatched hipped roofs. If these housed loft bedspace then eyebrow or gablet windows would be incorporated as at Fenaghy, Antrim - a lodge which owed its origin to John Nash and his assistant, George Stanley Repton, who had created the demonstration pieces at Blaise Hamlet, Somerset. This charming cottage at Fenaghy, now lacking its thatch, is derived from Blaise's Oak Cottage, replicating as it does the rustic sitting out area and the mock arrowloops. Similarites were to be found in the little dormered lodge to Oakfield, Donegal, now demolished.

The true Cottage Orné dwelling could rise from a simple rectangular or square plan as did the log cabin versions at Gosford Castle, Armagh, both of which were thatched and had tiny Gothick windows and surrounding verandahs. Alternatively, the mop head roof could disguise a deliberately complex plan such as at Heather Cottage, Castlecoole where the thatch reaches out, its eaves to be carried on timber posts. Here there is relief in a projecting bay with its own thatched topknot (introducing a continuing maintenance burden!)

The pretty example at Corcreevy, Tyrone is totally ruinous. Here was a cross, combining the English Cottage Orné with the Irish vernacular, a bucolic porch cum sitting area being confined to a recess on one external corner. The Cottage Orné was said to be an experiment in incorporating nature into architecture. Sadly at Corcreevy architecture has been incorporated rather too rapidly into nature, testifying to the vulnerability of the type which accounts for its scarcity in Ulster.

Uvedale Price, the Picturesque theorist, warned that anyone could throw up a conventional symmetrical house but a picturesque one, which would depend upon irregular elements tastefully disposed, would require a true architect. Francis Goodwin in his *Rural Architect* [1835] felt that:

*"In this age when Classic Architecture is so universally understood, whoever, thinking for himself, determines to build in the Old English style, may be pronounced a person of independent notions, superior to prejudice, and by inference a man of taste. Notwithstanding the prediliction for the classic or Italian style, he adopts that which poets and painters have always admired".*

The style embraces: gabled, steeply pitched roofs; a characteristic thatch, joined and angled together into an irregular silhouette; decorative curly carved barge-boards, complete with hipknobs; jettied overhanging upper floors; tall elaborate chimney stacks and dormers and diamond patterned windows. No doubt in deference to the local climate it was rare to find half timbering, an exception being at Tynan Abbey, Armagh where the lodge has striking similarities with the Apsley Wood lodge at Woburn Abbey, Bedfordshire. Designed by

Humphry Repton in 1811 this was probably the first recorded cottage in his Old English idiom. It may be no coincidence that Nash, Repton's partner, planned a transformation of Tynan Abbey about 1815.

The park at Tullydoey, Tyrone contains two of the most remarkable lodges of this type. At the north gate, if the improbable datestone of 1793 is to be taken at face value, is the most quaint and precocious of lodges; at the south entrance is another in this idiom, also obligingly dated (1841), which is in the best traditions of T.F. Hunt and P.F. Robinson.

The plans of these lodges often showed relative complexity laying greater emphasis on improving living spaces. The best of this type is to be seen at Rockhill, Donegal, Drumneaske, Monaghan, Cloverhill, Cavan, Willsborough and Moyola, Londonderry and in Antrim at Shane's Castle, Langford Lodge and Kilwaughter Castle. It was not strictly necessary to achieve the Picturesque through an irregularity of plan for some of the most charming lodges have the simplest rectangular plans, the best of which are, or were, at Drumcairne and Martray in Tyrone and Dartrey, Monaghan.

Based on the example of the Tudor manor house or a Cotswold cottage, the Tudor Revival Cottage is a more serious version of the Old English Cottage. On the same informal plan, it had a slated roof, dispensing with flamboyant bargeboards. Instead a skewtable gable of cut stone, for weathering purposes, rose from moulded kneelers to sculpted apex finials, sometimes as ornate as barber's poles. Being more expensive the style was associated with the more aristocratic and wealthier estates. It provided a symbol of wealth, power and taste of the landowner it served. Its extended gable areas were a suitable setting for a family crest, a motto, or often a full-blown coat-of-arms to advertise the status of the owner.

For these reasons many of these lodges were designed by architects. The earliest was that of 1835 by William Henry Playfair, the great Edinburgh architect, to Brownlow House, Armagh, once complete with its buttressed Tudor carriage archway. Other fine examples are at Necarne, Fermanagh probably by William Farrell, at Groomsport, Down by James Sands who possibly also designed those at Carncastle Lodge, Antrim. Other outstanding examples are Anthony Salvin's Bangor Castle lodge, Weightman and Hadfield's for Dunmoyle Lodge, Tyrone, Benjamin Ferrey's Belfast lodge to the Clandeboye estate, and those at The Cottage, Fermanagh and Lough Fea, Monaghan probably by George Sudden.

Another distinctive feature peculiar to the type was the gablet which would be applied in contrived mock form to break the eaves line of single storey cottages. Alternatively on one and a half storey versions the gablet would house an attic window as at P.F. Robinson's Parkanaur lodge, Edward Blore's at Ballydrain, William Burn's Bangor lodge to Clandeboye, and North Lodge at Gosford possibly by John Millar.

The Tudor cottage in the 1840s began to develop curvilinear gables in the Jacobean style. The most ostentatious example can be seen in duplicate at Loughgall Manor, Armagh. William Burn also in 1846 designed two such luxurious lodges for the Dartrey demesne but, sadly, they remain only as seductive perspective illustrations. The local firm of Lanyon, Lynn and Lanyon provided the shaped gables for the lodges at Kintullagh, Antrim and Castle Leslie, Monaghan and it was also to be seen at Fenaghy, Antrim, and on the lodge to the Deaf, Dumb and Blind Institution in Belfast, now demolished.

The Tudor Revival Cottage style was to remain popular until late in the century and beyond. It is perpetuated in William Hastings' two 1876 entrances to Drum Manor, Tyrone, and Young and Mackenzie's at Culloden, Down of 1875. This practice even carried the fancy curved gable into this century on their lodges to the Belvoir Hospital, Down of c1905.

Georgian Gothick ended in a burst of neat symmetry with such lodges as that at Friar's Bush Graveyard. Formality began to be discarded in favour of the irregular outline of real medieval castles. Whilst the earlier Gothick tended to produce flat facades with applied detail, the Romantic Castellated style introduced a refreshing variety of profile and light hearted whimsy to three dimensional exteriors.

Nash again had a pioneering influence in Ulster. The lodge at Killymoon was a composition derived from Humphry Repton's Blaise Castle entrance near Bristol. A simple two-storey castellated lodge was part of a Tudor arched double gateway. Such Regency Gothick entrances tended towards the sensational without regard to authentic medieval forms. This suggests that Nash's most accomplished antiquarian draughtsman, A.C. Pugin, was responsible for the vast castle style entrance to Tynan Abbey, Armagh. Here are rather more correct details in the Irish crenellations to defensive, battered screen walls culminating in square and octagonal towers. On the whole there was little demand for antiquarian correctness it being more important that the castle's outline suggested recognisable motifs such as towers, turrets, battlements, machicolated archways and blind arrowloops.

Lodges were not always a priority in Romantic castle screens. J.B. Keane at Camlin Castle, Donegal (1838) simply tagged one on behind the screen wall. The fairy tale entrance of about 1806 to Convoy House, Donegal, appears to be earlier than the gate lodge alongside. In contrast is the unique lodge to

Norwood Tower, Down, which was a little castle in its own right with incongruous gate piers near by. This exotic style, thought to be in keeping with the rugged Irish scenery, is vividly evoked in William Vitruvius Morrison's remarkable Barbican gatehouse of 1824 at Glenarm Castle, Antrim, which includes porter's accommodation and, with the bridge over the Glenarm river, forms a most dramatic composition.

The Romantic Castellated style reached a climax in the Randalstown Gate to Shane's Castle. Its curtain walls, widespread to terminate in corbelled bartizans, frame the main carriage archway with its portcullis, machicolations and ramparts above. To one side is a huge asymmetrically dominant octagonal watchtower which contains spiral stairs. This, as was a similar unexecuted design by Alfred Jones for Castle Leslie, was clearly influenced by Francis Goodwin's famed entrance to Markree Castle in Co. Sligo where the architect was at pains to justify such a tower on the grounds that it provided a means of telegraphic communications with adjoining estates! They also tended to be designated as flagstaff towers and now serve as very effective television aerials.

Many young English architects had undertaken modest Grand Tours after the Napoleonic wars and sketched in the Tuscan countryside in the 1820s. A consequence was the publication of pattern books such as T.F. Hunt's *Architettura Campestre* [1827] and Charles Parker's *Villa Rustica* [1832-41] which resulted in a passion for the Vernacular Italianate style manifest at the likes of Edensor and Alton Towers in England.

Popular for its loggias, arched entrances, balconies, chunky stone fretwork, belvedere towers, and low pitched roofs, it never gained great popularity as a style for lodges in Ulster. The closest approximations are the single storey lodges to Martlett Towers and Crebilly in Antrim which both have informal plans. At Killadeas, Fermanagh, the strong Italianate style of the big house is only slightly reflected in its lodges as is also the case at nearby Waterfoot and Lisgoole Abbey. Narrow round-headed windows were applied to standard symmetrical structures.

Charles Lanyon and his assistants adapted the loggia to a kind of miniature porte-cochère but fronting a perfectly formal plan. Decorative features were generally confined to exposed rafter ends. The Ulster landowner was not yet ready for the prominent look out tower and it did not make an appearance, and then in High Victorian Gothic vein, until the late 19th century.

The Swiss Chalet style is a Picturesque variant conspicuous for its absence in Ireland. The Ulster landowner and his architect clearly recognised the impracticalities of the Tyrolean low-pitched roofs and timber boarding in the Irish climate and were not influenced by Robinson's *Rural Architecture* [1837] or the design by R. Varden in Loudon's *Designs for Ornamental Cottages* [1846].

In the Faughan Valley, Londonderry, is to be found the most singular gate lodge in the Province. It defies categorisation. It is built in the style of a grotto giving rise to images of the gatekeeper as cave dweller or recluse. There are many such follies on Irish demesnes but, apart from another one at Kilronan Castle, Roscommon, no others conspicuously sited as gate lodges. It is built in rough limestone rather as at Rock Cottage, Baronscourt and Dublin Gate, Lough Fea but was a lot less comfortable with its square one-roomed accommodation. Not surprisingly it lies vacant - a unique eye-catcher with its incongruously sophisticated chimney pot of a later date.

Despite the wealth in choice of styles available, many lodges remained modest. Like the big houses, the number designed by known architects is greatly surpassed by the number of lodges of anonymous authorship particularly up to 1850. Lesser gentry lacking resources to indulge in elaborate lodge building would not seek architectural advice and had no need to fully understand the new styles. They simply applied some Tudor style trappings to the standard Georgian box - label mouldings to openings or exposed rafter toes as at Ballylintagh or Oakley in Down. Other structures were revitalised by the addition of an oversized decorated porch or the insertion of diamond-paned lights as at the neighbouring lodges of Fort Frederick and Virginia Lodge, Cavan.

The traditional lodge was still obstinately being erected in conservative Ulster well into the 1870s. It lingered on, mongrel fashion, at Donaghcloney, Down, with its Tudor cum Classical mix. At Coxtown, Donegal, however, J.B. Keane seems consciously to have created a delightful concoction of medieval windows framing a projecting pedimental hall. Naive innovation is sometimes encountered as at Creevanagh, Tyrone, with its all-embracing label moulding across the three bay front elevation.

In these early Victorian lodges, the main concession to progress was the adoption of gables rather than hips accommodating fancy bargeboards and bedrooms in the attics but not compromising the essentially symmetrical front facade as seen at the main entrance to Dartrey and at John Hargrave's Favour Royal lodge in Tyrone. This solution provided improved accommodation but less generous plans still persisted as at White Hall, Antrim which has two rooms of spartan dimensions and no sign of ostentation. Some architects did concern themselves with the gatekeeper's lot as at Antrim Castle and Seaforde lodges which were fitted with machinery to enable the gates to be opened remotely.

The mid-Victorian period saw both the emergence of new wealth with mill owners, especially in the Bann and

Lagan valleys, requiring lodges for their parks and also the established gentry indulging in the new sport of competitive lodge building. Many large demesnes were expanding the number of entrances from one or two to five or six as at Church Hill, Armagh, Pellipar, Londonderry, Cecil Manor, Tyrone, Ballywalter, Down and Lough Fea, Monaghan. The Shirleys of Lough Fea vied with their neighbours, the Rossmores, both in the size of their houses and also the number of entrances. Lough Fea emerged the winner with a total of seven lodges. The purpose was as much to provide interest in the landscape as to serve a practical end.

The larger properties often required additional lodges to cope with parts of the estate being separated by country roads as at Lough Fea and Purdysburn. Boundary revisions, as at Necarne and Ballywalter, meant the original lodges were superseded by distant replacements. Some landowners, however, simply indulged their architectural taste by opening up a new access and such improvements often date from the succession of an heir or the arrival of a bride, complete with dowry to make it all possible. Hundreds of designs in a bewildering variety of styles were trotted out to meet the frantic and increasing demand.

The 1830s in Ireland saw a rising, young architectural profession including W.V. Morrison, John Hargrave, J.B. Keane, William Farrell and Thomas J. Duff all of whom established thriving country house, and therefore gate lodge, practices. Duff deserves credit for being the first Ulsterman to compete not only with southern counterparts but also with such distinguished practitioners from across the water as Hopper, Blore, Burn and Playfair who continued to pick up important commissions.

All had to respond to the challenge of creating grandeur on a small scale and designing in a mood of deadly seriousness or sloppy sentiment. A choice was required between the orderly and systematic and Romanticism. Eclecticism had become the order of the day, and there was no greater exponent than Thomas Hopper. He was at pains to prove that in matters of style he was not doctrinaire - *"It is an architect's business to understand all styles and to be prejudiced in favour of none"*. At Purdysburn, Down for Narcisius Batt he complemented his pinnacled Tudor Gothick villa with a remarkable gate screen in the same idiom, whilst at the scene of his vast impenetrable neo-Norman castle at Gosford, he was probably responsible by contrast for two flimsy primitive rustic cabins.

At Castle Upton, Antrim the English practitioner Edward Blore coordinated work to the big house with an appropriate formal castellated entrance arch and at Ballydrain, for the Montgomerys, he designed a Tudor Revival lodge in harmony with the contemporary house. On the other hand he paid little heed to the style of Francis Johnston's classical villa of Cloverhill, Cavan or his own castellated Tudor pile of Crom Castle; for both he provided little decorative English cottages at the gates.

Two Edinburgh architects also had Ulster clients. W.H. Playfair furnished complementary lodges for his two Armagh commissions, the Italianate Drumbanagher and Tudorbethan Brownlow. The prolific William Burn was predictably most active of all with work at Clandeboye and Castlewellan in Down and at Dartrey, Monaghan. For Lord Cremorne at Dartrey he had preferred two rich neo-Jacobean designs presented to the client in two appetising perspectives. This was an example of how often the most spectacular proposals remained dreams on paper and it was probably for economic reasons that two relatively modest but attractively bargeboarded cottages were substituted on site. Expense would also seem to have been the reason for local architects Turner and Drew's grandiose suggestions for Montalto, Down being rejected. That landowners agonised over designs for estate entrances is known. The Fordes of Seaforde had proposals prepared in about 1798 by Samuel Woolley for a gate screen, to be updated by Charles Lilly a few years later, but both to be discarded in favour of P.F. Robinson's magnificent triumphal arch and lodge in 1833.

None of these architects, no matter how big the name or busy the practice, found a gate lodge design too menial and most plans are in the principal's hand. One such was the ageing Sir Richard Morrison who came back from a period of obscurity after his son's death to re-enter the architectural fray and prove himself as eclectic as the rest. He produced classical temples, triumphal arches and Tudor Revival cottage designs for Baronscourt and Castlecoole none of which were built, although the Greek rustic cottage at the Thomastown gate and the delightful Cottage Orné Heather Cottage at Castlecoole may be attributed to him.

Very few early estates established before 1850 displayed a consistency of architecture in all their buildings. They did not develop from any overall design concept but rather evolved over many years piecemeal. Succeeding heirs pursued their own personal whims, which usually reflected the fashion of their day, as can be seen at Caledon, Dartrey (or Dawson Grove) and Castle Leslie. Generally only in the smaller estates where lodges were contemporary with the house would they have accorded in style as at Tamnaharry, Down, Parkanaur, Tyrone and at many of Thomas Jackson's villas.

An early exception was Tollymore Park with its plethora of contemporary follies, gate pillars and entrance gates but this was because it changed little from the end of the 18th century, being mainly a summer retreat. There would also be consistency when an architect received a commission to develop a demesne from scratch as William Murray did in classical style for the Earl of Charlemont at Roxborough, Tyrone in the 1840s. William Farrell was in a similarly fortunate situation at Ely Lodge and also at Colebrooke where his buildings are a mixture of classical and Tudor style.

Not only was this apparent haphazard building a reflection of the relative prosperity of a demesne and its continuing expansion but also indicated that both client and architect had experienced a problem in style selection. Humphry Repton had in his *Landscape Gardening* [1803] admitted:

*"I am not ashamed to confess, that I have often experienced more difficulty in determining the form and size of a hovel, or a park entrance, than in arranging the several apartments of a large mansion, indeed, there is no subject on which I have so seldom satisfied my own judgement, as in that of an entrance to a park".*

There was considerable difference of opinion between contemporary writers as to whether there should be compatibility of style in the house and its lodges. P.F. Robinson in the introduction to his *Designs for Lodges and Park Entrances* [1833] states:

*"The Gate Lodge is a feature of considerable importance, in as much as it should indicate the character of the structure to which it affords an approach".*

He was as good as his word at Seaforde, but not so at Baronscourt if, indeed, he was directly involved there. Despite his predilection, like Robinson, for the Picturesque, J.C. Loudon in his *The Suburban and Villa Companion* [1838] is in accord:

*"Good sense dictates that the architecture of the entrance lodge and gates should be in harmony with that of the house ..."* but warns that *" ... in every case the lodge ought to be in a humbler style of design than the more important buildings of the place ..."* and that *"Independently altogether of style, care should be taken that the magnitude and seeming importance of the lodge be not such as to raise false expectations of the magnitude and importance of the house".*

That other pioneer of the Picturesque, T.F. Hunt, was as adamant that the architecture of the house was irrelevant when it came to gate lodge design for in his *Half a Dozen Hints* [1825] he prefaces his designs by stating:

*"... the Old English Domestic style has been preferred to every other as admitting of greater variety of form and outline, and as being better suited to the scenery of this country, than a Greek Temple or Italian Villa".*

There were other theorists of the Picturesque who also believed that the lodge should be designed in sympathy with its own location rather than in style with the big house.

In order that the great landed proprietor could announce his status and aesthetic good taste to the passer by, it was imperative that his entrance gates be so positioned as to have maximum impact. One way of achieving this objective was to locate the access to his demesne at a road junction. At Castledillon the twin lodges are apparent from afar on the approach to a T junction. Most impressive of all is William Hasting's main arched entrance to Drum Manor stopping a long straight vista on the road from Cookstown before it divides in two directions to skirt the estate.

Alternatively the gate screen could be situated at a bend in the carriageway which would be aligned on an axis with the demesne avenue before diverting away. This is a contrivance seen to best effect at the massive castellated access to the Tynan Abbey grounds on the road from Middletown and on a rather reduced scale in Francis Johnston's triumphal arch at Cloverhill, Cavan. The most modest example may be the gates to White Hall with their tiny lodge at the Broughshane approach.

Most impressive of all is the use of the main street as a continuation of the estate road where the proprietor's gates act as a focal point. The best and most convincing examples are at Town Gate, Carrowdore Castle, Down and Seaforde where the great Greek triumphal arch appears to have formed part of an overall estate strategy when much of the village was rebuilt concurrently. The maturing of the tree-lined avenue approach has somewhat reduced the original impact. In Castleblayney, Monaghan, access to the Hope demesne is between two estate houses flanking the entrance at the head of West Street which continues on to the big house.

Apart from the information given about the Baronscourt estate in the Abercorn papers, the identity of the people who lived in these early lodges is rarely known. The lodges were normally held rent-free, and only in rare cases in Griffith's Valuation in the mid 19th century are they named, most being included with the 'big house', the rates being paid by the landlord. The use to which lodges were put is not always as obvious as one would first think, many having had a dual function. For all their diminutive dimensions some were used as schools. The Doric temple lodge at Caledon was probably originally envisaged and built to serve as a school. This may also have been the case at Murvagh, Donegal. 'Logan's Lodge' at Drenagh, Londonderry may also have been pushed into service for that purpose after its erection c1830. The Ordnance Survey for that period tells us that from 1832 the schoolmistress was the gatekeeper's wife, Sarah McAfee. Doubtless this was when the Tudor Gothick building was extended. The decorative cottage at the secondary entrance to Tyrella, Down may first and foremost have been a 'smithy' as it is so noted on the second Ordnance Survey map.

Almost without exception these little structures are

devoid of any internal ornamentation unless it resulted from the all-important external appearance. The prettiest of effects is created by the decorative glazing patterns of William Farrell's secondary lodge to Colebrooke. Again at 'Logan's Lodge', Drenagh the latticed lancet windows are enhanced with panelled wooden reveals. Occasionally a moulded coving was permitted as in the early Castledillon pair, and, much later on, at W.H. Lynn's lodges to Campbell College, Down and in the Milford Manor building, Armagh.

The coming of the railways from the 1840s onwards had an impact on the estates. The first rush of enthusiasm for the railways meant some gate lodges were swept away where the track skirted a demesne as at Greenmount, Antrim. Another example is Castleblayney, Monaghan but here the line was laid along an estate avenue. Sometimes a new lodge was built to supersede an original as at Glenmore, Antrim around 1840, or in Castlecaldwell, Fermanagh. There in about 1866 the lodge was constructed along with the railway embankment and the composition incorporated a bridge as carriage arch with a pedestrian access tunnel alongside - a unique solution probably subsidised by the railway company by way of compensation. Another spin off of the arrival of the train was that it opened up remoter parts of the country encouraging previously absentee landlords who owned estates to build on them.

There was also the phenomenon of the provision of 'unnecessary' stations as at Helen's Bay, Down where the Blackwoods of Clandeboye erected a remarkable structure designed by the English architect Benjamin Ferrey in c1855; a station which could be seen as being an additional estate building or lodge. This was approached by a lengthy avenue which, where it crossed the Belfast to Bangor road, necessitated a set of gates and a gate lodge, 'Belfast Lodge', to house the porter.

Until the 1830s gate lodges proliferated where land was most productive and wherever the aristocracy and gentry established themselves and enclosed their demesnes. They were located by lough sides and river valleys which had provided the principal places for settlement and areas for better building. Here also the water power produced great mills, owners' houses and porters' lodges.

By the 1850s the middle and upper classes in Ulster were, unlike the rest of Ireland, enjoying a period of prosperity and expansion despite frequent famines. The disaster of the Great Famine (1845-49) whilst casting a dreadful shadow over the country as a whole, affected mainly the south and west of the Province. Donegal, being the most backward and poorest county, and south Armagh, where the standard of living was as low, suffered most. The prosperous north-east escaped relatively unscathed. In any case building activities were not greatly affected, for many works were carried out by landlords as famine relief schemes.

Many new fortunes were made in the industrial cities. The new linen, ship-building and iron founding magnates wanted to live outside the town. They aspired to grand suburban villas within easy travelling distance of the city, and to which they might ultimately retire. In the mid-19th century the new mercantile class was within reach of the new centres of industry, where, outside Belfast, they formed enclaves like Strandtown and ribbon developments along the Malone, Holywood and Shore roads, and at Londonderry on both banks of Lough Foyle. In this period lodge building was at its height. In the thirty years between the two Ordnance Surveys in Londonderry, Down and Antrim, where land was most fertile and industry was booming, the number of gate lodges trebled. Even in Armagh, Fermanagh, Monaghan and Tyrone they doubled. In the poorer counties of Donegal and Cavan there was a thirty percent increase.

By this time many architects who practiced in the first half of the century had disappeared from the scene. John Hargrave had drowned in 1833; William Vitruvius Morrison had predeceased his father by eleven years, Sir Richard having died in 1849. The previous year Thomas Duff had also passed away prematurely and J.B. Keane and William Farrell became less productive. This clean sweep left the field open for a new generation of home-grown practitioners to emerge and follow Duff's lead.

Victorian architects such as Charles Lanyon, Thomas Turner, W.H. Lynn as well as Thomas Jackson came to the fore. Jackson was the single most prolific of Ulster's architects who, after putting aside the Tudor Gothick influence of his short-term partner Thomas Duff, designed in neo-classical mode for thirty years. Although the Picturesque style had been taken up with enthusiasm elsewhere, there remained an unwillingness to break with the architecture of Greece and Rome particularly among the new conservative mercantile class. Jackson continued to find patrons, particularly in the Quaker community, convinced of the old classical values. His villas with their stuccoed walls had matching lodges in strict symmetry, and can be found over half the Province, the embodiment of the commercial wealth and seriousness of mid-Victorian Ulster. Only later in the century under the influence of his sons in the practice did his work lose some of its stiffness, as seen in the irregular Italianate lodges of Lismachan and Drum House, Down.

Alongside Jackson, dominating the architectural scene, was Charles Lanyon who pioneered the Italian Palazzo style modelled on the example of Charles Barry in London. He produced his cruciform planned lodges with their distinctive porte-cochères in harmony with his mansions of Dunderave and Moneyglass in Antrim and Ballywalter and Eglantine in Down. Lanyon had as young assistants Thomas Turner and W.H. Lynn who were to branch out on their own in 1851 and 1872 respectively. It may have been the latter who devised a hipped roof version of this genre at Lismara, Cromore and Gardenvale, all in Antrim whilst Turner designed a beautifully sculpted variant at Craigavad, Down. As Sir Charles Lanyon began to follow other pursuits, his son John from 1860 exerted considerable influence in the practice. A master of the smaller lodge composition, he was probably responsible for the greater flexibility of plan in the curly-gabled Jacobean style lodges of Castle Leslie, Monaghan and Kintullagh, Fenaghy and the Deaf, Dumb and Blind Institution, all in Antrim.

After the 1860s as land within easy commuting distance of Belfast became expensive, the entrepreneurs or their sons saw the opportunity for further money to be made, selling off portions of their parks, often as little as an acre at a time, for yet another villa to materialize complete with its obligatory status symbol, the porter's lodge. Many were simply objects of ostentatious pomposity. They were built on modest plots of land close to the main house and so began to lose their original function. The street directories of the day often record the occupants to be coachmen or gardeners.

Neo-Classicism remained popular in an increasingly robust and rich form to be found in Thomas Jackson's lodges to Seapark, Antrim and Trewmount, Tyrone and at Thornhill, Antrim and Strathearn, Down both probably by Young and Mackenzie. The English Domestic Cottage style lived on at Murlough, Down and at Stranmillis House, Antrim with its variety of finishes to the design of Lanyon, Lynn and Lanyon. A new range of building materials made possible a new style to rival those already established - the High Victorian Gothick. Its Revivalist proponents found it worked not only for churches but also for smaller domestic buildings. There is no finer example of this than the lodge and archway to Kilmore Cathedral, Cavan by the English architect William Slater.

The most prominent Ulster architects to be influenced by the writings of John Ruskin were W.J. Barre and W.H. Lynn. They drew on many medieval sources from the Lombardic Romanesque at Weir's Bridge lodge, Castlecoole to the Venetian in Barre's pioneering work in polychromatic brick at Belmont Church lodge in Belfast. He also designed an exuberant pointed entrance screen in cast iron and imported sandstone at the Antrim Road access to Fortwilliam Park. Inside these gates Barre placed an innovative lodge with dominant tower over the entrance hall, complete with belfry stage below a step pyramidal road which was to be imitated by many architects after his untimely death in 1867.

Perhaps the purest and richest Venetian Gothick lodges to be found in Ulster are the immaculately finished buildings at the Roman Catholic cathedrals of St. Patrick's, Armagh and St. Macarten's, Monaghan. These depended less upon contrasting materials for effect than on a subtle use of various stone finishes and sculpted bas-relief overpanels to openings. Lynn's pretty, unexecuted proposal, like a chapel in miniature, and the one probably by Thomas Drew that was built at Ballydrain, were both in a typical pointed manner.

In the last quarter of the century there were signs of increasing popularity of idiosyncratic eclecticism. The late Victorian architects acquired a cold-blooded facility to imitate and mix every style. Lodges began to appear in bewildering varieties that defy classification. In all shapes and sizes, colours and textures, they often failed to relate to their settings. The Tudor Revival cum Classical combination at Coolnafranky, Tyrone and Thomas Turner's Scots Baronial Italianate mixture at Stormont are examples. Although the Tudor Revival carried on in the short-lived gate lodge to Queen's College, Belfast and in W.H. Lynn's masterpiece at the main entrance to Campbell College, it tended to be absorbed in the Scots Baronial fervour of the 1870s.

Along with all this affectation there was a tendency for the lodge to be heavier and more monumental. The result was an increase in the scale of the structure sufficient to apply all these new-found devices. This meant not just an increase in ceiling heights but a greater generosity in accommodation. A more responsible attitude to working class living conditions became apparent. Most gatehouses now boasted two bedrooms and more than one living room in addition to the kitchen. The rich had begun to express their wealth in concern for their employees.

As noted earlier, no longer was detailing dependent upon locally available materials. They were supplemented by many imported stones, employed in combination with local brick to provide a polychrome effect. Affectionately called 'streaky bacon' such banding could be repeated by using both Bangor Blue and Westmoreland Green slates to enhance steeply pitched roofs as seen on William Batt's lodges to Bladon Park and Botanic Gardens, Antrim. In the latter asymmetry was of the essence, and was achieved by a dominant tower with its French Renaissance roof. Rarely at this scale could such a vertical emphasis accommodate a staircase. Rather it gave emphasis to the entrance porch and perhaps housed aloft a water tank, or in the case of the Botanic Gardens example, a clock and machinery. Similar features were applied to lodges at Clanwilliam, Antrim, Tandragee, Armagh and Thomas Turner's Stormont Castle lodge, Down. All terminated in distinctively tall pyramidal cappings.

Further technological innovations saw the emergence of special decorative bricks and tiles employed to effect in enhancing lodges such as William Fennell's exercise in red at Finnebrogue, Down, and to the gables of the commodious gabled affair to Drumglass, Antrim.

The Picturesque English Cottage style persisted in robust fashion at Moyallon, Down and two lodges at Larchfield in the same county but augmented by a squashed French Gothic column at each porch, a feature repeated on John Lanyon's otherwise Scots Baronial Belfast Castle lodge. These continental Gothick features appeared also in colonettes to windows at Clanwilliam and on gate pillars at Alexandra Park, Belfast. Bargeboards tended to be larger and more vigorously carved often in bas-relief as at Wilmont, Antrim.

At Bloomhill, Tyrone is the most singular of lodges with its combination of High Victorian Gothick fenestration below sturdy decorative bargeboards to hipped gables, a magnificent piece of conceit by an unknown architect. Another tour-de-force is John Lanyon's exquisite little lodge to Methodist College, Belfast, another variation on the theme with its conical-roofed brick stair turret.

The 1870s saw a resurgence of the Classical style. To vie with the new Gothick of northern Italy with its pointed openings there was a renaissance of rounded arches from the south the reintroduction of which seems to have been principally due to a Glaswegian architect, James Hamilton. He had been successful in an architectural competition for the Ulster Bank in Waring Street, Belfast in a sumptuous Palladian style. This has been repeated in the triumphal Shore Road entrance to Fortwilliam Park. Old photographs give glimpses of an arcaded Italianate lodge alongside, both here and to the nearby gates of Dunlambert, Antrim, both sadly gone. Also within the park, still surviving, is the lodge to Walton displaying further stylistic similarities. Hamilton's other large work in Belfast is the Ewart's warehouse where he displays Greek influence. Also in Fortwilliam Park is the lodge to Kileen which is reminiscent of the work of Alexander "Greek" Thomson, a compatriot of Hamilton to whom it can be attributed. These examples all tended to be applied to an informal plan as are those at Galwally, Down of about 1885 and Ballywalter, a design probably by William Fennell c1900, the completion of which signalled the end of this style in the Province. Ten years previously was built the most sumptuous of all classical lodges in Ulster in the columned excesses of the Dunville Park lodge, Antrim, which was in the form of an octagonal Ionic temple and is now tragically demolished.

Alexander "Greek" Thomson's influence is felt more directly in his 'fairy tale' mood at Ballygarvey, Antrim, Drumindoney, Down and Beech Hill, Londonderry, all probably copied by local architects. The Picturesque cottage of his later years is also to be seen at Ballykillaire, Down and Redburn in the same county, the latter probably adapted by John Lanyon with its prettily fretted gable apex spandrels and essential low pitched roofs.

It is in the work of the younger Lanyon and his partner W.H. Lynn that we see the sheer versatility that was expected of the Victorian architect, for they were to become masters of another new stylistic fashion, the Scots Baronial. Small wonder that the style was to prove a most popular import given the history in Ulster of the Scottish planters. It was clearly acceptable here more than in the rest of Ireland. The style had evolved during the Jacobean Revival in England and it is evident in two early examples here by Scottish practitioners. William Spence furnished just such a lodge to his miniature baronial castle at Elmfield, Down and in the same county David Bryce of Edinburgh probably designed another to complement his mansion, Ormiston. Both, unlike their respective big houses, were perfectly symmetrical but characteristically displaying prominent crow-stepped gables. It was left to local architects to show just how a picturesque outline could be applied to the small dwelling.

A prerequisite of the genre was that it be composed of rugged quarry-faced masonry to complement all the essential ingredients of crenellations, machicolations, corbelled bartizans and turrets. These latter features can be seen with their round 'candle-snuffer' conical roofs at the delightful Lanyon, Lynn and Lanyon compositions at Belfast Castle, Killyleagh Castle and the People's Park, Ballymena, all contrived to give the most exciting of silhouettes. The practice also designed the semi-detached twin-gable cottages at Castle Leslie. Another good example was to be found at Kincraig on Belfast's Antrim Road. At Magherintemple, Antrim, the architect (probably Samuel Pepys Close) contented himself with hewn stone and crow-stepped gables on a standard plan. Thomas Turner, although he had first-hand knowledge of the style being briefly in practice in Glasgow, was almost as subdued in his informal structures for Stormont and Thornhill, Londonderry.

The final style that the Victorian architect was to add to his repertoire was that based on the English domestic Elizabethan vernacular cottage. Distinctive for its half timbered or 'black and white' work usually to gabled upper storeys jettied out beyond the ground floor, it had originated in the Low Countries before spreading to England and even beyond to Ulster with the Elizabethan settlers. Whilst all of these have either been destroyed or rendered over when no longer in vogue, it was to be a style which was to become a forerunner of umpteen suburban bungalows popular in the early part of this century. Dubbed 'Stockbroker Tudor' it is enjoying yet another revival today but not as authentically as in the hands of the Victorians.

Pioneered by English architects Richard Norman Shaw, Eden Nesfield and John Douglas, it was popularised through exposure in architectural journals. Although there were early examples in the Province at Lemnagore lodge, Tynan Abbey and Lanyon, Lynn and Lanyon's Stranmillis cottage of c1860, it did not come into vogue until the 1880s. John Birch's White Lodge at Tollymore of 1876 slightly predates the period. The style was marked also by its tall modelled, red brick chimneys, oriel windows and verandahed porches with their turned wooden posts and balustrades. Another feature was the earthenware tile for roof covering and vertical hanging along with its accessories in ornamental ridge cresting, sawtoothed, lobbed or perforated with decorative apex finials. All these characteristics are seen at their best at Dullerton, Londonderry and the Manor House, Milford, Armagh but the purest example is at Sion, Tyrone for this is a copy of the medieval gate house to Stokesay Castle, Shropshire by another English architect William F. Unsworth.

The style was to endure into the Edwardian era and beyond in the hands of Henry Hobart at Conway Antrim and in identical gate lodges to the Cowan Herron Hospital, Down and his Lurgan Park, Armagh and in Watt and Tulloch's design for Crawfordsburn. At Ashfield, Cavan, McCurdy and Mitchell as late as 1932, produced a notable example of this style.

The 20th century in Ulster inevitably saw a dramatic scaling down of lodge building. The nobility and gentry were worse off than they had ever been; the Industrial Revolution had passed to give way to the slump; cheap labour was no longer available and the traditional skills of craftsmen were being lost. However, a handful of lodges were added to the landed estates although the gate lodge was now chiefly represented at the entrances to public buildings, particularly to schools. In these a new image was sought far from the brashness of the late Victorian era. Gone were Ruskinian Gothick, Italianate and the Scots Baronial, their vocabularies exhausted. This was a period of elegance and simplicity, its inspiration being found in the classical. Perfect symmetry was again universally accepted for the first time for three-quarters of a century.

The Queen Anne style saw a '... renaissance' in the perfectly balanced three bay lodge of 1938 to Clifton House, Antrim, a design with its correct broken pediment highlighted by mutules carried around as eavesbrackets. At Malone, Antrim is Blackwood and Jury's little masterpiece of 1921, one and a half storey with symmetrical chimneys and dormers, in Ulster pebbledash with classical trim. At Eldon Green (c1901) by Vincent Craig for himself and Carrowshane (c1930) both in Down the style is applied to rather less formal plans.

The neo-Georgian fashion with its fine lines and subtlety of detail was in greatest demand when allied to the popular new rustic clay brick and matching roof tiles. Here is a rebirth of the mid-Georgian cube pavilion to be seen at Ventnor, Antrim and Purdysburn hospital, T.F.O. Rippingham's Stranmillis Training College, Antrim and Arnold Thornley's delicate Portland stone essays at the gates to Parliament Buildings, Stormont. In the same vein, below their pyramidal roofs, is a series of lodges built in the interwar years to public elementary schools at Avoniel, Elmgrove and Nettlefield all in east Belfast and by the Ministry of Education architect R.S. Wilshere.

Evidence of the Arts and Crafts movement in Ulster is most noticeable in Robert Graeme Watt's structures for Kirkassock, Down and in the distinctive gate piers and gate house to Loughanmore, Antrim by an unknown architect. The influence of notable English practitioners of this period can be detected in James Hanna's novel creation at Glenganagh, Down where C.F.A. Voysey's favourite combination of sandstone and whitewashed roughcast is evident, although he would hardly have approved of the inclusion of the classical porch.
In the same vein is the charming cottage at Marble Hill, Donegal.

In 1916 Roland Ingelby-Smith introduced a flavour of Edwin Lutyens to the Province in the impressive pair of sturdy stone lodges to Greenmount Agricultural College, Antrim. John McGeagh's formal interpretation of Lutyens' famous vernacular cottage style of Munstead Wood, in 1953 at Tudor Hill, Antrim with its sensitive handling of brick and leaded lights, is a fitting finale to gate lodge building in Ulster.

# Guide to the Gazetteer

Entries are numbered and listed county by county for ease of reference. Each heading gives the *NAME* of the property with its *LOCATION*. This heading (or subheading where there is more than one lodge) is followed by a *DATE* of the building's construction its *ARCHITECT* and, should there be little or nothing evident on site, its *CONDITION*. Proposals which remain *UNEXECUTED* are also indicated. An *ILLUSTRATION* generally precedes the *DESCRIPTION* and *REFERENCES* complete the entry.

*NAME*
Title of house, demesne or institution with which a lodge is associated.

*LOCATION*
The nearest town or village. Entries in proximity of Londonderry city are labelled East or West depending upon their situation in relation to the Foyle river. Similarly those within the greater Belfast area in the counties of Antrim and Down are categorised North or South of a line of longitude passing through the City Hall.

*DATE*
Where a datestone or documentary evidence is lacking, the date of construction is deduced from visual assessment. If the lodge has been demolished, or is so ruinous or altered as to be unrecognisable, a date is given as "pre" that of the earliest Ordnance Survey map on which it appears. Occasionally if a gate lodge is referred to in the Griffith Valuation offering a more accurate date of erection this is noted. (For publication dates of the Ordnance Survey Maps and Griffith valuations see the bibliography).

*ARCHITECT*
In the absence of a documentary source, attributions are made on stylistic grounds or on the evidence of other associated building activities. Such ascriptions are made with varying degrees of certainty ranging from "perhaps" through "possibly" to "probably". "Architect not known" indicates a design sufficiently sophisticated to suggest the hand of a professional architect or talented amateur but with no attribution possible.

*CONDITION*
This is recorded solely where a lodge was discovered to be demolished or ruinous at the time of the visit although some may have gone or deteriorated since.

*ILLUSTRATIONS*
Photographs and drawings are by the author unless otherwise credited. Note of the original architect, artist or photographer is followed (in parenthesis) by the owner or holder of such material. Most architecturally important lodges are illustrated. Some of lesser merit have been included because they are now demolished and any record is considered of importance.

*DESCRIPTION*
In addition to describing the structure in detail an attempt has been made to relate it to other building phases on the estate, the big house and to the family, proprietor or patron responsible. Over 2000 sites have been visited in the course of this study and some have, of necessity, not been surveyed for some time. Changes may have occurred in the interval especially in urban areas.

*REFERENCES*
Abbreviated sources refer to the main bibliography.

*ABBREVIATIONS:-*

| | |
|---|---|
| A.J. | The Architect's Journal |
| B.N. | The Building News |
| B.N.L. | Belfast Newsletter |
| B.T. | Belfast Telegraph |
| D.B. | The Dublin Builder |
| H.M.B.B. | Historic Monuments and Buildings Branch, Dept. of the Environment for Northern Ireland |
| I.A.A. | Irish Architectural Archive |
| I.B. | The Irish Builder |
| N.L.I. | National Library of Ireland |
| N.T. | National Trust |
| O.S.M. | Ordnance Survey Memoirs |
| P.R.O.N.I. | Public Record Office of Northern Ireland |
| R.I.B.A. | Royal Institute of British Architects; Drawings Collection |
| R.P.B. | Royal Pavilion Museum and Art Gallery, Brighton |
| U.A.H.S. | Ulster Architectural Heritage Society |
| U.F.T.M. | Ulster Folk and Transport Museum |
| U.J.A. | Ulster Journal of Archaeology |
| U.M. | Ulster Museum |

# COUNTY ANTRIM

**1. THE ABBEY, Whiteabbey**
pre 1832; *demolished*
A lodge to the house of Richard Davison. Later the residence of Sir Charles Lanyon.

**2. ABBEYDENE, Newtownabbey**
(see LISMARA)

**3. ABBEYLANDS, Whiteabbey (2)**
Since its acquisition from the Haslet family in 1803 the property has seen a succession of houses for the McCalmonts, the present one a rebuild of that burnt by the suffragettes early this century.
**South Lodge** pre 1832; *demolished*
**North Lodge** pre 1857; *demolished*
The lodges fell victim to the Roads Service widening of the Shore Road. Both built by Hugh McCalmont.
O.S.M.; YOUNG (1909); McTEAR (1898)

**4. ABBEYVALE, Jordanstown**
pre 1857; *demolished*
The property in 1860 of Gilbert Vance.

**5. ABBEYVILLE, Whiteabbey**
pre 1857; *demolished*
The house was erected in 1826 by Maxwell Lepper. Passed from a Mrs Sinclair to the Bland family who built the lodge.
McTEAR (1898)

**6. ABBOTSCROFT, Newtownabbey**
pre 1857; *demolished*
A lodge for the McTear family.

**7. ABERDELGHY COTTAGE, Lambeg (2)**
At the heart of the Lagan valley once made prosperous by the linen industry, Mr Henry Bell, linen merchant, built the house in 1815 and subsequently improved the premises with the addition of a gate lodge.
**Lambeg Lodge** c1833; architects probably Thomas J Duff & Thomas Jackson; *demolished*
A delightful, Picturesque Tudor style cottage on the main road. This was in the P. F. Robinson manner adopted by Thomas J. Duff the Newry architect, seen also at Tamnaharry and Narrowater, (qqv) both in Co. Down. Of standard plan with slated gabled roof and porch, all decorated with pretty fretwork bargeboards which abound in Lambeg culminating in hipknobs. Rendered walls had label mouldings over the mullioned windows of small square panes. Clearly a hybrid of the brief architectural liaison between Duff and Thomas Jackson between 1830 and 1835, the fine stone hexagonal gate pillars, which alone survive, have "helmet" caps and recessed panels, much favoured by the latter, but cuspidated to reflect the lodge. Nice plain gates and spear-topped wrought iron railings in an ogee sweep. Not long after this Jackson was busy designing gate lodges for the neighbouring Glenmore House (qv) in his Neo-Classical style. Sadly only a council rosebed in memorium marks the site, with the "handsome winding avenue" noted in the 1837 O.S. memoirs, to this once charming small park, disused and leading nowhere in particular.
**Bell's Lane Gate** pre 1900; *demolished*
The lodge opposite the gates built by Alexander Airth Richardson after he came by the property.
B.N.L PHOTOGRAPH 19/7/1961; O.S.M.

**8. AHOGHILL GLEBE, Ahoghill** c1840
To an earlier glebe-house of 1815 a simple little three bay, hipped roof Georgian style lodge. Notable for its unusually sensitive modern extension in the form of a twin with a flat-roofed link. Probably built for Rev. George Kirkpatrick.
LEWIS (1837)

**9. ALEXANDRA PARK, Belfast North**
c1885; architect probably J C Bretland

Named in honour of the Princess of Wales' visit, this 20 acre public park was laid out in 1885 by J C Bretland, the Borough Surveyor who may also have designed the superintendant's lodge and gates. The lodge is one and a half storey, T shaped on plan in sooty uncoursed squared quarry-faced limestone. All openings have dressed stone shouldered arches. Single storey canted bay and lean-to hall, below a dinky dormer in a steeply-pitched roof behind skewtable gables. Four superb Gothic Revival square piers in pink sandstone dressed with smooth limestone. Engaged colonettes, each having a variety of exquisitely sculpted capitals of foliage, roses, convolvulus, ferns, berries, nuts, fruit and things; culminating in buff sandstone poppy finials over cappings with lancet gablets. The lodge a shell. There are plainer versions of both at Falls Park. (qv)
LAWRENCE PHOTOGRAPH (NLI).
Refs 3863(R) and 3866(R)

**10. ALLENBROOK, Larne**
(See MILLBROOK LODGE)

**11. ANNAVILLE, Ballycastle**
(see CARNSAMPSON)

**12. ANTRIM CASTLE, Antrim (3)**
**Main Entrance** 1818; architect probably John Bowden

The main entrance from the town, through a "Hampton Court" Tudor style gatehouse of 1818. A dramatic piece of street scenery, long associated with and crucial to Antrim town. Now dilapidated and shown scant respect. In squared uncoursed basalt rubble with limestone dressings. Heavy, iron-studded double doors below a Tudor archway with label moulding. Flanking it octagonal turrets, each housing a spiral stairs, pierced by loopholes topped by crenellated parapets enclosing conical roofs, now gone. These stairs led to accommodation over a stuccoed ribbed vault, from which the porter could observe approaching visitors through a wide quartered window and operate the doors by means of a wheel mechanism, with a minimum of disturbance. The Dublin architect John Bowden largely rebuilt the castle in 1813 for Chichester, 4th Earl Massereene but upon his death three years later the Viscountcy devolved upon his daughter Harriet who carried on the building work. She married the 2nd Viscount Ferrard, and a sketch for a gateway among the Ferrard papers suggests that Bowden was retained to design the gateway, sufficient to incorporate the arms of the united families over the arch.
**Randalstown Road Gate**
c1825; *demolished*
Off the Randalstown road a standard plan, three bay lodge with label mouldings to openings, demolished by the local council.

Postcard (A. Rankin)

*Antrim Castle, Main Entrance*

The Irish Builder

**Proposed Lodge** 1885;
W. J. Fennell; *unexecuted*
In 1885 William J Fennell, a Belfast architect, had a design published in the Irish Builder, possibly intended to replace the secondary lodge for the 11th Viscount of Massereene and Ferrard. It shows an irregular Picturesque one and a half storey High Victorian composition in stone with Scottish overtones. Armorial bearings decorate crowstepped gables, one of which is topped by a coronet finial; dominated by a bracketed pyramidal-roofed square tower rising above the entrance hallway.
ANTRIM & BALLYMENA; U.A.H.S. (1969); O.S.M.; PILSON (1846); I.B. (1885)

**13. ANTRIM NEW CEMETERY, Antrim**
c1880
In the main one and a half storey, a single storey projection to the road forms a T plan. Gabled roof carried down over the internal corner in a catslide to form an open porch, now enclosed. Roughcast walls with brick dressings to chamfered openings and quoins. Good solid perimeter wall and three square entrance pillars in squared uncoursed quarry-faced basalt with sandstone friezed cappings. Fine no nonsense spear-topped cast iron gates.

**14. ANTRIM R.C. CHURCH, Antrim**
pre 1832; *demolished*
Probably demolished in 1870 when the present church replaced the previous 1818 structure on Bow Lane.

**15. AQUINAS HALL, Belfast South**
(see DUNARNON)

**16. ARDNABREEN, Ballymena** c1920
Modest, half-timbered effect building.

**17. ARDNAVEIGH, Antrim**
(see BIRCH HILL)

**18. ARDOYNE, Belfast North**
pre 1901; *demolished*
Once the seat of the Andrews family.

**19. ASHLEIGH/ARLINGTON, Belfast South** c1856; *demolished*
Once a long straight private avenue from the Lisburn Road led to a pair of large semidetached mid-Victorian villas. Probably a speculative venture by the building contractor James Henry. Later combined to house Ashleigh House School before their recent demolition.

**20. AVONMORE LODGE, Lisburn**
pre 1900; *demolished*
Built by Henry John Garrett.

**21. BALLEE, Ballymena**
pre 1857; *demolished*
A property in 1856 of Thomas Casement.

**22. BALLINLIG, Cushendall** pre 1857
A lodge for the McDonnell family in the valley of Glenariff. Latterally called Kilmore. Opposite the gates a single storey, three bay symmetrical structure with a gabled roof. Constructed of rubble stone it now lies derelict serving as a sheep shelter.

**23. BALLYDIVITY, Derrykeighan**
pre 1932; *demolished*
Built for James Stewart Moore perhaps when additions to the house were carried out in about 1810.
O.S.M.

**24. BALLYDRAIN, Dunmurry (3)**
When Hugh Montgomery acquired this Stewart estate in the early 1830s he set about building here a house more stately than he found and chose the eminent English architect Edward Blore to design it. From 1834 to 1839, whilst also working at Castle Upton (qv) in the same county and Crom Castle, Co. Fermanagh (qv), he visited the site four times to liaise with his client and supervise the works which later ran to designs for gates and a lodge (to replace an older one across the avenue) in the same Tudor Revival style as the house.
**Belfast Lodge** c1838;
architect Edward Blore; *demolished*

K. Brown

One and a half storey, two up three down, on an informal plan identical to the one also employed at Crom Castle Co. Fermanagh (qv), although the latter is in the English ornamental cottage mode. In squared coursed quarry-faced basalt, the skewtable gables, window mullions and transoms were in dressed sandstone. The large external chimney-breast rose up to terminate in a pair of diagonal stacks just like the house. From the living room sight of the gates was from a stone roofed canted bay with a gablet over. Alongside projected a little gabled hallway, over the Tudor doorway of which was a crest with the motto "Gardez Bien". A peculiar tower pierced the single storey roof to give staircase landing headroom. Gable apexes had Blore's favourite "top-knot" finial features as had the gate pillars, two of which did not survive World War II requisition. Upon the demesne's acquisition for a golf course, not only were appalling indignities inflicted on the house, with removal of mullions, transoms, balustrading and chimney stack features, but the lodge was unaccountably demolished in 1966 - ironic considering present security problems. (For floor plans see under Crom Castle, Co. Fermanagh).
The estate wall was erected in 1841.
**Proposed Lisburn Lodge** c1876;
architect W H Lynn; *unexecuted*

W. H. Lynn drawing (P.R.O.N.I.)

In 1876 W H Lynn extended the house and drew up a proposal for a lodge at the stableyard avenue entrance. A charming ecclesiastical Tudor Gothick essay with buttresses and lattice-paned windows. He nevertheless shows a disgraceful disregard for basic comforts in his ladder access from a ground floor cupboard to the minute attic bedroom over.
**Lisburn Lodge** c1880; architect probably Sir Thomas Drew; *demolished*

P. Rankin

This tiny mid-Victorian Gothick building, which may have been adapted by Sir Thomas Drew from an earlier unexecuted design to suit this awkward sloping site, had one room up and the other below as a basement room. Again in quarry-faced basalt squared and uncoursed, with sandstone skewtable gables and window dressings carried up as pointed relieving arches. The shamrock motif in the front door spandrel repeated in the terracotta ridge cresting. The pair of brick chimney stacks were octagonal, matching the fine wooden gate posts, with ornamental gate. Very pretty but predictably unappreciated by its new owner, it was taken down in yet another piece of vandalism in 1964.
BLORE; BLACK (1984); COLVIN (1978); P.R.O.N.I. D1954/7/2;

**25. BALLYGARVEY, Ballymena**
**Old Main Entrance** c1850; architect possibly Thomas Jackson; *demolished*
The lodge, to what was the previous and now disused entrance, has gone. The isolated, surviving octagonal gate piers with recessed panels and helmet cappings are typical of Thomas Jackson's work.
**New Main Entrance** c1870; architects probably Young & MacKenzie
The reworked house is of about 1870 for the Currell family, as are the unusual stone piers at the present main entrance. These fairytale rustic Gothick piers of proportionately differing sizes to take carriage and wicket gates (now removed) are a design by A & G Thomson of Glasgow. Examples of these can also be seen at Beech Hill, Co Londonderry (qv) and Drumindoney, Co Down (qv). Perhaps cribbed by Young & Mackenzie of Belfast.
BLACKIE (1863); P.R.O.N.I. D2194

**26. BALLYGOLAN LODGE, Whitehouse**
pre 1858; *demolished*
The property in 1860 of James Aitken.

**27. BALLYHARVEY, Muckamore** c1857
Sturdy one and a half storey two up two down symmetrical lodge, constructed of squared coursed basalt with brick dressings. Gabled with carved and incised wooden ornamental bargeboards, repeated on a little breakfront hall, which are probably a more recent addition.

**28. BALLYLOUGH, Bushmills (2)**
**West Lodge** c1800

C.E.B. Brett

A unique and pretty two storey drum lodge. Now minus their Y tracery, the Gothick windows and also the doorway are in harled walls surmounted by a castellated parapet. Over the front door a tiny bull's eye window lights the landing, to which the stairs wind up from beside the

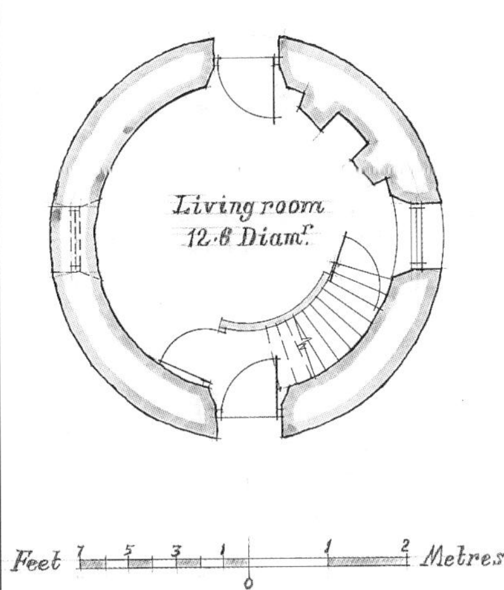


fireplace. The circular theme is repeated in the later piers and iron gates. Built by the Traill family soon after they acquired the estate in 1789, it is now derelict.
**East Lodge** c1840
The secondary lodge is gabled, a one and a half storey harled two up, two down cottage, memorable only for its eaves with curved brackets, one each per rafter projection. Spoilt by a nasty porch.
NORTH ANTRIM; U.A.H.S. (1972)

**29. BALLYMACASH, Lisburn**
pre 1857; *demolished*
A lodge for the Johnston family. Traditional single storey structure, three bay below a hipped roof. Symmetrical front elevation with Georgian squared pane sliding sash windows.

**30. BALLYMENA CASTLE, Ballymena (2)**
**Main Entrance** c1870; architects Lanyon, Lynn and Lanyon

Lanyon, Lynn and Lanyon's vast Scottish Baronial pile has tragically gone, the town's last landmark, to be survived on a less than imposing scale by its gate lodge. In the same uncoursed squared quarry-faced basalt with red sandstone ashlar dressings. Basically square on plan, single storey it has a pyramidal roof from which sprouts a four flue stack. Crowstepped gable projections on two elevations, one the hall with semicircular-headed door, the other a bay. Sturdy gate piers and concave sweep to match, all from 1870, it succeeded an earlier lodge on the same site. A much more innovative example of the Lanyon office's commission for Sir Shafto Adair (later Lord Waveney) is at the Peoples' Park (qv) in the town.
**Secondary Gate** c1870; architects Lanyon Lynn and Lanyon; *demolished*
At the entrance to the castle forecourt were more refined classical ashlar gate piers. Niched, square with fluted friezes below curved cappings.
ADAMS (1985)

**31. BALLYMENA GRAVEYARD, Ballymena** c1880;
architects Young and MacKenzie
A dreary composition one and a half storey on an L plan. Skewtable gables, one roof pitch carried down in a catslide to form a front door canopy with wooden brackets. In black basalt with yellow brick dressings and arrow shaped single storey bay window to one gable.
P.R.O.N.I. D2194

**32. BALLYMONEY GLEBE, Ballymoney**
pre 1832; *demolished*

**33. BALLYNACREE, Ballymoney** c1850
architect perhaps Charles Lanyon
Small stuccoed Gothick lodge earlier than, and in contrast to, Fitzgibbon Louch's 1861 Italianate rework of the house, having replaced an earlier pre 1832 lodge on the same site. Dressed stone lancet openings with hood mouldings and Y tracery. Standard plan, three bay under a hipped roof with emphatic oversailing eaves, almost identical to those at Clare Park (qv) and

Balnamore (qv) nearby. Built for Henry Anderson who, perhaps significantly, was on the Ballymoney railway committee with Charles Lanyon. Four highly ornate secondary iron gate pillars, similar to those at nearby Moorefort (qv), are flanked by Greek stellae stone piers, beyond which are convex sweeps. A most impressive entrance complex. The lodge deserted.

**34. BALNAMORE, Ballymoney (2)**
In 1832 a house called Harmony Hill here, was entered through a pair of rectangular lodges. Sometime before 1855 the house became Balnamore and two separate replacement lodges were built.
**Yard Entrance** c1850; *demolished*
The lodge situated opposite the gates.
**Main Entrance** c1850

C.E.B. Brett

To the main avenue a charming little Gothic style single storey three bay building. Stuccoed walls with solid hood mouldings to the lancet openings housing Y tracery. Stone quoins. Its hipped roof looks too big with its projecting eaves. A nice pair of octagonal stone chimney pots have gone in a recent well-intentioned extension in which the lodge has lost its quaintness. There are almost identical lodges at adjacent Ballynacree and Clare Park, Co Antrim (qqv). Built for Mr James Thomson owner of the mills on the demesne. Sometime later the house, on changing hands, became Millicent.
NORTH ANTRIM; U.A.H.S. (1972)

**35. BARN COTTAGE, Carrickfergus**
c1855; architect Thomas Jackson
James Taylor established the Barn Flax Spinning Mills in 1852 designed by his architect Thomas Jackson of Belfast. Sometime before 1857 he built for his client a small Neo-Classical three bay gate lodge in buff sandstone with segmentally-headed openings in similar recesses.

Pilastered quoins, bracketed cills and coupled eaves brackets to the hipped roof, crowned by a chimney stack again having brackets to the cornice. All typical Jackson though slightly less ornate that his lodge at Trewmount, Co. Tyrone. (qv). Now a hospital entrance, well maintained.
BASSETT'S CO ANTRIM (1888); CARRICKFERGUS; U.A.H.S. (1978)

**36. BARNETT'S PARK, Belfast South**
(see MALONE)

**37. BEARDIVILLE, Bushmills (2)**
**South Entrance** c1810;
architect perhaps Richard Elsam

Delightfully naive Classical composition in basalt rubble dressed in granite. Twin single storey porters' rooms each having large matching Diocletian windows, only the centre portions lights with Georgian squared panes. Hipped roofs against a semicircular-headed carriage archway below a pediment with an oculus in the tympanum, surmounted by three ball finial acroteria. The double gates were of unusual geometric pattern, now gone. Chimney flues carried over the archway to emerge magically from the central ridge. Flanked by curved walls the design of about 1810 akin to Coleraine market gateway, and may be by the architect Richard Elsam who had escaped from irate English clients about then. Although unoccupied, it is well maintained by its present owners as an entrance folly.

**North Entrance** c1790

Earlier, at what may once have been the main approach to the McNaghten family residence, another charming pair of single roomed lodges. Set forward of the gates they face each other across the entrance linked by concave wall sweeps, like those at the Lion Gate, Downhill, Co Londonderry (qv). Matching cubed pavilions in basalt rubble, capped by pyramidal roofs with little "pom-pom" wooden balls at the peaks. Now derelict and choked in undergrowth.
YOUNG (1909); COLVIN (1978); NORTH ANTRIM; U.A.H.S. (1972); COLERAINE & PORTSTEWART; U.A.H.S. (1972); P.R.O.N.I. D2134/1/7

**38. BEAUMONT, Belfast South**
c1880; architect not known

Built for the now demolished house of 1862, which was the home of Robert Atkinson, agent for Guinness & Co. Tall, single storey, three bay Classical lodge in orange brick with buff sandstone dressings and breakfront hall which has a heavy wooden pediment with dentil brackets, as has the hipped roof. Clever unobtrusive one and a half storey extension in the same style. Square sandstone gate piers, panelled with big caps over a foliated frieze. Ogee gate sweep. The lodge now independent, the avenue severed.
MALONE AND STRANMILLIS; U.A.H.S. (1991)

*Beaumont*

**39. BEECHMOUNT, Belfast South**
pre 1832; *demolished*

To an antique house of the Wallace family a lodge directly opposite the entrance to Willowbank Cottage (qv). Later a property of the Riddel family and now a convent.

**40. BEECH PARK, Belfast North**
pre 1857; *demolished*

The property in 1846 of John and Robert Getty.

**41. BELFAST CASTLE, Belfast North**
c1870; architect John Lanyon

John Lanyon's design for the 3rd Marquess of Donegall is a magnificent tour de force and an apt introduction to Lanyon, Lynn and Lanyon's similarly styled mansion on the Cavehill foothills beyond. A High Victorian Picturesque essay principally in the then fashionable Scots Baronial style with its riot of steep crowstepped gables embellished with coats-of-arms and topped by ball finials. The one and a half storey gable to the road is dominated by a tall four flue chimney stack cluster, set diagonally for even greater impact. Below, a conical-roofed bow window projection kept watch. Between these a sculpted

*J.J. Phillips drawing (U.M.)*

*Belfast Castle*

gargoyle in the form of a whimsical wolf poised to pounce. The porch behind the gates is carried on a squat column with medieval foliated capital. A hood-moulded semicircular-arched pedestrian gateway also under a crowstepped gable. To one side the grand octagonal carriageway piers were surmounted by more perky Donegall wolves, each holding an armorial shield. These and the equally decorative iron and wooden gates have been taken away, as have concave wall sweeps and the estate wall. The whole composition in uncoursed squared quarry-faced sandstone, honey-coloured with pink ashlar dressings, once formed an impressive landmark, but now imposed upon by an ever-widening road and second-rate post-war housing.
LARMOUR (1987); U.M. PHOTOGRAPHS Refs: ID/62 (PERSPECTIVE VIEW BY J J PHILLIPS) AND 10/39/1

**42. BELFAST GENERAL HOSPITAL, Belfast North** 1869; architects Thomas Jackson & Son; *demolished*
Founded in 1815 the main hospital building, probably designed by David McBlain, was a sedate pedimented Classical block. In 1869-70 the ground in front of the hospital was levelled, its surface asphalted, a stone gate lodge built and a new set of railings with two carriageways set up before the main entrance. Messrs Thomas Jackson & Son, architects, gave their services without charge and the stone, which came from Scrabo, was a gift of Messrs Ritchie, Jackson, the contractors. Along the Frederick Street frontage a perfectly symmetrical railed entrance screen, the lodge situated centrally on an axis of the old avenue approach. A typical Jackson creation in his favourite Neo-Classical manner. Single storey three bay, below a hipped roof hidden behind an entablatured parapet. Openings segmentally-headed, with moulded architraves, a flagpole projected from the fanlight. Quoins, and a chimney stack to each side elevation. Tall square gate pillars with friezed cappings. Briefly renamed the Belfast Royal Hospital and the Royal Victoria Hospital before the facility was moved to its present site when main block and gate lodge were demolished.
ALLISON (1972); CENTRAL BELFAST; U.A.H.S. (1993); BARDON (1982); U.M.; FRANK McKELVEY painting

**43. BELLMOUNT, Antrim**
pre 1832; *demolished*
A lodge for the Cunningham family, now gone along with the house.

**44. BEN EADAN, Belfast**
pre 1857; *demolished*
A lodge, cruciform on plan built for George Alexander Whitla of the Gobrana (qv) family. Gone as is the house, to have been replaced by St Clement's Retreat Home in about 1960.

**45. BEN NEAGH, Crumlin**
c1790; *demolished*
Simple square Georgian lodge. Pyramidal roof with a tiny single flue stack centrally placed. The harled walls had one small opening on each elevation. Built by Mr R McCauley who then owned the most extensive flour mills in the country.

**46. BENVARDEN, Derrykeighan (3)**
**North-east Entrance** c1830
Cute, single storey, three bay lodge with whitewashed harled walls and hipped roof. "Mouth organ" fanlight to doorway, flanked by "popeye" canted oriel windows on wooden brackets. All windows cast iron lattice-paned. Now disfigured by a flat-roofed porch. Well maintained ironwork to gates and ogee railings between chunky stone octagonal piers. Built for

John Montgomery upon succeeding to the estate after his brother Hugh moved to Ballydrain (qv).
**North-west Entrance** pre 1832; *demolished*
**South Entrance** pre 1832; *demolished*

**47. BERTHA, Belfast South** 1877; architects Thomas Jackson & Son
House of 1853 for Sir David Taylor by Thomas Jackson, followed twenty-four years later by a single storey three bay lodge with an ornamental bracketed front door canopy and hipped roof, designed by Thomas Jackson and Son. Widening of the Malone Road in 1927 necessitated its rebuilding when it gained an extra bay. In routine Neo-Classical style with segmentally-headed architraved openings in stuccoed walls. High Victorian chamfered gate piers crowned by good iron lampholders, their globe shades recently renewed.
CARLTON (1967); MALONE AND STRANMILLIS; U.A.H.S. (1991); BELFAST CORPORATION APPLICATION Ref 3773

**48. BILLY GLEBE, Bushmills**
pre 1857; *demolished*
A lodge which postdated the glebe house of 1810.

**49. BIRCH HILL, Antrim (3)** c1838
**Steeple Road Gate** c1838
Of the three original lodges, but one remains. Once a standard three bay single storey building it was built for Thomas Montgomery. Flanking the front door pretty tripartite windows under label mouldings. Hexagonal- shaped iron glazing bars to windows including the canted bay to the leading gable. Above it an ornamental cusped bargeboard stopped at the eaves in quatrefoils. Now improved and extended it is all that survives of the demesne's buildings. James Boyle in his O.S. Memoir of 1838 makes mention of the office houses only recently being finished. The gate lodges may have been part of this improvement. The property alternatively called Ardnaveigh.
**South-east Gates** both pre 1840; *both demolished*
O.S.M.

**50. BLADON PARK, Belfast South**
1877; architect William Batt
Much as illustrated in the Irish Builder, a design for Robert Atkinson of Beaumont (qv). An attractive one and a half storey gabled High Victorian lodge on a standard plan. Polychrome red and blue brick and geometric ornamental bargeboards to a steep roof. Intricately cut pink sandstone shouldered heads to door, paired windows and single storey canted bay. The brick stack carries fine cream terracotta pots (one of four missing). The gate piers heavy and ornate with foliated friezes below complex cappings with cast iron lamp holders.
MALONE AND STRANMILLIS; U.A.H.S. (1991); I.B. (1877 and 1880)

**51. BOG HEAD, Muckamore**
pre 1832; *demolished*
A quaint little lodge with pyramidal roof rising to a central chimney stack, located opposite the gate. In 1827 the occupant was the Rev Dr George McCartney.

**52. BOHILL, Dundrod**
pre 1832; *demolished*
On a bleak hillside of the same name a pleasant single storey, gabled, three bay lodge constructed of boulders. Both house and lodge of the McClarnan family, who succeeded to the property of William Gregg. Replaced in 1993 by a modern bungalow.

**53. BOTANIC GARDENS Belfast South (2)**
Another piece of 1960s vandalism saw the inexcusable destruction of the substantial Ruskinian, Venetian Gothic style lodge which presided over the gardens' entrance and also served as a public toilet - sorely missed. To quote Hugh Dixon:- "The demolition of the lodge in 1965 was unnecessary in that the site remains empty; it was also unfortunate in removing an important architectural focus for this busy junction, and a feature which gave arrival at the Botanic gardens a sense of occasion".
**Stranmillis Road Gate** 1877; architect William Batt; *demolished*
A tall single storey building designed in polychrome brickwork, red with Staffordshire blue bands, foiled stone pointed arches to all openings. The windows were arranged in pairs as were the arches of the portico from which rose a buttressed clock tower with medieval style carved capitals to engaged columns. The tower capped by a steep "French" roof, it and the hipped roof to the lodge had strongly bracketed eaves, scalloped slate courses and ornate cast iron cresting. In fact the clock tower was a later addition of 1880 thanks to public subscription, looking particularly spectacular when its faces

W.M. Lawrence (N.L.I.)

*Botanic Gardens, Stranmillis Road Gate*

were illuminated at night. The stone gates survive with lamps and poppy finials, part of the original composition.

**Botanic Avenue Gate** c1880; architect probably William Batt

This survivor is more modest, but probably also has polychrome brickwork under its paintwork. Tall single storey three bay symmetrical below a half-hipped roof. Barge and fascia boards with sawtooth carving supported on big sturdy wooden brackets. Window openings chamfered and arranged in pairs, those to the gables semicircular-headed. Front windows segmentally-headed flanking a gabled breakfront containing a round-headed front door, now missing its original door and fanlight. Two storey addition to rear.

LAWRENCE PHOTOGRAPH (NLI) Ref 310(R); QUEEN'S UNIVERSITY; U.A.H.S.; (1975); DIXON & WALKER (1983); BELFAST CITY COUNCIL, PARKS DEPARTMENT

**54. BRECART LODGE Toome** c1848; architect probably James Sands

One of a series of pretty lodges built for the O'Neill estates in the 1840s here and on the Shane's Castle demesne (qv) using the Tudor Picturesque English cottage style, then at the height of its popularity. Freely copied was

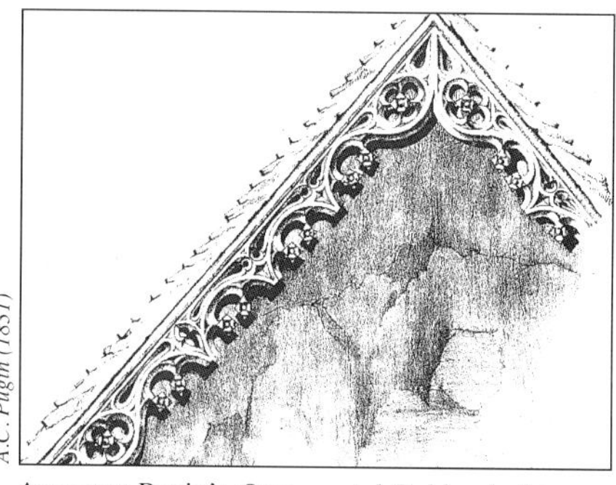

*A.C. Pugin (1831)*

Augustus Pugin's *Ornamental Gables*, in this instance Plate 21, an elaborate chamfered, cusped and foiled bargeboard from Leicester Hospital, Warwick. Single storey on an unusual T plan, the walls stuccoed punctuated with label-moulded windows, now unfortunately minus lattice panes. In the gables blank shields. On one elevation a canted bay with castellated parapet, over which is a mock dormer with its own little fretted bargeboards. The diagonal pair of stone chimney stacks have gone, a symbol of the general decay of house, lodge and gates. It is the latter which point to the architect's identity. An octagonal stone gate pier with carved coronet capping survives, identical to those at Groomsport House, County Down (qv). These were designed by James Sands, an English architect, who settled in Ireland and in correspondence with Perceval Maxwell of Finnebrogue, County Down (qv) in 1848 writes of having to visit Lord O'Neill. The elaborate cast iron gate screen has disappeared.

P.R.O.N.I. D1556; PUGIN (1831);

**55. BRIGADIE, Ballymena** pre 1857; *demolished*

Property early in the 19th century of the Tracey family.

**56. BROCKLEMONT or BROCKLAMONT, Ballymena**

Now the location of gates taken from Macedon (qv).

**57. BROOKHALL, Magheragall** 1871; architect probably Thomas Jackson

Mrs Holmes-Campbell took an existing plain and antique cottage, raised it to one and a half storeys, refaced it in a sort of Classical Picturesque confection and at the same time gave it a gate lodge in similar vein. It seems to have been a case of keeping up with the Joneses, or rather in this case the Richardsons of Springfield (qv) nearby. Many of the characteristics of the house are repeated in the single storey stuccoed four bay lodge which suggests that the architect Thomas Jackson was also employed here. The hipped roof has a plinthed and heavily corniced chimney stack. Window surrounds moulded, quoins and a plinth. There is a projecting gabled hall.

**58. BROOKHILL, Magheragall**

An historic but little known demesne acquired in the late 1860s from the Watson family when William Thomas Bristow Lyons removed here from Oldpark (qv). He set about extensive rebuilding including replacement of an earlier lodge not of long standing.

**West Lodge** pre 1832; *demolished*

A building for the older house of the Watsons had gone by 1857.

**East Lodge** c1870; architect not known

Large one and a half storey, two up two down building, its gable end with single storey canted bay, piercing and espying the gate sweep alongside. To further convenience the porter the gabled porch forms part of the screen with door access to front and rear. The three massive piers and porch had ball finials. In uncoursed squared quarry-faced basalt with distinctive smooth limestone dressings and quoins, it has heavily bracketed eaves and a conspicuous four-flued chimney stack. Sturdy and commodious with potential for extension, the whole a sorry dilapidated mess, going the way of the big house.

**59. BROOKLANDS, Belfast South** pre 1857; *demolished*

A stuccoed Neo-Classical villa built c1840 by John Owden on an old farm which fronted the present Malone Road but was broken up by the intrusion of the new Lisburn Road in 1819 and the Belfast-Dublin railway in 1839. Later tenanted by William Richardson with whose family Owden was in partnership in Richardson, Sons, and Owden, Linen Manufacturers. All had gone by the turn of the century.

BENCE-JONES (1988); CARLETON (1967)

**60. BROOKVALE, Belfast North** pre 1832; *demolished*

House and lodge built for Mr William Sinclair gone by c1878 to make way for Belfast Royal Academy.

**61. BROOMMOUNT, Aghalee** c1810

Standard single storey, three bay symmetrical cottage. Basalt with lancet windows, built for Stafford Gorman Esq. Blocked up.

**62. BURLEIGH HILL, Carrickfergus** c1860

Built by John Robinson, a small gabled plain single storey lodge now extended to form a modern bungalow. The house so called after the family which established its home here.

**63. BUSHBANK, Bushmills** pre 1832; *demolished*

Property in 1817 of John Gage Leckey, thereafter going through a succession of occupants before its burning in 1833. Its lodge had gone before 1856.

**64. BUSHMILLS DISTILLERY, Bushmills** pre 1858; *demolished*

The lodge of the Anderson family to the world famous distillery.

**65. BUSHMILLS** (See DUNDERAVE)

**66. CAIRNDHU, Larne (2)**

Soon after Charles Lanyon's Antrim Coast Road opened up the east coast in about 1849, the Agnew brothers of Larne set up the neighbouring estates of Carncastle Lodge (see below) and Seaview. The latter was purchased about 1878 by John Stewart Clark, thread manufacturer of Paisley. In 1896 he set about completely transforming the house and building gate lodges at both entrances, choosing as his architect Samuel Pepys Close who had worked for his uncle at Drumalis (qv).

**Main Entrance** c1898; architect S P Close

For the main entrance Close chose as a model the nearby main Carncastle gate lodge, although on a more generous scale and in High Victorian style. Single storey, it forms an impressive lengthy frontage to the road with yard wall, outhouses and gate sweep beyond. A solid uncoursed squared, quarry-faced sandstone composition with commanding steeply-pitched gables, heavy bargeboards and exposed rafter toes. On the leading gable a bow window, with half-conical roof, watches over the gates. These in sturdy wood with a diagonal cross motif repeated in the delightful verandahed porch with chamfered posts supporting a half-hipped roof.

**Side Entrance** c1898; architect S P Close

This porch is reproduced as the sole decorative feature on an otherwise plain three bay rear lodge.

**67. CARNCASTLE LODGE, Larne (2)**

Two important and decorative Tudorbethan lodges, in a style which reflected that of the house (demolished 1937), were erected by James Agnew. Both one and a half storey, in warm buff coursed Dungannon sandstone having distinctive skewtable gables with stepped kneelers and ornate barley twist pole finials and chimney-pots. Label and hood mouldings adorn openings that mix square, round and lancet heads to mullioned and transomed windows.

**Secondary Lodge** c1850; architect possibly James Sands

Akin to that at Groomsport House, County Down (qv), is this simple three bay two up, two down with projecting hall. The gable embellished with the Agnew arms and motto, CONSILIO NON IMPETU.

**Shore Lodge** c1850; architect possibly James Sands

Opposite the gates on a T plan made irregular by

a canted bay, projecting gabled porch and cute catslide roof. This is based on the East lodge at Lilburn Towers, Northumberland by English architect John Dobson, which was illustrated in J C Loudon's *Designs for Ornamental Cottages*

J.C. Loudon (1846)

(1846). At Shane's Castle (qv) is the same lodge, though a Picturesque English Cottage variant and probably the work of architect James Sands, to whom work at Carncastle may be attributed. To the bracing seaward side a cute detached round building houses the privy. Both lodges now deprived of their entrance gates.
LOUDON (1846)

**68. CARNFUNNOCK, Larne**
(See CARNCASTLE LODGE)

**69. CARNSAMPSON, Ballycastle** c1880
Symmetrical three bay with hipped roof, projecting gabled breakfront hall. Mildly ornamental fascia boards. In basalt with limestone dressings and quoins. Two banded chimney stacks. Built for the White family and now derelict. The house previously called ANNAVILLE.

**70. CASTLE DOBBS, Carrickfergus (4)**
Proposed Design 1875; architect S P Close; *unexecuted*
A surviving drawing shows a simple three bay symmetrical design to contain a bedroom and livingroom, a catslide-roofed rear return with a second bedroom and scullery. Fretted woodwork to spandrels of gables and carved door canopy. Lattice paned windows mullioned below Tudor label mouldings. Intended to be executed in stone, the front door under a depressed arch, relieving lancets to the gable windows. The design for C R Dobbs.

**Kilroot Entrance** c1875; architect probably S P Close

Now dilapidated, not as Close's surviving drawing proposal. Single storey, three bay symmetrical in uncoursed squared quarry-faced basalt with limestone dressings and quoins. Mixed architectural styles having Tudor label mouldings to windows, and a door set between Classical columns in antis. Polychromatic brick chimney stack on a hipped roof. Fine cast iron entrance gates and railings from BROWNLIE & MURRAY Ironworks, Glasgow.

**Tongue Lane Lodge** c1875; architect probably S P Close

A stuccoed variation of the above. There were another two lodges from c1840, simple standard plan one of which was plain, the other mildly Italianate in its architraved semicircular-headed openings and quoins. Both three bay single storey below hipped roofs, and now demolished. All in all, rather disappointingly modest introductions to a little known but grand Palladian style mansion.
H.M.B. PHOTOGRAPHS; P.R.O.N.I. T3020

**71. CASTLE ROCKLANDS, Carrickfergus**
c1870
Neo-Classical stuccoed three bay. Architraved opening surrounds and quoins. Hipped roof with two chimney stacks, unusually rising off the rear walls. Minimal ball finials to square stone gate pillars. For a Mr Warwick or R L Gilmour who were both listed as resident here in 1888.

**72. CASTLETON, Belfast North**
(see JENNYMOUNT)

**73. CASTLEUPTON, Templepatrick (2)**
**Old Main Entrance** c1810
Cowering behind the estate wall at the original main approach is a simple little two roomed lodge. The hipped gable elevation to the avenue has both a sheeted half door and a window of 28 square panes below seven lancet lights. Surrounding this a sub-frame of a central segmental arch flanked by two semicircular-headed ones. Coursed rubble basalt walls with some snecking. A modest but charming

introduction to the sophistication of Robert Adam's stables and mausoleum.

**Village Entrance** c1837; architect Edward Blore

In 1837 the 3rd Viscount Templetown employed English architect Edward Blore to restore the castle and put up a somewhat less than modest castellated gatehouse. The semicircular-headed carriage archways protected by machicolations supporting a crenellated parapet. Flanking this, and hidden from the road by tall castellated, buttressed walls, two single porter's rooms face one another under the covered archway. All in uncoursed squared basalt with ashlar dressings and loopholes in a symmetrical Romantic manner.
WEST ANTRIM; U.A.H.S. (1970); BLORE; COLVIN (1978)

**74. CEDARS, THE, Antrim**
pre 1902; *demolished*

**75. CHERRYVALLEY, Crumlin (2)**
both pre 1832; *both demolished*
The lodges had disappeared before 1858. The western one was round. Seat of the Gorman family before being acquired in the early 19th century by the Armstrongs.

**76. CHICHESTER PARK, Belfast**
c1860; architect not known; *demolished*
All that remain of the once distinctive entrance to this residential development are four grand square pillars, with recessed, raised and fielded panels, topped by ball finials. But even these are in a state of advanced decay, the highly decorative "Great Exhibition" cast iron carriage and pedestrian gates and splendid gas lamp holders with glass globes have gone. No less conspicuous was a lodge of imaginative Classical detailing on an informal plan. Stuccoed elevations framed in plain pilastered quoins carried up below moulded gables, ornamented with blank shields. Eccentrically placed pedimented doorway and aedicule window.
Its prominent location made it an irresistible provocation to vandals and it finally succumbed in 1988.
LAWRENCE PHOTOGRAPH (NLI.)
Ref 2408(C)

**77. CHURCHFIELD, Ballycastle**
(see MAGHERINTEMPLE)

**78. CITY CEMETERY, Belfast South (2)**
**Main Lodge** 1870; architects probably Lanyon, Lynn & Lanyon

The cemetery laid out 1866-69, gates and superintendent's office-cum-gatehouse built not long after. This is a one and a half storey double-pile house in uncoursed rubble, with ashlar dressings to skewtable gables culminating in spiky fleur-de-lys finials, and chamfered window-dressings. The dominant feature is a single storey rectangular bay window built diagonally across one corner, to survey both sides. Not so obvious to the rear, a catslide roof projects over an arcade forming a verandah with pretty wooden fretwork spandrels. Above this a dinky dormer with slate cheeks and pyramidal hat in steeply-pitched roof with alternate blue and green slate bands crowned by sawtooth crestings. There is a sculpted gargoyle griffin which clings above the hopper. Late Victorian Gothick gate piers in mixed quarry-faced basalt and ashlar sandstone. The large inner piers have dwarf buttresses to a square base broaching to an octagonal capping with eight gablets. The flanking outer piers smaller with shamrock motifs abounding.

**Whiterock Road Lodge** c1870
Plainer single pile version of above. Derelict.

**79. CITY HOSPITAL, Belfast South** c1850; architect probably Charles Lanyon; *demolished*

(H.M.B.B.)

Originally at the entrance to the Union Hospital, a stone lodge doubtless by Charles Lanyon. Distinctive with a very steeply-pitched roof and skewtables to main gables and that above the front door. A novel four-gabled Tudor Gothick chimney stack sat on a plinth. The square chamfered gate screen piers had Tudor cusped tops to recessed panels on two faces. Dentil course below cappings with gablets, which once carried swan neck lamp supports.
"... It is apparently and deservedly to be retained by the hospital", a forlorn hope expressed in the 1975 U.A.H.S. list.
QUEEN'S UNIVERSITY; U.A.H.S.; (1975);

**80. CLANWILLIAM, Belfast South**
(now DANESFORT) c1875; architects probably Young & MacKenzie

P. Larmour

At the entrance to W J Barre's "French-Italian-English Chateau" (Brett), a vigorous High Victorian Neo- Romanesque-Gothick miniature Schloss-like composition with irregular plan and roofscape. All in squared uncoursed quarry-faced limestone, the one and a half storey gable to the main road has pointed batement windows expressing the stairwell, whilst the two storey avenue elevation displays paired windows to living room and bedroom divided by colonettes with flowery capitals. In the internal angle a square tower rises from a buttressed open porch, above which is a bedroom closet. Over that again

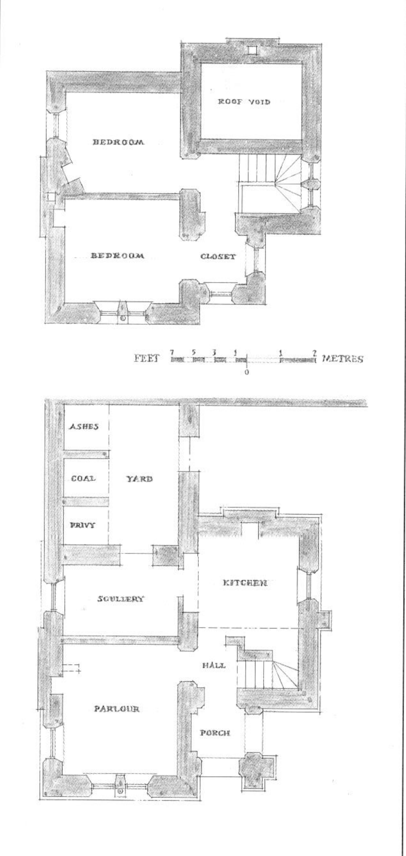


the second floor tank room is lit by two quatrefoils with hood mouldings carried around as a string course. Crowning it all a steeply-pitched pyramidal roof with cast iron finial, all carried off a heavily bracketed eaves. A remarkably ornamental chimney breast on the rear elevation embellished by a round plaque bears the Barbour crest (in dexter hand across pattee, fitched, gu), hood moulded as the quatrefoils. It culminates in a trio of cut stone chimney pots with foliated capital outlets. The single storey return doubtless had a single pot stack in similar vein, now replaced. Within, the plan contrives with the help of steel beams to give the effect without, deceitful but worthwhile. The two gate sweep piers that survive the road widening, of a style with the lodge, each having banded marble-shafted colonettes at their four corners with little sculpted heads over. Recessed panels below quatrefoil roundels echo the lodge. The gableted cappings are missing their cast iron finials, but these can be seen intact on identical piers at Manor House, Milford, County Armagh (qv). Commissioned in the late 1870s by Samuel Barbour from proceeds of the great Linen Thread Manufactory at Hilden and probably designed by Young and MacKenzie. The big house maintained by Northern Ireland Electricity - the lodge forgotten.
MALONE AND STRANMILLIS; U.A.H.S. (1991); BRETT (1985); DUNLOP (1868); P.R.O.N.I. D2194

**81. CLAREMOUNT, Andersonstown**
pre 1901; *demolished*

**82. CLARE PARK, Ballycastle**
c1860; *ruinous*

A.R. Hogg (U.M.)

A single storey symmetrical three bay lodge with hipped roof rising to an octagonal chimney. Dating from soon after 1855, the hooded lancet windows in stuccoed walls had Y tracery. Stone quoins. The lodge's similarity to those at Balnamore and Ballynacree (qqv) and its decorative cast iron gate posts suggest a common architect. Built for the McGildowny family. The photograph dated 22 October 1936.
HOGG PHOTOGRAPH COLLECTION (U.M.) Ref H01/66/1; GLENS OF ANTRIM; U.A.H.S. (1971)

**83. CLEARSTREAM COTTAGE, Belfast North** 1876;
architects Young & MacKenzie
A rare survival in the city's urban spread this Picturesque standard three bay lodge. Fish-scale slates to the hipped roof, with diagonal chimneys. In stuccoed walls, wide segmentally-headed twelve paned windows. Semicircular fanlight to front door in gabled projecting hall below rather crude decorative bargeboards. Surprisingly late in date. For Mr E Blair as at Wheatfield (qv). Architect's estimate £100. Known as "Rhubarb Cottage". House and avenue have disappeared.
P.R.O.N.I. D2194

**84. CLEGGAN LODGE, Broughshane (2)**
**Main Entrance** pre 1857
Plain single storey three bay cottage with a hipped roof and clipped eaves. Later extended to an L plan. Big plain stone gate pillars and concave quadrants.

**Secondary Lodge** pre 1857; *demolished*
To what was once the "beautiful hunting seat of Earl O'Neill's".
FRASER (1838)

**85. CLIFTON HOUSE, Belfast North** 1938; architect Godfrey Ferguson

Refined little Classical composition in dark brick which harmonises well with the 1771 Poor House. The square four room lodge has a pyramidal roof rising to a central chimney off a dentil bracket eaves. The hall projects in an open pediment gable, below which is a semicircular fanlight to the front door that is spoilt by a recent off-the-shelf door with a fanlight of its own. Rectangular-paned window openings have brick soldier courses. Built to replace a pre 1832 predecessor on the same site.

**86. CLONARD, Belfast North**
pre 1858; architect probably Thomas Jackson; *demolished*
A lodge to the property of James Kennedy of the nearby Falls Flax Spinning Company, gone along with the rest. The surviving house is a fine Neo-Classical villa of c1843 by Thomas Jackson as, one may speculate, was the porter's accommodation.
LARMOUR (1987)

**87. CLONAVON, Ballymena (2)**
both pre 1857; *both demolished*
Seat in 1856 of Andrew Gihon.

**88. CLONMORE, Lambeg** c1905; architect Henry Seaver
To a house and stables also by Henry Seaver as part of the same commission. Now improved, it was a simple three bay, rendered three roomed bungalow in Classical Arts-and-Crafts style. Wide tripartite square-paned windows on each side of a projecting hipped roof porch. Exposed rafter toe eaves of a hipped roof which rises to two banded chimneys.

**89. CLOUGH LODGE, Greencastle**
pre 1857; *demolished*
By the lough shore, house and gate lodge of George Gray.

**90. CONNOR RECTORY, Kells** pre 1900
Nondescript, to a glebe house of 1820.
LEWIS (1837)

**91. CONWAY, Dunmurry (2)**
**Lisburn Road Entrance** c1870; architect not known
At the main entrance a stuccoed lodge of spacious cruciform plan, with vestiges of its original Italianate style despite modern plate glass window insertions and a nasty flat roof porch. The chimney stacks were heavily corniced with deep recessed panels, one elegant Regency pot having survived. Eaves and bargeboards once carried on modillion brackets, in pairs. Two of the gate piers remain intact, with recessed panel shafts and semicircular pediment cappings. There is fine cast iron railing also of c1870.
Built for Mr Edward Charley.

**River Road Entrance** c1900; architect Henry Hobart

Off the pretty River Road at the rear of a once beautifully landscaped demesne a "Stockbroker Tudor" composition in the Eden Nesfield manner, the most opulent of the architect's known executed works. One and a half storey with all the Arts-and-Crafts trappings of ornamental half-timbered jettying projecting over one of the two canted bay windows, lights leaded as the rest. Ground floor walls in red brick as is the powerful chimney stack which pierces red terracotta scalloped roof tiles with matching cresting and finials. The main roof cascades down as a catslide over a decorative wooden porch with tile hung spandrel over. A fine design, proudly maintained, for which original drawings survive, irritatingly neither signed nor dated. However the recognisable hand, tall modelled chimney stack, plan and a distant pillar with its distinctive scalloped cap identify it as being a more ornate variant of that at Lurgan Park Co Armagh (qv) by Henry Hobart, for John D Barbour. What survives of the fancy cast iron gates is contemporary.
CORBETT (1990)

**92. COOLAVIN, Belfast South**
pre 1901; *demolished*
To an 1856 house once called Vipont Villa, the lodge for David Corbett, wine and spirit merchant.

**93. THE COPPINS, Carrickfergus**
(see CASTLEROCKLANDS)

**94. THE COTTAGE, Ballymena**
pre 1903; *demolished*
A modest gabled single storey composition.
ADAMS (1989)

**95. CRAIGDUNN CASTLE, Cullybackey**
(2) both pre 1903; *both demolished*
To the big Scots Baronial house for Edmund McNeill.

**96. CREBILLY, Broughshane** 1879; architect probably Timothy Hevey
A Picturesque building T shaped on plan. Stuccoed with low pitched roof decorated by scallop slate courses. Stone plinth, quoins and dressings to the semicircular-headed windows give an Italianate flavour. The main feature is an attractive open porch with nice latticed woodwork balustrade, posts and brackets. Obligingly the principal gable bears a shield with the date 1879 and the monogram of General M J Wardlow, who had married the last of the O'Haras to live at Crebilly. Probably the work

of Timothy Hevey, it now lies pitifully derelict, despite in scale lending itself to extension and rehabilitation.

**97. CROMAC COTTAGE, Belfast South**
pre 1858; *demolished*
A property on Donegall Pass of the Brown family no trace of which remains.

**98. CROMAC PARK, Belfast South**
pre 1832
Remarkable for being the closest surviving lodge of a country park to the city centre. Simple two roomed three bay under a hipped roof. Semicircular-headed windows. Now much abused and on its last legs serving as a shop. Once the property of the Glenfields.

**99. CROSSKENNAN, Antrim** c1855
A sturdy one and a half storey gabled structure, two bay to the avenue, an extensive single storey return to the rear. In squared uncoursed basalt quarry-faced, the openings are brick dressed with sculpted label mouldings over. Probably built by the Clarke family to replace a previous pre 1832 lodge across the road.

**100. CULMORE LODGE, Kilrea**
pre 1857; *demolished*
Built for James William Armstrong to a house described in 1831 as modern.
O.S.M.

**101. THE CURRAN, Larne** pre 1902; *demolished*
Property of the McNeill family.

**102. CUSHENDUN, Cushendun**
pre 1857; *demolished*
Built for Edmund A McNeill.

**103. DALRIADA, Jordanstown**
c1855; architect possibly Thomas Turner

A simple symmetrical three bay two roomed lodge dressed up as an elegant stuccoed Classical temple. A tetrastyle portico of slender Roman Doric twinned columns, the entablature to the pediment carried around as an eaves course. Antae corresponding to the columns flank the front doors which is architraved like the Georgian style paned windows. The contemporary house has details akin to those at Tullyhinan House, County Down (qv)

which point to Thomas Turner as architect probably influenced by the lodge of his sometime master, Charles Lanyon, at Drenagh, County Londonderry (qv). Erected for the Johnston family, wealthy grocers and flaxspinners. Extended to an L shape on plan in matching style.

**104. DEAF, DUMB & BLIND INSTITUTE, Belfast South** c1850; architect probably Charles Lanyon; *demolished*

Perhaps Belfast's greatest architectural loss has been Charles Lanyon's great Neo-Jacobean building of 1843, so tragically demolished by Queen's University in 1965. At the base of its approach avenue, past terraced lawns, in like style and symmetry, a little single storey gate lodge with curvilinear gables of its own culminating in spiky finials. Simply three bay on a cruciform plan it was of brick with dressed stone to openings, that to the Lisburn Road elevation sporting a stepped label moulding to a mullioned tripartite window. In the gables hood moulded decorative slits. The prominent chimney stack had a pair of very tall stone octagonal pots resting on a similar section brick base. Built in about 1850 it is easy to ascribe it to Charles Lanyon being similar to lodge and gates at Fenaghy (qv). The salt-cellar-like stone gate piers were octagonal broached from square plinths, each face having lancet recesses below a frieze with corresponding square indentations, repeated in the reduced caps.

LAWRENCE STEREOGRAPHIC COLLECTION (NLI.) Ref 382; POSTCARD VIEW, BARRY WATSON; DIXON AND WALKER (1984)

**105. DANESFORT Belfast South**
(see CLANWILLIAM)

**106. DANTE HALL, Whiteabbey**
pre 1857; *demolished*
A lodge for the Grainger family.

**107. DEMIVILLE, Lisburn** c1890

At the foot of a straight tree-lined avenue a plain single storey gabled lodge. Now extended to 5 bays, a flat-roofed hall projects. Roughcast.

**108. DERRYVOLGIE, Belfast South** c1858; architect Thomas Jackson

A view of about 1900 from the house across a manicured lawn with formal beds, shows a single storey lodge with hipped roof three bay, with on the corner furthest from the room, a projecting part-octagonal bay window from which to spy visitors. The eaves heavily bracketed like the corniced chimney stacks. The front door had a canopy with ornamental bargeboards, supported on carved wooden brackets. Presumably, like the house of 1856-58, by Thomas Jackson for Cranston Gregg. His distinctive panelled, corniced and capped hexagonal entrance pillars survive but the lodge was either reworked or rebuilt in 1931 by Munce and Kennedy to facilitate road realignment. Simpler in style but still Jacksonesque in feel with its architraved segmentally-headed windows. Classical door surround and matching pilasters.

BELFAST CORPORATION APPLICATION Ref 6938; YOUNG (1909); CARLETON (1978)

**109. DERRYVOLGIE, Lisburn (3)**

A house for William Gregg, agent to Lord Hertford, of about 1835, not long after which two lodges were erected on the Lisburn-Belfast road, neither of which survive.

**The Belfast lodge** c1840; *demolished*

First to be removed, by most accounts Classical in style with columned portico, the gate piers hexagonal.

**The Lisburn Lodge** c1840; *demolished*

In contrast, Tudor in style having label mouldings over the windows of a simple three bay symmetrical single storey building, stuccoed with a hipped roof. Its concave entrance sweeps had Greek stellae stone gate piers, tapering upwards to projecting cornices topped by semicircular-pedimented cappings.

**Bellsize Road Lodge** pre 1901

A surviving lodge developed into a sizeable bungalow.

**110. DRENTA, Dunmurry** c1900

L shaped lodge with large bow window. All in shocking yellow fireclay brick, a timely warning of the big house beyond. Both built for a Major Cowan.

**111. DRUMALIS, Larne (2)**

**Glenarm Road Lodge** c1890; architect S P Close

Single storey of irregular plan below hipped roofs, eaves projecting to form a shallow verandah with cast iron trellis for climbing plants. Roughcast walls with stone plinth, stringcourses, corners and segmentally-headed windows and dressings. Above the door a canopy with fretworked gable, carried on wooden brackets.

**Curran Road Lodge** c1890; architect perhaps S P Close; *demolished*

Cast iron railings and stone piers with pyramid cappings, typical of Close, remain at both entrances. He had previously extensively remodelled the house for Sir Hugh Houston Smiley.

YOUNG (1909)

**112. DRUMGLASS, Belfast South** c1882; architect perhaps Young and MacKenzie

An extravagant design in the Queen Anne Revival style contrasting with the earlier Classical villa of 1854. For Sir James Musgrave of iron-foundry fame, by an architect unrecorded. One and a half storey symmetrical, gabled and cruciform on plan, it cleverly disguises two dwellings. Subjected to rendering and a succession of paint colour schemes its red brickwork and terracotta tiled gables long forgotten. The ground floor windows framed by Classical pilasters as at the corners which support a panelled frieze. Each of the gables embraces an oriel window. Deep bargeboards decorated with rosettes rise to hipknobs, behind which are pretty ridge crestings. Above one doorway the Musgrave monogram, repeated on the cube of sandstone which sits on the great squat piers, heavily rusticated in projecting limestone bands. Convex dwarf walls sweep to similar outer piers this time crowned with strapwork ball finials. Modest cast iron railings and gates replaced something more elaborate removed during World War II. A forthright enough design to have been by Young & MacKenzie.

MALONE AND STRANMILLIS; U.A.H.S. (1991)

**113. DRUMNAGESSAN, Bushmills** pre 1855

A standard plan, Georgian style lodge with hipped roof and clipped eaves. Lions to pier cappings. The house occupied in 1862 by John Dunlop.

**114. DRUMNAGREAGH, Glenarm** pre 1903

Like the house on the hill above, unprepossessing. Built for George McFerran, now a hotel.

**115. DRUMNASOLE, Carnlough** c1860

Strikingly Picturesque lodge of standard plan on the Antrim Coast road. The exuberant cast iron entrance screen with spiky finialed piers, leafy railing tops, and arched polychrome brick chimney stack. Gabled with robust wave and foil bargeboards and hipknobs, there is a projecting hall to match which has a shouldered door head to the side and a round-headed niche on the opposing elevation to the road. In coursed basalt a mixture of segmental and semicircular-headed openings with limestone dressings and quoins making a nice contrast. Canted bay to roadside and blank shield in the gable over. A seat of the Turnly family.

**116. DRUMRAYMOND, Toome** c1835

On an eminence overlooking the gates from outside, at the end of a long laneway off the main road, a large whitewashed 'pepperpot' lodge, octagonal under its umbrello roof and central stone chimney pot. Most of the original tiny windows to each face now replaced with larger plate-glass openings. To an O'Neill demesne now neglected, which once possessed the most Picturesque Cottage Orné hunting lodge on the shores of Lough Beg.

MALINS (1980)

**117. DUNARNON, Belfast South** c1890; architect probably Samuel Stevenson; *demolished*

Indelicate Italianate villa of 1889 for James Johnston, JP, merchant, designed by Samuel Stevenson as no doubt was the tiny lodge now gone, marked only by a patch of tarmac. It was stuccoed with deeply rusticated quoins, survived by tall octagonal gate piers with ball finials over a dentil course. Now known as Aquinas Hall.

MALONE AND STRANMILLIS; U.A.H.S. (1991)

**118. DUNCAIRNE, Belfast North**
(see FORTFIELD)

**119. DUNCAIRNE HOUSE, Belfast North**
pre 1832; *demolished*
A seat of the Macrory family.

**120. DUNDERAVE, Bushmills (4)**
**Main Entrance** c1850; architect Charles Lanyon

A simply planned, symmetrical stuccoed lodge, but on a large scale. A mini-palazzo, given its impact by high ceilings, and its grand "porte cochère" a statement which the big house lacks. The approach is up steps below the three semicircular- arched porch, each of its four square piers complete with imposts from which spring archivolts, meeting in acones. Flat, shouldered arches return to the respond abutments. A simple string course at impost height embraces the whole composition, where the quoins stop and from which the paired gable window arches spring. These openings have a delightful bracketed balconette with stone fretwork balustrade, repeated in the portico sides. The low-pitched gables, carried on pairs of scrolled purlin ends, boast blind oculi. Slit windows flank the double leaf entrance doors. Over the big recessed panel chimney stack, a frieze with brackets below the corniced capping. A design by the master of the Italianate style in the Province - Charles Lanyon. For Sir Edmund Workman-McNaghten not long after building of the house in 1847. This cruciform planned lodge is a type which Lanyon repeated, there being variants at Moneyglass (qv) in the same county and Ballywalter and Eglantine, County Down (qqv). On a suitable scale nearby an extensive gate screen of tall square sandstone piers with restrained friezes below moulded cappings. Wide double cast iron carriage gates flanked by wicket gates and concave sweeps beyond. At the time of writing, the gates looking permanently locked, the lodge deserted and site overgrown.

**Rear Entrance** c1850
To the rear of the estate a less sophisticated lodge notable only for a projecting hall with broken-pedimented gable and channelled rustication carried up as voussoirs to semicircular-headed side openings, framing margined windows. Ball finials on big basic square gate piers.

**Secondary Entrances** both c1840
Two plain lodges to the short-lived 1837 Bushmills House.
BENCE-JONES (1988); NORTH ANTRIM; U.A.H.S. (1972); LEWIS (1837); McNAGHTEN (1951)

**121. DUNEIRA, Larne** 1880
In stone with some Tudor features. Datestone. Built for John Watt Smyth.

**122. DUNLAMBERT, Belfast North** c1873; architect probably James Hamilton; *demolished*
In the Fortwilliam Park was another large villa, by the Glasgow architect James Hamilton for Henry Matier, linen merchant. The Lawrence photograph the only record shows a mere glimpse of the lodge with projecting dentilled pediment topped by an anthemion acroteria. Below it an entablatured aedicule, pilasters with Corinthian capitals frame an arcaded tripartite window with rounded-headed openings. To a

*W.M. Lawrence (N.L.I.)*

backdrop of the Cavehill and Belfast Castle, were elegant square stone gate piers, within concave railed sweeps, tapering gracefully up to cappings with an anthemion on each face. Below, rectangular raised and fielded panels sandwiched between a band of roundels and another of Greek key pattern. The two central piers carried lamps.
LAWRENCE PHOTOGRAPHIC COLLECTION (NLI) Ref 2399(C); LARMOUR (1987)

**123. DUNLESKEN, Carrickfergus** pre 1901; *demolished*
A lodge for J Godfrey Echlin.

**124. DUNMINNING, Glarryford** pre 1857; *demolished*
In 1816 the house "a handsome modern edifice" with the extensive bleach greens nearby, the property of Thomas M Birnie, Esq. The lodge does not seem to have been built opposite the gates until John Patrick came by the house in the mid-19th century.
ATKINSON (1823)

**125. DUNMORE COTTAGE, Belfast North** pre 1857; *demolished*
Built by John Preston.

**126. DUNMURRY, Dunmurry (2)**
Two plain lodges built by James D Boyd following acquisition of a property previously called The Fort long in the possession of the Hunter family. The original entrances were worthy of mention in the O.S. Memoirs as having "good iron gates".

**Main Entrance** c1900
Standard plan, hipped roof with corniced chimney. Flat roofed hall with entablature.

**Secondary Entrance** c1900; *demolished*
O.S.M.

**127. DUNRAVEN, Belfast South** c1870; architect probably John Corry; *demolished*
Large house, and presumably lodge, in Italianate style by the architect John Corry in 1870 for his brother Sir James Porter Corry, timber merchant and ship owner. All removed in 1937 to make way for suburbia.
B.T. PHOTOGRAPH 4/2/1936

**128. DUNSONA, Whiteabbey** pre 1857; *demolished*
The home in 1856 of a Captain Fitzsimmons. Later the home of Nicholas Fitzsimmons, architect.

**129. DUNVILLE PARK, Belfast South** c1891; architect possibly Samuel Stevenson; *demolished*
In 1891 Robert Grimshaw Dunville presented 4 acres to be used as a public park for the populace in an increasingly built up area and primarily for the workforce from the little streets who manned his nearby whiskey distillery. This benevolence extended to landscaping, a highly decorative terracotta fountain and superintendent's

*A.R. Hogg (U.M.)*

*Dunville Park*

accommodation. The latter was in the form of an octagonal Ionic temple in buff ashlar sandstone. On three faces aedicule windows framed by columns and from a fourth projected a pedimented portico supported each side by clusters of three columns with corresponding antae. On alternate elevations architraved windows with bracketed cills and blank panels over. The whole sat on pedestals and plinth, surmounted by a dentilled entablature with balustrade over. The construction was at the then considerable cost of £1,150. Such opulence inevitably attracted the attentions of the vandals and the lodge has gone, the fountain destroyed. The massive sets of entrance piers alone stand defiant. They being V-channel rusticated with moulded projecting cappings. The family seat was at Redburn, Co Down (qv). DIXON AND WALKER (1983); BELFAST CITY COUNCIL; PARKS DEPARTMENT; HOGG PHOTOGRAPH COLLECTION (U.M.) Ref H10/36/25

**130. EDENDERRY MILL, Belfast North** 1914; architect Edwin Riddell Kennedy
A plucky little Arts-and-Crafts lodge dwarfed by the surrounding might of vast Victorian five storey mill buildings. In a crisp red brick with matching earthenware roof tiles. One and a half storey, its three bay symmetrical front facade with high eaves spoilt by later alterations. Two bay side elevations with segmentally-arched relieving heads to window openings below hipped gables. Still in use.
LARMOUR (1987)

**131. EDENMORE, Jordanstown (2)** both c1865; architects probably Lanyon, Lynn & Lanyon; *both demolished*
Only the house and one set of gate pillars survive to suggest the architects' work. Built for Mr James Torrens.

**132. EDEN-NA-GRANA, Belfast South** c1885; architect probably Robert Graeme Watt; *demolished*
To a large late Victorian Queen Anne Revival red brick house a contemporary lodge doubtless part of the architect's commission but now gone. For John Rogers, felt, wire and grease manufacturer.
MALONE AND STRANMILLIS; U.A.H.S. (1991)

**133. EGLANTINE HILL, Belfast South** pre 1832; *demolished*
One of the earliest villas in proximity to Belfast town, it and its gate lodge built for Hugh Hyndman. Demolished c1885.
CARLETON (1978)

**134. ELMWOOD, Belfast South** c1845; architect probably Charles Lanyon; *demolished*
An early residence of the late 18th century was replaced by a stuccoed Neo-Classical house for Edward F Clarke, vitriol manufacturer. The contemporary lodge was demolished c1875.
CARLETON (1978)

**135. EVERTON, Belfast North** pre 1901; *demolished*
The property in 1870 of James R Beck.

**136. FALLS PARK, Belfast South** 1879; architect probably J C Bretland
Public park of 44 acres opened in 1873. The lodge a watered down version of that at Alexandra Park (qv). One and a half storey on an irregular plan. In orange brick with buff sandstone cills, lintels, and skewtable to steeply-pitched gables. Sawtooth crestings. Lean-to single storey hall. Its mild Tudor Revival manner is in contrast to the High Victorian Gothick of the two gate piers, each having engaged colonettes to their four corners with good foliated capitals. Semicircular gablets break the pyramidal cappings which are crowned by poppy finials, almost identical to those at Alexandra Park. The lodge for the ranger was constructed in 1879 at a cost of £230 perhaps to a design by J C Bretland, the Borough Surveyor.
BELFAST CITY COUNCIL, PARKS DEPARTMENT

**137. THE FARM, Belfast North** pre 1901; *demolished*
Originally the property of the Bruce family as were neighbouring Thorndale and Benburb Manor, Co Tyrone (qv).

**138. FARM LODGE, Ballymena** pre 1857; *demolished*
Probably built when the Adair family, later resident at nearby Ballymena Castle (qv), was in occupation.

**139. FAUNORAN, Greenisland** pre 1857; *demolished*
Built by the Allen family.

**140. FELDEN, Whitehouse** pre 1901; architect probably Joseph Bell; *demolished*
The seat of the Bells.

**141. FENAGHY, Cullybackey (2)**
Delightfully situated on the bank of the River Main, the house and each of its gate lodges all contemporary in vastly differing styles. The house is extravagant Italianate looking very like the work of Thomas Jackson who is known to have worked for a Mr Young in the Ballymena area.

**Secondary Entrance** c1855; architect probably Thomas Jackson

*J. Horner drawing*

A copy of John Nash's Oak Cottage at Blaise Hamlet in Gloucestershire. Jackson was articled to George Dymond in Bristol until 1828 and would have been familiar with these cottages which popularised the English Cottage Picturesque style. Basically a two up two down one and a half storey L shaped cottage. Originally thatched, its hipped roof has ornamental scalloped slates and sawtooth cresting, the attic rooms with gablet dormers. Coved eaves. Across the entrance elevation a single storey pent roof over a rustic sitting area flanked by a store and the hall, each lit by

arrowslit lights, Nash's tree trunk and branch supports replaced by wrot timber brackets. Lattice paned windows in white roughcast walls paint a quaint picture which would be complete with a pair of tall diagonal brick chimney stacks. Recent restoration briefly exposed rubble stone walls with orange brick dressings which may have been the original facing.

**Main Entrance** c1855; architect probably Charles Lanyon

To the main entrance another caprice, this time Tudorbethan, with four shaped and pinnacled gables on a cruciform plan. The lovely little porch has Tudor arches with hood mouldings ending in cauliflower dripstones and in the gable a multi-foiled lozenge motif. Windows latticed under label mouldings. On the road gable a canted bay with blind lancet over. Walls stuccoed with stone dressings. Again the roof has scallop slates and an unfortunate modern chimney stack. There are unusual wooden picket fence concave sweeps to stone 'salt-cellar' piers. These have square bases broaching to octagons with cusped heads to recessed panels. All very nice. Having confidently attributed house and Picturesque cottage to Thomas Jackson, the main lodge and gate piers are clearly and disconcertingly by the same hand as those at the Deaf, Dumb & Blind Institute, Belfast (qv), accepted as being by Charles Lanyon - or are they?
COLVIN (1978)

**142. FERNAGH, Whiteabbey (2)**
**Main Entrance** c1880
Originally a gabled three bay single storey structure. Sometime early this century extended with a one and a half storey addition. The whole now pebble-dashed with crude rendered window dressings intended to match the earlier stone quoins. Fussy wave and foil bargeboards, fleur-de-lys crestings and odd flat-roofed buttressed hall in internal angle.

**Side Entrance** c1880
Plain, with red and cream polychromatic brickwork. Built for Mr E Malcolmson. Both avenues now public roads.

**143. FERNHILL, Belfast North** 1864; architect H Young; *demolished*
A bye-law submission for a lodge was made in 17 June 1864 by the architect. The floor plan shows a standard two roomed cottage with scullery, WC and yard out the back. A 1962 aeriel survey photograph reveals something rather grander than that proposed, at the base of a sweeping avenue. Cruciform on plan, three roof projections were hipped and that over the front door gabled. Presumably by the same architect and contemporary with the house. For Samuel Cunningham, youngest son of Josias from the neighbouring park of Glencairn (qv).
BELFAST CORPORATION APPLICATION; B.K.S. AIR SURVEY; YOUNG (1909)

**144. FIRGROVE, Muckamore** c1850;
*demolished*
Pretty, standard single storey three bay lodge. Tudor label mouldings and wide overhanging eaves of hipped roof. All that remains are two square stuccoed piers each with little "beret" cappings.
ANTRIM AND BALLYMENA; U.A.H.S. (1969)

**145. FIRMOUNT, Belfast North** pre 1901;
*demolished*
A lodge for Richard W Pring of Grattan and Co.

**146. FISHERWICK LODGE, Doagh (2)**
**South Lodge** c1845
One derelict survivor to the Marquess of Donegall's old hunting seat. Standard, three bay, plain. Basalt walls under a hipped roof with low eaves.
**North Lodge** pre 1857; *demolished*

**147. THE FORT Dunmurry**
(see DUNMURRY HOUSE)

**148. THE FORT, Lisburn** c1860; *demolished*
Lodge and house contemporary, built for Robert Barbour one of three brothers who carried on the largest tailor's and shoemaker's thread manufactory in the world, founded by their grandfather John of Plantation (qv). Presumably the lodge was, like the house, a stuccoed Neo-Classical affair, despite the distinguished Gothic Revival architect Sir Alfred Waterhouse having carried out work here.
BASSETT'S CO ANTRIM (1888); WATERHOUSE (1992)

**149. FORTFIELD, Belfast North** pre 1832;
*demolished*
A lodge, to the house renamed Duncairn before 1857, built for W Johnson.

**150. FORTWILLIAM, Belfast North**
(see below)

**151. FORTWILLIAM PARK, Belfast North (2)**
**The Early Lodges** two pre 1832, one pre 1857
Around 1810 George Langtry acquired the large estate on the northern shore of Belfast Lough which had belonged to the Lendrick family. There he resided, building two gate lodges on the Shore Road (both of which were demolished before the turn of the century). A third lodge of c1850 remarkably survives on the Antrim Road. A much improved single storey three bay building with mildly ornamental bargeboards. In 1863 the estate was broken up by James William Valentine and Henry Langtry into smaller lots, to house such superior residences as Dunlambert, Kileen and Walton (qqqv) each sporting its own obligatory lodge. All these were accessed off a private avenue which ran between the Shore and Antrim Roads at the junctions of which were grand entrances and porters' lodges.
**Shore Road Entrance** c1864; architect possibly James Hamilton; *demolished*
At the Shore Road was a once majestic entrance screen, in style wholly appropriate to the Italianate villas beyond. Over both footpaths triumphal archways, each rich in Classical detailing; niches with anthemions, dentil courses, decorative friezes, shields, pilasters and banding. Each semicircular arch below a projecting cornice crowned by a sculpted group of maiden, cupid and urn. In the centre of the carriageway was a matching pillar (now removed to Musgrave Park) which contains the monogram of Valentine and at the top of which a putti threesome held aloft a trio of globe gaslights. This decorative ironwork and that of both pairs of carriage gates, pedestrian gates, spandrels and

W.M. Lawrence (N.L.I.)

railings have gone. The photograph of about 1890 indicates beautifully carved crisp masonry, but it is in a buff sandstone totally inadequate to resist the vagaries of vandals and weather, and is now hopelessly eroded. Behind and to the right a glimpse of a short-lived Italianate lodge with parapeted low-pitched roof and arcaded "porte-cochère". All from about 1864 and perhaps by the Glaswegian architect James Hamilton who had other commissions in the city.
**Antrim Road Entrance** 1864;
architect William J Barre

Photograph from D. Dunlop's W.J. Barre (1868)

At the Antrim Road end, in total contrast, an early French Gothick concoction also commissioned by Valentine. Framing the gate screen, sexfoil-pierced dwarf concave walls lead into two pairs of large sandstone piers flanking

pedestrian gates. These are basically square, but embellished on each corner with three slender engaged columns having medieval capitals from which spring foiled pointed arches. Curved friezes support pyramidal cappings with unusual foliated finials. The quaint pier central to the carriageway, resembling a Chinese lantern, was in cast iron as were the decorative gates and wicket overthrows. All lost, put to warlike use. Happily unscathed is Barre's charming and innovative entrance lodge. On an L plan in uncoursed squared quarry-faced sandstone with smooth dressings to coupled and tripartite openings in a mixture of lancet and square heads. Gabled, its eaves are given support by curved wooden brackets arranged in threes. The composition dominated by a nice square belfry rising from the entrance hall, a perforated plinth separated from the slated spire by an open wooden lattice stage. The octagonal stone chimney rather apologetic in scale.
LAWRENCE PHOTOGRAPHS (NLI.) Refs 2400(C), 2402(C); DIXON AND WALKER (1983); DUNLOP (1868)

**152. FRIAR'S BUSH GRAVEYARD, Belfast South** 1829; architect not known
In 1828 the Marquess of Donegall gave the Roman Catholics of Belfast two acres as a burial ground, the whole of which was enclosed by a sturdy 8ft wall. This was superseded in 1869 by

Milltown cemetery. There is stuccoed late Georgian Gothick caretaker's accommodation flanking the arched entrance. Single storey cottages under hipped roofs face each other under the covered archway with its gable ends, through which access was gained below pointed arches. The lancet windows are now minus their Y tracery. The composition framed by four buttresses topped by simple spiked finials, features also to be found at Rosemount and Mountstewart, County Down (qqv), Hillsborough Parish Church in the same County (qv) and Downhill, County Londonderry (qv). Flanked by tall concave quadrant walls on the busy Stranmillis Road, it is now badly in need of care and attention.
QUEEN'S UNIVERSITY; U.A.H.S. (1975)

**153. FRUITHILL, Andersonstown**
pre 1901; *demolished*
Built for William Telford.

**154. GALGORM CASTLE, Galgorm** c1852
A lodge, compared to the big house, plain. In basalt, solid three bay below a hipped roof. It replaced an earlier pre 1832 building. Built for Dr William Young after his purchase of the property from the Earls of Mount Cashell in 1851.

**155. GARDENVALE, Moss Side** c1873;
architect probably W H Lynn

Another Italianate lodge of a pattern much used by the Lanyon, Lynn and Lanyon office, for Mr Alexander McNeill. Presumably by W H Lynn after he had left the practice, as drawings by the architect survive for rebuilding the house dated 1873. Standard plan, hipped roof and gabled "porte-cochère", with two main semicircular-headed arches, as are those to the slit windows, tripartite to the side elevations. Essentially the same as the lodges to Cromore, County Londonderry (qv) and Lismara (qv), but lacking some of its original decorative features removed in some twentieth century 'improvements'. Nice convex sweep of simple hooped railings.
NORTH ANTRIM; U.A.H.S. (1972)

**156. GARRON TOWER, Carnlough**
**Main Entrance** 1854; architect
probably Fitzsimmons
At the main entrance to the previous Londonderrys' estate, an unusual and once pretty ivy-clad lodge. Single storey two roomed octagon with a low-pitched roof behind a battlemented parapet. All in coursed squared

*(U.M.)*

quarry-faced basalt having smooth stone dressings to openings and fancy Tudor label mouldings to paired lattice-paned windows. Similar treatment of pointed-head doors in the projecting front and back halls. Now destroyed, blocked up, the parapet replaced by a concrete flat roof. A pity. Good Gothick octagonal cast iron piers, gates and railings, much as at Downpatrick lodge, Castleward, County Down (qv).
U.M.; PHOTOGRAPH Ref 01/29/21;
MAGILL (1990)

**157. GLANDORE, Kilrea** c1858
Plain, rendered with hipped gables. Three bay, its margined windows from the late 1850s. Nice hooped railings, centre piers removed. Built for William Anderson.

**158. THE GLEN, Whiteabbey** pre 1857;
architect probably Thomas Jackson;
*demolished*
Single storey three bay under a hipped roof with paired, bracket support. Corniced chimney. Flat-headed openings in semicircular-arched recesses. Gate piers with recessed panels, corniced with "helmet" cappings and railed ogee quadrants beyond, one terminating in a tall corniced screen wall which contained another round-headed and pilastered wicket gate opening. Clearly by Thomas Jackson, for the Pim family. Similar to the lodge at Lisnagarvey (qv) which also had Pim connections. Apparently at a shared access and avenue to neighbouring Glenavna (qv). All now removed, the site remembered most for the notorious murder of Patricia Curran.
B.T. PHOTOGRAPH 13/11/1952

**159. GLENARM CASTLE Glenarm (5)**
**Barbican Gate** 1824; architect William
Vitruvius Morrison
Beloved of photographers and Victorian illustrators for its dramatic architecture and romantic setting. Approached across a two arched bridge spanning the Glenarm river the "Barbican" is a three storey castellated gatehouse. Above its entrance archway the inscription, "This Gateway was built and the Castle restored by Edmund McDonnell Esquire and his wife Anne Katherine, in her own right Countess of Antrim and Viscountess Dunluce AD 1825". Designed the previous year by William Vitruvius Morrison as part of his brief which included transforming the house from a winged and pavilioned Georgian affair into a square Tudorbethan pile. Two grand buttresses with pockmarked vermiculation flank the great portcullised doors with their iron studding. Over them spans a four centred arch with hood moulding, also evident on the narrow windows to the first floor office. The second floor room is lit by a tripartite semicircular-arched window

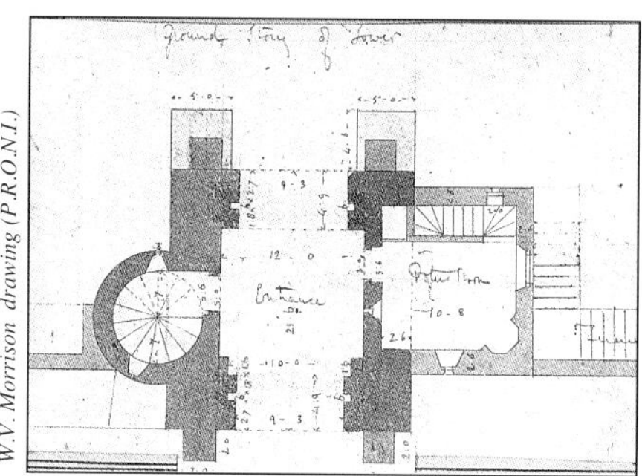

*W.V. Morrison drawing (P.R.O.N.I.)*

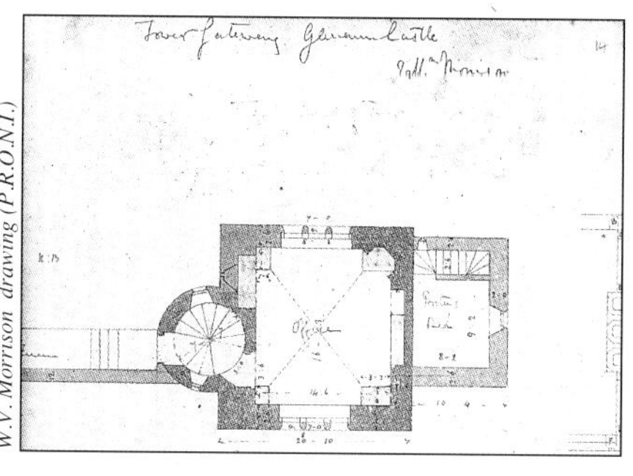

*W.V. Morrison drawing (P.R.O.N.I.)*

over which project the crenellated machicolations. Embrasured arrowloops pierce walls, merlons and the spiral stair turret which

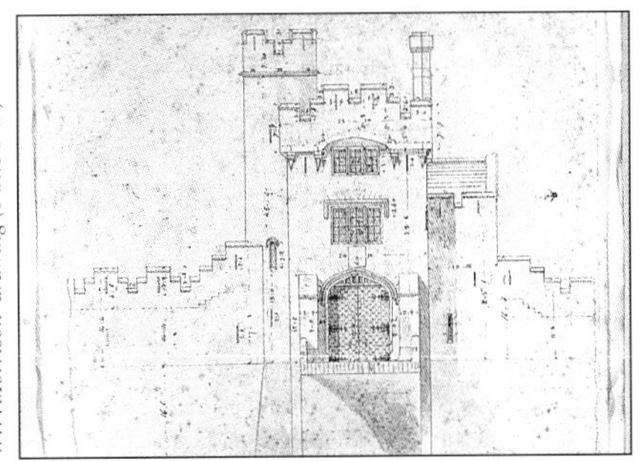
W.V. Morrison drawing (P.R.O.N.I.)

rises a storey above the rest and gives access to the upper storeys from ground and allure levels. To the other side, set into the Irish crenellated estate wall, two storey porter's accommodation, one up one down, with crowstepped gable. A three flue chimney corbels out and rises above the parapets. All in coursed squared quarry-faced basalt with pink galleted sandstone by the Irish master of the Romantic. A scrapbook of Morrison's drawings for the gate survives. There are similar designs by him at Borris, County Carlow and Thomastown Castle, County Tipperary.

**Town Lodge** c1845
In similar style and probably also by Morrison at the head of Main Street a four-centred Tudor style carriage archway with stepped parapet over and blank shield. Beyond, small square turrets as flankers with arrowloops. Behind is "Town Lodge". Two storey, painted stone walls with label mouldings to double sashed windows. Gabled with stone quoins.

**Farm Lodge** pre 1857
On the Ballymena road, single storey, gabled built in very black basalt, notable only for its stepped label moulding and mini gable over one window.

**Lothian Lodge** c1870
At the Ballymena and Carnlough Roads junction, opposite the stable yard gate a gabled one and a half storey lodge on a T plan. The elevation facing it two bay, a single storey hall projects behind from a corner of the back return. Between each of the label-moulded window openings and a high eaves is a blank shield ornament. The walls now pebble-dashed with toothed quoins.

**Holme Lodge** pre 1857; *demolished*
Deep in the estate at the entrance to the Great Deer Park a lodge now replaced by a sheep pen.
GLENS OF ANTRIM; U.A.H.S. (1971); BENCE-JONES (1988); McPARLAND (1989); P.R.O.N.I. D3560

**160. GLENARM CEMETERY, Glenarm** 1882
A distinctive building in very white coursed limestone with cream fireclay brick dressings to segmentally-headed openings, quoins and chimney stack. Single storey on an L plan with a hipped roof, the leading elevation gabled and sporting a big slate shield datestone. Now functioning also as a public toilet.

**161. GLENAVNA, Whiteabbey (3)** c1870; architect John Lanyon; *unexecuted*

J.J. Phillips drawing (U.M.)

An illustration by James J Phillips of a lodge for Mr Valentine the mining and railway magnate. Highly ornate wood fretwork to main gables and spandrels of catslide roof over arcaded verandah. Balustrade to latter repeated in entrance sweeps. Fancy brackets and finials on gable. Semicircular pediment caps to square piers. Intended location unclear, perhaps to replace the lodge at the shared entrance with The Glen (qv) on the Shore Road.

**North Lodge** pre 1857
Altered and extended out of all recognition, its avenue severed when the demesne was sold off in part for housing development, to be replaced by the Old Manse Road porter's accommodation.

**Old Manse Road** Lodge c1900
A very pretty little exercise in polychromatic brick, red and white fireclay. Single storey three bay below a hipped roof. The left hand bay in the form of a recessed entrance porch now enclosed as a glazed hallway. Mullioned windows with intricate margined and latticed lights.
U.M. PHOTOGRAPH, Ref IIA1/WHITEABBEY 10/6A; (ILLUSTRATION BY J J PHILLIPS)

**162. GLENAVY GLEBE, GLENAVY** c1820

Standard plan hipped roof roughcast walls and sheeted door. Very plain but for the most pretty pairs of latticed lights with trefoiled heads. A very appropriate ecclesiastical feel. The glebe house was built in 1819, the lodge coeval.

**163. GLENBANK, Ligoniel** c1875; *demolished*
The lodge built for Lavens M Ewart, of the vast flax spinning company, when the property was purchased from Robert Thompson. Demolished along with the house after the grounds were presented to Belfast Corporation in 1920 for use as a public park.

**164. GLENBURN, Dunmurry (2)** both c1835; *both demolished*
These lodges can be accurately dated, as neither appear on the 1833 O.S. Map and Thomas Fagan in his Ordnance Survey Memoir notes of November 1837 records considerable improvement on the premises by Edward Curtis, Esq; "there are 2 entrances to the house, one from the turnpike road by a very handsome winding avenue, and a second from the old Malone Road between Belfast and Lisburn. At each entrance is a neat porter's lodge." Neither lodges nor avenues remain, the demesne having been broken up, though the elegant house is immaculately maintained.
O.S.M.; DIXON AND HEATLEY (1983)

**165. GLENCAIRN, Belfast North** c1860; *demolished*
A photograph of c1900 shows a highly ornate and extensive cast iron sweep with gates hung on piers, much as at Trewmount, County Tyrone (qv). A 1962 aerial survey photograph shows the lodge opposite to have been a simple rectangular gabled structure with similar breakfront located symmetrically. Josias Cunningham who bought the property in 1855, or his eldest son James, greatly extended the original house, realigned the avenue and added the lodge sometime after 1857.
YOUNG (1909); B.K.S. AIR SURVEY

**166. GLENCAIRN, Broughshane** pre 1857; *demolished*
The property in 1837 and 1856 of Rev W Crawford.

**167. GLENCONWAY, Glenavy** pre 1832; *demolished*
In 1816, "Mr Whittle's cottage".
ATKINSON (1823)

**168. GLENDARRAGH, Crumlin (2)** both pre 1832; *both demolished*
"... the beautiful cottage and highly embellished grounds" of Lieut-Col Langford Heyland who may have erected the lodges. He had succeeded to the fifty acre demesne after the death of his father Rowley, the builder in 1765 of the most extensive and complete flour mills in the country, the first to be erected in the north of Ireland. These were later to be acquired by Robert Macauley of the neighbouring Ben Neagh (qv). Neither lodge survives, that at the main entrance having been taken down to make way for a railway cutting.
LEWIS (1837)

**169. GLENGORMLEY HOUSE AND BLEACHWORKS, Glengormley (2)** both pre 1857; *both demolished*
The house built in 1834 for Allen Gardner Brown.

**170. GLENMONA LODGE, Cushendun** pre 1857; *demolished*
Built for Mr M Harrison.

**171. GLENMORE, Lambeg (2)**
In 1835 James Nicholson Richardson, founder of Richardson Sons and Owden Ltd., purchased from Alexander Williamson Lambeg House, as it was then known, complete with two gate lodges, one in the village, the other opposite the Belfast-Lisburn Road entrance. Richardson embarked on extensive improvements and the Belfast architect Thomas Jackson was to benefit from the first of many commissions from the family. The house was to be transformed in more than name and both "East" and "West" lodges were replaced.

**West Lodge** c1840; architect Thomas Jackson; *demolished*

P. Rankin

This rebuilding was enforced by the intrusion of a large railway embankment carrying the Belfast-Dublin line within the estate, and soon after 1839 the realigned avenue passed below a bridge via two gates which flanked a new lodge on the main road. The new lodge had all the hallmarks of Jackson's hand, the canted bays on each gable to be seen at Longwood in the same county (qv) and Huntley, Co. Down (qv). Segmentally-headed paired and margined casement windows, set into recesses with architraved surrounds, and bracketed cills. Pilastered corners and paired brackets to the eaves of a hipped roof - all typical. The front door of this stuccoed cottage turned its back on the road. Chimney stack of two stone octagonal flues. Demolished to make way for road improvements in the 1970s.

**East Lodge** c1840; architect probably Thomas Jackson; *demolished*

This was similar in style and has suffered the same fate as its counterpart.

O.S.M.; DIXON AND HEATLEY (1983)

**172. GLENNALINA MILL, Belfast South** pre 1832; *demolished*

Part of a complex of bleach green, mills and owner's house of Mr William Orr. All now gone.

**173. GLEN OAK, Crumlin** c1840

Once a typical Georgian style lodge. Single storey three bay symmetrical below a hipped roof. Now cleverly extended and reorientated into a small villa in its own right, but spoiled by an inharmonious sun room planted on the original entrance facade. A seat of the Macauley family, mill owners.

**174. GLENSIDE, Belfast North (2)**

**Main Entrance** c1860; architect perhaps Thomas Jackson

Previously a perky little Neo-Classical building now forlorn, shorn of its big house, park and avenue. Single storey, symmetrical and stuccoed it has large double casement windows in architraved surrounds with diamond keystones, set off in channelled rustication, framed in turn with smooth bands as crude pilasters plinth and frieze. A mutuled eaves cornice is carried around the pediment, pluckily supported on two slender Roman Doric columns and corresponding antae. Hipped roof and corniced chimney stack. Just visible in the deep-set tympanum a crest, a rampant lion wielding a battleaxe, identifies the lodge as having been built by the Emerson family of the Glenbank and Ballysillan Flax Spinning Mills. An entrance sweep with ogee quadrants survives.

**Secondary Entrance** c1860; *demolished*

A modest version of the above without any of the architectural detailing.

BKS AIR SURVEY

**175. GLENVALE, Belfast North** pre 1857; *demolished*

**176. GLENVILLE, Andersonstown** pre 1901; *demolished*

The property in 1870 of James McAuley, having previously been that of the Stoupes.

**177. GLENVILLE, Cushendall** c1810

A once trim and typical little late Georgian Gothick cottage, which had lancet-headed openings with Y tracery glazing bars. Hipped, wide-eaved roof, stuccoed walls painted white. Now much extended though not quite having suffered the plate glass indignities of the main house. Built for Alexander Macauley.

H.M.B.B. PHOTOGRAPH

*(R. Huffam)*

*W.A. Green (U.F.T.M.)*

**178. GLYNN HOUSE, Carrickfergus** c1820

The delightful pencil drawing, precisely dated 10 April 1843, depicts a nice symmetrical Georgian Gothick composition. A box lodge with castellated parapet above a cornice and stringcourse. Two square recesses in the front elevation each frame tripartite pointed windows, balanced to the other side of the gates by a facade with neither windows nor lodge behind. Perhaps a twin was intended and the money ran out. Between, two large pilastered stone pillars crowned by splendid sphinxes with operatic busts. Probably dating from 1820 when major alterations were carried out to the house by the Legg family. The Green photograph of a century later shows the lodge transformed into something a little less sophisticated with a late Victorian Tudor Gothick cloak, having developed a steeply-pitched roof with ornamental bargeboards, cruder fenestration, label mouldings and a canted bay. To the rear sprouts a return with arcaded wooden verandah over a relocated front door. The lamp standards mark the abode of the Mayor of Belfast, W F Coates, to whom the demesne was then let. Sadly the sphinxes have disappeared and the lodge severed from the house by yet another DOE road.

GREEN PHOTOGRAPH (U.F.T.M.)
Ref W.A.G. 1080

**179. GOBRANA, Glenavy** pre 1832; *demolished*

Probably built by James Whitla on acquiring the property from Thomas Daniel.

**180. GOREMOUNT, Glenavy** pre 1832

Originally a pair, one of which survives. Rather plain, three bay and gabled. Once the demesne of the Gores.

**181. GRAYMOUNT, Greencastle** pre 1857; architect possible Thomas Jackson; *demolished*

An early c1835 Regency house by Thomas Jackson for William Gray, linen merchant who redeveloped the old Greencastle House and built the neighbouring bleach mill. The lodge demolished to make way for a modern bungalow at what is now the entrance to Cedar Lodge Special School.

LARMOUR (1987)

**182. GREENFIELD, Kells** pre 1857; *demolished*

In 1833 the residence of a Mr Maxwell.

**183. GREENISLAND HOSPITAL, Jordanstown** (see VENTNOR)

**184. GREENMOUNT, Belfast North**
pre 1857; *demolished*
Originally a property belonging to John Bell.

**185. GREENMOUNT, Muckamore (3)**
**West Entrance** pre 1832; *demolished*
Atkinson in about 1816 remarks, "... In the style of modern beauty, this is one of the handsomest villas in the neighbourhood of Antrim; an effect, to which the approach, guarded by a gatehouse of the first elegance, largely contributes ...". This villa was built for Robert Thompson Esq and designed by the English architect C R Cockerell and it is interesting to speculate whether he was also responsible for the gatehouse, which was probably taken away before 1857 to make way for a railway cutting.
**Inner Lodges** pre 1832; *demolished*
A pair of round lodges within the estate, little more than pill-boxes.
**East Entrance** 1925;
architect Roland Ingelby-Smith
The present Classical Arts-and-Crafts pair of lodges flank the new entrance to the agricultural college. Solid two storey, hipped roofs with big chimney stacks aloft. Single storey projections reduce the scale to the road. In black coursed rubble basalt, a chunky granite stringcourse becomes a Palladian lintel over small square-paned windows.
COLVIN (1978); ATKINSON (1823)
ARCHITECT'S JOURNAL (1925)

**186. GREENVILLE, Ballymoney** pre 1857;
*demolished*
Built by J R Moore.

**187. GRETTON VILLAS, Belfast South**
(see BLADON PARK)

**188. GROVE GREEN COTTAGE, Lisburn**
pre 1833; *demolished*
Built by Samuel Kennedy after purchasing the property here in 1817 from Fulton, Wightman and Co, converting the premises to flour mills. The O.S. Memoir mentions "iron gates to the different entrances" but fails to notice the porter's lodge.
O.S.M.

**189. THE GROVE, Belfast North** pre 1832;
*demolished*
Built for the Simms family, after purchasing the property from a James Carson c1810. Connop's 1863 painting shows a simple square or rectangular single storey lodge with a hipped roof.
CONNOP (1863)

**190. HAMPTON, Belfast South** 1896;
architects Young & MacKenzie
Built along with two semidetached cottages the lodge one and a half storey, originally in red facing brick. Single storey hall projection, gablet and main gables have timber collar and post features carried on carved brackets, fascias moulded. Flat-roofed arrow bay window on main road gable. Much extended, now rendered over, only the brick stringcourses expressed, chimney stack no longer decorative. It survives the earlier house of 1855 which has been demolished to make way for the Public Record Office of Northern Ireland.
LARMOUR (1987)

**191. HARBOUR COMMISSIONERS OFFICES, Belfast North** pre 1860;
architect possibly George Smith;
*demolished*
There is now no sign of the porter's lodge recorded in the Griffith Valuation. It would seem to have been contemporary with the original Italianate style offices by the Harbour Engineer. Perhaps swept away during W H Lynn's alterations and enlargements thirty years later.
LARMOUR (1987); GRIFFITH

**192. HARMONY HILL, Ballymoney**
(see BALNAMORE)

**193. HAZELBANK, Newtownabbey**
pre 1832; *demolished*
A lodge which sat back-to-back with that of Macedon (qv) and which suffered a similar fate. Built by David McTear before he sold the park to James Thompson.
McTEAR (1898)

**194. HENRYFIELD, Ballyclare** pre 1857;
*demolished*
A lodge which was removed before 1902. Built for John Johnston Kirkpatrick.

**195. HILLHEAD, Ballymena**
(see KINTULLAGH)

**196. HILLMOUNT, Cullybackey (2)**
both pre 1857; *both demolished*
One lodge was sited opposite the gates. Built by Messrs James and Robert Young of the nearby bleach works founded by their predecessors the Hill family.
BASSETT'S CO ANTRIM (1888)

**197. HILLMOUNT, Larne** c1800

Alluring, unsophisticated Georgian lodge in whitewashed harling. Single storey three bay two roomed, one opening off an open semicircular-recessed alcove. Hipped roof and precarious heightened stack seeking draw as the trees grow taller. Simpler than those at Derramore, County Down (qv) and Ely Lodge, County Fermanagh (qv) which have the same exposed porch arrangement. One-time owner was Lieutenant D McN Beatty, RN.

**198. HOLESTONE, Doagh (3)**
Only one of the entrances survives, all for James Owens
**Main Entrance** c1850
Fine octagonal granite gate piers with recessed panels, cornices and ball finials. Spear-topped gates. Plain three bay lodge.
**Secondary Entrances** both pre 1832;
*both demolished*

**199. HOLLYROOD, Belfast South** c1850

Perky little symmetrical three bay lodge with square window openings which had multi-rectangular panes. Sheeted door with Tudor style spandrelled head. Paired gutter support brackets to a clipped eaves below a hipped roof which has circular twin-flued stone stacks. Now expertly improved but no longer rose-embowered and missing its cottage garden. It sat back-to-back with the lodge to Coolavin (qv). Mysteriously, its avenue seems never to have led anywhere in particular.

**200. HUGOMONT, Ballymena** pre 1857;
*demolished*
Built by Captain Hugh Harrison.

**201. HUNTLEY COTTAGE, Dunmurry**
(see RATHMORE)

**202. HUNTLEY LODGE, Dunmurry**
pre 1858; *demolished*
The lodge survived by two good iron gate sweeps. Octagonal gate posts with recessed panels. A fine Neo-Classical villa built by the Hunters, a linen family from Dunmurry.

**203. INGRAM, Lisburn** pre 1901; *demolished*
Yet another house of the Richardsons. The lodge built by Jonathan of that family.

**204. INVER, Larne** c1860; *demolished*
An early photograph shows an idyllic scene, the little standard three bay lodge, gable-on sitting alongside the church lychgate. The low-pitched hipped roof extends to form a creepered trellis verandah. Probably roughcast with Georgian-paned windows framed by louvred shutters. There was a very tall plinthed and corniced chimney stack. To the other side, by the gates an unusual arcaded screen. For the Barklie family.
LAWRENCE PHOTOGRAPH COLLECTION (NLI.) Ref 5038(C)

**205. JENNYMOUNT, Belfast North**
pre 1832; *demolished*
Both lodge and the Romantic Gothick mansion of the Thomson family pulled down and the grounds made into small streets, the old driveway now Alexandra Park Avenue. J H Connop's "Bird's Eye View of Belfast" in 1863 suggests the lodge to have been circular or ovoid. In 1847 the house was renamed Castleton by Robert Thomson, director of the Belfast Banking Company.
McTEAR (1898); CONNOP (1863);
DIXON AND HEATLEY (1983)

**206. JOYMOUNT PALACE, Carrickfergus**
c1615; *demolished*

(British Museum)

In 1634 an anonymous English traveller relates "... the only grace of this town is the Lord Chichester's house, which is a very stately house, or rather like a prince's palace, whereunto there belongs a stately gatehouse and graceful terrace, and walk before the house ...". Sir Arthur Chichester had erected upon the site of an ancient friary in 1611-18 his palace of Joymount in honour of his patron Lord Mountjoy. Unique to Ireland at this time with its large windows and

early disregard for defence, secure as it was in the shadow of Carrickfergus Castle. In the manner of Longleat and Hardwicke, a 1680 view and map in the British Museum show what Mon Jorevin de Rochford describes following his visit of 1666 "... Another day I went to see the Great Palace, which is at one of the ends of the town, - it is a great square pavilion, having, I think, as many windows as there are days in the year; the top is turreted, and defended with balustrades: the entry is handsome. You just come into the outer great court, surrounded with the officers' lodgings, having a gallery over it, from whence there is a view of the sea, and all over the town; then you advance to a drawbridge, between the little turrets, which accompany a small pavilion rising over the gate of the drawbridge; this leads from the first to the second court, and faces the grand edifice". The turrets at each of the four corners of the gatehouse circular and topped by onion-shaped cupolas. The Chichesters, raised to the Marquisate of Donegall, lived here until 1724, but by 1760 Joymount was a ruin and eight years later was demolished.
BRITISH MUSEUM ILLUSTRATION; Ref K51.42; SWANSTON (1895); BIGGAR (1909); DIXON (1975)

**207. KILDRUM, Kells** pre 1832; *demolished*
Long time residence of the bleach green owner, Jesse Millar.

**208. KILEEN, Belfast North** c1870; architect possibly James Hamilton
Built off an L plan, a patchy honey-coloured sandstone lodge of single storey. Aedicule windows in the gables below a low-pitched roof, one of which is carried down in a catslide over the internal corner hall. Missing are the original ornate gable brackets and glazing bars. Like the house, in a style reminiscent of Glasgow's "Greek" Thomson, probably by James Hamilton of the same city. One of the parks formed in the late 1860s upon the breaking up of the old Fortwilliam estates by James W Valentine for whom Kileen was built. Not long after Robert Porter, director of the York Street Mill lived here.
LARMOUR (1987)

**209. KILLOWEN, Lisburn (2)** both pre 1901; *both demolished*
Built for J T Richardson.

**210. KILWAUGHTER CASTLE, Larne (2)**
**Main Entrance Gateway** c1810; architect probably John Nash
"... The approach is through a fine stone gateway at a considerable distance from the house and flanked by 2 small octagonal towers". Thus wrote Lieut R Boteler for the OS Memoirs in August 1833. Without doubt this gateway was designed, as was the castle, by the famous English architect John Nash, not long after 1807. He was commissioned by Edward Jones Agnew. The charming Lawrence photograph shows the two castellated turrets flanking a four-centred archway, similarly crenellated. Now the coursed squared basalt archway has, like the avenue, gone, the once ornamental demesne destroyed and the castle a shell.
**Main Entrance Lodge** c1835; architects possibly Millar and Nelson
Happily the beautiful little English Picturesque cottage lodge is appreciated and recently improved. One and a half storey two up three down, the single storey hall projects from below a gablet, all gables having lovely trefoiled bargeboards with onion-topped hipknobs. Latticed windows with unusual 'awning' hoods over, in random basalt walls. Dating from the late 1830s, perhaps by Millar and Nelson of Belfast, too late to have been by Nash and replacing a predecessor on the same site.

W.M. Lawrence (N.L.I.)

*Main Entrance*

**Secondary Entrance Lodge** c1830
Alongside the gateway, a tiny rectangular two bay lodge. In big chunky coursed stone, gabled, the high eaves housing minimal loft bedspace.
MANSBRIDGE (1991); DAVIS (1973); LAWRENCE PHOTOGRAPH (NLI.) Ref 9194(R); O.S.M.; SUMMERSON (1980)

**211. KILWAUGHTER CEMETERY, Larne** 1887
Three bay gabled lodge with projecting central hall. Paired segmentally-headed windows with chamfered stone reveals and a stringcourse wrapped around at springline. To the roof relieving bands of octagonal toed slates, crowned by sawtooth earthenware cresting. There is an informative shield in the leading gable:- "Built by David Nelson Esq JP of Larne, 1887."

**212. KINCRAIG, Belfast North** c1870; *demolished*

A.R. Hogg (U.M.)

An early photograph shows a distant view of a Picturesque Scots Baronial style lodge. One and a half storey with steeply-pitched crowstepped gables and ball finials. On one corner a circular turreted projection with "candle-snuffer" conical roof stands guard over the gates. All very much in the manner of Lanyon, Lynn and Lanyons' Belfast Castle lodge (qv) nearby, probably for N McVicar Gourlie. Both his lodge and contemporary big house now gone.
HOGG PHOTOGRAPH (U.M.) Ref H10/12/3

**213. KINTULLAGH, Ballymena (2)**
**South Entrance** c1862; architects Lanyon Lynn and Lanyon
A chip off the Victorian Jacobean buff ashlar sandstone main block, right down to its shaped gables, but swapping an amusing pyramidal porch canopy for the belfry. This is now unfortunately without its decorated wooden brackets and original carved post support. On an L plan it has apex finials identical to those on the Castle Leslie, Co Monaghan lodge (qv), for which it was a prototype. Concave walls sweep to stone pillars, well wrapped up in strapwork crowned with fleurs-de-lys. The two inner pillars now replaced by modern posts. All built about 1862 for William A Young and designed by Messrs Lanyon, Lynn and Lanyon, superseding a

pre 1857 lodge across the road for the previous house on the site known as Hillhead, when it belonged to the Gihon family.
**Secondary Lodge** pre 1903; *demolished*
Now a St Louis Convent.
BENCE-JONES (1988); ANTRIM AND BALLYMENA; U.A.H.S. (1969); DIXON (1975)

**214. THE KNOCKAGH, Greenisland** pre 1858; *demolished*
A seat in 1858 of James Walker.

**215. KNOCKANURE, Ballymena** c1858; *demolished*
Belfast architect Thomas Jackson built the house here in 1856 and perhaps was also responsible for the lodge. All cleared away in 1964. For William Dunseath. Previously called Mount Pleasant.
DIXON (1978)

**216. KNOCKMORE, Moss-side** c1860; *demolished*
Noted by Griffith in his valuation of 1864 as a property of Hugh B MacKay.
GRIFFITH

**217. LAKE VIEW, Upper Ballinderry** c1860; *demolished*
A lodge for William Addison.

**218. LAMBEG, Lambeg** (see GLENMORE)

**219. LAMBEG COTTAGE, Lambeg** (see ABERDELGHY COTTAGE)

**220. LANGFORD LODGE, Crumlin (3)**
**Whitegate Entrance Gates** c1825; architect probably Richard Morrison
The entrance gates are a design taken from J B Papworth's *Rural Residences* (1818) and an idea habitually employed by Sir Richard Morrison, to be found at at least five other locations in Ireland and in one of his unexecuted proposals for Baronscourt, County Tyrone (qv). The sturdy Greek stellae piers also boast his favourite laurel

J.B. Papworth (1818)

wreath motif. Papworth's design is faithfully copied down to the wrought iron secondary posts which carry the gates, now missing. The piers are now almost unrecognisable. Built for Major General the Hon Hercules Robert Pakenham between 1820 and 1825 at the time that the house was rebuilt when the property passed by marriage from the Rowley family (Barons Langford).

**Whitegate Entrance Lodge** c1840; architect possibly Richard Morrison

W.A. Green (U.F.T.M.)

The porter's lodge dates from the 1840s, a one and a half storey, commodious ornamental multi-gabled Tudor style villa with clusters of tall octagonal chimney pots. Bold lobed trefoil bargeboards, stopped at the eaves with "kiss curls". Nice single storey porch, all in coursed basalt rubble and rendered quoins. There is a smaller version of this by the same hand across the lough on the Shanes Castle estate (qv), possibly both by the ageing Morrison.

**Greengate Lodge** c1850

Another ornamental cottage with steeply pitched roofs and decorative bargeboards. Rising off a T plan the main body of the lodge one and a half storey with a single storey projection, the gable of which is relieved by a blank shield with sturdy label moulding over. The bargeboards are novel with repeating chamfered "continuous bracket" trim and fretted with mouchettes and tiny trefoils. Rendered over and spoiled by discordant additions and modern windows. It retains its original function at the entrance to an industrial complex.

**Gartree Lodge** pre 1858; *demolished*

A lodge opposite the entrance archway to the pretty Gartree church. The big house was bulldozed into the lough as part of the destruction of this once fine demesne.

WEST ANTRIM; U.A.H.S. (1970); PAPWORTH (1818); P.R.O.N.I. D.2134/1/3; GREEN PHOTOGRAPH (U.F.T.M.)

Ref W.A.G. 1221

**221. LARKFIELD, Dunmurry** pre 1858; *demolished*

A house of the McCance family. It and lodge gone.

**222. LARNE RECTORY, Larne** pre 1902; *demolished*

The lodge to an 1824 glebe house.

**223. LAUREL LODGE, Belfast North** pre 1857; *demolished*

Built for Charles William Lepper and situated by Trainfield (qv) of the same family who owned the adjacent Lodge Mill.

**224. LEGHINMORE, Ballymena** pre 1857; *demolished*

Built for John Dickey.

**225. LEGONIEL, Belfast North** pre 1832/pre 1857; *demolished*

A pair of lodges for Thomas Ferguson. Replaced before 1857 by James Bodell, flax spinner, by a single lodge since also demolished.

DIXON AND HEATLEY (1983)

**226. LEGONIEL VILLA, Belfast North**

Shared a common entrance with Legoniel House (see above).

**227. LESLIE HILL, Ballymoney (3)**

**Early Main Entrance** pre 1832; *demolished*

The imposing mansion and demesne of the Leslie family was once entered between a pair of round lodges but these were taken away before 1857 when the previous public road was absorbed into the estates.

**Modern Main Entrance** 1911

Off the old Coleraine Road a relatively recent lodge disguised as something earlier. An Italianate portico with Tuscan columns and corresponding pilasters carry the arches which front a stuccoed single storey building with narrow paired semicircular-headed windows. Hipped roof and squat central stack of four flues which reflect the accommodation within. The channelled gate pillars are earlier and in Georgian manner. The lodge deserted and blocked up.

**Farmyard Entrance** c1790

Within the demesne, protected from the world, at the entrance to the farmyard a pretty little three bay clipped eaves gabled Georgian Gothick building with Y traceried lancet windows in whitewashed harled walls. At the other side of two vernacular round gate posts with cone caps, the composition is almost balanced but not quite, for by a pond, the one-roomed payhouse is a scaled down version of the lodge, like a doll's house. All well maintained.

NORTH ANTRIM; U.A.H.S. (1972)

**228. LILLIPUT, Belfast North** pre 1857; *demolished*

The occupant in 1856 Captain Thomas Verner.

**229. LINFIELD FLAX SPINNING COMPANY, Belfast South** c1850

The concern of John Murphy, flax spinner, is remarkably survived by its gatehouse. It seems to have been a three by two bay two storey structure below a hipped roof with clipped eaves. In a pleasant mellow brown brick, openings to both floors semicircular-headed in similar recesses, now lacking their original Georgian style glazing pattern. The leading elevation has had its ground floor faced in quarry-faced stone, resulting in the loss of its openings and probably executed when a new gate screen was added. This has three tall octagonal stone pillars and sturdy spear-topped cast iron gates. The lodge still performs its original function.

**230. LISBURN CASTLE, Lisburn**

To Lord Conway's house an old red sandstone entrance gate with 1677 carved on it.

**231. LISBURN CEMETERY, Lisburn** c1880

One and a half storey symmetrical, gabled with label mouldings. The tall projecting hipped roof hall is incongruous.

**232. LISMARA, Newtownabbey** c1855; architects probably Lanyon and Lynn; *demolished*

(H.M.B.B.)

Another Italianate lodge almost identical to that at Cromore, County Londonderry (qv), but slightly more elaborate. For the Finlay family it was in buff coloured sandstone ashlar like the house. Symmetrical, three bay with a hipped roof carried on eaves brackets. Narrow windows, semicircular-headed, as are the arches to the "porte-cochère" which has moulded archivolts springing from square pillars, the side arches balustraded. Nice sculpted keystones and cartouche in the gable. Unlike Charles Lanyon's earlier gabled Italianate lodges at Moneyglass and Dunderave in the same county (qqv), and Eglantine and Ballywalter in County Down (qqv), the "porte-cochère" was two bay and the centre pillar sat uncomfortably on the front door axis. Another victim of road widening.
H.M.B.B. PHOTOGRAPHS

**233. LISMOYNE, Dunmurry (2)**
Lewis in 1837 talks of the demesne of Mrs Caldwell presenting one of the finest landscapes in the neighbourhood of Belfast. George Caldwell upon acquiring Lismoyne from his brother Robert around 1840 set about further embellishing it, with the addition of two delightful lodges, both simple three bay, Neo-Classical.

**Belfast Lodge** c1845; architect perhaps Thomas Jackson

That at the main gate more ornate with the hipped roof behind a stone parapet which crowns rough-cast walls. Windows, set into segmentally-arched recesses, have margined panes as has the double leaf front door. The portico entablature is carried on slender Roman Doric columns with corresponding antae. The gable bay windows, though modern, inoffensive. Panelled chimney stack and the glazing pattern have much reminiscent of the work of Thomas Jackson as at Longwood (qv). Some square gate piers survive with raised and fielded panels below a fluted frieze and moulded projecting caps. Good contemporary ironwork.

**Lisburn Lodge** c1845; architect perhaps Thomas Jackson

At the stableyard entrance a less pretentious but no less pleasing building. This time a projecting hipped roof has paired modillion brackets to the eaves. Walls roughcast and recessed as before

but the windows have only squared panes. Double panelled door but no portico. The fine proportions unimpaired by the extension which is a repeat of the lodge with a flat roofed link, showing how it can and should be done, much as at Ahoghill Rectory (qv). Now avenueless, the original gates have gone. Remarkably both lodges remain, well maintained, as sole survivors from a once fine small demesne now minus its big house and artificial lake, and gradually being split up into ever-decreasing plots for executive housing.
LEWIS (1837); HEATLEY AND DIXON (1983)

**234. LISNAGARVEY, Lisburn** c1855; architect Thomas Jackson; *demolished*

P. Rankin

Sarah Malcolmson was a Richardson girl who had married into the family of Portlaw - Quakers and cotton spinners. After being widowed she returned home to establish this small park with villa and gate lodge designed by the family architect. Ogee sweeps between octagonal piers with recessed panels and corniced caps all, like the little lodge, a well tried Jackson formula repeated at nearby Glenmore, Longwood, The Glen and Lissue (qqqv) in the same county and Dunbarton and Huntley in County Down (qqv). The Glen was a Pim family property and Anna R Pim lived at Lisnagarvey after her older sister Sarah's death in 1864. Single storey, three bay symmetrical front elevation by one bay deep. Hipped roof, paired eaves brackets, corner pilasters, moulded segmentally-headed surrounds to openings with margined casement windows. Standard plan and stuccoed walls in Neo-Classical style - all typical. Sadly, demesne and buildings swept away in 1968 to make way for a housing development.

**235. LISSANOURE CASTLE, Cloghmills (3)**

**East Entrance** c1790; *demolished*

In 1789 Lord Macartney, diplomat and Colonial Governor, received a lengthy report from his agent Richard Jackson stating that the estate wall was almost complete and declaring it to be "exceedingly well built". There was also built about then a porter's lodge on the east side of the demesne and a driveway put down from there to the castle. The only evidence of this today is two large square gate pillars.

**North Entrance** c1830; architect probably J B Keane

Around 1829 George Hume Macartney employed the architect J B Keane to design

sundry embellishments, those to the big house proceeding at a leisurely pace before their abandonment in 1847 following an accidental explosion, whereupon the family retired to the "elegant cottage" nearby. The commission included a remarkably commodious gate lodge at the north gate. The solid central one and a half storey cube has a gablet in the middle piercing a hipped roof. Below it a large panelled door with a simple "mouth organ" fanlight. Flanking are single storey, hipped roof wings each with double French doors. Built in coursed basalt with ashlar quoins and dressings. Avenue and entrance long disused.

**South Entrance** c1860

To the south entrance to Lissanoure Cottage, a large irregular stuccoed one and a half storey lodge, gabled with pretty serrated bargeboards and fascias, as has the projecting single storey hall. Segmentally-headed ground floor openings. The chimney stack with its diamond motifs and trio of octagonal pots too shyly located to contribute to the overall Picturesque effect. Outer stone octagonal piers linked to inner iron bullet-shaped posts by modern railings.
P.R.O.N.I. D.572/9/44; ROEBUCK (1983); NORTH ANTRIM; U.A.H.S. (1972); BENCE-JONES (1988); LEWIS (1837)

**236. LISSUE, Lisburn (2)**

**East Gate** c1855; architect Thomas Jackson

For all the world like that to Lisnagarvey (qv), but on entering an L plan is revealed.

**West Gate** c1855; architect Thomas Jackson

In identical style, a sympathetically extended building disguises its previous shape. Two Neo-Classical lodges for James Nicholson Richardson Esq. As with most of Jackson's lodges instantly recognisable, both with corniced chimney stacks, hipped roofs and paired eaves brackets. To a

three bay front, pilastered corners and margined windows with bracketed cills in segmentally-headed moulded surrounds to recesses, the walls stuccoed.
DIXON (1978)

**237. THE LODGE or LODGE COTTAGE, Belfast North** pre 1857; *demolished*
In 1846 the property of James Hind, partner of St C K Mulholland of Eglantine, Co Down (qv) in the flax spinning and linen manufactory of Mulholland and Hind. Villa and lodge gone.

**238. LONGWOOD, Whitehouse (2)**
A house and demesne complete with its own gate lodge were already established in 1772 by Nicholas Grimshaw. In about 1860 his descendant, Robert, engaged the fashionable Belfast architect Thomas Jackson who was already designing villas along the Malone and Shore Roads for the new mercantile class. His brief was to revamp the house and provide a replacement gate lodge from a new access.
**Old Entrance** pre 1832; *demolished*
**New Entrance** c1860; architect Thomas Jackson

Typical Jackson Neo-Classical, though here graced by an Ionic pedimented portico with matching antae. This is the frontispiece of a symmetrical composition flanked by margined windows with bracketed cills set into segmentally-headed recesses with moulded surrounds. Standard plan and stuccoed walls with pilastered corners. Strangely the canted bay is on the side elevation away from the gates (something that is put right at Huntley, Co Down (qv), where an identical lodge is located at the opposite side of the entrance). The hipped roof has a corniced chimney-stack with recessed panels to match those below the windows. The gates have gone and the lodge has recently been extended sensitively.
DIXON (1978); McTEAR (1898); O.S.M.

**239. LONSDALE, Jordanstown** c1858; *demolished*
By the lough shore with its back to the road a modest single storey gabled lodge built for Matthew Stothard.
GRIFFITH

**240. LOUGHANMORE or LOUGHERMORE, Templepatrick (4)**
**Side Entrance** pre 1832
A lodge opposite the gates much changed and insignificant.
**West Entrance** pre 1832
On the road to Parkgate the first lodge altered, with hipped gables, two storey basalt.
**Middle Entrance** c1910; architect possibly Robert Graeme Watt
An excellent Arts-and-Crafts design by an unrecorded architect, for the Adair family. The latest of three buildings on this site, the earliest being a pre 1832 circular lodge. Peculiarly turning its back on the road, one and a half storey in coursed basalt rubble with Classical Lutyens type windows, multi-squared with segmental heads. A symmetrical three bay elevation has dormer windows piercing the eaves line and gutters carried across. The rear elevation has a wide central dormer, with leaded segmentally-headed roof, like the others. Chimneys to both gables. The granite gate piers in nice Art-Nouveau manner have caps like those at Kircassock, Co Down (qv) by architect Robert Graeme Watt. Unaccountably lying empty.
**East Entrance** pre 1832; *demolished*
The third lodge on the same road swept away by the M2 motorway.

**241. LOWWOOD, Greencastle** pre 1832; *demolished*
Probably built by John Thomson on acquiring the property from Thomas Cunningham in 1811.

**242. LUCYVILLE, Whitehouse** pre 1857; *demolished*
A property in 1861 of Richard Bell.

**243. LUNATIC ASYLUM, Belfast South** c1830; architects Francis Johnston and William Murray; *demolished*
One of a series of nine such institutions built throughout Ireland to a standard plan, in this case dating from 1829. Doubtless its gate lodge was to the same pattern as those at Londonderry (qv) and the sole survivor at Armagh (qv). Both asylum and lodge long gone.

**244. MACEDON, Newtownabbey (2)**
**Old Lodge** pre 1832; *demolished*
**New Lodge** c1855; *demolished*

(H.M.B.B.)

Replacing the earlier pre 1832 lodge which sat at the other side of the avenue back-to-back with that to Hazelbank (qv). A solid building in ashlar, brick dressings and segmental arches, with keystones to windows. Like the house, it had a delicate ironwork verandah below a projecting eaves. Hipped roof, alternate slate courses laid diagonally, topped by an unusual three-flue cluster stack in corniced stonework sitting rather uneasily. By contrast the gates, piers and railings in the most extravagant style with a riot of fleurs-de-lys. All of about 1870 for John Cunningham Esq, but taken down, like much by the lough shore, to accommodate road improvements. The gates were salvaged and re-erected at Brocklemont, Ballymena (qv).
McTEAR (1898); H.M.B.B. PHOTOGRAPHS

**245. MAGHERAMORNE, Glynn (3)**
**Old Main Entrance** c1840; *ruinous*
John Irving was proprietor of the largest limestone works in the United Kingdom and built himself "a new mansion" about 1835 along with, on the high road, a simple hipped roof three bay gate lodge having quoins and Tudor label mouldings to openings. This lodge is now a shell. The house was replaced in 1880 by the First Lord Magheramorne on inheriting the estate from his brother-in-law Charles McGarel who had previously acquired it from the Irvings. His Lordship was not short of funds, having married into the immensely wealthy Douglas-Pennant family, slate magnates of Penrhyn Castle, North Wales. He set about continuing the transformation of the demesne that McGarel had begun, with the help of his architect S P Close, whose commission comprised the replacement mansion and a gate lodge to the new main entrance off the Shore Road.
**New Main Entrance** c1880; architect S P Close

An apt introduction to the big house, the lodge is primarily one and a half storey on an irregular plan with single storey wing and projecting hall. In uncoursed quarry-faced basalt rubble highlighted with red Scottish sandstone to plinth, stringcourses, window dressings, relieving arches, shield ornaments and steep skewtable gables terminating in ball finials. There are matching finials to the pyramidal caps on the square gate piers, the gates taken away to allow hotel traffic past.
**South Lodge** c1870
Nondescript.
LEWIS (1837); BASSETT'S CO ANTRIM (1888)

**246. MAGHERINTEMPLE, Ballycastle** 1874; architect possibly S P Close

A fitting prelude to the house, with which it is contemporary and in the same style - Scottish Baronial. The lodge of simple three bay format, one and a half storey having a highly-pitched roof with sawtooth cresting. Uncoursed squared limestone walls rising to crowsteps on main gables and that of projecting hall, all culminating in ball finials. Datestone over the front door. Chamfered surrounds to openings with sash windows not as appropriate as one would expect for this, the seat of the Casement family. Concave dwarf wall sweeps topped by ornate iron railings with repeated circular motifs. Gate pillars octagonal, having dome-shaped cappings and ball finials. The architect may have been Samuel Pepys Close for John Casement, father of Sir Roger. There was an older pre 1857 lodge at the other side of the gates for the previous family home known as Churchfield.

**247. MALONE, Belfast South (3)**
**Early West Lodge** pre 1832; *demolished*
**Early East Lodge** pre 1832; *demolished*
An old photograph shows the lodge presumably

built by William Wallace Legge in about 1840. He is said to have been his own architect for the graceful house but there was nothing elegant about this naive design. Three bay single storey with Georgian windows. Flat roofed as was the projecting hallway.

**New Lodge** 1921; architects Blackwood & Jury

*P. Larmour*

In total contrast the surviving gate lodge for James McGugan is a fine William and Mary Revival composition. One and a half storey three bay symmetrical, it has a hipped roof with a very high bracketed eaves and similar treatment of the flat-roofed dormers to the attic storey. The main feature is an open semicircular-pedimented portico with curved shell soffit supported on two Tuscan columns. Square-paned windows in moulded surrounds with lugs and bracketed cills, set off by nice Ulster pebble-dashed walls. The similarly rendered prominent chimney stacks, so crucial to the original concept, have tragically been removed in an ill-judged renovation that provides an extension in sympathetic style but which destroyed the overall form.
MALONE HOUSE; U.A.H.S. (1983); DIXON AND HEATLEY (1983); MALONE AND STRANMILLIS; U.A.H.S. (1991)

**248. MALONE PARK, Belfast South (2)**
both c1871; architects perhaps Thomas Jackson & Son
At Malone and Lisburn Road ends, standing guard over this private residential avenue, identical gate sweeps and lodges. Both L plan, but presenting symmetrical three bay elevations to the avenue. In red facing brick with glossy paint to emphatically raised quoins, moulded window surrounds and door entablatures carried on acanthus leafed console brackets. Small-paned Georgian style windows, hipped roofs. The cornices to chimney stacks survive on the Lisburn Road lodge only. Tall square chamfered sandstone piers with corniced tops suggestive of Thomas Jackson & Son. Identical gate sweep on Balmoral Avenue. There was a similar lodge at Glenmachan, Co Down (qv).
MALONE AND STRANMILLIS; U.A.H.S. (1991)

**249. MALONE PROTESTANT REFORMATORY, Belfast South** c1860; architects probably Lanyon and Lynn; *demolished*
Later named Malone Training School, its contemporary gate lodge presumably a small scale version of the main block in similar Gothic style. The complex closed down in 1968 and was demolished to make way for an industrial estate.
MALONE AND STRANMILLIS; U.A.H.S. (1991)

**250. MALONE ROAD, No 143, Belfast South**
1897; architect perhaps W H Lynn
Within a stone's throw of the house, similarly stuccoed but having none of its Classical symmetry, the L plan porter's lodge, mildly Picturesque. Simple timber collar member to the

gables, heavily corniced chimney stacks, quoins and chamfered openings. Both for Frank Kerr, solicitor. House and architect anonymous. Immaculately maintained by the Construction Employers Federation.

**251. MANOR HOUSE, Lisburn (2)**
**Main Entrance** c1860; architect not known

Lovely one and a half storey symmetrical three bay Picturesque Tudor essay in honey coloured sandstone ashlar. Showy heavily carved bargeboards to main gables and to projecting hall support sharply pointed hipknobs with pendants. Two and three light pointed windows under label mouldings. Lattice panes and original chimney stack missing, but otherwise beautifully restored and the sensitive modern return an object lesson. Built at the entrance to a rather plain Regency villa in about 1860 for the Stannus family, whose splendid crest (a talbot's head catching a dove) and motto ET VI ET VIRTUTE decorate the hall gable.

**Chapel Hill Lodge** pre 1900; *demolished*
House, park and lodge gone.

**252. MARTELLO TOWERS or MARTLETT TOWERS, Belfast North** c1855/c1880; architect perhaps R M Young or Charles West

Restrained Italianate design with low-pitched roof, gables supported on carved purlin ends. Walls in coursed squared quarry-faced basalt with smooth sandstone dressings to narrow semicircular-headed openings. To the parlour a Venetian window. Fine raised and fielded door. Built alongside an earlier pre 1857 lodge.

**253. MEADOWBANK, Whitehouse** c1845; *demolished*
George Kennedy Smith, solicitor, probably built this lodge upon acquiring the property from Mrs James Cunningham.

**254. MERVILLE, Whitehouse** 1838; architect probably Thomas Jackson; *demolished*
"Porter's lodge is very neat and of a modern style, built in 1838". This replaced a pre 1832 lodge to the park. Built by Major John Rowan who married the widow of the previous owner James Blair. The house was reworked about then by Thomas Jackson who presumably also designed the lodge.
O.S.M.; DIXON (1978); DIXON AND HEATLEY (1983)

**255. METHODIST COLLEGE, Belfast South**
1879; architect John Lanyon

*J.J. Phillips drawing (U.M.)*

An exquisite High Victorian Gothick masterpiece by John Lanyon. One and a half storey on an asymmetrical plan, gabled with steeply-pitched skewtables to a roof having alternate bands of green scalloped and blue slates topped with sawtooth cresting. Over the turreted stairs a fairytale "candle-snuffer" conical roof with fish-scale slates and iron finial. The chimneys a pair of octagonal stone pots. Built in orange brick, all its soft sandstone dressings have eroded badly. The J J Phillips illustration shows the lodge as it must have been before the ravages of time robbed it of features such as foliated apex finials, gargoyle, first floor hood mouldings, quoins, dressings and stringcourses. Much has been patched with cement render. Windows to ground floor shouldered, those on first floor pointed and foiled, one bipartite, all originally had leaded lights. The canted single storey bay with its own slated roof once had a miniature "balcony" rail. By the decorative buttress a nice herring-bone sheeted door with decorative hinges. There is a quatrefoil panel with the monogram "WMC" for Wesleyan Methodist College. The Lisburn Road pillars with finialed "pixie hats" badly eroded, those to the Malone Road taken down.
LAWRENCE PHOTOGRAPH (NLI.) Ref N.S.2430; U.M. PHOTOGRAPH; Ref ID/6a (Illustration by J J Phillips); QUEEN'S UNIVERSITY; U.A.H.S. (1975)

**256. MIDDLEPARK, Whitehouse** pre 1857; *demolished*
One time the seat of William Clarence Smyth.

**257. MILLBROOK LODGE, Larne (2)**
**Main Entrance** c1790; *demolished*
Delightful pair of umbrello lodges of c1790 the front doors of which once confronted each other across the avenue. On octagonal plan, whitewashed walls with Georgian Gothick lancet openings which would have had Y tracery. Roofs rose to central brick stacks, whilst skylights reveal what must have been very little more than garrets over two roomed ground floors.

(Larne Historical Society)

**Secondary Entrance** pre 1832; *demolished*
The extensive cotton factory of Samuel Allen, and all lodges have disappeared. The house was previously known as Allenbrook.
LARNE HISTORICAL SOCIETY PHOTOGRAPH

**258. MILLICENT, Ballymoney**
(see BALNAMORE)

**259. MILLTOWN, Belfast South** pre 1832; *demolished*
The property early in the 19th century of Robert Hamilton became in 1869 the city's Roman Catholic burial ground in succession to Friar's Bush (qv) when Timothy Hevey's bold High Victorian Romanesque arched gateway was built.

**260. MOAT PARK, Dunmurry**
(see THE PARK)

**261. MONEYGLASS, Toome (3)**
**Old Main Entrance** c1820
The original main entrance lodge survives, just. Three bay with high eaves, label mouldings to openings. Otherwise plain, it served the first Georgian house. Sometime around 1850 Kenrick Morres Hamilton-Jones called in Charles Lanyon to reconstruct the house and design two new gatekeepers' lodges.
**Rear Entrance** c1855; architect probably Charles Lanyon

At the rear gate, a pleasant three bay lodge, mildly Italianate, on the site of an earlier building. Hipped roof with an outsized chimney stack. To the front elevation semicircular-headed openings, banded with keystones. On the side wall a flat arched tripartite window. The stuccoed wall has quoins, deeply vermiculated like the gate piers which have moulded cappings and basic boulder finials. Derelict.
**New Main Entrance** c1855; architect: Charles Lanyon
On the Ballymena road an example of Lanyon's unrestrained Italianate style which is also to be found in similar lodges at Dunderave in Co Antrim (qv) and Ballywalter and Eglantine in Co Down (qqv). Though fundamentally a three bay symmetrical building, it is on a grand scale, with high ceilings and three step approach below an arcaded "porte-cochère". From four square piers spring semicircular-headed arches, archivolted

with acones. The stuccoed walls have little more than slit windows flanking the "porte-cochère", but enhanced with decorative Baroque surrounds and bracketed cills. Beyond the quoins the side elevation displays a large tripartite window with its cill projecting to platform proportions, carried on large scrolled brackets. In the gables, cartouches below a low-pitched roof carried on carved purlin ends. The scrolled bracket motif is used again to support the chimney stack cornice. Very grand sandstone octagonal entrance piers have deeply recessed panels to the shafts and to the friezes under big cappings. Its ironwork, like the mansion, now gone.
WEST ANTRIM; U.A.H.S. (1970)

**262. MOORE FORT, Ballymoney (2)**
both pre 1855; *both demolished*
Nice ironwork of around 1850, like that at Clare Park (qv) and nearby Ballynacree (qv). Built for J Moore Esq.

**263. MOOREFIELDS, Kells** pre 1857; *demolished*
Built for David Kirk.

**264. MORVEN, Belfast North** (see WALTON)

**265. MOSSLEY, Mossley** c1865; architects possibly Lanyon, Lynn and Lanyon
To the mills and manager's house a three bay single storey lodge with high-pitched main roof and projecting porch. Walls in red and yellow diapered brickwork. Sandstone plinth, quoins, dressings and hood and label mouldings to a variety of round, four-centred and square-arched openings. Arrow slits to main gables, and over the front door a sculpted shield in quatrefoil. Windows had geometric pattern glazing bars. Once a very attractive Tudor style cottage, now "improved" with plate glass windows and cement rendered walls. Perhaps by Lanyon, Lynn and Lanyon. The seat in 1839 of Edmund Grimshaw.
ANTRIM and BALLYMENA; U.A.H.S. (1969)

**266. THE MOUNT, Carrickfergus**
(see WOODBURN COTTAGE)

**267. MOUNT DAVYS, Cullybackey** pre 1857; *demolished*
The lodge opposite the gates built by Alexander McManus to his house, described as modern in 1833.
O.S.M.

**268. MOUNT EDWARDS, Cushendall** c1845
Standard single storey, hipped roof. Three bay with nice octagonal lattice glazing bar pattern to windows. For the Cuppage family. Seemingly the survivor of a pair of lodges.
GLENS OF ANTRIM; U.A.H.S. (1971)

**269. MOUNT PLEASANT, Ballymena**
(see KNOCKANURE)

**270. MOUNT PROSPECT, Belfast South** pre 1858; *demolished*
A villa belonging to Alexander Crawford. Both it and lodge gone.

**271. MOUNT VERNON, Belfast North** pre 1857; *demolished*
Built for Hill Hamilton Esq.

**272. MOUNTCOLLIER, Belfast North** pre 1832; *demolished*
The lodge built for Andrew Mulholland after coming by the property from Christopher Hudson.

**273. MOYARD, Andersonstown** c1880; architect not known
Late Victorian stuccoed single storey lodge on an L plan. Segmentally-headed openings with keystones, the drip mouldings and cills carried around as stringcourses. Canted bay window. Brackets to eaves of hipped roof and chimney stack cornice. For the Stringer family.

**274. MUCKAMORE HOUSE, Muckamore** c1880; architect not known
Irregular one and a half storey stuccoed lodge with fretted bargeboards to main gables and gablet. Smooth surrounds to openings and heavy label mouldings over. Scalloped slate courses to roof. Now extended in harmony to form a double pile. For Mr Samuel Thompson at the entrance to an earlier house probably by W H Lynn.

**275. MUCKAMORE LODGE, Muckamore** pre 1832; *demolished*
An early round lodge which did not survive to see the 20th century. Probably for Mr John Thompson.

**276. MUSGRAVE PARK HOSPITAL, Belfast South** (see NATIONAL MODEL AGRICULTURAL SCHOOL)

**277. NATIONAL MODEL AGRICULTURAL SCHOOL, Belfast South** 1859; architect Frederick Darley; *demolished*
The Dublin architect designed this rather drab Neo-Jacobean building with curved gables and a belfry constructed in red brick and stone dressings c1852. The lodge was presumably in matching manner. Tenders were invited for its construction in August 1859. At the Stockman's Lane gate, it has disappeared without trace. The complex now absorbed into the Musgrave Park Hospital and a Belfast City Council public park.
MALONE AND STRANMILLIS; U.A.H.S. (1991)

**278. NEWBRIDGE, Dunmurry**
(see LISMOYNE)

**279. OAKFIELD, Carrickfergus** c1860; *demolished*
Built for Thomas Battersby.

**280. OATLAND, Upper Ballinderry** c1860
Neat single storey three bay under a hipped roof. Georgian paned windows in very black basalt with contrasting red brick dressings. Well maintained. Built for Thomas Walkington.

**281. O'HARABROOK, Ballymoney (2)**
**South Lodge** pre 1832; *demolished*
Situated opposite the gates.
**North Lodge** c1840
Pleasant late Georgian survivor of standard plan. Both built by C O'Hara.

**282. OLD FORGE, Dunmurry** c1880; architects probably Thomas Jackson & Son; *demolished*
House for Joshua Richardson by Thomas Jackson in c1855. The lodge of about 25 years later probably from the same practice. In red and yellow polychrome brickwork. Both house and lodge demolished to make way for a golf club.
DIXON (1978)

**283. OLD LODGE, Belfast North** pre 1857; *demolished*

A lodge built by John Lytle.

**284. OLD PARK, Belfast North** pre 1832; *demolished*

Once belonging to the Lyons family "... a beautiful rural home, with fine gardens and trees and a convenient distance from the 'madding crowd'. Now, in our time, the forty-two acres of which the demesne consists are advertised to be let in lots for villas or streets, which will doubtless be the case in due time". Thus wrote Benn prophetically in 1877. Swept away was the graceful mid-Georgian villa, along with its pair of octagonal inkpot lodges flanking the main entrance.

DIXON AND HEATLEY (1983); BENN (1877)

**285. ORANMORE, Ballymena** pre 1900; *demolished*

**286. ORLANDS, Carrickfergus (2)**

**East Lodge** pre 1857; *demolished*

A one and a half storey Neo-Tudor building for the Smith family.

**West Lodge** pre 1901; *demolished*

The Archers on acquiring the property extended the house into a huge Classical mansion and built a late Victorian basalt lodge with gabled porch and lattice windows. Both now gone, the former having been burnt down by the suffragettes.

**287. THE PARK Dunmurry (2)**

A property founded in the 1840s as Moat Park by Robert Moat who built a lodge.

**North Lodge** pre 1858

This structure may have been incorporated into an existing house on the site, no longer recognisable.

**South Lodge** c1875

Originally a lofty single storey gabled lodge, three roomed on an L plan. Stone to window surrounds, plinth and corniced chimney stacks. Flat-roofed hall in the internal angle. Mildly Italianate feel about the leading gables with low-pitched bargeboards carried on scrolled brackets over blanks shields and coupled openings in stuccoed walls. Probably built for a John Boyle the lodge is now lost in transformation into a modern bungalow. The very fine surviving gate screen is earlier with corniced pillars and funerary urn finials to ironwork of gates.

**288. PARK COTTAGE, Antrim**

(see SKEFFINGTON LODGE)

**289. PARKMOUNT, Greencastle** pre 1832; *demolished*

Once a hunting lodge of the Donegall family, it was rebuilt in about 1796 by Hugh Cairns, and the lodge either dated from then or around 1828/9 when the property was bought by John McNeill.

DIXON AND HEATLEY (1983)

**290. PEOPLES' PARK, Ballymena**

1870; architects probably Lanyon, Lynn and Lanyon

A highly Picturesque multi-gabled irregular building in Scottish Baronial style. Its rugged romantic outline emphasised by the combination of one and a half and single storey crowstepped gables culminating in Jacobean strapped ball finials. The high pitched roofs have terracotta cresting and a prominent chimney stack. In squared coursed quarry-faced basalt the road elevation is liberally scattered with informative plaques telling us the construction date, the monogram of benefactor and squire Sir Shafto Adair, his family crest and a shield portraying the seven towers of Ballymena the central one clearly that of Ballymena Castle (qv). Strangely

the most articulate elevation is that facing the park. The canted single storey bay is in red Scottish sandstone as are all the other features including quoins and chamfered dressings to window openings. To the single storey office outshoot are distinctive Baroque "orangery" windows below gables back and front. On its side elevation a bell hangs to signal closing time. There are dated cast iron hopper heads. A gem, clearly the work of Lanyon, Lynn and Lanyon, reminiscent of John Lanyon's work at Belfast Castle (qv).

**291. PORTGLENONE, Portglenone (2)**

A house of 1823 for Bishop Alexander is postdated by both lodges.

**Side Entrance** c1870

A one and a half storey gabled structure built off an L plan with a fancy wooden verandah in the internal angle. Rendered. Built for J S Alexander.

**Front Entrance** c1850

An eccentric single storey building, standard three bay. To the windows large Tudor label mouldings with pendant dripstones. Stone quoins to roughcast walls. Hipped roof with trio of outsized diagonally-placed chimney stacks. Later Victorian open timber porch under a lean-to roof. Built for Nathaniel Alexander when a wing and porch were added to the house.

O.S.M.; BENCE-JONES (1988)

**292. POTTERS WALLS, Antrim** pre 1835; *demolished*

Alexander Montgomery built himself a residence in 1833 "somewhat in the cottage style and neat and modern in its appearance". He was the third of four brothers, all of whom resided in the county. John was of Benvarden (qv), Hugh of Ballydrain (qv) and Thomas had his seat at Birch Hill (qv).

O.S.M.

**293. PROSPECT, Carrickfergus** c1872; architect Timothy Hevey

For Daniel O'Rourke a particularly undistinguished lodge. This replaced a pair of round Georgian "salt and pepper" lodges closer to the town where a contemporary basalt and red brick archway survives, more appropriate to the house, and built by the Ellis family.

CARRICKFERGUS; U.A.H.S. (1978)

**294. PROSPECT COTTAGE, Lisburn** pre 1901; *demolished*

**295. QUEEN'S COLLEGE, Belfast South** 1906; architect Robert Cochrane; *demolished*

This porter's gate lodge and tower was known as Hamilton Tower in honour of the Rev Thomas Hamilton, President of the College (1889-1908) later Vice-Chancellor of the University (1908-1923). Thus remarkably it was built (1906) and removed (1922) in his lifetime. Designed by Dr Robert Cochrane, architect to the Board of Works in Dublin, in the Tudor Revival style. Single storey lodge with hipped roof behind a parapet, a gabled breakfront framed the label-moulded, mullioned and transomed living room window. The entrance door with quatrefoiled spandrel over like that to the four-centred carriage arch alongside in the two storey entrance tower. An octagonal turret to the rear housed spiral stairs to the crenellated parapets and a first floor of doubtful function. The whole composition in brick with stone dressings, quoins and plaque features. Its loss would have been lamented had it been located elsewhere and not obscured Charles Lanyon's masterpiece beyond.

LAWRENCE PHOTOGRAPH COLLECTION (NLI.) Ref 10096R; DIXON AND WALKER (1983)

**296. RACEVIEW, Broughshane** c1880; *demolished*

Probably built by J B Black upon acquiring the property from Alexander C Montgomery.

**297. RANTALARD, Whitehouse** pre 1857; *demolished*

Once the property of John Thomson.

**298. RATHFERN, Whiteabbey** pre 1857; *demolished*

A lodge, cruciform on plan, probably for George Mitchell.

**299. RATHMORE, Dunmurry (2)**

**Dunmurry Gate** c1875; architect probably W H Lynn; *demolished*

On a park previously occupied by Huntley Cottage, Victor Coates, ironfounder, built himself an Italianate mansion and matching lodge. On an L plan, three room below a low-

*W M Lawrence (N.L.I)*

*Queen's College*

pitched roof, it had a semicircular bow-ended living room, and projecting from the internal angle a Tuscan pilastered hallway in honey coloured ashlar sandstone. Similar dressings to windows, plinth, cill course and deep frieze to eaves. Otherwise in coursed squared quarry-faced sandstone. The frieze feature, repeated on the ashlar chimney stack and gate pillars, is typical of the work of Lanyon, Lynn and Lanyon, to be seen also at Redburn, Co Down (qv). Remains of extensive ogee gate sweeps survive but the lodge was allowed to rot until finally demolished in 1991.

**Finaghy Gate** c1875; *demolished*

**300. RAVENHILL, Greenisland**
pre 1832/c1910; *demolished*

For the Forbes family. An innovative early 20th century lodge on a square plan with hipped roof. Stuccoed single storey, it had an oriel window "suspended" from the projecting eaves. Entrance door in heavily voussoired semicircular recess springing from ground level. The previous pre 1832 lodge built by the Gilmore family served as an annex. All now replaced by a modern bungalow.

**301. RAYMOND COTTAGE, Toome**
(see DRUMRAYMOND)

**302. REDHALL, Ballycarry (3)**
**Main Entrance** c1870; architect Thomas Allason

John Claudius Loudon published one of his many pattern books, *Cottage, Farm and Villa Architecture,* in 1833. In it a collection of gate lodge designs from various contributors, one by Thomas Allason (1790-1852) a castellated Tudor style concoction. This has been faithfully reproduced on the Carrickfergus-Larne road differing only in the front door emerging from behind the gate sweep. An irregular composition of interlocking boxes and octagonal stair turret displays a Romantic outline. All in uncoursed squared quarry-faced basalt with red sandstone label mouldings and dressings. The minuscule hallway block leads to a taller single storey kitchen and the parlour occupies the ground floor of the two storey cube from which access is gained to the bedroom over by spiral stairs. Across the avenue, once linked by a gate screen with a pair of ball finialed pillars, is a battlemented coal shed completing the effect. Built about 1870 for John Macauley, perhaps under the supervision of architect Alexander McAlister. Ironwork long removed, the lodge now in a pitifully neglected state.

**Ballycarry Lodge** c1850

On the back road at Ballycarry, a standard hipped roof three bay lodge with projecting eaves and label mouldings.

**North Lodge** c1830/c1870

As the above but with a clipped eaves and lattice paned windows replaced after about forty years by an irregular one and a half storey cottage now lacking any architectural pretensions. Both the early lodges built by the Kerr family.
LOUDON (1833); LARNE HISTORICAL SOCIETY PHOTOGRAPH

**303. RHANBUOY, Carrickfergus** c1880

Nice little L plan lodge with hipped roof and chimneys to end elevations. Three bay stuccoed in a confusion of styles. Tudor label moulding to windows and a Classical doorcase with moulded surround to the semicircular fanlight and heavily vermiculated quoins. Unfortunately the otherwise commendable rehabilitation included insertion of nasty slim concrete cills and plate glass windows. Resident in 1880, John McKee.

**304. RIDDEL HALL Belfast South** c1915; architect W H Lynn or S P Close

The large gaunt Tudor Revival female hostel for Queen's University was designed in 1913 by W H Lynn. At the entrance a lodge in identical style and materials - red brick with sandstone dressings, relieved by Virginia creeper. One and a half storey on an L plan with a single storey canted hall at the internal angle and gablet window over. Stone mullioned and transomed windows, steep skewtables crowned by prickly fleur-de-lys finials, a feature to be found also at Campbell College (qv) by the same architect. It is difficult to distinguish between originator and

executant as Lynn shared offices with S P Close and his son in his final years, lodge and gates having been built after his death. The gate piers octagonal with a shield ornament band, have steep cappings and finial almost matching those on lodge and main building.

**305. ROCKLANDS, Belfast South** pre 1857; *demolished*

Once a pleasant country seat, now a housing development. Both house and lodge gone and the avenue between now forms New Barnsley Parade. A property in 1858 of George Coates.

**306. ROSE COTTAGE or ROSEMOUNT, Greenisland** c1850; *demolished*

Replacing a pre 1832 lodge at a revised access. Notable simply for its tall gabled three bay front elevation.

**307. ROSGANNA MANOR, Carrickfergus** pre 1901; *demolished*

Both house and lodge by the lough shore gone. Built for Mr W Higgin.

**308. ROSSTULLA, Whiteabbey** pre 1857; *demolished*

The lodge opposite the gates built for Samuel Gelston.

**309. RUSH PARK, Newtownabbey (2)**
**Early Lodge** pre 1832; *demolished*

Built for the Joice family.

**Later Lodge** pre 1857; *demolished*

Built for John McNeal or his successor Robert James Tennent.

**310. ST CATHERINE'S, Greenisland**
pre 1857; *demolished*

Probably built for James Hanson.

**311. ST HELENA, Toome** pre 1829; *demolished*

The lodge perhaps contemporary with the house

*J. C Loudon (1833)*

*Redhall, Main Entrance*

built c1802 by David Babington on the shores of Lough Beg.
O.S.M.

**312. ST LOUIS CONVENT SCHOOL, Ballymena** (see KINTULLAGH)

**313. ST MALACHY'S ROMAN CATHOLIC CHURCH, Belfast South** c1850; architect probably Thomas Jackson; *demolished*
In 1841 Thomas Jackson's design won the competition for the Tudor Gothic style church. The extensive iron railed screen has three double carriage gates all hung on squat stone octagonal piers, each with recessed panels to shafts and frieze, below cappings bearing gas lamps. These survive to this day, but not so the little lodge with shaped, finialed gable to the road, below which was a large oculus over a label moulded "window", both blind. In brick with stone plinth, quoins and other dressed features, it also had the mark of Jackson's hand, dating from c1850.
DIXON AND WALKER (1984); LAWRENCE STEREOGRAPH (NLI.) Ref 457

**314. ST MARY'S TEACHER TRAINING COLLEGE, Finaghy** (see TRENCH HOUSE)

**315. SANDYMOUNT, Belfast South** pre 1858; *demolished*
A lodge and house of William Watson, wholesale clothier, on what was Friar's Bush Road. Both gone, the property remembered only by a street of the same name, off what is now Stranmillis Road.

**316. SANS SOUCI, Belfast South** pre 1857; *demolished*
One time home of the Lindsay family.

**317. SCOUT BUSH, Carrickfergus (2)** both c1930
Both one and a half storey with hipped gables, built to replace early 19th century lodges of the Forsythes. For the McAuliffe family.

**318. SEAPARK, Greenisland** c1865; architect Thomas Jackson
The architect in his richest Neo-Classical/ Italianate mood. On a solid plinth the large, well-proportioned three bay lodge has stuccoed

horizontally channelled rustication punctuated by semicircular-headed windows (bipartite to the end elevations) with framed surrounds carried down to embrace recessed panels below cills. Quoins and keystones of diamond pattern. A frieze of scrolled modillion brackets carries the eaves and continues about the hipped roof portico entablature. This portico has two Ionic columns flanked by square Tuscan piers. The hipped roof is crowned by an equally high relief chimney stack with recessed panels and bracketed cornice. All glossily well kept. Road widening has removed the entrance screen. Built for Thomas Greer in the mid-1860s along with a new villa to replace a previous lodge of the Owdens on the same site which in turn had superseded a Georgian "ink-pot" porter's accommodation.

**319. SEAPORT LODGE, Portballintrae** c1790; *demolished*

J.F. Leslie

P. Rankin

A lovely pair of "Strawberry Hill" Gothick buildings which faced each other outside the entrance gates to a "bathing lodge" of Mr James Leslie of Leslie Hill (qv). Each of simple two room plan, three bay with curved leading corners to avoid carriage wheels. Lancet-headed windows on either side of ogee-arched doorways. In crude coursed basalt with snecking, they would seem to have spent their latter years whitewashed, the roof pitches carried up to ball finials curiously placed asymmetrically. Chimney stacks taken off elevations to park.

**320. SEAVIEW COTTAGE, Belfast North** pre 1857; *demolished*
There is no trace of residence or its lodge. 1860 occupant James Ritchie probably lessee of the Simms family.

**321. SEAVIEW, Belfast North** pre 1832; *demolished*
A pair built by James Boomer, prominent cotton spinner and linen manufacturer. Before 1835 work here by Thomas Jackson, architect. Both house and lodges gone.
DIXON AND HEATLEY (1983)

**322. SEAVIEW, Larne** (see CAIRNDHU)

**323. SEYMOUR HILL, Dunmurry** c1835; architect not known; *demolished*

Emily Charley (Moyne Ramsey)

Seymour Hill

"... seat of William Charley, Esq ... at the entrance ... a very handsome and extensive railing and neat wrought iron gate, together with a handsome porter's lodge ...". This description by Thomas Fagan, an early connoisseur of gate lodges, in his Ordnance Survey Memoir of 1837 neatly dates the entrance as it does not appear on the 1832-3 Ordnance Survey Map. William Charley had purchased the property in 1825 and set about rebuilding and reconstructing it, expending £5,000 in the process. The ogee sweeps between square piers flanked an inner screen with panelled and corniced hexagonal piers carrying double carriage gates. The stuccoed symmetrical three bay lodge had an entablatured parapet, behind which the hipped roof was crowned with a corniced "Vanbrugh" chimney stack. Wide segmentally-headed window openings had decorative festoon reliefs over. The margined glazing had roundels with painted scenes. The entablatured portico carried on two Tuscan columns with corresponding antae. Although sadly long gone an identical entrance can be seen at Ballybeen, Co Down (qv). No architect is recorded but the gate piers are of a type as favoured by Thomas Jackson.
O.S.M.; PHOTOGRAPH TAKEN BY EMILY CHARLEY C1910; DIXON AND HEATLEY (1983)

**324. SHAMROCK LODGE, Belfast North** pre 1857; *demolished*
A seat of the Young family, partners with the Coates of Glentoran, Co Down (qv) in the ironfoundry business.

**325. SHANE'S CASTLE, Randalstown (6)**
For the 3rd and last Viscount O'Neill of the first creation, a collection of very fine entrances and porter's lodges, unsurpassed in Ireland. These were clearly a response to the appalling state of the demesne perimeter that he inherited. It was so run down as to move James Boyle in 1838 to devote a description in his Ordnance Survey notes. "The entrance to the demesne, 2 in number, one being near its western and the other near its eastern end (on the Randalstown and

Antrim road), are not all in character with the place or the ideas associated with it. The one near Antrim [Sandgate Lodge] merely consists of a miserable and ruinous wooded gate without pillars or lodge, there being merely a plain cottage on the opposite side of the road in which the gatekeeper resides. The other gateway is somewhat better. A large iron gate with wickets is swung from a pair of plain brick pillars. In a cabin nearly opposite, the person who opens the gate resides. His lordship is now erecting a 6 foot stone wall with Welsh coping along the demesne, on the road from Antrim to Randalstown. About half a mile has already been completed." Now the estates lack a great house, both Nash's castle creation and Lanyon, Lynn and Lanyon's mansion were destroyed by fires in 1816 and 1922 and with them much valuable information on the estate's buildings. However, correspondence of the Maxwells of Finnebrogue (qv) reveals that the architect James Sands visited Lord O'Neill in 1848 and this may be a clue as to authorship of all entrances bar Ballealy Cottage and Sandgate lodge. Certainly Antrim and Whitegate lodges here have much in common with that to Brecart (qv), another O'Neill demesne which has gate pillars identical to those by Sands at the Maxwells' Groomsport House, Co Down (qv).

**Ballealy Cottage** c1835;
architect perhaps Richard Morrison

Down a muddy track by a stream this secret Picturesque one and a half storey cottage on an irregular plan has an abnormally extensive range of outbuildings. This might be explained by James Boyle's O.S. notes of 1838 in which he refers to two lodges in the deerpark, one "... the residence of the park-keeper and is built of stone, in miniature imitation of the lodge of the ranger of Windsor Forest. Attached to it is an aviary on a small scale, in which are some gold and silver pheasants". Clearly by the same hand as Whitegate Lodge on the Langford demesne (qv) nearby, it has unsophisticated lobed trefoil bargeboards right down to the "kiss-curl" toes which also feature there. Tall octagonal chimney pots, timber mullioned and transomed windows and crude coursed basalt walls are identical. Here though some of the gables are hipped with fascias matching bargeboards. The little hipped canopies to windows and front door are missing.

**Sandgate Lodge** pre 1829; *demolished*
Located opposite the entrance.
(See O.S. Memoir description above.)

**Dunmore Lodge** c1850; architect probably James Sands

The most decorative of the Picturesque lodges, one and a half storey gabled on an L plan. It has beautifully carved bargeboards to main gables and the single storey porch adapted from Augustus Pugin's *Ornamental Gables* rising to wooden hipknobs with pendants. Brackets to eaves. The attic rooms had tiny lattice paned lights whilst the ground floor windows had octagonal pattern glazing bars with flowery tops all with cuspidated timber frames. Both main gables boasted canted bays with crenellated parapets. The stuccoed walls had quoins and label and hood mouldings to openings. Two tall octagonal chimney pots pierce the scalloped slate roof. The lodge is unrecognisable now, having suffered the most outrageous transformation into a bland two storey house. The only clue to its identity is the entrance sweep which is intact. The two wicket and double carriage gates are hung on secondary cast iron piers with ball finials. Main pillars square stone with recessed panels and moulded caps.

W.A. Green (U.F.T.M.)

*Dunmore Lodge*

R.J. Welch (U.M.)

*Antrim Lodge*

**Antrim Lodge** c1848; architect probably James Sands

Very much as Dunmore Lodge in form and plan but a single storey variant. Three gables display the O'Neill coat-of-arms below fancy bargeboards copied from Pugin's *Ornamental Gables* (Plate 20: Butcher's Row, Coventry). A row of three octagonal chimney pots and lattice window panes unfortunately removed. This is a variation on Shore Lodge at Carncastle Lodge (qv) which is based on an illustration in Loudon's *Designs for Ornamental Cottages* (1846). Fine decorative cast iron gate piers with coronet tops.

**Whitegate or Ballygrooby Lodge** c1848; architect probably James Sands

Unlike Antrim Lodge this is symmetrical, stuccoed three bay with a wide quoined entrance breakfront, again with the O'Neill coat-of-arms below another Pugin bargeboard from his *Ornamental Gables* (Plate 12: Wells Street, Coventry). The front door has a nice fanlight below a hood moulding to the four-centred Tudor arch. Windows have label mouldings but lack their original lattice glazing. Two diagonally-set stone chimney stacks. Pretty Gothick garden railings and main entrance screen.

**Randalstown Gate** c1848; architect probably James Sands

The pièce de résistance of the estate and the most impressive entrance complex in the Province. A vast Tudor Revival fantasy of flamboyant castellated outline. All in squared coursed basalt rubble dressed in contrasting granite. Dominating is a huge octagonal arrow-looped flagstaff tower set asymmetrically and housing spiral stairs which lead firstly to ramparts across the entrance archway and ultimately to a machicolated and crenellated top. Main access under a Tudor archway is

R.J. Welch (U.M.)

*White Gate or Ballygrooby Lodge*

W.M. Lawrence (N.L.I.)

*Randalstown Gate*

surmounted by more machicolations, the grand gates with raised diamond panels below a mock portcullis. To the left, as you approach, a shed (battlemented of course) with a small square tower, repeated to the right on the porter's lodge which peers out through a cuspidated tripartite window. The lodge, three bay with rear return has a low-pitched roof behind a parapet. A pair of octagonal stone chimney pots. Over the front door a carved O'Neill coat-of-arms also to be seen in the stepped main archway ramparts, both coming and going lest you forget. The whole powerful impregnable approach between extensive concave outworks terminating in corbelled bartizans. Now severed from the estate by a motorway it again seems to show James Sands' dependence upon pattern books, showing as it does similarities with Francis Goodwin's entrance to Markree Castle, Co Sligo, published in his *Rural Architecture* 1835.
LAWRENCE PHOTOGRAPH (NLI) 7704(C); WELCH PHOTOGRAPH (UM) W.01/82/28, W.01/82/29; GREEN PHOTOGRAPH (UFTM) WAG 1738; PUGIN (1831); P.R.O.N.I. D1556; WEST ANTRIM; U.A.H.S. (1970); O.S.M.

**326. SINCLAIR SEAMEN'S CHURCH AND SAILORS' HOME, Belfast North** c1858; architects probably Lanyon and Lynn; *demolished*
Regrettably there is no sign of a gate lodge recorded in the Griffith Valuation of 1860, doubtless part of the architects' commission. One may speculate that it was in the manner of the Lombardic style Presbyterian church or the contemporary Gothic Revival Sailor's Home.
LARMOUR (1987); GRIFFITH

**327. SKEFFINGTON LODGE (Deer Park), Antrim (2)**
**Outer Lodge** c1910
Single storey red brick lodge with catslide roof over verandahed canopy supported by turned posts.
**Inner Lodge** pre 1857; *demolished*
To what was then known as Park Cottage. In 1862 the residence of Hon Rev James Agar.

**328. SKEGONEIL, Belfast North** pre 1832; *demolished*
The property in 1816 of Samuel Wolsey.

**329. SLIEVE-NA-FAILTE, Whiteabbey** c1860; *demolished*
A property of Elias Thompson.

**330. SNUGVILLE, Belfast North** pre 1832; *demolished*
House and lodge demolished late last century to make way for the spread of Belfast. A victim of the Industrial Revolution. A seat of the Walkington family.

**331. SPRING FARM, Antrim** pre 1832; *demolished*
A lodge which had disappeared by 1857. A seat in 1837 of Lewis Reford.

**332. SPRINGFIELD, Belfast North (2)**
both pre 1857; *both demolished*
The lodge probably built for William Coates after acquiring a property of the Stevenson family.
GRIFFITH

**333. SPRINGFIELD, Magheragall (2)**
**Ballinderry Lodge** c1845
An entrance described by the gate lodge-conscious Thomas Fagan in his 1837 Ordnance Survey Memoir as "... a neat wrought iron gate, at which stands a neat porter's lodge ...". Built to replace a predecessor on the same site probably for Edward Wakefield, from whom the Houghtons came by the property in 1811. Single storey three bay symmetrical below a hipped roof. Breakfront gabled hall with a doorway segmentally-headed as are the other openings, all having moulded architraves. The road facade contains an unusual bipartite window embraced by a wide segmental arch. Now rendered with quoins and with modern windows. Many of these architectural features may have been applied as part of Thomas Jackson's commission some fifteen years later. The architect benefited from the patronage of the Richardson family working at many of their seats such as Glenmore, Old Forge and Lissue (qqqv). By marrying the daughter of Major Richard Rolls Houghton in 1850, Joseph Richardson acquired the Springfield demesne and engaged Jackson to design a new villa and gate lodge both in his recognisable stuccoed Neo-Classical manner.
**Lisburn Lodge** c1860; architect Thomas Jackson
Single storey three bay, hipped roof with gabled projecting hall. Quoins, segmentally-headed openings with moulded surrounds, panelled and corniced chimney stack - all typical Jackson. It has sprouted a large extension in matching style, the original front door blocked up and repositioned. All done up in gloss paint. The gate pillars to both entrances are identical but probably earlier than the lodges. Slender granite with recessed panels, fluted frieze, corniced capping and unusual tops having delicate anthemion motifs. The ironwork has all gone. Jackson's villa and the former single storey long gentry cottage both survive.
DIXON (1978); O.S.M.

**334. SPRINGMOUNT, Clogh** c1860
A pleasant lodge, modest and looking earlier than its date. Two roomed, three bay the right hand of which is the front door. High eaves below a pyramidal roof and central brick stack. Segmentally-headed openings in harled cream-washed walls. The simplest of square stone piers have, to one side, a rustic stile for pedestrian access. Probably built for John O'Neill Higginson.

**335. THE STEEPLE, Antrim (2)**
Two lodges for George Jackson Clarke Esq to a restrained Neo-Classical house of 1827.
**North Lodge** c1845
Unusually commodious single storey lodge. Two wings advance towards the outbuildings approach to form a C plan. Simple sash windows in stuccoed walls below hipped roofs with rafter toes carved into scrolled ends.
**South Lodge** c1845
Square single storey structure below a pyramidal roof rising to a central chimney stack. Three bay front elevation, that to the right hand side a recessed porch. Segmentally-headed windows. All now rendered bland in modernisation.
ANTRIM & BALLYMENA; U.A.H.S. (1969)

**336. STONE POINT, Greenisland** c1860
A miniature single storey two bay gabled lodge. Built of rubble stone, the openings brick dressed. Blocked up.

**337. STRANMILLIS/STRANMILLIS TRAINING COLLEGE, Belfast South (4)**
In 1857 Thomas G Batt acquired the demesne from the Black family and proceeded to transform it into a landscaped park, and commissioned Messrs Lanyon and Lynn to design buildings more befitting a Director of the Belfast Bank. The house is in the Jacobean manner but at the main gate was to be a composition which shows the versatility expected of the Victorian architect and the eclecticism of this particular practice.

**Main House Entrance** c1860; architects Lanyon & Lynn; *demolished*

(*Linenhall Library*)

This was a highly Picturesque essay using a variety of devices and materials. One and a half storey on an L plan with a single storey living room projecting from the main block in uncoursed ashlar like the rest of the ground floor. The windows transomed and mullioned with Tudor heads and lattice panes. Jettied out on stone corbels a half-timbered attic storey with polychrome brick nogging below most intricately carved Puginesque bargeboards. The steeply-pitched roof had a tiny "Benjamin Woodward" hipped dormer, scalloped slate courses and metal cresting crowning the ridge. The stone appears again in the prominent chimney stack. In the internal angle a mono-pitch canopy, supported on carved posts and brackets, over the front door. In 1922 the demesne was acquired by the Ministry of Finance and by 1930 a piece of official vandalism was complete - the house spoilt and the lodge demolished. Two squat vermiculated sandstone piers survive as thankfully does much of the park following its being put to use as a teacher training college.

**Main College Entrance** c1933; architect probably T P O Rippingham
The replacement front gateway is by architect Roland Ingelby-Smith in the form of tall Portland stone pillars with moulded capstones surmounted by urns. The Neo-Classical Arts-and-Crafts gate lodge is a low rustic brick bungalow with small-paned windows behind a curved screen wall. Green glazed pantiles to the hipped roof.

**Side Entrance** c1949; architect probably T P O Rippingham
To replace another lodge to Stranmillis House is a sensitively handled Queen Anne Arts-and-Crafts exercise in clay facing brick and rosemary tiled roof with bonnet hip tiles. One and a half storey on a square plan, a stone stringcourse, forming a frieze below the eaves, carried around as a parapet to the projecting bowed hall. The pyramidal roof rises steeply to the brick chimney

stack. There are centrally placed copper clad dormers. Clearly influenced by the lodges to Parliament Buildings, Co Down (qv).
LINENHALL LIBRARY PHOTOGRAPH; LARMOUR (1987); WELCH PHOTOGRAPH (U.M.) Ref W10/72/10; MALONE & STRANMILLIS; U.A.H.S. (1991)

**338. STRANOCUM, Stranocum** pre 1903; *demolished*
Built for F W Hutchinson.

**339. STRATHEARN, Finaghy (2)**
**Later Main Entrance** c1900; architect perhaps Vincent Craig

A fine stuccoed lodge of about 1900, when the house seems to have been revamped upon its acquisition by Harold Adrian Milne Barbour. Perhaps by architect Vincent Craig, it is much gabled with that of the living room projection sporting a Venetian window, a collar tied feature over carried on moulded purlin brackets. A lower gable to the hall advances alongside. Pilastered frames to openings, exposed rafter toes. Good iron gatesweep.

**Original Entrance** c1870
Back-to-back with the above is a modest earlier lodge to the original house built for Philip Fletcher Richardson.
The estate now a girl's school.
WELCH PHOTOGRAPH (UM) Ref W10/37/11

**340. SUFFOLK, Dunmurry** pre 1901; *demolished*
John McCance in 1824 built the house, as it stood until recently, in proximity to his extensive bleach greens. The lodge, which was a modest affair with a hipped roof, may have dated from when the house was refaced in about 1870 by Finlay McCance. Both now gone.

**341. TAWNYBRACK, Kells** pre 1857
Nondescript. One time property of the Refords.

**342. THISTLEBOROUGH, Glenavy** pre 1832; *demolished*
Gone before 1901. Built by the Whittle family.

**343. THORNFIELD, Carrickfergus** pre 1832; architect perhaps J B Keane; *demolished*
House and lodge both gone, the former having born an uncanny resemblance to Coxtown, Co Donegal (qv) probably by the architect J B Keane.

**344. THORNHILL, Belfast South** c1865; architects probably Young & MacKenzie

A seat of the Wilson family who built the house 1854-6 and attached this ornate little Italianate porter's lodge about ten years later. Simple stuccoed three bay and hipped roof, but with vigorous moulded features. Strong channelled quoins to corners and hall breakfront with architraved door. Windows (coupled to gables) having bracketed cills, plain pilastered jambs and moulded semicircular heads broken by diamond keystones. Ogee eaves gutters carried on paired modillions. Solid chimney stack with frieze and cornice. The house has been swept away to make way for a new housing development but the lodge is intact and well kept. Very much akin to those at Strathearn, Co Down (qv).
CARLTON (1978)

**345. THORNLEA, Larne** c1880
Made plain in revamping by the raising of roofline.

**346. THRUSHFIELD, Templepatrick** pre 1857; *demolished*
A pair to the property of John Ferguson.

**347. TILDARG, Ballyclare** c1860
Three bay standard plan single storey. Basalt with high eaves line. Solid mid-Victorian, built to replace an earlier building of pre 1832 for the Messrs J and J Owens.

**348. TRAINFIELD, Belfast North** pre 1857; *demolished*
Built for Robert Stewart Lepper of the family which owned neighbouring Laurel Lodge (qv) and the Lodge Mill nearby. Now the only trace of family and house is preserved in the names of the little red-brick terrace streets which succeeded them in the 1890s.

**349. TRENCH, Andersonstown** 1880; architect Alexander McAlister
House and lodge built for Arthur Hamill to designs by Alexander McAlister. Three bay single storey with central projecting Queen Anne Revival hall, its pediment having emphatic mutules carried around from the eaves of a hipped roof. Segmentally-arched main windows, those lights to the side of the hall semicircular-headed and only they retain their original vertical sliding sashes. Also rendered in recent improvements. Tall chimney stack corniced and friezed off a plinth. Now St Mary's Teacher Training College.
LARMOUR (1987)

**350. TRUMMERY, Moira** pre 1900
Nondescript. One time seat of the Conran family.

**351. TUDOR HILL, Belfast South** 1953; architect John McGeagh
Pretty symmetrical three bay Arts-and-Crafts chalet bungalow designed by John McGeagh

sixteen years after he had planned the house for Sir Cecil McKee. Camera-shy behind a rampant laurel hedge, all in warm clay finishes. Orange rustic brick to walls and bulky central corbelled chimney. Leaded-light windows, the sheeted wooden front door has a canopy carried on timber brackets, like the main roof and dormers hipped and finished in clay rosemary tiles complete with hip bonnets. The roof has gambrels echoed by nice anthemion stops to dormer ridge tiles. Round gate piers with "noddy" caps, in brick and tiles to match the lodge. Sturdy timber gates.
MALONE & STRANMILLIS; U.A.H.S. (1991); BELFAST CORPORATION APPLICATION; Ref 28052

**352. TULLYMORE LODGE, Broughshane** pre 1832; *demolished*
Gone before the turn of the century, the porter's accommodation to a hunting lodge and dower house of the O'Neill family.

**353. UNION HOSPITAL, Belfast South** (see CITY HOSPITAL)

**354. UPPER BALLINDERRY GLEBE, Ballinderry** pre 1857
Plain. Contemporary with the glebe-house.

**355. VENTNOR, Whiteabbey** c1920; architect probably W J W Roome

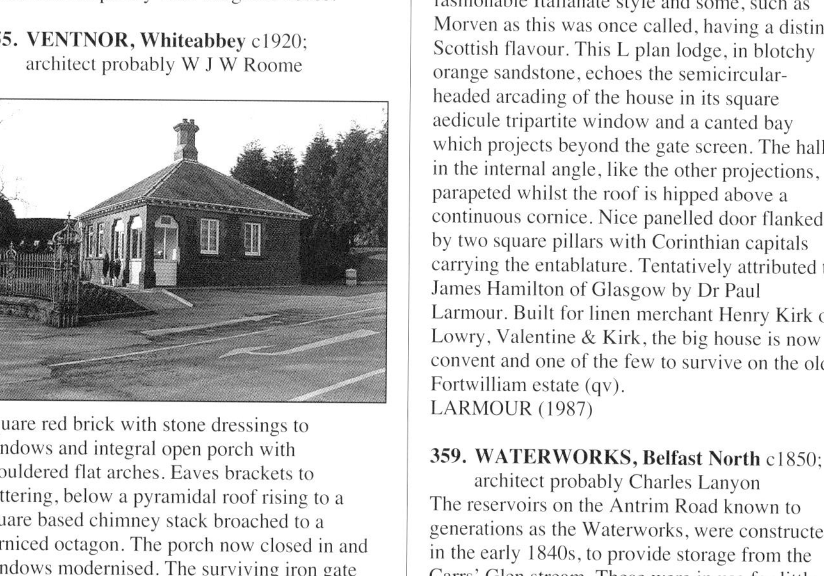

Square red brick with stone dressings to windows and integral open porch with shouldered flat arches. Eaves brackets to guttering, below a pyramidal roof rising to a square based chimney stack broached to a corniced octagon. The porch now closed in and windows modernised. The surviving iron gate piers and concave railing sweeps look like those to Kircassock, Co Down (qv). A house, of 1920 for the McClean family, which became Greenisland Hospital in 1941.

**356. VIPONT VILLA, Belfast South** (see Coolavin)

**357. WALLACE PARK, Lisburn (2)** both 1884; architect John McHenry
Two identical single storey lodges to each end of the park. Typical late Victorian Neo-Classical with no embellishment spared. On an L plan a canted projection to the front elevation all under a hipped roof with spiky wooden hipknobs. The park facade has a flat-roofed canted bay, balanced by a square hall projection to the road with a strapwork balustrade over. Mainly in red brick, openings architraved, the whole sits solidly on a stuccoed plinth, heavily rusticated up to a moulded cill course. A stringcourse forms a frieze below the ogee gutter. Chimney stack similarly vigorously handled with wide cornice. Early this century extended in matching style to form a C on plan to enclose a yard, losing the balustraded hall in the process and gaining another chimney stack. The ogee entrance sweep lost its railings and four fine cast iron piers for the war effort. Presented to the people of Lisburn as the "People's Park" by Sir Richard Wallace (he of the Wallace collection).
LISBURN MUSEUM (postcard view)

**358. WALTON, Belfast North** c1870; architect perhaps James Hamilton
One of the parks formed from breaking up the old Fortwilliam estate. Many of the new mansions of the late 1860s were in the fashionable Italianate style and some, such as Morven as this was once called, having a distinct Scottish flavour. This L plan lodge, in blotchy orange sandstone, echoes the semicircular-headed arcading of the house in its square aedicule tripartite window and a canted bay which projects beyond the gate screen. The hall in the internal angle, like the other projections, parapeted whilst the roof is hipped above a continuous cornice. Nice panelled door flanked by two square pillars with Corinthian capitals carrying the entablature. Tentatively attributed to James Hamilton of Glasgow by Dr Paul Larmour. Built for linen merchant Henry Kirk of Lowry, Valentine & Kirk, the big house is now a convent and one of the few to survive on the old Fortwilliam estate (qv).
LARMOUR (1987)

**359. WATERWORKS, Belfast North** c1850; architect probably Charles Lanyon
The reservoirs on the Antrim Road known to generations as the Waterworks, were constructed in the early 1840s, to provide storage from the Carrs' Glen stream. These were in use for little more than twenty years when the catchment became inadequate, but not before the completion of a fine porters' lodge. Stuccoed, single storey on a cruciform plan, very much in Lanyon's Baroque Italianate style which he also employed at Dunderave and Moneyglass in this county (qqv) and Eglantine, Co Down (qv). Here he substituted hipped roofs for gabled, and hallway for "porte-cochère". With similarly generous ceiling heights the eaves has a series of

Postcard (Lisburn Museum)

paired curved brackets. On the side gables the architect's distinctive stepped Venetian window which also featured on his demolished curator's house at Stranmillis, Belfast and a Muckamore villa. The taller centre light sheltered by an entablature carried on two big crossettes. The other openings of varying widths all semicircular-headed with smooth raised surrounds, the cills moulded and carried on scrolled brackets. The front doorways have heavy acones. Toothed quoins, a smooth raised stringcourse unites the composition. Heavily corniced central chimney stack. Along the Antrim Road frontage was an impressive range of big squat piers with recessed panels each surmounted by fancy urns. The two piers flanking the entrance supported two grand cube-shaped lanterns. Now all replaced with something more mundane.

**360. WELLINGTON PARK, Belfast South** c1865; *demolished*
A typical villa of the nouveau riche, stuccoed Italianate for George Tate, timber merchant who had acquired an old farm here in 1850. The house survives as an hotel whilst the contemporary obligatory porter's lodge has been demolished.
CARLETON (1978); MALONE & STRANMILLIS; U.A.H.S. (1991)

**361. WESTONCROFTS, Ballymoney** c1860; *demolished*
House of c1860 in the late Georgian tradition, stuccoed, the small gate lodge in the same style.
NORTH ANTRIM; U.A.H.S. (1972)

**362. WHEATFIELD, Belfast North** 1876; architects Young & MacKenzie; *demolished*
Lodge and house designed 1876 by Young and Mackenzie, as at Clearstream Cottage (qv) for Mr E Blair. The lodge quoted by the architects to cost £190 has been demolished. Replaced an earlier lodge extant 1862.
P.R.O.N.I. D2194

**363. WHITEHALL, Broughshane** c1850
Tiny cottage, three bay built in big basalt lumps laid in white joints. Located outside the gates from which two square piers are missing. Devoid of any architectural pretensions but none the worse for that. Stone soldier courses to openings. Projecting eaves to an unusually steeply-hipped roof. Comprised of two main rooms each 3.3m by 2.3m (11ft 0in by 7ft 6in) further reduced by chimney breasts. On a gate pillar a commemorative plate to Sir George White (1835-1912), hero of Ladysmith, who lived here. Built for James Robert White. Now derelict.

**364. WHITEPARK, Ballyclare** pre 1857; demolished
A lodge for the Fergusons.

**365. WILLOWBANK COTTAGE, Belfast South** pre 1832; *demolished*
Directly opposite the old entrance and lodge to Beechmount (qv) porter's accommodation built by Mr Sharman Moore.

**366. WILMONT, Dunmurry (3)**

**Original Entrance** pre 1832; *demolished*

A lodge, or pair of lodges, down by the Lagan canal was at the entrance to the Stewart estate. This and the big house which had been abandoned, were removed and replaced by a new mansion and "Belfast Lodge" upon acquisition of Wilmont in 1859 by James Bristow of the Northern Banking Company.

**"Belfast" Lodge** c1860; architect probably Thomas Jackson; *demolished*

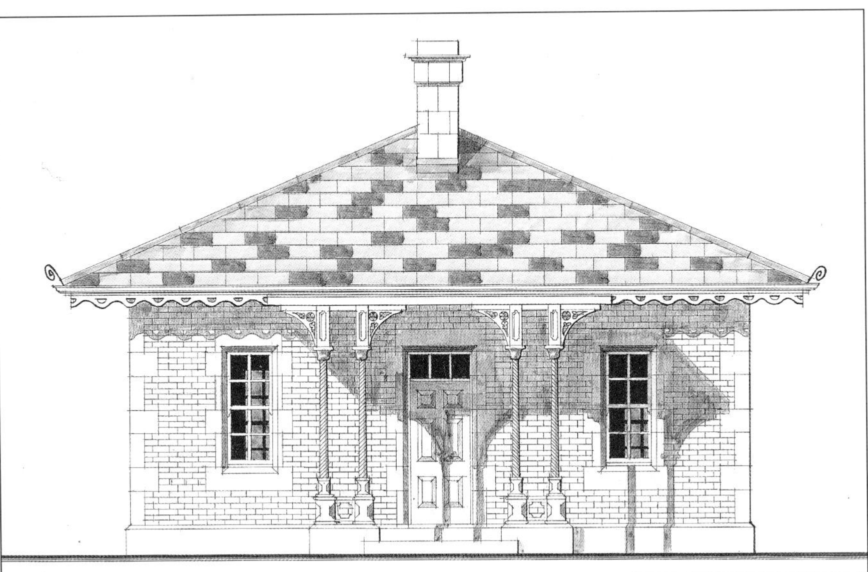

Spacious single storey in materials much as the new house - brick with grey stone plinth quoins, toothed opening dressings and corniced chimney stack. Four roomed to generous proportions with ceilings as high as the eaves which projected with wavy fascia boards to its hipped roof. The projecting porch had a flat lead roof supported on slender cast iron twinned barley twist columns and brackets. Eminently extendible but mysteriously taken down to make way for a banal bungalow after being presented to Belfast Corporation. The lodge doubtless by Thomas Jackson, as was the house, not long after 1859. Original gates replaced.

**"Lisburn" Lodge** c1880; architect not known

(R.H. Reade)

Surviving intact, having been built soon after Wilmont was bought in 1879 by Robert Henry Sturrock Reade, flaxspinner. Three bay symmetrical, two up two down one and a half storey. In polychrome brick, red with yellow quoins, toothed opening dressings and diamond chimney stack motifs. Windows and door heads segmentally- arched, chamfered like the jambs. Gabled with wooden bargeboards carved in relief and curved corner eaves brackets now lacking their turned pendants. Timber picket fence and square chamfered gate posts now gone to make way for ludicrous replacement brick piers with concrete ball finials.

**367. WOLFHILL, Belfast North** pre 1901; *demolished*

Resident in 1888, Frederick William Finlay.

**368. WOOD COTTAGE, Dunmurry** pre 1856; *demolished*

The lodge to a seat of William Woods.

**369. WOODBANK, Whiteabbey** c1837; architect probably Thomas Jackson; *demolished*

Simplest of gabled symmetrical lodges with central chimney. The young architect Thomas Jackson altered the house in 1837 and undoubtedly designed the lodge also. Roughcast, the leading gable had a Picturesque canted bay guarding the entrance, in the manner of Thomas J Duff his erstwhile partner. Squared panes and projecting rafter toes. Built for Rev Robert W Bland and removed to make way for an encroaching road, which never did.
O.S.M.

**370. WOODBURN, Dunmurry** pre 1858; *demolished*

A seat in the mid-19th century of M Charley Esq.

**371. WOODBURN COTTAGE, Carrickfergus (2)** both pre 1857; *both demolished*

Leased in 1858 by Richard Thompson to a Dr McGee. House later known as The Mount.

**372. WOODBURN MILLS, Carrickfergus** pre 1858; *demolished*

**373. WOODVALE, Broughshane** pre 1857; *demolished*

**374. WOODVALE PARK, Belfast North** c1885; architect probably J C Bretland

A public park formed from the grounds of Woodville House. The four excellent Gothic Revival carved stone pillars to carriage and wicket gates are a variation on those at Falls and Alexandra Parks (qqv). Nicely sculpted capitals to engaged colonettes at the four corners of each. Proud poppy finials to gableted cappings. The superintendent's lodge a square two storey house in red brick. Double gabled front elevation. Good brick specials form label mouldings and ornament the chimney stacks.
BELFAST CITY COUNCIL; PARKS DEPARTMENT

# COUNTY ARMAGH

**1. ABBEY PARK, Armagh** pre 1905;
*demolished*

**2. ACTON, Acton (2)** both pre 1860;
*both demolished*
A demesne founded by the Poyntz family of Iron Acton in Gloucestershire. The fine Georgian villa of 1790 went through a succession of owners one of whom, Robert Quinn Alexander, built both lodges.

**3. ALTAVALLEN, Armagh** pre 1905;
*demolished*

**4. ALTAVILLA, Portadown** pre 1864;
*demolished*
The seat in 1864 of Averell Shillington. Now Nazareth House.
GRIFFITH

**5. ANNAMOY, Blackwatertown** pre 1834;
*demolished*

**6. ANNESBOROUGH, Lurgan**
(See WOODVILLE)

**7. ANNVALE, Keady** c1855
Seat of the Kirk family of the vast flax spinning manufactory of Wm M Kirk and Partners. A single storey lodge on an irregular T plan with Classical features. A big square eaves bracket course is carried beyond as mutules to open pediment gables, in one of which is a canted bay with half-umbrello roof. "Improved" this century with pebble-dashed walls and synthetic slates.

**8. ARCHIEPISCOPAL PALACE, Armagh (3)**
Richard Robinson from his elevation to the primacy in 1765 until his death as the 1st Lord Rokeby in 1794 set about the redevelopment of Armagh to create an environment more suitable to a primatial city. This included an appropriate palace and by 1769 Parliament had passed an Act for the enclosure of the demesne. In the following year, to designs of a young English architect Thomas Cooley, the mansion was complete. The commission included at least one of the entrances.

**Main Entrance, Newry Road** 1771; architect Thomas Cooley
The drawing which survives was executed almost in its entirety. The four grand piers were built from grey limestone quarried at the southern end of the demesne and carried two flanking timber wicket gates and double wrought iron carriage gates with spear tops. The two central ashlar piers in V-jointed quoins are embellished with simple Greek key pattern bands above which the friezes have swag motifs. The cornices above carry ball finials on curved pedestals (the drawings have more hospitable pineapples) all framed by convex quadrants in a wall to the landscaped park which was completed in 1822 by Robinson's successor Primate Stuart at a cost of £20,000. The gates have been removed and rebuilt to the new See House at Cathedral Close. The unpretentious lodge of pre 1835 which lurked behind the high wall was demolished in the 1960s.

**Dobbin Street Entrance** pre 1835;
*demolished*

**Newtownhamilton Road Entrance** pre 1835
A dilapidated, plain late Georgian lodge.

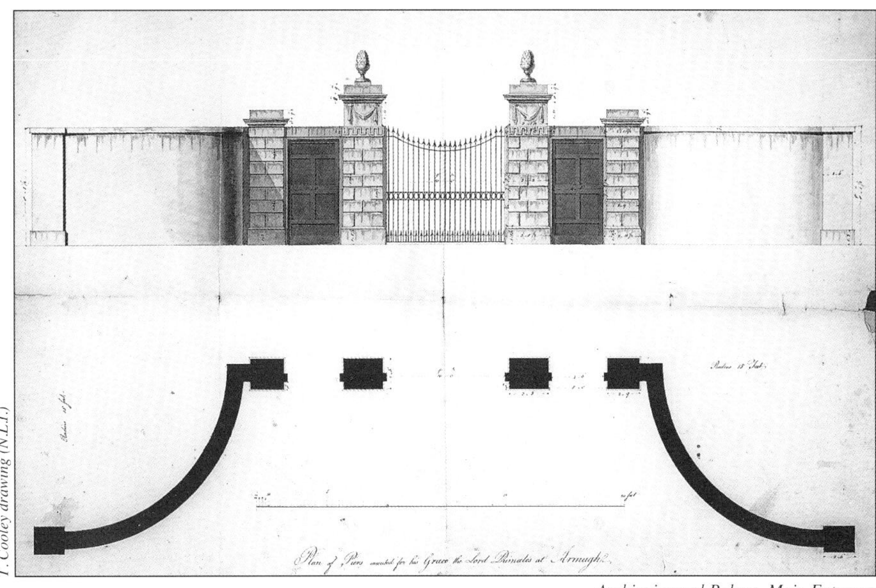
*T. Cooley drawing (N.L.I.)*

*Archiepiscopal Palace, Main Entrance*

The two gate piers, simpler versions of those at Cooley's main gate, have the same Greek key pattern bands.
NLI; Drawings Collection AD 2598

**9. ARDMORE COTTAGE, Armagh** pre 1905; *demolished*

**10. ARDRESS, Loughgall** pre 1834;
*demolished*
Good square limestone ashlar pillars survive the lodge, which was located opposite and built for George Ensor. Now a property of The National Trust.

**11. THE ARGORY, Moy (3)**
Between 1819 and 1824 Walter MacGeough transformed the old Derrycaw demesne by building the Greek Revival house and handsome offices, now known as the Argory. These were to the designs of A & J Williamson, the latter at least having been assistant and cousin of Francis Johnston. They may have been responsible for the first lodge to be built.

**"Conlon's Cottage"** c1825; architects perhaps A & J Williamson

It was quite common for a lodge to be known by the name of one of its gatekeepers, even long after his death, and this is a case in point. Symmetrical three bay hipped roof lodge, unusual in having a "highbrow" eaves housing two attic rooms lit by a pair of oculi. The lofty eaves sports bracket supports. Now cement rendered, the lodge has later buttresses and iron ties testifying to its structural instability. Unoccupied and sealed up.

**Derrycaw Lodge** c1835; architect probably T J Duff

The Newry architect, Thomas J Duff, acted as superintending architect here for the Williamsons and correspondence points to him having designed the two later lodges. Symmetrical three bay single storey, gabled with mild Picturesque style serrated bargeboards - no sign of the P F Robinson influence yet. Intricately patterned cast iron casement windows, like Georgian cabinet doors, on either side of a primitive portico with granite columns and entablature, over which is another serrated bargeboard gable. Nice mellow brick walls and chimney stack. Across the road the entrance gates.

**Stonefield Lodge** c1835; architect probably T J Duff

Differing only from Derrycaw lodge in having Georgian style rectangular-paned sash windows and quoins. Alongside square ashlar pillars, with gates to the field, from the same source as those

at Knappagh in the same county (qv). The main gate screen to the demesne opposite has lovely flanking fan railings akin to those at Tullyvin, Co Cavan (qv). Both these lodges built for the same Walter MacGeough as the house, who by now had assumed the added surname of Bond.
JACKSON-STOPS (1983)

**12. ASHFORT, Middletown** pre 1835; *demolished*
A fine set of square late Georgian gate pillars survive the lodge. A property in 1837 of Hugh Harris.

**13. ASHTON PARK, Newry** pre 1835; *demolished*
A lodge to the seat of the Ogles.

**14. BALLINTAGGART, Portadown (2)**
**West Lodge** pre 1835
Undistinguished
**East Lodge** pre 1835
Peculiar in having one blind opening to what should have been a three bay symmetrical front facade, the window moved to the roadside elevation to watch over the gates. Two roomed with a hipped roof. Rendered with quoins and a slight hall projection under a catslide roof. Derelict. Both for a Mr Todd, absentee landlord.

**15. BALLINTEMPLE CHURCHYARD, Forkhill** pre 1835; *demolished*

**16. BALLINTATE, Newtownhamilton** pre 1834
Another seat of the Synnot family of Ballymoyer and Lurgana (qqv). Some cut stone, otherwise nondescript.

**17. BALLYARDS CASTLE, Milford (2)**
A house of the Simpson family was on the demesne prior to the building of the present vaguely Scots Baronial pile on a new site in 1868.
**Keady Road Entrance** c1870; architect Charles Sherry

The lodge and gates contemporary with the new "Castle" and in matching quarry-faced coursed limestone rubble, turned a mellow pinkish brown. On a charming site, a gabled rectangular building with conspicuous canted bay windows now lacking character after recent "improvements". Banded rugged gate piers with distinctive tiered pyramidal cappings.
**Milford Entrance** c1870
At the original main access by the Callan River, square ashlar Georgian piers contemporary with the old family home. Alongside a much later, rather plainer two storey gabled lodge.

**18. BALLYGASEY COTTAGE, Loughgall** pre 1834; *demolished*
One time property of Edward Robinson

**19. BALLYMORE GLEBE, Tanderagee (2)**
**Rear Entrance** pre 1834; *demolished*
**Front Entrance** pre 1834; *ruinous*
A two roomed lodge with its gable projecting beyond two tall square piers. All in random rubble. Spear-topped gates also survive. This old tree-lined avenue has not been used since the main entrance was moved to the foot of the hill and nearer town, when the new rectory was built in about 1890. Of the old square rectory, with its glebe which comprised 520 acres, nothing survives.
LEWIS (1837)

**20. BALLYMOYER, Newtownhamilton** pre 1835; *demolished*
A large three storey mansion built in 1778 by Sir Walter Synnot. Demolished as is its lodge. Acquired along with avenue and glen by the National Trust in 1938.
BENCE-JONES (1988); LEWIS (1837)

**21. BALLYNAHONE, Armagh** pre 1835; *demolished*
The house survives much as altered by Henry Cust in the late 18th century but its lodge has gone.

**22. BEECH HILL** c1825; architect perhaps J B Keane

Built for Thomas Simpson Esq, the lodge is simple two roomed single storey over a part basement. The front elevation single bay gabled with a crude pediment over a recessed elliptical archway, which may originally have framed the front door, now blank. Perhaps once faced in rubble stone like the house, it is now roughcast with elegant Soanean incised pilaster strips as quoins. The windows have shelf-like stone drips above. The chimney stack as built has since been twice raised to ziggurat form in search of a better draw. It seems that this was once quite a sophisticated little composition, now defaced and deserted. Relatively unspoilt are two impressive stone Greek stellae type gate pillars with key pattern to the friezes below semicircular-pedimented cappings, seemingly on the wrong way round. Nice sturdy basic iron gates. Many features here - gate pillars, "gable-on" lodge, pilasters and not least the pretty villa itself - show characteristics of the Morrison practice, if not one of the principals then J B Keane, their erstwhile assistant, in his own right.

**23. BELLEVUE, Lurgan (2)** both c1855; *both demolished*
House and main lodge Neo-Classical, for Samuel A Bell of the Lurgan Weaving Company. The house a shell, the lodges lost without trace.

**24. BELLEVUE, Newry** pre 1860; *demolished*
A property of James McMahon for whom local architect William J Barre carried out work here.
DUNLOP (1868)

**25. BELMOUNT RECTORY, Forkhill** pre 1835
Standard plan, gabled and plain.

**26. BONDVILLE, Middletown** c1830
Opposite the old entrance, now gateless, the lodge is apparently standard single storey three bay symmetrical below a hipped roof. In fact it is two up two down with basement rooms below road level. Constructed in brick, whitewashed, with carved brackets to a wide eaves. Two broad square brick chimney stacks are carried off a rectangular plinth. Front window openings since enlarged from the small sashed originals. Built for Henry Coote Bond.

**27. BROWNLOW, Lurgan (4)**
William Henry Playfair of Edinburgh was the most fastidious of architects but even he found Charles Brownlow the most frustrating of clients, the new house having a long and slow gestation thanks to indecision. Playfair eventually enlisted the help of the future Baron Lurgan's brother-in-law Maxwell Close of Drumbanagher (qv) and in 1837 Samuel Lewis was able to report, "near the town is Lurgan House, the residence of the Rt Hon Charles Brownlow, now being rebuilt on an extensive scale and in the Elizabethan style, with freestone brought from Scotland; the approach is by a handsome lodge and gateway of the same character ...".
**Town Lodge and Archway** 1834; architect W H Playfair; *demolished*

A.R. Hogg (U.M.)

The architect produced the most meticulous and comprehensive set of drawings (twenty-two in all) for the lodge and archway. A dumpy little single storey building of two main rooms, a bed closet return to the rear and projecting gabled front porch with a tiny closet alongside under a catslide roof. Otherwise it is all skewtables and kneelers, apexes topped by tall chimney stacks with octagonal pots. The front window gablet crowned like other projections with spiked ball finials. Windows mullioned with label mouldings, the porch Tudor-arched and drip-moulded with a blank shield over.
The grand Tudor archway again label-moulded and surmounted by stepped crenellations housed the Brownlow coat-of-arms and motto "ESSE QUAM VIDERI" both sides. All well buttressed back and front, the 12'6" (3.8m) high convex wall sweeps had a little wicket door opening in matching style. Sturdy studded wooden double and single doors. All in soft golden sandstone like the house, the whole complex mindlessly swept away.
**Belfast Road Entrance** c1835; architect W H Playfair; demolished

K. Clendenning

A similar fate has befallen this charming little lodge which was a Picturesque cottage version of the Town Lodge. On a similar plan, handed, it swapped skewtables for a steeply-pitched hipped roof, the chimney flues carried up in a central corbelled stack. The projecting hall with side door had carved bargeboards and a hipknob. Stuccoed walls with hefty quoins and label

W.H. Playfair drawing (P.R.O.N.I.)

*Town Lodge, Brownlow House*

mouldings over openings. Another needless loss along with its gates. One should be thankful for the mansion's survival within what is now a public park.

**School Entrance** c1840; architect probably W H Playfair

Off North Street on the perimeter of the demesne is a substantial single storey school building in a solid Picturesque gabled style constructed with sandstone ashlar like the mansion. There are sturdy ornamental carved wooded bargeboards and large hipknobs. Label mouldings, transoms and mullions to the windows all in Tudor vein suggest that this was also part of Playfair's commission and its location at an access to the demesne, point to a secondary function as a porters' lodge.

**Rear Entrance** pre 1834; *demolished*

The fourth lodge, much earlier than the others and to the "antique castle" predecessor, has also gone, without record. At the turn of the century most of the demesne was given to the town for use as a public park (see Lurgan Park).
P.R.O.N.I. Drawings D1928/P/8/C; HOGG Photograph (UM) HO2/26/4&5; LEWIS (1837)

**28. CARRICKBROAD, Forkhill (2)**
both pre 1832; *both demolished*

One time property of the Johnston family, some rubble marks the sites, with plain gate piers.

**29. CASTLEDILLON Armagh (3)**
**Main Entrance** 1760; architect probably Sir William Chambers

Sir Capel Molyneux, MP, and 3rd Baronet erected in 1760 "... the most costly park gates, perhaps at that time in the three kingdoms". So enthused a visitor of 1811. Costly indeed for the time, being noted in 1782 as having cost £2,000. By 1786 the Post Chaise Companion recorded "In fine, the park gates and offices are in the best style of architecture and elegance and a suitable mansion house in the room of the present old one would render this seat one of the most agreeable in the Kingdom". Tradition has it that these remarkable lodges and gates were designed by the celebrated English architect Sir William Chambers (1723-96) and this was always the belief of the late T G F Patterson. No documentary evidence has come to light to support this but there are elements such as the springing voussoirs and contrasting smooth keystones to openings which are similar to some on Charlemont House, Dublin, and Somerset House, London, both by Chambers. He had also designed Marino Casino for Lord Charlemont with whom Molyneux was an ardent Irish Volunteer. Sir Capel was an inveterate improver and eccentric and he had many statues disposed about the park and in 1787 erected the 60' (18m) obelisk. One can imagine him, as recorded, driving to and from Armagh between the gargantuan gate piers every Sunday in a coach and six with three postilions. Just why these pillars, all of 21' (6.4m) high and crowned with cornice and blocking caps, were so disproportionate to the lodges is a mystery but they were reduced to reasonable proportions sometime this century. These "Day and Night" lodges are on a substantial scale in their own right. Each room measures 14' 3" (4.35m) square with an 11' 4" (3.45m) high ceiling, with moulded covings. Authoritative and monumental Roman Palladian in style, built in large limestone rubble blocks deeply rusticated with V-jointed channelling, the walls amply support grand ashlar pediments spanning full width. The windows almost to ground level are mullioned and transomed in timber and further divided into rectangular panes. To the road, blind openings which may always have been architectural features. With their limestone mellowed to a pleasant pinkish brown these unique lodges are now derelict and crucially in need of restoration and preservation.

W. M. Lawrence (P.R.O.N.I.)

**Hockley Entrance** pre 1835; architect perhaps Thomas Cooley

A plain Georgian lodge. The gate sweep is probably contemporary with it. Four large square pillars with ball finials on elegant stems. Concave wall sweeps. Perhaps of about 1780 when Thomas Cooley designed the stable range.

**Armagh Entrance** pre 1835; *demolished*

CROOKSHANK (1963); POST CHAISE COMPANION (1786); PLAYFAIR'S BARONETAGE (1811); LAWRENCE PHOTOGRAPH (P.R.O.N.I.) 5885(R);

**30. CHARLEMONT FORT, Moy** 1673; architect probably Sir William Robinson

Commanding the Blackwater River crossing, the remains of a fort erected during Mountjoy's 1602 campaign. Situated in a position of strategic importance are starfort earthworks with pointed bastions and a governor's residence. During its turbulent history it was occupied by a garrison and used as an ordnance depot for the north of Ireland. The fort was long associated with the Caulfields, Earls of Charlemont, who intermittently held the Governorship until 1858 the year following which they purchased the fort for a private residence. There clearly was a gatehouse to the fort since its foundation and there were several references to it through time, the earliest in 1665: "Gatehouse new roofed and shingled, had new made the drawbridge". It may not have assumed its present form until 1673 when Viscount Conway was Governor. A letter from the Surveyor General of Ireland, Sir William Robinson (fl c1643-1712), on April 26th indicates extensive improvements to the fort being carried out as evidenced by "we are now cutting a graft [trench or foss] before the ravelin and preparing for a new drawbridge and entrance" (Conway papers). The contractor was recorded as being a Mr Johnson. It is also significant that in 1746 an estimate was prepared for certain works including a gate wicket, and two stone bridges, in place of the ruinous drawbridge. Although it is not known if the latter work was carried out, drawbridge pulleys and chains survive to this day and Observations by the Commissioners on their view of the several Barracks throughout the Kingdom of Ireland

(1760) still mentions a drawbridge at the entrance of the south curtain and "... the Watch-Tower over gateway new roofed and slated". On 15 February 1858 the artillery garrison occupying the barracks was withdrawn, the Government deeming the fort no longer necessary, and one year later Francis William Caulfield, Earl of Charlemont purchased it from the Crown. On its passing into civilian use the outbuildings and defences were levelled, only the central building and gateway being retained. The filling in of the moat and planting of the beech-lined avenue approach which survive to this day, date from c1859. From this point onwards only a caretaker was in residence, Lord Charlemont seemingly preoccupied with his grand building works across the river at Roxborough, Co Tyrone (qv). The gatehouse as it appears today is substantially Robinson's design of 1673 but probably refaced in sandstone ashlar upon its assuming a more decorative rather than a defensive role. Then the large plaque bearing the Caulfield arms was incorporated above the semicircular-headed entrance archway which springs from a stringcourse that continues through the flanking wings from the frontispiece. These screen walls each have three loopholes at rampart level. On either side of the arms a chamfered slit for observation from the watchroom, over which are pediments on back and front elevations. The tympana display fine clock faces. Pulleys and chains remain from the old drawbridge now replaced by two pairs of large wooden doors. Over the front archway a wrought iron lamp bracket and on a side elevation what is perhaps a mason's monogram "EW". The Governor's fort was burnt down in 1920 and demolished the following year leaving the once handsome gateway neglected and looking uneasy in isolation, its flanks exposed.
MARSHALL (1921); JOPE (1960);
LOEBER (1981)

**31. CHURCH HILL Moy (6);** *all demolished*
The fine demesne of the Verners now only remarkable for its almost total disappearance. The elegant house of c1830 for Colonel William Verner probably by William Farrell has vanished, along with no less than six gate lodges, all of which were in position by 1859. Half of these were built before 1834. Now the Peatlands Theme Park.
OSM

**32. CLONCARNEY CASTLE, Markethill**
(see GOSFORD CASTLE)

**33. CORCRAIN, Portadown** c1850; *demolished*
Linen manufacturing was begun here in 1840 by Mr Joseph Druitt who built stores, offices, thirty workers' houses and the porter's lodge. In 1872 the seat and works became the Linen and Cambric Handkerchief Manufactory of Thomas Dawson. Demolished to make way for a housing estate one century later.
BASSETT'S CO ARMAGH (1888)

**34. CORCRAIN VILLA, Portadown** pre 1864; *demolished*
The property in 1864 of Charles F Wakefield.
GRIFFITH

**35. CRANAGILL, Loughgall (2)**
both pre 1834; *both demolished*
Two lodges for the Nicholson family.

**36. CREGGAN LODGE, Crossmaglen (2)**
one pre 1835 one pre 1860; *both demolished*

**37. CROWHILL, Loughgall (2)**
both pre 1834; *both demolished*
Lodges to a villa of the Atkinson family.

**38. DARKLEY, Keady** c1840
The most undistinguished standard plan, single storey, three bay symmetrical gabled whitewashed cottage now incorporated within a modern bungalow. A property in 1837 of H McKean.

**39. DARTEN, Killylea** 1870

Mid-Victorian single storey gabled lodge on an L plan. Set diagonally across the internal angle a canted hall with a peculiar parapet over. All window lights semicircular-headed in a variety of tri- and bipartite openings. The canted bay has a sort of Venetian window, the front door under a pointed head. Wavy bargeboards with sawtooth fillet overlay. There is a slender gawky one flue chimney stack. Datestone in gable. An amateurish composition in coursed Armagh limestone rubble quarry-faced, as is the gate sweep. The ogee quadrants have crude crenellated copings. Beyond, square chamfered piers with battered bases and cappings with gablets. Highly decorative pair of cast iron carriage gates in curly-wurly pattern. Built by Mr William Cross on the site of its pre 1834 predecessor.

**40. THE DEANERY, Armagh (2)** c1845
A quaint Cottage Orné in Nash/Repton manner, from its approach apparently single storey, but on sloping ground the cross of the T plan over a basement room. Gables and gablet have simple foiled bargeboards and hipknobs recently restored. Casement windows below label mouldings in rubble walls with punched ashlar quoins. On top a row of three square brick stacks, previously nicely inebriated, now rebuilt and upright. It replaced a pre 1835 lodge across the road which may have been contemporary with the existing gate pillars. These are in punched ashlar stone, square and Classical with cornices and block cappings, only stems survive of the ball finials. Designed c1790, the gates have been removed. Two concave wing walls of rough stone, built after 1950s road widening, terminate in smaller piers.

**41. DEER PARK, Belleek** c1800
At the entrance to Lord Gosford's remote deerpark a pitifully dilapidated lodge and entrance archway, the main elliptical carriage arch of which has collapsed. The little wicket gate opening with lancet head has a moulded surround in a smooth coursed whinstone rubble wall. Behind, the lodge is single storey three bay the openings not quite symmetrical and the precarious stack off-centre on a tall hipped roof. In harled walls, small window openings with square Georgian panes, the doorway wide. The irregular fenestration and high eaves line give a quaint rustic feel.

**42. DERRYCAW, Moy** (see THE ARGORY)

**43. DERRYESKER, Loughgall** pre 1862; *demolished*
The property in 1862 of George Beggs.
GRIFFITH

**44. DERRYMORE, Bessbrook (4)**
All lodges to this delightful seat of the Corry family disappointingly nondescript. The original main entrance has a pre 1834 lodge, two built prior to 1861 and the most recent before 1906.

**45. DERRYNOOSE GLEBE, Middletown** c1860
A modest gabled one and a half storey three bay building opposite the entrance to a mid-Georgian rectory, all now deserted. Also known as Madden. Probably built for Rev Samuel Simpson.

**46. DRUMALANE, Newry** pre 1859; *demolished*
The lodge to a house acquired by Hill Irvine in the early 1850s. He also built up the big Bessbrook Spinning Co Ltd nearby.
BASSETT'S CO DOWN (1886)

**47. DRUMBANAGHER, Poyntzpass (3)**
In 1951 the Edinburgh architect W H Playfair's magnificent Italianate masterpiece of Drumbanagher for Lieut-Col Maxwell Close was demolished succumbing to death duties, maintenance costs and other financial difficulties. Commenced in 1830 to replace a previous house of the Moore family from whom the estates were bought in 1818. It was to the later house that two gate lodges belonged, neither having survived. £80,000 was spent on building the mansion and outbuildings and there seems to have been little left in the coffers to provide an appropriate lodge at the time.

**North Entrance** pre 1835; *demolished*
**South Entrance** pre 1835; *demolished*
**West Entrance** c1847; architect perhaps W H Playfair

The above situation would appear not to have been put to rights until 1847 when the estate wall was built to provide employment for victims of the Famine. This beautiful little lodge has all the architectural details of the big house but in the Edinburgh University Library, where rest the usual plentiful and meticulous collection of drawings one would expect of Playfair, there is no record of a lodge. Yet it is too able and compatible a design to look beyond him for an attribution. Single storey but with high ceilings, it was simply two roomed and three bay though somewhat short of symmetrical, having a variety of window openings in stuccoed walls with stone quoins. The right hand window is bipartite with an architraved surround surmounted by a moulded entablature carried on two crossettes. To the left a semicircular-headed window with architraved surround which contains little engaged colonettes with flowery capitals. Margined glazing. Below the bracketed cill a recessed balustrade, a feature repeated below the tripartite gable window. Here again outer engaged colonettes carry round-headed mouldings springing from two crossettes on the

dividing mullions. The building is bound on the three main elevations by a cornice surmounted by a criss-cross balustrade decorated with flowerheads, central to which is a round-topped block with anthemion motif. At external corners, acroteria. Hidden behind is a low-pitched roof with a corniced chimney stack and terracotta pots. The projecting hall has a matching balustrade with small urns adorning both corners, below which are two Close family crests within wreaths: a demi-lion vert holding a battle-axe, or headed arg, and incorporating on one side the Close motto FORTIS ET FIDELIS and on the other that of the Maxwells, SINE CRUCE, SINE LUCE. Within the semicircular-headed and moulded surround, nice panelled double leaf doors. To the sides little round-headed lights with their own balustraded cills. It is to be hoped that this charming lodge does not suffer the same fate as the house, already having been subjected to ill-considered renovations despite being listed.
DOYLE (1854)

**48. DRUMCREE RECTORY Portadown** pre 1835; *demolished*
A lodge opposite the gates was built along with the glebe house in 1828 for Rev Charles Alexander, long time incumbent.
LEWIS (1837)

**49. DRUMILLY, Loughgall (3)**
The antique mansion of the Copes and its magnificent "Great Exhibition" conservatory have gone along with all its gate lodges. Hardly a vestige of this beautiful demesne remains intact. Early entrances both pre 1834; both demolished Two pairs of porters' lodges have not survived to see this century.

**Later Entrance** c1845; *demolished*
A modest three bay lodge, below a hipped roof, built into a screen wall. In rough Armagh limestone, small square-paned sash windows with decorative cast iron overpanels the same pattern as on an Argory (qv) lodge. The big square piers had, over plain cornices, concave pyramid cappings as outsized pedestals for bulbous urns. A nice little sheeted wicket door between pier and lodge matched the front door.

**50. DRUMSILL, Armagh (2)**
The other seat of the MacGeough family of the Argory. (q.v.)

**Dungannon Lodge** c1840/c1880
Two roomed with gable to the avenue. Extended to a single storey "double pile" late last century with polychrome brick chimney stack. Further additions to the rear more recently. Good square Georgian gate piers.

**Armagh Lodge** c1880
Unprepossessing two storey building, also having a polychrome brick chimney.

**51. EDENDERRY, Benburb**
(see EGLISH GLEBE)

**52. EDEN HALL, Benburb** pre 1860; *demolished*
Built for Thomas Armstrong.

**53. EGLISH GLEBE, Benburb** pre 1860; *demolished*
Probably built for Rev St John Thomas Blacker. More recently called Edenderry.

**54. ELM PARK, Killylea (4)**
The once dignified mansion house now lies empty, having served as a boys' school and more recently as a deep-litter poultry farm. Originally the seat of the Maxwell-Close family.

**Inner Lodge** pre 1834; *demolished*
The earliest lodge, which was situated well within the later estate boundary, has disappeared.

**East Lodge** c1803/c1830

A fine entrance screen of four quatrefoil stone cluster piers with moulded plinths and stem cappings to ball finials (now missing). Identical to those at Derrybard, Co Tyrone (qv) perhaps based on the grander versions at Portumna, Co Galway. These probably date from 1803 when major rebuilding of the house was carried out. Some thirty years later the piers were complemented by a simple three bay, single storey lodge in a confusion of styles. Picturesque "double-diamond" chimney stack on a hipped roof with paired eaves brackets. Now cement rendered, there are crude pilaster quoins which frame wide casement windows that may once have been label moulded. Deserted.

**South Lodge** 1867; architect perhaps J Rawson Carroll
Gabled, one and a half storey, three bay in uncoursed quarry-faced Armagh limestone rubble. Chamfered dressings to mullioned windows, both bi- and tripartite. In one gable a diamond shaped window to an attic room and a corresponding datestone on the gable of the projecting hall. Large widely-spaced brackets to the eaves, below a scallop-slated roof. Probably by J Rawson Carroll, architect of Dublin, who produced drawings for work to the house about this time.

**North Lodge** c1890
By 1870 the seat had passed by marriage to St J T Blacker- Douglass of Grace Hall, Co Down (qv) who built this substantial lodge on the Knappagh Road. A one and a half storey house on an L plan, roughcast with facing brick window dressings, quoins and battered corbelled chimney stack. Vigorous late Victorian carved timber bargeboards, foiled and waved with quatrefoil toes and spandrels which support tall hipknobs. Exposed rafter toes to main roof and the decorative foil-arched lean-to porch-cum-verandah over the entrance door. It surprisingly lies empty.

**55. ENNISCLARE, Milford** c1850

A once perky little building for the Barcroft family. Single storey, symmetrical three bay. Gabled, as is the predominant breakfront with its keystoned oculus over the front door. All openings have semicircular heads, echoed in the tall "Vanbrugh" type chimney stack, the two flues arching across to meet. A very pleasing Italianate composition now a forlorn shell, the windows empty and staring.

**56. FAIRVIEW, Tynan**
(see TYNAN ABBEY)

**57. FATHOM PARK, Newry** pre 1864; *demolished*
A gate lodge noted here by Griffith in his valuation as being the property of the Benson family.
GRIFFITH

**58. FELLOWS HALL, Killylea (2)**
**North Lodge** pre 1834
Plain and abandoned.

**South Lodges** pre 1860; *demolished*
Semidetached with some Gothick windows. Both built by the Armstrong family the seat having derived its name through belonging at one time to Trinity College Dublin.
YOUNG (1909)

**59. FEVER HOSPITAL, Armagh** c1827; architect probably William Farrell; *demolished*
The lodge appears from the OS map to have been contemporary with the hospital building designed by Farrell and Carroll in 1827. Constructed in stone, it was later raised a storey in brick with an outsized chimney. The Macan Asylum for the Blind as it later became known has, along with the lodge, been cleared away to make way for a housing estate.

**60. THE FOLLY, Armagh (2)**
**Barrick Hill Lodge** pre 1835; *demolished*
**Newry Road Lodge** pre 1835; *demolished*
A property in 1858 of Leonard Dobbin.
GRIFFITH

**61. FORKILL, Forkill** pre 1835/c1845/c1880
The Jackson family had a lodge built here sometime before 1835, originally of standard plan. This was subsequently extended by a bay, when cast iron lattice panes were inserted in lancet windows to the projecting hall, around 1840 when Henry Alexander bought the estate. Bargeboards with a repeating perforated cross motif were added in the 1880s by Henry's son Captain Granville Henry Jackson Alexander. A rectangular slab of coursed rubble masonry, once harled, is pierced by a Tudor carriage archway and dressed, quoined and coped with granite. The cast iron gates have fleur-de-lys finials and an alert row of flower heads at waist height. Probably dating from the 1840 improvements.
LEIGH (1832); BASSETT'S CO ARMAGH (1888); YOUNG (1909)

**62. FORKHILL RECTORY, Forkhill**
(see Belmount Rectory)

**63. THE GLEN, Newry**
(see TURNER HILL)

**64. GLENANNE, Newtownhamilton** c1830
In 1818 Mr William Atkinson settled here and erected extensive cotton spinning and weaving mills. By the entrance to the house he added a little lodge with a quirky leading gable hipped in eyebrow fashion. Below it the front door, which leads directly into one of two rooms, flanked by small lattice-paned sidelights in roughcast walls. Now deserted.
BASSETT'S CO ARMAGH (1888)

**65. GLENAUL PARK, Benburb**
(see MULLYLOUGHAN)

**66. GLEN EYRE, Portadown** pre 1905; *demolished*
The lodge probably built for William Henry Atkinson sometime after acquiring a property previously belonging to Thomas C Wakefield.

**67. GOSFORD CASTLE, Markethill (5)**
The old Cloncarney Castle was destroyed in the rebellion of 1641 and it was not until comparative peace arrived after the Williamite wars that a new manor house was built by Sir Nicholas Acheson, 4th Baronet. It was either he, or his son Arthur who succeeded him in 1701, who erected the oldest surviving non-defensive gate lodges in the Province.

**Old Cloncarney Entrance** c1700

Off the old county road, now absorbed into the enlarged Gosford estates, lie two large ornamental ponds between which the avenue to the manor house led over a causeway. The access is below a semicircular-headed carriage archway in a large wall of roughly carved rubble whinstone dressed in Classically-moulded carved limestone. At springing level impost blocks, the arch crowned by a keystone. To each side blind "openings" on a smaller scale similarly moulded. Luxuriant creeper makes further description impossible. Behind these blank openings a pair of commodious one roomed 16' 3" x 10' 0" (4.9m x 3.0m) porters' lodges face each other. Each has a gable shaped in the Dutch style then in fashion and significantly echoing those at Richill Castle (qv) but five miles distant. At their peaks rest arched chimney stacks in Vanbrugh style, like little belfries. Round-headed window openings overlook the ponds, in uncoursed random rubble 21" (0.5m) thick. Here it is said that Dean Swift often lingered on his visits to the Achesons in the 1720s. It is comforting to know that though only roofed shells, they are preserved as public shelters by the Department of Agriculture.

**Drumlack and Tanderagee Lodges** both c1840; architect probably Thomas Hopper

No less unique in Ulster are these two lodges erected not long after completion of, and in striking contrast to, Thomas Hopper's vast and solid essay in the Neo-Norman style for Archibald Acheson, 2nd Lord Gosford. Each is in the form of a rustic log cabin with a steeply-pitched hipped roof within which is an attic bedroom lit by a little dormer window. The original thatch was replaced in 1939 by hexagonal asbestos slates thus losing much of its picturesque effect. The eaves extend to form a verandah right round, originally carried on tree trunks. The external walls are of vertical logs relieved below cill level by a herring-bone pattern band. The openings have pointed arches. These little delights are reminiscent of Smoothway Lodge, Ugbrooke Park, Devon and may have been a whimsy of Hopper's or of his assistant John Millar. Drumlack lodge has gone but Tanderagee lodge remains well tended, slates replaced in diamond pattern and the posts now metal.

**North Lodge** c1850; architect perhaps John Millar.

(R. Bryson)

Opposite the Drumlack gate a substantial and informal Tudor Revival style building originally stone faced, now rendered over. One and a half storey on a T plan it is all skewtables and kneelers to main gables, a gablet and projecting single storey hall. The front door semicircular-headed with hood moulding and blank shield above that again. Other ground floor openings have splayed jambs and label mouldings over. Roof hexagonally slated with a pair of tall octagonal stone chimney pots. Very ornate but now somewhat spoiled by removal of many of those features in an insensitive "improvement" scheme. John Millar seems to have been sent across to superintend the construction of the castle and stayed, setting up in practice in Belfast.

**Garden Lodge** c1850

To the eastern boundary a relatively inept exercise in a jumble of styles. One and a half storey three bay symmetrical with hipped gables, one pierced by a Georgian-paned window in a gablet. Rendered walls with quoins have transomed and mullioned windows with label mouldings. The front door has lattice-paned sidelights. Stumps of a pair of diagonal chimney stacks.

LEWIS (1837); MINISTRY OF AGRICULTURE GUIDE (1970); DIXON (1972); MALINS (1976)

**68. GREEN HALL, Loughgall**
(see HAYES HALL)

**69. HARRYBROOK, Tanderagee** pre 1834
A commonplace lodge of square plan under a wide-eaved hipped roof. Probably built for Robert Harden.

**70. HAWTHORN HILL, Forkhill** c1845

Opposite the entrance a pretty, three bay lodge, single storey with paired bracketed eaves to a pyramidal roof. In granite there are brick relieving arches over openings. Distinctive chiefly for very pretty geometric patterned cast iron glazing bars to windows. Simple granite gate posts. It apparently replaced an earlier lodge on the same site, built not long after the house of 1815 for Hunt Walsh Chambre.

SEAVER (1950)

**71. HAYES HALL, Loughgall** pre 1860; *demolished*
A lodge probably for the Cowdy family.

**72. HEATH HALL, Newry (2)**

**West Lodge** pre 1835; *demolished*

Thomas Seaver upon acquiring the property built a two storey thatched house in 1769 and afterwards a lodge to the western boundary on the Armagh-Dundalk road approach via a beech-lined avenue which was utilised until the early 1830s. Then the introduction of turnpike gates at this access necessitated the laying down of a shorter drive to the north, and the building of a new porter's lodge opposite this new exit, for Thomas's grandson Jonathan.

**North Lodge** c1834/c1897; architect Henry Seaver

The estate was sold by the family in 1853 but bought back in 1897 when another Jonathan secured the services of his second cousin Henry Seaver, a rising young Belfast architect, to restore or replace the existing lodge and inflict a most inappropriate castellated tower on the pleasant old Georgian house. The unremarkable lodge survives with mildly Picturesque bargeboards and pebble-dashed walls, the house ruinous.

SEAVER (1950)

**73. HOCKLEY LODGE, Armagh (3)**

(R. Bryson)

The Honourable Henry Caulfield, younger son of the 1st "Volunteer" Earl of Charlemont, in the 1830s added to the house an extension in the Regency style and sundry other improvements. These included pretty outbuildings, and to the demesne boundary, three porters' lodges all principally deriving their picturesque appearance from lattice-paned cast iron windows.

**Main Entrance** c1836

Severed from the demesne by recent realignment of the Belfast-Armagh Road, a harled L plan one and a half storey two up two down building with simple clipped verges to gables. Now boarded up, its gate piers repositioned across the carriageway.

**Drumilly Lodge** c1836

Simple three bay symmetrical single storey and gabled. Built in stone with brick window dressings. Deserted.

**Middle Lodge** c1834; architect not known

The earliest and most distinctive of the three. Single storey three roomed on a cruciform plan. All four gables are hipped, as is the little rectangular bay on the leading elevation. A diagonal single flue chimney stack is broached from a square base. Now unoccupied like the others, there are the remains of a pretty cottage garden and a rustic stile by the side of the vehicular access. Very pleasant. Akin to the lodge at Green Gate, Mourne Park, Co Down (qv). Architect not identified for either.

OSM; BENCE-JONES (1988)

**74. KILCLOONEY RECTORY, Tanderagee** pre 1835

Nondescript.

**75. KILLEVY CASTLE, Forkhill (2)**

Killevy Lodge was transformed into a symmetrical Gothick castle in 1836 for Powell Foxall Esq, by the architect George Papworth.

**South Lodge** c1837 architect probably George Papworth; *demolished*

A painting in the Armagh Museum indicates what was a contemporary and unassuming gate lodge at the end of a straight avenue on an axis with the front door of the "castle".

**North Lodge** c1837; architect probably George Papworth; *ruinous*

Single storey three bay gabled with a projecting eaves, the door asymmetrically placed. On the gable to the road two mock arrowslits and on the other a mysterious corbelled "shelf" at high level.

PAINTING IN THE ARMAGH MUSEUM; CRAIG (1970)

**76. KILLEVY CHURCHES, Forkhill**

(see BALLINTEMPLE CHURCHYARD)

**77. KILLYCOMAIN, Portadown** pre 1905; *demolished*

A lodge to the property in 1888 of John Collen JP, timber merchant.

**78. KILMORE, Loughgall** c1820; architect perhaps Francis Johnston

A typically modest and pleasant late Georgian

A.C.W. Merrick

lodge. Three bay single storey with hipped roof and projecting eaves. Constructed in lovely random rubble with brick dressings to square window openings. At the end of a short drive was the glebe house (1793). Much added to early in the 19th century as the seat of the Johnston family, one of whom was the architect Francis Johnston. He may have been responsible for the gate lodge for its proportions are much akin to those of the Lunatic Asylum lodge, Armagh (qv).

YOUNG (1909)

**79. KNAPPAGH, Killylea (2)**

Another residence of the Johnston family whose most famous son was the architect Francis Johnston and who probably designed the house in 1790. By the time James Johnston decided that lodges were a requirement Francis had retired but it must have been he that recommended Alexander McLeish to prepare plans. A pupil of J C Loudon, he came to Ireland in 1813 principally as a landscape architect but had, like his master, developed into a jack-of-all-trades. He had worked with Francis Johnston at Ballynagall, Co Westmeath.

**Main Entrance** 1827; architect Alexander McLeish; *demolished*

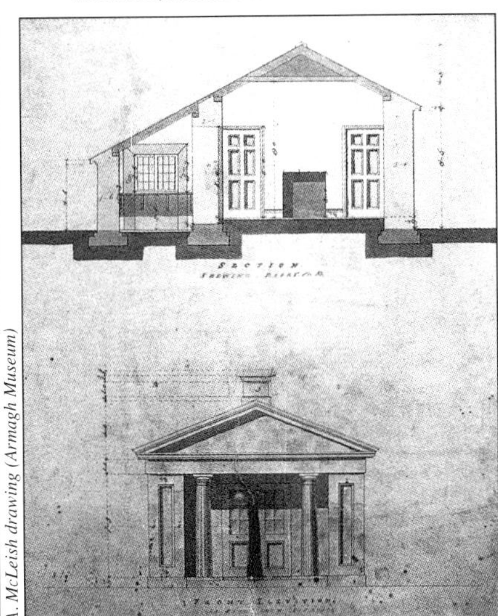
A. McLeish drawing (Armagh Museum)

McLeish prepared a chaste little Classical design, really only one sophisticated elevation which was the leading gable of a single storey two roomed main block with a single roomed outshoot below a catslide roof to the rear. In Armagh limestone ashlar the pediment full width carried, on either side of a double leaf panelled

and glazed front door, by two Doric columns in antis, the antae broad with recessed panels. Otherwise the other elevations were simply harled. Drawings for the lodge, showing a competent drafting technique, survive in the Armagh Museum. The convex wall sweeps, in similar ashlar to the lodge, flank entablatured wicket gates on either side of double carriage gates. The gates are intact but the lodge disgracefully removed in favour of a bland bungalow.

**Knappagh Road Entrance** c1827; architect probably Alexander McLeish

OS maps and appearance point to the lodges being of an age and likely to be McLeish's Picturesque style. Commodious, single storey on an L plan, with a hipped roof advancing at the front to form a verandah carried on five wrought iron columns. A gabled projection (perhaps a later extension) has serrated bargeboards with carved patera motifs to the toes. Below the gable a rectangular bay with its own hipped roof. The windows small squared panes, in harled walls. Across the road the tall square corniced ashlar piers carry similar iron gates to the main entrance, and of a pattern used at The Argory, Moy (qv).

DRAWINGS IN THE ARMAGH MUSEUM; MALINS (1980)

**80. LONGSTONE, Armagh** pre 1860; *demolished*

**81. LOUGHGALL MANOR, Loughgall (2)**

**Main Entrance** c1842; architect perhaps William Murray

In the midst of this sleepy village of graceful Georgian architecture, a most striking Neo-Jacobean extravaganza in the form of an extensive entrance screen and a pair of elaborate lodges behind. The stone ogee sweep is a semicircular-arched balustrade of tapering columns on a band of polygonal rubble walling over a moulded ashlar plinth. Its carved coping is crowned with intermittent tubby urns. The terminating and four inner pillars square on heavily rusticated bases are built up in alternate courses of prismatic bands and pecked ones with central diamond pointed stones. The corniced cappings have prettily carved arabesque friezes below, and are crowned with the Copes' dragons breathing fire and rising from fleurs-de-lys. The two wicket and double carriage gates suitably elaborate and obligingly signed and dated by the whitesmith "R.MARSHALL CALEDON 1842". Unfortunately the fine overthrow was toppled by a lorry in the 1960s and has not been replaced despite promises which have proved empty. The identical porters' lodges facing each other across the avenue are lavishly embellished, disguising simple two roomed, single storey L plans. Built of more polygonal rubble walling, framed by a tall plinth and quoins in ashlar, the gables suitably shaped in Jacobean fashion, providing shelves for a series of square pinnacles with onion pendants and finials. The apex finials were originally a variety of wild animals, a lion and a bear identifiable, but all now removed. In the internal angle a flat-roofed porch with all the Neo-Jacobean trappings in flamboyantly carved stone. A tapered outer column and two matching pilasters on block bases with diamond pointed features, have shafts banded and strapped, expanding to squashed Ionic capitals. These support deeply scrolled brackets, from which spring elliptical arches with alternate voussoirs again having diamond pointed motifs, all carrying a moulded cornice with ogee guttering. The front door panelled in a Tudor surround. The two leading gables have oriel windows with hipped and rolled lead roofs, one rectangular on scrolled brackets, the other canted on a corbel. As if this were not enough, the slates are

W.M. Lawrence (N.L.I.)

scalloped and there are, or rather were, luxurious tall cream terracotta Tudor chimney pots. In the same material each gable is decorated with the Cope coat-of-arms and motto, EQUO ADESTE ANIMO. The evidence of the gate inscription shows all to have been commissioned before the death of Arthur Cope at the age of thirty in 1844 without issue. The estate was bequeathed to his cousin Robert Wright Cope Doolan who changed his surname to Cope and incorporated his arms into each gable. This dramatic introduction does little to prepare one for the comparatively modest rambling Tudor Revival manor house. The late T G F Patterson speculated that all may have been the work of William Murray with considerable assistance from Italian craftsmen who were already employed in building nearby Roxborough House, Moy Co Tyrone (qv) for Lord Charlemont. No corroborating evidence has come to light.

**Rear Entrance** c1850; *demolished*
On the East boundary a rather more crude but equally extensive sweep. A tall wall in coursed random limestone quarry-faced interrupted by square pillars with crenellated tops. Decorative carriage gates. The lodge opposite now replaced by a modern residence.
LAWRENCE PHOTOGRAPH (NLI) Refs 3623(C), 3624(C); BURKE (1904)

**82. LOUGHGILLY RECTORY, Markethill (2)** both pre 1834; *both demolished*
Two lodges to the glebe house of 1782.
LEWIS (1837)

**83. LOWER DARKLEY, Keady** pre 1864; *demolished*
A gate lodge identified by the Griffith Valuation as being to a house and beetling mill of the Kirk family.
GRIFFITH

**84. LUNATIC ASYLUM, Armagh** c1829; architects Francis Johnston and William Murray

Johnston and Murray's wide-winged institution is the only one of three on a standard plan to have survived in the Province, those at Belfast (qv) and Londonderry (qv) having been demolished. As Superintendent to the Board of Works Johnston's design was complete by 1825 and the gate lodge finished not long afterwards. Itself a standard plan no doubt used at the other two locations, it was three bay symmetrical and two roomed. Under a hipped roof with a chubby central chimney stack, the walls in coursed Armagh limestone rubble with dressed quoins. Extended by another bay and chimney to match sometime since, it is now sealed up and looks likely to share the fate of its Londonderry and Belfast counterparts. The gates and piers are missing. A later screen wall with chamfered end is echoed in a reworked corner of the lodge.
ARMAGH; UAHS (1992)

**85. LURGAN CASTLE, Lurgan**
(see BROWNLOW)

**86. LURGAN PARK, Lurgan** 1908; architects Hobart and Heron
A public park, formed from part of the Brownlow estate (qv), opened in 1909 by Lord Aberdeen. In May 1908 the Lurgan Urban District Council appointed Henry Hobart to design a new gate lodge, to be built at the Windsor Avenue entrance. The Irish Builder and Engineer of 27 June 1908 records: "At the mid monthly meeting of the Council the Public Park Committee reported that Mr H Hobart, CE, had submitted two or three sketch plans of gate lodges which he considered would be suitable for erecting at the entrance to the proposed Public Park, including one similar to that erected at the Cowan Heron Hospital grounds at Dromore, [Co Down, qv] at a cost of £300 and it was agreed to inspect this building and if thought suitable to have plans drawn up in accordance therewith". The committee was suitably impressed. An opulent Edwardian design constructed in red Seagoe brick off an L plan. Subtle use is made of "black and white" work confined to leading gables. The main block is one and a half storey its gable advancing and containing a rectangular bay window. Alongside projects the gabled hallway with semicircular head having a terracotta keystone over the spoked fanlight. At right angles is the single storey wing with its canted bay window surveying the entrance. The windows are wooden transomed and mullioned with leaded lights and the roof finish continues the emphasis on clay finish with rosemary tiles. Above is a tall modelled chimney stack in red brick. There is also a more elaborate version at Conway, Co Antrim (qv). The entrance screen differs in being grander with four tall red brick pillars the inner ones carrying lamps, those beyond crowned with ball finials. Scalloped decoration to the cappings. Rich contemporary cast-iron carriage and wicket gates.
CORBETT (1990)

**87. LURGANA, Newtownhamilton** pre 1860; *demolished*
A lodge for Marcus Synnot of the same family as nearby Ballymoyer (qv).

**88. MACAN ASYLUM, Armagh**
(see FEVER HOSPITAL)

**89. MADDEN RECTORY, Middletown**
(see DERRYNOOSE GLEBE)

**90. MANOR HOUSE, Milford** c1880; architects probably Young & MacKenzie

A little red brick mill village which sprang up by the damask manufacturing works of Messrs McCrum, Watson amd Mercer, the wide main street of which leads to the impressive entrance of the McCrum family demesne. The long main avenue was once noted for being one of the first in Ireland to be lit electrically, visitors travelling from far and wide to stare agog at the phenomenon. The remarkably durable geometric pattern teak concave fence sweeps are flanked by High Victorian limestone pillars virtually identical to those at Clanwilliam, Co Antrim (qv), differing only in being surmounted by ornamental metal fan-shaped electric light holders. The rugged square pillars rise from smooth bases, the body with engaged and banded polished marble colonettes at each corner. Over, the cappings are gabled with quartrefoil motifs as are the semicircular gablets to the two side faces. Two big stone balls act as buffer protection to the central piers which never had gates. In contrasting hard red raw brick is the single storey T plan lodge, its three steeply-pitched gables clad in diamond terracotta tile hanging and decorated with simple bargeboards with collar tie. The slate roof, with red earthenware cresting and fleur-de-lys apex finials, carries down in a catslide over a nicely carved timber arcaded entrance hall. On the main gable a tall canted timber bay with hipped roof awaits visitors. Red brick corbelled chimney on a plinth. The lodge is well maintained, the avenue now sealed off. At the rear entrance an off-the-shelf cast iron gate sweep from Musgrave & Co Ltd, of Belfast. The gate posts "roofed". Since the death of Mr Robert Garmany McCrum, for whom the buildings were designed, the house has served as a girls' school and now as a special care home.
P.R.O.N.I. D2194

**91. MIDDLETOWN RECTORY, Middletown** pre 1835; *demolished*
A lodge to St John's Church and the 1812 glebe house. Also known as Shantally Lodge.
LEWIS (1837)

**92. MILLMOUNT, Keady** c1840
To a house, flour and beetling mill of the Kirk family. A standard single storey three bay lodge below a hipped roof. Central projecting hipped roof hall. Now pebble-dashed and extended.
GRIFFITH

**93. MOORE VALE, Newry** pre 1834; *demolished*

**94. MOUNTAIN LODGE, Keady** pre 1834; *ruinous*
Remains of a red brick lodge on an L plan, with two canted ends. The whole structure arcaded with semicircular-headed recesses. Most unusual Attractive little decorative iron gate posts. For the Garmany family.

**95. MOUNT CAULFIELD, Bessbrook (2)**
Two nondescript lodges, one pre 1861, long and low with a shallow-pitched roof and wide eaves. The other pre 1906 in red brick. Probably both for James N Richardson of the Bessbrook Spinning Co Ltd.

**96. MOUNT IRWIN, Tynan** c1800
Quaint little Georgian Gothick two roomed single storey lodge for the Irwin family. The front elevation is canted almost creating an octagon on plan, the three main faces of which have lancet-headed openings. The sash windows once had Y tracery. Hipped umbrello roof with exposed rafter toes. The walls now rendered may have been in facing brick. Plain square Georgian gate pillars with later gates.

*Mount Irwin*

**97. MOUNT ST CATHERINE CONVENT, Armagh** c1900
A two storey three bay gabled lodge of late Victorian polychromatic brick design. All in red facings with yellow fireclay brick as window dressings and stringcourses with dogtooth specials. The first floor gable window to the road has a pointed relieving arch, the tympanum of which is decorated in herring-bone pattern. Basic wavy bargeboards and terracotta ridge cresting.

**98. MULLAGHBRACK RECTORY, Markethill** pre 1860; *demolished*
A lodge which postdated an 1829 glebe house.
LEWIS (1837)

**99. MULLYLOUGHAN, Benburb (2)** pre 1834
Fine Georgian stone gate pillars. The lodges plain semidetached. Formerly known as Glenaul Park, the seat of Joseph Johnston in 1837.

**100. NEW PARK, Lurgan**
(see LURGAN PARK)

**101. THE OBSERVATORY, Armagh** c1791; architect Francis Johnston
Following the death of Thomas Cooley in 1784 Francis Johnston, Armagh's distinguished architect son, carried on Primate Richard Robinson's grand plan to convert Armagh from little better than a village into the cultural capital of Ireland. Part of this plan included designing the Observatory in 1789 followed shortly after by entrance gates and a gate lodge at the base of College Hill. The modest hipped roof single storey lodge remarkably has survived with its gable foremost projecting beyond the gate screen. Hardly on the scale of Johnston's alternative Gothic style to be seen at Markree, Charleville and Slane Castles, it is nevertheless the only example to be found in Armagh - a single little lancet window with Y tracery and original pointed shutters to fit. The walls in local pink random rubble limestone. The standard two roomed plan extended behind the gates to form a T plan. The gate piers square, of punched ashlar stone with a frieze of studded banding below corniced cappings. Simple contemporary wrought iron gates and domed octagonal stone bollards.
WATERCOLOUR IN ARMAGH MUSEUM (1810); LETTER: JOHNSTON (1820)

**102. THE PALACE, Armagh**
(see ARCHIEPISCOPAL PALACE)

**103. THE PAVILION, Armagh (2)**
Just as Brighton has its Regency Pavilion so did Armagh, a delightful villa of various dates. Commenced in about 1805, probably to designs of Francis Johnston for Captain William W Algeo who lived there until his death in 1845. Tucked away modestly behind the courthouse it was tragically demolished c1960 to make way for a school. "... the house is pulled down, the gardens have gone, and a secondary school is being built. Pressure brought on the Education Authority has obtained the promise that railings and lodge will be restored ...". Thus recorded the late T G F Patterson in 1964. The lodge was demolished a few years later.

**The Mall Entrance** c1840; *demolished*

*(Armagh Museum)*

A boxy little composition of standard plan, three bay symmetrical and single storey. Elevations framed with simple corner pilasters and parapet entablature to form recesses in which the windows had pretty cast iron octagonal glazing bars. The corniced parapet hid a very low-pitched roof. It seems to have spent its final years cement rendered. The railings remain, perhaps of c1820, as intricate wrought iron gate piers surmounted by tall lamp holders. Almost identical to those at Francis Johnston's Bank of Ireland in Armagh.

**Lisanally Lane Entrance** 1846; architect probably William Murray

The four-face pedimented gate pillar cappings here are identical to those by William Murray at the main entrance of Roxborough, Co Tyrone (qv) for the Earl of Charlemont. It is conceivable that this lodge was commissioned from Murray by William Algeo just before his death, he having married the daughter of the Earl of Charlemont's agent. A track led from here to the Pavilion but it seems was never developed as an avenue after the client's death. Replacing an earlier building on the site, in coursed squared rubble stone on a T plan. It has steeply pitched roofs with unsophisticated fretted bargeboards, repeated on the single storey projecting hall, which has a Tudor-arched doorway. On the two main gables, arrowslit ornaments and to the road a quatrefoil window below which is the datestone. Only some of the windows, which have been modernised, have label mouldings over. The bargeboards are repeated at lodges to Castle Leslie Co Monaghan and Learmont Castle, Co Londonderry (qqv).
ARMAGH MUSEUM PHOTOGRAPH

**104. PORT NELLIGAN, Middletown (2)**
**Rear Lodge** pre 1835; *demolished*
**Front Lodge** c1840
On the Armagh-Monaghan Road a single storey, three bay lodge noteworthy for its pretty diagonally-set pair of brick chimneys on a hipped roof. The square window openings have a pair of sliding sashes each. Once in facing brick now whitewashed over, it lies unoccupied. The two surviving square piers have ball finials, the original gates missing. Built for Mr Alexander Cross.

**105. RAUGLAN Lurgan (2)** *both demolished*
Beautifully situated on the shores of Lough Neagh both lodges, one pre 1834 and the other pre 1861 built for the Fforde family.

**106. RICHHILL CASTLE, Richhill** pre 1835

A.R. Hogg

A major house in the village for the Richardson family, its main gates being within a stone's throw of the front door. Built c1665 it was one of the first big houses in the country to display little regard for defence, depending upon its U plan with flanking wings covering the front door. Nevertheless, in 1804 the demesne is reported as having been "well enclosed" and in 1835 the 188 acres are described as being surrounded by a 10ft (3m) high wall. The magnificent Baroque wrought iron gate screen is generally assumed to date from 1745 and to have been the work of the Thornberry brothers, originally of Falmouth, for Mr William Richardson. The Thornberrys who had settled locally may have derived inspiration from James Gibbs' A Book of Architecture (1728) a useful pattern book of the time. In their original location with painted black livery they were wholly appropriate, silhouetted with the Dutch gables as a backdrop. Highly ornate, there is a beautiful overthrow which incorporates the Richardson's coat-of- arms in beaten copper, surmounting which is their crest - an armoured arm wielding a sword. The gates were the pride of the place, and no little controversy arose when they were moved in 1936 to glorify the front of the new Government House, Hillsborough (see Hillsborough House, Co Down). It would be churlish now to criticise this transplant since the gates are maintained in mint condition, and are now the pride of their new place. They had not been opened in their original location since the 1850s. The gate lodge is of little interest.
MINISTRY OF FINANCE (1963); COOTE (1804); OSM; A R HOGG Photograph

**107. ST COLEMAN'S COLLEGE, Newry**
(see VIOLET HILL)

**108. ST LUKE'S HOSPITAL, Armagh**
(see LUNATIC ASYLUM)

**109. ST MARK'S PARISH CHURCH, Armagh** c1845; architect probably William Farrell
From the Victoria Street approach a pleasant entrance of simple iron railings and gates, four octagonal stone pillars with domed corniced cappings. The one and a half storey lodge on an L plan, gabled now has simple modern bargeboards. In uncoursed and coursed limestone rubble, the openings are chamfered as are the external wall corners, squinching to the square at first floor level with ogee-carved corbels. The chimney stack is not original. The front door has a Tudor head in an otherwise pleasant no-nonsense composition.

**110. ST PATRICK'S R C CATHEDRAL, Armagh** 1884; architects: Ashlin & Coleman
Below the great terraced and stepped approach to McCarthy's pointed spires, there is a solid single storey lodge on an L plan with a back return. Gabled with steeply-pitched roofs, in squared and coursed limestone rubble, quarry-faced. Skewtables, moulded kneelers, quoins, plinth coping, eaves cornice and friezed chimneys all in dressed limestone. The little gabled hall,

advancing flush with the main avenue gable, has a roll-moulded and shouldered door opening with a recessed trefoiled overpanel which has, in bas-relief, a depiction of Christ as the Good Shepherd in a bed of shamrocks. The apex is surmounted by a foliated finial. The square-headed mullioned windows to main gables chamfered and shouldered, have pointed relieving arches, the tympana of which are richly carved in bas-relief. That to the avenue contains the date "A.D. 1884" in a cinquefoil supported on a pair of pointed trefoil heads containing more shamrock foliage. Hood-moulded with carved dripstones possibly of St Malachy and St Coleman. Over the roadside window the arch frames a single pointed trefoil containing the arms of Primate McGettigan with his motto "PRO DEO ET ECCLESIA". Here the dripstones may be St Brigid and St Patrick. There are two carved panels. That facing the

cathedral has a Papal tiara and keys of St Peter, the other towards the avenue, has an Irish harp. The main gable apexes had metal finials. Each of the gate pillars is in complementary High Victorian Gothick with marble-shafted colonettes to each of their four corners and cusped trefoil heads to recessed panels. A moulded plinth and layered cappings are topped by decorative metal lanterns. Highly ornate gates flanked by railed screens in cast iron on ogee dwarf walls.
YOUNG (1909); ARMAGH; UAHS (1992)

**111. SALEM LODGE, Moy** pre 1859
Standard plain lodge, derelict. Built by David R Goldlatte.

**112. SANDYMOUNT, Richill** pre 1835
Standard plan hipped roof late Georgian lodge with a side entrance. A property of the Redmond family.

**113. SHANTALLY LODGE Middletown**
(see MIDDLETOWN RECTORY)

**114. SILVERBRIDGE, Crossmaglen (2)**
Two lodges for the Mullen family, the earlier pre 1861 replaced by a modern bungalow, that of pre 1906 undistinguished.

**115. SILVERWOOD, Lurgan (2)**
*both demolished*
Nothing remains of the charming Georgian house and the two gate lodges, one pre 1834, the other pre 1859. A property of the Cuppage family.

**116. SUMMER ISLAND, Loughgall** c1820
The prettiest pair of surviving Georgian Gothick porters' lodges in the Province. Situated to the back of a segmental lay-by approach, they rather contrarily have bow-fronted elevations. Each three bay, basically single storey the two ground floor rooms giving ladder access to loft bedspace over. Gabled with slate roofs perhaps originally thatched. In whitewashed harled walls, the windows have high cills, their pointed heads forming "lancettes" with typical Y tracery. The sheeted doors arched to match. Brick dentil course to eaves. Some fifty yards distant a detached privy. The cottages flank four square Classical pillars contrastingly refined in ashlar stone, V-jointed with moulded cornices and a shallow concave capping. Painted white to match. Built by the Clarke family as an introduction to their elegant Classical villa. Though now empty they are well maintained as popular cotoneaster-clad follies by the Cowdys.

*Summer Island*

**117. TALLBRIDGE, Loughgall** c1845

Pleasant symmetrical three bay on a standard plan under a hipped roof with a central chimney. The walls roughcast distinguished by the windows, each divided by timber mullion and transom forming two semicircular- arched heads, glazing prettily margined. The stone gate piers octagonal with plain friezes and caps. Concave sweeps and chunky carriage gates of the same period. Built for John Nicholson Esq.

**118. TANDERAGEE CASTLE, Tanderagee (3)**

Situated in pleasant undulating countryside the castle rises in dramatic outline on a "bold and abrupt eminence". Once the Irish seat of the Montagu family, Dukes of Manchester now reduced to a shell, surplus to the needs of potato crisp production. The old house of the Sparrow family was replaced in 1835 by a highly innovative Tudor Revival manor house passing as it had by marriage to the Montagus. Designed by Isaac Farrell. Improvements continued in the 1850s and 60s to include a grand machicolated tower extension to the house and two new entrances with more subtle romantic avenue approaches, one crossing a stream and in its gradual ascent, producing "charming scenic effects". Two lodges were located at these points, each approach, along with the Town Gate, through solid timber "portcullis" gates below Tudor style archways in basalt, dressed with granite.

**Town Gate** c1850; architect probably Issac Farrell

In 1837 Charlotte Elizabeth writes of "..... a large dark, ponderous-looking gate facing you, with rather a frowning aspect, overhung by trees of immense growth......". Behind this gate was a pre 1834 lodge, since demolished. At the head of the steep main street, the original main entrance is now down-graded to provide an entrance for the extensive outbuildings, and is rather less ponderous than that which confronted the 1837 visitor. In the high screen wall a large Tudor carriage archway chamfered and toothed in dressed stone as is the flat coping over. Alongside, the pedestrian door similarly dressed with a label moulding.

**Clare Road Gate** 1865; architect probably Isaac Farrell

The high screen wall in random rubble uncoursed with crenellations carried over the carriage archway as a shallow stepped gable. The wicket doorway simply flat-arched. Behind, a one and a half storey, two up two down lodge under a high pitched roof with skewtables in granite as are the fancy fleur-de-lys apex stones and clustered four-flue chimney stack. The windows mullioned to form bipartite slits, the doorway set off centre. Datestone.

**Markethill Road Gate** 1852; architect probably Isaac Farrell

Basically as the above but rendered more Picturesque in outline by taking out the stairs into a projecting square tower, crowned by a bracketed steeple over a "belfry" storey with peculiar fretted slate screens to each of the paired openings. Slit windows light the staircase and one panel displays the Montagu monogram, another the date of construction. Alongside a verandahed porch shelters the front door, its

lean-to roof supported by good decorative timber posts and carved brackets. High in the gables are quatrefoil features again crowned by fleur-de-lys apex stones. A pair of windows keep watch outside the gateway. The gates here have a much steeper stepped gable over. The entrance has the distinct misfortune to be associated with a golf club, the lodge lies empty, the fine gates removed and the archway partially demolished. An opportunity lost for this group of buildings to form a distinctive advertisement for the club.
COOTE (1804); TONNA (1838);
DOYLE (1854)

**119. TANDERAGEE RECTORY, Tanderagee** (see BALLYMORE GLEBE)

**120. TULLYELMER, Armagh** pre 1864; *demolished*

A lodge is listed by Griffith to the property of William F Cardwell.
GRIFFITH

**121. TULLYMORE, Armagh** pre 1905; *demolished*

A property in 1864 of Osborne Kidd.
GRIFFITH

**122. TURNER HILL, Newry** pre 1834; *demolished*

A lodge built for the Turner family. The park later became known as The Glen upon its acquisition by Baron Frederick Ludwig von Stieglitz. Subsequently purchased by Henry Barcroft of the Bessbrook Spinning Company.
BASSETT'S COUNTY DOWN (1886)

**123. TYNAN ABBEY, Tynan (3)**

Contiguous with the other big estates of Glaslough Co Monaghan (q.v.) and Caledon Co Tyrone (q.v.) which are so rich in a variety of gate lodges, as if the landowners were in competition. Tynan is no exception and must also have benefited from the visits of the architect John Nash to Caledon. The recent tragic fire which destroyed the mansion also consumed a set of architectural perspectives by A.C. Pugin of the Nash office for proposals to rebuild the previous house on the site. These were unexecuted but there is much of the house as carried out to make a confident attribution. In 1813 Sir James Matthew Stronge (2nd Bart) had commenced the transformation of his house "Fairview" into the mansion that was Tynan Abbey, in a Tudor Gothic style. Mrs Calvert, Stronge's future mother-in-law in September 1810 visited Tynan; "Sir James drives down four beautiful horses which Isabella admires very much. His carriage is built like a stage coach with a railing round the top. He is very near-sighted, and I should tremble at being drove by him".

**Castle Gate** 1817; architect probably John Nash

It must have been in deference to his eyesight that he conceived such a powerful Romantic castellated Gothick set-piece. The gate is in the form of a double "portcullis" in a Tudor archway recessed below machicolations. All framed by a tall 23' (7m) high screen wall, L-shaped 55'

*Tynan Abbey, Castle Lodge*

(16.75m) x 50' (15.25m) and located on a right angle bend on the Middletown Road. Flanked by a square turret and an octagonal tower on the extremities, the latter housed the gatekeeper's accommodation. All in random squared uncoursed quarry-faced limestone, crowned by Irish crenellations with "arrowloops". The solidity of the whole composition is increased by battering of the wall base. The porter's room is approached up a flight of steps from the forecourt. Lit by two windows, with segmentally-pointed heads, from one of which he could overlook the distant gate. His spartan accommodation was supplemented sometime later by an additional building against the ramparts.

**Lemnagore Lodge** c.1817; architect possibly John Nash

An initial impression is of a Victorian "stockbroker Tudor" dwelling, but a lodge existed on this site prior to 1835. Humphry Repton and his son John Adey had left the Nash practice in 1802 and pioneered similar half-timbered work in a lodge at Aspley Wood, Bedfordshire in about 1811, so perhaps as there, this lodge belies it true age. A nice gabled design of informal outline, the one and a half storey portion is two bay with a two storey projection and a single storey three bay wing, which may be a later addition. Mainly in greywacke stone with orange brick window dressing. The projecting porch, in brick with a Tudor archway, carries a jettied half-timbered bedroom over. Incorporated below the pair of latticed casement lights are two ceramic tiles set diagonally which depict the Stronge family coat-of-arms and monogram. The ground floor windows are also latticed casements, that to the attic gable square pane. The steeply-pitched roofs now in diagonally-set red asbestos slates. Two chimney stacks carry decorative cream terracotta "chess-piece" pots as if in further imitation of Aspley Wood. Quite why a lodge so spacious as this, so visually desirable and in such an idyllic setting lies deserted is a mystery. Two low wooden "portcullis" carriage gates are carried on squat Armagh limestone dressed piers chamfered under steep four-gabled cappings with roll tops. Perhaps c.1870 by W.H. Lynn.

**South Lodge** c.1860; architect perhaps W J Barre

On the Middletown Road something less prepossessing in smooth grey limestone with dressed stone to quoins, window and door surrounds. Substantial, gabled on an L plan there is a tripartite single storey bay. Two diagonally-set square pillars survive with ball finials.
For Sir John Calvert Stronge 4th Bt.
STROUD (1962); MARSHALL (1932).

**124. TYNAN RECTORY, Tynan** c.1820

To the glebe house built in 1777 a single storey lodge, square on plan with pyramidal roof rising to a central brick chimney stack. Segmentally-headed openings to tripartite window in harled stone walls. There is a later hall below a catslide roof. The fine square ashlar piers are probably contemporary with the rectory. Below the cornice and block capping a fluted frieze. The gates later, there are nice tapered octagonal stone carriage buffers.
LEWIS (1837)

**125. VIOLET HILL, Newry (2)**
**North Lodge** pre 1834; *demolished.*
**South Lodge** c.1879

Single storey lodge below a hipped roof with its rear to the road. Three bay, not quite symmetrical with a gabled breakfront hall under a high eaves. Stuccoed walls. Probably built when the new avenue was constructed on the opening of the school buildings of St. Colman's College. The entrance also gives access to the Bishop's palace which shares the grounds.
BASSETT'S COUNTY DOWN (1886)

**126 WOODFORD, Armagh** c.1840

A building of confused styles and age probably originating as a single storey semidetached pair of two bays each, handed identically. Later raised to house an attic storey. In faintly ornamental gable style with foiled bargeboards and two gawky dormer windows. Later still converted to one dwelling and cement rendered. Mixture of hexagonal cast iron and squared Georgian style window glazing patterns.

**127. WOODHOUSE, Bessbrook** c. 1880; architect probably Thomas Jackson and Son

For Mr John Grubb Richardson of the Bessbrook Spinning Co Ltd., a one and a half storey gabled three bay lodge. Random rubble walls with quoins left quarry-faced. Cream fireclay brick dressings to openings and in a band to the red brick chimney stack. Margined windows. The eaves carried on five big scrolled wooden brackets. Distinctive slate roof laid in single-lap pattern, a feature of two lodges at Moyallon, County Down (q.v.) another property of J G Richardson. Nice sturdy pair of "portcullis" carriage gates and matching wicket gate at right angles, all hung on chunky quarry-faced stone pillars and screen walls.
An attribution to Thomas Jackson and Son would be reinforced by the long-lasting Quaker relationship between family and architect.
BASSETT'S CO ARMAGH (1888)

**128. WOODPARK, Tynan (2)** both pre 1860

To this once pretty little park of Captain Acheson St George one lodge is converted out of all recognition, the other plain square, standard plan and single storey lies derelict and overgrown.

**129. WOODVILLE, Lurgan (3)**
*all demolished*

For the Greer family, one lodge pre 1834 to Annesborough as the house was once known. The other two lodges pre 1859. Everything, including the house, swept away.

# COUNTY CAVAN

**1. ANNE'S FORT, Cootehill** pre 1836; *demolished*
A lodge for George Powell, Esq.

**2. ARLEY COTTAGE, Mount Nugent** pre 1878
An ordinary two storey lodge with a hipped roof and bracketed eaves, much improved. Opposite the entrance to the shooting lodge and occasional residence of the Maxwells, Earls of Farnham.

**3. ARNMORE, Cavan** pre 1881; *demolished*

**4. ASHFIELD GLEBE, Cootehill (2)**
**Cootehill Gate** c1830
A minuscule one and a half storey gabled lodge.
**Redhills Gate** pre 1836; *demolished.*

**5. ASHFIELD LODGE, Cootehill (4)**
The fine old house of the Clements family and two pre 1836 lodges have gone, the latter to be replaced by something more fashionable of their time.
**Redhills Road Lodge** c1890; architect Sir Thomas Drew

(I.A.A.)

(I.A.A.)

For Henry Theophilus Clements, irregular High Victorian in outline but fundamentally the main body a two up two down lodge. Gabled, one and a half storey with a canted single storey living room projection under a hipped roof, alongside which the main roof is carried down as a catslide to form a porch. On the opposing elevation a rear return. The steeply pitched roofs in red earthenware plain tiles with matching cresting and ball finial to the hipped projection. At the roofs junction a prominent red brick corbelled

chimney stack. Walls in squared uncoursed rubble basalt, quarry-faced dressed in a combination of red brick to plinth, windows and stringcourses, and red sandstone quarry-faced quoins, exquisite carving to the squat little column support to the porch and a scrolled bracket nearby with enveloping flowers and foliage. The sculpted scrolled cartouche on the canted elevation frames a panel displaying the Clements coat-of-arms. Surrounded by egg and dart moulding, a hawk perches proudly on a shield askew, perhaps foreseeing the estate's impending demise. Intertwined with flamelike acanthus mantling the motto "PATRIIS VIRTUTIBUS". Windows leaded in minute squares. On the rear elevation an arrow shaped bay window. The iron finials to main apexes have gone as has any sign of the gates and avenue. The Clements had already employed Drew on their other property of Lough Rynn, Co Leitrim.
**River Lodge** c1932; architects probably McCurdy and Mitchell

Here, beautifully situated on the banks of the Dromore River, another surprise in this Eden Nesfield Arts-and- Crafts design away off the beaten track looking as if it has escaped from suburbia. On an L plan this gabled house has its first floor hung in earthenware tiles to match the roof. The avenue gable tiles bellcast above the bedroom window, the whole jettying out on carved wooden brackets over the canted bay below, with squared panes aplenty. The other gable displays a black and white half-timbered spandrel above a horizontal panel of two casement windows divided by a sculpted stone cartouche of the Clements family bearings. The ground floor elevations in more solid squared uncoursed grey rubble with some red brick dressings. The main gable catslides alongside to form a canopy to the front door. All well maintained, the gateway gone.
I.A.A. Photographs, Refs S/353/11 and 12 S/354/1 and 2

**6. ASHGROVE, Belturbet** pre 1878
To a graceful Palladian style villa of the Baker family, a plain little single storey lodge opposite the gates. Three bay with the front door asymmetrically positioned. Two roomed with a wide-eaved hipped roof.

**7. AUBAWN, Killashandra (2)**
**North Entrance** c1840
Standard single storey two roomed lodge with two bay front elevation of tiny windows in harled whitewashed walls. Hipped roof refinished in asbestos slates and perforated earthenware cresting. Later entrance gate screen with cast iron piers topped by ball finials.
**South Entrance** c1840
Standard single storey two roomed three bay structure, gabled. Extended by another bay. Undistinguished. Both lodges perhaps for Rev J Vernon.

**8. BAILIEBOROUGH CASTLE, Bailieborough (2)**
**West Lodge** pre 1836
Located opposite the entrance a basic late Georgian building with extended eaves. Built by Sir William Young Bart., who bought the property about 1814 from Mr Stewart Corry, it has developed a later one and a half storey incongruous bargeboard extension.
**Town Lodge** pre 1878; *demolished*
McCOLLUM (1856); MASON (1814-16)

**9. BALLYCONNELL, Ballyconnell (3)**
The estates changed hands on a number of occasions and successive owners left their marks. George Montgomery was responsible for the elegant gate screen at the previous main entrance.
**Early Belturbet Lodge** pre 1836; *demolished*
The lodge opposite this gate, supplanted by a modern bungalow, may have been contemporary with this fine gate screen of c1780. Flanked by relatively simple secondary piers with ball finialed tops, from which concave quadrants lead to the main ashlar pillars. Each nicely blotched with lichen they have a semicircular headed niche resting on the plinth. Over is a frieze of alternate patera and fluting pattern, and a moulded cornice with dentil course. The blocked capping crowned by a fluted vase with serrated rim (one now missing). These are almost identical to those at Belleville, (qv) in this county.

**Later Belturbet Lodge** c1890
This screen is in stark contrast to the nasty gatehouse behind. In polychromatic brickwork, two storey, the roof has serrated crestings and apologetic foil and wave timber bargeboards. A canopy above the front door is supported by a turned timber post. Probably built for Mr Samuel Black Roe it has now been stripped of roof slates and like the fine gates doomed, now being the access to a building site.

**Town Lodge** c1830
On the banks of the Woodford River a derelict and overgrown lodge built by William Hamilton Enery who had acquired the property from the Montgomerys. Three roomed on an L plan, its gable to the avenue in the form of a bow with a tripartite window which is dressed stone, in rough cast walls. The hipped roof is low pitched with paired bracket eaves support. Dressed stone chimney stack over. Simple slender stone chamfered gate posts.

**10. BALLYHAISE, Ballyhaise** c1830; architect possibly William Farrell

The fine house by Richard Cassels was sold by the Newburgh family in about 1800 to the Humphreys. Sometime later wings were added with Wyatt windows typical of William Farrell's work, an attribution made easier by the entrance gates. These are akin to those at Ely Lodge, Co Fermanagh (qv), in the form of Greek stellae, the stone piers repeated to a smaller scale at the gate lodge across the road. With its back to the Annalee River the single storey building a graceful piece of duality. Three roomed with a hipped roof, bracketed eaves and two stunted little corniced chimney stacks. The central doorway is flanked by two narrow semicircular headed lights all set within a covered porch behind a latticed cast iron arcade. On each side a room projects with simple square headed windows in their own recesses, all in stucco work. Two good gate screens, the railings with spear heads. The main gates to what is now an Agricultural College are missing.
BENCE-JONES (1988)

**11. BALLYMACHUGH, Kilnaleek** c1840
An almost square plan, single storey lodge. Once three bay, two windows retain their original semicircular- headed recesses in rendered finish. Pyramidal roof with paired brackets to eaves. Stone octagonal gate posts have fluted friezes. Previously called "The Cottage".

**12. BAWNBOY, Bawnboy** pre 1836
Originally built by John Hassard upon acquisition of the demesne from the Enerys when the latter moved to Ballyconnell House (qv). The lodge seems to have been given a crude mid- Victorian face-lift to its three bay front, with smooth rendered opening surrounds.

**13. BEAGH GLEBE, Bailieborough** pre 1836; *demolished*
A lodge opposite the entrance.

**14. BEHERNAGH TOWNLAND, Virginia** c1850
A lodge to the property of Patrick McInroe identified in the Griffith Valuation of 1856. A three bay asymmetrical single storey structure in random coursed rubble. Hipped roof.
GRIFFITH

**15. BELLAMONT GLEBE, Cootehill** pre 1836; *demolished*

**16. BELLAMONT FOREST, Cootehill (4)**
"From the town one drives nearly a mile on a fine gravelled road, a cut hedge on each side, and rows of old oak and ash trees, to Mr Coote's house. Within two hundred yards of the house is a handsome gateway, which is built in great taste, with a fine arch to drive through". Thus recorded Mrs Delaney in her diary on August 24th 1732 not long after Ireland's finest Palladian villa was complete. Doubtless by Sir Edward Lovett Pearce like the house. Nothing of this archway remains today. In a beautiful setting surrounded by lakeland both lodges noted on the 1836 OS Map, "Bawn Gate" and "Bog Gate" have disappeared. Today what survives are two comparatively modest lodges of more recent vintage. These are a reflection of the Coote family's diminishing fortunes eventually resulting in them living in relative obscurity. The estate was sold in 1874 to the Dorman-Smiths.

**Rockcorry Road Entrance** c1820

Built for Charles Coote, an illegitimate son, when the Bellamont title had become extinct after 1800, it is a single storey, two roomed lodge having only a door opening on the main elevation. The roof at each gable terminates in a half umbrello under which is a canted end elevation, each face of which has a round-headed window with low cills. These are set into similarly arched recesses carried down to ground level to form arcades. How distinctive this must have appeared in its original mellow brickwork, now painted over. There is a rear return. It lies sealed up awaiting its fate. The modest gate sweep looks later, perhaps 1850. Stone outer piers flank inner cast iron posts, railings and gates.

**Town Lodge** c1840/c1875
Straightforward late Georgian style lodge for Richard Coote. Single storey, three bay to a standard plan. Now rough cast below a hipped roof with a bracketed eaves. Squared sash windows. Extended somewhat later by the Dorman-Smiths with matching windows and wall finish. Otherwise incongruous one and a half storey with foiled bargeboard to the gable. This extension has developed an out of scale minuscule addition of its own. Octagonal cast iron gate posts and gates.
DELANY (1861-62); BENCE-JONES (1988); GEORGIAN SOCIETY RECORDS, Vol. V (1913)

**17. BELLEVILLE, Bellananagh** pre 1836
An entrance notable not for the nondescript harled single storey, three bay gabled lodge but for the two fine ashlar gate pillars of about 1780, almost identical to those at Ballyconnell House (qv) in the same county. Tall, each with a semicircular-headed niche above which is a Classical swag. A moulded capping is surmounted by a small fluted vase with serrated rim. Rather pathetically the vases have been replaced upside down and the pillars carry a farm gate. Once the demesne of the Fleming family.

**18. BELLGREEN, Cootehill** pre 1836; *demolished*
A lodge of the Brunkers.

**19. BELTURBET GLEBE, Belturbet** pre 1834; *demolished*

**20. BINGFIELD, Crossdoney** pre 1836; *ruinous*
Engulfed in undergrowth and derelict. Probably built for a Henry T Kilbee upon acquiring the demesne and graceful Palladian style house from the Story family.

**21. BOB'S GROVE, Mount Nugent** (see FARRENCONNELL)

**22. BRACKLAGH, Granard** pre 1836; *demolished*
The lodge survived by the gates. These have round topped posts with nice anthemion decoration.

**23. BRUCE HALL, Arvagh** pre 1836; *demolished*
A seat of the Warren family.

**24. CABRA CASTLE, Kingscourt (3)**
Colonel Joseph Pratt bought Cormey Castle from the Fosters and by 1837 had transformed it into a grand rambling romantic Gothick castle. The pre 1836 lodge to the old castle has gone but Pratt erected two lodges to grace the newly furnished demesne.

**Kingscourt Lodge** c1840; *demolished*
Situated near the railway station, now gone leaving no trace.

**East Lodge** c1840
Suitably in Picturesque Gothick style to reflect the castle, the one and a half storey, two up two down, two bay lodge has lost much in "improvement". The bargeboards are modest wavy replacements and on the gable to the avenue can be detected evidence of there having been a single storey projecting canted bay window. Above this a bipartite attic window with twin lancet heads. The front elevation has two pretty windows with pointed heads and small square panes, in rough cast walls.

**Racecourse Lodge** 1857; architect not known
Where the Pratt property was divided by the Kingscourt to Carrickmacross road are to be found the most distinctive pair of gate screens, one to Cabra Cottage (qv) which became a

dower-house, the other the main entrance to the castle, erected by the same Joseph Pratt. In the most exuberant cast iron Gothick, the railings spill over with trefoils, quatrefoils and cusped arcading, repeated in the square posts. These have gablet caps similarly foiled, topped by foliated finials and crowned by crocketed pinnacles with their own finials. The screens terminate in pretty fan features. Not quite in keeping with the castle is the fine Tudor Revival lodge in high quality dressed stonework laid squared and uncoursed. Gabled single storey, the front three-bay elevation to the avenue has a breakfront hall with skewtables and big kneelers to match the main gables. The front door has a pointed overpanel with datestone above. The main windows mullioned with label mouldings over. On the road elevation is a canted bay window with half umbrello roof and a mock loophole relieving the gable above. An extensive rear return renders the lodge commodious, and is further lengthened by a yard screen wall stopped by an ornamental octagonal turret with castellated parapet. The main chimney stack of channelled stone culminates in a simple frieze below the capping. All very impressive and given a new lease of life at the entrance to Cabra Castle Hotel.
BENCE-JONES (1988)

**25. CABRA COTTAGE, Kingscourt**
pre 1836; *demolished*

A lodge to the old house of the Pratts off the Shercock Road. To the east the fine gatesweep described under Cabra Castle (qv).

**26. CARN, Ballyconnell** pre 1835; *ruinous*

A three bay building quite spacious with two loft rooms in a hipped roof. Now overgrown and derelict like the house of the Benson family which overlooks it.

**27. CARRIG HILL, Belturbet**
pre 1835; *demolished*
A lodge built for Captain James Bailie JP.

**28. CASTLE COSBY, Crossdoney**
pre 1836/1856

Originally a routine two roomed lodge for the Nesbitt family which seems to have been embellished with a segmental bow to the avenue gable elevation in 1856, the date inscribed on a gate pillar. The bow has three openings, the central one having been the front door but now a window, all of which have moulded surrounds, lugged at cill and springline, carried around the semicircular heads to meet heavily vermiculated keystones. Channelled pilaster quoins . The half cone gable roof is finished in big scallop slates. Low square granite gate piers V-jointed blocks have cast iron urn finials. Contemporary decorative railings link these to simpler outer piers.

**29. CASTLE HAMILTON, Killashandra (4)**
The property descended through marriage from the Hamiltons to Lieut-Col Robert Henry Southwell and it seems to have been he that built "... the new mansion ..." recorded in 1818, and further improved it with a series of gate lodges.
**South Lodge** pre 1836; *demolished*
**North Lodge** pre 1836; *demolished*
**Middle Lodge** pre 1836
A simple harled single storey lodge now notable only for its Tudor label mouldings. Derelict.
**Town Lodge** c1840

A single storey Georgian Gothic style lodge of three bays, the projecting hall with its own hipped roof not quite central. This and the main body of the lodge have lancet openings the windows with lattice glazing. The hipped roof on a paired bracket eaves has the chimney stack asymmetrically located. Walls harled and whitewashed. Quaint. The elaborate cast iron gates are c1860. The whole once fine estate now distinctly down-at-heel.
KING (1892); AN IRISH GENTLEMAN (1818)

**30. CASTLE SAUNDERSON, Belturbet (2)**
**Belturbet Road Gate** pre 1835;
*demolished*
The lodge opposite the gates has gone but the latter remain as testimony to the architectural good taste of Francis Saunderson, owner of the previous Georgian house. Four tall square ashlar pillars with V-jointed blocks each surmounted by a moulded cornice with frieze below ornamented by an elegant ovoid fan pattern. Dating from about 1800, they are almost identical to those at Ballyward Lodge, Co Down (qv).
**Legakelly Lodge** c1840; architect (gates) probably Edward Blore.
The gate lodge is a plain two storey house with hipped roof and harled walls. The Georgian house was either dramatically reworked or replaced about 1835 in castellated Tudor style, with such a striking resemblance to nearby Crom Castle, Co Fermanagh (qv) that it must be attributed to the English architect Edward Blore, working for Francis' son Alexander Saunderson. The architect's signature is to be detected in the "top-knot" capping finials on otherwise crude quarry-faced block entrance pillars. There are sparsely spaced rails with fleur-de-lys finials on an extensive entrance screen, now spoiled by general dilapidation and a commercial intrusion. There are identical entrance pillars to be found at the other Saunderson seat at Cloverhill (q.v.) a couple of miles south.
KING (1892); SAUNDERSON (1936)

**31. CASTLETERRA RECTORY, Ballyhaise**
pre 1878; *demolished*
A lodge which postdated the 1829 rectory.

**32. CAVAN CEMETERY, Cavan** c1890
A late Victorian single storey three bay symmetrical lodge in red brick with fairly ornate bargeboards to main gables and that to the projecting hallway. Segmentally-headed openings.

**33. CAVAN PLEASURE GROUND, Cavan**
pre 1835; *demolished*
A pleasure ground described by Lewis as "A large garden handsomely laid out in walks and planted, was left by the will of the late Lady Farnham, under certain restrictions, as a promenade for the inhabitants". The park was gradually built over from the beginning of this century, its gate lodge off Wesley Street taken down. Only portions of later 19th century railings survive.
LEWIS (1837); CAVAN; U.A.H.S. (1978)

**34. CAVAN ROYAL SCHOOL, Cavan**
pre 1835; *demolished;* architect probably either Francis Johnston or John Bowden
Cavan Endowed College, as it was then called, was completed in 1819 to plans by Francis Johnston. Its approach alongside a branch of the River Erne once had a gate lodge at the access from College Street. The appearance on the first O.S. Map suggests it may have been designed by the Armagh man or the supervising architect John Bowden.
CAVAN, U.A.H.S. (1978)

**35. CAVAN UNION WORKHOUSE, Cavan**
1841; architect probably George Wilkinson
A vast complex has a substantial building at the entrance, a portion of which accommodated the gatekeeper. Two storey five bay symmetrical, the terminating bays form gabled breakfronts with ornamental carved foil and wave bargeboards above label-moulded widely chamfered window openings. Between, the upper floor has three mock dormers each with decorative bargeboards. The main central double leafed panelled doorway is set below a Tudor archway flanked by mullioned windows all embraced by linked label mouldings. At each extremity single storey subsidiary hallways both of which had Tudor entrance doors. Dormers to rear elevation, chimneys missing. Now St Felim's Hospital.
CAVAN, U.A.H.S. (1978)

**36. CLONKEIFFY, Oldcastle** pre 1836;
*ruinous*
A single storey three bay symmetrical gabled cottage traditional in form. A property in 1856 of William Love.

**37. CLOVERHILL, Redhills (3)**
The house, now derelict, was designed to replace an earlier one in 1799-1804 by the architect Francis Johnston, for James Saunderson.

**Village Entrance** c1800;
architect (entrance archway) probably Francis Johnston

A modest, but impressive entrance archway lacking any sophisticated architectural embellishment other than the pediment over a semicircular carriage arch springing from basic impost course. In similar ashlar stone the terminating piers are square and frame two small flat arched wicket gates below connecting cappings. The cast iron gates look later. The lodge somewhat distant on the approach to the entrance arch is, in its present form, a substantial two storey structure in contrasting Tudor manner. Cruder rubble stone and quoins to the upper floor suggest the lodge may have originated c1840 as a one and a half storey gabled structure with low eaves. This alteration may have occurred when a single storey hall and porch projection was added c1860. Gabled, it has very fine fretwork to bargeboards and spandrel with nicely carved chamfered and tapering timber posts. Three bay, two up two down below a hipped roof with eaves well extended on brackets. In random rubble with dressed stone quoins, the windows dressed in toothed brick with label mouldings over. The lights, transomed and mullioned in wood, have lattice panes. Upstairs the rooms are lit by gable windows, the front elevation having recessed blank panels as relief, corresponding to the windows below.

**Middle Lodge** pre 1836; *demolished*
The original main road took a more direct north-south course but was realigned when the demesne was increased, rendering this entrance redundant. Of the lodge which was opposite there is no trace.

**North Lodge** c1837; architect probably Edward Blore

Sandwiched between Corrarod and Drumgorry Loughs, a solid Picturesque lodge design. The English architect Edward Blore seems to have been employed by the other branch of the family at Castle Saunderson (qv) but two miles north and these are identical gate pillars to the Legakelly entrance there, less their "top knot" finials which have been removed. The lodge is basically a simple two up two down building but given an irregular outline by a tall gabled projecting hall positioned asymmetrically on the avenue elevation. On the facade to the road a castellated canted bay and over it a blank shield surmounted by a Saunderson Spur crest. Above this a rotting, wave and foil decorative bargeboard. The window openings, dressed with mullions and label mouldings framing lattice glazing bars, in quarry-faced walls that are a mixture of coursed and uncoursed squared rubble. The hall bargeboard replaced in something plainer, the chimney stack rebuilt.Despite the plight of the house, both lodges are occupied.
BENCE-JONES (1988); KING (1892)

**38. CORBY GLEBE, Bawnboy** pre 1836
Nondescript.

**39. CORNASHECK, Virginia** c1850
Plain, three bay gabled with matching projecting hall. Derelict. Probably built by David Kellett.

**40. CORR, Arvagh** pre 1836; *demolished*
Opposite the entrance the lodge had gone by 1879. To a seat in 1856 of John Alexander Faris.

**41. CORRANEARY LODGE, Arvagh** pre 1836; *demolished*

**42. CORRAVAHAN, Ballyhaise** pre 1856
A seat in 1856 of Rev Charles Leslie. Nice ogee wall quadrants flank two square stone carriage pillars each carrying good gates with pretty palmette motifs. The lodge across the road now modernised out of all recognition. It may have been a Classical composition a gable elevation facing the entrance.

**43. CORRINSHIGO, or CORINSECA, Kingscourt** pre 1836; *demolished*
A lodge for another branch of the Pratts of Cabra Castle (qv).

**44. CORVILLE, Bawnboy** pre 1836
A nondescript building built for the Finlay family.

**45. CRANAGHAN, Ballyconnell** c1825; architect possibly Alexander McLeish; *demolished*
The gate lodge had gone by 1877 but the entrance screen on a large scale survived until recently. From big square outer corniced stone pillars a convex wall swept to a pair of heavily entablatured pedestrian gates which flanked the carriage gate opening. In fine ashlar work, an unusual arrangement which can also be found at Drenagh, Co Londonderry (qv) and more closely at Knappagh, Co Armagh (qv). So close in fact to the latter as to suggest the involvement of Alexander McLeish, architect. This seems to have been for a prosperous Church of Ireland incumbent, the Rev Joseph Storey. The distinctive gate screen along with a pretty wooded stretch of road and the fine villa have all been swept away to make way for a gross and intrusive hotel complex, a major blot on the landscape.

**46. CROVER, Mount Nugent** pre 1836; *demolished*
Sometime seat of the Cuming family.

**47. CULLIES, Cavan** c1880
There was originally a pre 1835 lodge here built for the Moore family. This two storey, red brick, gabled gatehouse supplanted the above after the demesne was taken over in about 1869 from Nathaniel Montgomery to form St Patrick's College. There dates from this time a pretentious and widespread gate screen manufactured by Kennan & Sons of Dublin. The otherthrow to the carriage gates looks more recent.
CAVAN, U.A.H.S. (1978)

**48. DANESFORT or DEANSFORT, Cavan** c1850; *demolished*
This lodge to what was previously the Deanery of Kilmore diocese was built for Lord Fitzgerald and Vesey.

**49. DENN GLEBE, Stradone** pre 1836; *demolished*
The lodge was contemporary with the rectory.

**50. DRUMCARBAN, Crossdoney** c1800

A charming Georgian Gothick porter's lodge with a canted gable elevation to the avenue with a half-umbrello roof over and hipped to the rear. Its front face has a simple flat-arched doorway with lancet windows on each side now boarded up. Whitewashed harled walls, central chimney and exposed rafter toes. There are two slender octagonal stone entrance posts with fluted friezes and matching buffers. Built for Mr George Thomas Booth.

**51. DRUMCROW, Redhills** pre 1836; *demolished*

**52. DRUMELTAN, Kill** pre 1836
A rectangular standard plan lodge extended to L shape by a rear return. High hipped roofs gave loft bed space lit by skylights. Most openings are sealed up but some simple brick label mouldings survive. Off-centre door and chimney. Apparently built for Richard Adams.

**53. DRUMHEEL, Crossdoney** pre 1836; *demolished*
A lodge for Mr Ralf Bell.

**54. DRUMKEEN, Cavan** pre 1835; *demolished*
The property in 1856 of Colonel Alexander Saunderson.

**55. DRUMMULLY, Killashandra** c1870

A one and a half storey, three bay, two up two down lodge under a very steep gabled roof with ornate bargeboards of alternate quatrefoil and trefoil design. The roof has bands of slates laid diagonally, earthenware cresting and an octagonal stone chimney stack. Perhaps originally in facing brick, the walls now rough cast. Openings have label mouldings and smooth banded surrounds repeated as quoins. Modern glazing inserted. The breakfront hallway roofed to match the main roof. On the road gable a single storey, flat roofed canted bay watches the gates. The big square stone pillars in contrary Classical vein, with intermittent fluting to the friezes below the cornices. There is a flat arched wicket gate alongside and dwarf convex wall sweeps. All built for Albert Hutton, Esq.

**56. DRUMRORA LODGE, Ballyjamesduff** pre 1855; *demolished*

A property until 1855 of Pierce Morton also of Kilnacroft (qv), who sold it then to Anthony J Tatlow. The property deteriorated before house and gate lodge were demolished by 1939. LYONS (1993)

**57. DRUMSHEIL, Cootehill** pre 1836

An unpretentious building.

**58. DUNOWEN, Oldcastle** c1850

A substantial two storey brick lodge with a hipped roof. Its front elevation having openings irregularly arranged. Built for Edward Plunkett.

**59. ERNE HILL, Belturbet** c1840; architect possibly J B Keane

An elegant lodge embodying many of the characteristics of Sir Richard Morrison's practice. Symmetrical about the leading gable elevation with balancing hall outshoots on opposing side walls, a formula often used outside the Province as well as at the Thomastown entrance, Castlecoole, Co Fermanagh (qv) and in a Morrison proposal for Baronscourt, Co Tyrone (qv). Here the lodge was situated facing the gates across the road. It is probably too late to have been by the Morrisons but could be to the designs of J B Keane, as a one time assistant of theirs. He certainly used this format at Stradone (qv) and perhaps at Beech Hill, Co Armagh (qv). What lends weight to such an attribution are the incised pilaster strips which owe much to Sir John Soane's influence, so evident in Morrison's work. What a pity the gates and the big house have gone, removing vital clues, but they had to make way for a golf club. Single storey, standard plan under a low pitched roof of extended eaves with paired brackets. The front elevation is flanked by pilasters in the manner of Sir John Soane. Projecting to form a recess from which advances a living room window bay with tripartite margined lights each having semicircular heads, the same as at Redhills (qv) nearby. In the spandrels little decorative flowerheads, the cills supported on four brackets. The side doors were each framed by attractive crested ironwork screens. The walls stuccoed, the fine design crowned by a central chimney stack. Built for Mr George M Knipe. At the time of writing this lodge is undergoing improvements and it would be churlish to criticise too strongly the loss of ironwork and the regularity of the new synthetic slates.

**60. ERRIGAL, Cootehill**
(see FORTWILLIAM)

**61. FARNHAM, Cavan (3)**

C.B. Wynne painting (I.A.A.)

All the lodges for the Maxwells, Earls of Farnham, through time have been to the deerpark, divided by a public road from the demesne of beautiful undulating countryside richly planted, and boasting four lakes. Clearly the need to retain three hundred head of deer was once a priority. C B Wynne's attractive late eighteenth century watercolour shows what may have been an archway bridge, below a road embankment, as access to the deerpark. Its location is no longer obvious. Flanked by circular castellated turrets with pointed openings, is a segmental arch with what look like boulder voussoirs. Above it all a crenellated parapet to the road. By the 1830s there were two lodged gates.

**Kilmore Lodge** c1780; *demolished*

A plain mid-Georgian lodge now gone but its proud contemporary gate screen alongside survives. Two grand stone pillars are flanked by tall rubble wing walls which house two little wicket gate openings. All now rather run down.

**Cavan Lodge** c1855; architect not known

This replaced the other pre 1835 lodge and is a highly decorative and substantial stuccoed one and a half storey building, gabled but now minus the previous ornate bargeboards. The Classical front door case is framed in a breakfront with its own gable sporting a spiky hipknob, below which the window is a modern replacement like the others to the attic rooms. Canted bay windows each flank the central doorway, parapeted, transomed and mullioned with highly decorative hexagonal glazing bar pattern. Even this is put in the shade by the magnificent gate screen. On each of the moulded stone plinths rest bundles of fasces crowned by battleaxe heads, to be held together with guilloche patterned binding, all to signify the entrance to a magistrate's property. The gates are a riot of repetitive floral and foliated effects.

**Deerpark Lodge** c1839

This must be part of the improvements instigated by Henry Maxwell, 7th Lord Farnham. Wasting little time after the death of his father he built a new stable range and enlarged the house. Behind a high wall, a two storey house with a perky hipped 'hat' roof and extensive bracketed eaves, the chimney stack rising off the rear wall. In mellow coursed squared rubble stone, the openings are dressed with orange brick. The two bay front elevation has tall bipartite ground floor windows recessed below segmental arches, those to the first floor shallower, having similarly divided casements with squared panes. Very pleasant. The entrance is via the side elevation. MORRIS (1880); BENCE-JONES (1988)

**62. FARREN CONNELL, Mount Nugent (3)**

**North Lodge** pre 1836; demolished

The demesne of the Nugent family was known as Bobsgrove, the earlier lodge to which is not to be found today.

**South Lodge** c1870

This lodge which survives, but only just, had a pre 1836 predecessor at the other side of the avenue. Single storey on a spacious plan, it is built in excellent quality coursed squared masonry. From the main hipped roof a half-umbrello projects over a canted bay window to the living room, access to which is from a recessed porch. Below the main roof, its support is from carved ogee stone brackets and a wooden corner post which carry timber beams. From the generous living room a corridor leads to four further rooms. An impressive lodge, though derelict, still having potential for rehabilitation.

**63. FAYBROOK, Cootehill**
(see THE RETREAT)

**64. FORT FREDERICK, Virginia (2)**

Two typical rustic late Georgian lodges, simple three bay, two roomed below a hipped roof. Both showing the emergence of the Picturesque fashion in their lattice paned windows.

**Virginia Lodge** c1830

The original lodge obscured by the efforts of some mid-Victorian improver. There is an out-of-scale projecting gable hallway added with ugly naive bargeboards and of an age is the crude red brick chimney stack with sawtooth band.

**Oldcastle Lodge** c1830

Displaying the transition between Classical and Picturesque values, the front elevation has lattice panes to windows whilst that to the road has the squared Georgian type. Four stone gate posts broached from a square base to octagonal section. Spear-topped iron gates. The main house has been demolished and both lodges, for the Scott family, lie empty.

**65. FORT GEORGE GLEBE** pre 1836; *demolished*

Also known as Lurgan glebe.

**66. FORTLAND, Kilnaleck (2)**

One of the many "cottage villas" clustered around Lough Sheelin, this one built by the Maxwells of Farnham (qv).

**West Entrance** pre 1836; *demolished*

**East Entrance** c1830

Facing the road alongside the ogee gate sweep, a one and a half storey building with a high eaves to the low pitched gable roof. The simple bargeboards carried on exposed purlin brackets. In harled walls the front elevation should have been three bay but the right hand wall is blind beside a barely projecting porch below a lean-to roof. Just a suspicion of an acquaintance with the new-fangled Picturesque style. The OS map of 1836 suggests that this is the survivor of a pair.

**67. FORTWILLIAM, Cootehill** c1840
Now so overgrown as to be invisible from the main road, it nestles opposite the entrance gates. A standard two roomed three bay lodge with lean-to roofed accommodation behind. There are carved modillion brackets to the oversailing eaves of the hipped roof, which housed two mean loft bed spaces. The harled walls do not display any surviving architectural detailing. This, and the old villa across the road probably of an age, for Mr Thomas Coote a son of the Bellamont Forest (qv) family. The villa and its big Tudor Revival addition of the 1880s, later called Errigal, lie vacant.

**68. GARTINARDRESS or GARTONARDIS, Crossdoney** pre 1836; *demolished*
Once the seat of the Veitch family the lodge was probably built by the Youngs upon their acquiring the estate. It would seem also to have served as lodge to Lakeville (qv) which also belonged to the Youngs.

**69. GARTNANOUL COTTAGE, Killashandra** pre 1836; *demolished*

**70. GLAN LODGE, Swanlinbar** pre 1856; *demolished*
In a bleak mountainous area the property in 1856 of Lord Annesley noted in that year by Griffith as being vacant. No trace remains of a gate lodge.
GRIFFITH

**71. GREENVILLE, Ballyconnell** pre 1856; *demolished*
This lodge for Mr Perrott Thornton has been demolished at the entrance to a property which included the house, corn mill, kiln and offices.
GRIFFITH

**72. HACKWOOD, Killashandra** pre 1836; *demolished*
The lodge probably for a branch of the Godley family of nearby Killigar (qv) has disappeared without trace.

**73. HEATH LODGE, Kingscourt** pre 1836; *demolished*
A seat of the Nesbitts, the house and outbuildings lie derelict.

**74. HOLYWELL COTTAGE, Kilnaleck**
(see TARA COTTAGE)

**75. KILDALLAN GLEBE, Ballyconnell** pre 1835; *demolished*
The lodge was probably coeval with the 1821 rectory.

**76. KILLICAR, Belturbet (2)**
Two lodges both pre 1877 and both opposite their entrances. One has gone, the other nondescript. Built for Mr Arthur Nesbitt.

**77. KILLIGAR, Killashandra** c1845

The house in Co Leitrim but the lodge in Co Cavan. A pretty building in pristine condition for Mr John Godley. Three bay, two roomed, single storey under a hipped roof with paired brackets. All now rough cast, the openings are unusually dressed in smooth channelled stone, untoothed. The windows lattice-paned with label mouldings over. The present family representative another John Godley, Lord Kilbracken.

**78. KILLYCONNY, Mullagh** pre 1856
A gabled single storey lodge now with a corrugated iron roof and put to farming use. The seat of Richard Fisher.
GRIFFITH

**79. KILLYKEEN COTTAGE, Cavan** pre 1835; *demolished*
The entrance, once beautifully situated behind a bridged approach on the shores of Lough Oughter, has gone the way of much good architecture at the hands of Forestry Departments whether north or south of the border.

**80. KILMORE PALACE and CATHEDRAL, Cavan (2)**
The palace of the Church of Ireland Bishops of Kilmore was designed by William Farrell in about 1833.

**Palace Gate** c1840; architect possibly William Farrell
A simple three bay, single storey lodge below a hipped roof. In ashlar stone without embellishment but for the centre bay entrance door in a gabled breakfront which has a skewtable returned to form an open pediment. A once pleasant unassuming little building it has now suffered the most grotesque extension to the front elevation.

**Cathedral Gate** c1860; architect probably William Slater

The cathedral was designed in 1857 by the English architect William Slater (1819-72) and it seems safe to attribute the fine lodge and entrance archway group to him, being in sympathetic Ruskinian Gothick style. The lodge meets the visitor gable-on, a projecting canted bay on this elevation has good trefoil headed windows like the rest in dressed stone. Its own half umbrello roof advances from a steeply pitched hipped main roof with central chimney. The doorway behind the gate has a lancet head with a simple roll-moulding carried around the reveal. All is otherwise in uncoursed squared rubble, as is the tall archway alongside linked by a low wall, in which is a little wicket gate. Over the segmental pointed carriage arch, dressed similarly to the front door, a skewtable gable which displays the Episcopal coat-of-arms and motto. Although little more than a two roomed lodge, it and its archway a design which succeeds in making a considerable impact and a fitting introduction to the cathedral beyond.
CRAIG (1989)

**81. KILNACROTT, Mount Nugent** c1840
Overlooking the shores of Lough Sheelin the lodge, for Mr Pierce Morton also of Drumrora Lodge (qv), has suffered at the hands of improvers. Signs nevertheless survive of its Tudor Picturesque style, a finialed gable here, an ornamental bargeboard there and a shield above the doorway. The house looks to be contemporary, in a similar pinnacled Tudor Revival style.
LYONS (1993)

**82. KILNAHARD, Kilnaleck** c1835
Small two bay, two roomed cottage, rough cast below a hipped roof with extended eaves. The entrance door to an end elevation. Tall concave rubble stone entrance wall sweeps lead to square ashlar pillars. Built for Mr Andrew Bell.

**83. LAKEVIEW, Arvagh** pre 1878
A plain, minute lodge opposite the gates. For Mr Hugh McManus, standard single storey with a hipped roof and clipped eaves.

**84. LAKEVIEW Mullagh** c1850
Across the road from the entrance, its back to Mullagh Lough, a very plain building probably for a Mr Mortimer.

**85. LAKEVIEW, Virginia** c1800
A tiny standard plan single storey lodge, its main elevation two bay with miniscule windows in harled walls. Hipped roof.

**86. LAKEVILLE, Crossdoney** pre 1836; *demolished*
This lodge was to the park of Mr Richard Young whose family also owned the neighbouring demesne of Gartinardress (qv).

**87. LANESBOROUGH LODGE, Belturbet** 1859; architect perhaps William Hague

Built for George John Danvers Butler, 5th Earl of Lanesborough, a substantial one and a half storey gabled lodge, three bay with the projecting gabled porch placed asymmetrically. In uncoursed, squared quarry-faced stone with dressed chamfered and label-moulded windows and quoins, of excellent quality masonry. Over the Tudor porch archway a dated shield and on the high eaved main elevation a sculpted stone quarter embracing the Butler coat-of-arms with the motto "LIBERTIE TOUTE ENTIERE". All windows nicely latticed. The foils of the bargeboards are carried around as an ornamental fascia. Hipknobs at the apexes and at the toes, onion- shaped pendants. The four panelled entrance door is nicely studded. Also known as Quivey Lodge, Lanesborough phased improvements to the demesne from his succession in 1847. He first built a Tudor Revival manor house, followed by a church in 1855 by the youthful Cavan architect William Hague later to become one of the most prolific interdenominational church architects in Ireland. The lodge is well maintained.

**88. LARCHFIELD GLEBE, Kingscourt** pre 1836; *demolished*

**89. LAURELBANK, Arvagh** pre 1879
One and a half storey with mildly ornamental bargeboards, otherwise plain.

**90. LISMORE CASTLE, Crossdoney** pre 1836; *demolished*
The Nesbitts' lodge and the bulk of the house have gone.

**91. LISNAMANDRA, Crossdoney** pre 1836; *demolished*
A lodge built for the Elliott family.

**92. LISSANOVER, Bawnboy** pre 1836; *demolished*
The Armstrong family lodge was located opposite the gates.

**93. THE LODGE, Virginia** (see VIRGINIA LODGE)

**94. LURGAN GLEBE, Virginia** (see FORT GEORGE GLEBE)

**95. MARSHWOOD, Newtowngore** pre 1877; *demolished*
Previously known as Woodford House, a site of one of the ancient seats of the Gore family. The lodge by Ballymagauran Lough has gone.

**96. MOUNT PROSPECT, Mount Nugent** pre 1836; *demolished*
A lodge for T Nugent Esq.

**97. NEWGROVE, Cootehill** pre 1836; *demolished*
Mr Mayne's lodge has gone.

**98. NORTHLANDS, Shercock** pre 1836; *demolished*
The seat of the Adams family. The house was built in 1822 by the Very Rev Samuel Allen Adams, Dean of Cashel. The lodge was erected not long after but has not survived.
BURKE (1855)

**99. OWENDOON, Bawnboy** pre 1877; *demolished*
The lodge was probably built by George Henry L'Estrange after he moved from Lisnamandra House (qv).

**100. PALMIRA, Virginia** pre 1836; *demolished*

**101. PORTALIFF GLEBE, Killashandra** c1850
A standard single storey structure, symmetrical three bay constructed in rubble stone with red brick prominent as dressings to openings, eaves course to the hipped roof and chimney stack. Probably built for the Venerable Archdeacon Martin.
GRIFFITH

**102. PROSPECT, Redhills** pre 1836; *demolished*

**103. QUIVEY LODGE, Belturbet** (see LANESBOROUGH LODGE)

**104. RAHARDRUM (Townland of), Virginia** pre 1835; *demolished*
The 1878 OS map suggests that this lodge was by then a shell.

**105. RAKENNY, Cootehill** c1840; architect probably William Farrell
Here is the most minimal of accommodation. Only the lodge at Killcatten Lodge, Co Londonderry (qv) is quite so small. Little more than a sentry box, the one main room 12' 0" x 10' 0" (3.6m x 3.3m). Its survival is a wonder

too, being of little use now other than as a pretty little summerhouse. Novel also in retaining its original facing brick without requiring the protection of later rendering. In pleasant mellowed orange brick, the side walls project in piers to form a recessed front elevation of two bays - the entrance door and a wide lattice paned casement window. The pyramidal roof has paired carved eaves brackets, but the chimney stack rises off the rear wall in a way which Farrell employed at his Ely Lodge and Colebrook lodges, Co Fermanagh (qqv). Now not surprisingly unoccupied but well tended. A beautifully wooded estate of 500 acres by the Annalee River for which Farrell designed a Classical house, the gates strangely insignificant and the lodge oddly distant from them. The client was Theophilus Edward Lucas Clements.

**106. REDHILLS, Redhills (3)**
The fine antique demesne of the Whyte family had three lodges perhaps of mid-Georgian vintage none of which survives. Only the gate pillars remain at two entrances, each with more fashionable lodge replacements.

**Town Lodge** c1840
This one and a half storey lodge has now lost much of its original Picturesque character in modern improvements. Gone are the Tudor label mouldings, lattice paned windows, fanciful bargeboards and ornamental chimney stack. Its cement rendering perhaps hides facing brick. It has retained its gablet window on the hipped roof elevation to the road, bands of fishscale slates and its irregular form. Occupied. The square gate piers older, plain in pleasant random rubble.

**Cootehill Road Entrance** c1845

Magnificent ashlar pillars of c1790 whose crowning glories are the pinecone finials fitting neatly into foliated carved "egg cups". Below the blocked cornice a plain frieze. To the gate stops a

scrolled top. All the same as the entrance pillars at Thomastown Gate, Castlecoole, Co Fermanagh (qv). A common link has not been established. Hiding behind the high wall screen with its back to a pretty stream, a charming stuccoed Italianate lodge rich in architectural detailing. Framed by two Irish yews, its gable-on elevation, single storey, two roomed. The hipped roof projects in a half umbrello over a canted hall, each face of which features a semicircular headed arch. The doorway flanked by recesses which house tiny square openings which in turn frame round headed windows with margined glazing, the same as at Erne Hill, Belturbet (qv). The side windows flat arched and architraved each with a pair of matching sashed lights. Reticulated quoins and a highly ornate carved modillion bracketed eaves. A very desirable little building, which is, at the time of writing, undergoing restoration.

**107. THE RETREAT, Cootehill (2)** both pre 1836; *both demolished*
A pleasant seat, on the banks of the winding Annalee River, to which Charles James Adams provided two gate lodges, neither of which are there today. The house was later renamed Faybrook.

**108. ROCK, Kilnaleck** pre 1836; *demolished*
A lodge opposite the entrance.

**109. ROEBUCK, Mount Nugent** pre 1878; *demolished*
A lodge to the Reilly demesne.

**110. SAINT PATRICK'S COLLEGE, Cavan** (see CULLIES)

**111. SHINAN, Shercock** pre 1836; *demolished*
Another property of the Adams family.

**112. STRADONE, Stradone (2)**
In 1828 the architect J B Keane designed a new house here for Major F Burrows, "a modern handsome building, quadrangular in form" and contemporary with it a porter's lodge.

**Cavan Lodge** c1830; architect J B Keane; *demolished*

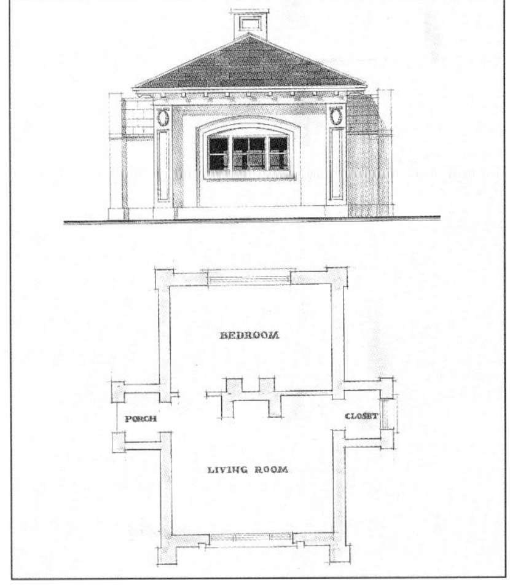

An important Grecian style lodge in the Sir Richard Morrison manner. Keane had worked as assistant in this office which pioneered this gable-on approach. A graceful composition which is repeated at Mount Richard, Carrick-on-Suir, Co Tipperary. The gate piers were again in 'Papworth' Greek stellae mode but they, with the elegant lodge, were swept away by a European-funded road scheme. Simple single storey, two roomed under a low hipped roof. Finished in stucco, the side elevations extend in the form of antae (although without columns in antis) each stone face of which had a recessed panel crowned by a bas-relief laurel wreath, a motif repeated from the portico on the big house. These frame a wide square paned window with a segmental head, in a similarly arched recess. The high extended eaves is supported on brackets. A low gabled entrance hall on a long elevation is balanced by a small projection to the opposing facade. The house was also demolished some years earlier, all a sad loss to the county.

**Village Lodge** c1845; architect perhaps J B Keane

Very much along the lines of the above in form and orientation to the road. The flat-arched window to the avenue tripartite having the most intricate glazing bar pattern, almost Art Nouveau in style, and similar in feel to those at Tullyvin House (qv) nearby and Glaslough, Co Monaghan (qv). Simple smooth banded quoins in rough cast walls. Flat roofed porch projection. Good stone central chimney to the low pitched hipped roof. Intact and occupied.

BENCE-JONES (1988); O.S.M.

**113. SUMMERVILLE, Kilnaleck** pre 1836; *demolished*

Away off the beaten track, at the entrance to another fishing lodge on the banks of Lough Sheelin, was a round gate keeper's residence. For the Webb family.

**114. TARA COTTAGE, Kilnaleck** pre 1879

A plain and "improved" lodge.

**115. TULLY, Killashandra** pre 1835

A tiny, standard two roomed, single storey building with a steeply hipped roof, its eaves decorated by paired scrolled brackets. A semicircular-headed door opening in brick walls with stone quoins. Two square squat ashlar piers. Built for Major Randall Stafford.

**116. TULLYCOE TOWNLAND, Stradone** pre 1856; *demolished*

A property of a Thomas Nesbitt identified by Griffith in his valuation. Not located, presumed gone.

GRIFFITH

**117. TULLYVIN, Cootehill (2)**

A demesne acquired from the Moore family early in the 19th century by Maxwell J Boyle who, having rebuilt the house, scarcely lived in it. Whilst being apparently under-enamoured by his acquisition, he nevertheless saw fit to further improve the park by the furnishing of two porters' lodges.

**Cootehill Gate** c1840

A very modest little single storey standard plan lodge. Harled with a hipped roof and clipped eaves.

**Village Gate** c1845; architect not known

More pretentious, lording it over the entrance gates from across the road. Whilst appearing a fairly standard three bay lodge it disguises a spacious four room plan with front and back hallways. Single storey stuccoed under a hipped roof with paired bracket eaves ornament. The window openings large and tripartite with intricate and flamboyant cast iron glazing, partly fishscale pattern, much as at Glaslough, Co Monaghan (qv) and Stradone House (qv) nearby. Tudor label mouldings over the windows. In contrast the doorway has a Classical surround of pilasters and entablature, framing a two-leaf, three-panelled door over which is a semicircular teardrop fanlight with a central eight petalled flower, a throwback to an English fanlight of a quarter of a century before. Corniced stone central chimney. Facing the front hall door within is a niche. Screening the front garden a low railing and gates with lovely cast iron posts topped with lancets containing anthemions. The rails have spur or etoile finials. The screen across the road to the demesne similar but stopped by pretty fan-shaped terminals, all nicely picked out in silver paint. The lodge lies inexplicably empty and rejected.

**118. TURE LODGE, Ballyconnell** pre 1835; *demolished*

A pair of lodges perhaps for a Mr John Jones, now gone.

**119. VICAR'S HILL Cootehill** pre 1836; *demolished*

**120. VIRGINIA LODGE, Virginia (3)**

On the banks of Ramor Lough, a beautiful park where the Marquis of Headfort had a hunting lodge in plain rambling Picturesque cottage style "where he delights to spend the autumnal months". In complementary vein two little gate lodges, a third rather later and grander.

**Town Lodge** c1835

Single storey, two bay and gable-on to the avenue, the walls now rough cast. The gables have ornamental bargeboards with lobed foils and hipknobs, the ridge crested on either side of nice brick octagonal chimney stacks. Cast iron lattice paned windows.

**Ballyjamesduff Lodge** c1835

Much as the above in materials and style but three bay to the avenue and one and a half storey. A pair of coupled octagonal brick stacks to each ornamental gable. Shamrock motif to bargeboard toes, the high eaves supported on pairs of scrolled timber brackets. There is an unfortunate projecting hall in brick, of later date, which is out of scale. Similar to the nearby lodge of Fort Frederick (qv) and probably by the same "inspired" jobbing builder.

**Oldcastle Lodge** c1880; architect not known

An impressive High Victorian one and a half storey, two up two down lodge. In coursed squared rubble quarry- faced. Dressed stone to quoins, windows which have roll-moulded heads and chamfered reveals, and the skewtables to a very steeply-pitched roof. The gable thrust forward of the gate screen has a single storey canted bay with hipped roof. Above this to the attic bedroom, a tripartite window with cut stone dripshelf, over which is a relieving arch. Behind the gates on the avenue facade a bipartite window. Alongside is a lofty carved ornamental timber porch with chamfered posts, curved brackets, decorative bargeboards to its steeply-pitched canopy roof and, behind the cross patterned balustrades, quaint bench seats. From the rear wall rises a very tall, stone, three flue chimney stack with moulded cornice. Suitably extensive and robust gate screen, the big dressed stone pillars gabled on four faces, those to the road having recessed trefoil features. Of the gates only a fancy wood and iron wicket survives.

COOTE (1802)

**121. WOODFORD Newtowngore** (see MARSHWOOD)

# COUNTY DONEGAL

**1. AGHNAGADDY, Ramelton** c1830
Described as a "... large glebe-house and demesne ..." in 1836, it became a private residence early this century and was recently burned down. A drawing of 1826 held in the Irish Architectural Archive shows a proposal for the house seemingly signed by P Nugent, Architect. It was complete by 1828 at a cost of £6,000. The lodge of squarish plan, two roomed with two bay elevations under a hipped roof. In harled walls the windows small and square each having a pair of casements with decorative upper glazing bar pattern. All with vigorous stone label mouldings over. Sturdy central chimney stack.
FRASER (1838); LEWIS (1837); I.A.A.

**2. ARDARAVAN, Buncrana** pre 1900; *demolished*

**3. ARDNAMONA, Donegal** c1840
Beautifully situated on the banks of Lough Eske, the property when the lodge was built of George C Wray. A single storey gabled building with its back turned impolitely to the road, the doorway the left hand opening of three bays. Label mouldings to lattice glazed windows. The pretty bargeboards carried through the catslide rear extension roof. Dilapidated, deserted and overgrown.

**4. ARDRUMMAN, Ramelton** c1840; *demolished*
By the shores of Lough Swilly, the seat of Francis Mansfield of Castlewray (qv). The lodge opposite the gates did not survive until this century. Contemporary with, and probably in the same gabled Tudor Revival manner as, the main house.

**5. ARDS, Creeslough (4)**
The Wrays once owned these lands of upwards of 2000 acres, remote before the arrival of the motor car. Of an early entrance to the estate Charlotte Violet Trench writes, "The 'grand gate' of Ards. A high mound of rock overgrown with brushwood stood there, and William Wray had tunnelled through the rock for about thirty yards to make an entrance. On the inner side backed by rock had once stood a gate-keeper's lodge. This entrance is no longer used. The iron gate is closed and barred and overgrown ...". In 1781 the property was purchased by Alexander Stewart, younger brother of the 1st Marquess of Londonderry of Mount Stewart, Co Down (qv) who had John Hargrave build a new house in 1830.

**Ballymore Gate** c1820; architect perhaps W V Morrison

Clearly the same designer was employed by the Stewart brothers for here is the same building as the two which form a pair at Mountstewart (qv). A copy right down to the naive Y-tracery in the lancet windows. The architect is likely to have been associated with the County Down property where W V Morrison was employed. The canted gables under half-umbrello roofs and Gothick windows are also to be found at Montalto and Florida Manor (qqv) both in Co Down. Single storey, two bay to the front elevation, the walls are stuccoed with stone quoins. There is a later rear return. Occupied and well kept.

**Cashelmore Gate** c1810
Also off the beaten track, a pleasant single storey Irish Georgian cottage with hipped gables. Three bay on a standard plan in harled walls, the windows squared sash. Later back return wing and ornamental timber gabled porch at the front door. Both lodges survive the house which was sold to the Franciscan Order in 1937 and later demolished.

**Farm Lodge** pre 1902; *demolished*
BENCE-JONES (1988); TRENCH (1945)

**6. BALLYARR, Ramelton** pre 1903; *demolished*
Seat of Lord George A Hill.

**7. BALLYBRACK, Greencastle** pre 1833
Unnoteworthy lodge for George Hill Boggs.

**8. BALLYCONNELL, Falcarragh (2)**
When the house was enlarged about 1840 it was dressed up with Tudor embellishments by the Ophert family. Two lodges were added to the estate around this time.

**East Lodge** c1840; architect possibly J B Keane
In a sort of Classical Tudor mix, now much improved and extended into a two storey house, stuccoed with stone quoins. The lodge was probably originally exactly like that to Coxtown (qv), single storey three bay symmetrical under a hipped roof. Raised another storey under the same hipped type roof with paired brackets to the eaves. The single storey hall projection survives having its open pediment over a rounded door opening with hood moulding. The ground floor windows have label mouldings like the house and perhaps had ornamental glazing bars like Coxtown. Cast iron gate sweep and octagonal posts with finialed cappings.

**West Lodge** c1840
A nondescript lodge. A nice low cast iron screen with decorative posts.
ROWAN (1979)

**9. BALLYDUFF, Lifford** c1910
A three bay symmetrical bungalow with two canted bay windows on either side of the enlarged front door opening. A banal introduction to a rather more pleasant villa.

**10. BALLYMACOOL, Letterkenny (2)**
A tall mid-Georgian house of the Span family which underwent a startling Tudor Revival face-lift on its acquisition by Major John Boyd. He also built two appropriate and identical lodges in Tudor Picturesque manner in the most notable of settings as described by Mrs Tonna in 1837: "You would delight in this situation it is so completely shut in that you need not unless you choose to think about it, know that there is any visible world beyond its limits". And again in 1909: "Surrounded by a broad grass terrace, and near the house is a pine walk comprising a variety of conifers, among which are the finest specimen in Ireland". Both lodges lie empty and the demesne is now run down.

**East Gate** c1835; architect perhaps W V Morrison

One and a half storey, stuccoed, three bay and symmetrical with coved eaves to gabled roofs. All gables including those of the projecting porches have lost their fanciful decorative bargeboards, the steeply-pitched roof of one lodge has the remnants of pretty cresting and retains large scalloped slates. There is a variety of openings, those to the front elevation flat-arched mullioned with three wooden latticed lights. The porch side windows, chamfered with Venetian-arched heads, have traceried bipartite lights. The entrance arch is Tudor four-centred. On the leading gables, facing the gates, canted oriels also mullioned and transomed with lattice panes to round headed lights.

**West Gate** c1835; architect perhaps W V Morrison

Identical to East Gate. The form of these lodges and particularly the treatment of openings are identical to the lodge at Milltown Lodge, Co Tyrone (qv) by William Vitruvius Morrison. There is also a replica lodge to Drumboe Castle (qv) in the same county.
TONNA (1838); YOUNG (1909)

**11. BARNHILL, Letterkenny** pre 1834
Small standard plan late Georgian lodge, three bay with a hipped roof.

**12. BELLMONT, Lifford** c1840; *demolished*
Probably built by General Andrew Clarke.

**13. BIRDSTOWN, Burnfoot (2)**
Previously the property of the Bensons it passed by marriage to the Rev Peter Benson Maxwell who inherited in 1822. He clearly felt the need for improving the demesne as both lodges seem to date from then.

**Burnfoot Road Lodge** pre 1833; *demolished*
Replaced by a modern bungalow.

**Side Entrance** c1825
Probably an octagonal, two roomed, pepperpot lodge in its original form now extended by a rear return parallel to the road. Single storey below an umbrello roof with a central chimney. The walls roughcast with transomed and mullioned square-paned windows. Once typical of many late Georgian lodges in the country but no longer commonplace. Squat, square, contemporary ashlar gate piers with fluted friezes and simple corniced cappings.

**14. BOGAY, Newtowncunningham** pre 1833; *demolished*
Only crude gate piers survive with modern eagles above. Hardly in keeping with the elegant house.

**15. BONNYGLEN, Inver** pre 1835; *demolished*
A lodge for Murray Babington. Later the property of the Sinclairs of Holyhill, Co Tyrone (qv).

**16. BREAGHY GLEBE, Ramelton**
(see AGHNAGADDY)

**17. BROWN HALL, Ballintra (3)**
Robert Woodgate, Sir John Soane's clerk-of-works, settled in Ireland after supervising the rebuilding of Baronscourt, Co Tyrone (qv), and then designed Brown Hall for the Hamilton family in 1794. Only one lodge looks early enough to have been built by James Hamilton but perhaps too desperately plain to be by Woodgate. Two further lodges were built to help retain stock in the deerpark. One of c1830 standard plan, single storey with lattice-paned windows was likely to have been for the Rev Edward Michael Hamilton who had been ceded the property by his brother John. John Hamilton, grandson of James, had inherited as a child in 1811 but by 1825 he appears to have lost interest in the estate and moved to St Ernans (qv) with a newly-acquired wife. Edward Hamilton was rarely in residence and it seems the third lodge was built in about 1840 by his uncle Abraham Hamilton. This lodge has now gone.
DEERY (1948); BURKE (1904)

**18. BUNCRANA CASTLE, Buncrana (3)**
Three lodges seemingly built by the Todd family when the Vaughan male line became extinct. The park and fine antique house are now in the later stages of decay.

**North Lodge** pre 1900; *demolished*
**Middle Lodge** pre 1834; *ruinous*
A minute, single storey, standard plan lodge with a hipped roof.

**South Lodge** pre 1900; *demolished*

**19. BURT, Burnfoot** pre 1833; *demolished*
The property in 1836 of Andrew Ferguson.

**20. CAMLIN CASTLE, Ballyshannon (3)**
The Tredennick family moved here from lands near Bodmin, Cornwall upon their confiscation by the Commonwealth. Parts of their 17th century house were incorporated in a pretty battlemented and gabled Tudor Revival mansion by the architect J B Keane for John Arnold Tredennick in 1838, when a suitably impressive gateway was also built.

**Main Entrance** c1838; architect J B Keane

A Romantic castellated design in squared uncoursed ashlar, incorporating single storey one roomed porter's accommodation behind a high crenellated screen wall with a narrow hood-moulded slit window. Dominating the whole composition rises a tall circular flagstaff tower housing a spiral staircase leading from the porter's room to a machicolated and Irish-crenellated parapet. The tower is decorated with loopholes to light the stairs. To balance the design, a buttressed Tudor carriage archway with label moulding below a battlemented parapet displaying a blank shield. The original timber gates have gone. Castellations also crown the concave quadrant walls. This fine folly remains fairly intact but the pretty mansion was removed in expectation of flooding by the Ballyshannon hydroelectric scheme. The water level never endangered it. Two other lodges, both pre 1835 to the south-east, have gone.
YOUNG (1909)

**21. CARNAGARVE, Moville** c1850
Behind basic low ogee gate sweeps with octagonal piers are two little matching gabled lodges on guard, squinting at each other across the entrance. Each apparently single storey but skylights illuminate minimal bed space in the loft. They have a mild Tudor Picturesque feel through label mouldings to three bay fronts and pretty foiled bargeboards with pendant hipknobs. The walls now rendered and whitewashed. There was a diagonally-set chimney stack to each, broaching off a square base, but these are now replaced with slender terracotta pots. Apologetic pine cone finials to the gate piers. The house, renamed Ravenscliff, was in 1837 the property of Mr H Corbett of Londonderry.

**22. CARRALEENA, Rathmullan** pre 1903; *demolished*

**23. CARRICK LODGE, Carrick** c1865; architects possibly Young and Mackenzie

The family of Musgrave and Sons, the great Belfast Iron Manufactory, came here in the late 1860s to acquire this remote property on the edge of Glencolumbkille. They improved it by extending the house in a Tudor/Scots Baronial style and built a lodge in similar vein. Simple three bay two up two down but substantial and robust in its handling. One and a half storey, the roughcast walls highlighted in a suitably rugged quarry-faced boulder treatment of quoins, window dressings, cills, heads and crowstepped gables with great crude kneelers. Incongruously the apex finials are quite delicately carved and turned. The window glazing in cast iron with a mixture of bi- and tripartite mullioned casements. The projecting gabled hall similarly handled with the Musgrave monogram below a crowstepped gable. A lean-to room to the rear forms part of an extensive range of outbuildings. No architect has been established but Young and Mackenzie of Belfast carried out work for the family business. The Musgraves' main seat was Drumglass, Co Antrim (qv). Both house and lodge succeeded earlier buildings on the site built between 1835 and 1847. After years of dilapidation, house and lodge now renascent.
SLATER (1870)

**24. CARROWCANON, Falcarragh** pre 1903; *demolished.*

**25. CARROWNAFF LODGE, Moville (2)** both c1860; architect not known

Two identical lodges possibly built for the Haslett family. In Picturesque Tudor manner, one and a half storey gabled on a T plan. The

front elevation three bay asymmetrical, the left hand bay slightly advanced below its own gable. Ornately carved wave and foil bargeboards, hipknobs with sharp finials and paired brackets to eaves. In quoined stuccoed walls under label mouldings are pretty cast iron margined lattice windows with neatly pivoting openers. Within a mile is the same lodge, at Gortgowan (qv), differing only in having squared sash windows.

**26. CASTLECARY, Moville** pre 1900; *demolished*
A lodge for Arthur L Cary.

**27. CASTLEFINN, Castlefinn** pre 1835; *demolished*
Seat of the Taylor family.

**28. CASTLEFORWARD, Newtowncunningham (2)** both pre 1833; *both demolished*
Both lodges, built for William Forward-Howard, the 3rd Lord Wicklow of Shelton Abbey, Co Wicklow, are gone along with the house.

**29. CASTLEGROVE, Ramelton (2)**
For long the property of the Grove family, an elegant Georgian mansion beautifully situated on the shores of Lough Swilly.

**Inner Entrance** pre 1834; *demolished*
A pair of lodges within the present boundary gone, probably taken down upon the building of their successor on the Letterkenny Road.

**Outer Entrance** c1863
Two square stuccoed carriage gate piers have small ball finials with tall stems on simple moulded blocked cappings. Flanking are high concave wall quadrants each housing wicket gates. Behind is an astylar lodge without embellishment, elegant in its simplicity. Single storey, three bay under a hipped roof with an entablatured parapet to the front elevation only. Square window openings with Georgian style panes in stuccoed walls, all looking to be from forty years earlier but seemingly built by James Grove Wood Grove upon his inheriting the 2,000 acre estates in 1863.
BURKE (1855)

**30. CASTLEWRAY, Ramelton** pre 1834; *demolished*
The lodge for Francis Mansfield did not survive into the present century, just like that to his other property of Ardrumman (qv) further north.

**31. CAVANCOR, Ballydrait** c1850
Set at a slight angle to, and casually supervising, the gates opposite is a two storey three bay gatehouse, gabled with harled walls. The ground floor windows unfortunately enlarged to take modern casements with DIY louvre shutters. The windows over as original, wide openings with tiny rectangular panes. Very homely. Plain square rubble gateposts and sweep. Built by Benjamin Geale Humfrey upon marrying Mary, only daughter of William Keys.

**32. CAVANGARDEN, Ballyshannon (2)**; *both demolished*
One pre 1835 probably superseded by that of c1840, the latter built by Thomas John Atkinson.

**33. CHERRYMOUNT, Ballyshannon** pre 1835; *demolished*
A small property on the banks of Assaroe Lake. Owned in the early nineteenth century by the Jones family.

**34. CLARAGH, Ramelton** c1830
A lodge built by Mr James Watt in a pleasant rustic Georgian style. Originally built for an earlier house on the demesne, it now serves as an introduction to something completely different, eccentric and late Victorian. Beautifully secluded, it is on a simple two up two down plan, one and a half storey, but given an irregular outline with two single storey hall outshots with lean-to roofs. Basically two bay having square Georgian paned windows in harled walls. The roof is hipped gable with clipped verges and eaves. Access to the bedrooms is from a staircase open to the living room. A very attractive little building.

**35. CLIFF, Ballyshannon (2)** both c1840
On an elevated site overlooking the River Erne the summer residence of the Conollys of Castletown, Celbridge, Co Kildare. One of the lodges survives built for Colonel Edward Conolly MP, a modest standard two roomed three bay affair with a hipped roof and deep soffited eaves.
DOYLE (1854)

**36. CLOGHAN LODGE**
A lodge to Sir Thomas Charles Style's romantic shooting lodge.

**37. CLONLEIGH, Ballindrait** c1863; architects probably Welland & Gillespie

Set obliquely to the road, a highly distinctive and unique lodge with an obvious ecclesiastical feel, contrasting with the modest Georgian house of the Knox family. There is no documentary evidence to connect Welland and Gillespie with the lodge but it is probably no coincidence that they were working on the local parish church in 1863. Mainly faced in random uncoursed rubble it has dressed stone to skewtable gables, sculpted kneelers and shamrock motif apexes. Single storey commodious on a T plan, a two roomed "nave" with another room in each of the "transepts", both of which have a tripartite window, each light with a pointed head in dressed stone. As in all of the three main gables, above is a relieving arch and little trefoil window over. Main windows have margined lattice-paned cast iron church windows. Below the trefoil on the leading gable the "west" window is in the form of a rectangular bay, with lights shouldered in cut stone, under a half hipped roof. Giving a sense of informality is a gabled hall projecting off the side elevation, having a lancet-headed door with blank shield over. Some roof pitches retain bands of diagonally laid slates, the chimney stacks crudely rebuilt. Built by William Knox to replace an earlier lodge on the same site. Low, cast iron gateposts and railings with fleur-de-lys tops. Lion finials like those at Cloverhill (qv) were taken away to Rash, Co Tyrone (qv).
ROWAN (1979)

**38. CLOVERHILL, Inver** c1900
The lodge, if lodge it is, is a large gabled house of random rubble with red brick quoins and window dressings. Otherwise not notable but the tall plain ashlar gate pillars each support a proud stone lion, guarding unpretentious wrought iron gates, perhaps for Mr Hugh Montgomery, a century or so before the lodge. Similar lion figures were at Clonleigh (qv)
ROWAN (1979)

**39. CONVOY, Convoy** 1806/c1850; architect possibly Sir Thomas Forster

(I.A.A.)

A plain Classical house and contrasting entrance complex built by Robert Montgomery, said to have been designed by the amateur architect Sir Thomas Forster. Described by Alistair Rowan as "... a nice piece of castle-style nonsense in the manner of Francis Johnston". Consisting of a carriage gate under a castellated parapet with shallow pointed archway flanked by a pair of round turrets, in turn framed by concave quadrant walls also battlemented. Here the symmetry ends, for to one side is a square watch tower rising over a pointed arched pedestrian gate buttressed to the fore by two tiny square turrets. Access to the upper level is by way of external steps curving up behind a quadrant wall. Crowning the tower is a fundamental machicolated parapet with round corbelled bartizans to each corner, three having little "candle-snuffer" conical roofs, the fourth crenellated and taller to carry the flagstaff. Further beyond and completing an irregular composition is a single storey lodge dating from about 1850. The elevation to the road, two bay with lancet windows below a hipped roof, the Gothick tracery now boarded up. In rustic random rubble the walls incorporate salvaged pieces from the previous house on the site. Over the main gate, as a keystone, a coat-of-arms with the date "1693" and the monogram "RM". On the watch-tower a primitive face grins down. A photograph from early this century shows this first floor tower room to have been glazed with cast iron lattice windows. A delightful folly now unkempt and ivy-infested.
MONTGOMERY (1887); COOPER PHOTOGRAPH; PRONI D/1422/21/13; ROWAN (1979); I.A.A. PHOTOGRAPH

**40. COOLBEG, Ballyshannon** c1840
An unpretentious lodge suffering from recent "improvements". Low-pitched hipped roof. Built by John Reynolds.

**41. CORCAM, Stranorlar** c1840; *demolished*
Gone before the turn of this century. A seat of Mr Henry Stewart in 1837.

**42. THE COTTAGE, Buncrana** c1840; *demolished*
A lodge probably built by a Dr Evans.

**43. COXTOWN, Ballintra** c1835; architect probably J B Keane
A Neo-Classical villa of about 1830 for Mr Alexander E Hamilton displaying many features typical of the work of J B Keane. A miniature version of the house but with a Tudor slant. Single storey, standard plan, three bay below a hipped roof from which projects a hall gabled to form an open pediment over. It, and the eaves, carried on pairs of brackets. Sometime roughcast with dressed stone quoins, plinth, opening surrounds and label mouldings. The front door is double-leafed under a Tudor hood-moulded arch. The windows used to be paired with beautiful cuspidated pointed heads and lattice glazed. All now somewhat blemished by modern hardwood window intrusions and smooth rendering. A sturdy nicely proportioned little composition,

A. Rowan
Coxtown

something similar to one at Ballyconnell (qv). Gate sweep with square stone piers, recessed panels to each face and projecting cappings. Pleasant low ornamental cast iron railings.
ALISTAIR ROWAN, Photograph Ref. B0964 3A; ROWAN (1979)

**44. CROAGHAN, Portsalon** pre 1835; *demolished*

**45. CROGHAN LODGE, Lifford** c1840; *demolished*
A small property belonging to James Cochrane.

**46. CRUMMIN, Muff** c1840; *demolished*

**47. CULDAFF, Culdaff (2)**
"In this remote but lovely situation it is pleasant to see the well-improved and elegant demesne of Mr Young of Culdaff". It was probably George Young, upon his father's death in 1823, who built the first lodge.

**Moville Gate** c1825
A pleasant late Georgian lodge with satisfying low lines. Single storey, three bay below a shallow-pitched roof and extended eaves. It is harled with ashlar quoins, dressed stone to casement windows having small squared panes. Below the eaves is a tiny breakfront door with a little rustic pediment. Simple contemporary square stone gate piers.

**Village Lodge** c1900
Bland, single storey, roughcast bungalow lodge. Hipped roof catsliding as a front door canopy. Living room with canted projection under a half umbrello roof. Built for George Lawrence Young. The gate sweep older, its wicket with low flat arch for "little people" only.
DOYLE (1854); YOUNG (1929)

**48. DANBY, Ballyshannon** pre 1904
Built to replace an earlier lodge of pre 1835 to the house of Mr James Forbes. The present building on an L plan. Verandah with trellis work. Probably built upon Mr Thomas Troubridge Stubbs acquiring the property in 1870.
YOUNG (1909)

**49. DANEVILLE LODGE, Bundoran** pre 1836
To one of many early 19th century bathing villas overlooking Donegal Bay, a plain miniature gabled three bay, single storey building to a park previously known as Fairview. Similar in appearance to the neighbouring lodge at Rochfort (qv). Occupied by the Rev Herbert M Nash in 1824 and 1837.

**50. DAWROS BAY, Ardara** pre 1903; *demolished*

**51. DINGLE-I-COUSH, Bundoran**
(see ROSE LODGE)

**52. DOE CASTLE, Creeslough** pre 1834;
Before the causeway approach, a modest single storey three bay structure, gabled with harled walls. Probably for General George Vaughan Hart of Kilderry (q.v.) who inherited the property around 1800.

**53. DONAGHMORE GLEBE, Castlefinn (2)** both c1840
Two lodges clearly the result of a prosperous living. Both Georgian style three bay, each having a hipped roof with projecting eaves, one with a high "brow" housing bed spaces in the loft, just as at The Bawn, Co Tyrone (qv) and The Argory, Co Armagh (qv). All in contrast to the present High Victorian house which replaced the old rectory.

**54. DRUMBOE CASTLE, Ballybofey (4)**
Once a fine demesne now run down and being encroached upon by modern housing and commercial development. The big house of the Basil family has gone.

**East Lodge** pre 1836; *demolished*
**Inner Lodge** pre 1836; *demolished*
**West Lodge** pre 1836; *demolished*
**Town Lodge** 1870;
design by W V Morrison

The one surviving entrance was built by Sir Samuel Hercules Hayes whose great-great grandfather Samuel had come by the property through marriage with a daughter of William Basil. This lodge is identical in every respect to those at Ballymacool (qv) which can be explained by the connection through marriage in 1799 of Major John Boyd of that place, to Frances a daughter of Sir Samuel Hayes. Were it not for the datestone one would assume the lodge to be from forty years earlier, like the Ballymacool versions. These in turn are so akin to the lodge to Milltown Lodge, Co Tyrone (qv) that they can be attributed to William Vitruvius Morrison. This must be a copy. One and a half storey three bay gabled with a steeply- pitched roof. The principal ground floor windows tripartite with big timber lattice glazing bars, repeated on the canted oriel window (now a bay) with half hipped roof on the gable away from the road. The gabled projecting hall has side lights with simple tracery under Venetian arches, the front door Tudor arched with the datestone over. On the road gable, delicate wooden carved wave bargeboards and hipknob survive. The hall gable bargeboards a somewhat more geometric pattern. These and the coved eaves detail and window features are identical to those at Milltown lodge. Narrow round- headed lights to attic rooms. Contemporary square cast iron gateposts with big cappings are all that can be detected of the former gate sweep.
BURKE (1904)

**55. DRUMBRISTAN GLEBE, Ballintra** c1830
Formerly identical to the lodge at Inver Rectory (qv). Single storey three bay below a hipped roof. Notable for its tripartite windows with pointed heads in unusual stone lintels. A similar head forms a fanlight to the front door. In squared coursed stone, the lodge has been raised to one and a half storey with gable ends, and a canopy on timber post support added across the front elevation to form a verandah. At one time served also as a schoolhouse.

**56. DUNFANAGHY, Dunfanaghy** c1845
In stone, but otherwise an ordinary standard plan, single storey, three bay structure with a hipped roof.

**57. DUNLEWY, Dunlewy** c1810

Described by James Frazer in 1836 as "The occasional residence of J Dombrain, Esq", with the spectacular backdrop of Errigal, snug in a beautiful glen overlooking Dunlewy Lough. Formerly a simple two roomed single storey lodge gable-on to the avenue having pretty Georgian Gothick lancet sash windows with Y-tracery. Sometime later it was extended by an identical addition alongside to form a double pile, the front door moved from side to front facade. The walls harled, it also acquired mildly Picturesque wavy bargeboards. This later work carried out by the Russell family.
FRAZER (1838)

**58. DUNMORE, Carrigans (2)** both pre 1835; *both demolished*
To a graceful house of the McClintock family.

**59. EDENMORE, Stranorlar (2)** *both demolished*
On the banks of the River Finn an elegant late Georgian villa had one contemporary lodge, the other slightly later (c1840). Both for Mr John Cochrane.

**60. FAHAN GLEBE, Buncrana** c1840; *demolished*
To a glebe house of 1822 a lodge which postdates it. Built for the Rev William Hawkshaw. Surviving are pretty iron gates and square posts with ball ornaments to each corner. All in striking white paint.
LEWIS (1837); LESLIE (1940)

**61. FAIR VIEW, Bundoran**
(see DANEVILLE LODGE)

**62. FARM HILL, Donegal** pre 1835; *demolished*
The lodge to a property comprising house, offices, kiln, corn and flax mills belonging to the Earl of Arran. The lessee Adam McBride.
GRIFFITH

**63. FERN HILL, Kilmacrennan** pre 1834
A very small standard plan three bay single storey lodge. Late Georgian with hipped roof and tiny windows. Entry directly into living room, the chimney stack on an end elevation. In 1858 occupied by Thomas Stephenson. The lessor the Earl of Leitrim.

**64. FORT ROYAL, Rathmullan (2)**
Another seat of the Wrays of Donegal is now a hotel.
**North Lodge** c1840; *ruinous*
**South Lodge** c1845
Opposite the gates is a one and a half storey three bay two up two down lodge. Simple bargeboards with sharp finials to hipknobs repeated on the dainty little timber porch to the double-leafed front door with semicircular fanlight. The windows to the main elevation bipartite with dressed stone surrounds and plain label-moulded lintels, just like those to the side gate lodge at Eglantine, Co Down (qv). Neat, harled and whitewashed. Low framing quadrant walls. Both lodges for Mr Charles Wray.

**65. FORT STEWART, Ramelton** pre 1834; *ruinous*
The lodge reduced to a shell. Two roomed single storey, its main two bay elevation parallel to the road and forward of the gates beyond. The entrance looks to be of an age that would coincide with the time when Sir James Stewart employed the architect John Hargrave to carry out minor works in 1823. A big mid-Georgian pile surrounded by good plantations beautifully situated on the shores of Lough Swilly.

**66. FORT WILLIAM, Ballyshannon** pre 1834; *demolished*
Probably built for John Tredennick but gone by late in the 19th century. Contiguous with the other seat of the family at Camlin (qv).

**67. FOX HALL, Letterkenny** pre 1834/pre 1903; *ruinous*
The first lodge on the site was probably built just after the Neo-Classical house for Mr John Chambers in about 1830. Its successor was perhaps erected when the property passed to Mr Philip Doyne in 1865.

**68. GLENALLA, Rathmullan** c1860
Built by Thomas B Hart. On the evidence of Picturesque estate cottages and the school in the vicinity, the lodge has been shorn of many of its decorative features. One and a half storey in pleasant uncoursed rubble stone, its bargeboards are plain, the windows lacking attractive glazing bars.

**69. GLEN GOLLAN, Buncrana** pre 1833
A pretty, small Georgian single storey three bay building with a hipped roof, which has been tastefully extended. Good big square stone piers and dwarf wall quadrants to smaller outer piers. Elegant contemporary gates and railings. Probably built for a Mr Thomas Norman before his death in 1833.

**70. GLENMORE, Ballybofey (2)**
Unlike the Georgian house which was reworked in half timbered Elizabethan fashion the lodges are unpretentious, one dating from before 1835, the other c1840. Both for a Charles Style, from a junior branch of the family which owned nearby Cloghan Lodge (qv).
ROWAN (1979)

**71. GLENVEAGH CASTLE, Kilmacrennan (2)**
The notable gardens and fairy tale Baronial castle of 1870 for the Adair family in a beautifully wild and once remote estate with a deerpark, has no lodges worthy of, or contemporary with, the castle. All rather derisory.
**Outer Lodge** c1920
Formerly a single storey two bay gabled structure, it has a later inept extension with thatch, probably applied to corrugated asbestos which remains exposed on the original structure. Georgian style squared sash windows in roughcast walls. Moulded string courses below high eaves. Very strange.
**Inner Lodge** c1920
Single storey three bay symmetrical with low pitch of the gabled roof matched by the bracketed canopy over the front door. Roughcast and plain.

**72. GOOREY LODGE, Malin** pre 1834; *demolished*
Built by the Harveys of Malin Hall (qv), the lodge had gone before 1848.

**73. GORTGOWAN, Moville** c1860
Apart from having squared pane sash windows, a lodge identical in every respect to those at Carrownaff Lodge (qv) further south. Postdating an attractive Regency villa. Once a rectory, the lodge may have been built for the prosperous incumbent Rev Charles Seymour. One and a half storey three bay, the left hand bay a breakfront gabled like the side elevations with wave and foil carved bargeboards. The walls stuccoed with quoins and Tudor style label mouldings to Classical windows.

**74. GORTLEE, Letterkenny** pre 1834; *demolished*
The lodge built for the Boyd family had disappeared by the late 19th century.

**75. GREENCASTLE, Greencastle** c 1845;
Plain one and a half storey two up two down with a projecting central hall similarly gabled. Possibly built by Sir Francis Chichester.

**76. GREENFIELD, Stranorlar** pre 1835; *demolished*
A short-lived building disappearing before the 1845 Ordnance Survey.

**77. GREENFORT, Portsalon** c1810
A late Georgian style lodge now lying exposed to the Atlantic gales, with neither tree nor avenue. Little single storey, two roomed building with a hipped roof. Two bay, the right hand one the front door. Walls harled, the side elevation has a later bay window. Once the seat of Humphrey Babington. Deserted.

**78. GREENHILLS, Convoy (2)**
**Rear Lodge** pre 1835; *demolished*
**Front Lodge** pre 1835; *ruinous*
William Fenwick may have built the lodges upon acquiring the property through marriage to Rebecca Sophia Nesbitt, daughter of the previous owner.

**79. HIGGINSTOWN, Ballyshannon** pre 1904; *demolished*
A lodge opposite the gates now gone.

**80. HOLYMOUNT, Rathmullan** pre 1834; *demolished*
Narcissus Batt must have built this lodge before he bought The Lodge (qv) nearby in 1832. Upon the estate passing to a John McGhee, the lodge fell into ruin and had gone before 1900.

**81. HORNHEAD, Dunfanaghy** pre 1834
Standard three bay single storey lodge now almost unrecognisable through extensions. Probably for Captain William Stewart at the entrance to the sad afforested remnants of the park which passed out of Stewarts' hands in 1936
TRENCH (1945)

**82. INCHENAGH, Lifford** pre 1904; *demolished*

**83. INVER RECTORY, Inver** c1830
A quaint little building for the Rev Alexander Montgomery. Simply a standard single storey, three bay building with harled walls below a hipped roof and bracketed eaves. Ordinary but for its wide tripartite window openings with three-pointed arch stone lintels, repeated over the door opening to form a fanlight. These singlular square-paned windows can be seen on a once identical lodge to Drumbristan glebe (qv) across Donegal Bay. Boarded up it seems to owe its survival to a resident colony of bats. Unremarkable square stone gate piers.

**84. KILDERRY, Muff** pre 1831; *demolished*
A lodge perhaps erected by General George Vaughan Hart for his "straggling, amusing, intriguing, lady-like" mansion.
HART (1907)

**85. KILLAGHTEE GLEBE, Inver** pre 1834; *demolished*
The lodge had gone before 1904.

**86. KILLCADDAN, Killygordon** pre 1836; *demolished*
A seat once of the Knox family.

**87. KILLINDARRAGH, Lifford (2)**
both pre 1840; *both demolished*
To a property previously called Nassau Hall of the Stewart family leased from the Earl of Erne.

**88. KILLYGORDON, Killygordon** pre 1836
Abandoned standard Georgian single storey, three bay lodge below a hipped roof. To an unassuming Georgian gentry farmer's house formerly another property of the Mansfield family.

**89. KILMACREDDAN, Inver** pre 1834; *demolished*
Built by the Nesbitt family, the lodge had gone before the end of the 19th century.

**90. KILTOY LODGE, Letterkenny** pre 1834; *demolished*
Described by Alistair Rowan as a "pretty thatched lodge opposite the gates" in 1979. Now swept away by road widening. The house occupant in 1836 was the Rev William Boyd. No photographic record known to survive.
ROWAN (1979)

**91. LAPUTA, Ballyshannon** pre 1835; *demolished*
The lodge to this pretty Georgian villa for Mr George Johnston.

**92. LAUREL HILL, Castlefinn** pre 1906; *demolished*

**93. THE LODGE, Rathmullan (2)**
The house built by Lieut-Col. Andrew Knox of Prehen, Co Londonderry (qv) "whose family went there for the sea bathing in the summer" was sold in 1832 to Mr Narcissus Batt of Purdysburn Co Down (qv). Upon his death in 1840 his son Robert set about improving the property, having moved from Holymount (qv) nearby. He enlarged the house and provided the estate with two gate lodges and changed its name to Rathmullan House.

**Secondary Entrance** ("Rose Cottage") c1841
Opposite the gates to the stableyard entrance a modest but pleasantly proportioned lodge of low lines. Standard plan, three bay, single storey with a hipped roof and a tiny central chimney stack. A small hall projection has an open pediment. Georgian style squared sash windows in harled walls nicely maintained in whitewash to set off pretty climbing roses.

**Main Entrance** c1841

More self-conscious is this single storey three bay lodge on a square plan with pyramidal roof rising to a small chimney stack aloft having recessed panels. Below the extended bracketed eaves, the walls stuccoed with squared Georgian style sash windows. In dressed stone are plinth, quoins and little pedimented distyle Roman Doric portico to the front door. On the facade to the road is a canted bay eyeing the gates from below a half-umbrello roof. There are many features here reminiscent of the work of the architect Thomas Jackson. Good extensive railed ogee gate sweep with plain corniced square stone piers. The house is now an hotel.
TRENCH (1945)

**94. LOUGH ESKE CASTLE, Donegal (3)**
**West Lodge** pre 1835; *demolished*
In an exquisite location by the banks of the lough, Thomas Brooke built himself a house here in 1751, the lodge to which has gone. A replacement mansion for this earlier dwelling was built in the Elizabethan Revival style 1859-61 for a later Thomas Brooke to designs by the architect Fitzgibbon Louch. Two new porters' lodges date from this time.

**Boat-house Lodge** c1861; architect probably Fitzgibbon Louch
A two storey house over a vaulted basement at water level which provided storage for the family boats. Two up two down, gabled with stuccoed walls and stone quoins. The ground floor windows are bipartite with lintel stones forming a pair of lancet heads framing Y tracery, the lights to the upper floor Georgian style squared pane. The eaves have an eccentric decorative fretted fascia in the form of rows of large pendulous onions. This is repeated on the single storey projecting hallway which also features carved bargeboards, ornate collar tie, purlin ends

and pendant hipknob, much as the main gables. Corbelled three flue brick chimney stack. The stucco appears to have been applied later, over what may have been exposed stonework.

**Crossroads Lodge** c1860; architect possibly Fitzgibbon Louch
One and a half storey two up two down symmetrical three bay structure opposite the gates. In rubble masonry there are wave and foil carved timber bargeboards to main gables and projecting hall, the pattern used also as decorative fascias. Spiky hipknob to the hall and fancy cresting to all ridges. The windows square paned sash. Now whitewashed over, the chimney stack as the other lodge.
ROWAN (1979)

**95. LURGYVALE RECTORY, Kilmacrennan (2)**
**North Lodge** c1840; *demolished*
**South Lodge** pre 1834; *demolished*
Earlier of the two lodges, opposite the gate probably built not long after the 1815 rectory.

**96. LYRTLE'S GROVE, Letterkenny** pre 1834; *demolished*
Gone before the end of the 19th century.

**97. MALIN HALL, Malin (2)**
A house built in 1758 for the Harvey family by the shores of Trawbeaga Bay on the outskirts of the village.

**Village Gate** c1830
Late Georgian lodge of standard two room plan three bay under a hipped roof. Single storey, the windows displaying in their label mouldings the novelty of the Tudor Picturesque movement.

**North Lodge** c1825
Another late Georgian lodge of standard plan three bay single storey but having a hipped-gable roof. Chiefly memorable for being the most northerly lodge in the country. Both built for John Harvey who inherited in 1820.
YOUNG (1929)

**98. MARBLE HILL, Portnablagh (2)** pre 1834/c1895

There was a lodge here before 1834 probably to the earlier house on the site for the Babington family. The estate passed to Mr G Barclay early in the nineteenth century and he built the present elegant villa probably by either Sir Richard Morrison or J B Keane. The surviving lodge, however, is a replacement of more recent times. A pretty Arts-and-Crafts Classical style building having a steep hipped roof bellcast at the eaves, with secret hip flashings. Single storey, the front three bay roughcast elevation has a projecting porch under its own hipped roof carried on timber posts. On the avenue elevation is a bow window with square- paned casement lights like the rest. For Hugh Law who purchased the estate in 1894. The low concave quadrant walls similarly roughcast with square stone gate piers, crowned with small pine cone finials probably from the earlier entrance.
BENCE-JONES (1988)

**99. MEENGLASS, Ballybofey** pre 1904; *demolished*
The lodge to the demesne once of the Hewitt family, Viscounts Lifford.

**100. MILLFIELD, Buncrana** c1880; architects possibly Turner and Babington
Probably built by John Brice Mullin, a three bay single storey symmetrical building with a pyramidal roof and central chimney stack. Gabled breakfront hall, the windows paired with segmental heads. Toothed brick dressings and quoins. Three recessed panel piers with ball finials carry ornate carriage gates and one wicket gate in ornate cast iron. There is an identical lodge at St Mura's (qv) nearby.
YOUNG (1909)

**101. MONELLAN, Killygordon** pre 1836
An unremarkable little building for Samuel Delap.

**102. MOUNT CHARLES HALL, Mount Charles (3)**
A seat of the Marquess of Conyngham of Slane Castle, Co Meath. These lodges are relatively plain and it is a pity that Francis Nathaniel Conyngham, the 2nd Marquess, did not see fit to employ the architect T F Hunt here, as he had done on his English property Bifrons in Kent, where he designed in his pioneering cottage Picturesque manner.

**Shore Lodge** pre 1834
Dull and "improved".

**West Lodge** pre 1834
A peculiar building, one and a half storey two up two down three bay symmetrical with an extremely steep roof pitch. Carved wave and foil bargeboards. The attic room windows are Georgian style squared sash whereas those below are transomed and mullioned with Picturesque diamond pattern casements. Simple sheeted front door, a mouth organ fanlight over. Walls harled. Basic square ashlar piers with nice plain spear-topped iron gates.

**East Lodge** c1840
Modest one and a half storey three bay lodge with Tudor label mouldings.

**103. MULROY HOUSE, Carrigart** c1865; architect perhaps William Burn

For the 3rd Earl of Leitrim, William Sydney Clements, one of the most oppressive and hated landlords in the country, who was murdered not far from here in 1878. A commodious essay in the mid-Victorian Picturesque Tudor Revival style. The Scottish architect William Burn, specialist in the Neo-Jacobean manor house style, is thought by Mark Bence-Jones to have worked for the family both here and at their other seat at Lough Rynn, Co Leitrim. This would have been one of his last commissions. A one and a half storey irregular lodge on an L plan in uncoursed rubble with red brick dressings and quoins. On the front gable a single storey ashlar canted bay with a flat roof, and alongside, over the internal angle the main roof carries down in a catslide to form a front door canopy. All windows small square-paned sash, those to the attic rooms bipartite. Bargeboards simply carved with decorative collar ties and hangers. Sawtooth earthenware crestings and finials.
WARD & LOCK (1894); BENCE-JONES (1988)

**104. MURVAGH, Ballintra**
(see DRUMBRISTAN GLEBE)

**105. NASSAU HALL, Lifford**
(see KILLINDARRAGH)

**106. OAKFIELD, Raphoe (2)**
Sometime early in the nineteenth century this delightful Queen Anne style villa of 1739 ceased to be a deanery for the Diocese of Raphoe and was acquired by the Johnston family who furnished the park and added two gate lodges.

**Rear Lodge** pre 1835; *demolished*

**Front Lodge** pre 1835; *demolished*

An amusing little design which attempted to mimic the house with its dormer windows to the front and the side pitches of its hipped roof. In the Cottage Orné vogue, one and a half storey with a two bay front facade. In 1985 the roof was in corrugated iron with decorative metal cresting, probably replacing the original thatch. Sadly it has recently been demolished to make way for a modern bungalow, which at least has dormer windows in the same vein.
I.A.A., CO DONEGAL PHOTOGRAPHS REFS: 11/0 AND 11/1

**107. OAK PARK, Letterkenny (2)**
both pre 1834; *both demolished*
Two lodges built by the Wray family, one had gone by 1845 the other before 1903.

**108. PORTHALL, Ballymagorry** pre 1834; *demolished*
The lodge to Michael Priestley's refined house for Robert Vaughan had gone before 1903.

**109. PORTNASON, Ballyshannon (2)**
Two Neo-Classical lodges for a Robert Johnston.

**Secondary Entrance** c1880

Off a square plan a single storey three bay stuccoed lodge. From the hipped roof rises a row of four diagonally-set cream brick chimney stacks. Openings with banded surrounds, the walls quoined. Modern plate glass windows. Looks like the lodge at Rhanbuoy, Co Antrim (qv). Square cast iron gate posts with spiky ball finials.

**Main Entrance** c1870

Single storey three bay lodge under a hipped roof. A gabled central breakfront frames the front door with an incongruous hood moulding to the semicircular fanlight. Quoins to breakfront and corners. Segmentally-headed architraved windows in stuccoed walls. The eaves has paired brackets. Gates and pillars removed.

**110. PORT VILLA, Greencastle** pre 1900; *demolished*

**111. PROSPECT HILL, Carrigans** pre 1835
Unnoteworthy lodge to another seat of the McClintocks of Dunmore (qv).

**112. RAPHOE PALACE, Raphoe (2)**
Originally erected as a fortress in about 1661 the palace was occupied by the Church of Ireland bishops until the 1830s. Beautified and repaired in the late eighteenth century by Bishop Oswald who walled in fifty acres of demesne between 1763 and 1780, which he planted with oak, ash and laburnum, as well as making some improvements to the house, adding a new kitchen and offices. It would be at this time that the town lodge was built.

**Town Lodge** c1770

Flanking the gateway are two ivy-clad octagonal turrets with mock loopholes and crenellated parapets, in coursed rubble. To the right a wicket gate with segmentally- headed arch in a battlemented wall. To the left a balancing short wing wall connects to the lodge. This Romantic castellated entrance is of later date, c1800. The lodge is a one and a half storey antique looking building with a traditional mid-Georgian look. Under an undulating hipped roof of thick aged slates, from which a bulky decrepit chimney stack of four flues projects, is a sizeable building with very low eaves and ceilings. The gable-on elevation alongside the gateway has a basic gablet window over a dreadful modern ground floor window insertion. The whole a delightful whitewashed, harled relic. In 1834 it is described as a "School House", by which time the palace had become a private residence which it remained until its final demise in the 1870s.

**Ballindrait Lodge** pre 1834; *demolished*

POST CHAISE COMPANION (1786); FFOLLIOTT (1975)

**113. RATHMULLAN, Rathmullan**
(see THE LODGE)

**114. RAYMUNTERDONEY GLEBE, Falcarragh** pre 1858; *demolished*
Noted by Griffith in his valuation of 1858, a gate lodge to an unoccupied property of Rev Alexander Nixon which was probably the rectory house of 1815. Not located, assumed gone.
GRIFFITH

**115. REDCASTLE, Moville (2)**
One of the most substantial older houses in Donegal, a description which is also appropriate for the surviving lodge.

**West Lodge** c1830

Between the road and the gates is a late Georgian lodge, typical in form but on an unusually grand scale. Single storey three bay with a hipped roof on an extended eaves with the inevitable bracket support. The central doorway later reduced to a window, the openings sealed up in whitewashed walls. Two gate pillars roughcast with pyramidal cappings and ball finials, the gates contemporary. Deserted.

**East Lodge** pre 1834; *demolished*

Both lodges built for Mr Atkinson Wray.
ROWAN (1979)

**116. REDFORD GLEBE, Culdaff** c1840; *demolished*
Built for the rector Rev R Hamilton.

**117. ROCHFORT LODGE, Bundoran** pre 1836
Like the neighbouring lodge to Daneville (qv) a tiny, plain single storey gabled building. Three bay asymmetrical, the front door to the left. Probably originally thatched. Named after the Rochfort family.

**118. ROCKFORT, Buncrana** pre 1834; *demolished*
The seat of Rev Hamilton Stewart, incumbent of Lower Fahan and "... a respectable feature of improvement on the property of Daniel Todd, Esq, of Buncrana Castle ... It comprehends a good mansion-house, and eighteen acres of a handsome lawn, whose base is washed by the waters of Lough Swilly". Thus did Atkinson describe the demesne but failed to notice the gate lodge which would then have been in existence.
ATKINSON (1833)

**119. ROCKHILL, Letterkenny (3)**
This estate belonged to the Chambers family until the early 1830s when it was acquired by John Vandeleur Stewart, of Ards House (qv). He set about altering and greatly enlarging the house.

**North-west Lodge** pre 1835; *demolished*

**North-east Lodge** pre 1846; *demolished*

Opposite the gates.

**Back Lodge** c1840;
architect perhaps John Hargrave

Far off the beaten track is a most surprising essay in the Picturesque style. A most forlorn sight this large "Hansel and Gretel" pattern book lodge lies rotting and empty. One and a half storey on an L

*Rockhill, Back Lodge*

plan, three up three down with a spacious dog leg staircase hall and landing, it boasts all sorts of Picturesque devices. Stuccoed, most of the windows are label moulded with cast iron lattice panes having pivoted openers. To two gable elevations are single storey flat-roofed chamfered rectangular bays with tripartite windows and castellated parapets. The front door has a pointed, diamond-paned fanlight and on the wall projecting alongside a round- headed niche. The eaves projects considerably over big curved brackets which also carry a dormer on the front elevation, jetty fashion. On a side facade is a curious miniature blind oriel feature high up, seemingly serving no purpose other than to relieve a blank gable. The steeply- pitched roofs decorated with the prettiest of fretted bargeboards in the form of ornamental teardrops, weeping for its demise. Sharp finials and nice pendants to hipknobs, the roof finished in big scalloped slates, on the ridge of which are two stone bases each supporting the most precarious pairs of brick chimney stacks, three octagonal, one square. Despite its dilapidation in 1987, the generous accommodation would have made repair and rehabilitation worth while. Its architect is not recorded but John Hargrave had worked here for the Chambers earlier as he had for the Stewarts at Ards and it is conceivable that he may have been responsible for the design before his untimely death by drowning in 1833.
FRAZER (1838); YOUNG (1909); ROWAN (1979)

**120. ROCKVILLE, Ballyshannon** c1840; *demolished*
A lodge which had disappeared before the turn of the century. Probably built by T W Crawford and coeval with the pretty Picturesque villa residence.

**121. ROSE LODGE, Bundoran** pre 1836; *demolished*
Latterly rather quaintly called Dingle-i-coush, the lodge had gone before the end of the nineteenth century.

**122. ROXBOROUGH GLEBE, Carrick** pre 1847; *demolished*
The lodge would appear also to have had the function of a "Sewing School".

**123. ST CATHERINE'S, Killybegs** c1840; *demolished*

**124. ST ERNAN'S, Donegal** c1845
A pretty lodge delightfully situated defending the entrance "to a furlong of causeway built by his grateful tenantry" for John Hamilton, to save him from Atlantic tides on his approach to a retreat which he built in 1825. He had become disenchanted with Brown Hall (qv) which he had inherited on his father's death in 1811. A one and a half storey two up two down Picturesque cottage with ornamental serrated bargeboard to gables. One elevation aligned obtusely with the entrance gates, a single storey canted bay window looks on. In uncoursed squared masonry now painted over, a flat- roofed rear return and entrance hall recently added are hardly compatible. John Hamilton enjoyed his island idyll until his death in 1884 when it passed to A H Foster his daughter's husband.
HAMILTON (1894); DEERY (1948); BURKE (1904)

**125. ST MURAS, Buncrana (2)** c1880; architects probably Turner and Babington
A house of 1870 in Neo-Classical style for D M Colquhoun by the practice of Turner and Williamson. Sometime later two lodges appear. That which survives is a three bay, single storey symmetrical building, under a pyramidal roof with a central chimney. Gabled breakfront hall with simple decorative bargeboards over a door with segmental head to the fanlight. Pairs of windows each side have identical heads. Red brick dressings and quoins. Piers with ball finials. An identical lodge was built at Millfield (qv) nearby. Now a special care home.
ROWAN (1979)

**126. SALTHILL, Mount Charles** c1840
The graceful house built as a land agent's house to the neighbouring Marquess of Conyngham's estate of Mount Hall (qv). The lodge's evolution is rather difficult to assess, but it was initially probably a one and a half storey three bay two up two down affair in Tudor Picturesque manner. Two windows with label mouldings remain but the front door has been replaced by an ugly projecting chimney, the entrance now via a single storey gabled hall tacked on to a rear extension gable which forms a double pile. All windows may formerly have had pretty little pointed Gothick glazing bars, now only evident to the attic bedrooms. The ground floor windows now square paned, paired sashes in roughcast rendered walls.

**127. SEAVIEW, Bundoran** c1880
The Neo-Classical lodge a smaller version of the villa, but a stone's throw distant by the shore. Single storey stuccoed with plinth and channelled pilaster quoins. Moulded window surrounds with segmental heads. Two bay deep by three bay front elevation, the fanlit doorway, with Doric pilaster casing, away off centre. Hipped roof with yellow brick chimney stack. Now called VILLA NOVA and a convent of the Sisters of Mercy.

**128. SHANNON, Raphoe** c1840; *demolished*
A lodge built by James C Ball.

**129. SHARON GLEBE, Newtowncunningham** c1840
A lodge located opposite the entrance, derelict and nondescript.

**130. STONEWOLD, Ballyshannon** pre 1904; *demolished*
Gone as is the house, the site of which was submerged by the River Erne hydroelectric scheme. Perhaps built by Mr Robert Crawford who came to the property after Edward Allingham.
YOUNG (1909)

**131. TIRNALEAGUE, Carndonagh (2)**
**Rear Lodge** pre 1840; *demolished*

A charming standard lodge, boxy, its hipped roof with high bracketed eaves. Eccentric "drape" heads to latticed pane lights set into round arched recesses in roughcast walls.
**Front Lodge** pre 1840
A simple single storey structure with a bracketed eaves to hipped roof. Whitewashed rendered walls. Both lodges for the Carey family.

**132. TYRCALLAN, Stranorlar** pre 1835; *demolished*
A shooting lodge built here by Henry Stewart in about 1800, in a demesne where he "... exceeds all this county, and perhaps any individual of Ireland for planting", still obvious to this day. Among the improvements were an observatory and a gate lodge which no longer survive.
McPARLAN (1802); LEWIS (1837); ROWAN (1979)

**133. VILLA NOVA, Bundoran**
(see SEAVIEW)

**134. WHITECASTLE, Moville** pre 1833; *demolished*
A short-lived lodge, having disappeared before 1848, to a pretty mid-Georgian villa in a miniature park, for the Carey family.
ROWAN (1979)

**135. WOODHILL, Ardara (2)** both pre 1834; *both demolished*
Both lodges to this venerable property of the Nesbitt family have gone. They were probably built by James Ezekiel Nesbitt or his father George. The seat passed by marriage to the Tredennicks of Camlin (qv) who rebuilt the house in 1886.
YOUNG (1929)

**136. WOODLANDS, Stranorlar (2)**
Both lodges built by James Johnston Esq who had also erected the house not long before.
**Clady Road Lodge** c1840; *demolished*
**Rear Lodge** c1840
A type of late Georgian style building which was widespread. Symmetrical three bay single storey with a hipped roof.
ATKINSON (1833)

# COUNTY DOWN

**1. AGHADERG GLEBE, Loughbrickland** pre 1859; *demolished*
To the rectory of 1801 for Rev Geoffrey Lefroy.

**2. ANNADALE HALL, Newtownbreda** pre 1858; *demolished*
Formerly known as Galwally and occupied by a George McCartney Portis it was renamed after Lady Anne Mornington, mother of the Duke of Wellington, who lived here for a period. The big square Georgian mansion passed into the hands of Alexander McDonnell in about 1840 and on his death in 1855 to his son-in-law Robert Calwell. It was one of these two who built the gate lodge which was demolished early this century after the house was destroyed by fire in 1921 and the park sold up for the Hampton Park housing development.
DEANE (1977)

**3. ANNADALE, Newtownbreda** c1860; architect not known; *demolished*

(*U.M.*)

There was also a pre 1834 lodge on this site. A tantalising glimpse of the later lodge can be seen in a late Victorian photograph which shows the multi-gabled Picturesque Italianate house in the background. The proud top-hatted gatekeeper stands outside the projecting hallway of the lodge, sufficient of it showing to give a clue to its considerable architectural pretensions. In ashlar its eaves were decorated with a sculpted foliated corbel course, the gable rose to an ornate cast iron apex finial, the ridge embellished with fleur-de-lys cresting. Two outer square stone pillars to the gate sweep had recessed panel shafts and ball finials over. These flanked very decorative cast iron carriage gates with a pair of wickets on each side separated by two "chinese-lantern" type piers with arabesque ornamentation. The 1863 occupant David McConnell. Both lodge and house long demolished to make way for suburban spread.
PHOTOGRAPH (U.M.) Ref 10/62/4

**4. ANNA'S COTTAGE, Belfast South** pre 1834; *demolished*
A lodge on the Saintfield Road access has gone, the drive to the house now Haypark Avenue. The property in 1823 of a Christopher Strong.

**5. ANNSBOROUGH COTTAGE, Castlewellan** pre 1834/c1860; architect possibly Thomas Turner
The early O.S. map indicates a tiny square lodge built by James Murland who had founded the great neighbouring linen mills. Clearly this became outdated, for the present lodge looks to be mid-Victorian and was doubtless built by Charles Murland on his succession to the property when the house received a face-lift and was renamed Ardnabannon. Single storey three bay symmetrical with a gabled roof. Delicate moulded surrounds to openings and a corniced chimney stack in similar Neo-Classical vein. Extended to four bay later with an additional room. Deserted.
MOURNE; U.A.H.S. (1975)

**6. ARDENZA, Belfast South**
(see LANEVAN)

**7. ARDIGON, Killyleagh** pre 1859; *demolished*
To an elegant early Victorian Neo-Classical house Robert Heron built a contemporary gate lodge across the road from the entrance.

**8. ARDMAINE, Newry** c1900
A modest building with Georgian style squared windows. One and a half storey gabled, granite window surrounds and quoins. Three bay symmetrical.

**9. ARDS HOSPITAL, Newtownards**
(see NEWTOWNARDS WORKHOUSE)

**10. ARDMORE, Ballygowan** pre 1901; *demolished*

**11. ARDMORE, Downpatrick**
(see THE HILL)

**12. ARDNAGREENA, Belfast North** c1890
Built for Charles W Black (solicitor) a peculiar Classical Picturesque mixture. Single storey stuccoed on an L plan but with a symmetrical three bay front elevation. From the hipped roof projects a gabled hallway with carved bargeboards, fretted with fleur-de-lys and fancy hipknob. To segmentally-headed windows moulded surrounds with keystones. Quoins. Disfigured by modern windows and chimney stack. Now severed from the Neo-Classical house later called Lake View.

**13. ARDNALEA, Holywood** c1870
Facing the road alongside a vanished gateway the three bay symmetrical front of a standard plan lodge. Single storey with a hipped roof it is constructed of rubble stone having toothed brick dressings to the windows. These have lost much in modernisation, their paired sashes with central box mullions removed. Balancing the entrance is a watchman's cottage in similar fashion, also built by the Crawford family.

**14. ARDTULLAGH, Crawfordsburn**
(see WOODLANDS)

**15. ARDVARNA, Belfast North**
(see BALLYNISERT)

**16. ARDVIEW, Killinchy** pre 1858
A long low single storey gabled cottage opposite the gates, now much renovated. Built by Robert Potter.

**17. ARDVILLE, Holywood (2)**
Built by James Lemon to an earlier house, two late Victorian gate lodges one of which survives. (c1880). A two storey house roughcast with an eaves band on which are delicate carved timber brackets. Rows of scalloped slates to roof. This must be a replacement for one of two lodges recorded in the Griffith Valuation of 1863.
GRIFFITH

**18. ARNO'S VALE, Rostrevor** pre 1834; *demolished*
A late 18th century marine cottage named after a Tuscan river valley, built by John Darley. It saw a succession of owners one of whom added a gate lodge but it is difficult to say which as the lodge has gone. Lord Lifford was in residence in 1820 followed three years later by James Moore after he moved from nearby Green Park (qv).
CROWE (1973)

**19. ASHDENE, Comber** c1900
A chunky little lodge built in the same materials as the contemporary big house. In uncoursed squared quarry-faced sandstone, the segmentally-headed openings of the three bay symmetrical front elevation in orange brick dressings. The brick is further used to emphasise the clipped verge gables. There are good English Arts-and-Crafts gate piers in matching stone and brick, each with its little tiled roof. For George P Culverwell

**20. ASHFIELD, Dromore** c1860; *demolished*
A lodge opposite the gate built for Maurice Lindsay. His father, a scion of the Tullyhinan (qv) family, had set up a factory for weaving heavy fabrics here in 1828.
GREEN (1963)

**21. ASH GROVE, Newry** pre 1834; *demolished*
For the Boyd family, later the Moorheads, and now a school.

**22. AVONIEL, Belfast South** pre 1858; *demolished*
House and lodge demolished c1933 to make way for a new school development (see below).

**23. AVONIEL P E SCHOOL, Belfast South** c1935; architect R S Wilshere
To a distinguished and extensive classroom and administrative building an equally notable little gate house in the same pleasant mellow brown rustic brick. Two storey, below a steeply pitched hipped roof with a clipped eaves highlighted by a course of brick-on-end. Boxy and rectangular on plan two bay deep by a three bay front elevation with very narrow windows. The central front door in brick surround and low semi-octagonal arch over. Soldier brick repeated to window heads and chimney stack. There are similar gate houses by the same architect at the nearby contemporary public elementary schools at Nettlefield and Elmgrove. (qqv). The finest little house in the district, vandalised and derelict.
LARMOUR (1987)

**24. BALLOO, Bangor** pre 1833; *demolished*
The lodge had gone before 1858 probably having been built by William Steele Nicholson.

**25. BALLYALOLLY, Comber (2)**
**Front Lodge** pre 1833
A standard plain single storey three bay lodge with a hipped roof. Sash windows in harled walls.
**Side Lodge** c1792
Of more consequence is this single storey, three bay symmetrical building having a tall eaves, with unusual moulded cornice, steeply pitched roof and canted ends. Much as the lodges to Florida Manor (qv) but Classical rather than Gothic. The squared Georgian sash windows are

framed by pilasters at each corner with recessed panels. Over the doorway an elliptical spoked fanlight. Roughcast walls. Recently immaculately renovated and extended after earlier work, probably in 1935 when architects Blackwood and Jury rebuilt the house for Rt Hon Captain Herbert Dixon. Located opposite nice contemporary wrought iron gates. Both lodges probably built for the Hamilton family.

**26. BALLYALTON, Newtownards** pre 1858; *demolished*
Although the lodge to this delightful Tudor Gothic style house has gone, fine contemporary octagonal gate piers with cusped top panels in similar manner survive. Probably for the Farrell family.

**27. BALLYBEEN, Comber** c1835; architect not known

The big house for long a seat of James Birch was burnt down early this century, the entrance gates and lodge in pristine condition. These are identical to those which once graced Seymour Hill, Co Antrim (qv). From two outer square piers sweep railed ogee quadrants to four inner hexagonal ones all with panelled shafts and corniced cappings. The robust ironwork by Shaw of Belfast. Stuccoed single storey symmetrical Classical lodge with an entablatured parapet. Behind this a hipped roof rises to a corniced chimney stack bridged in the manner devised by Sir John Vanbrugh. Segmentally-headed wide windows with decorative festooned panels over. The margined glazing is repeated in the double leaf door. Entablatured Tuscan portico of two columns.

**28. BALLYDUGGAN, Downpatrick** pre 1834; *ruinous*
The lodge now a shell on a redundant road, severed from the big house built in 1781 by Capt Henry Webb. Probably erected by John Aynsworth Auchinleck a later owner who owed much of his wealth to smuggling. Basalt construction with brick dressings it probably dates from the period 1810-20 when additions were made to the house.
MINISTRY OF FINANCE (1966)

**29. BALLYEDMOND CASTLE, Rostrevor (2)** pre 1834; *demolished*
The lodges predated the present mansion of c1855 for Alexander Stewart who probably employed Charles Lanyon as his architect. This replaced an earlier "... good plain 2-storey house" of which it is significant to note Maria Edgeworth's description on a visit here in 1806. The house called Fort Hamilton had wings and pavilions one of which she says in a letter to her mother "... looks like any square porter's lodge". At the present entrance off the new road is a pair of "off the shelf" cast iron posts just like those at Beech Hill, Co Monaghan (qv) and Trewmount, Co Tyrone (qv). They have pyramidal "tiled" roofs complete with ogee "dormers" and arabesque shafts.
O.S.M.; EDGEWORTH (1806)

**30. BALLYGOWAN, Dunmurry (2)**
In 1864 the gentleman farmer George Macklin rebuilt the old Drum Cottage as a Neo-Classical villa changing its name in the process and adding a gate lodge.

**Drumbo Entrance** c1864
A simple single storey gabled cottage, two bay to the road. Ornamental carved wavy bargeboards. Spoilt by later metal windows and pebble-dash to the walls.

**Drumbeg Entrance** c1890
In typical late Victorian polychromatic brick, red with cream dressings to doorway, quoins and eaves corbel courses. A distinctive single storey three bay symmetrical design with a steeply pitched hipped roof, the chimney also in decorative brick. The projecting gabled hallway has fretted ornamental bargeboards and hipknob. Softened by Clematis Montana. To the rear a gabled extension in matching materials, dating from c1925. (William Macklin having sold the property in 1894). The entrance piers are probably contemporary with the house, stone octagon with corniced caps. Durable Swedish ironwork designed by the proprietor.

**31. BALLYHOSSETT, Ardglass** c1840
A modest lodge built for the Gracey family. Single storey, three bay not quite symmetrical with clipped verge gables. Built in rubble stone, whitewashed with cast iron lattice paned casement windows. Unoccupied but nicely maintained. A pair of fine Classical gate pillars probably late Georgian. Square with rusticated V-jointing and corniced cappings.

**32. BALLYKILAIRE, Bangor** c1880; architect possibly James Hamilton
A house and gate lodge with a distinctly Scottish feel, the former looking like the work of Glaswegian James Hamilton, the latter very much a smaller version of Alexander "Greek" Thomson's "Croyland", Newton Mearns, Renfrewshire of 1875. Built for Capt A M Henderson. A decorative little single storey building on an L plan. Gabled, in the apexes of which are delicately fretted panels copying the big house. The verandahed porch is formed by a catslide roof supported on timber posts and a fretwork bracket. On the leading gable a bow window in rendered walls. Unusual stone piers, chamfered shafts, lobed frieze and capping block ornate with recessed roundel motifs.
BANGOR AND GROOMSPORT; U.A.H.S. (1984)

**33. BALLYLEIDY, Bangor**
(see CLANDEBOYE)

**34. BALLYLINTAGH, Annahilt** c1850
Standard two roomed three bay symmetrical single storey lodge below a hipped roof. Stone construction with brick window dressings. There are paltry label mouldings to openings which contain bipartite lights with segmental heads. Originally the seat of the Cowan family, the lodge probably built for James Smith a later owner. Now derelict, the demesne run down. Grand Classical gate pillars, with channel jointed rustication. Layered pyramidal caps carry coronets with unicorn crests (lacking their horns). The date 1874 inscribed.

**35. BALLYMENOCH, Holywood (2)** c1805; *both demolished*
A property originally of the Hamiltons was acquired by Cunningham Gregg of Macedon, Co Antrim (qv) in 1802. It is likely that he built the house and lodges not long after. These charming lodges and the old house are things of the past. Known affectionately as the "ink-wells" each was single storey, two roomed ovoid on plan below a conical roof with central circular stone chimney stack. In basalt rubble laid haphazardly by contrast was a moulded stone eaves course. The panelled front door had a doorcase of Tuscan pilasters and a fanlight with Gothic glazing pattern in moulded surround. Flanking also under elliptical heads two little

*Ballymenoch*

squared pane windows. Similarly arched recesses at each end contained larger windows. One lodge was taken down in the 1930s the other in 1971. The demesne now a public park.
DIXON AND HEATLEY (1983)

**36. BALLYNISERT, Belfast North**
pre 1902; *demolished*
The lodge gone to a park of John Vernon, later called Ardvarna.

**37. BALLYVALLY, Banbridge** c1825
Below a pyramidal roof a painted brick lodge. Single storey on a square plan, two bay deep by three bay symmetrical elevation fronting the road. Square paned Georgian sash windows under elliptical arches. Plain stone gate posts alongside. In 1820 the property of Moses and James Wood.

**38. BALLYWALTER, Ballywalter (7)**
Previously Springvale the seat of the Matthews family, it was purchased in 1846 by Andrew Mulholland. He was made prosperous by the vast York Street linen mills in Belfast and rose to become mayor of that city. He had as a fellow councillor Charles Lanyon who as his architect was to transform the house into a great Italian palazzo and provide two gate lodge designs in similar manner. It is these two buildings and one of late Victorian date which are worthy of notice. The other four of the period 1834-1858 are insignificant.
**Main Entrance** c1850;
architect Charles Lanyon

As an appetizer for the big house the architect supplied a beautiful little Italianate lodge. This was a model that Lanyon also used at Eglantine (qv) in the same county for a younger brother of Andrew and at Moneyglass and Dunderave (qqv) both in Co Antrim. A perfectly symmetrical suave building on a cruciform plan in fawn-coloured sandstone and stucco. Dominating is the three semicircular-arched "porte-cochère", with archivolts springing from square piers to scrolled keystones. In the gable over a roundel with the Mulholland crest, an escallop gules. The sides of the porch have shouldered arches and pretty pierced balustrades. There are paired scrolled brackets to eaves, repeated as purlin ends to gables. To the side elevations are tall semicircular headed windows with margined glazing set into recesses. Flanking are smaller subsidiary lights in Venetian vein. Uniting the composition a moulded stringcourse at arch springing level. At the junction of ridges is a big square panelled chimney stack with bracketed cornice. There is an equally impressive entrance sweep. Extensive walled quadrants are contained by big stone pillars. These frame iron railings containing wicket gates which flank the big carriage gates in matching robust and decorative cast iron. Each sandstone pillar is built up with deeply rusticated panelled blocks off a carved plinth. A plain frieze is surmounted by a moulded capping. Pretty scrolled volutes to the gate stops as at Cromore, Co Londonderry (qv).
**Holland's Lodge** c1850; architect probably Charles Lanyon; *demolished*
The lodge was sited on the original western perimeter of the estate but it became isolated when the neighbouring Ballyatwood property was acquired and the public road was re-routed around the new boundary. Contemporary with the main entrance, it may have been identical, its outline on the O.S Map shows it also to have been cruciform on plan. There are some remnants of its cut sandstone to be seen. The gate screen, which has been reconstructed at the new West Gate, is also the same as that main gate.
**West Entrance** c1900; architect probably William J Fennell

A forthright Neo-Classical design in sandstone and stucco. Single storey on an L plan each arm of which is gabled with a mutule pediment containing the Mulholland coat-of-arms and their motto SEMPER PRAECINCTUS. To each apex an acroterion moulding. On the road elevation a canted bay window surveys the gates, its openings architraved and parapet balustraded. The avenue elevation contains a semicircular-headed window framed with pilasters and a keystoned archivolt. In the internal angle a porch with a bowed entablature carried on a pair of Tuscan columns and responds resting on a base which is carried around the lodge as a stringcourse which corresponds with the cills. Rusticated quoins. Puny chimney stack. On this dull, flat eastern side of the Ards peninsula the Mulhollands, raised to be Barons Dunleath in 1893, landscaped the estate to become the beautiful plantation to be found today.
ROWAN (1967)

**39. BALLYWARD LODGE, Castlewellan**
c1825

"Ballyward is a good 2 storey house pleasantly situated and surrounded by belts of planting tastefully laid out. It was built in 1811 by the father of the present resident proprietor Francis Charles Beers, Esq JP." It was this gentleman who built the lodge slightly later in contrast to the pretty Classical villa, an essay in the Gothic taste. Single storey under a hipped roof, its three bay front elevation dominated by the projecting canted hallway with its half umbrello roof. The door has a semicircular fanlight, the sidelights lattice paned with lancet heads. Flanking are two larger windows also with pointed arches which have Y-tracery glazing. Walls stuccoed and whitewashed. Probably of an age with the house are the graceful square ashlar pillars. These have pretty fan shaped "Adam" rosettes to their friezes identical to those at Castle Saunderson, Co Monaghan (qv). Corniced cappings.
O.S.M.

**40. BALLYWHITE, Portaferry** c1870
The old house was enlarged and the gate lodge added in the Italianate style by Mr Warnock, a Downpatrick solicitor. One and a half storey, two up two down symmetrical with a gabled roof. Its high eaves has a moulded course returned to the side elevations to form an open pediment. The projecting gabled hallway is flanked by flat arched windows with entablatures on supporting crossettes. Attic bedroom windows semicircular headed with hood mouldings. Walls stuccoed.
BENCE-JONES (1988)

**41. BALLYWILLIAM COTTAGE,**
**Donaghadee** pre 1863; *demolished*
Probably built when Nicholas Delacherois succeeded to the property after Lady Charlotte Jocelyn's death.

**42. BALLYWILLWILL, Castlewellan**
A pleasant long low mansion house in Classical style was built by Rev George Henry McDowell Johnston in 1815. As the U.A.H.S. observed in 1975 the demesne is now a shadow of its former self, having suffered from World War Two requisitioning and the loss of many of its trees.
**Main Entrance** c1815
Off the Ballylough road, now without an avenue but with big late Georgian square granite gate pillars, ashlar with fluted tops which have been almost completely removed. There never was a lodge here.
**Clonvaraghan Gate** c1845

A durable little lodge constructed in coursed, squared rubble galleted, with dressed granite quoins. Single storey three bay symmetrical below a hipped roof. Windows of tiny squared cast iron pattern flank a canted hall projection with a half umbrello roof. The sheeted door has a sophisticated surround comprised of recessed panel pilasters on plinth blocks and a flat entablature over. On the ridge a trio of diagonally set chimney stacks.
MOURNE; U.A.H.S. (1975); O.S.M.

**43. BANBRIDGE CEMETERY, Banbridge**
1883; architects probably
Young and Mackenzie
Big robust late Victorian gatehouse in coursed squared basalt conspicuously dressed with yellow brick. One and a half storey gabled with carved timber brackets to bargeboards and mono-pitch canopy over the front door. Below the front eaves a sandstone panel with the Banbridge coat-of-arms, the motto PER DEUM ET INDUSTRIAM and the date of construction. Convex entrance quadrants terminate in square quarry-faced sandstone pillars with steeply pitched sculpted cappings, gabled to each face with trefoil motifs.

**44. BANFORD, Lawrencetown (2)**
both pre 1833; *both demolished*
A mid-Georgian house built by Robert Jeffrey Nicholson who may also have been responsible for the lodges marked on the 1833 O.S map. Both have gone but Bassett in 1886 states that one of them was in fact a structure known as "Black Castle", a look-out tower built c1772 to warn against the approach of the "Hearts of Steel". This was used as gatekeeper's accommodation by Thomas Haughton of the Banford Bleach Works whose family had purchased the demesne in 1815. A similar tower survives at Stramore House (qv).
BASSETT'S CO DOWN (1886)

**45. BANGOR CASTLE, Bangor (2)**
The Wards of Castle Ward (qv) came by the property through marriage with the Hamilton family in 1709. In 1779 they were recorded as living in a "... low moderate structure" but by 1832 a contemporary view shows a substantial Romantic castellated Gothick mansion. Robert Edward Ward, grandson of the 1st Marquis of Bangor, replaced this with the Jacobean style house that survives to this day as the town hall. His architect in 1847 was the prolific Scot William Burn, although Anthony Salvin is also recorded as having worked here at around the same time. It is not easy to differentiate between their respective roles, but what is obvious is that the big house is essential Burn, whilst the two gate lodges are clearly by a different hand. It seems likely that the English architect was called in to complete Burn's work and it would seem safe to credit Salvin with the lodges on stylistic grounds.
**Abbey Street Lodge** 1852; architect probably Anthony Salvin

At this previous main entrance the function of this fine lodge is no longer evident having been left exposed by the removal of the demesne wall in the 1950s. In pleasant yellow sandstone ashlar it is an irregular Tudor Gothic style building one and a half storey on an L plan, dominated by skewtable gables, kneelers and poppy finials. The gable that projects towards the old avenue contains a canted bay window with a narrow label moulded attic light over. Advancing still further alongside, the hallway has an elegant Tudor arched and panelled front door below a stepped label moulding which frames a sculpted monogram R.E.W. This is a device to be found in many of Salvin's designs. Windows are arranged under label mouldings singly or bipartite with very fine foiled and cusped heads, though now lacking Picturesque glazing. To the road elevation is a sculpted lion gargoyle. Unsympathetic modern chimney stack replacement.
**Castle Street Lodge** c1852; architect probably Anthony Salvin

Similar to the main lodge but spoiled by modernisation. It differs in one wing being single storey and being part built in inferior stuccoed finish. The canted bay window has an arcade design to the parapet whilst the front door has a pointed arch. All windows, now lacking their label mouldings, and the ludicrous fanlighted "takeaway" door are recent intrusions. Very tall chimney stack. Again there is nothing to be seen of the entrance gates.
BANGOR AND GROOMSPORT; U.A.H.S. (1984); LUCKOMBE (1780); DIXON AND HEATLEY (1983); POST CHAISE COMPANION (1786); BINGHAM (1975); ALLIBONE (1988)

**46. BANN VALE, Gilford (2)**
Two lodges for the Uprichard family of the Springvale Bleach Works.
**South Gate** c1850
Opposite the entrance a standard plan single storey three bay symmetrical lodge with a steeply pitched hipped roof. Constructed in basalt with granite quoins and dressings to segmentally-headed openings. Pair of diagonally set brick chimney stacks. Deserted.
**North Gate** c1880
A distinctive lodge in very black basalt with yellow fireclay brick dressings and quoins in stark contrast. Unlike the other lodge irregular on an L plan. Single storey gabled with paired purlin projections. A little gabled hall advances alongside and beyond that to the avenue. Tall chimney stack corniced on a plinth. Squared pane sash windows.

**47. BANVILLE, Lawrencetown** c1810
A typical Georgian Tudor Gothick gate lodge. Single storey below a wide brimmed hipped roof with a high eaves. The stuccoed wall three bay front elevation comprised of a central door with label moulding flanked by two lancet windows each set into a semicircular-headed recess. The chimney stack rises off the rear wall. Very fine entrance sweep of basalt ogee quadrant walls containing wicket openings with granite

dressings and original wrought iron spear topped gates. Two big square stone pillars have friezes with plaques indicating the name of the property and an illegible date. For James Foote owner of the local bleach mill.
GREEN (1963)

**48. BEACONFIELD, Belfast South** c1870; *demolished*
Lodge and house gone, the latter having looked like a late Lanyon and Lanyon Neo-Classical effort. Resident in 1880 Joseph Millar.

**49. BEECHCROFT, Belfast North** pre 1902; *demolished*
A lodge built for Alexander Knox.

**50. BEECHMOUNT, Lisburn** 1880
A real oddity: a house which became a gate lodge. The Todd family built themselves a replacement cottage in the fashionable Neo-Classical style. A comparatively generous five bay symmetrical single storey structure, gabled with exposed rafter toes. Stuccoed with quoins, ornamental doorcase and moulded window surrounds containing original square sashes. Still discontented with this accommodation they created a larger house on an elevated site beyond and their second house became its gate lodge.

**51. BELLEVUE, Banbridge** pre 1860/c1900; *demolished*
For Robert Hayes a lodge which was reworked or rebuilt early this century.

**52. BELMONT, Banbridge** c1860; architect perhaps Thomas Jackson
Attributed to the architect Thomas Jackson, an elegant sandstone ashlar Greek Revival house now an hotel. For Robert McClelland of the Bann Weaving Company. A contemporary somewhat less elegant gate lodge. A solid Neo-Classical design with central hipped roof porch flanked by Doric columns with equivalent pilasters as quoins. Single storey with a hipped roof, a frieze surrounds the building below the eaves. Three bay symmetrical the windows with moulded surrounds in stuccoed walls. Deserted. Convex railed quadrants framed by stone piers, those to the carriage opening taper upwards with recessed panels to projecting cappings.

**53. BELMONT PRESBYTERIAN CHURCH, Belfast North** c1861; architect W J Barre
A beautiful early example of the use of polychromatic brickwork in a Ruskinian Gothick design by one of the most talented and short lived of Ulster's mid-Victorian architects. Barre succeeds in enlivening a rather square lump of a lodge with irregular fenestration and handling of colours. Effective use is made of tripartite arcades of slit lights alternating with bipartite windows about three elevations with a combination of lancet heads and segmental pointed heads. On the front facade each window of the trio has a corresponding diamond light over, a feature repeated singly to each gable. Centrally the front door has its own segmental pointed arch. All windows are dressed in cream

brick on a pink background with a continuous stringcourse of Staffordshire Blues carried up to hood the openings. The eaves is highlighted with a double corbel course of cream canted brick. On the ridge a paired chimney stack distinctively buttressed.

**54. BELMONT, Belfast North (2)**
both pre 1834; *demolished*
Two entrances with lodges built by James Orr, director of the Northern Bank. Both the southern pair and that to the north were swept away in about 1890 after being sold up by Sir Thomas McClure to make way for the grounds of Campbell College. Connop's view though distant shows the north lodge to have been a standard single storey gabled affair.
CONNOP (1864)

**55. BELVOIR PARK HOSPITAL, Newtownbreda** c1905;
architects Young and Mackenzie
Like the main hospital blocks in red brick with sandstone dressings. Single storey having to the road an ornamental shaped gable with nice scrolled stops containing a bow window with a sculpted coat-of-arms over. In matching materials five large entrance pillars with friezes below cappings in the form of four sided pediments. Concave railed quadrants to dwarf walls.
LARMOUR (1987)

**56. BELVOIR PARK, Newtownbreda (4)**
Over centuries a gathering place for the nobility, an estate over which admiring visitors eulogised lies today broken up and built over. In 1758 Mrs Delany wrote of "... a charming place, a very good house ... much enriched with bleachyards, farmhouses and pretty dwellings". The big house dating originally from the 1740s and probably by the German-Irish architect Richard Cassels was unceremoniously blown up in 1961 because it was suffering an attack of dry rot. It was principally the Hills, of whom Arthur was created Viscount Dungannon in 1765, that were responsible for beautifying the place. His eldest daughter was to become mother of the Duke of Wellington and he spent much of his childhood here. The family eventually turned its attentions to property in Dublin and Bath and the property was purchased c1811 by Thomas Bateson later the 2nd Baronet. It was his son Robert who succeeded to Belvoir in 1818 and carried out further improvements which included the provision of gate lodges to four entrances. None of these have survived but illustrations are available of two.

**Newtownbreda Gate** c1820; *demolished*
"A short distance below the village is the first entrance ... The entrance is rather neat: on both sides of the gate are 2 porter's lodges built so as to make them have a circular appearance. They are covered with ivy, which give it rather an old appearance. The approach to the house winds through the beautifully laid off pleasure grounds and lands ...". Thus recorded J Heather in the Ordnance Survey Memoirs of 1837. Each of this pair of "salt and pepper" lodges was in fact octagonal, built of a lovely dark mellow brick laid in Flemish bond. Below flat soldier arches on each of the leading three faces Georgian squared sash windows. Behind the gate screen the doorways had rectangular spoked fanlights. Above octahedral domed roofs were stone chimney pots of similar section. Linking the lodges a grand gate screen with two square stone pillars in channelled rusticated sandstone, each with fluted friezes and ball finials to cappings. On each side brick walls with sandstone dressed wicket openings. An elegant composition demolished in 1963 to make way for a spanking new road.

**Galwally Gate or "Low Lodge"** c1820; *demolished*

Somewhat less sophisticated but no less endearing. The photograph shows the little lodge in its required ivy livery, in the foreground Mr Thomas Harper, the proud gate porter cloth-capped, waistcoated and watch-chained stands to attention. A standard rectangular, single storey, three bay, symmetrical, hipped roof lodge. Lifted from the ordinary by the two tall chimney stacks rising from the back corners, and the unusual segmental pedimented portico supported on two spindly columns. To each side a Georgian squared sash window.
Demolished c1930, part of a lost demesne.
PHOTOGRAPHS: Lisburn Museum, B.N.L. April 4 1923, Mrs Helen Elliott, Mrs A A Frost; MINISTRY OF FINANCE (1966); P.R.O.N.I. D2585/4/2; DELANY (1861-62); O.S.M.; BENN (1880); WALKER (1980)

**57. BENVENU, Rostrevor c1840**
For the Bruce family, a nondescript single storey gabled lodge, two bay to the avenue, a small gabled porch projects from the road facade.

**58. BESSMOUNT, Dundonald** c1840;
*demolished*
A single storey three bay symmetrical Georgian Gothic style lodge with a wide eaved hipped roof. Lancet-headed openings. Demolished to make way for Ulster Hospital development. A property in 1837 of T S Corry.

**59. BISHOP'S PALACE, Holywood**
pre 1834; *demolished*
In 1827 the Rt Rev Richard Mant, Bishop of

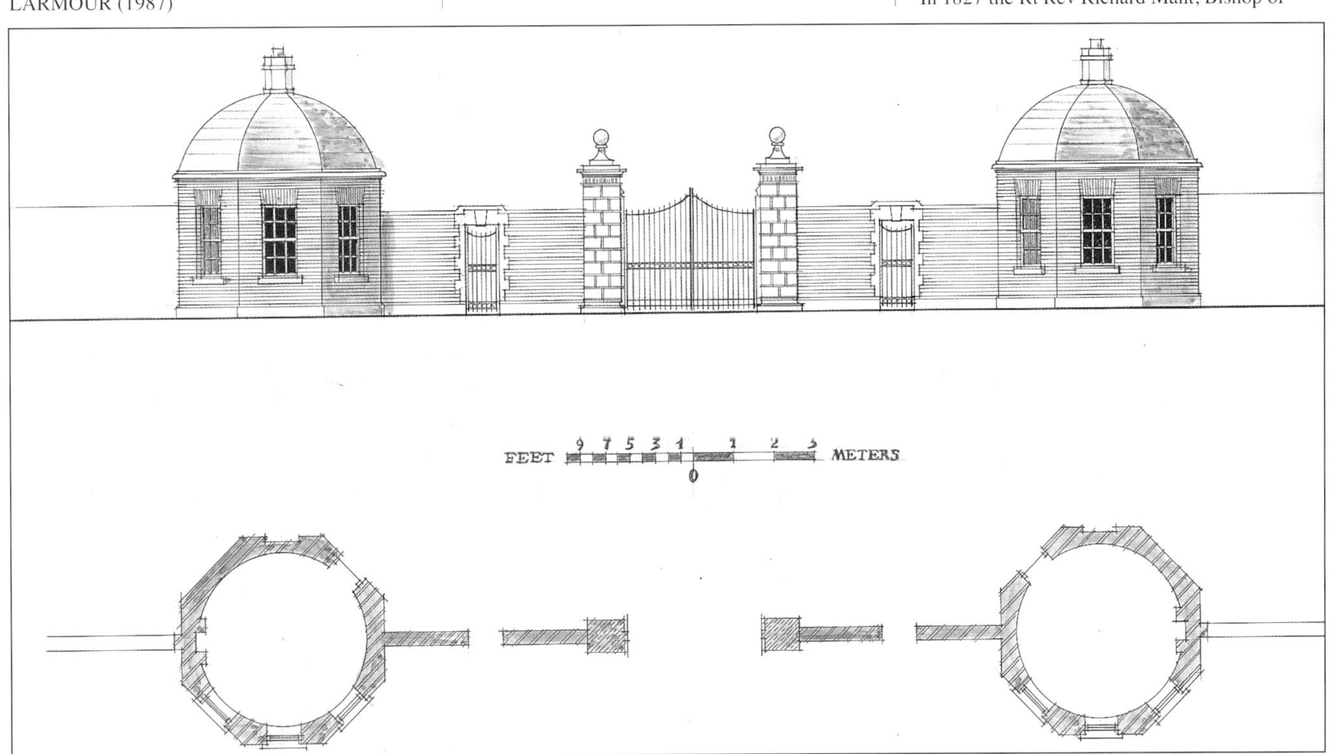


*Belvoir Park, Newtownbreda Gate*

Down and Connor, built the house which remained a palace until 1887 when the Church of Ireland sold it and their bishops removed briefly to Culloden (qv). The contemporary lodge has been demolished as was the big house in c1890 to make way for the Palace Barracks.
MERRICK (1986)

**60. BISHOP'S PALACE, Dromore**
pre 1834; *demolished*
A large plain palace of the Bishops of Dromore of 1781 variously called Bishopscourt, Beechmount or Loyola after being sold into lay hands in 1842 when the Diocese of Dromore was merged with that of Down and Connor. Some remnants of the planting for this impressively sited palace can still be detected, but no trace remains of the house or its gate lodge.
MINISTRY OF FINANCE (1966); BENCE-JONES (1988)

**61. BLOOMFIELD, Belfast South** c1820; *demolished*
A lodge which gave way to the Bloomfield roundabout in 1954. Known alternatively as "Ivy" or "Rose" Cottage and built by Arthur Crawford it was located opposite the entrance on the northern approach to the neighbouring demesne of Orangefield (qv). A standard late Georgian lodge, single storey three bay symmetrical with squared pane sashes in harled walls. Hipped roof with wide eaves and a chimney stack rising off the rear wall.
PHOTOGRAPH: B.N.L. 24 AUG 1954

**62. BROOKFIELD, Banbridge** c1830
A modest pair of lodges facing each other across the avenue between inner and outer gate screens. Simply single storey three bay symmetrical with hardly a vestige of architectural pretension. From each hipped roof a catslide projects over a front door breakfront. Modern windows and doors in rendered walls with quoins. Built by John Smyth of the Milltown Bleach Works, at Lenaderg. The family purchased this big concern in 1825 and presumably also developed this small demesne then.
BASSETT'S CO DOWN (1886)

**63. BROOKLYN, Belfast** c1903; *demolished*
An Edwardian lodge for an older Neo-Classical villa. Daniel Jaffe noted as occupant in 1860.

**64. BUNKER'S HILL, Belfast North (3)**
Three lodges for William Radcliffe, all visible on Connop's view of 1864, two off the Holywood Road.

**Belfast Lodge** c1840; *demolished*
Little more than a pill-box, one roomed single storey below a pyramidal roof.

**Holywood Lodge** c1840
Remarkably this pleasant little lodge has resisted road widening and housing development. Simple single storey square on plan below a shallow hipped roof with an extended eaves. Two bay elevation to the old main avenue which is now a public road. Nicely extended, roughcast and in apple-pie order.

**Station Road Lodge** c1860
Portions of this lodge are also to be found. Originally three bay single storey with quoins and a gabled roof. Built for the convenience of the proprietor when the road was constructed to the new Sydenham Halt.
CONNOP (1864)

**65. CABIN HILL, Belfast South** c1940; *demolished*
R.J. McMordie in 1903 commenced extending and transforming the house he had purchased from John Dinnen, solicitor. This work to the designs of Hugh Brown did not include a gate lodge. Strangely the lodge does not seem to have been built until after 1932 by which time the property had become Campbell College preparatory school and must qualify as the shortest-lived porter's accommodation in the province.
WILSON (1979)

**66. CABRAGH, Rathfriland** c1845
An unusually spacious gatekeeper's accommodation, two storey below a hipped roof with wide bracketed eaves. One bay deep by three bay symmetrical front each one set into full height recesses with segmental heads. Now all roughcast with banal modern windows and minus its chimney stack. Of an age are good iron railings and gates hung on square stone piers. These have incised panel shafts below corniced cappings. Stone buffers. Post-dating a fine Regency house by about twenty years and all probably for Alexander McMullen.

**67. CAIRN HILL, Newry** c1860;
Architect possibly W J Watson

The house previously known as Emy Ville was acquired from the Hendersons and rebuilt in its present form by Henry W Wallace who was also responsible for the pretty lodge. Looking like a Picturesque cottage from a quarter of a century earlier, one and a half storey on an L plan. Ground floor windows paired, its two leading gables have decorative foiled bargeboards. Now deserted and blocked up. There is an attractive pair of cast iron gate posts looking like Chinese lanterns with ornamental quatrefoils, and trefoils to the four sided gabled cappings.

**68. CAMP LODGE, Lisburn** c1855
A rugged little single storey three bay lodge constructed in basalt coursed rubble with toothed brick dressings and quoins all glossily painted. On the hipped roof a diagonally set Picturesque brick stack. Extended by another bay in matching style. Two elegant slender cast iron gate posts with pyramidal tops and fleur-de-lys finials.

**69. CAMPBELL COLLEGE, Belfast North (3)**
An estate called Belmont (qv), later the seat of Sir Thomas McClure, was purchased under the will of Henry James Campbell who left about £200,000 to build and endow a high class boys school in the neighbourhood of Belfast. It opened in September 1894. The extensive school buildings are in a restrained Tudor Revival manner, of red brick with sandstone dressings. There are two co-ordinating porters' lodges.

**Belmont Gate** c1894;
architect W H Lynn
A highly distinctive and innovative design of irregular outline and generous accommodation. Dominated by a large square three storey "watch-tower" scaled down from that of the College. Surmounted by a parapet, with a big chimney to one corner, it contains a pyramidal roof crowned by a ball finial. From one face of the tower projects a one and a half storey wing with breakfront gablet and at right angles a single storey projection. Tucked into one corner behind the gates a tiny flat roofed and parapeted hall with Tudor doorway. Abounding in skewtable gables with big kneelers rising to spiky fleur-de-lys finials. All dressed in red sandstone in raw red brick, an array of single and bipartite transomed and mullioned slit windows. One of Lynn's finest compositions which he was not to equal, as he was by then sixty-five. In matching materials two big octagonal gate pillars topped by domed ogee cappings and more fleur-de-lys finials, much as those at Riddell Hall, Co Antrim (qv), looking to have suffered from schoolboy target practice. Extensive stretch of railings with intermediate piers having Gothick gableted caps.

**Hawthornden Gate** c1894;
architect W H Lynn
Another essay in red brick and sandstone, this one in the restrained Picturesque gable manner. One and a half storey on an L plan a tiny gabled hall advances alongside the main avenue projection. Plain bargeboards with dainty hipknobs. Segmental headed openings and a large breakfront four flue chimney stack. In the same mood as the architect's lodge at Benburb Manor, Co Tyrone (qv). The lodge survived a road realignment but not so the fine gate sweep. Here the pillars were as at the main entrance but crowned with globe lantern lights.

**Holywood Road Lodge** c1894;
*demolished*
Only the gate screen survives.
LARMOUR (1987); YOUNG (1909); EARLY POSTCARD VIEWS, LINENHALL LIBRARY; WELCH PHOTOGRAPH (U.M.) Ref. W10/70/1

*R.J. Welch (U.M.)*

*Campbell College, Belmont Gate*

**70. CARNALEA, Bangor** pre 1901, *demolished*
A short-lived lodge to a beautifully situated house of the Higginson family.

**71. CARNESURE, Comber** c1920
A house built by the Andrews family of flour mills and linen industry fame has been burnt down to be survived by the lodge. A mildly Arts-and-Crafts style building, part single and part one and a half storey gabled, with squared leaded lights in roughcast walls.

**72. CARNMEEN, Newry (2)**
**Down Gate** pre 1859; *demolished*
To an elegant Classical farmhouse of 1756 a seat of the Coulter family, the lodge which postdated it by about a century has gone.
**Armagh Gate** pre 1862; *demolished*
The 1862 Valuation of Co Armagh notes another lodge to the west
GRIFFITH

**73. CARPENHAM, Rostrevor** pre 1834; *demolished*
A beautiful villa in the Elizabethan Cottage style of William Vitruvius Morrison. Extensions built onto an older house for Henry Hamilton, brother-in-law of the Duke of Wellington. Completed in 1826 and renamed after his wife Caroline Penelope Hamilton. It is not known if the lodge was by the same architect.
McPARLAND (1989); CROWE (1973)

**74. CARRICKBAWN, Rostrevor**
pre 1834/c1870
Originally quaintly known as Topsy-Turvy it was developed into a multi-gabled Tudor Revival mansion to plans of the Dublin architect William Deane Butler c1836. It became the property of the Ross-of-Bladensburgh family who developed the grounds and acquired one of the finest collections of non- indigenous shrubs and trees in these islands. The previous pre 1834 gate lodge to the original house for William Maguire. The surviving lodge on the same site is a mid-Victorian replacement either for Lady Balfour or the next owner Colonel Roxburgh. Single storey gabled its three bay front elevation accentuated by a row of mock gablets breaking the eaves line. There is a mono-pitch bracketed canopy above the front door and canted bay windows to opposing end facades. One of these projects through the gate screen which looks to be contemporary with the house. Modern windows in roughcast walls. Large back return. Shamrock perforated earthenware ridge cresting. Now a convent.
CROWE (1973)

**75. CARROWDORE CASTLE, Carrowdore (2)**
The Huguenots fled French persecution in 1685 and introduced the linen industry to Ulster. There is a tower here dated 1690 with the name Delacherois Crommelin upon it. The family was responsible for a charming group of buildings in a rustic castellated Gothic style which included two lodged entrances.
**Millisle Gate or Lower Lodge** c1818; architect not known; *ruinous*
A lovely symmetrical composition uncannily like the architect John Carr of York's two estate entrance gates in Lincolnshire, Redbourne Hall and Raby Castle, but seemingly too late to have been by him. All in random rubble basalt with orange brick dressings to openings. The tall central carriage archway semicircular under a battlemented parapet between two square towers embellished with recessed Cross-of-Lorraine motifs. Flanking, two lower similarly arched and crenellated pedestrian gates are linked to the lodges beyond. Single storey rectangular boxes with castellated parapets present their single bay fronts to the approach, the openings had Georgian squared sash windows. The composition now no more than a stage set at the base of the avenue, the lodges reduced to shells.
**Upper, Town or Barbican Gate** c1818; *demolished*
Another delightful folly entrance sited as a focus at the end of the main street. Again symmetrical Romantic in similar materials to the Lower Lodge. Here the central carriage archway had double segmental heads which carried a room over with crow-stepped gables front and back. To each corner slender square towers rising two storeys and decorated with more arrowloops. This watchroom, with a Georgian squared sash window back and front, can only have been approached by ladder from one of the two ground floor rooms. Each of these in the form of a lean-to with their own crowstepped gables and little square corner turrets. A building of considerable charm and importance to the village which has now been replaced by a piece of pretentious modern Classicism at a different location.
MINISTRY OF FINANCE (1966); O.S.M.; MOWL (1984); GREEN PHOTOGRAPH (U.F.T.M.) Ref W.A.G. 1855

*Carrowdore Castle, Millisle Gate*

*Carrowdore Castle, Upper Gate*

**76. CARROWSHANE, Belfast South** c1930; architects perhaps Hobart and Heron
A distinctive lodge in the Arts-and-Crafts Queen Anne Revival style. The main body of this single storey building presents a wide open pedimented gable to the avenue, with moulded mutules carried around from the eaves. From this elevation projects a canted bay window flanked by narrow lights. From each side extends a gabled wing to complete the cruciform plan. The walls are roughcast on a brick plinth. Westmoreland green roof slates, earthenware cresting and scrolled apex finials. Central bracketed chimney stack. Contemporary with and in the same manner as the house for John E Wellwood.

**77. THE CASTLE, Newry**
(see TOWER HILL)

**78. CASTLEWARD, Strangford (4)**
In 1759 Bernard Ward, MP for Co Down and the future 1st Viscount Bangor, inherited the estate and immediately set about replacing the old tower house by Strangford Lough as a residence. Much has been written of the eccentric design of his new mansion, but nothing of the age or styles of it are to be found in its gate lodges. Though simple rectangular buildings which may have been porters' lodges are shown on the earliest estate map of c1800 inside the gates of the Downpatrick and Ballyculter avenues, those in evidence today date from later in the 19th century. Henry Ward, who was later to become the 5th Viscount, married in 1854 the talented Mary King, naturalist, astronomer, pioneer of the microscope and amateur watercolourist. It is in her latter role that she has left valuable records of the estate in the 1860s. Two of her paintings illustrate Ballyculter and Downpatrick lodges.
**Ballyculter Lodge** c1830/1870; architect probably Francis Stirrat
Mary Ward's painting of c1862 portrays a simple rectangular three bay single storey lodge with a hipped roof. This forms the nucleus of the present building which was extended into a T plan. This was probably when the entrance to the big house was relocated in 1870 by Francis Stirrat the Irish partner of James Hamilton of Glasgow. Stuccoed, the openings and semicircular-headed niches are label moulded with cauliflower-like bosses as dripstones. The windows Georgian style squared sashes. Quoins. The main entrance screen comprises four large square pillars. Those flanking the carriage opening crowned by ball finials, below the cornice of each of which is a frieze with triglyphs, the shafts of heavily reticulated rusticated masonry on plain bases. Fleur-de-lys tops to good iron gates and concave railed quadrants. Probably contemporary with the 1830 lodge.

**Downpatrick Gate** c1845;
architect not known

At an access not used, which may formerly have been the principal approach, is a Picturesque Tudor style lodge. Three bay, single storey, stuccoed it has steeply-pitched gables decorated with carved wave and foil bargeboards. This is repeated on the little projecting gabled hall with its Tudor arched front door. Mary Ward's view of 1862 shows square-paned lights to the front elevation and the canted bay on the leading gable. Also shown are highly ornamental hipknobs recently restored and a lancet recess relieving the gable is now replaced by a remarkable sculpted coat-of-arms of the Wards. The present brick diagonally-set pair of chimney stacks are modern replacements for stone originals. Now excellently restored. The widespread curved entrance screen in a richly ornate Gothic manner with ogee tops and foliated finials complete with cusps, crockets and quatrefoils. The hollow octagonal piers are similarly treated, terminating in crenellated tops and poppy finials - the same as at Garron Tower, Co Antrim (qv).

**Strangford Lodge** pre 1859
A gabled building of little interest.

**North Lodge** c1880

Leading to the kitchen garden is an attractive late Victorian lodge in random uncoursed rubble with brick dressings. Two bay side elevations, its gabled front to the road contains a small hall projection. Ornamental bargeboards, hipknobs and decorative wooden fretwork pendant fascias. Over the windows simple brick label mouldings. Crowning the ridges highly ornate crestings and a chimney stack in polychromatic brickwork. Recently admirably restored.
REEVES-SMYTH and McERLEAN (1990); PORTAFERRY AND STRANGFORD; U.A.H.S. (1969); BENCE-JONES (1988); FFOLLIOTT (1975); GIROUARD (1961)

**79. CASTLEWELLAN CASTLE, Castlewellan (2)**

Nestling at the foot of the Mourne Mountains is this magnificently wooded estate once of the Annesleys, now belonging to the Forestry Service. The lands around about were purchased by the family in 1741 from the Magennis clan, not long later building a low Georgian cottage residence. There is no evidence of there having been any early porters' lodges but Mrs Mary Delany reports that the Annesleys had walled in and planted 350 acres for a park by 1751. It was not until 1856 that the 4th Earl Annesley, William Richard built a dwelling he considered more worthy of the place. He engaged the Scots architect William Burn to design him a castle in the Baronial style, a diversion from his favourite Tudor Revival manner to be seen at Dartrey, Co Monaghan and Bangor Castle in the same county (qqv). In contrast to this dull but appropriate granite pile Burn provided plans for the main entrance to the estate from the town.

W. Burn drawing (P.R.O.N.I.)

*Castlewellan Castle, Town Gate*

**Town Gate** 1861; architect William Burn

A remarkably flamboyant Picturesque villa as gate lodge, in advance of its time. A double-fronted single storey building three bay, each bay with a prominent gable having the most luxuriantly carved timber bargeboards with intricate repeating foliated scrolls. These rise to hipknobs with pendants and collar ties. The central gable advances as a porch to the front door, carried on two pairs of slender carved posts tapering downwards. Burn employed a two post version of this porch on his lodge to Clandeboye (qv). Flanking in stuccoed walls are bipartite windows with dressed granite surrounds and segmental keystoned relieving arches over. In the gables over, panels with Annesley monograms. On the main ridge a pair of tall balancing granite chimney stacks. Immaculately maintained. The gate screen by way of further variety in Classical style. Two big handsome granite pillars built up in heavily rusticated blocks, each with smooth surrounds to quarry faced finish and having channelled joints. Above moulded corniced caps support heavily swagged urns. To each side screen walls in common grey granite ashlar with a plinth of Newcastle light granite carried around the wicket openings. These have lugged tops and a central monogram feature with coronet. Rich contemporary cast iron gates. As ever the meticulous Burn provided copious drawings leaving little scope for local interpretation and ensuring a result exactly as intended. These survive in the Public Record Office of Northern Ireland.

**Drumbuck Entrance** c1860; architect Henry Roberts

Relatively plain one and a half storey semidetached gabled workers' cottages. In harled walls the ground floor openings label moulded, the windows to the two bay front have central sash boxes. The high eaves is broken by gablet windows to the attic storey. Big shared Picturesque chimney stacks, a combination of square and diagonally set flues identify the cottages as being designs of Henry Roberts, English architect and evangelical and presumably copied from his *Dwellings of the Labouring Classes*. Modest semicircular quadrant walls to simple granite piers. Both entrances for the 4th Earl Annesley who with his successor created one of the finest arboreta in these islands.
DELANY (1861-62); MOURNE; U.A.H.S. (1975); P.R.O.N.I. D1503/10/35, 37 and 38; MALINS (1980); CURL (1983); ROBERTS (1850)

**80. CHERRYVALE, Belfast South** c1880
An inconsequential two storey gabled lodge for Samuel McCausland.

**81. CHERRYVALLEY, Comber** pre 1858; *ruinous*
Now forming part of a tumble-down barn.

**82. CHINAULEY, Banbridge** c1855;
architect probably Thomas Turner

A good Greek Revival villa for a Mr Wadsworth lies dilapidated with its contemporary gate lodge a shell. The single storey building lies behind a tall convex quadrant wall. That formed part of a screen of which only an entablatured wicket opening remains. The three bay stuccoed lodge

was once of some sophistication although little of its Classical detailing survives intact. Three bay symmetrical below a hipped roof, its windows have architraves carried down to contain underpanels. Over each an entablature. Between is a flat-roofed portico with cornice and square pillared support. Below the eaves a continuous cornice moulding.

**83. CHROME HILL, Lambeg** pre 1858; *demolished*

Richard Nevin acquired this property from the Wolfenden family and established the nearby works for the printing of muslin in which process he invented bichrome from which the house derives its name. There are two earlier mid-Georgian entrances each with good rusticated stone pillars one with ball finials, both from the Wolfenden period when the house was known as Lambeg House.

**84. CLANDEBOYE, Bangor (7)**

John Blackwood early in the 17th century acquired considerable property in and around Bangor and it was his grandson, also John, later to be created the 1st Baronet, who built Clandeboye in 1801 to designs by Robert Woodgate. Building on the estate within the lifetimes of the 2nd, 3rd and 4th Barons, (James, Hans and Price) was of a low-key nature. Sir Richard Morrison carried out a modest remodelling of the house but there is no evidence of any other work on the estate by him. There were in this period three gatekeepers' lodges one of which survives on the line of a former public road that was absorbed into the property.

**Early Lodge** c1830

Single storey three bay symmetrical on a square plan below a pyramidal roof rising to a central chimney stack. Applied to harled walls are simple pilasters defining the bays. Openings with plain banded surrounds. Paired brackets to the high eaves. Lying decayed and forgotten on one of the original approaches to the house, it was rendered redundant by the grand ideas of the 5th Baron who succeeded in 1841. The young Frederick Temple Blackwood was to become one of Ulster's most famous sons. A Victorian statesman, diplomat, Governor-General of Canada and Viceroy of India, for his services being honoured in 1871 as Viscount Clandeboye and Earl of Dufferin and in 1888 as Marquis of Dufferin and Ava. He was also a romantic with a passion for building and that none of his grandiose schemes for transforming the house or rebuilding it bore fruit may be due to his commitments abroad. He contented himself with embellishing his estate with follies such as Helen's Tower, a fanciful schoolhouse, Helen's Bay railway station and a series of gate lodges. The first couple of these were of a modest nature before he began commissioning designs from notable architects.

**Inner Lodge** c1845

On the same redundant public road mentioned above another lodge constructed in basalt. Plain single storey gabled three bay with small squared pane windows flanking a breakfront porch below a catslide roof.

**Cloister Lodge** c1845

A pleasant one and a half storey mildly Picturesque gabled affair with rendered walls. Initially the future Marquis was to have as his chosen architect the prolific domestic architect, the Scot William Burn. He was to provide numerous abortive schemes, between 1848 and 1853, to reface the house in his favourite Neo-Jacobean style and also produced plans for a schoolhouse and a bridge neither of which was executed. His persistence was however rewarded in the shape of Helen's Tower (1848), Ballymullen farmhouse (1851) and a gate lodge.

*W. Burn perspective (R.I.B.A.)*

*Bangor Lodge*

**Bangor Lodge** 1849;
architect William Burn; *demolished*

The architect's intention was that this one and a half storey Tudor Revival cottage be built in a rubble stone. In reality it was constructed in brick with certain other modifications. A surviving perspective view and working drawings show it to have been a two up two down skewtable gabled affair. The two bay elevation to the road irregular with an asymmetrically located gablet and decoratively carved wooden porch to the front door. This porch design Burn was to use twelve years later at Castlewellan except that here it was reduced to two post support each tapering downwards. The windows mullioned in a variety of tripartite, bipartite and single lights, those to the ground floor label moulded, all to be lattice glazed. From the avenue gable facade a canted bay window with stone roof projected and a tall Picturesque diagonally set pair of chimney stacks rose off the rear wall. The lodge formed part of the overall entrance composition and it was framed by convex wall quadrants. Alongside was a Tudor arched pedestrian doorway beside two big carriage gateway pillars. These were to be crowned with "Morgenstern" spiky ball finials as the architect also proposed at Dartrey Castle, Co Monaghan (qv). This was what Burn proposed, what was realised were modest piers surmounted by stone eagles. This fine lodge, which also served as a post office, was demolished in 1960 allegedly to make way for the widening of the Belfast-Bangor road, though it never seems to have encroached. There is now a mundane modern bungalow in its stead. Meanwhile the 5th Baron was transforming the surrounding fields of his estates into a vast and idyllic park landscape in so doing forming a huge lake with islands. This flooding necessitated new roads to bound the demesne's perimeter all of which provided much needed employment following the Famine. Blackwood also embraced the coming of the railway as an excuse to construct a grand 2 mile tree-lined avenue to a new railway station for his own private use, and in so doing founded the village of Helen's Bay. This station is in a sort of exuberant Baronial Gothic style designed by the English architect Benjamin Ferrey to whom the client switched his allegiance between 1854 and 1865. Ferry also designed a pretty gate lodge where the new avenue crossed the Belfast to Bangor road.

**"Belfast" or "Ava" Lodge** 1855;
architect Benjamin Ferrey

A special little Tudor Revival design. Single storey on a symmetrical L plan from the internal angle of which springs a hall gabled, as the rest, at an angle of 45°. Dressed in stone, skewtables rise from big kneelers to lucarned apex stones all to contrast with brick walls. Ashlar also surrounds timber transomed and mullioned windows with lattice glazing. The front door sheeted with cast iron studding and ornamental strap hinges has a Tudor archway over which is a sculpted panel containing a coronet, Dufferin and Ava monogram and the date. From over the ridge appears a pair of diagonally set chimney stacks. After 1865 the Belfast architect W H Lynn was commissioned to provide schemes for transforming the mansion but all remained flights of fancy. Later another lodge was erected to replace a predecessor of pre 1834 where the avenue was to bridge the Newtownards road.

**Bridge Lodge** c1875;
architect perhaps W H Lynn

Relatively plain, a solid standard square three bay lodge below a shallow pitched hipped roof with central chimney. Constructed in basalt rubble curiously it lies empty.

**South or Newtownards Lodge** c1890

The last lodge to be commissioned by the Marquess, and a disappointing lumpish affair it is. Commodious one and a half storey "stockbroker Tudor" suffering from a lack of timber in its "black and white" attic storey. Very large brick chimney stack. In contrast delicate Tudor Gothick gate piers with recessed panels and conical cappings.

R.I.B.A.; B.N.L. PHOTOGRAPH; July 14 1960; CLANDEBOYE; U.A.H.S. (1985); BENCE-JONES (1970); BENCE-JONES(1988)

**85. CLANMURRAY, Dromore** c1840
A most unremarkable lodge of standard plan single storey three bay symmetrical with harled walls and hipped roof with clipped eaves. Built by William McClelland.

**86. CLIFTON LODGE, Holywood (2)**
Formerly a seat of the Hallidays the lodges may have been built when the property was acquired by the Finley family in the mid-1850s.

**Holywood Lodge** c1855; *demolished*
**Belfast Lodge** c1855; *ruinous*

Single storey three bay symmetrical built in Tudor Picturesque manner. Single gable ends repeated on the projecting hall which has a roundel relief over the doorway. In stuccoed walls label-moulded openings, the windows had fancy lattice glazing. Two diagonally-set chimney stacks. Sometime later extended to a double pile. Vacated, subsequently burnt down and now a crumbling shell. The house was demolished in the 1880s by the McCance family from Suffolk, Co Antrim (qv) who built the present red brick pile that is Knocknagoney House in the manner of W H Lynn.
MERRICK (1986)

**87. CLONAVER, Belfast North** pre 1900; *demolished*
The property in 1870 of James Girdwood.

**88. CLOONEAVIN, Rostrevor**
(see RICHMOND)

**89. COMBER CEMETERY, Comber** c1880
One and a half storey gabled and symmetrical. Three bay stuccoed front elevation the ground floor windows with moulded surrounds, the doorway entablatured with crossettes. The corresponding bedroom windows over semicircular headed in a row of gablets breaking the eaves line.

**90. CONN'SBROOK, Belfast North** pre 1834; *demolished*
A round lodge long since disappeared along with the house. In 1819 for John Martin, "merchant of Belfast".
MASON (1814-1819)

**91. COOSE VALE, Lawrencetown** pre 1834; *demolished*
The Law family built one of the oldest spinning mills in the country and owned both this house later named Glenbanna and Hazelbank close by. Although the gate lodge has gone an avenue through two rows of giant beech trees survives.

**92. THE COTTAGE, Banbridge** pre 1860; *demolished*
A pair of lodges to a property of the Lindsay family.

**93. CORRYWOOD, Castlewellan**
(see WOODLAWN)

**94. THE COURT, Lisburn** c1840; *demolished*
Located at the entrance to Peter Hill's house and bawn of c1630 and a later gentleman farmer's villa, the lodge may have been built by the 1856 resident John Harrison. A single storey square two roomed building with a pyramidal roof and clipped eaves. Singularly inconsequential but infinitely preferable to the incongruous and pretentious "replacement dwelling".

**95. COWAN HERON HOSPITAL, Dromore** c1904; architect Henry Hobart

Nicely reflecting the style of the 1898 hospital building beyond is this lodge on an informal L plan. Subtle use of "black and white" work applied to leading upper gables. The main block one and a half storey its leading gable having a rectangular bay window. Alongside advances a gabled hallway with semicircular fanlight and ornamental terracotta keystone. At right angles projects a single storey wing having a canted bay overlooking the gates. Constructed in red brick. Leaded lights. There is a handed version of this design at Lurgan Park, County Armagh (qv). The entrance pillars in big square rusticated red sandstone blocks with "pock-marked" finish. Cappings have four sided pediments. Designed by local man Henry Hobart (1858-1938) who in 1904 went into partnership with Samuel Heron to form the well-known architectural practice.
McMILLAN (1991); DOLOUGHAN (1991)

**96. CRAIGAVAD, Cultra (3)**
Following the death of Arthur Forbes in 1847 John Mulholland bought the property. He erected a restrained Neo-Classical house to designs of Thomas Turner part of whose commission was also to provide plans for at least two gate lodges. The central of three porters' lodges had disappeared before 1900, those that survive are delightful set-pieces.

**Belfast Lodge** c 1851; architect probably Thomas Turner

A single storey building showing the influence of John Nash's Picturesque Cottage Orné style. On a T plan the wing towards the road bow-ended below a semiconical roof, projects to form a verandahed sitting out area or pent in the best rustic style. Advancing towards the old avenue the gabled hallway with restrained sawtooth pattern bargeboard and sharp hipknob. Below a semicircular headed doorway with moulded surrounds. In the gable a Mulholland crest - an escallop shell. Windows Georgian squared with moulded surrounds carried down to contain underpanels. All stuccoed with quoins. Sensitively extended by the present owners to provide modern accommodation. The original entrance gates and avenue have gone.

**Central Lodge** c1851; *demolished*
**Bangor Lodge** c 1851; architect Thomas Turner

A sophisticated Italianate composition in good buff coloured sandstone like the house. Raised on a tall plinth this single storey symmetrical gabled lodge has much sculpted masonry and carved timber to admire. The projecting "porte-cochère" of two semicircular arches is carried on a central column and two outer ones engaged to square piers. The innovative capitals are composite with acanthus leaves embracing escallop shells. In the spandrel an ornamental bracket supported by a sculpted maiden. Beneath a fine panelled door is approached up a flight of steps flanked by fretted stone balustrades. On each side a window with semicircular head, bead moulded and banded surround with engaged colonnette reveals. To the road gable similar windows paired below a roundel, again displaying the family's escallop shell. A stringcourse continues about the structure at cill level. At the junction of ridges a slender ashlar chimney stack with plinth, friezed cornice and pretty scroll moulding. To the rear an awful flat roofed extension which demands a judicious planting screen. Again the gate screen and avenue have gone, the house now a golf clubhouse. John Mulholland who later moved to Ballywalter (qv) upon his father's death and in 1892 was raised to the peerage as the 1st Baron Dunleath.

**97. CRAIGAVON, Belfast North (2)**
A large Italianate house of 1870 was built to designs by Thomas Jackson for James Craig one of whose sons, another James, was to become Lord Craigavon 1st Prime Minister of Northern Ireland and another Vincent was to be a respected Ulster architect.

**Circular Road Lodge** c1880; architect probably W H Lynn

Sturdy little lodge displaying most of the architectural details of the house. Tall, single storey and perfectly symmetrical three bay below a hipped roof. Below its own hipped roof is a projecting porch with an opening treated like the rest. A semicircular-headed arch with moulded surround, springing from a cornice stringcourse, rises to a diamond panelled keystone. To all reveals are engaged colonnettes with composite capitals resting on another moulded stringcourse. Below the windows recessed panels. The side elevation to the road has paired windows. The eaves is highlighted by a repetitive bracket course. The squat chimney stack has a capping with delicate sawtooth course. All beautifully maintained, its stuccoed walls and detailing enhanced by contrasting colours.

**Holywood Road Lodge** c1880; *demolished*

**98. CRAIGDARRAGH, Helen's Bay** c1870; architect not known

A big stone and stucco house designed by Charles Lanyon in his Italianate palazzo style c1850 for Francis Gordon. It seems that the client ran short of funds for he never occupied the place, it being tenanted for many years. Nor could he afford a gate lodge because what stands today was built by Thomas Workman upon his purchasing the property. In contrast is this mid-Victorian Picturesque lodge on a typical informal L plan with steeply pitched gables. On the avenue projection was a canted bay window with mock arrowloop over. Alongside advanced from the internal angle, a little gabled hallway. Prettily fretted bargeboards with hipknobs. All disgracefully abused having two garage door openings inserted where the windows should be, its banal bungalow successor adjacent. Roman fasces incorporated in the gate screen.

**99. CRAWFORDSBURN, Crawfordsburn (3)**

Three fine gate lodges to the old Sharman-Crawford estate, of differing styles and ages.

**Burn Lodge** c1812; architect John Nash

*G.S. Repton drawing (R.P.B.)*

In the Royal Pavilion Art Gallery and Museum, Brighton is held one of the notebooks of George Stanley Repton. This Repton was the son of the noted landscape architect and partner of John Nash, Humphry Repton. George had remained with the Regency architect after his father's acrimonious break up from the partnership c1802. This notebook contains fifty drawings of subjects, executed or otherwise, for many of which neither location nor client has been identified. Three of these drawings are perspectives for Classical park entrance lodges, all variations on a theme and all perhaps proposals for the same locus. One of these has been established as having been erected here on the old Crawford estate. There is no evidence of Nash or his young assistant's work elsewhere on the demesne, the previous house having been little more than a typically modest villa of c1780 for an Irish gentleman. So how did this "building of extreme individual distinction" come to be here? The answer is genealogical. Anne, daughter of James Crawford of this place, was mother of Du Pre Alexander, 2nd Earl of Caledon who in the early 19th century was employing Nash to transform his mansion of Caledon (qv) and provide designs for gate lodges. One of these proposals is very much a variant of those in the notebook. The architect would have met Crawford on one of his visits to Co Tyrone and he was never one to forgo the opportunity of another commission, no matter how small. A unique design, two storey, presenting a symmetrical elevation to the public road. The ground floor plan of one main square living room 4.4m x 4.4m (14ft 6ins x 14ft 6ins) is flanked by two small single storey pedimented wings one advancing to the avenue as the hallway, the other balancing it a small kitchen. The double leaf front door semicircular headed with a spoked fanlight which is in a moulded surround to a stringcourse at spring level. To the side elevations semicircular-headed niches similarly treated but without their urns as Nash envisaged. On the living room elevation a breakfront containing a simple flat-arched window in a recess, arched and treated as before. The ground floor is surmounted by an entablature on which rests an octagonal first floor the shelves thus formed again minus urns as depicted in the notebook illustration. The bedroom approached by stairs from the living room is lit back and front by an oeil-de-boeuf window. Each external corner is emphasised by a Tuscan colonnette carrying the entablature of an octahedral roof which rises to a central finial. All now roughcast and well tended but demanding the urn decoration as the architect intended, return of its squared glazing bars and reinstatement of its gate pillars. To the rear, thankfully inconspicuously positioned, an extension of c1910. Dominated by a canted bay with segmentally-headed windows. There is a cartouche ornament in a pedimented gable. Probably built to designs of Vincent Craig c1910 who designed the monstrous replacement house.

**Helen's Bay Lodge** c1870; architect not known

A distinctive two up two down one and a half storey lodge with single storey return, gabled as the main body. To each main gable a lean-to structure, one a pretty glazed hall with fretted foil timber fascia. On the road elevation an unusual "arrowhead" bay window. Constructed in random uncoursed quarry-faced basalt dressed with smooth masonry, there are highly decorative carved foiled and waved bargeboards. To the rear an extravagant ashlar chimney stack chamfered, with an exaggerated coved frieze to its capping.

**Home Farm Lodge** c1900; architects Watt and Tulloch

To an ornamental Edwardian farmyard complex this complementary one and a half storey lodge in similar half timbered Arts-and-Crafts style. From a pyramidal roofed main body projects a "black and white" gabled upper attic storey jettying out beyond the red brick ground floor. To the front door a porch with nicely turned post support. Exposed rafter toes to eaves and a big ornate brick chimney with vertical ribs. A pleasant composition now lacking its multi-glazed window pattern. Little remains of the fine big wooden gate and solid piers.

TEMPLE (1993); BURKE(1921); WELCH PHOTOGRAPH (U.M.) Ref W05/31/18).

*R.J. Welch (U.M.)*

*Crawfordsburn, Home Farm Lodge*

**100. CREEVY, Belfast North** pre 1863; *demolished*
A property about which little is known beyond a distant view in J H Connop's watercolour at which time it was unoccupied. There appears a typical single storey lodge on a square plan with a hipped roof. In 1898 the house still lay vacant and after the First World War the grounds were built over.
CONNOP (1864)

**101. CROFTON HALL, Holywood** c1870; architect not known;*demolished*

A.C.W. Merrick

The lodge for William Murland once faced the public road, the widening of which swept it away in 1970. Stuccoed one and a half storey, three bay symmetrical and gabled. Highly unusual decoratively fretted wavy bargeboards rising from carved pendant toes to ornamental hipknobs with spiky finials. Openings to front elevation arranged in pairs below semicircular heads and coupled hood mouldings, that to the recessed porch forming a central pendant dripstone. Bracketed cills. Single lights to attic windows. Two chimney stacks with moulded cornice cappings and octagonal terracotta pots. In keeping very fancy Tudor Gothick gate piers. Square chamfered with lancet recesses below sculpted four gable cappings carrying curly cast iron lanterns.

**102. CROSSGAR, Crossgar**
(see TOBAR MHUIRE)

**103. CULCAVY COTTAGE, Hillsborough** pre 1858; *demolished*
Griffith in his valuation of 1863 records a gate lodge here, the proprietor Hercules Bradshaw. Neither the delightful Cottage Orné of c1826 nor the lodge overlooking the lake survives.
MINISTRY OF FINANCE (1966)

**104. CULLODEN, Holywood (2)**
William Auchinleck Robinson, a Scot, came with his wife to Ireland in the 1850s to make his fortune as a stockbroker, settling on Belfast's Antrim road. The extent of his success can be seen in this big mansion and outbuildings in appropriate Scots Baronial style. Built in 1876 to designs by the Belfast practice of Young and Mackenzie. Most of the stone came from Scotland by boat, landed at Portaferry and brought by horse and cart to the Craigavad site. It took 2 years to build during which time the client resided in a small cottage in the gardens. For a while, after Robinson's death in 1884 the residence of the Bishops of Down, Dromore and Connor to whom it was conveyed by his wife Elizabeth Jane Robinson (nee Culloden). Now an hotel. There were two gate lodges as part of the original architects' commission one of which survives.

**Belfast Lodge** c1875; architects Young and Mackenzie
Clearly the architect was familiar with Edward

Blore's lodge at Ballydrain, Co Antrim (qv) with which it has a marked resemblance. One and a half storey with steeply pitched roofs, skewtable gables, moulded kneelers and sculpted apex finials in the form of shamrocks. Constructed in squared uncoursed quarry-faced sandstone with smooth dressings. On the road gable a feature chimney stack culminating in a pair of octagonal pots. To the avenue a canted bay window over which a gablet with shouldered window opening breaks the eaves line. Extending from the main block a single storey wing from which projects a tiny gabled porchway with lancet archway. A pleasant composition well maintained and extended but lacking its former glazing pattern. Octagonal ashlar pillars with nice foliated corbelling to layered octahedral caps. The central carriage pillars gone along with all ironwork.

**Bangor Lodge** c1875; architects Young and Mackenzie; *demolished*
At the "back avenue" to the outbuildings a lodge very much a variation on the above but its gable to the avenue, from which the hall projected. Taken down to make way for road realignment.
PHOTOGRAPH: B.N.L. June 7, 1952;
P.R.O.N.I. D2194/101

**105. CULTRA, Holywood (2)** both pre 1833; *both demolished*
The Kennedy family resided here from 1671 and built a castellated Tudor Revival house. Both lodges built for Hugh Kennedy opposite their gates, one cruciform on plan.
DIXON AND HEATLEY (1983)

**106. CULTRA MANOR, Holywood** c1905
House and lodge built for Robert John Kennedy, British diplomat and grandson of Hugh, to replace old Cultra House (qv). To a big Edwardian Classical house, now the headquarters of the Ulster Folk and Transport Museum, a modest single storey three bay by two bay deep rendered gate lodge below a pyramidal roof.
DIXON AND HEATLEY (1983);
YOUNG (1909)

**107. DAISY HILL, Rostrevor** pre 1859
A humble two bay roughcast single storey building with a pyramidal roof. Minuscule and derelict.

**108. DALCHOOLIN, Holywood (2)**
A property leased by Hugh Kennedy in 1832 to William Crawford who built the house called Wellington Lodge and an attendant gate lodge. Crawford purchased the land in 1847 and erected another porter's house prior to its purchase in 1867 by James Moore who extensively renovated and altered the house into a striking Tudor Revival affair, rambling with multiple pinnacled gables, turrets, castellations and barley sugar chimney pots. Both lodges were by the Lough shore.

**North Lodge** pre 1834; *demolished*
**South Lodge** c1855; *demolished*
Symmetrical three bay structure with stuccoed walls, the gables decorated with serrated timber bargeboards. Single storey, the openings with label mouldings, door panelled, windows with margined glazing. Demolished like the big house to make way for Ulster Folk and Transport Museum expansion and executive housing.
MERRICK PHOTOGRAPH

**109. DELAMONT, Killyleagh (2)**
A park of about 200 acres acquired in the late 18th century by David Gordon of the Florida Manor (qv) family, a property he was to inherit on his elder brother's death.

**Main Entrance** c1855
Opposite the gates a sturdy lodge constructed of rubble stone with decorative red brick window dressings, door surround and simple banded pilaster quoins. Single storey on a standard plan, three bay symmetrical below a hipped roof. Square granite pillars to the entrance screen each with incised panels, friezes and plinths. Good contemporary ironwork to wide quadrants, wicket and carriage gates all with repeating diagonal cross pattern.

**Secondary Entrance** c1855
Alongside a simple gateway facing the road a one and a half storey lodge conspicuous for its very steeply pitched breakfront to the front door. Built in rough basalt squared and coursed with contrasting dressed stone skewtables and big corbelled kneelers. Three bay symmetrical its windows margined sashes. Above the front door a mock lancet slit. All framed by ogee quadrant walls. Both lodges built for Robert Gordon.
YOUNG (1909)

**110. DERRAMORE, Newtownbreda (2)**
Lodges stood at the end of two drives to a house acquired from Thomas Verner in 1824 by Lawson Annesley part owner of the local bleachgreen of New Forge. Both pre 1834 lodges may originate from after that conveyance. One of these survived until recently.

**Ardnavally gate** c1825; architect not known; *demolished*

P. Rankin

Basically a single storey standard plan building below a hipped roof but distinguished through its elegant three bay symmetrical front facade. Georgian squared sash windows with spoked heads within semicircular arches in stuccoed walls flank the central portico. This projects as a semicircular bow carried into an equivalent recess to describe a circle. Entablatured and supported on two half fluted Tuscan columns with corresponding pilasters. An arrangement much as at Ely Lodge, Co Fermanagh (qv), here access between the two rooms was via the open portico, the doorways flanking a central semicircular-headed niche. Taken down in 1970. The demesne was eventually absorbed by the neighbouring Bateson estates of Belvoir Park (qv) which family chose its title from Derramore when raised to the peerage in 1885.
DIXON AND HEATLEY (1983);
GREEN (1963)

**111. DONAGHCLONEY, Donacloney** c1855
An impressive Tudor Revival gabled brick villa of about 1840 for James Brown after whose death in 1851 the land was sold to Robert G Nicholson who showed less taste than his predecessor in building this gawky Tudor Classical mixture. Its lodge single storey stuccoed on a T plan the main three bay symmetrical front elevation faces the gates across a road junction. Below a hipped roof its entrance with Classical doorcase is flanked by mullioned windows under Tudor label mouldings. Quoins. The big square channelled ashlar entrance pillars pure Classical.
GREEN (1963)

**112. DONARD LODGE, Newcastle** 1836; architect Thomas J Duff

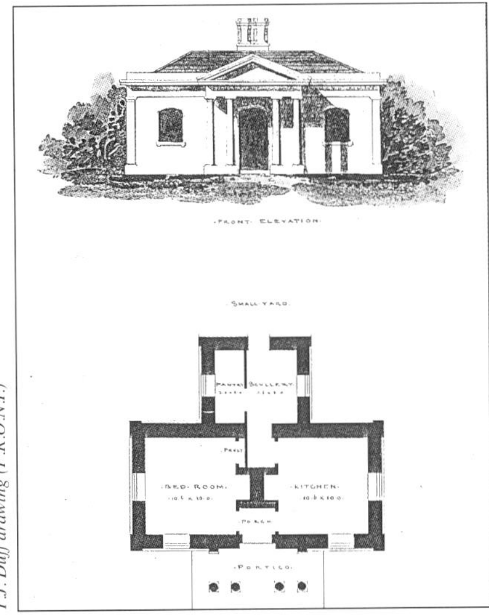

*T.J. Duff drawing (P.R.O.N.I.)*

Built as a "marine residence" or "bathing villa" for the Annesleys of Castlewellan (qv) it was in fact for many years a dower house. The house built from 1830 onwards in which architects John Lynn, Thomas Jackson and Thomas Duff were all involved, has been demolished along with its fine conservatory. Once a landmark on the foothills of Slieve Donard it is survived by its gate lodge, drawings of which are held in the Public Record Office of Northern Ireland showing a chaste design by Duff. This initial proposal shows a simple two roomed single storey structure with living room and bedroom and a rear return housing scullery and pantry. Neo-Classical in style with an entablatured parapet to the hipped roof and a pedimented portico projecting centrally supported on two pairs of Doric columns repeated as pilasters to the corners. The windows were to be segmentally headed with bracketed cills. A second drawing probably indicates what was finally agreed, having alterations to the chimney stack arrangement. What was in fact executed is but a disappointingly watered down version of what the Newry architect intended. Elevated and approached up a flight of steps it lacks a portico and entablature and is constructed in crude granite blocks with very basic pilasters flanking the doorway and as quoins. The margined window pattern and a pair of octagonal chimney pots are all that appear as envisaged. Plain granite gate piers with wicket gates.
MOURNE; U.A.H.S. (1975); P.R.O.N.I. D1503/10/16 AND 212; BENCE-JONES (1988)

**113. DOWNSHIRE HOSPITAL, Downpatrick** c1885; architect probably Henry Smith
An extensive hospital block in red brick dating 1883-1898 to designs by Henry Smith. Another brick building obscured by paint. In Italianate manner it may also have been extended since its original building. Formerly single storey three bay symmetrical and gabled, it was enlarged to form a T plan with a big wing built at right angles in similar style. There is also a back return added to the roadside gable. The semicircular-headed door opening is flanked by windows with brick surrounds and cills carried around as a stringcourse to unite the composition. Liberal use is made of bullseye windows. To a very shallow pitched roof are extended eaves and bargeboards carried on exaggerated brackets. There are three sturdy stone chimney stacks with plinths and cornices. Now the Norman Thompson Hostel.
DOWNPATRICK; U.A.H.S. (1970)

**114. DRAPER HILL, Seaforde** c1830
A plain lodge, single storey with its gable-on elevation to the avenue canted below a half umbrello roof. Built for John Cromie, who set up business in 1815 and was one of the largest of the early 19th century linen manufacturers in the country.
GREEN (1963)

**115. DRUM, Dunmurry** c1870; architects Thomas Jackson and Son
An antique seat with many occupants over the years but probably founded by James Hamilton Maxwell in 1725. Pleasantly located by a meander in the river Lagan, John Arnott Taylor came here in the 1870s and fronted the old house with a late Victorian stuccoed Neo-Classical villa repeating the exercise to a smaller scale at the main gate. Single storey on an L plan its stuccoed decoration in forthright Italianate style. Rusticated quoins frame horizontally channelled walls, this emphasis repeated in a moulded cill course and plinth which embrace the lodge. Below the eaves a frieze course with paired brackets, a feature carried up each of the main gables, which are in the form of open pediments crowned by ball finials. In each gable twin narrow windows framed by fluted pilasters and semicircular heads. Over a roundel containing the Arnott crest, in hand a dagger, erect, proper. In the internal angle a once pretty verandah unfortunately enclosed with inappropriate glazed screens. The ridge has "fang" cresting and a tall plinthed chimney stack with bracketed cornice and a peculiar curved block capping. Only two of the former gate piers remain. Square with distinctive triglyphed friezes complete with guttae. The double pedestal cappings surmounted by ball finials. Congruous modern carriage gates.
DIXON AND HEATLEY (1983)

**116. DRUMANTINE, Poyntzpass (2)**
Long the seat of the Innes family, one lodge pre 1834 the other late Victorian, but neither of any merit.

**117. DRUMBEG RECTORY, Dunmurry** c1895; *demolished*
The original glebe house of 1826 at Hillhall was abandoned in favour of one built in 1895 in closer proximity to the church. To complement this red brick rectory a simple little single storey lodge in the same material. Gabled three bay symmetrical with a gabled breakfront hallway. Swept away by road widening.

**118. DRUMNASCAMPH, Rathfriland** pre 1860
An unprepossessing building. Single storey, two roomed, with outshoot hall, gable-on to the road. One time resident Rev James Cargins.

**119. DRUMINDONEY, Kilkeel** c1870; architects possibly Young and MacKenzie
The lodge to a dower house of the Needhams, Earls of Kilmorey of nearby Mourne Park (qv) seems originally to have been a little single storey cube with a pyramidal roof, and, to the road a pair of segmentally-headed windows. To the avenue a carved timber porch with semicircular arches. Sometime later a two storey house was tacked on with some sympathetic detailing. Perhaps contemporary with the first lodge building a distinctive gate sweep adapted from a design by Alexander "Greek" Thomson the Glasgow architect as illustrated in *Villa and Cottage Architecture* published in 1863. Framed by hexagonal granite masonry walls are round gate pillars of differing sizes, one the smaller to carry the wicket gate, the wide carriage leaf hung on the larger "To obviate a common defect of sagging". The domed cappings a diversion from the original design, the sturdy carved gates much as envisaged. There are entrances akin to this at Beech Hill, Co Londonderry (qv) and Ballygarvey, Co Antrim (qv), for the latter at least the Belfast practice of Young and Mackenzie were involved as could be the case here. The avenue now severed, the house since 1900 was for many years Mourne Grange School.
MOURNE; U.A.H.S. (1975); BLACKIE (1863)

*Drum*

**120. DUFFERIN VILLAS, Groomsport** c1875

Stuccoed one and a half storey two up two down gabled cottage. From its symmetrical three bay front extends a little gabled hallway. Scroll ended rafter toes and earthenware apex finials. Now extended into a double pile. To a series of semidetached villas built for Rev Issac Mack, Groomsport Presbyterian Minister.
BANGOR AND GROOMSPORT; U.A.H.S. (1984)

**121. DUNBARTON, Gilford** 1845; architect Thomas Jackson

A very typical Thomas Jackson Neo-Classical gate lodge similar to those to Longwood, Co Antrim (qv) and nearby Huntley Glen (qv) from whence the builder Hugh Dunbar had moved in 1845. He was the vastly prosperous founder of Dunbar, McMaster & Co, flax spinners of Gilford. This house was one of the many villas that sprang up along the Bann in the linen boom years. After Hugh Dunbar's death in 1847 much of his property was purchased by his partner John McMaster, including Dunbarton. A perky pretentious composition. Single storey with a high eaves below a hipped roof. Symmetrical three bay with a central distyle Ionic portico with heavily entablatured pediment. Framed by Doric pilasters, the walls channelled horizontally and carried down to form voussoirs to segmentally headed recesses. These contain similarly arched windows with margined casements, a pattern repeated in the front door. Brackets to cills and eaves course. On a corniced chimney stack two octagonal pots. The lodge now no longer associated with avenue or house.
BASSETT'S CO DOWN (1886); CAMPBELL (1990)

**122. DUNDRUM BATH HOUSE, Dundrum** c1840

Financed by the Marquis of Downshire as part of his hot and cold bath and pleasure ground novelty of c1835. A simple two roomed lodge with a hipped roof and two diagonally set chimney stacks. Parallel to the public road and situated behind a tall walled screen containing big square masonry pillars. Contemporary carriage gates alongside a lancet headed wicket opening in the concave screen wall.
LEWIS (1837); EAST DOWN; U.A.H.S. (1973)

**123. ECHLINVILLE, Kircubbin**

There never was a gate lodge at this old demesne of the Echlin family but there are some fine ashlar gate pillars to be seen, dating from the mid-Georgian period. The property more recently called Rubane.

**124. EDENVALE, Belfast North** c1860; *demolished*

The proprietor in 1863 Arabella Greer.

**125. EDGECUMBE, Belfast North (2)** both pre 1858; *both demolished*

The original house was built by 1837 for John Wallace, solicitor. In 1854 it was acquired by John Workman, manufacturer, who enlarged and refaced it in stuccoed Neo-Classical style probably to designs by Young and Mackenzie. One of these owners built two lodges. Connop's distant view of 1864 shows one of these to have been square, single storey below a hipped roof. The house suffered the fate of its lodges in 1992.
CONNOP (1864)

**126. EGLANTINE, Hillsborough (2)**

"This beautiful feature of the Hillsborough property, the seat of Hugh Moore, Esq from the elegant arrangement of its gate, avenue and plantation ...". Thus Atkinson in 1817 set the scene for a pair of little lodges flanking the gate. By c1845 the house and land had passed to St Clair Kenburne Mulholland of the York Street Mill, younger brother of Andrew of Ballywalter Park (qv). Like his brother he was to employ Charles Lanyon as his architect to reface or rebuild the house and replace the old lodges with one in his favourite Italianate palazzo style.

**Main Lodge** c1845; architect Charles Lanyon

The most ostentatious and innovative of this series of lodges by the architect. The others all on a similar cruciform plan are at Ballwalter Park in the same county and Dunderave and Moneyglass (qqv) both in Co Antrim. Taller than the other examples and containing an attic storey, it is in stucco with dressed stone detailing. The front elevation has a central breakfront which extends further by a bay to form a three arched "porte-cochère". Each semicircular arch springs from square piers, archivolted with a central acone. In the gable over a keystoned oculus for relief. The shallow pitched gabled roof advances over carved purlin ends with deeply moulded wooden brackets supporting the eaves. The "porte-cochère" arcade is repeated on the front elevation within, the central front door having a spoked fanlight over. To each side of the breakfront projection a novel oblong shaped window framed by V-channelled quoin blocks. The main side elevations have equally unusual windows, Lanyon interpretations of Venetian lights with Baroque surrounds. The whole remarkable composition embellished further by a strong plinth and stringcourse at arch springing level. It is gratifying to note that this important lodge even at a late stage in its decline is being saved from complete dereliction by a restoration scheme, which includes an accompanying garage in matching style. The gate screen is no less impressive. The outer concave quadrant walls have delicate sculpted scroll motifs against and in contrast with the robust sandstone pillars. These are built of deeply reticulated blocks, those flanking the carriage opening crowned by a peculiar corniced octagonal block finial supported on a bracketed frieze. The carriage and wicket gates in sturdy cast iron with a repeating circular pattern.

**Side Lodge** c1855

A comparatively straightforward Tudor Picturesque lodge, one and a half storey and gabled. Three bay symmetrical built in rounded basalt bounders, dressed stone highlights as quoins and window surrounds with expressed lintels incorporating label mouldings just as at Fort Royal, Co Donegal (qv). Below the high bracketed eaves a pedimented breakfront hall with little decorative cusped bargeboards. Much extended in matching fashion, the avenue no longer leading to the house which is in any case now a burnt out shell.
ATKINSON (1823)

**127. ELDON GREEN, Helen's Bay** c1901; architect Vincent Craig

A big house on an elevated site overlooking Belfast Lough for the architect who also designed the gate lodge. It is a pleasant long low composition on an informal plan, roughcast walls below a hipped roof of earthenware tiles. To the avenue projects the living room with half timbered effect gable jettied on scrolled stone brackets. Advancing flush alongside a little flat roofed hallway with bullseye window. Exposed rafter toes and battered chimney stack. Ball finialed gate pillars also in early Edwardian Arts-and-Crafts manner.

**128. ELMFIELD, Gilford (2)**

A small Scots Baronial style castle of 1856 for James Dickson who employed the Scottish architect William Spence, just as his brother Benjamin had done at Gilford Castle (qv) close by. The brothers had become wealthy through the linen boom in the mid-19th century in association with Hugh Dunbar of Dunbar

*Main Entrance*

Dickson and Co, a partnership which ended acrimoniously in 1866.

**Main Entrance** c1860;
architect probably William Spence

Lost in laurel is this shell of a lodge built in the highest quality punched sandstone ashlar with much fine sculpted detailing. Single storey but commodious four roomed accommodation over a part basement. Three bay symmetrical with crowsteps to main gables and to that of its steeply pitched projecting hallway, all culminating in ball finials. Relieving these gables mock arrowloops and over the sheeted front door a Dickson crest, the shield sculpted, in dexter hand a sword, in bent, proper. Semicircular headed slit lights to hallway, openings otherwise flat arched. To the high eaves a course of moulded brackets stopped against panelled scroll topped kneelers. Aloft a moulded stone chimney stack. Later stuccoed extension. A jaunty little building which though probably past rehabilitation could conceivably be stabilised and exposed as a pleasing eyecatcher.

**Rear Lodge** pre 1833

Much modernised into a plain two storey house, three bay with pyramidal roof. The gates to an earlier house the property of James Wilson. Square pillars of channelled rusticated stone with corniced cappings.

**129. ELM GROVE, Belfast South**
pre 1902; *demolished*

House and lodge gone, the grounds since 1930 redeveloped for school use (see opposite).

**130. ELM GROVE PE SCHOOL, Belfast South** c1933;
architect Reginald S Wilshere

One of a series of originally designed schools by the same architect built in the inter-war years in the Belfast area. There is a porter's lodge in similar pleasant mellow rustic brick, Edwin Lutyens influenced. Proud and lofty on an elevated site, the two storey gate house rises from a double plinth to a wide eaved pyramidal roof with red pantiled finish. Symmetrical front elevation dominated by a central projecting flat roomed hall with chamfered corners and semicircular arched doorway. Flanking, two tiny slit windows and above a single wide casement light with squared panes. Tall chimney stack rising from a side elevation. There are other gate houses of the same genre at nearby Nettlefield and Avoniel PE Schools (qqv).
LARMOUR (1987)

**131. ELSINORE, Bangor** c1874; architects possibly Young and Mackenzie

A stuccoed Neo-Classical lodge built for Daniel Joseph Jaffe. Single storey under a hipped roof with a gabled breakfront hall central to the three bay symmetrical front elevation. Segmentally-headed windows with moulded cills, surrounds and plain keystones. Front door with semicircular headed fanlight. To the eaves a continuous frieze with multi-moulded bracket support. Quoins. Big chimney stack with bracketed cornice. Whimsically called Hamlet Hill. Square base ashlar gate screen pillars broach to octagonal shafts with corniced cappings.
BANGOR AND GROOMSPORT; U.A.H.S. (1984)

**132. ENNISKEEN, Newcastle** c1894;
architect probably William Batt

To a faintly Scots Baronial roughcast pile, a contrasting Picturesque/Neo-Classical stuccoed gate lodge. One and a half storey gabled three bay symmetrical with a high eaves. Front door and fanlight below a gabled canopy with fretted foil bargeboards. On each side a pair of windows with moulded surround to upper third which springs from a continuous stringcourse. Similar treatment of gable attic windows. Corniced chimney stacks. Built for Robert Wallace Murray of the Belfast Tobacco Company. The house now an hotel.
MOURNE; U.A.H.S. (1975)

**133. FAIRMOUNT, Magheralin** pre 1903;
*demolished*

Probably built for Thomas Hall.

**134. FAIRVIEW, Drumbo** pre 1834;
*demolished*

Formerly a pretty harled single storey gate lodge under a thatched hipped roof. A victim of replacement dwelling approval. Once a property of a branch of the Echlin family, the house has more recently been called Rokeby Hall.

**135. FINNEBROGUE, Downpatrick**

An antique mansion thought to originate from about 1635 owes much of its appearance today to extensive restoration by Dorothea Maxwell in 1789-95. Gate piers from this time can still be traced in the undergrowth a few yards north of the gate lodge. Square in section the big dressed sandstone pillars with plinths and full entablatures have breakfronts or pilasters on three faces, one forming a gate stop. That gates in 1837 were a rarity at Finnebrogue is observed by Binns who comments of the grounds that there were "no gates in any part of them (even the lawn and flower-garden lying open as the fields), the most perfect order is maintained". John Waring Maxwell clearly felt this deficiency around this time for he commissioned a gate lodge design for an unknown location.

**Proposed Design** c1836;
architect John Lynn; *unexecuted*

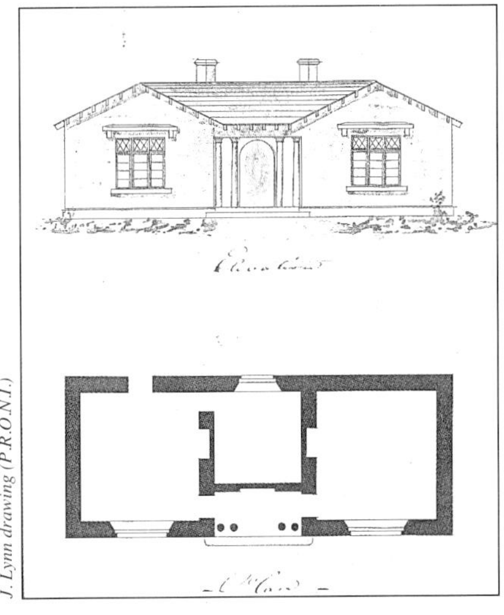

*J. Lynn drawing (P.R.O.N.I.)*

A nice piece of duality more in the form of a school than a gate lodge. Central is a wide recessed porch behind a screen of paired classical columns on the rear wall of which is a semicircular headed recess. The eaves over is highlighted by brackets continued up each of the gables beyond. These flanking bays are in the form of wide window openings transomed and mullioned. The upper lights with their distinctive lattice pattern and the basic shelf moulding over are typical of many buildings in Seaforde and no doubt signify P F Robinson's influence on Lynn, the latter probably having been the Englishman's executant architect there. Two diagonally set stacks rise from behind the ridge. It was not until half a century later that the first and only lodge was built on the estate.

**Main Entrance** c1888;
architect William J Fennell

For Major R R Maxwell a highly commodious and individual design in smooth raw red brick as pristine as the day it was erected, it is liberally decorated with terracotta ornament, quite a shock in this rural location. The one and a half storey main body has a single storey rear return. Tucked into the internal angle thus formed is a flat roofed hallway with a repeating quatrefoil perforated parapet, the front door semicircular-headed with brick special hood moulding. In the

W.M. Lawrence (N.L.I.)

return gable a big tripartite window, with relieving arch, overlooks the estate. Advancing towards the road a large gabled rectangular bay with bipartite window over which is an ornamental band of repeating earthenware roundels. Both eaves and verges throughout accentuated by brick corbelling. At the rear roofs junction a huge breakfront brick chimney stack. Perforated terracotta crestings and fleur-de-lys apex finials. In contrast, but of an age, square sandstone carriage pillars with friezes, moulded pyramidal cappings and ball finials. These are repeated on a smaller scale in the outer piers, linked by sturdy late Victorian Gothick cast iron railings to match the gates. Stone ball buffers in the Lawrence view now missing.
MINISTRY OF FINANCE (1966); P.R.O.N.I. D3244/E/5/17; LAWRENCE PHOTOGRAPH (N.L.I.) Ref 5726(C)

**136. THE FIRS, Holywood** 1893
To a house of 1889 built by the Payne family an exercise in red, brick walls and earthenware tiled roof. Single storey on a cruciform plan, the gables contain windows with squared upper glazing pattern. Vertically ribbed brick chimney stack.

**137. FLORIDA MANOR, Killinchy (2)**
To a fine classical mansion of c1796 for the Gordon family, two Georgian Gothic style lodges of later date.
**West Lodge** c1840

Facing a road junction with its back to the estate the lodge is framed by concave quadrant walls one of which contains the carriage gate. Built in random rubble three bay symmetrical its end elevations canted. Lancet openings the overpanels of which are blank to disguise the floor of an attic storey within the high eaved hipped roof. These may have been painted with Y-tracery effect. Nasty modern metal windows inserted in whitewashed walls.
**East Lodge** c1840; *ruinous*
Much as the above but located alongside the gate screen. One and a half storey as before with the same overpanels but on a plan closer to an octagon. Crude gate pillars with semblance of contemporary spear topped railings. Now totally dilapidated and overgrown. Both lodges for David Gordon director of the Belfast Bank and of the same family as Delamont and Summerfield (qqv).
YOUNG (1909)

**138. FORSTER GREEN HOSPITAL, Newtownbreda (3)** all c1900
A hospital for consumption formed in 1897 from the Fortbreda demesne (qv) with three Edwardian lodges one of which survives. Red brick two storey cube below a pyramidal roof with ball finial top. Mock gables to two elevations. From the avenue facade projects a single storey canted bay asymmetrically placed under a roof extending beyond as a canopy to the front door alongside. Bracket and wooden post support.

**139. FORTBREDA, Newtownbreda (2)**
*both demolished*
A fine villa in Classical Ionic style probably for the Boyd family who built a pre 1834 lodge. On being acquired by the Crawfords of Crawfordsburn (qv) another lodge was added pre 1858. Both of these were supplanted by later structures when the demesne was sold to accommodate Forster Green Hospital (qv).

**140. FORT HAMILTON, Rostrevor**
(see BALLYEDMOND)

**141. FORTWILLIAM, Annahilt** c1860
Modest single storey three bay symmetrical lodge. Windows with decorative "Ulster" banded surrounds in roughcast walls. Hipped roof with high eaves.

**142. FOX LODGE, Belfast South** pre 1834;
*demolished*
Previously Lagan Vale and recently renamed Nazareth Lodge in 1823 the seat of William Fox. The gate lodge which did not survive the turn of the century appears from the 1858 OS to have been circular.

**143. FRAZERVILLE, Newry** c1890
A late Victorian Picturesque gate lodge to a large ostentatious stuccoed Neo-Classical house built by W Frazer, a local grain merchant. Terminating the outbuildings at the foot of a steep approach to the house the two storey stuccoed lodge dominated in its leading gable by a full height canted bay window with half-umbrello roof below a fanciful fretted timber bargeboard with quatrefoil motifs. Two up two down each side elevation has a mock gable with similarly treated bargeboards. To the rear was the appropriate gabled porch now relocated and replaced by something less suitable. Perforated earthenware cresting and apex finials. Decorative corbelling to chimney stack. The lodge is occupied and resplendent in bright green livery. The house later became the property of the Quinn family and recently the Ardmore Hotel, now destroyed.

**144. GALWALLY, Newtownbreda** c1885;
architect possibly W H Lynn

B. R. Cobain

A big aggressive Classical house for John Martin of the building firm of H & J Martin. At the gate a chip off the main block. In matching materials and detailing as the house is this fine late Victorian set-piece. In red sandstone ashlar with contrasting dressed stone quoins, window surrounds, stringcourse and multi-bracketed high eaves. Single storey on an L plan below a hipped roof which terminates in a half umbrello over the canted avenue projection. From the internal angle a little hallway advances under its own hipped roof, the front doorcase with pilasters and fluted frieze. All raised on a quarry-faced stone plinth, there is a tall friezed and corniced chimney stack. Now immaculately restored and expertly extended. It may be no coincidence that architect and builder were involved together on the new central library in Belfast at this time, using the same Dumfries sandstone.

**145. GARNERVILLE, Belfast North**
pre 1834; *demolished*
Connop's distant view of 1864 suggests a standard single storey lodge below a hipped roof facing the avenue which led from the Holywood road. Flanking an entrance screen with wicket openings, convex quadrant walls. For the Garner family.
CONNOP (1864)

**146. GARRANARD, Belfast North** c1880;
architect not known
A delightful and neat late Victorian Neo-Classical lodge. Constructed in quarry-faced basalt with contrasting orange brick quoins toothed dressings and segmental arches to openings. Single storey three bay to the now severed avenue. To the hipped roof a distinctive eaves with big carved brackets. Large stuccoed chimney stack having an outsized cornice capping. Lodge and house for William Hugh Patterson.

**147. GILFORD CASTLE, Gilford**
For long the estate of the Johnston family, it was purchased about 1855 by Benjamin Dickson who, with his brother James, had benefited from the linen boom. Each built his own castle to designs by the Scottish architect William Spence, James at Elmfield (qv) and Benjamin here on a different site from the old dilapidated earlier house. There are two entrances, only one with a lodge.
**Banbridge Gate** c1860;
architect perhaps William Spence
The big Neo-Classical gate pillars in sandstone ashlar with V-jointing in contrast to the mildly Picturesque lodge. Single storey gabled, three bay symmetrical front elevation dominated by a tall gabled breakfront containing the front door and slit light over. All openings have segmental arches with pretty fretted fascia boards over. Lofty proportions like those lodges at Elmfield and Straw Hill (qv).
**Gilford Gate** 1902;
architects Young and Mackenzie
Tall gate piers in sandstone. Square with rebated angles rising to four sided pediment cappings, each of the leading ones carry a shield with the monogram 'C' of the Carletons. From each capping springs an octagonal base for a curly lamp standard. There never was a lodge at this entrance but when Miss Carleton came to the property it was her intention that this be remedied. She was impressed by the lodge and gates at Fowey Hall in England for a Mr Hanson by the architect C E Sayer and permission was granted by him to replicate the latter at Gilford. In the event the ironwork was not by the Coalbrookdale Company as the original, but manufactured by Musgrave and Company of Belfast. The piers were by Richard Lutton of Portadown to designs of Young and Mackenzie. The Hansons also provided photographs of their gate lodge, a typical Edwardian half timbered design with balustraded entrance porch much as at Dullerton, Co Tyrone (qv). It never materialised.
P.R.O.N.I. D2194 (Box 59)

**148. GILLHALL, Dromore (2)**
The historic haunted house of Captain John Magill was unceremoniously blown up by the army recently after years of decay. The seat probably owed its appearance to the architect Richard Cassels who was commissioned by Robert Hawkins Magill to carry out alterations and additions c1736. It passed through marriage in 1774 to the Earls of Clanwilliam who would have been responsible for adding both lodges.

**North Lodge** pre 1834; *demolished*
**South Lodge** c1845
Pleasant one and a half storey gabled structure, built in basalt rubble with galleting. Brick dressings to windows. Canted bay to leading gable. Modern squared windows.
FFOLLIOTT (1975); BENCE-JONES (1988)

**149. GLENALMOND, Belfast North** 1938; architect John McGeagh
A late Arts-and-Crafts style house of 1932 for the McConnell family to designs by John McGeagh. There is a gate lodge in complementary vein. In mellow rustic brick with earthenware tiled roof. The main body one and a half storey gabled, a two storey hipped roof projection from the front elevation houses a bedroom over the hallway. To the left hand side an elongated octagonal light. Windows square leaded casements.

**150. GLENBANK, Bangor** c1890; architect not known
A big rambling late Victorian Neo-Classical house in red brick, sandstone dressed, for the Connor family. There is a contemporary lodge in like style and materials. Spoiled by a jumble of extensions and alterations its former shape barely detectable, its character destroyed. Originally an octagon with two extended elevations, single storey below a Westmoreland green slate roof with half umbrello ends. A succession of semicircular-headed moulded openings (some blind) surrounded the lodge united by sculpted stringcourses at cill and spring levels. Big aggressive chimney as on the big house, red brick with stone plinths, moulded bands and curved cornice cappings. Good sandstone quarry faced pillars contain ogee sweeps now minus carved wooden screens and gates.
BANGOR AND GROOMSPORT; U.A.H.S. (1984)

**151. GLENBANNA, Belfast South** pre 1834; *demolished*

**152. GLENBANNA, Lawrencetown** (see COOSE VALE)

**153. GLENBROOK, Newtownbreda** pre 1901; *demolished*
A lodge for William Hinder, coal merchant and ship owner.

**154. GLENCRAIG, Helen's Bay** c1840
A lodge rather less ambitious than the Tudor Revival house, all pinnacles, gables and crenellations built in 1833 for Miss Mary Symes. Three bay symmetrical with label moulded openings. One and a half storey gabled. Walls stuccoed with quoins.

**155. GLENDHU, Belfast North** pre 1902; *demolished*

**156. GLEN EBOR, Belfast North** c1865; architect probably Thomas Jackson
A gauche stuccoed lodge on a rectangular plan of three bays, the left hand one in the form of a breakfront all under the hipped roof. Projecting centrally a small flat roofed hall with bracketed entablature. Segmentally-headed windows with keystones breaking a hood moulding carried

down and around as a stringcourse. Lofty eaves with paired brackets. Bulky chimney stack. Like the house, built for Jonathan Cordukes, renamed Hampton.
DIXON (1978)

**157. GLENGANAGH or GLENGHANA, Groomsport** c1900; architect James Hanna

To what is thought to have been a dower house for the Blackwoods of Clandeboye (qv) was a pre 1834 gate lodge. This was replaced by an exceptional Arts-and-Crafts building in Voysey manner, for the Kingan family who came here in about 1880. Raised on a basement is this unique and innovative design. Finished in white roughcast with red sandstone dressings to corner buttresses and classical portico asymmetrically placed on the three bay front elevation. A pair of stylised columns support a simple flat entablatured roof. Windows Georgian style squared pattern as is the oriel to the road elevation. Square on plan the pyramidal roof rises to a tall central chimney. To the eaves a continuous sandstone dentil-course. Ball finialed sandstone gate pillars.
BANGOR AND GROOMSPORT; U.A.H.S. (1984)

**158. GLENMACHAN, Belfast North** c1862; architect probably Thomas Jackson; *demolished*
To a large villa by the architect Thomas Jackson for himself but promptly purchased by Sir William Ewart. The house was the first of many on this hillside to be designed by the architect giving rise to the name of Jacksonville. Were it not for Connop's painting and a surviving photograph, its porter's lodge could not be identified as it is not noted on either 1858 or 1902 OS Maps. Simple standard plan single storey lodge with a hipped roof. Segmentally-headed windows with toothed dressed surrounds and quoins in contrast to its brick facings. Corbelled eaves. Enclosed yard.
CONNOP (1864); DIXON (1978); LINENHALL LIBRARY PHOTOGRAPH

**159. GLENMACHAN TOWER, Belfast North** c1863; architect probably Thomas Jackson; *demolished*
Yet another Italianate villa, for Sir Thomas McClure. The only clue to the existence of this now demolished lodge is from Connop's view. It appears to have been a simple square single storey building with hipped roof doubtless in Jackson's habitual Neo-Classical manner.
CONNOP (1864); DIXON (1978)

**160. GLENMAKIERAN, Holywood** 1928
Single storey, like a suburban bungalow with earthenware tiled roof and roughcast walls. Canted bay to road elevation.

**161. GLENTORAN, Belfast South** pre 1858; *demolished*
The park disappeared to be replaced by little streets c1880. The seat of William Coates of the Coates and Young iron foundry.

**162. GLENVILLE, Newry** pre 1860; *demolished*
An early Victorian lodge replaced this century. Its successor also demolished. For the Glenny family, mill owners in the district. Now a Carmelite monastery.

**163. GOOD SHEPHERD CONVENT, Belfast South** 1868/1895; architects Sherry and Hughes/J J McDonnell
To an extensive red brick and stone Catholic Gothic Revival complex a substantial gabled one and a half storey lodge probably in the same materials but now stuccoed over. Parallel to the public footway it was formerly two bay rectangular but later enlarged by a bay, in matching manner, to form an L plan. Left hand bay in the form of a recessed porch-cum-pedestrian access via two segmental pointed arches, with quatrefoil roundel light over. Alongside two pairs of segmentally headed ground floor windows below similar single sashes in gablets breaking an eaves with ogee gutter and exposed rafter toes. Secondary gutter at first floor cill as stringcourse. Big brutal chamfered chimney stack with corbelled capping.
LARMOUR (1987)

**164. GOVERNMENT HOUSE, Hillsborough** (see HILLSBOROUGH CASTLE)

**165. GRACE HALL, Magheralin (2)**
A big Regency villa attached to an earlier house for the Douglass family.

**Lurgan Road Gate** pre 1833; *demolished*
A lodge for Thomas Douglass.
**Side Entrance** c1845
For Charles Douglass a typical modest Tudor Revival style lodge located outside the gates with their crude pillars. Single storey naive with a high bracketed eaves to its hipped roof. The long elevation to the road two bay with wide label moulded openings. Short elevation three bay with central doorway flanked by a pair of minute lights. Walls stuccoed with reticulated and channelled quoins.

**166. GREENAN LODGE, Newry** pre 1859; *demolished*

**167. GREENMOUNT, Cultra** pre 1858; *demolished*

**168. GREENPARK Rostrevor** pre 1834; *demolished*
Probably built by Francis Carleton after the departure of James Moore to Arno's Vale (qv) in about 1820.
CROWE (1973)

**169. GREENVALE, Castlewellan** pre 1901; *demolished*
A lodge to a much earlier Georgian house built for William H Murland of the neighbouring flax spinning and linen manufactory.
GREEN (1963)

**170. GREENVILLE, Belfast South** pre 1834; *demolished*

A pair of lodges once south of the Beersbridge Road, demolished before the turn of the century to make way for red brick terraced housing. John Holmes Houston of the Belfast Bank moved to neighbouring Orangefield (qv) about 1830 and it was probably his successor here, one Thomas Ferguson, that built these lodges.

**171. GREENWOOD PARK, Newry** pre 1870

Lodge to a Picturesque sham castle for long the property of Ross Thompson and his widow. Built after the latter's death by the new owner. One and a half storey, originally three bay having projecting central hall with basic wavy bargeboards, a repeat of those on the main gables. Most of its previous Picturesque features lost in modernisation and extension.

**172. GREYABBEY, Greyabbey (3)**

A very fine estate of the Montgomerys. The house, alternatively known as Rosemount, in the main 1760-70 part Classical part Gothick as at Castleward (qv). None of the lodges are of that vintage.

**Abbey Entrance** c1825; architect not known

Facing the visitor across the gate screen a pretty single storey Georgian Gothick lodge. Its leading gable canted under a half umbrello roof, each face having a little lancet window with Y-tracery in dressed stone surround. Otherwise constructed in coursed basalt rubble with galleting just as at the Mountstewart (qv) pair, pointing to the same local mason. In the same manner and materials an impressive gate screen comprised of four large square pillars crowned with spiky pinnacles of dressed stone. These frame wing walls containing wicket openings with pointed heads. Good decorative ironwork in appropriate style.

**Early Town Gate** c1820

A simple hipped roof single storey Classical cottage. Three bay asymmetrical, the left hand one the entrance door with spoked fanlight. The windows in harled walls, their heads similarly treated with semicircular arches. Lacking its gates this entrance was made redundant by a mid-19th century road realignment. Both lodges built by William Montgomery not long after his succession in 1815.

**Later Town Gate** c1860

A pleasant Classical/Picturesque mixture. One and a half storey on a square plan, each elevation gabled containing an attic window. Front facade three bay built in greywacke with red brick dressings to semicircular headed openings. A gabled porch with similar archway advances from the left hand side, the composition balanced here by a single storey lean-to outshoot.
MINISTRY OF FINANCE (1966);
BENCE-JONES (1988)

**173. GROOMSPORT, Groomsport** c1848; architect James Sands

A Tudor Revival finialed and turreted stone villa which had a long gestation period. First mention of a new house was as early as 1841 but it did not materialise until about 1848. For John Waring Maxwell of Finnebrogue (qv) to designs

of the immigrant Englishman James Sands, architect to the Marquis of Downshire. His commission also included plans for a gate lodge and screen. A delightful little ashlar building in the same style as the house. A letter of 1841 from Sands to his client refers to plans for the house and "The Gate House". What was built is certainly not as described, being tiny single storey accommodation in sandstone ashlar. Very steep roof with dressed skewtable gables rising off deep sculpted kneelers. This is repeated in the hallway that projects from the symmetrical three bay front facade, the front door with chamfered reveals, hood moulded pointed arch and a blank shield relieving the gable over. Windows bipartite with central sash boxes. An octagonal pair of chimney pots repeated in the gate pillars. The pillars with their sculpted coronet finials are akin to those at Brecart Lodge, Co Antrim (qv). Both lodge and gates disgracefully neglected.
P.R.O.N.I. D1556; BANGOR AND GROOMSPORT; U.A.H.S. (1984)

**174. THE GROVE, Gilford**
(see ROSE COTTAGE)

**175. THE HALL, Donacloney**
(see STRAWHILL)

**176. HAMILTON VILLA, Bangor** c1875

Simple one and a half storey gabled, stuccoed, three bay symmetrical cottage.

**177. HAMPTON, Belfast North**
(see GLEN EBOR)

**178. HARRYMOUNT, Lurgan** pre 1833; *demolished*

**179. HAWTHORNDEN, Belfast North** c1890

Both house and lodge look twenty years older, the former a typical stuccoed Neo-Classical villa of the nouveau riche, the latter a modest cottage in complementary vein. Formerly three bay single storey and gabled. The door in a gabled projecting porch, openings segmentally arched. Stuccoed with quoins. Sometime later extended by two bays at one end.

**180. THE HILL, Downpatrick** c1860; *demolished*

Lodge to a house originating from 1791, which was built by John Potter who made his fortune smuggling. It was reworked c1860 by Rev Samuel Craig Nelson. The lodge though coeval looks older, a most unprepossessing affair. Built in rubble, single storey on a square plan, three bay symmetrical below a pyramidal roof with central chimney stack. Georgian style squared sash windows with shutters. The old postcard view shows the gatekeeper relaxing on his front step. The house, more recently called Ardmore has been demolished along with its lodge.
POSTCARD VIEW, LINENHALL LIBRARY

**181. HILLBROOK, Holywood** 1852; architect Thomas Turner; *unexecuted*

Designs were prepared for a house, outbuildings and a gate porter's lodge for William Bankhead. That the latter was not executed is explained by correspondence of 1854 which mentions Turner calling on his client en route to Craigavad (qv) probably in the hopes of effecting payment which seems not to have been forthcoming. In any case the house was divided into a pair of semidetached villas not long after and no trace of the drawing is to be found.
P.R.O.N.I. D1905/2/1470

**182. HILLHALL, Lisburn** c1840

The essential Irish Georgian style gate lodge to a decent Ulster farmhouse of 1775. The standard single storey, two roomed, three bay structure below a wide brimmed hipped roof. Walls now roughcast and windows enlarged but well tended. Concave quadrant harled walls flank the two survivors of four octagonal granite piers with friezes and cappings. Gates gone. Built by William Malcolm, there is a similar lodge and gate screen at New Grove (qv) nearby which suggest the same jobbing builder to have been responsible.

**183. HILLSBOROUGH ARCHDEACONRY, Hillsborough** c1830; *demolished*

The rectory first came into being in 1762 when Wills Hill gave a lease of 20 acres and a dwelling house to Francis Hutchinson, Archdeacon of Down and his successors for ever. It was extended in 1803, 1825 and 1830 the first of these three dates probably being when a porter's lodge and gate screen were built. In contrast to the accommodation of the noble three storey house with its extended eaves hipped roof was this little standard single storey three bay lodge, its hipped roof clipped. At right angles to the road its end elevation formed part of one of the wing walls each of which contained a semicircular-arched wicket opening. The two big square gate pillars harled like the rest of the composition. Probably built by Archdeacon John Dickson.
BARRY (1962)

**184. HILLSBOROUGH CASTLE, Hillsborough (5)**

A pleasant English-looking village with the big house, long and low at the top of the street integrated with it. A foundation of the Hill family of whom the 1st Marquis of Downshire engaged the English architect Robert William Furze Brettingham to rework and enlarge an earlier house on the site. This was complete by 1797. That the architect's brief extended to the provision of plans for a gate lodge is indicated in a letter from Thomas Lane to Lord Downshire: "Hillsborough Aug 31 1795. Mr B [Brettingham] is decided against the rooms over the kitchen. The additional building there is up - so is the porter's lodge - but no roof yet on either tho preparing". Quite where this was located is not clear for there is no evidence of it either on site or on the 1834 OS Map. That lodged entrances were contemplated along with the realignment of the Moira road can be seen from an estate map of 1810 which appears to be little more than a proposal. The actual rerouting did not occur until the 1830s and the proposed pair of lodges at an entrance to the Market Square never materialised although Peter Rankin in his Hillsborough Castle (U.A.H.S.) speculates that one of these was built to form the surviving Doric temple. Further alterations and additions were made to the mansion in the 1820s by Thomas J Duff but it was not until about twenty years later that a new gate screen to the Market Square appears to have been provided and the present demesne wall constructed in 1841.

**Town Lodge** c1840; architect probably William or James Sands

By 1858 the little Classical gate lodge fronting the guardhouse had appeared. Little more than a single storey sentrybox on duty alongside the gates. Two roomed on a square plan with a pyramidal roof and central chimney. Built in a blotchy sandstone ashlar, the one bay front has a squared pane sash window in a recess with dentilled and entablatured parapet over. The tall square corniced pillars built up of V-jointed rusticated masonry, today frame the magnificent gate screen all acquired from their rightful setting at Richhill, Co Armagh (qv). Taken from there in 1936 amongst much controversy to glorify the new residence of the Governor of Northern Ireland.

**Garden Lodge** pre 1858; *demolished*

On the second OS Map a "gate-lodge" is shown at the walled garden entrance. Probably built to accommodate a head gardener. Across the street separated from the demesne by the town is the park. One and a half miles square, surrounded by a high wall there are two unremarkable lodges. One "Park Street Lodge" by the town (pre 1858) the other "Upper Lodge" (c1860).
MID DOWN; U.A.H.S. (1974);
HILLSBOROUGH CASTLE; U.A.H.S. (1993);
P.R.O.N.I. DOD 607/566; GREEN (1961-2)

**185. HILLSBOROUGH FORT, Hillsborough** c1650/1758; architect probably Sanderson Miller

A star shaped artillery fort of c1650 the outer ramparts of which were built by Colonel Arthur Hill. What was a plain and functional gate house to the north west owes its present appearance to the 1st Lord Hillsborough who converted it into a charming mock castle in 1758. The former rectangular building was remodelled with the addition of four square corner towers each rising from a battered ground floor storey, incorporating slit windows with ogee heads, and extended to beyond the adjoining parapets. The latter were also heightened and crenellated, the first floor room on opposing elevations having three lancet windows inserted, each Y-traceried below hood mouldings. At ground level the old semicircular-arched gate openings were filled with tripartite doorway and sidelight screens, also with pointed heads. Ground floor constructed in rubble masonry with brickwork in English bond above a moulded stringcourse. This is one of the first instances of the Gothic Revival in Ireland and extends to the

*Hillsborough Fort, Gatehouse and Gazebo Gate*

contemporary and charming little gazebo entrance in the north-east rampart. Both buildings are thought to be examples of the work of the architect Sanderson Miller. At ground level the round headed archways are surmounted by traceried ogival windows in dressed sandstone. This upper storey gives access to the ramparts. Walls are raised to a corbelled parapet or mock machicolation at roof level.
MINISTRY OF FINANCE (1966); MID DOWN; U.A.H.S. (1974)

**186. HOLLYMOUNT, Downpatrick** c1820; *ruinous*

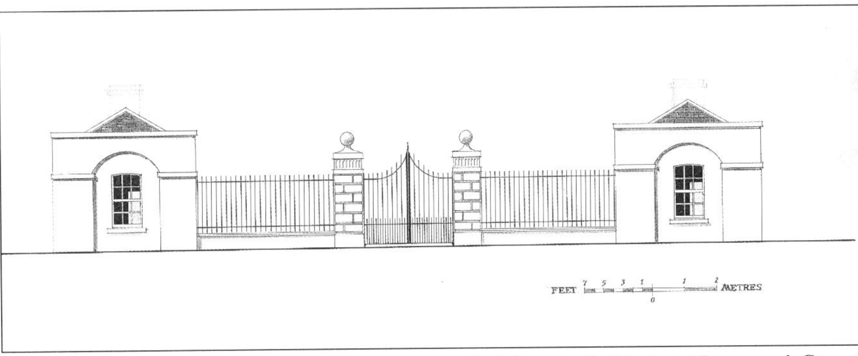


A pair of astylar Neo-Classical pavilions flanking the gates to a graceful house of 1781 built for Cromwell Price MP. The lodges were built for a later occupant Francis Savage. Single storey three bay they presented their single bay elevations to the visitor. Square paned sash windows framed by segmentally-arched recesses below parapets concealing hipped roofs. Simple stringcourse at spring level in stuccoed walls. There were two square ashlar pillars linked to the lodges by straight railed screens. This once fine demesne, like its house and lodges, has almost completely disappeared.
MINISTRY OF FINANCE (1966)

**187. HOLYWOOD, Holywood** pre 1858; *demolished*

Lodge to a house, now gone, which passed through a succession of owners after being built by Simon Isaac. The lodge was probably built for Henry Harrison on his acquisition of the property from J McCartney.
MERRICK (1986)

**188. HOMRA, Hillsborough** pre 1834/1920

The former lodge here probably built by Colonel Marcus Corry has been replaced by an early twentieth century affair, pebble-dashed with smooth lugged opening surrounds. Gabled and single storey.

**189. THE HOWE, Dromara** c1880

Replacing an earlier pre 1834 structure is this single storey four bay building, the right hand bay blind. Constructed of random basalt rubble with red brick dressings. The hipped roof has its eaves decorated by a continuous perforated wavy fascia board. Deserted and dilapidated.

**190. HUNTLEY, Gilford** c1837; architect Thomas Jackson; *demolished*

In 1835 Hugh Dunbar acquired the property and founded the large yarn spinning mill which opened in 1839. Sometime before he had built this decent Neo-Classical villa with gate lodge.

A building identical to that at Longwood, Co Antrim (qv) by the same architect. Identical that is in all but the parapeted roof which is substituted here for the projecting eaves there. Single storey three bay in style to match the house but more ostentatious with its central distyle Ionic pedimented portico. In stucco dressed in stone, its segmentally-arched openings

in corresponding recesses their architraves carried down to plinth level. Door and windows were margined in a manner Jackson employed at Glenmore, Co Antrim (qv) Dunbarton (qv) nearby and elsewhere. Doric pilasters as quoins. To the road a canted bay. Surviving are typical Jacksonesque octagonal gate piers with recessed

panels and corniced "helmet" cappings. Spear topped gates and matching railings on ogee quadrants. Hugh Dunbar was to move from here, leaving his four sisters in occupation, to build Dunbarton in 1845 with similar porter's lodge.
BASSETT'S CO DOWN (1886);
CAMPBELL (1990)

**191. INCH ABBEY HOUSE, Downpatrick**
pre 1834; *ruinous*
A humble lodge now ruinous and over-grown probably to the herd's house mentioned in Griffith's valuation on the property of John Waring Maxwell of Finnebrogue (qv). The lodge has a three bay front to the road by one deep. Single storey in rubble stone below a hipped roof with clipped eaves.
GRIFFITH

**192. ISLAND SPINNING COMPANY, Lisburn** pre 1834; *demolished*
On an island formed by the Lagan river and navigation canal was the sulphuric acid works established here by Thomas Gregg and Waddell Cunningham in 1764 which gave the name of Vitriol Island until 1828. Green states the entrance gate pillars and walls of basalt masonry probably to be of this early period. An 1888 illustration shows the approach across a bridge at the twelfth lock to a gabled lodge alongside the gates. The front elevation was two bay with Gothick lancet windows. The works became a concern of Jonathan Joseph Richardson of Kirkassock (qv). The whole island site was recently completely cleared of buildings.
BASSETT'S CO ANTRIM (1888);
GREEN (1963)

**193. KILBRONEY PARK, Rostrevor** c1845; architect probably Thomas J Duff

Lodge to a pleasant rambling Picturesque house of the Martin family. The gate lodge an apposite fancy bargeboard introduction. Very much from the architect's P F Robinson period which he also displayed at nearby Narrow Water Castle (qv) and Tamnaharry (qv) with their ornamental gables. More generous in scale, one and a half storey on an L plan. Roughcast walls with granite quoins, the gables decorated with carved foiled bargeboards with quatrefoil toes. To the road elevation a dormer window and to vary the outline a gablet faces the avenue, all with squared sash windows. Big paired chamfered chimney stacks. Plain stone carriage gate piers.

**194. KILLAIRE, Bangor**
(see BALLYKILLAIRE)

**195. KILLINCHY RECTORY, Killinchy** c1840
Built for the long serving incumbent Rev Henry Ward to the earlier tall Georgian rectory. A tiny single storey two bay gabled lodge. Advancing to the avenue a breakfront porch with crudely carved bargeboards and stunted hipknob. Bipartite sash window to the road in harled walls. Quaint and uninhabited.
EAST DOWN; U.A.H.S. (1973)

**196. KILLYLEAGH CASTLE, Killyleagh (2)**
By the shores of Strangford Lough, like a chateau on the Loire, rising above the trees is the romantic outline of the castle with its crenellated and conically-roofed towers. Founded in the late 12th century it owes its present appearance to James Hamilton who rebuilt it c1610, and to the architect Charles Lanyon who was responsible for a major reconstruction in 1847-51. At the head of the main street is the entrance screen which fronts an enclosure 100 yards by 50 yards, an area which formed the former bawn. It is this screen which represents a fascinating tale of intrigue, for in consequence of a contested will and a twenty year legal battle the property was divided in 1697. The castle remained in Hamilton hands but the entrance accommodation had passed by marriage to the Blackwood family of Ballyleidy, later Lords Dufferin of Clandeboye. By the 1830s the situation was unchanged and the gate house was not sufficiently commodious to house the younger Blackwood sons. The architects Duff and Jackson, then in brief partnership, were to produce the most ponderous and repetitive castellated Gothick design to close access to the old bawn. This was to prove short-lived thanks to Lord Dufferin who in 1849 buried his differences and restored the gate house to the Hamiltons. His generosity extended far beyond this for he was to offer his architect Benjamin Ferrey, already employed at Clandeboye (qv), to provide plans for a singularly more appropriate entrance screen and gate house than that which it replaced, and all at his own expense.

**Town Gate** 1860;
architect Benjamin Ferrey
Between the original 17th century flankers the architect planned tall curtain walls leading to a fortified entrance gatehouse suitable in all but materials. In a crisp grey, squared and uncoursed basalt which contrasts with the older rubble and harled construction beyond. Irregular in outline, it is basically a pair of rectangular towers rising from battered bases on either side of the entrance carriageway, the bedroom accommodation spanning overhead. The left hand ground floor "lodge" gives spiral access to the sleeping storey over and continues a further two floors into a machicolated and crenellated watch-tower. The central bedroom has a similarly treated parapet and has an ornamental oriel window overlooking the castle forecourt. At this level is access to the curtain wall ramparts. The right hand ground floor room is designated "Tools" by the architect, for his drawings survive at Clandeboye. The whole composition employs dressed stone to a surplus of sculpted machicolations, single and bipartite mullioned windows and the Hamilton coat-of-arms with a heart over three cinquefoils. Below the moulded and pointed carriage archway are modern iron gates much too flimsy in such an otherwise indestructible display. Lord Dufferin duly presented the gatehouse to the Hamiltons by way of atonement for the family feud, and two years later proceeded to marry the Hamilton daughter. In 1869 an indenture of friendship was drawn up between the two families and the Hamiltons agreed to pay annual rent for the gate house of a golden rose and a pair of silver spurs.

**Side Gate** 1870; architects Lanyon, Lynn and Lanyon
On the Shrigley approach, later than Lanyon's mid-19th century work to the castle, is this very picturesque gateway and screen wall owing much to his partner W H Lynn. There are two "candle snuffer" conical roofs, one to a round tower on the right of the semicircular arched carriage access, the other on a corbelled bartizan

W.A. Green (U.F.T.M.)

*Killyleagh Castle, Side Gate*

B. Ferrey drawing (Marchioness of Dufferin & Ava)

*Killyleagh Castle, Town Gate*

to the left. In the archway spandrels suitable monograms and the datestone, all surmounted by a stepped crenellated parapet which contains a plaque with sculpted coat-of-arms. All in coursed squared quarry-faced basalt with dressed sandstone to slit windows, mock arrowloops, corbel stringcourse and moulded arch surround. Beyond, the screen wall extends stepping up to terminate in another fairy tale bartizan.
GIROUARD (1979); ROWAN (1970); DIXON (1972); EAST DOWN; U.A.H.S. (1973); GREEN PHOTOGRAPH (U.F.T.M.)
Ref W.A.G. 1700

**197. KILMOOD CHURCH OF IRELAND, Killinchy** c1830

Whether a gate lodge or sexton's accommodation or both, is not clear but it has the quintessential shape of the former. A pretty single storey three bay symmetrical building with wide oversailing eaves to its hipped roof. Georgian Gothick lancet heads to openings with small squared sash windows and blind overpanels which probably conceal the attic floor as at nearby Florida Manor (qv). All whitewashed and harled as are its wing walls. Probably built for Rev John Robert Moore.
EAST DOWN; U.A.H.S. (1973)

**198. KILWARLIN MORAVIAN CHURCH, Hillsborough** c1855

At the entrance to the unique grounds and church founded in 1755 is a Classical gatescreen comprised of central carriage opening flanked by wickets, all with iron uprights topped by pine cones. The square stone pillars are surmounted by ball finials each with unusual Greek key pattern bands. These perhaps reflect the advent of the Greek minister, Basil Patras Zula, who effected a revitalisation of the church from 1834. Outside a little single storey gabled lodge surveys the entrance alongside spoiled by the insertion of a steel beam and garage doors over which survives an oval plaque with the inscription OF THINE OWN HAVE WE GIVEN THEE O LORD, 1 Chrons. 29.14. Just visible through the undergrowth in harled walls, lancet windows on the side elevations are glazed with margined lattice pattern lights suggesting a mid-Victorian date.

**199. KINGHILL, Rathfriland** c1850

Once the property of William Wynstead Newell Barron who built the lodge, now a sorry sight lying derelict, the demesne run down. Single storey, three bay gabled in stucco with brick dressings. The road gable now minus its canted bay window, a roundel relief over. Fine contemporary gate screen with four square granite pillars with panelled shafts and pyramidal cappings over a frieze.

**200. KIRKASSOCK, Donacloney (3)**

The seat in the early 19th century of John Christie who had two gate lodges, one pre 1834 to the south west boundary of the demesne the other pre 1858 to the north east. Both superseded. In about 1866 the property passed to Jonathan Joseph Richardson of the Island Flax Spinning Company (qv). For once the family's architect Thomas Jackson and his habitual Neo-Classical style were forsaken for the great English Gothicist Sir Alfred Waterhouse. He designed his client a tall multi-gabled mansion with mullioned and transomed windows in Ruskinian Gothick manner. Richardson had probably met the English architect through the other big linen family, the Barbours who had commissioned Waterhouse at The Fort, Lisburn (qv) in 1861. He also provided plans for a new lodge and gates to the north west entrance at Lismaine, none of which were executed. By 1889 the estate had been inherited by Wakefield Christie- Miller who engaged the local architect Robert Watt to design two porters' lodges.

**Main Entrance** 1889; architect Robert Watt

A good Arts-and-Crafts two storey gatehouse, an essay in red brick with matching earthenware tiled gabled roofs. Three bay symmetrical with skewtable gables, that to the road with quadripartite windows, above which is a bullseye light to the roof space. The avenue facade with very high eaves has a three bay semicircular-headed arcade, once an open porch under its own hipped roof. Squat corbelled chimney stack. Extensive entrance gates with pretty round stone pillars and secondary curvilinear cast iron carriage piers much as at Greenisland Hospital, Co Antrim (qv).

**Lismaine Lodge** c1890; architect Robert Watt

A prettier variation on the above to smaller scale and in polychromatic red and yellow brick, the front porch projection reduced to a single bay.
P.R.O.N.I. D1031; WATERHOUSE (1992)

**201. KNOCKBARRAGH PARK, Rostrevor** pre 1860; architect perhaps W J Barre; *demolished*

A lodge for Charles A Von Stieglitz for whom the youthful Newry architect is recorded as having worked in the late 1850s.
DUNLOP (1868)

**202. KNOCKBREDA RECTORY, Newtownbreda** pre 1834; *demolished*

A lodge probably built by the incumbent Rev John Kinahan long gone, having been overrun by late Victorian city spread.

**203. KNOCKNAGONEY, Belfast North** (see CLIFTON HALL)

**204. LAGAN VALE, Belfast South** (see FOX LODGE)

**205. LAKEVIEW, Lurgan** c1853; architect possibly Thomas Jackson; *demolished*

A lodge to a big blousy Neo-Classical villa for Francis Watson by Thomas Jackson.
DIXON (1978)

**206. LAMB'S ISLAND, Waringstown** pre 1834

To a pleasant Regency gentleman farmer's villa is an entrance through a pair of grand round, conical-topped Ulster field pillars. These are flanked by an ogee quadrant to one side and a shorter wing wall to the other pierced by a rustic stile and stopped by a simple lodge. With a chimney stack to each gable its main elevation to the roadside was previous asymmetrical three bay with its door to the left. A delightful group of structures appropriately whitewashed. Probably for the Rev John Sherrard, the 1823 proprietor. The lodge having been delisted is being subjected to plastic Georgianisation.
H.M.B. PHOTOGRAPH Ref. UB/14/16/34; MINISTRY OF FINANCE (1966);

**207. LANEVAN, Belfast South** pre 1900; *demolished*

A house which has undergone numerous name changes probably originating as Cumingville for George Cuming. Subsequently called Lanevan, briefly Washington and, since the turn of this century, Ardenza. The house now appears as a wealthy merchant's double fronted stuccoed villa of c1880, its little three bay gate lodge demolished in the late 1970s, perhaps contemporary.

**208. LARCHFIELD, Annahilt (4)**

Daniel Mussenden, a founder of the Belfast Bank, built this fine mid-Georgian house c1756. Opposite the entrances were pre 1834 gate lodges to which only the elegant gate pillars remain. Square with V-jointed masonry each is decorated with a delicate frieze, fluted with sculpted "cobweb" motifs central to three faces. The corniced cappings have the simplest of ball finials. The cast iron gates later, probably of an age with the replacement lodges. The property passed in 1868 from the Mussendens to the Graham family of whom Ogilvie Blair Graham ten years later replaced both lodges in a new fashionable robust late Victorian Picturesque style.

**Lisburn Lodge** 1878; architect probably John Lanyon

In squared uncoursed basalt contrasting starkly with "white" fireclay brick dressings, quoins and stringcourses. One and a half storey on a simple rectangular plan, the gable elevation facing the gates contains a single storey canted bay, also in yellow brick, offset to accommodate a recessed corner porch alongside. Manfully carrying the external corner a banded column with foliated capital, much as that to the Belfast Castle (qv) lodge by John Lanyon. The main gables have lost their ornamental bargeboards but a wavy one does survive on a dormer window. Ground floor windows have segmental heads enhanced with canted bricks. High on the leading gable the Graham crest (a falcon killing a stork) and the motto MEMOR ESTO with the date on a sculpted plaque. By the huge squat yellow brick chimney stack earthenware sawtooth cresting.

**Hillsborough Lodge** 1878; architect probably John Lanyon

Identical to the above except that sandstone is substituted for yellow brick and the better for it.
MASON (1814-19)

**209. LARGYMORE DAMASK FACTORY, Lisburn** pre 1858; *demolished*
A lodge to the bleachworks built in 1823 by William Coulson & Sons. Most of the surviving buildings on the site are post 1870 when the company was bought out. There remains a gabled single storey structure with segmentally headed windows in polychrome brickwork c1880 which may be replacement porter's accommodation for that recorded by Griffith in his valuation of 1863.
GREEN (1963); GRIFFITH

**210. LAWRENCETOWN, Lawrencetown (2)**
Alexander John Robert Stewart of Ards, Co Donegal (qv) came by the property from Hugh Lyons Montgomery who had built the house. Neither of the lodges survive.

**East Gate** pre 1834; *ruinous*
The lodge survived by a fine symmetrical Classical gate screen of square granite ashlar pillars with fluted friezes and corniced cappings. Flanking are straight wing walls each containing a wicket opening. Good contemporary late Georgian spear topped wrought iron gates.

**West Gate** c1860; *demolished*
Gate pillars like those above, rebuilt in stunted state. The house occupied by the Bowen family for many years, presumably as Stewart agents.

**211. LEAWOOD, Belfast North** pre 1898; *demolished*
In 1898 the occupant was the architect R Graeme Watt who was to become partner of Frederick H Tulloch three years earlier.

**212. LEGMORE, Moira** pre 1903
A long nondescript lodge, in 1870 the property of Thomas McDade.

**213. LISBURN FLAX SPINNING MILL, Lisburn**
(see ISLAND SPINNING COMPANY)

**214. LISMACHAN, Belfast North** 1872; architect A T Jackson

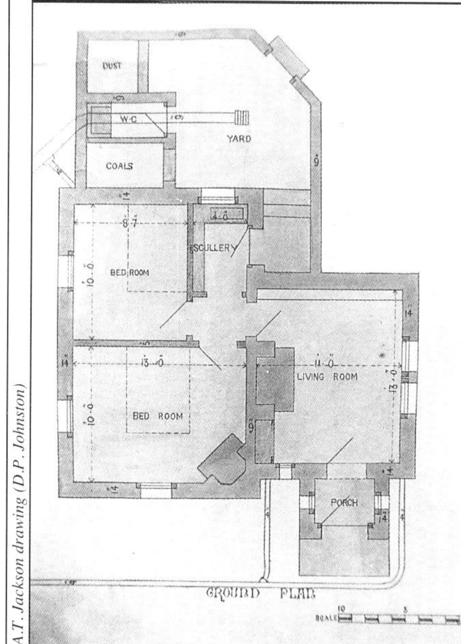


*A.T. Jackson drawing (D.P. Johnston)*

One of many large villas in the Glenmachan area by Thomas Jackson, architect to rich merchants and Quakers. This example of 1869 for James Shaw. The lodge in complementary style by the architect's son. For T M Greeves, a competent informal Italianate style lodge. Single storey stuccoed, with shallow pitched gables, on an irregular plan. Semicircular-headed openings with stringcourses at spring and cill levels. Advancing towards the avenue a small hallway with sidelights. Quoins expressed in the stucco with recessed joints. There is a typical Jackson chimney stack, with a plinth and moulded brackets in the cornice. The original drawing which survives shows accommodation of living room, two bedrooms, scullery and integral yard space to the rear.

**215. LISNABRAQUE LODGE, Poyntzpass**
(see UNION LODGE)

**216. LISNABREENY, Newtownbreda** pre 1834; *demolished*
The seat in 1817 of H S Harvey.

**217. LISNACREE, Rostrevor**
(see MOUNT LOFTUS)

**218. LISNAGADE, Scarva** pre 1833; *demolished*
A pair of lodges which did not survive the end of the century. A property in 1836 of E H Trevor.

**219. LISNASTREAN, Lisburn** c1840
A modest two roomed single storey lodge with a hipped roof. Gable-on outside the gates. Built for the Graham family. Abandoned.

**220. LITTLE CLANDEBOYE, Newtownards** c1865; architect not known

In the village of Conlig a Tudor Gothick villa on an elevated site, now a shell. The lodge is later. A solid design constructed in quarry-faced basalt with distinctive contrasting ashlar quoins, plinth and chamfered openings with hood moulded pointed heads. Pendant dripstones. Single storey gabled, as is the projecting hall with basic wavy bargeboards. Spoiled by modern window intrusions and puny brick chimney stack. One time seat of James Alexander Pirrie after having served as a Blackwood dower house.

**221. THE LODGE, Rostrevor** pre 1834; *demolished*
The porter's accommodation and the house both gone. In 1836 "... the seat of David Ross, Esq, whose seat, The Lodge is distinguished from the smaller villas by the extent of its grounds and plantations". The family was to move to Carrick Bawn (qv) not long after this was written. Now a public park.
FRASER (1838)

**222. THE LODGE, Strangford** c1865

A pretty Picturesque mid-Victorian cottage built by James Blackwood Price. Single storey stuccoed and gabled with delicately fretted bargeboards and slender hipknobs. A gabled hallway projects from the symmetrical three bay front facade, with a segmental arch and narrow sidelights. On the road elevation a canted bay window with semicircular-headed niche over. Quoins, the windows modern. Chimney stack with dentil course to cornice. Thin octagonal cast iron posts with recessed panel shafts and "morgenstern" ball finials. Delicate palmette topped railed sweeps.

**223. LOUGHBRICKLAND, Loughbrickland (2)**
Although the architect Thomas J Duff worked for Mrs Whyte here in 1826 there is nothing at the gates pretentious enough to be by him.

**North Lodge** pre 1833; *demolished*

**Town Lodge** pre 1833
The archetypal Irish vernacular lodge. Single storey three bay symmetrical below a wide shallow hipped roof with eaves brackets. Harled walls. Deserted.

**224. LOYOLA, Dromore**
(see DROMORE PALACE)

**225. MARMONT, Belfast North** 1886; architect not known
W C Mitchell of Glasgow came to Belfast in 1863 as manager of Dunville and Co, Distillers.

He built his house in 1886 in an Italianate manner with a gate lodge to match. On an irregular plan a single storey lodge of generous accommodation. Under a hipped roof, the wing to the road canted, from the face of which rose a chimney stack. The wing to the avenue in the form of a rectangular breakfront bay window. In an internal angle a flat roofed porch with semicircular-headed arches. Below the continuous eaves frieze of moulded brackets, windows were arranged in pairs with chamfered reveals. Stringcourse at cill level. Three corniced chimney stacks. The lodge has now undergone the most remarkable and surreal transformation into a modern butterfly-roofed house. Extensive gates with concave railed quadrants all swept away. Very decorative ironwork to carriage gates and pair of flanking wickets. Now the Mitchell House school.
P.R.O.N.I. D3624/2/29 Photographs

**226. MARYFIELD, Holywood** c1830; *demolished*
To a house, the first known resident of which was John Kennedy, a contemporary and highly original gate lodge. Single storey on an octagonal plan from alternate faces of which projected rectangular bay windows and an entrance porch. Windows had semicircular heads in stuccoed walls below the conventional eaves of the slated octahedral roof which rose to a central chimney stack. The house was burnt down in 1969 and the lodge demolished two years later.

**227. MAYFIELD, Dromara** c1845
Outside the gates a Gothick lodge of one and a half storeys. Constructed in basalt rubble with red brick dressings to lancet openings. Its gabled roof later raised. In 1846 the property of James Birch Gilmore. Abandoned.

**228. MERTOUN HALL, Holywood** pre 1858; *demolished*
The lodge to a house of c1835 built by its occupant for a short time, Dr James Taggart. It then passed to John Harrison, ship owner, who added the lodge.
MERRICK (1986)

**229. MILECROSS, Newtownards** c1855
A Picturesque stuccoed formal one and a half storey three bay lodge. Main gables and that to the projecting hall decorated with pretty foiled bargeboards and trefoil toes. Slender carved hipknobs with finials and pendants. In the hall gable a shield displaying the monogram of the proprietor George Dickson. Now restored after years of neglect.

**230. MILLMOUNT, Banbridge** pre 1903; architect perhaps Thomas Turner; *demolished*
Although nothing remains of the lodge the architect is known to have carried out work here for the Hayes family. They were owners of the huge Seapatrick Mills of the Linen Thread Manufactory, F W Hayes and Co.
P.R.O.N.I. D1905/2/147; BASSETT'S CO DOWN (1886)

**231. THE MOATE, Belfast North** pre 1834; *demolished*
The 1863 house belonging to John L Bell had a gate lodge. In that year the property was purchased by the linen merchant Thomas Valentine who replaced the old house with a remarkable new Italianate mansion by the architect W J Barre. The old lodge continued to serve until its demolition this century.
DUNLOP (1868)

**232. MONTALTO, Ballynahinch (3)**
The estates previously of the Rawdons, Earls of Moira were purchased in 1802 by David Ker of Portavo (qv). He was to make the house his "occasional residence" and in 1813 is recorded as not having spent much on its improvement. It was probably his son of the same name who provided two gate lodges.

**Spa Gate** c1825; architect perhaps W V Morrison
A Georgian Gothick cottage much in the form of those at Florida Manor (qv), with canted ends. Perhaps of greater significance is the incorrect Y-tracery glazing pattern to the lancet windows which is also to be found at Mountstewart (qv) and Ards, Co Donegal (qv), two Stewart estates. David Ker in 1814 had married Lady Selina Sarah Stewart daughter of the 1st Marquis of Londonderry. Charles Brett (UAHS 1974) has noticed work in the house resembling that of William Vitruvius Morrison and this could be another pointer to the author of the twin lodges at Mountstewart. Now stuccoed the lodge has been greatly modernised and extended with the addition of an ornamental bargeboarded hallway. Hidden from the road at the end of a long avenue approach.

**West Gate** pre 1834
The present uninteresting building looks to be a mid-Victorian successor to an earlier lodge. Two storey with modern windows. It is curious that there was no entrance of any pretension from the town in the first half of the 19th century, a state of affairs that David Stewart Ker was at pains to remedy. Between 1860 and 1867 he was to commission the most remarkable series of ostentatious designs before settling upon something rather less than remarkable.

**Town Gate** Design No 1 1867; architect George Aitchison the Younger; *unexecuted*
Perhaps the most outrageous of the plans submitted. Clearly a product of the architect's Grand Tour is this medieval Tuscan palazzo. A four square two storey gatehouse with a heavily machicolated parapet with "cloven hoof" crenellations straight from the Palazzo Vecchio in Florence. The ground floor has a pointed arch entrance door surmounted by a band of shields at first floor cill level. This upper storey displays a series of window openings rendered bipartite by colonettes, below semicircular heads with sculpted spandrels. Rising off one corner a tall crenellated campanile tower. That the client considered this to be a viable proposal is clear from its appearance in the background of two perspective drawings for an accompanying gate screen designed by Thomas Turner and Thomas Drew during their brief architectural liaison. Neither design makes the remotest effort to be congruous.

**Town Gate** Design No 2 c1867; architects Turner and Drew; *unexecuted*
A fantastic and monumental Neo-Classical design for a triumphal archway. With vermiculated voussoirs to its semicircular carriage opening, it is flanked by Vitruvian openings on rusticated podia from which rise paired Corinthian columns to a balustraded parapet decorated with urns. Above the arch a three bay stage with oculi supports a pediment, its tympanum having sculpted anthemion over. As if this were not enough, beyond are extensive concave screens, eight bays each separated by pairs of rusticated Ionic columns. The bays perforated by more oculi. The wicket openings, triumphal arches in their own right, are crowned by segmental pediments. The screen wall has an entablatured coping decorated with urns, goddesses gracing the terminating bays.

G. Aitchinson drawing (Capt. D.J.R. Kerr)

*Town Gate, Design 1*

Turner & Drew drawing (Capt. D.J.R. Kerr)

Town Gate, Design 2

Turner & Drew drawing (Capt. D.J.R. Kerr)

Town Gate, Design 3

**Town Lodge** c1870; *demolished*
An early 20th century postcard view shows a gate lodge. A single storey four bay gabled building the walls ivy-clad. There were narrow lancet windows and a projecting gabled porch with mildly fancy bargeboards. It would be interesting to know if the respective architects were suitably remunerated for their pains particularly after having been supplanted by a relative amateur.
DRAWINGS IN POSSESSION CAPT D J R KER; DIXON (1972); BURKE (1904); D.B. (1961); POSTCARD VIEW, BARRY WATSON; MID-DOWN; U.A.H.S. (1974)

**233. MOORE LODGE, Newry** c1914
To match the contemporary house, a one and a half storey, roughcast gabled gate lodge, Arts-and-Crafts style. On an L plan formed by a breakfront with canted bay window. Alongside a verandah over the front door extended to cover a nice rustic bench, part of the architect's concept. Earthenware tiled roof. Built for a local solicitor J Hunter-Moore.

**234. MOUNT HALL, Warrenpoint**
(see NARROW WATER)

**Town Gate** Design No 3 c1867;
architects Turner and Drew; *unexecuted*
Not quite as grandiose as the previous design. In the form of six huge ornamental Italianate pillars which frame concave outer railed sweeps, a pair of wicket gates and the central carriage opening. All the ironwork excessively decorative in keeping with the sculpted masonry. Each pillar would appear to boast a low level lionhead drinking fountain, the shaft above containing an ornamental roundel in the shape of a modern "hub-cap". The "lucarned" cappings over carry clusters of five globe lanterns. At this point Ker seems to have abandoned his castle-in-the- air, for the next proposal has gatekeeper's accommodation incorporated in the entrance screen.

**Town Gate** Design No 4 c1867;
architects Turner and Drew; *unexecuted*
Comprising a pair of boxy lodges with panelled parapets crowned by rows of acroteria. Front elevations blind and pilastered. Uniting these buildings two pedimented pedestrian doorways which flank a grand carriage arch, heavily rusticated with attached Tuscan columns. These support an open segmental pediment its tympanum containing a sculpted coat-of-arms. Framing all this, relatively plain vermiculated stone concave walls terminating in pairs of pillars similarly treated, as copied in the eventual successful design. In the background of the drawing rises a mysterious Italianate villa with fluttering flag.

**Town Gate** Design No 5 c1867;
architect William Brown
An extensive screen 118ft 6ins (36m) wide is here proposed. A crude drawing probably by a jobbing builder. Two large carriage pillars with quarry-faced stone shafts have contrasting ashlar plinths, fluted friezes and corniced cappings crowned by swagged urns. The concave screen and octagonal secondary posts had a variety of domed and onion finials all in wood with ornamental fencing. The timber was replaced early this century by cast iron railings and gates. Much as executed.

Turner & Drew drawing (Capt. D.J.R. Kerr)

Town Gate, Design 4

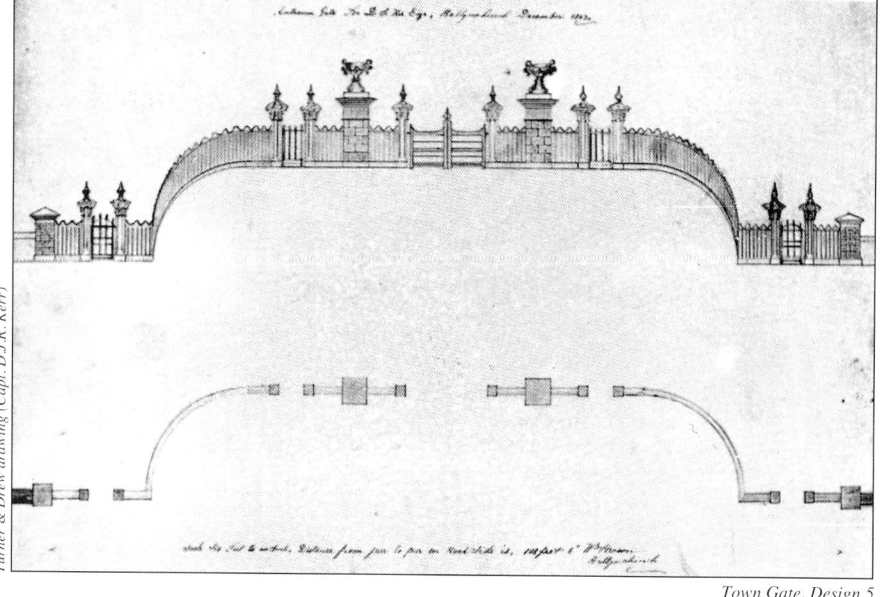
Turner & Drew drawing (Capt. D.J.R. Kerr)

Town Gate, Design 5

**235. MOUNT KEARNY, Newry** c1830;
*ruinous*

Opposite the gates a charming lodge for James Parker. A single storey two roomed two bay structure with ornamental lobed bargeboard gables. The elevation to the road had windows framed by elliptical arched recesses. Constructed in stone rubble, a charming 1959 photograph shows it in its heyday clothed in ivy. Entrance door to side elevation.
B.N.L. Photograph (20th November 1959)

**236. MOUNT LOFTUS, Rostrevor** pre 1834;
*demolished*
By 1859 this lodge had gone, the house renamed Lisnacree.

**237. MOUNT PANTHER, Dundrum (4)**

One of Ulster's most important Georgian houses today lies a sad shell in the final stages of decay. Rented by Dean and Mrs Delany it was rebuilt in 1770 by Lord Glerawley of the Annesley family. It is probably from this time that the two earlier gate lodges date, one of which survived until around 1970. This was a square building with an open porch recessed on one corner. Very plain, harled and whitewashed walls below a pyramidal roof, located opposite the gates like its counterpart. These early lodges were replaced by John R Allen who acquired the seat from Hugh Moore.

**Newcastle Lodge** c1830
A simple two roomed single storey lodge below a hipped roof. Gable-on to the avenue this elevation has a central doorway with integral slit sidelights all framed with dressed granite in harled walls. Ornate pillars and ironwork look later.

**Side Lodge** c1830
Identical to the above behind crude entrance pillars.
MINISTRY OF FINANCE (1966);
DELANY (1861-62)

**238. MOUNT PLEASANT, Newtownards**
1846
The lodge appears as a simple rectangular plan on the 1858 OS Map when the proprietor was a Captain Morrison. Sometime later it was raised by the Mayne family to two storeys. Simply gabled, the walls roughcast with smooth banded opening surrounds. There is a further extension to the earlier breakfront, a datestone roundel relocated in the gable. The fine Scrabo stone entrance screen has four V-jointed ashlar pillars and concave quadrant walls. Probably coeval with the rebuilding of the house c1820. The pretty house which was burnt down in the 1789 rebellion was later rebuilt and became the home of the architect, John Millar, who had his offices in York Street, Belfast. It was enlarged probably in 1846 when the lodge was built.

**239. MOUNTSTEWART, Greyabbey (3)**
The *Post Chaise Companion* of 1786 tells us that the Right Honourable Robert Stewart was "... building a magnificent seat", something that Arthur Young in 1779 records that he was intent on. Additions to the house were made in 1804 by the architect George Dance and about twenty years later William Vitruvius Morrison was commissioned to greatly enlarge and re-orientate the mansion. The 1st Marquess of Londonderry, as he was created in 1816, was not to execute the designs until 1845, after the architect's death, perhaps due to his concentrating on the restoration of his English seat after a fire there. The 1st Marquess did nevertheless add three lodged entrances to the demesne before 1834.

**The Twin Lodges** c1825;
architect possibly W V Morrison

Aligned for maximum impact on the Newtownards road approach is this fine pair of single storey lodges with leading canted elevations below half umbrello roofs. Georgian Gothick with lancet openings the Y-tracery not quite correct, something to be found in an identical lodge on the other Stewart estate, Ards, Co Donegal (qv) and at Spa Lodge, Montalto (qv) where the daughter of the 1st Marquess had married David Ker. One original octagonal stone chimney stack remains, the other having been replaced in ugly brick. Constructed in squared coursed basalt with galleting as on the earlier house and also to be found on the Gothick Greyabbey (qv) gate lodge. Flanked by the lodges is a pair of pretty wrought iron carriage gates hung on simple square pillars with lanterns aloft.

**Greyabbey Gate** c1830

A highly distinctive building facing the road alongside the entrance. Constructed in unusual polygonal basalt, the openings have pointed heads and Y-tracery. Single storey three bay symmetrical the outer bays forming breakfronts below a parapet on each corner of which are hornlike spikey finials. Beautifully restored, it is flanked by curved wing walls.

**Rear Entrance** c1830/c1860/c1890
A lodge with a chronology to equal that of the house. Originally a simple gabled building with a columned Doric front. It lost its former elegance in the Picturesque period with the addition of a gabled wing at right angles, forming an L plan. Fretted foiled bargeboards over a rectangular bay window. Later still an extension with tall late Victorian red brick chimney stack. Now all roughcast.
YOUNG (1892); POST CHAISE COMPANION (1786); COLVIN (1978); McPARLAND (1989)

**240. MOUNT VILLA, Downpatrick** c1880
To a fine Neo-Classical villa of the Pilson family a late Victorian lodge post-dates it by some 150 years. Faced in "white" fireclay brick, single storey on an L plan. The gable to the road has a bow window, its lights separated by banded stylised Ionic colonettes over which is a dentil course. The projection to the avenue canted below a half umbrello roof with central finial. Terracotta sawtooth cresting and a big plinthed and chamfered chimney stack. Once characterful in a hotchpotch of styles and materials but now rendered mundane by a cloak of roughcast, and much extended. An elegant gate screen in the manner of the house. Square sandstone ashlar pillars, each decorated with a band of roundels below a Greek key pattern. Chamfered shafts have cappings with dogtooth motif surrounds. The original gates and railings to ogee sweeps are missing. Built for Conway Pilson, the house later became known as Rathdune.
DOWNPATRICK; U.A.H.S. (1970)

**241. MOURNE GRANGE SCHOOL, Kilkeel**
(see DRUMINDONEY)

**242. MOURNE PARK, Kilkeel (4)**
Once called Siberia and a seat of the Needhams Earls of Kilmorey, the estate is situated in fine scenery around the Whitewater river.

**East Lodge or Ballymaglogh Gate** c1820
A very simple rustic gabled cottage. Single storey three bay its windows tripartite casements in harled walls.

**West Lodge or Tullyframe Gate** c1840
By a ford a pleasant lodge now approached by a foot-bridge. Single storey stuccoed Regency style with a low pitched hipped roof.

**Whitewater Gate** c1830

By the same hand or from a common unidentified pattern book as the middle lodge at Hockley, Co Armagh (qv). An unusual single storey cottage on a T plan under hipped roofs. The arm advancing to the avenue contains a projecting canted bay window with a roof of its own. Raised on a basement there is a large five flue chimney stack. Now roughcast rendered which may disguise a previous rubble stone finish. The lodge presides over a good gate screen, Classical in style, which probably predates it by about 20 years. Four large square granite ashlar pillars with fluted friezes and corniced cappings. The screen railings have matching cast iron wicket gates flanking the carriage opening.

**Green Gate Lodge** c1890

At the present main entrance a hefty late Victorian house of two storeys in squared uncoursed quarry-faced granite with red brick dressings. On an L plan the gables have big straightforward robustly carved bargeboards. Brick used as eaves corbel course and as a continuation of window dressings to form semicircular overpanels at first floor. In the internal angle, to the front door, a very decoratively carved porch. To each leading gable a flat-roofed single storey canted bay window. The roof has scalloped slate coursings, earthenware cresting and banded red brick chimney stack. The large square granite gate pillars have fluted friezes and corniced cappings. Chunky cast iron gates undersized.
MOURNE; U.A.H.S. (1975)

**243. MOURNE RECTORY, Kilkeel**
pre 1859; *demolished*

A lodge built by Rev John Forbes Close. The house was renamed Mourne Wood.

**244. MOYALLON, Gilford** pre 1863;
*demolished*

A lodge noted in the Griffith Valuation to a seat of Joseph Dawson. Not a trace remains of house or lodge since an 1870s fire.
GRIFFITH

**245. MOYALLON HOUSE, Gilford (2)**

Formerly the estate of Thomas Christy Wakefield which passed through marriage to John Grubb Richardson of Woodhouse, Co Armagh (qv) and the Bessbrook Spinning Co Ltd. In contrast to the graceful Neo-Classical villa there are two sturdy late Victorian Picturesque gate lodges.

**Rear Lodge** c1880; architects probably Thomas Jackson and Son

A formal one and a half storey gabled three bay building. Constructed in squared uncoursed quarry faced basalt with liberal yellow brick as quoins, dressings and two chimney stacks. Over the semicircular-headed front door a gablet with shallow pointed arched window, repeated on the gables. Here as at the Woodhouse lodge is the distinctive single lap slate pattern to the roof. Big crude stone gate pillars to the adjacent outbuildings.

**Front Lodge** c1880; architects probably Thomas Jackson and Son

Similar in style to the above but on a T plan, its three bay front to the public road irregular in outline. The left hand bay emphasised by a quoined and gabled breakfront which contains a ground floor tripartite window with single attic light over both with Classical surrounds to Picturesque latticed panes. This fenestration is repeated on the right hand bay but with the upper window in a gablet breaking the eaves. Central is a semicircular-headed doorway with hood moulding and pendant dripstones to complete a fine confusion of architectural styles. In squared coursed basalt with white brick dressings to secondary elevations, the front facade stuccoed. The roof eccentrically slated as before. Alongside, the main carriage opening is flanked by tall slender square pillars with ball finials. Uniting the gates with the lodge, a screen wall containing a gabled wicket opening in sandstone. Gates vigorous, each in carved timber, portcullis fashion.

**246. MOYGANNON COTTAGE, Rostrevor**
pre 1834

A single storey lodge contemporary with a very pretty late Georgian marine cottage residence typical of the area. Cruciform on plan its main elevation gabled three bay from which projects a gabled hallway. Much modernised the replacement bargeboards simplified wave pattern. All now roughcast, the avenue realigned.

**247. MURLOUGH, Dundrum** c1877;
architect probably Fitzgibbon Louch

Lodge to a long low Neo-Classical bathing villa for the 4th Marquess of Downshire designed in 1858 by William Haywood of London. In contrasting style the porter's lodge is a very decorative mid-Victorian Picturesque gabled lodge in a wide variety of materials. One and a half storey of ample proportions on an L plan it is raised on a plinth, the ground storey faced in uncoursed quarry-faced granite with window reveals in chamfered dressed sandstone. Wooden mullioned and transomed casement windows, on one wing in the form of a canted bay. To the entrance door in the internal angle a very ornate carved timber porch with lean-to roof. The attic storey jetties out with the help of large carved timber brackets to be faced in pebble-dash rendering. In one gable a plaque with the Downshire coat-of-arms and on the other an oriel window with a shield over containing a coroneted monogram. Bargeboards perforated with tiny quatrefoils rise to sharp turned hipknobs. To the roof scalloped slate courses, sawtooth earthenware cresting and a big clustered breakfront chimney stack. Now the property of the Church of Ireland having been presented by the 7th Marquis.

**248. MUTTON HILL, Banbridge** c1820;
*demolished*

*A.C.W. Merrick*

To a charming Georgian cottage, once of the Evans family, an equally delightful and naive Georgian Gothick gate lodge. A simple single storey structure on a standard two roomed plan. Three bay symmetrical with lancet openings, the windows Y-traceried and a minuscule fanlight in similar fashion to the front door. Harled whitewashed walls below steeply pitched hipped roof and chimney stack off centre.

**249. MYRA CASTLE, Strangford**
pre 1834/c1860

A gatekeeper's lodge existed on this site to the late 16th century tower house of Walshestown Castle and some of this can still be detected in an arcaded feature to the rear of the present structure. The old castle was the property of Richard Anderson whose daughter married Rowland Craig-Laurie who built a modern castle called Myra in the 1850s, in a castellated Romantic manner. He also extended the lodge to two storeys below a hipped roof with exposed rafter toes. Alongside this he erected rather awkwardly a pretty Tudor Gothick gateway in the John Nash style. To the left a tall battlemented octagonal tower housing a spiral staircase which leads to ramparts over the carriage archway that spans onto the entrance hall. Rather boxy it has a Tudor arched doorway with blind quatrefoil motif over as relief. Archway and hall have lost their crenellations and the whole thing is now rendered.
PORTAFERRY AND STRANGFORD; U.A.H.S. (1969)

**250. NARROW WATER, Warrenpoint (4)**

A beautifully situated estate where Roger Hall between 1831 and 1837 let the local Newry architect Thomas J Duff give full vent to his Tudor Picturesque repertoire. Duff extended the old Mount Hall as it was then called into an extravagant Tudor Revival mansion with an array of bays, gables, pinnacles and ornamental chimneypots, all in granite hewn from a local quarry. The client also engaged the respected Sir Joseph Paxton and the local landscape architect Thomas Smith to enhance the undulating park with serpentine walks and create a formal garden. Two of the entrances can confidently be attributed to Duff.

**Castle Gate** c1837/1905; architects Thomas J Duff/Vincent Craig

A solid castellated Romantic entrance screen built in coursed squared granite appropriate to the tower house of Narrow Water Castle across the road. Originally comprised of tall curtain walls relieved with mock arrowloops, surmounted by Irish crenellations and terminating in square sham turrets similarly castellated and machicolated. The composition has suffered this century, firstly with the insertion of a one and a half storey lodge with crowstepped gables to one end, designed by the Belfast architect Vincent Craig. Then requisitioning in the Second World War resulted in the loss of gates and the right hand carriage turret. However, following a terrorist bomb, the design as first conceived was returned almost to its original appearance by demolition of the lodge and restoration of the entrance turret.

**Tudor Lodge** c1837;
architect Thomas J Duff

The architect was a known subscriber to architectural pattern books and this lodge is a direct consequence of the influence of P F

Narrow Water, Castle Gate

Narrow Water, Tudor Lodge

Robinson, a pioneer of the English Picturesque cottage style. A delightful one and a half storey lodge on an L-plan constructed in granite ashlar. The gables are suitably ornate with intricately fretted, lobed and cusped bargeboards. In the internal angle is a rustic pent across the front door, supported on granite columns, a variation of Robinson's favourite rustic posts. All windows of tiny square paned casements, transomed and mullioned. Two single storey canted bay windows enhance the informal effect. On the ridge a pair of diagonally set chimney stacks on a rectangular base. From almost terminal decay this important lodge has been miraculously rescued in an admirable restoration, with extensive but sympathetic additions by architect Dawson Stelfox. The gate screen of pretty ironwork by Samuel Weir, Whitesmith of Newry, had elegant outer piers. Quatrefoil in section and crowned by meringue-like cappings it is intended that these be restored to their previous location. There is a single storey variant of the lodge by the architect at Tamnaharry (qv) nearby.

**Newry Gate** c1831; architect perhaps Thomas J Duff; *demolished*

The earliest of the lodges can be described from a 1964 photograph. Single storey with harled walls and hipped gable roof. On the gable facing the visitor was a very pretty canted oriel window with hexagonal lozenge glazing pattern. To the avenue advanced a fancy gabled porch. The Tudor flavour of the house was suggested by the granite entrance piers with their incised panels and cusped tops. The extensive iron screen innovative in design with a repetitive crisscross pattern. Regrettably all now lost without trace.

**Rear Gate** c1835; *demolished*

A substantial one and a half storey gate lodge. Three bay symmetrical with harled walls and hipped roof. Ground floor windows with simple label mouldings flanked a projecting gabled hall. Interrupting the front eaves two balancing flat roofed gablets.

BENCE-JONES (1988); MALINS (1980)

**251. NETHERLEIGH, Belfast North** c1870; architects probably Lanyon, Lynn and Lanyon; *demolished*

A small park formed by Mr R Robertson from a portion of the old Belmont estate (qv). The lodge to the big Neo-Classical house has gone but the gate screen survives. Two big sandstone ashlar carriage pillars with fluted friezes and cappings with dentil courses. Name inscribed on the shafts.

**252. NETTLEFIELD, Belfast South** pre 1858; *demolished*

A property of Frederick H Lewis redeveloped c1934 and put to school use (see below).

**253. NETTLEFIELD PE SCHOOL, Belfast South** c1936; architect Reginald S Wilshere

To an innovatively designed school with a Scandinavian flavour, a distinctive gatehouse in a similar brown rustic brick, a relief from the red of the surrounding terraced streets. Generous gatekeeper's accommodation in the form of a cube below a pyramidal roof, finished in earthenware plain tiles, with a central chimney stack. Subtle use of projecting horizontal brick courses as rustication. Terracotta tiled drip course to window heads. Back return. There are similar Lutyensesque lodges by the same architect at Avoniel and Elm Grove PE Schools (qqv) nearby.

LARMOUR (1987)

**254. NEW COMBER, Comber** pre 1834; *demolished*

**255. NEW GROVE, Ballylesson** c1840

To a house of the Russell family, a typical late Georgian vernacular Irish lodge. Tiny two roomed, three bay symmetrical below a hipped roof with extended eaves. Now smartly rendered and engulfed in extensions all intended to be in sympathy. The lodge and octagonal granite piers similar to nearby Hillhall, and obviously by the same jobbing builder.

**256. NEWRY MANSE, Newry** pre 1858; *demolished*

**257. NEWRY WORKHOUSE, Newry** pre 1859; *demolished*

The lodge may have been of an age with the old Union Workhouse of 1841. Now Daisy Hill Hospital.

**258. NEWTOWNARDS WORKHOUSE, Newtownards** c1870; achitect not known

To the Union Workhouse of 1841 by George Wilkinson a later gate lodge in innovative irregular Picturesque style. An interplay of gables, catslides and dormers makes for an interesting outline from all angles. To the rear a curious half-canted garret dormer with a Scottish feel. One and a half storey, built of coursed, squared basalt with punched sandstone dressings. Now the Ards Hospital.

GOULD (1983)

**259. NORWOOD TOWER, Belfast North (2)**

Although there was a house here prior to 1834 it was not enlarged into a rambling Tudor Revival mansion until the 1840s by the Henderson family. 1864 paintings by J H Connop and Hugh Frazer show the house to have been dominated by a tall castellated tower, set in a landscaped park with a flimsy wooden summerhouse and an entrance from the Circular Road via a little battlemented gate lodge.

**West Lodge** c1845; architect possibly Thomas Jackson; *demolished*

Both artists' impressions tally in showing a two storey crenellated tower with a single storey wing alongside, an appropriate introduction to

H. Frazer painting (Capt. O.W.J. Henderson)

the big house. Passing the front door with its pointed head and hood moulding, is the family landau transporting finely attired Henderson ladies in wide brimmed hats. Behind, gate piers with "helmet" cappings as habitually employed by the architect Thomas Jackson. Could lodge and house be a rare diversion from his habitual Neo-Classical style?

**East Lodge** pre 1902; *demolished*

In 1934 the demesne passed from the family to a distant cousin, Sir Christopher Musgrave, signalling the start of a rapid decline ending in the demolition of the mansion in 1955 and the sale of the park for housing development.
CONNOP (1864)

**260. NURSERYVILLE, Comber (2)**
both c1860; *both demolished*

Two porters' lodges for William Campbell. Only the stumps of two very large V-jointed ashlar pillars remain at one entrance.

**261. NUTGROVE, Seaforde** pre 1834; *demolished*

The first OS Map indicates a smaller lodge than that in the 1964 photograph, probably having been extended by one room to the rear in the interim. Formerly two roomed, single storey with a canted end to the avenue. On the leading face the entrance flanked by windows, bipartite with a central sash box. Stuccoed.

**262. OAKLEY, Killough (2)**

A house now demolished, apparently built for Dean Annesley in 1789 with the Dublin architect Charles Lilly as consultant. At the Western entrance a gate lodge of an age with it.

**West Lodge** c1790;
architect possibly Charles Lilly

Originally a standard two roomed, three bay lodge with harled walls and central chimney stack on a hipped roof. Georgian Gothick with lancet openings, it was later enlarged by a room to one end in the form of a bow, a gabled hall added later. Very pretty. Two crude rubble stone gate pillars are surmounted by sculpted pineapple finials of Bath stone.

**East Gate** c1865

A typical Ulster gate lodge of mixed styles. Single storey three bay symmetrical below a steeply pitched hipped roof with pairs of slender carved eaves brackets. Georgian squared sash windows below Tudor label mouldings in stuccoed walls. One bay deep. Octagonal pair of chimneypots. Square granite pillars to an extensive gate screen with ogee railed quadrants and flanking wicket gates to the central carriage opening. For long the property of the Birney family.
MINISTRY OF FINANCE (1966)

**263. OLD COURT, Strangford (2)**

A house built in 1844 by the 23rd Lord de Ros in place of an earlier residence. It became the home of Dudley Charles Fitzgerald de Ros and in celebration of his marriage in 1853 his friend Frederick Temple, Lord Dufferin and Clandeboye presented him with a new avenue approach lined with lime trees. A unique wedding gift which seems to have included the first lodge here.

**Dufferin Lodge** 1853

Pretty one and a half storey gabled building. Symmetrical three bay front elevation with projecting gabled entrance porch, flanked by two tripartite casement windows with lattice panes, in whinstone walls. Since 1869 the avenue approached by a flight of steps, the road beyond having been lowered to facilitate transport to and from the port.

**Down Lodge** c1869; *demolished*

Built as a new access following the loss of Dufferin Avenue as a carriage approach. Also a one and a half storey symmetrical three bay lodge with a very steeply pitched gabled roof. Central gabled hallway. Windows squared pane with label mouldings.

**264. OLD HALL, Rostrevor** c1830;
*demolished*

W.M. Lawrence (N.L.I.)

Lodge to a building described by Bradshaw in 1819 "... Smithson Corry has lately fitted a lodge in a very elegant style". To this marine cottage of 1815 was added gatekeeper's accommodation, caught for posterity in a Lawrence photograph showing the approach to Rostrevor from the Warrenpoint Road at the turn of the century. Facing the road with its gabled three bay front elevation symmetrical. A pretty trellised porch to the front door is framed by two canted bay windows in harled walls. Paired verge brackets. Alongside a smaller gabled addition with diamond paned windows to match the original. A distinctive pair of squat fluted stone columns as gate piers, topped by unusual "bap" bounder finials. Elegant palmette ornament to iron carriage gates. Piers and gates are preserved at nearby Roseena.
BRADSHAW (1819); CROWE (1973); LAWRENCE PHOTOGRAPH (N.L.I.) Ref 7600(R)

**265. OLINDA, Holywood** c1905;
architect not known

A.C.W. Merrick

Built by the Mitchell family, the lodge masquerading as a Neo-Classical mid-Victorian stuccoed affair but in fact of Edwardian origin. Single storey on a square plan with a pyramidal roof and central chimney. The three bay by two elevations heavily stuccoed with segmentally-headed recesses, their surrounds carried down to contain panels below similarly arched openings with margined window glazing. Exaggerated raised quoins deeply reticulated. Much extended.

**266. ORANGEFIELD, Belfast South (4)**

These lodged entrances were to the 1779 dwelling of the Batesons which was found in 1817 to be " a handsome square edifice" after its acquisition by Hugh Crawford. It was the latter or his successor and fellow banker John Holmes Houston who was responsible for adding wings to the house and for the lodges. One lodge was to the west from the Castlereagh Road, another to the north on the Bloomfield approach and a third at the Knock Road.

**South Gate** pre 1858; *demolished*

Richard Bayley Blakiston-Houston succeeded to the estate of his father-in-law in 1844 assuming his name and adding a further gatekeeper's house also off the Castlereagh Road. About this time he replaced the northern lodge with a pair which have suffered the same fate as the rest.

**West, North and East Gates** all pre 1834;
*all demolished*

John Blakiston Blakiston-Houston replaced the previous old mansion with a brand new Neo-Classical pile not long after his father's death in 1857, probably to plans by Lanyon, Lynn and Lanyon.
DIXON AND HEATLEY (1983); ATKINSON (1823); BURKE (1904)

**267. ORMEAU, Belfast South (2)**
both pre 1834; *both demolished*

George Augustus Chichester, the debt-ridden 2nd Marquess of Donegall (1769-1844), greatly enlarged his Ormeau Cottage in 1823 to designs of William Vitruvius Morrison. This is one of the earliest examples of his Tudor Revival works of which he is reputed to have been a pioneer in this country. The two lodges, one in proximity to the old Long Bridge to the north and the other by the Ormeau Bridge, have both gone leaving no clues

as to whether they formed part of the architect's commission. The house was demolished in 1869 when the family moved to Belfast Castle (qv) and the demesne was presented to the public as a park.
McPARLAND (1989); MAGUIRE (1979)

**268. ORMISTON, Belfast North (4)**
A big Scots Baronial style house in sandstone ashlar designed by the Edinburgh architect David Bryce in 1865 for James Combe who had come here from that city. Of the four original lodges, two can still be traced.

**Hawthornden Road Lodge** c1867; architect probably David Bryce
A relatively plain three bay symmetrical single storey lodge built in squared uncoursed quarry faced sandstone. Steep gables with lapped skewtables and little kneelers. Deserted.

**Belmont Road Lodge** c1867; architect probably David Bryce

Much as the above but more architecturally pretentious. The gables crowstepped as is that to the little central projecting hallway. To the apexes emblems of each of the three kingdoms: sculpted rose, shamrock and thistle.
LARMOUR (1987)

**269. PARLIAMENT BUILDINGS, Belfast North (2)**
The huge and impressive Parliament building in white Portland stone at the head of a grand processional avenue is preceded by a giant entrance sweep and elegant lodge.

**Upper Newtownards Road Gate** c1932; architect Arnold Thornley

In Portland stone grandiose square carriage pillars are surmounted by large fluted urns raised on corniced cappings with acroteria to each corner. Below, framed by triglyphs with guttae, a frieze with bas relief bucrania and more acroteria. Each pillar is flanked by a breakfront with more bas relief and Greek key patterned bands, repeated on the secondary pillars which are crowned by octagonal lanterns. All these Classical motifs are carried through the extensive iron screen and gates. The two storey cube lodge has a very steep pyramidal roof finished in Westmoreland green slates rising to a central chimney stack. The composition co-ordinated in Portland stone with horizontal emphasis in the form of embracing moulded stringcourses below the eaves and at first floor cill level, the latter carried out as parapet to a segmental bow window facing the road. Squared leaded lights to windows. Ground floor openings between pilasters, the avenue elevation has a ground floor breakfront containing the entablatured front door.

**Massey Avenue Gate** c1932; architect Arnold Thornley

Lodge identical to above, the gates reduced in extent.
LARMOUR (1987)

**270. PINE LODGE, Belfast North** pre 1902; *demolished*
A seat in 1880 of Thomas Shaw, of Shaw Pollock, flour importers and general merchants.

**271. THE PINES, Newtownbreda** pre 1901
Single storey below a hipped roof much modernised and extended. Now six bay from which projects a gabled hall under the high eaves. Nice octagonal gate piers with concave cappings. The house demolished.

**272. PLANTATION, Lisburn** c1860; *demolished*
A house established by John Barbour of Paisley who founded a threadworks nearby in 1784. By 1863 it had passed to a John Sloan who presumably built the lodge.
GREEN (1963)

**273. PORTAFERRY, Portaferry (3)**
The original house on this beautifully situated estate was built about 1760 by Andrew Savage and was extensively enlarged between 1790 and 1820. Plans were prepared first by Charles Lilly and then William Farrell, both Dublin architects. The lodges appear to date from this later building period, all three in a mild-mannered Picturesque style but none showing the characteristics of Farrell's work.

**Shore Lodge** c1830
A long low four bay symmetrical single storey lodge of one and a half storeys. Half hipped gables contain tiny attic windows. Over the front door a semi-hexagonal gablet breaks the eaves line. Original pair of stone chimney stacks diagonally set on a rectangular base. Modern frilly bargeboards probably had more intricately carved predecessors. Recent squared window replacements.

**Town Lodge** c1830
Originally a two roomed single storey cottage with gabled roof, its bargeboards replicas of those on Shore Lodge. Three bay elevation to the avenue, the left hand bay being the doorway, all below a fancy wave and foil fascia board. Probably predating the lodge by a few years, large Classical V-jointed rusticated square stone pillars. Less than delicate fluted friezes below ball finialed cappings.

**Country Lodge** c1830
As Town Lodge but with harled walls, it also retains its diagonally set chimney stacks. Ornamental bargeboards as above. Here the eaves extends full length beyond the front elévation to form a rustic sitting out verandah with post support. Simple outer pillars with ball finials flank a cast iron gate screen continuing the ball motif with a repeating crisscross pattern. Inner iron carriage posts. All three lodges for Colonel Andrew Nugent whose family had changed its name from Savage.
PORTAFERRY AND STRANGFORD; U.A.H.S. (1969); ORAM (1992); MINISTRY OF FINANCE (1966)

**274. PORTAVOE, Donaghadee (2)**
James Ross is recorded as living here in 1740 but sometime later it passed to the Ker family who built a grandiose square Palladian mansion consumed in 1844 by a calamitous fire. Until that date David Ker had been in infrequent occupation of his other seat at Montalto (qv). As there the family indulged themselves in commissioning gate lodge designs, none of which materialised at Portavoe.

**Design No 1** c1810; architect not known; *unexecuted*

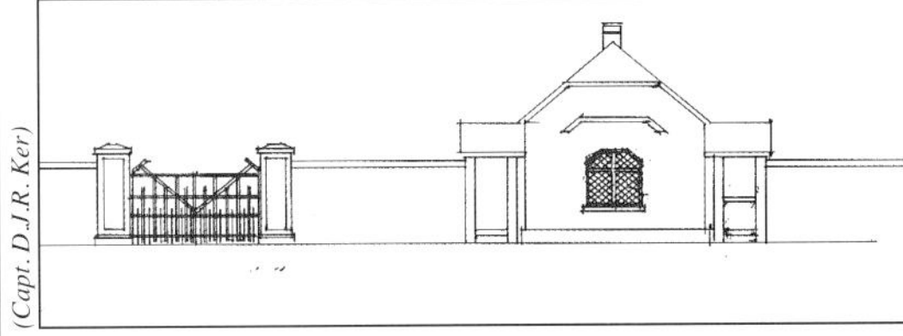

(Capt. D.J.R. Ker)

A lodge, one bay gable to the road with a half hip echoed in the window head below and its hood moulding. Single storey with latticed pane windows it was to have been flanked by a pair of porches to back and front doors integral with the walled screen and gates alongside. Square carriage piers with recessed panels.

**Design No 2** c1810; architect not known; *unexecuted*

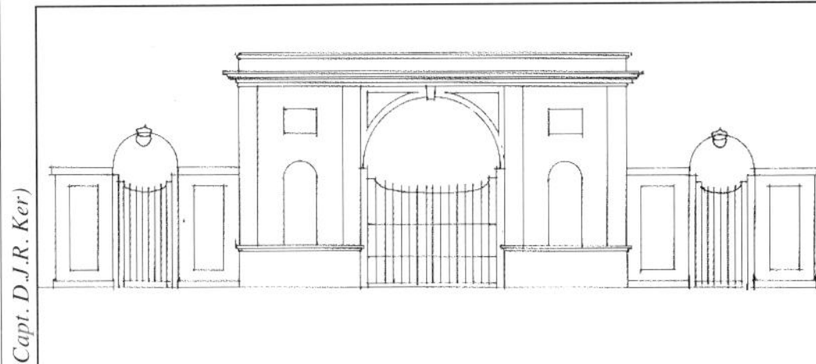

(Capt. D.J.R. Ker)

In contrast to the other rustic Tudor design is this Classical gateway perhaps incorporating twin porters' lodges. The central semicircular-arched carriage opening flanked by two storey accommodation. Each side contains a round arched opening or niche below a first floor window or plaque, both framed by plain pilasters resting on a high plinth. Uniting it all a full length entablature. To each side in lower panelled screen walls, wicket openings with iron overthrows carrying lantern lights. A drawing on paper which has an 1803 watermark.

**Seaward Lodge.** pre 1833; *demolished*
**Inland Lodge** pre 1833.
Within the estate to the west a single storey lodge with canted end elevation to the gate. Much improved and extended.
DRAWINGS IN POSSESSION OF CAPT D J R KER; DIXON (1972)

**275. PORTLOUGHAN, Strangford** c1860
Simple single storey two roomed, three bay cottage with gables. Constructed in rubble, harled having crude label mouldings. Built by Samuel Bailie. Deserted.

**276. PROSPECT, Belfast South** pre 1834; *demolished*
A lodge to the property of William Connor. The old drive to the house now Deramore Avenue.

**277. PURDYSBURN, Newtownbreda (5)**
Thomas Hopper had by 1825 succeeded John Nash as the Prince Regent's architect and had extended his practice to Ireland. In contrast to his remarkable gargantuan Norman Revival essay at Gosford, Co Armagh (qv) then under construction he displayed the eclecticism then required of an architect with this pretty Tudor Gothick house for Narcissus Batt founder of the Belfast Bank. In replacing an older house of Hill Wilson, Hopper's commission was to extend to the stable yard, probably the estate village, schoolhouse, and also two entrances to the demesne.

**Main Entrance** c1825; architect Thomas Hopper; *demolished*
In a manner complementary to the house an introductory Tudor Gothick gate screen and probably a lodge, cruciform on plan, which was demolished before it. From an old photograph can be detected four tall octagonal pinnacles, a repeat of those on the house but here employed as towering gate pillars similarly crowned with crocketed onion finials. The shafts had each face recessed with cusped Tudor heads and flanked two screen walls both containing Tudor arched wicket openings. Over, a parapet with a band of traceried quarters. The little pedestrian gates and the huge carriage leaves showing the whole repertoire of Gothick motifs including quatrefoils, poppy finials and Y-tracery. This dramatic prelude to the house was flanked by extensive concave-railed quadrants, the dwarf wall of which and terminal hexagonal piers are all that remain to be seen. There are similar gates at Margam Abbey, Glamorganshire by the same architect.

**Ballylesson Gate** c1825; architect Thomas Hopper
A gate screen on a reduced scale to the above survives with identical carriage gates. Tall hexagonal ashlar pillars with convex-domed cappings.

**Ballylesson Lodge** c1850; architect not known; *demolished*
A pretty lodge in the Tudor Picturesque manner. One and a half storey three bay symmetrical with a little gabled porch having a four centred entrance arch, and mock arrowloop over. Faced in red brick with stone quoins and dressings to wide transomed and mullioned windows with lattice panes. To gables spiky wave fretted bargeboards with ornate hipknobs.

**Purdysburn Village Entrance** pre 1858; *demolished.*

**Garden Entrance** pre 1858; *ruinous*
The remnants of a lodge built in rubble stone with brick dressings to segmentally-headed openings. The three bay front of this single storey building was flanked by pedestrian openings in extended screen walls.

**Milltown Lodge** pre 1858; *demolished.*
LEWIS (1837); DIXON AND HEATLEY (1983); P.R.O.N.I. D2585/4/2

**278. PURDYSBURN HOSPITAL, Carryduff** c1930; architect not known
A very fine Lutyensesque Arts-and-Crafts style lodge. Single storey on a cruciform plan the central body of which rises in a steep pyramidal roof of Westmoreland green slates to a central cluster of four diagonally set chimney flues in brick. Advancing from each flank, hipped roof wings, the left hand one containing the keystoned, rusticated doorway. Across the front elevation was the flat-roofed open verandah, now filled in. Originally having squared pane windows in red brick walls.

**279. QUILLY, Dromore** c1840
A pretty late Georgian style standard lodge. Single storey three bay symmetrical with stuccoed walls below a wide hipped roof and central corniced chimney stack. Segmentally-arched openings with small squared windows. There is a later catslide canopy to the front door and a rather crudely constructed two bay extension to one side. Big Classical gate pillars of recent date. Square with raised and fielded panels and corniced cappings proudly surmounted by eagles. For George Montgomery Vaughan who inherited the demesne in 1840 upon his father's death.

**280. QUINTIN CASTLE, Portaferry**
There is no lodge here but a charming folly gateway worthy of notice. Like a stage set in slaked rubble stone are a tall octagonal crenellated tower decorated with arrowloops and pointed pedestrian door giving access to a spiral

*Ballylesson Lodge*

*Main Entrance*

stair leading nowhere in particular. At the other side of the entrance the same but smaller and spanning the opening an unusual rectangular arch over sturdy timber "portcullis" gates. An early tower house beyond of the Smith family in the early to mid-19th century was enclosed and extended in the castellated Romantic style by the Rev Nicholson Calvert who had come by the property through marriage to the Ross heiress. There is a tradition that the architect William Vitruvius Morrison was employed here and if that is so these works may precede 1838.
SAVAGE (1906)

**281. RADEMON, Crossgar** pre 1858;
*demolished*
For John McRobert, millowner, a pretty one and a half storey gabled Picturesque lodge with diamond paned windows.

**282. RADEMON HOUSE, Crossgar** c1820;
*demolished*

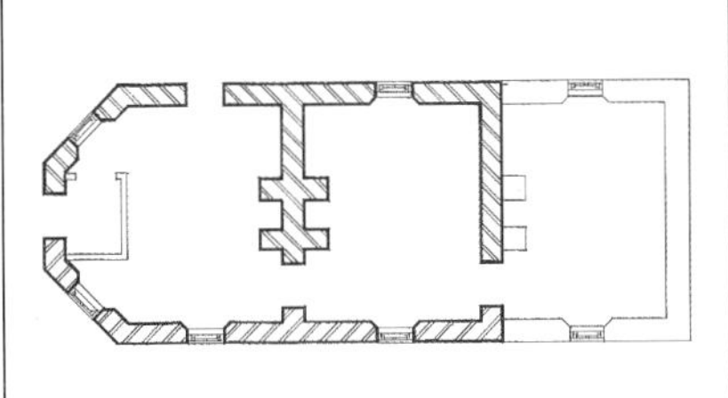

Formerly a two roomed, single storey lodge with canted end elevation with half umbrello roof. The simple sheeted doorway had a Y-traceried Georgian Gothick fanlight repeated in the pointed window heads. Later stuccoed and extended by a room, it was subsequently neglected and finally demolished c1970. There was a Georgian Classical version of this building at Nutgrove (qv). The gate screen is later, with vigorous square stone pillar panelled, the ironwork equally sturdy and the same as at Kilmore parish church close by. Sir Thomas Drew designed the latter in 1870. A house existed here as early as 1740, a seat of the Johnson family. It has undergone many alterations since then, not least when the property was acquired by James Crawford of Crawfordsburn who had married the Johnson daughter and heiress.
BURKE (1904); BENCE-JONES (1988)

**283. RATHDUNE, Downpatrick**
(see MOUNT VILLA)

**284. RATHGAEL, Bangor** pre 1900;
*demolished*
A house and demesne of the Cleland family which along with the late Victorian lodge have all been cleared.

**285. RATHMONA, Donaghadee** c1870;
*demolished*
An ample gatehouse probably for the Carmichaels. In the form of a cube stuccoed in Italianate style was this one and a half storey structure. Under a hipped roof with high eaves line interrupted by a central gablet with coat-of-arms over, is a pair of segmentally-headed attic windows. Below, the front elevation is relieved by an intermediate stringcourse over the three bay facade. The central door case elaborate, framed by Corinthian pilasters "supporting" a fanlighted overpanel flanked by little colonettes below a crowning pediment. Ground floor windows semicircular-arched with pilastered surrounds and diamond raised keystones.

**286. RATHMOYLE, Helen's Bay**
(see ELDON GREEN)

**287. RATHTURRET, Warrenpoint** c1936
To a highly ornate late Victorian house of 1883 probably designed by William Watson is a later lodge for the Richards family. A mildly ornate single storey bungalow, gabled with earthenware tiles and bonnets. Foiled bargeboards with tiny shamrock or trefoil perforations. Rectangular bay in roughcast walls.

**288. RAVENHILL, Belfast South** pre 1834;
*demolished*
Once a seat of the Sneyd family, in 1824 called Rookery. All long since swept away by urban expansion.

**289. REDBURN, Holywood** c1870;
architect probably John Lanyon

A.C.W. Merrick

A property of the Dunville family prosperous through their whiskey distilling business (see also Dunville Park, Co Antrim). In 1867 Robert Grimshaw Dunville built a large informal 70 roomed house to designs by Lanyon, Lynn and Lanyon. Contemporary with it is a lodge in similar materials with Picturesque features. A substantial lodge with a main body of one and a half storeys flanked by equal single storey wings, the composition rendered asymmetrical by an eccentrically positioned forestanding portico. Constructed in a squared uncoursed, quarry-faced Scrabo stone like the house. Quoins, roll-moulded window surrounds and large chimney stack in dressed masonry. All shallow-pitched gables decorated with frilly fretted spandrels, long hipknobs and carved purlin projections, the architect clearly influenced by Alexander "Greek" Thomson's later work, particularly 336 Albert Drive, Pollockshields, Glasgow completed by Robert Turnbull after his principal's death. The porch remarkable for its contrasting Classical style. Under its shallow gable, paired classical piers and corresponding pilasters carry semicircular arches with archivolts. Some of the entrance screen survives in the form of square pillars one with a steep concave pyramidal cap minus its finial.

**290. RICHMOND, Rostrevor** pre 1834;
*demolished*
A lodge, cruciform on plan to a demesne at one time of the Waring family of Waringstown (qv) by 1859 was called Clooneavin.

**291. RICHMOND LODGE, Belfast North (3)**
**Early Main Entrance** pre 1834;
*demolished*
Another seat of the Turnly family of Rockport and Drumnasole, Co. Antrim (qqv) of whom Francis probably built this early "inkpot" lodge on the Holywood Road perhaps similar to those at nearby Ballymenoch (qv).
**Secondary Lodge** pre 1858; *demolished*
After Francis Turnly's death in 1844 his widow Dorothea only survived him by two years before the property passed to John Dunville, founder of the whiskey distillery, who was responsible for this lodge off the Knocknagoney Road.
**Later Main Entrance** c1875; architects possibly Thomas Jackson and Son;
*demolished*

B.R. Cobain

Richmond Lodge remained in Dunville hands until 1874 when John's son William Dunville died and it was sold to James Kennedy. He set about considerable improvements which included a new avenue approach but 100yards south of the old main entrance.The new complementary lodge was a highly decorative single storey three bay symmetrical Neo-Classical composition very much a version of that at Seapark, Co. Antrim (qv), in form and in the style of its portico. The latter was a rather refined design comprising a pair of Ionic columns in antis supporting a flat entablature with delicate dentil course. This correctness lapses into something rather more inventive, the entablature extending beyond with a repeating modillion motif as a parapet to the hipped roof. All these details including raised quoins, windows with innovative surrounds, bracketed cills and underpanels as well as a breakfront bay window to the main road were highlighted in gloss paint contrasting starkly with sandstone walls.In similar masonry was a central lofty chimney stack and unusual gate screen piers with stout cable mouldings and gadroon sculpted cappings. The only vestige left of this neat demesne is the later avenue.
DIXON AND HEATLEY (1983);
MERRICK (1986)

**292. ROCKFIELD, Dundonald** c1850
An exceptionally plain lodge to a property in 1863 of a James Shaw. Two roomed, three bay

symmetrical, single storey with a hipped roof. Central projecting gabled hall. Roughcast walls, improved with new windows and increased by one bay.

**293. ROCKPORT, Helen's Bay** pre 1834; *demolished*
A lodge to a house described in 1819 as a modern built house for John Turnly, near a small harbour from which it derived its name.
DIXON AND HEATLEY (1983)

**294. ROCKVILLE or ROCKVIEW, Banbridge** c1860; *demolished*
At the entrance to the Rock Linen Factory, bleach green and proprietor's house, a pair of lodges. The property in 1863 of William Robinson.

**295. ROKEBY HALL, Drumbo**
(see FAIRVIEW)

**296. ROSE COTTAGE, Gilford** c1870; architect not known
There was a residence here in 1833 which was greatly enlarged before 1860 but remained lodgeless until about ten years later. A dapper structure in sturdy materials and forthright design. Single storey symmetrical three bay below a hipped roof with high eaves carried on paired carved brackets. Constructed in basalt with granite quoins and brick dressings to segmentally arched openings. Very like the lodge at Garranard (qv) and perhaps by the same hand. Probably built by the Park family. Now called The Grove, a replacement 20th century house.

**297. ROSE HALL, Lawrencetown** pre 1833; *demolished*
A lodge to a property in the early 19th century of the Stuart family.

**298. ROSEMOUNT, Greyabbey**
(see GREYABBEY)

**299. ROSETTA, Newtownbreda** pre 1858; *demolished*
A lodge for James Kennedy, muslin manufacturer.

**300. ROSETTA, Rostrevor** pre 1859
On a cruciform plan the lodge has been subjected to much modernisation which includes pebble-dashing to walls. Pyramidal roof and projecting gable hall to symmetrical three bay front. Formerly occupied by Rev Holt Waring of the Waringstown (qv) family it came into the possession of Samuel Reid by 1863.

**301. ROSSCONOR COTTAGE, Downpatrick** c1860
Set well back from the road a plain stone built lodge, single storey and now put to use as a garage. A property in 1863 of Matilda Kincaid.

**302. ROSSCONOR, Downpatrick** pre 1859; *demolished*
The lodge was located opposite the gates to the one time seat of Arthur Brown.

**303. THE ROSS MONUMENT, Rostrevor** c1830; architect probably Thomas J Duff; *demolished*
A massive granite obelisk built in 1826 to designs by William Vitruvius Morrison, its execution probably supervised by local architect Thomas J Duff. Erected to the memory of Major-General Robert Ross (1766-1814) the victor of Bradensburg. A pretty Picturesque lodge on an L plan. Single storey gabled with harled walls. On the road gable a canted bay window with squared panes. From the internal angle advanced a gabled porch with post support. Fronting the road at the base of the obelisk steps an extensive contemporary iron railed screen incorporating a Roman fasces feature.
McPARLAND (1989); LAWRENCE PHOTOGRAPH (N.L.I.); BELL (1989)

**304. RUBANE, Kircubbin**
(see ECHLINVILLE)

**305. SAINTFIELD, Saintfield (4)**
The family of Price descended from that of Hollymount (qv) has been here since c1700, the lofty mansion house dating from some fifty years later. It was Nicholas Price who installed gatekeepers at three entrances in the early 19th century.

**North Lodge** c1820
A plain late Georgian single storey lodge under a spreading hipped roof. Now much extended and modernised to lose most of its former character.

**West Lodge** c1820

(R. Bryson)

A once choice Georgian Gothick design now spoilt by inept "improvement". Previously a two roomed single storey cottage the hipped roof extending beyond the leading canted elevation, the roof supported at the corners by slender round columns. On the front face the entrance door with rusticated stone surround and Y-traceried lancet fanlight, replicated in the pointed window openings beyond in harled walls. Across the road a contemporary gate screen with big square Classical pillars.

**South, or Town Lodge** c1820

Situated alongside elegant square pillars with channelled ashlar masonry and fluted friezes is another Georgian Gothick lodge. An unusually commodious single storey structure with a wider than normal three bay symmetrical front elevation. Once more the canted feature is used, here as a central hall projection advancing under a half umbrello from the main hipped roof with wide eaves. Again the Y-traceried lancet windows in rendered walls. As at Montalto (qv) there is a connection with the Stewarts of Mountstewart (qv), Nicholas Price having married a sister of the 1st Marquis of Londonderry. All these Co Down estates have a tradition of Georgian Gothick lodges with canted features.

**Main Entrance** c1850; architect not known; *demolished*
A highly ornate Tudor Picturesque one and a half storey lodge. Gabled with outrageous and unique carved decorative bargeboards with a repetitive pendulous feature culminating in tall hipknobs.

(P. Larmour)

Constructed in squared uncoursed quarry-faced basalt the quoins in contrasting stone with similar finish. Three bay symmetrical the projecting hallway also displaying the icicle-like bargeboards. Like all openings the front door, in dressed stone surround under a hood moulded Tudor arch, was sheeted timber with iron studding. Mock arrowloop over and lancet sidelights similarly hooded. The main windows square, each mullioned with tripartite lights under Tudor heads, both embraced by label mouldings. Richly carved bracket eaves support. There is much in the form and proportions of this lodge akin to that at the secondary gate at Carncastle Lodge, Co Antrim (qv) probably by James Sands. Tragically lost without trace. The fine Tudor Gothick gate screen is now in the final stages of decay. The inner carriage piers octagonal, like the outer ones having recessed panel shafts with trefoil cusped heads. Wide layered caps over panelled friezes. Big stone convex wall quadrants. The sort of entrance pillars designed by both Lanyon and Jackson offices. Erected for James Charles Price.
POSTCARD VIEW, BARRY WATSON

**306. ST MALACHY'S CHURCH OF IRELAND, Hillsborough** 1773; architect James McBlain
A charming composition of Georgian Gothick in the manner of a pair of gate lodges but in fact founded as schoolhouses, one for boys, the other for girls and infants. Later they functioned as a parish room and sexton's house.

**307. ST PATRICK'S RC CHURCH, CONVENT, SCHOOLS AND PRESBYTERY, Downpatrick** c1875; architect probably Mortimer Thomson; *demolished*

O'Hanlon (1875)

A gate lodge contemporary with the Convent of Our Lady of Mercy begun in 1872 to designs by Mortimer Thomson of Belfast. A pleasant little Ruskinian Gothick lodge single storey gabled on an L plan constructed in brick with sandstone highlights. To each leading gable a pair of narrow windows both with trefoiled heads. Post and collar features in wood to both gables below apex finials. Round pillars reduced in stages to decorative lucarned caps with sculpted foliated finials. Secondary posts to carry the carriage gates.
O'HANLON (1875); DOWNPATRICK; U.A.H.S. (1970)

**308. SARAHFIELD, or SARAHVILLE, Helen's Bay** pre 1858; *demolished*

Lodge to a pretty Regency cottage. A property probably named after the 1863 occupant Sarah McDowell.

**309. SCARVAGH, Scarvagh (2)**

Burke in his *Visitation of Seats* in 1855 describes this seat of the Reilly family as being stables and offices put to residential use when a mansion to close a courtyard was abandoned. Formerly of 1717, alterations were carried out in the mid-18th century when the grand entrance from the village may date.

**Village Gate and Lodge** c1746/pre 1860

Classical pillars on a grand scale built up in rusticated ashlar. 3ft 0ins (900mm) square by 14ft 0ins (4.25m) high, they are crowned by urns sculpted with helical fluting. Below each cornice a Greek key pattern band and fluted surround. The flanking wing walls in basalt rubble curve up to meet the pillars and contain dressed stone wicket openings for little people. Good Georgian wrought ironwork. Across the road a building barely recognisable as a gate lodge now adapted to garage use. Built by J Lushington Reilly.

**North Lodge** c1870

A typical Victorian mix of styles in this one and a half storey structure with hipped gable roof. Below the high eaves a three bay symmetrical front elevation, the front door in Classical manner with pilastered door case and semicircular spoked fanlight. Above the attic windows naive wave and foil barge/fascia boards. Above a vertically ribbed squat brick chimney stack. Now spoilt by modern windows and roughcast walls. Built by John Temple Reilly.

BURKE (1855)

**310. SCHOMBERG, Belfast North** c1860; architect probably Thomas Jackson; *demolished*

Both big Italianate villa and its contemporary lodge gone. For Sir William Quartus Ewart who succeeded his father Sir William Ewart of Glenmachan, another Jackson house.

DIXON (1978)

**311. SCION HILL, Dromara** c1850

A standard single storey three bay lodge below a hipped roof with red brick corbel course to the clipped eaves. Basalt rubble construction with granite quoins and label mouldings to openings. A property of the Gilmour family.

**312. SCRABO COTTAGE, Newtownards** c1865; architect possibly John Lanyon

An unsophisticated little single storey Classical lodge. Gabled, that to the avenue in the form of a pediment, its tympanum containing a blank shield, an ornamental roundel equivalent on the opposing facade. Built of crudely worked squared coursed masonry, architectural features, including surrounds to the two bay front, in dressed stone. On the ridge a single octagonal stone chimneypot in the manner of John Lanyon perhaps not unrelated to the practice having planned Scrabo Tower close by. Two much more elegant square ashlar gate pillars with dentil courses below moulded cornices.

**313. SEACOURT, Bangor** c1920

Single storey lodge on a square plan with back return and side porch recessed behind chamfered reveals. To the avenue a pair of flat roofed bow windows project from roughcast walls.

Pyramidal roof. Earlier (c1865) is an innovative gate screen for Foster Connor, a Belfast linen merchant. In sandstone ashlar the inner carriage pillars square and beautifully sculpted in Greek Revival style with corner pilasters having anthemion capitals over rose motif friezes. The cappings similarly decorated with acroteria to each corner below a finial in the form of a casket on a dentil coursed base. In contrast the outer pillars more in a fairytale style. From a square base broach round shafts not unlike Alexander "Greek" Thomson's design for Ferndean Villa, Loch Long, Scotland. Perhaps by the Glasgow architect James Hamilton.

BANGOR AND GROOMSPORT; U.A.H.S. (1984)

**314. SEAFORDE, Seaforde (5)**

There has been a residence of the Forde family here since the 17th century when it was named Castle Navan but the house in its present form was not built until 1816. On the 9th June of that year it was burnt down only to be rebuilt by 1820. Years prior to this, Mathew Forde had been contemplating a grand gated approach to the demesne, for there are preserved in family records proposed designs, both built and unexecuted, by a number of architects over a forty year period.

**Design No 1** c1798; architect Samuel Woolley; *unexecuted*

Woolley had come to Ireland about 1798 to supervise restoration work at Downpatrick Cathedral for his master R W F Brettingham. This rather distorted watercolour perspective for a sumptuous Classical gate screen although not realised here was to be erected in its entirety at Glenanea, Co Westmeath for a Mr Smith. There liberal use was made of that new-fangled material Coade stone, and that was clearly the intent at Seaforde. The central semicircular carriage archway is flanked by Corinthian pilasters with husked margents below a frieze, fluted with a central swagged panel. On the entablature a unicorn couchant on a plinth decorated with festoons and flanked by a pair of urns. Beyond the gates railed screens punctuated by Ionic columns under an entablature, terminate in grand pillars. In each of these is a niche containing Greek goddesses, Flora and Pomona, below a decorative roundel over which is a corniced capping surmounted by another Chambers swagged urn.

**Design No 2** 1805; architect Charles Lilly; *unexecuted*

Very much a variation on the above but in this case incorporating a pair of flanking pavilion lodges. The Dublin architect was obviously influenced by Robert Adam's entrance screen to Syon Park, Middlesex, the design for which was published in his *Plans, Elevations and Sections of Buildings* (1778). Here the order is Tuscan and the centre-piece alternatively surmounted by a lion. Each of the terminating pavilions is a lodge in the form of a perfect cube. The recess to each incorporated a pair of columns in-antis which in turn frame a central semicircular headed blind opening. Crowning the entablature over is a squat swagged urn. The ground floor plan shows stair access to an attic room, the feasibility of which was not to be put to the test. These designs had been commissioned by Mathew Forde not long after he succeeded to the estates in 1796 on the death of his father of the same name. It was his son, another Mathew, who inherited in 1812 and set about building the mansion and its subsequent reinstatement. He was also, before his death in 1837, to leave the village of Seaforde much as we see it today. His architect for this considerable commission was the Englishman, Peter Frederick Robinson, who

*S. Woolley painting (P. Forde)*

*Seaforde, Design No. 1*

C. Lilly painting (P. Forde)

Seaforde, Design No. 2

P.F. Robinson drawing (P. Forde)

Seaforde, Design No. 3

P.F. Robinson drawing (P. Forde)

Seaforde, Design No. 6

besides designing the delightful almshouses in 1828 and perhaps the schoolhouse also planned the magnificent entrance archway and lodge. Robinson had been preparing proposals for this entrance from as early as 1825 producing many alternatives for his demanding patron. Six of these drawings, in the form of simple elevations, survive in estate records, the exact sequence of which is not clear.

**Design No 3** c1825; architect P F Robinson; *unexecuted*

By far the grandest design, the only one to incorporate lodge accommodation in the composition. Each of these outer pavilions has a hipped roof concealed behind an entablatured parapet which is supported at the corners by advancing piers which frame a tapered window with lugged surround. The screen walls have similarly treated wicket openings which connect to the central carriage gates. These are contained in a remarkable and impractical archway in the form of paired square columns at each corner to carry a deep entablature crowned by a "Pantheon" type dome. Drawing in pen and ink with subtle colour enhancement. This may have been the first of the architect's proposals following that of Lilly's both of which had integral lodges. Thereafter the decision must have been to separate porter's accommodation for all succeeding suggestions are for entrance screens alone.

**Design No. 4** c1825; architect P F Robinson; *unexecuted*

A single semicircular-arched carriage archway containing elaborate iron gates with cross motifs, framed by paired square columns carrying a flat entablature decorated with a simple dentil course. The tall flanking walls are without pedestrian access. Again in pen and ink and wash.

**Design No. 5** c1825; architect P F Robinson; *unexecuted*

Much as the above and in the same medium. Single pier support is substituted as support to the entablature which has a breakfront blocking course and patera ornament to spandrels. Flanking are lower wicket gates with their own flat arches. Gates as the preceding design.

**Design No. 6** c1825; architect P F Robinson; *unexecuted*

Another triumphal archway sketch. Pairs of Roman Doric columns carry a pediment with a deep frieze of outsize triglyphs. Big outer pillars terminate tall screen walls which contain wicket openings. These walls display an innovative "crested" coping, a device carried through to the carriage gates which also feature "wheel" motifs. Drawing in pen and ink and wash.

**Design No. 7** 1825; architect P F Robinson; *unexecuted*

A departure from Robinson's previous suggestions in that it lacks a pompous archway. The proposal is a pretty pencil and watercolour presentation, dated August 1825 and initialled by the architect. Four identical pillars punctuate the screen with heavily rusticated vermiculated alternative blocks supporting an obelisk each resting on balls to the corners, in the Vanbrugh Baroque manner. A central carriage opening is flanked by wicket gates in wing walls.

**Design No. 8** 1825; architect P F Robinson

In the same mellow medium as Design No. 7 this shows the archway almost as eventually executed, lacking only the crowning acroterion and Greek key pattern, but displaying sculpted bas-relief panels which were obviously victims of a cost-cutting exercise. A seductive little drawing initialled and dated August 1825 by the architect. Eight years were to elapse before Robinson had approval to submit the most beautifully drafted and meticulously annotated working drawings for both this entrance archway and a gate lodge.

P.F. Robinson painting (P. Forde)

*Seaforde, Design No. 7*

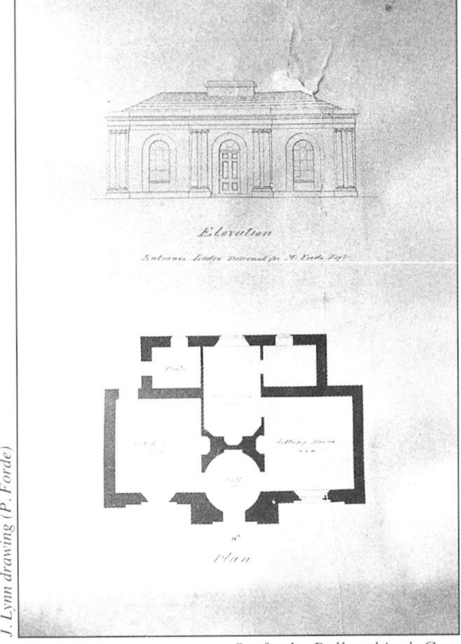
J. Lynn drawing (P. Forde)

*Seaforde, Ballynahinch Gate*

P.F. Robinson painting (P. Forde)

*Seaforde, Design No. 8*

**Main Entrance Archway** 1833; architect P F Robinson

Magnificently aligned on an axis with the main street and approach from Newcastle is a superb Greek Revival composition in rich golden sandstone. The archivolted semicircular arched carriage gate is surmounted by a blank panel below a heavily mutuled pediment with large deeply sculpted anthemion acroteria. On the central arch spring line is a course of Greek key pattern carried beyond to highlight the head of each flanking flat arched wicket opening. Over both of these are stages with more blank panel recesses crowned by basic entablatures with peculiar ball motifs. Bellpushes survive which alerted the gatekeeper who, from the shelter of his lodge, could open the gates with a wheel mechanism in the hallway. The carriage gates were mysteriously spirited away during Second World War requisitioning. The complex extends far beyond in concave railed quadrants, in ironwork matching the wicket gates, which terminate in high curtain walls flanked by large pillars with more key patterns. Robinson, who was a prolific producer of pattern books, had illustrated something similar in his *Rural Architecture* (1823).

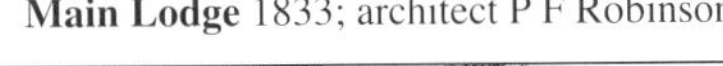
**Main Lodge** 1833; architect P F Robinson

Behind to one side a highly innovative and perfectly symmetrical gate lodge in similar sandstone ashlar. One and a half storey on a T plan the projection to the avenue is crowned by a pediment the tympanum of which never had the coat-of-arms that the architect envisaged. This projection houses a "lumber place" over the hallway and is flanked by Tuscan hipped roof porticoes in each internal angle. The main body of the lodge has basic two up two down accommodation. A single storey lean-to structure to the rear of pantry and scullery opens into a semicircular yard area constrained by a high wall enclosing storage, ash-pit and privy. All windows are Georgian squared sashes, that facing the avenue with a flat hood entablature. Off the rear wall rise two pairs of tall square chimney stacks. Well maintained.

**Ballynahinch or North Gate** c1830; architect John Lynn

A signed undated plan and elevation drawing depicts a gate lodge proposal which varies slightly from that built. Single storey three bay symmetrical below a hipped roof disguised by an entablatured parapet. In reality the breakfront front door surround was replaced by a flat entablatured portico with two pairs of Ionic columns. Semicircular-headed openings with spoked heads and fanlights set into equivalent recesses. Panelled front door and squared sash windows in fawn-coloured ashlar walls. Wide gate screen with square stone pillars which have recessed panelled shafts, repeated on the frieze below moulded corniced cappings.

**East Gate** c1860

Replacing an older lodge opposite the gates this building displays many of the features employed by P F Robinson in his Seaforde village designs. These include the diagonal cross pattern to the

*Seaforde, Ballynahinch Gate*

upper portion of windows and the crude shelf-like hood above the front door. Seemingly too late to be by John Lynn although he proposed a lodge akin to this for the Waring estate at Finnebrogue (qv). By 1840 William Moore of Belfast was the family architect. Perhaps it was executed posthumously. Single storey three bay symmetrical. In stuccoed walls, wide window openings tripartite with timber mullions and transoms below label mouldings. Hipped roof with a big squat chimney stack. Predating the lodge by about half a century are the huge stone carriage pillars, simple and square with ball finials. The fine ironwork looks coeval.

**West Gate** c1860

Identical to the above, similarly replacing a pre 1834 lodge across the road.

**"Pheasantry" Lodge** c1850

Perhaps originally a gate lodge as well as gamekeeper's accommodation is this one and a half storey building. Three bay symmetrical gabled as is the small hall projection. Mildly Picturesque, there is a big bulky chimney stack.
ROBINSON (1823); EAST DOWN; U.A.H.S. (1973); ADAM (1778)

**315. SEAPATRICK, Banbridge** pre 1860; *demolished*

The seat of the Hayes family whose great Linen Thread Mills were nearby. Founded in 1840 by

Frederick W Hayes, it was his son William who built a gate lodge to the house. Contemporary iron gates and good square gate piers with fluted shafts and ovoid cobweb motifs to friezes.
BASSETT'S CO DOWN (1886)

**316. SEAPATRICK RECTORY, Banbridge (2)** both pre 1860; *both demolished*
Built by the long-lived incumbent Rev Daniel Dickenson.

**317. SEAPOINT COTTAGE, Rostrevor** pre 1834; *demolished*

**318. SHRIGLEY HALL, Killyleagh (2)**
John Martin in 1824 built a cotton mill which was to become the largest of its kind in Ireland. In 1845 it was replaced by a flax spinning mill and the proprietor established himself in residence in the heart of the industrial village which had grown up. To both premises he set up lodged entrances.

**Mill Entrance** c1845; architect not known; *demolished*

Flanking the entrance a pair of two roomed Greek Revival cube lodges like tea caddies. Single storey in ashlar, the elevations to the footway single bay, both entrance doors with pilastered door cases. These pilasters were repeated on a larger scale on the corners. Eaves entablatures surrounded the shallow pitched pyramidal roofs each of which rose to a chimney stack with incised panels. Between the lodges two unusual gate piers in the form of circles of cast iron rails.

**House Entrance** c1850; architect not known; *demolished*

Built of basalt with red sandstone quoins and dressings a single storey building, three bay symmetrical. Below a hipped roof there was a similarly roofed projecting hallway. Openings architraved with segmentally headed arches, the window cills bracketed. Concave quadrant walls framed by simple square piers. Wicket openings had secondary iron posts with Greek anthemion cast tops. Carriage pillars in the form of truncated fluted columns surmounted by cast iron lantern lights. Both entrances like the Hall, with its ornamental conservatory, mill and village swept away in a remarkable orgy of uncontrolled vandalism.
GREEN (1963); EAST DOWN; U.A.H.S. (1973)

**319. SONOMA, Belfast North**
A matching gate lodge to an opulent high Victorian house for Robert J Crawford, wine merchant.

**Holly Cottage** c1895; architect not known
On an irregular plan, single storey in orange brick with big bargeboards. These are semicircular supported on big carved pairs of brackets, with a serrated motif to the verge. Exposed rafter toe eaves. Moulded stone stringcourse at spring level and carried around as a hood to semicircular opening heads. Round bay in leading gable. Much extended, liberated from the big house in its own garden and overshadowed by its variegated holly.

**320. SPRINGFIELD, Magheralin** c1830
A gate lodge to an older house on the site which was revamped as yet another Neo-Classical house of the Richardson family. In contrast to this stuccoed house is the roughcast single storey lodge. Standard three bay below a wide-brimmed hipped roof it now lies abandoned. It ceased to function as a lodge when the avenue was re-routed further west probably when the house was transformed c1850.

**321. SPRINGVALE, Ballywalter**
(see BALLYWALTER)

**322. STEADLY or STUDLEY, Rostrevor** c1855; architect probably W J Barre; *demolished*
A restrained stuccoed Italianate house, and presumably lodge, built for David Stead to designs by William J Barre in the 1850s.

**323. STORMONT CASTLE, Dundonald** c1860; architect Thomas Turner; *demolished*

*B.N.L.*

A property once of the Jackson family which passed by marriage to the infamous and unscrupulous Rev John Cleland (1755-1834). He amassed a fortune by dubious means and it was his grandson who set about extending and refacing the old square Georgian pile after his succession in 1842. Work was not underway until 1858, the transformation into a sort of Neo-Jacobean Scots Baronial being to plans by the architect Thomas Turner who may have adapted earlier drawings by the Scot, William Burn. Be that as it may the fine gate lodge was pure Turner. The lodge was an informal composition in Thomas Turner's Scots Baronial/Italianate/ Picturesque manner just as at his Magherafelt courthouse. Faced in squared, uncoursed quarry faced sandstone with ashlar dressings it appears to have been on an L plan. Rising to one and a half storeys it was dominated on its internal angle by a square entrance tower rising through a second storey lit by bullseye windows to a steep pyramidal roof. Crowstepped gables terminated in ball finials. The gate screen walls were framed by pillars reflecting the gate lodge tower their pyramidal cappings relieved with small "peaks" to each face. The shafts below had recessed roundels to echo the tower portholes. The 1962 photograph which records the tragic dismantling of the entrance had the caption stating that it was "... apparently interfering with the approach to the new Government building, Dundonald House", which of course it need not have done. A regrettable loss.
DIXON (1972); PHOTOGRAPH, B.N.L. 21 Aug 1962

**324. STRAMORE, Gilford** pre 1860; *demolished*
Built for the Purdon family.

**325. STRAMORE HOUSE, Gilford** c1865; *demolished*
A property formerly of the Croziers, it passed to the Nicholson family who sold it to Hugh Watson. He employed the architect Thomas Jackson to carry out alterations to the house c1865 and the lodge may date from then.
DIXON (1978)

**326. STRANGFORD, Strangford** c1790
Tiny single storey, two roomed lodge, two bay lancet windowed elevation to the avenue. A semi-bowed gable end projects beyond gate sweep alongside. Square Classical ashlar carriage pillars with fluted friezes. Wicket gate to one side and balancing dummy to other. Some contemporary ironwork. The house of 1789 built by a customs collector called Nelson who may also have provided the lodge in contrasting style in the manner of Castleward (qv) nearby.
PORTAFERRY & STRANGFORD; U.A.H.S. (1969)

**327. STRANDTOWN, Belfast North** pre 1834; *demolished*
A lodge in close proximity to the large five bay Tudor Gothick house of David Anderson also now demolished and replaced by a cinema.

**328. STRANGFORELAND TERRACE, Belfast North** pre 1858; *demolished*
What looks like a single storey pill-box lodge with a pyramidal roof on Connop's view now gone along with the terrace. The latter was also sometime called Yarrow Villas.
CONNOP (1864)

**329. STRATHEARN, Belfast North (2)**
House and two identical lodges in stuccoed Italianate style for James A Campbell. Now a girls' school.

**Front Lodge** c1880; architects probably Young and Mackenzie

A single storey standard plan three bay symmetrical building below a hipped roof. A gabled canopy projects over the doorway supported on a pair of ornate carved wooden brackets. The segmentally-arched front door has a moulded surround extending to a keystone with bullseye fanlight over. Windows with semicircular heads have chamfered raised surrounds and bracketed cills. There is the same robust detailing in the raised quoin stones and bracketed eaves course here as at Thornhill, Co Antrim (qv).

**Rear Lodge** c1880; architects probably Young and Mackenzie
As above.

**330. STRAWHILL, Donacloney** c1860; architect probably William Spence

Lodge to a big mid-Victorian Picturesque villa with vigorously detailed fancy bargeboards and sculpted ashlar stone for the Nicholson family. There is much about the architecture of the house reminiscent of the work of William Spence of Glasgow, also to be seen in the gate lodge. In the same sandstone ashlar as the house, the lodge in form is much akin to that at Elmfield (qv) where Spence was active. One and a half storey, two up two down and three bay symmetrical. Gables, including that to the front door breakfront, now lacking any decorative bargeboards. The door has a corbelled bracket course over and blank shield relieving the gable. Flanking are bipartite windows with chamfered reveals and label mouldings. To the road a canted bay with tiny lancet attic light over. Gate pillars also in good quality masonry with friezes decorated in raised quatrefoil motifs and each crowned by strapped ball finials. Good chunky cast iron gates. For William Nicholson.

**331. STREAMVILLE, Rathfriland** c1830
Probably built by the family of Swan is this now derelict and overgrown lodge. Opposite the gates a pretty Tudor Picturesque structure, its front elevation two bay with bipartite casement windows, lattice paned below label mouldings. Single storey below a hipped gable roof decorated with foiled fascia/bargeboards. Label moulded side entrance door in harled walls. There is a pair of diagonally set brick chimney stacks.

**332. STUDLEY, Rostrevor** (see STEADLY)

**333. SUMMERFIELD, Dundonald (2)**
both pre 1834; *both demolished*
Previously a seat of the Gordons also of Delamont and Florida (qqv) it is now a golf club. Built by Robert Gordon.

**334. SYDENHAM, Belfast North.** c1860; *demolished*
To a big Classical villa with a bow front was a gabled single storey lodge with another gable above the front door, visible on Connop's view. CONNOP (1864)

**335. SYDENHAM VILLA, Belfast North** c1860; *demolished*
The Connop painting suggests a tiny pill-box type lodge below a hipped roof.
CONNOP (1864)

**336. TAMNAHARRY, Warrenpoint (2)**
The present multi-gabled Picturesque bargeboard house was built by William Edmond Reilly, 2nd son of John Reilly of Scarvagh (qv). He had come by the property on his marriage to Harriett Hamilton whose family had been resident here for many years before. His architect was the Newry man Thomas J Duff who had recently discovered the Picturesque style and he added two gate lodges in similar manner.

**West Entrance** c1840; architect T J Duff
Once a pretty ornamental bargeboard cottage it has suffered in recent restoration which has robbed it of much of its former character. What was probably a simple single storey lodge with asymmetrical projecting hallway on a three bay front has been extended and had inappropriate modern windows inserted. Now rendered and painted in pleasant pastel shade the trefoil bargeboards and hipknobs probably fair facsimiles of the original. In a gable survives the family crest, a dexter hand supported by two lions and their motto FORTITUDINE ET PRUDENTIA. The entrance screen has been separated from the lodge and reassembled a few yards away. Unusual "salt-cellar" granite piers clearly by Duff have stylised Tudor Gothick recessed and jaunty corniced caps. Modern ironwork.

**East Lodge** c1840; architect T J Duff

*A. Rankin*

Here lies, deserted and deteriorating rapidly, a typical "P F Robinson" Picturesque cottage, a single storey version of Duff's Tudor Lodge at nearby Narrow Water (qv). On an informal L plan, three roomed with steep gables decorated with original trefoiled bargeboards, the hipknobs amputated. To the road gable a mullioned and transomed window with tiny squared glazing below a label moulding. The gable to the now disused avenue has a canted bay with chamfered granite surround. In the internal angle a mono-pitched rustic sitting-out verandah, the canopy supported on two and a half granite columns, rather than tree trunks as Robinson would have left. On the ridge off a rectangular base rise two diagonally set granite chimney stacks. A highly desirable building much in need of loving care and attention.

**337. TEMPLEGOWRAN, Newry** c1910
For long a property of the Parsons family whose flour mills of Gordon and Parsons were nearby. The lodge replaced an earlier pre 1860 building on the same site. One and a half storey on an L plan, gabled with roughcast walls. Unusually the internal angle, with trellised canopy faces the demesne. A single storey canted bay with squared pane sashes looks across a plain gate screen.

**338. THORNHILL, Belfast North** pre 1904; *demolished*
Listed as the residence in 1868 of one John Wood. The lodge may have been built by the Barnetts when they came here in the 1880s.

**339. TOBAR MHUIRE, Crossgar** 1875

There was a pre 1834 gate lodge on the site of the present one, to what was then Crossgar House. This residence had been purchased from an Edward Ruthven by the Thompson brothers, William and James. Subsequently the property was inherited by James Cleland who rebuilt the house and altered the name in 1864. It was his son John who succeeded in 1875 and wasted no time in further improving the estate with extensive outbuildings and replacement gate lodge all in sturdy construction. The lodge is a typically brash late Victorian design in contrasting materials. Slightly elevated from the avenue a single storey three bay symmetrical lodge with hipped roof from which projects a gabled hall. Constructed in coursed, squared quarry-faced basalt with yellow fireclay brick dressings and vermiculated stone quoins. Above the front door a slate datestone roundel with brick "sunburst" dressings. Over this again a skewtable gable its kneelers supporting cream terracotta urns and on the apex a proud eagle in similar material. The demesne now a Passionist Retreat Centre.

**340. TOLLYMORE PARK, Bryansford (5)**
Over the centuries there grew up here, in the foothills of the Mourne Mountains, the most beautiful landed estate in the north of Ireland. Eulogised over by countless visitors, Harris in 1740 found the Lord Limerick's "... two deer parks, finely wooded, watered and cut into Ridings or Vistos; where the Goats whey Drinkers, by Advice of Physicians, resort in the spring and summer seasons, and find health and amusement". Then there would have been little to marvel over in the way of building but by the time the Rev Daniel Augustus Beaufort, traveller and amateur architect, visited in 1787 he was able to pass through "a new handsome Gothic gateway" into a park where the quality and quantity of the architecture had evolved into something equally unrivalled. In 1806 Sir Richard Colt Hoare, he of the magnificent Stourhead gardens who rarely praised the seats of the Irish nobility, wrote "Few, if any nobleman, either in Ireland, or in the sister kingdom, can boast of a residence placed in so singular and romantic situation. The approach to it, under a Gothic gateway, is truly prepossessing". This remarkable entrance to the demesne from Bryansford village was one of a series of follies and like eyecatchers to embellish the property and mark it as one of the first in Ireland to show the influence of the Gothic Revival style. This can be attributed to James Hamilton, Lord Limerick who laid out the property as a summer retreat and who was the Irish patron of Thomas Wright, the "Wizard of Durham", mathematician, astronomer, architect and landscape gardener. He had visited Ireland at his patron's invitation in 1746 and is known to have spent eight days at Tollymore that summer, and it is from this year that a variety of follies, all in a very peculiar style, began to appear. That the two entrance archways are late 18th century in origin, the Bryansford example actually bearing the date of Wright's death, does not deter Michael McCarthy from attributing both to the Durham architect on stylistic grounds.

**The Bryansford or Gothick Gate** 1786; architect probably Thomas Wright
McCarthy cites a drawing c1750 for an eyecatcher in the *Avery Sketchbook* as being a preparatory design for the gateway and there certainly are strong similarities. The tall elegant pointed carriage arch is buttressed at ground level and its pinnacled, crenellated parapet restrained by foiled flying buttresses. Both these and finials are decorated with Ulster crockets or "bap" motifs, a peculiarity common to many of the follies about the estate. Below the dated frieze in the arch spandrels are unique trefoil

W.M. Lawrence (N.L.I.)

*Tollymore Park, Bryansford Gate*

W.A. Green (U.F.T.M.)

*Tollymore Park, Barbican Entrance*

ornaments again showing a baker's influence. Flanking the archway is a pair of pedestrian entrance structures each in the form of a lancet arch surmounted by the same crenellated and pinnacled parapet. Beyond this granite ashlar composition are tall quadrant walls. The turn of the century photograph shows a proud top-hatted gatekeeper resplendent in his war medals in front of less than appropriate later cast iron gates and a notice-board stating bye-laws for public entry to the demesne.

**The Bryansford Gate Lodge** 1802
Secreted to one side behind the estate wall with its back to the road is a pretty Georgian Gothick gate lodge. Single storey on a standard plan, three bay below the required hipped roof. Openings all with lancet heads the windows Y-traceried in walls now rendered over, the stone quoins still expressed. In immaculate order, it has been extended by one bay in matching style.

**Barbican Entrance** c1780; architect probably Thomas Wright
"A charming squat rough stone castle with an arch between two round towers with trefoils and arrowslits", as Barbara Jones describes it and even if the date is wrong this design is again spiritually Wright's. Once more there would appear to be a precedent in the *Avery Sketchbook* of a Thomas Wright elevation for a gateway c1750 displaying a distinct resemblance. Constructed in rubble stone lightly rendered, the circular towers contain granite dressed shamrock motifs over pointed arched openings, one permitting pedestrian access to the park the other leading to the spiral steps within, which rise to the battlemented rampart that surmounts the pointed carriage arch. The latter has a stringcourse at spring level and cross arrowloops to its spandrels. Plain wrought iron gates. There is a similar gateway at Wallington, Northumberland, another Wright design. An early photograph reveals a highly appropriate gate lodge nestling behind the archway.

**Barbican Lodge** c1810; *demolished*
A single storey three bay symmetrical lodge with castellated parapet disguising a hipped roof. Constructed in rubble stone the openings all with lancet heads, the windows had large diagonal glazing patterns. In 1798 the estate was inherited by the Jocelyns, Earls of Roden from the Hamiltons, Lord Limerick and Earls of Clanbrassil and they added further lodges in somewhat different vein.

**East Lodge** 1865
One and a half storey gabled lodge constructed in rubble stone with big crude granite quoins. Gabled three bay symmetrical the centre in the form of a gabled breakfront, over the front door of which is a recessed shamrock feature containing the datestone. Nasty modern steel windows spoil the effect. Chimney missing.

**White Lodge** 1876; architect John Birch

On the Hilltown road, past many of Lord Limerick's fairytale folly gate pillars in complete contrast to all that had gone before, a late Victorian gate house. A distinguished essay in half-timbered Tudor Revival manner by an architect who, apart from being a pioneer of the use of concrete, was a prolific author of cottage designs for which he suggested minimum sizes on humanitarian grounds. He published his *Picturesque Lodges* in 1879 which features this design for Tollymore, erected much as illustrated. A two up two down, one and a half storey, three bay symmetrical cottage with hipped gable roof finished in earthenware tiles complete with bonnets. On the central stone chimney a plaque with a Roden monogram below a coronet. The attic storey jettied out "in black and white" work sporting a datestone to the park gable and, facing the road, an oriel under a catslide. The ground floor in random basalt laid to course, the windows with unusual margined glazing pattern in brick dressed surrounds. Below the oriel is a canted bay window with a mono-pitch roof on brackets. Sheltering the front door is a fine carved timber gabled porch, like a lych gate. Birch intended this to have been constructed in rustic lattice tree trunks. There is perforated terracotta cresting and a metal finial to the ridge. Good carved wooden gates and decorative posts not quite as the architect envisaged.

HARRIS (1740); BEAUFORT (1787); HOARE (1806); McCARTHY (1987); JONES (1974); BIRCH (1879); LAWRENCE PHOTOGRAPHS (N.L.I.) Refs 2476(R), 2392(C) 423(1), 841(1); GREEN PHOTOGRAPH (U.F.T.M.) Ref W.A.G. 1859; MOURNE; U.A.H.S. (1975)

**341. TOWER HILL, Newry** pre 1834
To a residence previously "The Castle" a simple single storey lodge. Three bay symmetrical and gabled with nice pendulous carved bargeboard pattern, with shamrock or trefoil toes. Built in random rubble with harling. Derelict.

**342. TUBBER-NA-CARRIG, Kircubbin** c1860
Once called Summerhill, a property in 1856 of Colonel John Ward. Gable-on to the avenue, a pretty single storey lodge with steeply pitched roof having ornamental wavy bargeboards and carved hipknobs. Alongside the main gable with its canted bay presiding over the gates is a gabled hall like an afterthought, containing the Tudor arched front door. Margined windows in

roughcast walls. Very unusual gate piers, octagonal, tapering upwards, clustered vertical round ribs to each corner. Cappings with minuscule ball finials. Prickly topped wooden fence screens.

**343. TUDOR HALL, Holywood** c1850; *demolished*
Contemporary lodge on a markedly smaller scale to a tall gabled and chimneyed Tudor Revival pile of 1849 built for Henry Murney a Belfast Tobacco merchant.

**344. TULLYCARN, Magheralin** pre 1834; *demolished*
For the Magill family.

**345. TULLYHINAN, Banbridge** pre 1860; *demolished*
A chaste Neo-Classical villa designed in 1861 by the architect Thomas Turner. For John Lindsay, linen manufacturer of the Ballydown Mill.

**346. TULLYHUBBERT, Comber** pre 1833
A lodge for Robert Wilson. Single storey two bay gabled, a chimney stack to each gable. Plain and derelict.

**347. TULLYLISH, Lawrencetown** c1870
A very pleasant three bay cottage for James Greer Bell. Constructed in basalt rubble with mellow brick dressings. One and a half storey under a hipped gable roof with paired bracket support to its high eaves. Appropriate modern squared windows. Immaculately tended.

**348. TURF LODGE, Belfast South** pre 1858; *demolished*
A lodge probably built when the property was acquired from John Kane by James Davidson. House and lodge overtaken in the late 19th century by industrial Belfast.

**349. TWESKARD, Belfast North** pre 1901; architect perhaps Thomas Jackson & Son; *demolished*
A house by Thomas Jackson for T M Greeves.
DIXON (1978)

**350. TYRELLA, Clough** c1830/c1850

A cosy little lodge of two dates. Initially built by Arthur Hill Montgomery, 4th son of Hugh of Greyabbey (qv) not long after his marriage in 1825 and after he had acquired the property from Rev George Hamilton. Formerly a simple three

bay elevation to the road, two bay deep below a hipped roof, the older windows having lancet heads. Sometime later it was extended by the addition of a rear return with tripartite latticed window and to the avenue a big bowed enlargement containing two very wide windows each with intricate cast iron margined Tudor Gothic glazing. Roughcast walls. In contrast the entrance screen has sophisticated Greek stellae type gate pillars. In ashlar they taper upwards to four faced pediment cappings. To the west the old smithy looking like a Picturesque gabled gate lodge.
BURKE (1904)

**351. UNION LODGE, Scarvagh** pre 1833; *demolished*
The core of an 18th century residence of the Dawsons known as Lisnabraque Lodge survives but the pair of gate lodges within the demesne has not. The Fivey family after acquiring the property were responsible for the gate screen that remains on the edge of the estate. A variety of granite pillars, those flanking the central carriage opening grandest with V-jointed rustication, friezes and corniced caps.

**352. VIANSTOWN, Downpatrick**
No gate lodges but to the main road a late Georgian gate screen and at the access to the outbuildings from a minor road is a symmetrical castellated entrance arch. In squared uncoursed rubble the segmental carriage arch is dressed in brick with a keystone sculpted in the shape of a blank shield. Over is a crenellated parapet spanning between square turrets. Probably built by Hugh Cleland after the property passed from Bernard Ward c1850.

**353. WALSHESTOWN CASTLE, Strangford**
(see MYRA CASTLE)

**354. WARINGSTOWN, Waringstown** pre 1863; *demolished*
The lodge to this important mud-built house of 1667 was built by Rev Holt Waring or his cousin, son-in-law and heir Henry Waring.

**355. WELLINGTON LODGE, Holywood**
(see DALCHOOLIN)

**356. WESTBANK, Belfast North** pre 1902; *demolished*
A lodge built for William Holmes Smiles, a partner in the Belfast Ropework Company.
YOUNG (1909)

**357. WESTBROOK, Holywood** pre 1834; *demolished*
A villa of c1817 and its coeval lodge both built by Rev Edward May and both demolished to make way for the Palace Military Barracks.

**358. WINONA, Donacloney** c1890; architect possibly Henry Hobart
A small park developed as an occasional summer retreat by the Hilliard family, founders of the Waldorf Astoria Hotel, and named after a town in the central United States. In contrast to the rather drab red brick late Victorian house is a lighter hearted lodge in the same material but with "black and white work" to its gables. Part one and a half and part single storey on an informal plan. To the avenue advances a canted bay window with leaded lattice lights. Alongside, out of sight from the house, the stable and coach buildings. Good carved chamfered wooden posts and gates.

**359. WOODBANK, Gilford** c1840/c1880
Outside the gates a unique split level single storey structure which probably started life as a three bay lodge on one level with tiny bipartite sash windows below a hipped roof. The left hand bay, later raised in the late Victorian era to accommodate a higher floor, has a tall rectangular window with squared panes. This more recent work probably for George Gerald Turrell included red brick chimney stacks, earthenware ridge tiles and apex finials. Walls roughcast with quoins. Panelled front door. Contemporary with the original lodge octagonal stone entrance piers with friezed caps perhaps for an earlier owner, James Fivey who acquired the seat from William Dawson.

**360. WOODLODGE, Castlewellan** pre 1859; *demolished*
Near the town there was a simple standard plan single storey lodge opposite the gates. Built to the fine Regency villa of James Murland.

**361. WOOD LODGE, Castlewellan** pre 1859; *demolished*
Two miles north of the town at the entrance to Clonvaraghan Wood a lodge for the Rev James Anderson. Now gone, it was described by the U.A.H.S. in 1975 thus: "A nice 18th century plain iron gate into the wood, with square cut-stone gate piers, robust shallow pyramidal tops, a little Regency gate lodge of coursed rubble with little stones between three bay with shallow hipped roof, single chimney in centre. Plain late Georgian glazed windows in broad sash boxes either side of plain doorway."
MOURNE; U.A.H.S. (1975)

**362. WOODLANDS, Crawfordsburn** c1939; architects Blackwood and Jury
More recently known as Ardtullagh, a house, garage, chauffeur's accommodation and lodge for Lady Kelly late of Ballymenoch (qv), all in matching materials and all part of the architects' commission. The lodge is a pleasant late Arts-and-Crafts Picturesque composition. To the avenue a two storey gabled block with a single storey wing at right angles containing a sandstone door case in roughcast walls. Rectangular gabled bay projecting from the opposing facade. Westmoreland green slates with exposed rafter toe eaves.

**363. WOODLAWN, Castlewellan** c1840
A lodge built for Samuel Murland to one of many houses in the vicinity associated with the family and local linen mills of James Murland. Originally a single storey three bay standard cottage below a hipped roof it has since been extended many times to sprout many canted bay windows. Much of this work may have coincided with the house's transformation into an Italianate villa and its being renamed Corrywood. Now a residential home in a beautifully matured park.

**364. WOODVILLE, Loughbrickland** pre 1833; *demolished*
Lodge to a property in 1817 of John Howe and 1837 of R Boardman.

**365. YARROW VILLAS, Belfast North**
(see STRANGFORELAND TERRACE)

# COUNTY FERMANAGH

**1. AGHAMORE, Lisnaskea** pre 1834
Opposite the gates, an exceedingly plain lodge, three bay, single storey and gabled. Perhaps built for the Abbott family.

**2. AGHAVEA GLEBE, Brookeborough** pre 1834
A typical late Georgian gate lodge. Standard plan, three bay with a hipped roof. The incumbent in 1837, Rev Thomas Birney.

**3. AGHYOULE TOWNLAND, Derrylin** pre 1862; *demolished*
A lodge identified by Griffith in his valuation to a herd's house leased from a Robert Quinn by the incumbent of the neighbouring Kinawley Rectory (qv), Rev John J Fox. No trace of it can be found.
GRIFFITH

**4. ARDVARNY, Kesh (2)**
**East Lodge** pre 1834; *demolished*
A lodge to the former entrance now gone. This avenue approach was superseded by a new access from the west in the mid-19th century.
**West Lodge** c1860; *ruinous*

I.O.G. Perrott drawing

The overgrown ruin to be found today is of what was originally a pretty Gothick porter's lodge. Mainly single storey on an L plan, it is raised off a basement to address the avenue. Two roomed and gabled, constructed in rubble stone having brick dressings to lancet openings with cast iron latticed glazing pattern. Built for Edward Athill.

**5. ARDESS RECTORY, Kesh** pre 1834; *demolished*
The gate lodge to a 1780 glebe house.

**6. ASHBROOKE, Brookeborough** c1835; architect probably William Farrell
A dower house of the Brookes from neighbouring Colebrooke (qv). This seems to have formed part of a lucrative commission for the architect, there being many buildings of similar form in the vicinity by Farrell for the Brooke family. A gate lodge of generous accommodation, one and a half storey, two up two down, with a symmetrical three bay front elevation. The gables steeply-pitched, including that to a entrance door breakfront which is flanked by canted single storey bays under half umbrello roofs. A similar bay to one gable, the other openings have retained their Tudor label mouldings despite having suffered at the hands of the improvers. Now minus many of its original Picturesque features, such as fancy bargeboards and ornate window glazing which has been replaced by modern bland casements. The whole now rendered over in sand cement.
ROWAN (1979)

**7. BALLINDULLAGH, Killadeas** c1860
A most modest single storey, three bay symmetrical cottage, rendered with chimney stacks to each of its gables. Thought to have been built to another residence of the Irvines of Castle Irvine (qv)

**8. BELLEISLE, Lisbellaw (2)**
An historic and beautiful estate of the Gores, Earls of Ross on the banks of the Upper Lough Erne. The ruinous house was rebuilt around 1856 by John Grey Vesey Porter whose father, Rev John Grey Porter who was also the prosperous rector of Kilskeery, Co Tyrone (qv), had purchased the property for him c1818. Both lodges were built for J G V Porter
**Demesne Gate** c1856
Built to function both as a gatehouse and a schoolhouse, it had become a post office by the turn of the century. Two storey with square-paned windows in roughcast walls. Gables to upper floor windows.
**Causeway Gate** c1856
Also two storey, gabled three bay and plain, again with roughcast walls.
BINNS (1837); KING (1892);
BENCE-JONES (1988)

**9. BELLEVUE, Enniskillen** pre 1834; *demolished*
Probably contemporary with the house of c1830, a pair of lodges built by George Knox one having survived until this century when the property was owned by the Collum family.

**10. BINMORE GLEBE, Derrygonnelly** pre 1834; *demolished*
Opposite the gates, the lodge now gone.

**11. CALLOW HILL, Derrylin** c1860
Formerly a modest three bay single storey cottage with tiny sash windows under a hipped roof. A peculiar perforated brick chimney stack over was heightened when the lodge was later extended by a bay with a larger window, gable end to the road, an extra chimney and a disfiguring lean-to hall projecting towards the avenue. A property in 1860 of Robert Cockburn to whom it was leased by the Earl of Enniskillen. Deserted. Square gate piers with delicate cut stone ball finials.

**12. CARRA, Clones** pre 1834; *ruinous*
A Georgian Gothick lodge with pointed window. A seat in 1837 of Jason Hassard prior to which it was occupied by the Rev Mr Roper.

**13. CARRICK, Lisnaskea (2)**
A house built in 1802 by William Greydon subsequently passed to the Maguires of Munville (qv).
**Existing Entrance** pre 1908
A lodge, opposite the gates, now much 'improved' with disfiguring modern windows and pebble dash. One and a half storey gabled with matching breakfront hall.
**Early Entrance** pre 1834; *demolished*
An earlier lodge across the road from the gates.

**14. CASSIDY LODGE, Irvinestown** pre 1855; *ruinous*
The lodge, now a pile of rubble, was to a property which formed part of the greater Castle Irvine (qv) estate adjoining. It probably served as a dower house. The occupant in 1846 was William J D'Arcy.

**15. CASTLE ARCHDALE, Irvinestown (2)**
**North Lodge** pre 1856; *demolished*
Gone, tragically, as is the graceful 1773 mansion house. The lodge built by Lieut-Col William Archdall not long after succeeding to his eldest brother's estates in 1839.
**South Lodge** c1870
Built to supersede a pre 1834 lodge deeper in the demesne on the same avenue. Tudor Picturesque in style it has lost some of its features in subsequent alterations. One and a half storey, two up two down, three bay symmetrical and gabled. The main bargeboards, and those to the single storey hall projection, have wavy ornamental overlays, hipknobs and expressed collar ties. All very trim but now sand/cement rendered over and less its original decorative windows. Built for Captain Mervyn Edward Archdall.
O.S.M.

**16. CASTLECALDWELL, Belleek (2)**
A romantic estate on a once thickly-wooded promentary of Lower Lough Erne. Previously known as Castle Hassett and then Rossbeg before the 1792 rebuilding of the old residence in charming pasteboard Gothick by the Caldwells, who purchased the property about 1662 from the Blennerhassetts. It became a venue for the lavish hospitality of Sir James Caldwell once ending in disaster. The fall by a musician from "the 6-oared barge, with colours flying and a band playing" resulted in a giant five feet stone violin memorial, to the overindulgence of the fiddler Denis McCabe, propped against the surviving gatehouse. The 1834 Ordnance Survey Map shows a much more extensive estate than that which remains today. The present Enniskillen to Ballyshannon road had not then been

constructed, its predecessor skirting the property further north, from where there is thought to have been lodged access. The map also indicates a pair of circular buildings which flanked an avenue deep within a wooded area of the demesne, one of which is noted as a schoolhouse, the other may have been a balancing porter's lodge. In 1817 the property passed through the female line to the Bloomfields.

**Railway Gate** c1866; *ruinous*; architect either Robert William Armstrong or Thomas Brassie

John Caldwell Bloomfield was in 1857/8 a co-founder of the Belleek Pottery, with one Robert William Armstrong who, among other things, practiced as an architect. It is likely that the new lodge was financed by compensation received from the Irish North Western Railway Company rather than from proceeds of the business. Between 1862 and 1866 the INWRC laid a branch line from Bundoran Junction (Irvinestown) to Ballyshannon, within the northern boundary of the demense, to provide for seasonal tourist traffic to Bundoran and the regular pilgrimage to Lough Derg. The author of the lodge therefore was either Bloomfield's partner who had already been employed at Killadeas Manor (qv) or, as the quality of the design suggests, by Thomas Brassie, engineer and major shareholder in the railway company. Access to the demesne had to be achieved through the newly constructed embankment and the resultant bridge combined as an impressive carriage gateway which linked the gatehouse on one side and the pedestrian tunnel on the other in a unique solution in the Victorian Tudor Castellated style. Two storey, two up two down in squared uncoursed, quarry-faced limestone the embattled parapets corbelled out on mock machicolations to a secondary tower fronting the pedestrian access, the bridge and the gatehouse which boasts its own flagstaff tower. The latter has round headed slit lights whilst the other openings are elliptically headed. Each tower displays a blank shield. Irregular in outline to give a Romantic stage set feel. The hospitality must have continued unabated for the estates were eventually sold up and the castle and gatehouse are now mere shells, both barely discernable under their mantels of ivy. Despite being an amateurish two dimensional design the lodge has charm but the Forestry Service has thus far failed to realise its potential as an eyecatcher at the entrance to what is now a public park.

YOUNG (1780); TRIMBLE (1919-1921); McCUTCHEON (1980); ROWAN (1979)

**17. CASTLECOOLE, Enniskillen (4)**

Since 1655 the estates of the Corrys until coming by marriage to the Lowrys of Aghenis Co Tyrone (qv). As Lowry-Corry the family was raised to the peerage as Earls of Belmore in 1797, coinciding with the completion of James Wyatt's palatial house. Prior to this there had been a pleasant Queen Anne house dating from 1702 but no record of gate lodge provision until a new layout was planned for the park c1783 as a consequence of which this was remedied on the old Enniskillen approach.

**The Twin Lodges** c1785

This delightful pair has had a chequered career for as early as 1834 they were described as being "... plain and in bad repair". Two years later they were considered to be "... more fit for a country chapel than a Park and only just wide enough for the family carriage to pass through". Indeed on the O.S. Map of the same year one was not even considered worthy of recording such was their state of dilapidation. Although the lodges may have had their origin in the late 18th century what we see today is a result of extensive restoration or rebuilding sufficient for both to warrant mention on the 1857 O.S. Map. The lodges present themselves today to the visitor as a Georgian Gothick composition in pretty pink facing brick each leading gable having a large lancet window with Y tracery. Both are flanked by straight wing walls, one screening yard space the other joining a tall square stone pillar surmounted by a small ball finial on an outsized pedestal. Their three bay symmetrical elevations face each other behind the gates, simple square headed openings below an eaves so high as to give a gawky appearance and which once accommodated attic bedspace. A recent reworking has unfortunately seen the loss of the chimney stacks which were central to hipped roofs. The builder of these lodges, Armar Lowry-Corry the first Earl of Belmore, died in 1802 to be succeeded by his son Somerset who for almost forty years was to continue the energetic building programme where his father left off. A long and lasting relationship between Somerset and his contemporary the architect Sir Richard Morrison commenced. Not all his designs were to bear fruit but some such as the agent's house and the huge farm and office complex did materialise, and it was to the latter that a new lodge was designed.

**Thomastown Lodge** c1835; architects Richard and William V Morrison; *ruinous*

*J. Soane (1793)*

Based on a design from John Soane's *Sketches in Architecture* (1793) this is a design on a gable-on plan which the Morrisons were to pioneer and employ throughout the country. In a sort of rustic Greek style there was a slightly more ornate example to be seen at Kilruddery, Co Wicklow (demolished 1992) and in an unexecuted drawing for Baronscourt, Co Tyrone (qv). In random rubble the avenue elevation is dominated by a wide segmental headed tripartite window picked out by a broad band of ashlar which is used as a string course, plinth and quoins. Over the simple two-roomed plan is a very shallow pitched hipped roof on a high, bracketed eaves line. To the side elevation a small gabled hall projects although now lost amongst later additions, and on the opposing facade a balancing structure, perhaps the privy. The lodge had a predecessor on the same site the gates of which still remain. This fine screen has two square ashlar pillars with scroll-moulded tops to the gate stops and lovely pine cone finials as at Redhills, Co Monaghan (qv). Both gate screen and lodge have been allowed to fall into hopeless dilapidation, the fancy finials having been moved to a new location for safekeeping. The 2nd Earl was to retain the Morrisons until shortly before Sir Richard's death to produce many more designs in a variety of styles none of which were to materialise.

**Design for the "Enniskillen Approach"** c1834; architects Richard and William V Morrison; *unexecuted*

"His Lordship is at present in possession of a plan (by Morrison of Dublin) of a splendid gate and pair of Gatehouses in the Grecian Cottage style, which if executed accordingly will add much to the other embellishments of the place". Thus did Lieutenant Clayton in his 1834 O.S. Memoir describe a proposal which like most of Morrison's proposals never did embellish the place. A particularly suave design for which, unusual for Richard Morrison, there is no known source. A pair of matching cube lodges each of which is topped by a pyramidal roof set behind an entablatured parapet. Access to both is from the front approach through frontispiece porches of two Doric columns in antis, with triglyphed friezes and blocking courses supporting fine

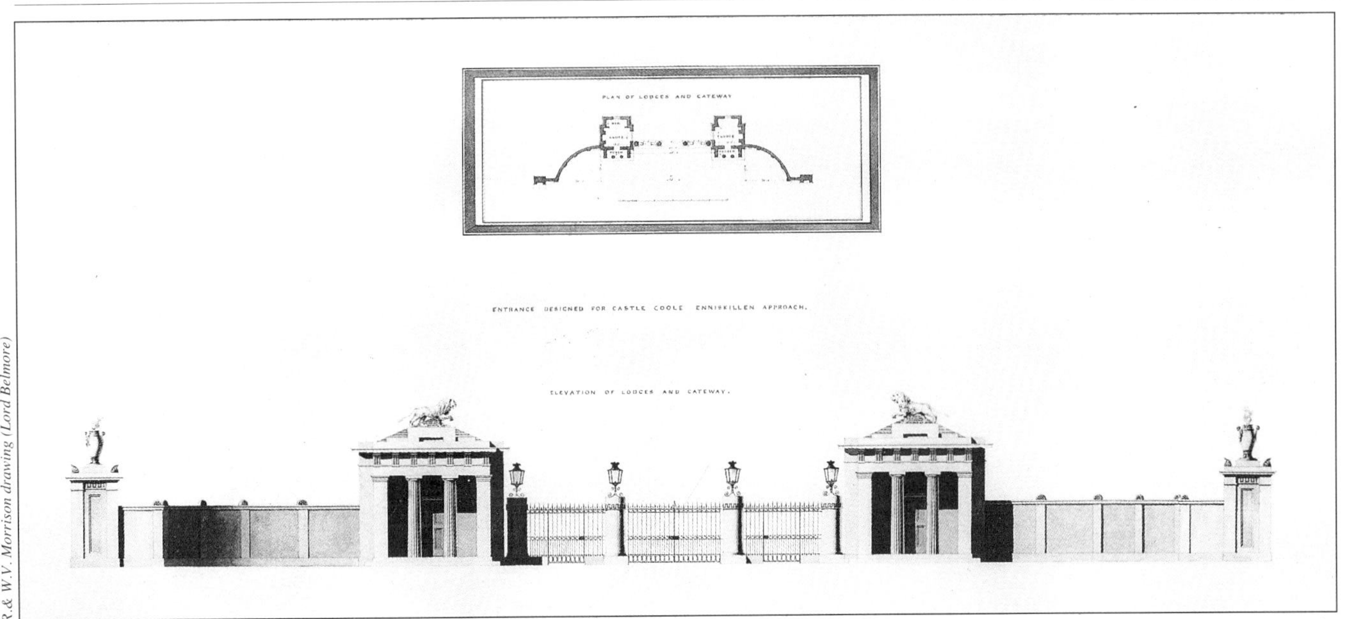


R.& W.V. Morrison drawing (Lord Belmore)

*"Enniskillen Approach"*

sculpted lions rampant facing each other across the face of the gates. Within each structure is a single room 13ft 6ins (4.1m) x 10ft (3m) with a 4ft (1.2m) bed outshoot to the rear balancing the porch. Between, wide central carriage gates and flanking wickets are framed by four cylindrical gate piers each decorated with a Greek key pattern and carrying an octagonal lantern light on scrolled brackets. Completing the impressive composition are concave quadrant walls, pilastered with acroteria to the copings, all terminating in grand aedicule pillars, panelled with more key patterns and acroteria and topped by tall elegant smoking urns.

**Design for the "Dublin Approach"** c1834; architects Richard and William V Morrison; *unexecuted*

Additional to the preceding design the long-suffering architects produced this grand scheme. They were to provide something almost identical for Baronscourt, Co Tyrone (qv) which was again destined not to be built, although a truncated version of the gateway was erected at Oak Park, Co Carlow. The drawing displays a triumphant archway, its semicircular head with a vast entablature over, crowned by a sculpted coat-of-arms, supported by two pairs of Ionic columns raised on pedestals. Flanking are brief colonnades of two Greek Doric columns, stopped by big niched aedicule piers surmounted by draped vases. Hardly coincidentally there are illustrations in Humphry Repton's *Landscape Gardening*, edited by J C Loudon in 1840, which indicate a similar archway and a gate lodge much as the Morrisons proposed. Probably intended to be located opposite the gate "from the Dublin approach" a sophisticated temple raised importantly on a stepped plinth with two Greek Doric columns in antis supporting a pediment. The accommodation comprises a large living-room (inadequately lit from a single window in the portico recess) and one bedroom with a small closet to the rear. Balancing on the side elevations project a gabled and pilastered privy with external approach, and matching entrance porch opposite. A plan not far removed from that of the Thomastown lodge. There were to follow many more delightful sketches from the Morrison pen for the estate, varying from Picturesque thatched cottages to a design for a gate lodge in the Tudor Revival manner, all of which remained unexecuted.

**The Tudor Revival Lodge** 1838; architect Richard Morrison; *unexecuted*

A design from the architect who was then in his seventy-second year is much in the style

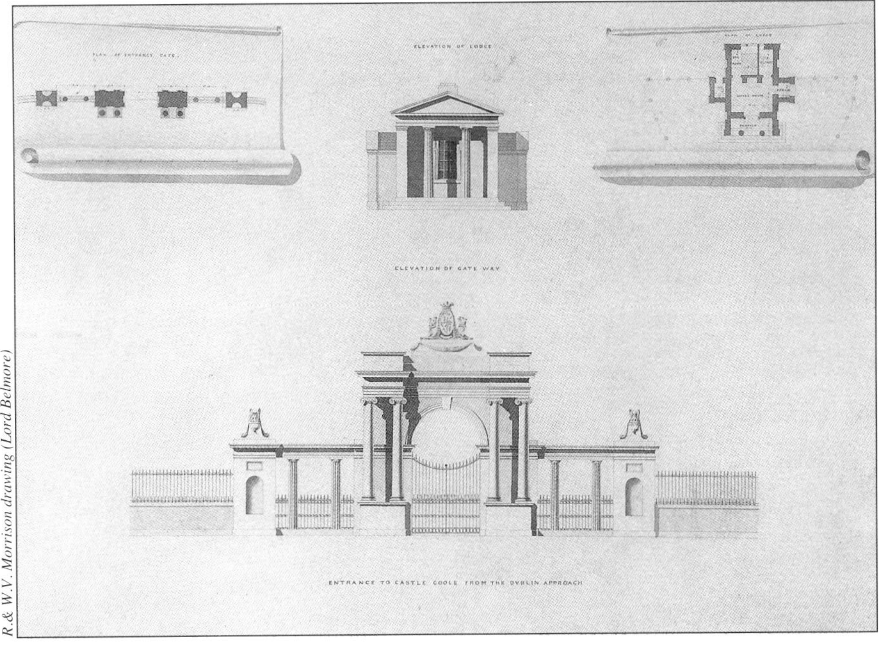


R.& W.V. Morrison drawing (Lord Belmore)

*"Dublin Approach"*

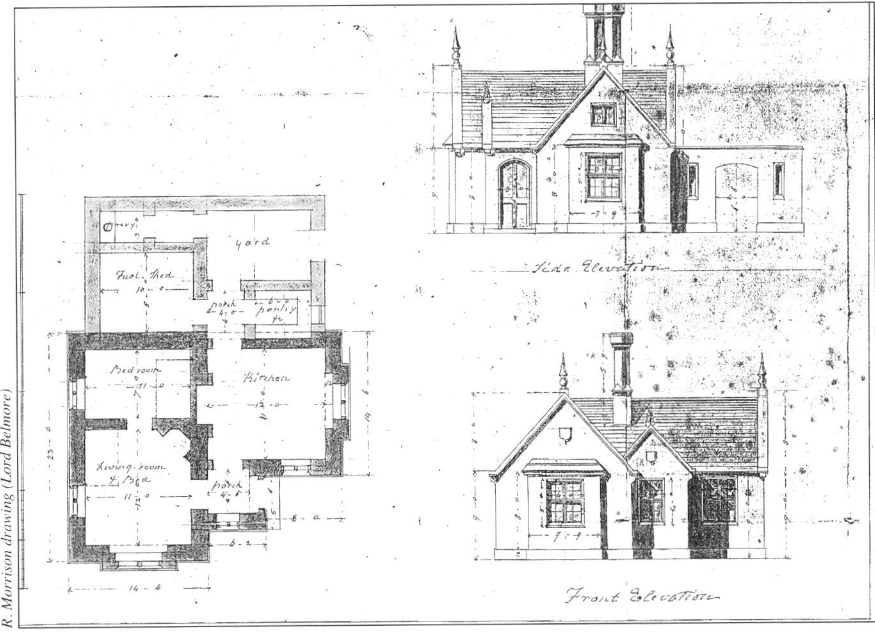


R. Morrison drawing (Lord Belmore)

*Tudor Revival Lodge*

pioneered by his son William Vitruvius who died that year. Simply three roomed and single storey on an L plan. Skewtables culminate in spikey finials below which are shield ornaments in the main gable elevations each of which has a small rectangular bay. The windows transomed and mullioned with square leaded lights. From the internal angle advances a little gabled hall with a pinecone finial aloft. Dominating the composition is a huge pair of diagonally set chimney stacks. Quite where these unexecuted designs were intended to be located is not clear but they may all have been discarded in favour of the eventual Cottage Orné solution.

**Heather Cottage Lodge** c1840; architect possibly Richard Morrison

To replace an earlier pre 1833 lodge situated opposite the previous gates on the old coach road is this delightful rustic concoction. Single storey on an irregular plan, roughly L shaped with a small rear return. Under a thatched roof a canted bay projects towards the avenue with a thatch of its own. From the bay the cottage is surrounded by a verandah formed by an extended eaves supported on rustic poles. In harled walls are mullioned lattice paned windows. Having four designed elevations it cannot be successfully extended to provide modern living accommodation in an aesthetically acceptable way. Unless an alternative function can be contrived it will remain a pretty but provocative ornament to the vandals. Nevertheless it survives as a credit to Lord Belmore for his persistent restorations.

**Weir's Bridge Lodge** c1880; architect unknown

A. Rankin

The construction of this new avenue approach dates from 185/ to 1860 as part of the last major change of the estate layout for the 4th Lord Belmore, Somerset Richard Lowry-Corry. The lodge would seem not to have been added until the building of Weirs Bridge in 1879, erected to carry the Enniskillen- Florence Court-Belcoo line of the Sligo, Leitrim and Northern Counties Railway. A very fine building in the Lombardic style of the highest quality ashlar sandstone with immaculately carved detailing. Single storey, four roomed on a T plan, the cross of the T extending to the avenue on a raised stepped platform to form a "porte-cochère" with semicircular-headed arches. The windows arranged singly and in pairs with similar heads, the surrounds beautifully sculpted in a variety of decorative geometric motifs. Flanking the entrance archway a pair of round headed niches with bracketed cills repeated under the windows. To the quoins an elegant rope pattern. The hipped roof is crowned by two pairs of unusual round squat studded terracotta chimney pots. The approach is marked by ogee quadrants framed by square piers, again intricately carved sandstone with decorative chamfering, studded plinths and sawtooth corbelled cappings. The inner carriage piers are surmounted by serpent-entwined vases. There are in the Public Record Office what appear to be preliminary sketches for the gates, unsigned and undated. No architect is recorded as having worked on this entrance and one can only speculate. John Lanyon was particularly adept in the picturesque design of smaller buildings and carried out much in this style for the railway companies. Alternatively John Corry is thought to have been a kinsman of the Lowry-Corrys and there is much here akin to his Elmwood Church in Belfast.

O.S.M.; ROWAN (1979); MORRIS (1880); McPARLAND (1989); SOANE (1793); LOUDON (1840); McCUTCHEON (1980); McERLEAN (1984)

**18. CASTLEHUME, Enniskillen** pre 1834; *demolished*

"One of ye most stately and sumptuous buildings in the north of Ireland, situate in a commodious and pleasant place bordering ye famous water of Lough Erne, encompassed with pleasant improvement and ornamental buildings." Whether the latter description included the gate lodge may never be known for all that remains are a dovecote and the stables. The big house for Sir Gustavus Hume in 1728 was the first commission in Ireland by the German architect Richard Cassels. On Hume's death in 1731 the demesne fell steadily into decline having passed through the female line to the Loftus family and thence to the Tottenhams, Marquesses of Ely who built Ely Lodge (qv) nearby. The mansion was demolished in 1810 the gate lodge surviving into the present century.

TRIMBLE (1919-1921)

**19. CASTLE IRVINE, Irvinestown (3)**

The castle of Nekarne near Lowtherstown, as property and town were previously called, originated in 1611 but went through a succession of owners before being bought by the Irvines in 1667. Portions of this original castle were incorporated by the architect J B Keane into a rather incongruous Tudor Revival symmetrical addition of 1833 for Major Gorges Marcus Irvine.

**Early Main Entrance** pre 1834; *demolished*

Opposite the original gates on the old Enniskillen Road this lodge was taken down to be superseded by the present entrance when the road was absorbed into the estate and the avenue extended accordingly.

**Existing Main Entrance** c1850; architect probably William Farrell

William D'Arcy Irvine inherited from his father, the major, in 1847 and this lavish entrance would seem to date from then, too late for J B Keane to have been responsible. Much points to William Farrell of Dublin as being the author. He had designed the Irvines' local Church of Ireland and perhaps of greater significance William D'Arcy Irvine in 1817 had married Maria, daughter of Sir Henry Brooke of Colebrooke (qv), Farrell's patron in a lengthy commission there. But it is the chimney stack which provides the strongest clue, rising off the rear wall as it does on the Colebrooke lodges and his two at Ely Lodge (qv). This is a hallmark of the architect's work at the time. Furthermore at the Omagh Lunatic Asylum lodge, Co Tyrone (qv) is the same vertically channelled paired stone stack. In an attractive Tudor style not unlike the house, the lodge is single storey on a T plan with a symmetrical three bay front elevation. Given an imposing appearance by its tall ceilings and steeply-pitched stone skewtable gables rising from big kneelers to fancy finials. The projecting hallway is similarly treated, its nice panelled door and matching overpanel under a Tudor arch. In stuccoed walls are stone dressed windows having pointed heads, the lights in pretty cast iron oblong pattern. To the road elevation a parapeted and canted bay with mullioned openings, and a blank shield relieving the gable above. The gate approach is truly striking, framed by widespread ogee railed sweeps on dwarf walls between big octagonal pillars with domed cappings. These in turn flank further railed screens and impressive carriage pillars in the form of Greek stellae which have recessed shafts below friezes with laurel wreath motifs. The cornices have Greek key patterns and semicircular cappings ornamented with carved anthemions. The whole complex, unlike Keane's house, now well maintained, the ironwork in distinctive white paint.

**Town Lodge** pre 1855; *demolished*

The lodge on this rundown approach to the farmyard has now gone.

ROWAN (1979); TRIMBLE (1919-1921); BURKE (1904)

**20. CASTLETOWN, Derrygonnelly (2)**

Two relatively plain lodges built for John Dawson Brien. Earlier than an extensive addition in 1869 to the original house which had succeeded Monea Castle nearby after the latter's burning in 1750.

**North Lodge** c1860; *demolished*

Survived by square gate pillars surmounted by concave cappings.

**West Lodge** c1860

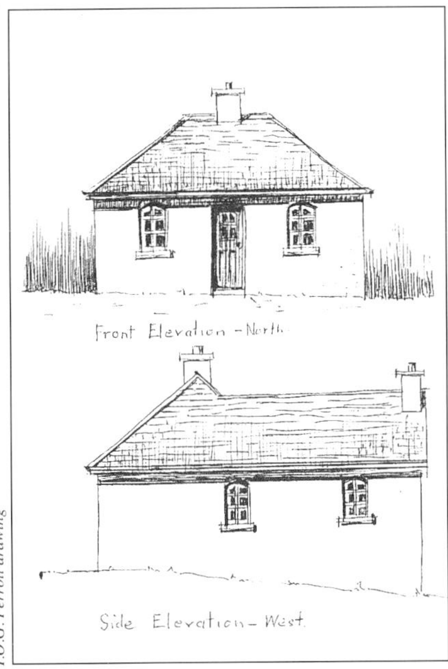


*I.O.G. Perrott drawing*

Before renovations and extensions of 1979 a modest single storey structure below a hipped roof projecting to an L plan with a gabled return. Three bay symmetrical front elevation with segmentally-headed openings.

**21. CHANTERHILL, Enniskillen** c1830

Opposite the gateway to a noteworthy glebe house built by Rev Thomas Smyth in 1784, an unnoteworthy lodge. Built for a later incumbent probably Rev J C Maude. It is single storey, three bay symmetrical on a standard plan. The hipped roof has exposed rafter toes over harled walls. Derelict in 1985.

DUNDAS (1916); O.S.M.

**22. CLABBY GLEBE, Fivemiletown** c1870

A very plain lodge to a mid-Victorian rectory. Probably built for the Rev Francis James Hurst.

**23. CLEENRIS, Lisnaskea** 1846; architect possibly George Sudden

A lodge considerably more pretentious than the plain house which predates it by a decade. Opposite the gates, it is symmetrical three bay, single storey. Under a steeply pitched roof, the gables to which have skewtables rising from grand kneelers to little capped octagonal finials akin to those at The Cottage (qv). All repeated on the breakfront hall which has a datestone in the form of an inverted heart. The walls newly roughcast with nasty modern windows and front door inserted as part of a misguided improvement scheme which has resulted in a watering down of its Tudor style. Dominating it all a monster plinthed and corniced chimney stack of cut stone. An early occupant was John Patterson, the lessor being the Earl of Erne which suggests the work of his architect George Sudden.

**24. CLIFTON LODGE, Lisnaskea (2)**

**Side Entrance** c1840

An unassuming building of one and a half storeys with minute attic windows, crudely detailed. Now deserted. Built for the house then called Sheebeg for Mr H Gresson.

**Main Entrance** c1850; architect not known

Opposite the gate screen a sturdy and distinctive building erected after the property had been acquired by Colonel Edward Archdall and renamed. Symmetrical three bay in very fine square coursed masonry, the quoins ashlar and dressed stone Tudor label mouldings. Brackets in

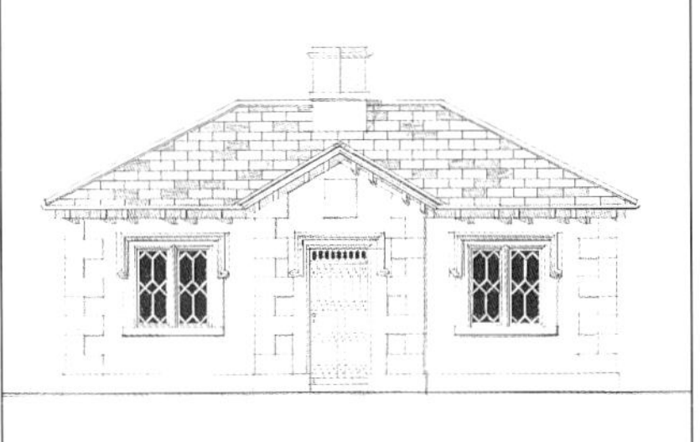

pairs to the eaves line carried beyond as mutules on the gabled breakfront hall. On the hipped roof ridge a pair of squat diagonally-set chimney stacks on a rectangular base. Most attractive are the bipartite windows with their octagonal lattice glazing pattern in cast iron, a feature repeated in the fanlight above the sheeted and studded front door over which is a large blank plaque which never quite got carved with a coat-of-arms. Three roomed, remarkably there was minimal loft accommodation in the roof space approached by a ladder from the hall. Now sadly derelict and choked in laurel. The gate sweep has good cast iron railings and gates. Square stone piers, panelled with cornices and domed caps.

**25. COLEBROOKE, Brookeborough (3)**

In 1786 the *Post Chaise Companion* describes "a very fine and delightful seat" here but clearly Sir Henry Brooke was not satisfied with this beautifully wooded demesne on the banks of the meandering river of the same name. From 1819 for a period of about twenty years the Dublin architect William Farrell was to benefit from the patronage of Sir Henry and, after 1834, his son Sir Arthur Brinsley Brooke. The commission was to include a dower house (see Ashbrooke), estate cottages, a school, a new mansion house and two gate lodges one with an ambitious entrance arch.

**The Triumphal Entrance** c1830; architect William Farrell; *ruinous*

Here is a statement in the grand manner expressed by a triumphal arch. In yellow sandstone ashlar, the semicircular-headed carriage entrance is surmounted by a big blocking course above an entablature which extends on each side to unite two secondary round headed wicket openings, all framed by Tuscan pilasters. Leading one in, a pair of extensive ogee railed quadrants of robust ironwork like the carriage gates which have meeting rails surmounted by a battleaxe. Behind all this, rather pathetically, is a lodge in the same style but in decline. Compared to the archway it was built in second rate materials and this has accelerated its deterioration. In stuccoed brickwork with its fair share of Tuscan pilasters rather a poor derivation of the chaste example at Ely Lodge (qv). Single storey building on a T plan, its three bay front elevation dominated by a bow-shaped hall projection. With its high ceilings and entablatured parapet concealing a hipped roof, it is truly an ungainly design. All the openings have classical surrounds but inexplicably the front door head does not line up with the rest. To compound an already unworthy design the pair of chimney stacks rise together diagonally in the most incongruous Picturesque manner. These chimneys are located at the junction of the back return and the main block, a favourite ploy of Farrell's which he first employed in the two lodges at Ely Lodge the provenance of which is explained under that heading.

**Church Lodge** c1835; architect perhaps William Farrell

On the approach from Aghalurcher church, fifty metres within the demesne facing the gates a simple single storey gabled lodge. Three bay symmetrical, having lancet windows with cast iron lattice glazing flanking a later ungainly projecting hall. Scrolled brackets to eaves. Harled walls. The chimney stack rises off the rear wall suggesting another William Farrell design.

**Secondary Entrance** c1835; architect: William Farrell

On an identical plan to the main entrance lodge but here the elevations are wrapped up in a Picturesque Tudor cloak. A flimsy gabled porch is positioned centrally supported on simple posts flanked by mullioned windows with label mouldings the lights of which have pretty octagonal lattice-paned glazing. The walls stuccoed below a hipped roof with bracketed eaves. Now deserted, its back return suffering from terminal subsidence. There is a fine entrance sweep with fleur-de-lys topped railings and matching gates.

O.S.M.; POST CHAISE COMPANION (1786); ROWAN (1979)

**26. CONVENT OF MERCY, Enniskillen** pre 1862

A lodge identified by Griffith in his valuation. It now appears as a commodious two storey gabled house, perhaps raised earlier this century from an earlier single storey structure, three bay symmetrical with a breakfront hall. Constructed originally in red brick with toothed quoins.

GRIFFITH

**27. THE COTTAGE, Newtownbutler**
**Mullynacoagh Lodge** c1838;
architect probably Edward Blore

On the Crom Castle (qv) estate on the west shore peninsula was a Picturesque Tudor style glebe house dating from c1840, since destroyed by terrorists. Blore paid at least twelve visits to the Crichton property between 1831 and 1838 providing designs for the whole range of estate buildings from Crom Castle itself, to the "two gate houses on demesne" costing the total of £600 mentioned in demesne accounts, doubtless referring to this lodge and that across Upper Lough Erne at the main entrance. An innovative Tudor Revival design, three roomed, single storey on an L plan with the hall projecting at 45° from the internal corner. Almost symmetrical it is all cut stone with skewtable gables, big kneelers and octagonal finials crowning the apexes. In one main gable is an unsculpted shield and over the hood-moulded Tudor front door is another blank shield surmounted by a carved coronet in bas-relief. The window openings are chamfered in dressed stone and label moulded set into walls of squared coursed masonry. Unfortunately the chimney stack is no longer ornamental, but extended and roughcast.

**Mullynacoagh Entrance** c1838;
architect Edward Blore; *demolished*

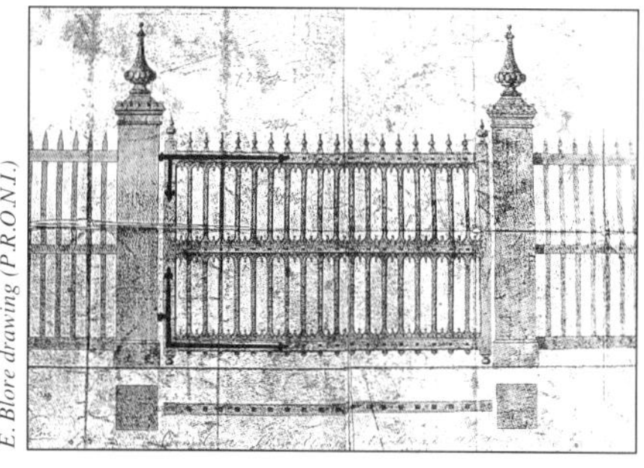

*E. Blore drawing (P.R.O.N.I.)*

A working drawing signed by the architect for an ornate Gothick gateway survives today in the Public Record Office of Northern Ireland. It was to be constructed in timber, which probably accounts for its disappearance. The drawing shows big carriage posts, with crenellated tops and crowned with fancy finials, one of which carried a single arcaded gate in Gothic style. It was decorated with iron studs and hung with great strap hinges in the same material. This was framed by a simple tall picket fence. The gate opening was to have been 13 feet (3.9m) wide by 9 feet (2.7m) high with 15 feet (4.5m) tall posts. That the client had doubts over the scale of the entrance is clear from a note in pencil on the back of the drawing to one Gillespie from John Hamilton, the Crom agent which requests that "Mr Crichton asks you to send him in a proposal for erecting this plan of gate to be only 6 feet high. In my other report according to plan the posts to be oak painted and furnished - send two estimates in old to provide the timber yourself the other Mr Crichton supplying you with all the materials. J P Hamilton."
P.R.O.N.I. D1939; ROWAN (1979)

**28. CROCKNACRIEVE, Ballinamallard (2)**
An elegant villa, built in 1817 by a Captain John Johnston, which shows characteristics associated with Sir Richard Morrison's office.

**Irvinestown Road Gate** c1840;
architect possibly J B Keane; *ruinous*

A stuccoed single storey two bay by three bay symmetrical front elevation lodge. Over the front door, projecting from the hipped roof is a pedimented portico supported on a pair of fundamental Doric columns. On either side, set into segmental headed recesses mimicking features on the house, are windows with pretty cast iron casement lights the glazing in octagonal pattern. Now derelict. This lodge is virtually identical to that at Inishmore Hall (qv) a house which also displays Morrison's influence. This suggests that his one time assistant J B Keane may have been the author. The estate passed on as a result of the marriage in 1834 of Johnston's widow to Henry M Richardson of Rossfad (qv) and Richhill Castle, Co Armagh (qv). He in turn handed them to his cousin Nicholas Archdall, 5th son of Mervyn Archdall of nearby Castle Archdale (qv) and it was Nicholas who was responsible for the other very much less pretentious lodge.

**Ballinamallard Road Entrance** c1850
Single storey, three bay symmetrical and gabled with a projecting hall to match.
BURKE (1904); O.S.M.

**29. CROM CASTLE, Newtownbutler (2)**
The Crichtons have been resident here from about 1655 when Colonel Abraham Crichton married a daughter of Bishop Spottiswoode. The fine Queen Anne house on the demesne beautifully situated amongst the islands on the southernmost tip of Upper Lough Erne was destroyed by fire in 1764. It was to this house that there was an early gate lodge in Aghadrum townland but 120m south of the present one.

**Old Lodge** pre 1834; *demolished*
The remains of a square building of which only the foundations are visible in the wood close to the stream. In the early 1830s a new avenue was formed to serve the Blore castle and its predecessor gradually passed out of use, the gate lodge abandoned. It was not until 1829 that the fashionable English Regency architect Edward Blore was approached by Colonel the Hon. John Crichton to design a new mansion. Blore was to be committed to the future 3rd Earl of Erne for a further decade until the vast castellated Tudor-Gothick house was virtually complete. The architect's commission was to include many lesser works on the estate amongst which were two gate lodges.

**Main Entrance Lodge** c1838;
architect Edward Blore
Despite the lack of documentary proof this design is obviously from the Blore office, for there was a lodge on an identical plan at Ballydrain, Co Antrim (qv) by him which was contemporary. This is an irregular Tudor Picturesque cottage variant of mainly one and a half storey. Here, as at Ballydrain, the elevation to the boundary is dominated by a tall chimney breast and stack, in yellow sandstone. The two main gables with pretty serrated bargeboards and

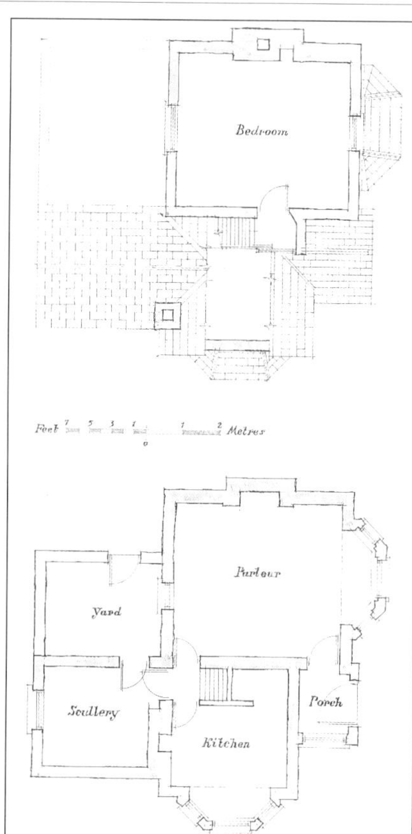

finialed hipknobs have rickety single storey canted bay window projections. A small gabled hall advances to the avenue, its window having the sole surviving lattice panes. Access to the upper floor bedroom was by way of very steep stairs and the awkward roof protuberance to give landing headroom smacks of an on-site solution, much better handled at Ballydrain. The walls are now rendered. In spite of, or perhaps because of, shoddy workmanship and slipshod design by the normally meticulous Blore it succeeds in being an endearing little building. Blore was also responsible for the stables, farm complex, forge yard and turf house. This may well be the last of his works at Crom, for upon the accidental burning of the nearly- completed castle his services were dispensed with in favour of the Dublin-based George Sudden (see Cleenris House).
ROWAN (1979); JACKSON-STOPS (1988); TRIMBLE (1919-1921);
REEVES-SMYTH AND McERLEAN (1990)

**30. THE CROSS, Enniskillen** pre 1834;
*demolished*
The lodge replaced by a modern bungalow. Once a property of the Frith family of whom one, William, was listed as an Enniskillen architect in 1846.
SLATER (1846)

**31. CURRAGH, Maguiresbridge** pre 1856;
*demolished*
A lodge to a house of Capt W Charters had been taken down before 1906.

**32. DERRYBRUSK, Lisbellaw**
(see INISHMORE HALL)

**33. DERRYGORE, Enniskillen** pre 1862; *demolished*

Griffith in his valuation notes a gate lodge of Edward Irwin. Trimble records the house to have been erected in 1850 to designs of Roderick Gray of Enniskillen. The location of the lodge has not been established, assumed demolished.
TRIMBLE (1919-1921); GRIFFITH

**34. DERRYVULLEN, Lisbellaw** c1860

A property which passed to the Denny family through marriage to Mary Rynd. A pleasantly proportioned one and a half storey building below a hipped roof. In rendered walls the front elevation three bay symmetrical, two sash windows flank a front door sheltered by an ornamental gabled porch with lobed bargeboards supported on bracketed and chamfered wooden posts. The porch looks to be a later addition of c1900 probably by Edward Mitchell who had recently purchased the estates. Access to the bedrooms is from a staircase rising from within the living room.
CRAWFORD (1992)

**35. DONAGH, Lisnaskea** c1840; *demolished*

A fine mid-Georgian double-pile farmhouse which lay unoccupied in 1835 after the death of its owner William Noble. The new residents, probably the Bamfords owners of the nearby corn mill, added a gate lodge to the property not long after acquiring it. This charming building is the nearest approach to an Irish Vernacular Picturesque style lodge in the Province, its age betrayed by the wide square window openings in a typical three bay symmetrical gate lodge elevation. A simple sheeted front door flanked by squared cast iron casements in traditional lime-washed rubble walls. Over its two rooms a hipped thatched roof with its chimney stack nicely located off centre. Sadly no more, the house derelict.
O.S.M.

**36. DRESTERNAN CASTLE, Derrylin (2)** both pre 1834

A survivor of two, this is something unique to Ulster - a gate lodge in the form of a vernacular linear Irish cottage. Single storey, three roomed, the four bay front elevation with narrow openings in whitewashed walls below a steeply pitched thatched roof of a type common to the county. The Winslows were clearly a family of few pretensions, not for them the need to make some statement in a foreign style at the gates.
ROWAN (1979)

**37. DRUMARD OR DROMARD, Lisbellaw** c1860

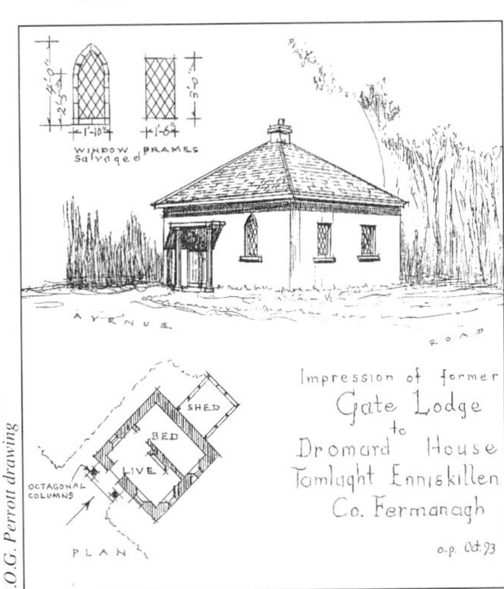


*I.O.G. Perrott drawing*

To an antique thatched gentleman farmer's residence a lodge, single storey, square on plan with a pyramidal roof rising to a central chimney stack. Two bay front elevation, that to the left the entrance door below a flat roofed porch with octagonal stone columned support. The right hand opening a pretty lancet window with margined cast iron lattice frame. Built for Rev Christopher Weir.

**38. DRUMBADMORE, Lisnaskea** pre 1862; *demolished*

A lodge identified by Griffith in his valuation to a house of one James Moore. Replaced 1993 by a modern bungalow.
GRIFFITH

**39. DRUMDERG, Tempo (2)** both pre 1906; *both demolished*

In 1870 the property of George Hurst.

**40. DRUMGOON, Maguiresbridge (2)** *both demolished*

Both lodges, one pre 1834 the other from before 1856, built by the Graham family.

**41. DRUMMUSKY, Newtownbutler** c1845

The Richardsons came here from Summerhill (qv) nearby, purchasing the lands from the Earl of Erne and built the house c1840, to be followed soon after by the gate lodge. A plain building of standard form. Larger than average single storey, two roomed with wide windows to the three bay symmetrical harled front elevation. Resplendent in its hipped corrugated asbestos roof. Abandoned.

**42. ELY LODGE, Enniskillen (2)**

A much visited and admired demesne by intrepid 19th century travellers. It spread to an island on the Lower Lough Erne, where the Loftus family moved after deserting the neighbouring Castle Hume (qv). It was Sir Charles Tottenham who assumed the arms and name of Loftus when the estates devolved upon him from his uncle. He was created Marquess of Ely in 1800 and it was his son the 2nd Marquess, John, who set about building what was variously described as an ordinary or small handsome villa where "... the situation is most enchanting and fairly entitled to be called a little Paradise". He employed as his architect the Dubliner William Farrell to design the new house and two porters' lodges.

**Main Entrance Lodge** c1820; architects Henry Hakewill and William Farrell

On the main Enniskillen-Ballyshannon road impressive entrance gates and an elegant Classical gate lodge in a design too sophisticated to have been by Farrell whose domestic architecture is not always noted for its excellence of proportion. The identity of the real author of this design is to be found at Blenheim Palace in Oxfordshire. At one of the entrances to the great park is Eagle Lodge, identical in every respect to the lodge here. This can be explained by the marriage in 1810 of the 2nd Marquess to Anna Maria, daughter of Sir H W Dashwood, who was a close friend of the 5th Duke of Marlborough and MP for the little town of Woodstock by Blenheim's gates. Eagle Lodge would date from c1815 when the architect Henry Hakewill was employed by the Churchills. The client was impressed enough to bring the idea back to be located at Ely Lodge and supervised by Farrell. A perfectly symmetrical single storey lodge on a T plan in grey ashlar below a hipped roof with an extended eaves. The windows are square paned Georgian in moulded surrounds set into recesses formed by a plinth, Tuscan pilasters and entablature. Central to the three bay front elevation is a bow fronted portico, supported on two Tuscan columns. The circle completed in a recess in which is the panelled entrance door delightfully flanked by semicircular-headed niches, each of which contains a Classical goddess (something which Eagle Lodge can not boast). The rear return and a trio of tapering chimney pots which rise off the party wall are a plan form and feature which Farrell was to copy at the other Ely Lodge gate, the two Colebrooke (qv) lodges and probably that to Castle Irvine (qv) all in Co Fermanagh. Alien extension to the rear. The extensive gate sweep approach has good ironwork culminating in cut stone pillars in the form of Greek stellae with tapering recessed panels and cappings of four-sided pediments. An important entrance its white ironwork contrasting nicely with the grey ashlar.

**Bridge Lodge** c1820; architect William Farrell

"The mansion is approached over a strait of the lough by a handsome bridge, at the end of which are massive iron gates, well barricaded, and committed to the custody of a porter." Thus recorded Binns in 1835. These gates are no

longer extant but the pretty little gate lodge survives. Again Farrell employs the plan form of the main lodge but here the elevations are dressed up in Tudor Picturesque guise. Another single storey cottage with a three bay front under a shallow hipped roof. In stuccoed walls are pretty label moulded window openings each of which contains a pair of pointed lights with latticed panes. The central doorway is sheltered below a gabled canopy supported on two quatrefoil section cluster posts. Characteristic of this period in the architect's career, the chimney stack rises from the back wall of the main lodge. The accommodation extends in a hipped roof structure to the rear. The guttering is carried on nice cast iron curled brackets. Farrell's house was destroyed by explosives in 1870, partly to mark the 21st birthday of the 4th Marquess, and never replaced as intended. The stables were converted into a residence but the family continued as absentee landlords residing at their main seat, Loftus Hall, Co Wexford. Both lodges remain well tended.
COLVIN (1978); BENCE-JONES (1988); BARROW (1836); ROWAN (1979); BINNS (1837)

**43. FAIRVIEW, Lisnaskea** c1860; *demolished*
A modest building. Single storey, three bay below a hipped roof. Ugly metal windows were inserted and the front door sealed up in modern renovations prior to its demolition in 1992.

**44. FAIRWOOD PARK, Enniskillen** (see NIXON HALL)

**45. FARMHILL, Scotshouse** pre 1857; *ruinous*
A lodge opposite the gates now engulfed in ivy. Standard plan, three bay single storey below a hipped roof. Probably for a Mr Charles Crowe.

**46. FLORENCE COURT, Belcoo (3)**
An important mid-18th century house of the Cole family built for the 1st Lord Mountflorence, completed with wings c1762. By this time there would have been in position the "Grand Avenue". It is about the gates of this approach that Rev John Wesley has in 1767, as ever, much to say. They were "... painted blue, green, and yellow, like a child's rattle" and "surely the owner has never seen the pretty bauble; but will no one inform him of it?" When Wesley paid a return visit eighteen years later it seems that the gates and their attendant pillars had been moved to their present position. Then he "observed the partly coloured gates (as they were some years since) to be painted red".

**Grand Gates and Lodges** c1778

At the time of rebuilding the gate screen apparently had the new pair of matching lodges incorporated into the layout with new rubble stone quadrant walls. Linking the porters' twin accommodation to form a symmetrical composition are the carriage gates hung on rusticated cut stone pillars surmounted by ball finials on pedestals, repeated beyond to carry wicket gates. A coping unites the pillars and screen walls to the lodges which are single storey of one room each. Their leading canted elevations advance beyond the screen with a window on three faces each in the form of a pair of sashes. These would previously have been Georgian squared-pane, although by c1840 they received the fashionable cast iron lattice inserts, further replaced by the present simplified style in 1920. The walls now cement rendered were previously harled below a high eaves to a roof gabled to the park and with half umbrellos to the fore. Access to each lodge was from behind the gates. The unfortunate loss of the chimney stacks in another improvement show the lodges to be no longer occupied. Built by William Willoughby Cole, created 1st Earl of Enniskillen in 1789.

**Secondary Entrance** c1800
Much improved and extended over the years into a rambling and incoherent form. Somewhere in the fabric is the original single storey three bay cottage which sat alongside the big square plain stone gate pillars with short wing walls.

**South Lodge** c1870
On the site of an earlier lodge a mid-Victorian Picturesque cottage. One and a half storey, and gabled, its three bay front given an informal feel with a projecting single storey gabled hallway. To the right hand side and below a gablet a canted bay window to the left hand bay. Windows now with simple modern glazing in dressed stone surrounds to rubble walls. Quatrefoil motifs to bargeboards.
P.C.C. (1786); BENCE-JONES (1988); I.A.A. Photograph Ref 3/93; REEVES-SMYTH (1990)

**47. FORTHILL PLEASURE GROUNDS, Enniskillen** pre 1862; *demolished*
A lodge listed by Griffith in his valuation seems not to have survived.
GRIFFITH

**48. GARDENHILL, Belcoo (3)** *all demolished*
An old house of varying dates of the Hassard family, now ruinous. Of the lodges, two pre 1834 (one opposite) the other pre 1856, nothing remains on the remnants of a once sizeable demesne.

**49. GORTORAL HOUSE, Kinawley** (see PROSPECT HILL)

**50. GREEN HILL, Brookeborough** pre 1856
To an earlier villa of the gentry a nondescript lodge for Major Hamilton Irvine.

**51. HALL CRAIG, Enniskillen** pre 1834; *demolished*
Only the pillars remaining to a fine house of 1721, all for the Weir family.

**52. INISHMORE HALL, Lisbellaw** c1840; architect probably J B Keane

(*Joy Duncan*)

A place called Derrybrusk, "a plain old-fashioned cottage with a thatched roof" was purchased from John Deering by Richard Hall in the late 1830s. It was given an imposing new house, a name to go with it and the obligatory gate lodge. This is a replica of that at Crocknacrieve (qv) and here as at the Johnston house are reminders of the work of the Morrison practice in the laurel wreaths which decorated the entablature of the house. The lodge, single storey, is deeper than the three bay front elevation. From the hipped roof projects a basic pedimented portico over the doorway supported on two naive Doric columns. Flanking are simple sash widows set into segmentally-headed recesses, in stuccoed walls. On a side elevation a cusp-headed window. At an unsociable distance is a comical Gothic Revival privy, square with a pyramidal roof. Its doorway and louvred opening have lancet heads in harled brickwork. The entrance gates in late Victorian cast iron.
The lodge is now abandoned, the house demolished, its big Corinthian columns now gracing the entrance to Portora Royal School in Enniskillen (qv).
O.S.M.; KING (1892)

**53. JOHNSTOWN, Newtownbutler** pre 1857; *demolished*
Probably built for C P Irvine.

**54. KILLADEAS MANOR, Killadeas (3)**
The Irvines lived here from 1691 building the house known as Rockfield in 1746. This Georgian block, with outbuildings arranged as balancing pavilions linked to it by tall wing walls, had an air of grandeur. Not grand enough for Colonel John Gerrard Irvine who between 1861 and 1868 transformed it into a huge Italianate "railway hotel". He embellished it with just about every motif in that style within the vocabulary of the architect Robert Armstrong. So when it came to the provision of gate lodges he had either run short of ideas or the coffers had run dry, for all three are relatively plain.

**Goblusk Lodge** c1870; architect probably R W Armstrong; *demolished*
The main entrance and the most architecturally pretentious. Single storey, three bay below a

Mrs M. K. Summerville

hipped roof. Mildly Italianate having semicircular-headed openings with moulded surrounds in stuccoed walls and rusticated quoins. The central porch was recessed giving access to the left hand livingroom. The windows gathered in pairs divided by mullions with capitals from which the arches spring. In the openings centre pivot lights. The eaves had closely spaced modillion brackets. Heavily ornate cast iron gates and screen with spearhead tops.

**Middle Lodge** c1870; architect probably R W Armstrong; *ruinous*

Simply a plainer edition of the above without the same architectural detailing other than the eaves brackets. Lacking moulded window surrounds and substituting a harled wall finish for stucco. Now a shell.

**North Lodge** c1870

An unremarkable building, single storey, three bay gabled, with a small gable above the front door. Looking much as the secondary lodge to Crocknacrieve (qv) nearby. The big house is now appropriately an hotel.

TRIMBLE (1919-1921); ROGERS (1967); ROWAN (1979);

**55. KILLYHEVLIN COTTAGE, Enniskillen (2)**

**Enniskillen or West Lodge** pre 1834; *demolished*

A three bay single storey lodge. Openings with lancet heads, the doorway to left-hand side.

**East Lodge** pre 1834; *demolished*

Only some remnants of the entrance gates are still to be found. Once the residence of Richard Dane, agent to Lord Belmore. The site now occupied by a fine Arts and Crafts house, since converted and extended for hotel use.

O.S.M.

**56. KILLYREAGH, Lisbellaw** pre 1906; *demolished*

The house was once another seat of the Dane family. Plain square masonry gate piers survive with a modern bungalow on the site.

**57. KINAWLEY RECTORY, Derrylin** pre 1834/c1840

The original little lodge in stone construction can still be seen parallel to the road, unusual in having half hipped and part gabled roof, just as the adjacent Callow Hill (qv) lodge. It now forms a back return to the later lodge which faces the avenue. The latter, on a slightly larger scale, under a hipped roof with corbelled eaves. Three bay front, the square windows with cast iron diamond panes in stuccoed walls. The window to the road slightly pretentious, being set into a segmentally-headed recess. Deserted, as is the fine old glebe house.

**58. LAKE VIEW, Enniskillen** pre 1834; *demolished*

One time resident a Captain Beaufoy.

**59. LAWNAKILLA, Enniskillen** pre 1905; *demolished*

To an earlier house of the Frith family, a simple three bay single storey lodge under a hipped roof. Central gabled porch projection. A pretty pair of latticed cast iron gates survive.

**60. LENAGHAN, Enniskillen (2)**

both c1870; *one demolished*

The surviving lodge rendered even plainer by a pebble dash finish and the intrusion of modern bland windows. Single storey, square on plan below a pyramidal roof, the eaves of which is decorated by a continuous fretted fascia. The central projecting gabled hall has a semicircular-headed side entrance door and pretty lobed bargeboards carried around as a fascia. The entrance approach is simple but impressive in the form of extensive railed concave quadrants framing two square ashlar piers, corniced with blocked cappings. All look to be c1870 for Maurice Ceely Maude.

**61. LEVALLY RECTORY, Enniskillen**

c1840

Almost identical to the lodge to Lisbofin (qv) not far distant. Single storey, standard plan, three bay without any notable architectural features but for a hipped gable roof. In harled walls the windows now spoilt with the loss of their previous Picturesque lattice-paned lights.

**62. LISBOFIN, Enniskillen** c1830

A standard single storey three bay cottage but with a hipped gable roof just like that at Levally Rectory (qv). Probably built by Charles Fausset.

**63. LISGOOLE ABBEY, Enniskillen** c1850

Standard three bay single storey lodge below a hipped roof. Mildly Italianate with its narrow semicircular-headed windows in rendered walls. To the front door a flat roofed stone porch with shouldered heads supported on chamfered pillars. To the rear a sympathetic modern extension, designed by architect Richard Pierce in 1979. To the beautiful Georgian Gothick villa of the Jones family, the lodge built by Captain Michael Jones or his successor William.

**64. LISMACSHEELA, Rosslea** c1845

I.O.G. Perrott

Opposite the entrance gates a chirpy little building which probably pre-dates the 1850s when the property went through many owners in rapid succession. To a backdrop of tall trees an almost square lodge, single storey, three bay symmetrical with a very steeply-pitched hipped roof. In harled walls the windows have semicircular heads, the central door opening has a timber doorcase inserted with a matching archway. With its previous thatched roof and wooden lattice paned lights it must have been truly quaint. Probably built by John Jackson. Abandoned.

**65. LURGANBRAE, Brookeborough** c1870; *demolished*

A short lived lodge built by Matthew Henry Sankey.

**66. MAGHERAMENAGH CASTLE, Belleek** c1840; architect J B Keane

Unlike his symmetrical Tudor Revival villa extensions at Camlin Castle, Co Donegal (qv) Learmount Castle, Co Londonderry (qv) and Castle Irvine (qv) in the same county Keane here designed a composition in more informal fashion as a replacement for Leurae House, to mark the

wedding of James Johnston. In contrast to the assembly of octagonal turrets, pinnacles, gables and finials the gate lodge is in a straightforward Gothic Revival manner. Secreted behind rampant shrubbery the gabled three bay building constructed in very fine uncoursed squared masonry in which the windows with lancet heads are arranged in pairs their chamfered reveals framing Y-traceried sashes. A central ornamental porch to the front door has been taken down. To the steep gables sturdy waved bargeboards and below the high eaves, closely spaced modillion brackets. Sturdy stone gate pillars with pyramidal cappings. The house is now a ruin, the lodge though occupied, run down.

ROWAN (1979)

**67. MUNVILLE, Lisnaskea** c1830

To an unusual Regency cottage of the Maguire family is a minute doll's house of a lodge. Single storey, symmetrical three bay with a clipped verge. In harled walls, the windows have big diamond panes repeated on the upper half of the door. Now secreted as a result of a road realignment, it was probably built by a Mr George Lloyd, the occupant in 1824.

**68. NIXON HALL, Enniskillen** pre 1834; *demolished*

Now in ruins this was a fine mid-Georgian house with its outbuildings arranged as wings to give a grandiose appearance. It was the seat of the Nixon family before being sublet to a Dr J Denham who changed its name to Fairwood Park. Accidentally burnt down in 1844. The lodge was off an old public road now long disused.

TRIMBLE (1919-1921)

**69. NUTFIELD, Maguiresbridge** pre 1856

Not quite opposite the entrance gates a pair of one and a half storey semidetached cottages, each three bay symmetrical and both having monopitched canopies to front doors with decorative spandrels and shamrock motifs. Otherwise plain. A property of the Brookes of Colebrooke (qv) who used it as a dower house. Thereafter let to the Leslie family of whom Blayney Leslie may have built these cottages.

**70. PORTORA ROYAL SCHOOL, Enniskillen** pre 1834; *demolished*

The single storey lodge with short elevation and projecting porch to the avenue and breakfronted facade to the approach was lost when the present grand entrance screen was erected in 1945 as a war memorial. Designed by architect Robert McKinstry it incorporated four Corinthian columns salvaged from the portico of Inishmore Hall (qv).

ENNISKILLEN; U.A.H.S. (1973)

**71. PROSPECT HILL, Swanlinbar**

pre 1834; *ruinous*

An early 19th century residence of the Maguire family its lodge probably contemporary. Remnants suggest it to have been Georgian Gothick with a pointed head to the doorway in the leading gable elevation. The house now called Gortoral.

**72. RIVERSDALE, Ballinamallard (2)**
A property long in the possession of the Archdall family was sold in 1947/8 to the Forestry Service who afforested the grounds and, inevitably, demolished the house in 1960, and both gate lodges.

**West Entrance** pre 1834; *demolished*

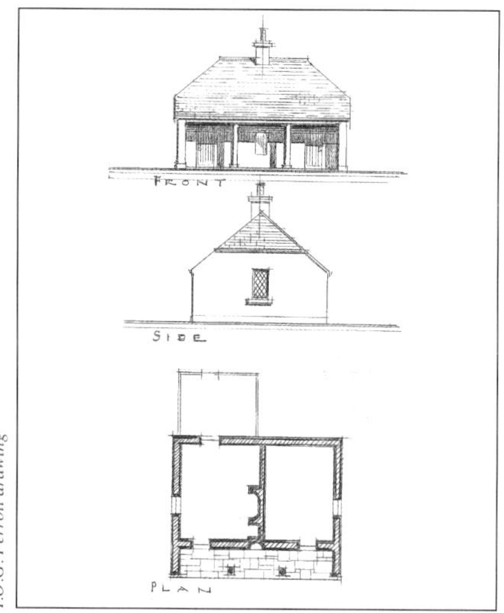


I.O.G. Perrott drawing

The sketch illustrated is based on local recollections and indicates a lodge of simple two roomed standard plan but innovatively elevated. Single storey below a hipped gable roof which is carried beyond the front facade to form a columned verandah. There being no direct communicating door between rooms, this provided sheltered access between two doorways which flanked a central niche. The interior was lit by latticed gable windows.

**East Entrance** pre 1834; *demolished*
ATKINSON (1833)

**73. ROCKFIELD, Killadeas**
(see KILLADEAS MANOR)

**74. ROSSCLARE, Irvinestown** c1830/c1850
To an early Victorian Italianate villa is a plain single storey building on an L plan but displaying a symmetrical three bay front to the avenue, from which advances a gabled hall. Roughcast walls below a hipped roof. The lodge as it appears today must be a replacement for a predecessor to a house successively owned by the Barton, D'Arcy Irvine and Richardson families. It may date from the acquisition of the property by James Armstrong, as does the gate screen. Two big chamfered square stone carriage piers with ogee domed cappings of similar section. Gates and railed screen heavily ornate with fleur-de-lys tops.

**75. ROSSFAD, Ballinamallard** pre 1834; *demolished*
The lodge opposite the gates, built by the Richardsons, taken down before 1855.

**76. ROSSLEA MANOR, Rosslea** c1820; *demolished*
Opposite the main gates at the base of a long avenue was a pretty Georgian Gothick lodge. Single storey of standard plan below a very wide eaved hipped roof. In a symmetrical three bay front elevation, lancet headed windows between a pedimented breakfront. Built by Captain S G Madden to a house then called Spring Grove. Both lodge and mansion have gone, the latter following an 1885 fire.
U.M. Photograph Ref 06/19/3;
BENCE-JONES (1988)

**77. RUSHIN, Enniskillen** c1840
Single storey symmetrical three bay lodge with a hipped roof built by a Capt Charles John Jones. Now deserted. Plain but for fashionable lattice-paned windows in harled walls below an eaves with dentil course formed of brick headers.

**78. ST ANGELO, Ballinamallard** pre 1834; *demolished*
There was a lodge here in 1834 to "... a spacious, old cottage with thatched roof, much like the residence of a respectable country farmer".
This residence of a Dr Johnston was transformed by the Lowrys of Pomeroy, Co Tyrone (qv) into a Picturesque half-timbered affair in the late 19th century.
O.S.M.; ROWAN (1979)

**79. SHEEBEG, Lisnaskea**
(see CLIFTON LODGE)

**80. SILVERHILL, Enniskillen** pre 1834; *demolished*
A lodge opposite the gates probably built by the Faussets.

**81. SKEA HALL, Enniskillen** pre 1834; *demolished*
Gone by 1906, the lodge would have been contemporary with the stylish Regency villa built by George Hassard.

**82. SNOW HILL, Lisbellaw** c1862; architect not known

Samuel Yates Johnstone succeeded to the property in 1862 upon the death of his nephew, and built this lovely Tudor Picturesque style lodge across the road from a new gate screen. Unusual in having a five bay front it is single storey under a hipped roof with fancy foiled and lobed bargeboards to the central projecting hallway. The front door is panelled with a hood-moulded four-centred fanlight. In the gable over, the Johnstone coat-of-arms with a winged spur crest above and their motto "NUNQUAM NON PARATUS" under. In white harled walls on either side of the hallway two window openings, each united by a continuous label moulding, both bipartite with latticed lights and cusped Tudor heads. Two chimney stacks positioned symmetrically. The gates opposite are no less decorative. Cast iron ogee railed sweeps framed by four stone piers surmounted by ornate iron urns with anthemion motifs. Matching gates with spear tops, not unlike those to Weir's Bridge lodge, Castlecoole (qv).
BURKE (1904)

**83. SPRING GROVE, Rosslea**
(see ROSSLEA MANOR)

**84. SUMMER HILL, Clones** c1850; *ruinous*
An interesting house which looks to be a late Georgian farmhouse with indiscreet mid-Victorian windows. These and the lodge probably date from the time when Joseph Richardson JP, was in residence. The lodge now an ivy-covered ruin.

**85. TAWNYREAGH, Lisbellaw** pre 1906; *demolished*
Once a property of the Betty family, the lodge probably built by a Patrick Curra, lessee.

**86. TEMPO MANOR, Tempo (3)**
Since c1611 the estate of the Maguires until it passed to Samuel Lyle in 1798 who sold it to William Tennent of Belfast in 1815. It was his son-in-law, Sir James Emerson Tennent, who in 1861 demolished the old house to make way for a delightful new low Jacobean style design by Lanyon, Lynn and Lanyon all curved gables on an informal plan in a beautiful park. Sadly neither of the surviving gate lodges is the equal of the house.

**Town Lodge** c1870; architects possibly Lanyon, Lynn and Lanyon
The lodge may have been more attractive prior to losing its original windows and bargeboards. Single storey on an L plan in irregular Picturesque English cottage manner. On the road gable is a canted bay window, whilst a little gabled hall projects from the internal angle. Now rendered in a recent improvement when label mouldings may have been removed from over the openings. Not unlike a lodge at Springhill, Co Londonderry (qv). This lodge had a pre 1834 predecessor at the opposite side of the avenue entrance. The entrance gates carried by big square stone pillars with lancet-headed recesses and fluted friezes over.

**North Lodge** pre 1834; *demolished*
**North-East Lodge** c1870
An unremarkable cottage.
O.S.M.; TRIMBLE (1919-1921);
MAGUIRE (1986)

**87. THOMASTOWN, Enniskillen (2)**
both pre 1834; *both demolished*
To a house of the Auchinleck family.

**88. THORNHILL GLEBE, Enniskillen**
pre 1862; *demolished*
Lodge noted by Sir Richard Griffith in his valuation. No trace of the lodge can be found.
GRIFFITH

**89. TULLYCLEAGH GLEBE, Ballinamallard** pre 1908; *demolished*
The 1870 incumbent Rev Richard Verschoyle.

**90. THE WATERFOOT, Pettigo** c1860; architect possibly R W Armstrong; *ruinous*
One and a half storey, two up two down with clipped verge gables. Faintly Italianate in style, the three bay symmetrical front elevation openings and attic windows have semicircular heads with banded surrounds in stuccoed walls. Reticulated quoins. To the eaves big solid square bracket supports. Built by Lieut-Col Hugh Barton later than the 1830s alterations to the house by J B Keane. There are similarities with Goblusk lodge at Killadeas Manor (qv) which may be the work of Robert William Armstrong.
ROWAN (1979)

**91. WHITE PARK, Brookeborough**
pre 1856; *demolished*
For A Bailey Esq.

# COUNTY LONDONDERRY

**1. ABERFOYLE, Londonderry West**
pre 1853; *demolished*
The lodge to a house which was later renamed Talbot. Then the house next door rather confusingly assumed the name Aberfoyle, it previously having been Richmond (qv).

**2. AGHADOWEY, Aghadowey** c1840
A lodge to the Hemphill family property.

**3. AGHANLOO GLEBE, Limavady** c1850
Described in 1975 as "a one and a half storey gate lodge with a half-hipped tiled roof. Partly Georgian glazed". Since modernised it appears as a mundane building having lost both features previously noted. Now gabled with asymmetrical three bay front elevation, pebble-dashed.
Built for the Rev George Craig.
NORTH DERRY; U.A.H.S. (1975)

**4. ALLA GLEBE, Claudy**
(see GLENALLA)

**5. AMPERTAINE, Maghera (3)**
**Early Lodges** both pre 1832;
*both demolished*
Two lodges of this period were probably built not long after 1830 when Alexander Clarke transformed his "... small thatched cottage ..." and "Third rate seat" from Upperlands House into the present big Regency dwelling. One of these gave way to that opposite the main gate.
**Main Gate** c1870
An undistinguished cement-rendered single storey lodge. Three bay, each of which projects in canted fashion under an extended eaves line of a hipped roof, two timber 'pop-eyed' oriels flanking a flimsy hallway. The gates and railing opposite have ogee swept approaches. All contemporary with the lodge, cast iron from Musgrave and Co Ltd of Belfast. Erected by a later Alexander Clarke.
OSM

**6. ANONYMOUS, Carrigans** c1830
Right on the border with County Donegal four miles south-west of Londonderry on the old Carrigans Road is a late 18th century house which in 1830 was nameless and remains so to this day. At an angle to the road the lodge has its gable elevation projecting alongside the now dilapidated gate sweep. Single storey in brick, below a hipped roof its leading facade has a canted bay below a half umbrello end supported by big timber brackets to an extended eaves. Derelict.

**7. ARDMORE, Drumahoe (2)**
A property of the Smyth family.
**North Lodge** c1830
Two storey three bay gatekeeper's accommodation with a hipped gable roof, the fascias and bargeboards of which have lobed overlay decoration perhaps from later in the century. There are also very big scrolled brackets which flank the surrounds to tiny first floor windows. Roughcast walls. The gate sweep looks c1810, with convex quadrants to a pair of square ashlar piers, blocks V-jointed, below nice pointed concave caps.
**South Lodge** c1830
Very much as the above but plainer and having a hipped roof.

**8. ARDMORE LODGE, Limavady**
pre 1904; *demolished*
The lodge to a property of the Macrory family.

**9. ARDNARGLE, Limavady** c1845
A lodge built not long before his death in 1849 by James Leslie to an old house of c1750. Later the property of the Ogilby family.
BURKE (1855)

**10. ASHBROOK, Drumahoe** pre 1853;
*demolished*
To an antique mansion long in the family's possession, William Hamilton Ash built a lodge.

**11. BALLYARNET, Londonderry West**
pre 1904; *demolished*
Formerly the demesne of the Gallaghers, the lodge was probably built for James Corscadden who acquired the property before 1870.

**12. BALLYDEVITT, Aghadowey (3)**
By the nearby beetling mill and bleach green the house here was built in 1806 "in the cottage style with a neat stone front and an avenue" and Thomas Bennett was in residence by 1812. These dates seem about right for the two early porters' lodges, one of which remains.
**West Entrance** c1810

*Mrs O. Cunningham*

A once charming and picturesque building of a type probably widespread in Ireland in Georgian times. Opposite the gates the Gothick lodge single storey three bay symmetrical and two roomed below a steeply-thatched hipped roof with outsized eaves. Lancet openings in whitewashed harled walls, it had low curved flanking walls. Known locally as the "wren's nest" it has sometime this century suffered the most disgraceful transformation to the extent that it is almost unrecognisable. Now one and a half storey gabled the eaves having been raised. Neatly smooth rendered it is now boarded up and deserted.
**Middle Entrance** pre 1831; *demolished*
The other lodge on the same side road has gone. Around 1865 Bennett moved on to Castleroe (qv) when he assigned Ballydevitt to John Adams and the house was converted from a cottage style residence to its present form, renamed Wigmore, and another lodge provided on the main road.
**East Entrance** c1865
In the Neo-Classical style, a stuccoed three bay single storey lodge in the Thomas Jackson manner. A perky little building with a conspicuous high eaves with carved brackets to the hipped roof. Segmentally-headed openings have architraved surrounds over a stringcourse

between plain pilasters. Central chimney on a plinth, chamfered, friezed and corniced. A low wall sweep leads to square stone piers in channelled ashlar with plain friezes below projecting cappings. The lodge lies empty, the windows sealed with corrugated iron.
OSM; MULLIN (1972)

**13. BALLYKELLY PRESBYTERIAN CHURCH, Ballykelly** 1827;
architect Richard Suter
In 1820 the Fishmongers' Company was moved to rescue the village from decay and embark upon a rebuilding programme which included this striking pedimented meeting-house and as part of the scheme its little porter's lodge. In a similar pinkish Dungiven sandstone rubble with raised ashlar quoins and window surrounds. Moulded surround to door and mouth organ fanlight. Well proportioned three bay symmetrical front elevation below a hipped roof. Designed by the Company's surveyor.
NORTH DERRY; U.A.H.S. (1975); CURL (1981)

**14. BALLYNACROSS, Londonderry West**
c1870
Off the beaten track a humdrum lodge, three bay, single storey under a hipped roof with clipped eaves. Now pebble-dashed. It sits between two avenues one having octagonal cast iron posts with ornate gates. Wicket gate with flat lintel over.

**15. BALLYNAGARD, Londonderry West (2)**
**Early Lodge** c1830
A nondescript affair built for Captain John Hart.
**Later Lodge** c1850
A single storey standard plan three bay symmetrical structure below a hipped roof. Unusual in its opening surrounds, those to the front elevation banded with a patera to each lintel. Conspicuous in its flat-roofed bowed hall projection. Faced in coursed rubble masonry. The family's other property of Kilderry, Co Donegal (qv) is nearby.
ATKINSON (1833); HART (1907)

**16. BALLYSALLY, Coleraine** c1840
A standard single storey late Georgian style lodge with a hipped roof. Built for the Black family. Abandoned.

**17. BALLYSCULLION, Bellaghy** c1880
Single storey, gabled as is the porch. Canted bay windows. An unnoteworthy building for Colonel H S B Bruce, built to a rather more dignified house of c1850 probably by Sir Charles Lanyon. Here also is the site of the Earl Bishop's great palace folly.

**18. BANNFIELD, Coleraine** c1840; *demolished*

The lodge was contemporary with the pleasant Neo-Classical villa built for Samuel Lawrence.
O'HAGAN (1845)

**19. BARLEY PARK, Limavady**

"Residence of Mr William Ross, built 1813 by William Ross, a handsome new entrance too heavy for the size of the grounds has been built in 1835." No lodge apparent from the OS maps.
OSM

**20. BAYVIEW HOUSE, Londonderry East** pre 1830

To a house previously called Seaview, Henry Nicholson built a lodge which may have assumed its present appearance in the mid-eighteenth century when it became the property of John Hamilton. A Picturesque style one and a half storey three bay symmetrical building with exceptionally steep roof repeated on the little projecting hall. All the gables have carved foil and wave bargeboards. Chimneys to the gables rather than central. In stuccoed walls the attic windows were in tiny squared pattern whilst those to the ground floor were in the most exquisite Gothick cusped tracery. Sadly the windows were replaced in plastic in 1993 after being vandalised.

**21. BEAUFORT LODGE, Claudy** (see CUMBER)

**22. BEECH HILL, Drumahoe (2)**
**Londonderry Gate** c1875;
architect Alexander Thomson and possibly Young and Mackenzie

*Blackie (1863)*

Here is a most unusual and original entrance composition, a design in a sort of Scottish fairy-tale Picturesque vein. Uncommon too in grouping secondary and principal accesses, at right angles to one another. Straight ahead facing the road is the stableyard gate below a semicircular-headed archway in a tall tower with a rustic machicolated eaves carrying a steeply-pitched hipped roof. The first floor watch room lit by gablet windows back and front. Above the archway in contrast to the random rubble construction is a nicely sculpted plaque displaying the Nicholson family coat of arms and the motto GENEROSITATE, SUB TEGMINE FAGI. Nestling alongside, behind the main gates, a pair of semi-detached one and a half storey gabled cottages, very picturesque in the same grey stone. Each is two bay, the ground floor windows mullioned four part, with the most ornate octagonal cast iron pattern, all gathered under basic label mouldings. On each side

*A. Rowan*

round-headed recessed porches, one sheltered by the main roof carried down as a catslide canopy supported on posts, the rafters extended exaggeratedly. Repeating the tower gablet, another pair both bipartite glazed as the ground floor. Like the fancy glazing, ornamental ridge cresting has not survived. If these cottages show a Scottish influence the entrance gates certainly have an identifiable provenance. These are a copy of a design by Alexander "Greek" Thomson, the celebrated Glasgow architect. It is tempting to speculate that there may have been a family connection between client and architect. The architect's wife was a Nicholson although no direct relationship has been established. Thomson had died in 1875, the same year that Edward Nicholson acquired Beech Hill from the Skipton family, but it is conceivable that Robert Turnbull, who carried on the practice after his principal's death, was responsible. Alternatively it could be that the Thomson design, which was published in Blackie's *Villa and Cottage Architecture* (Plate XXIV), was adapted by a local architect, perhaps Young and MacKenzie of Belfast who seem to have employed it at Ballygarvey, Co Antrim (qv). These contrasting round pillars and walls with mock loopholes are faithfully reproduced in all but the ball finials, for which miniature sculpted beech trees are substituted. Sadly the gates are missing.

**Claudy Gate** pre 1853

A nondescript cottage, at the earlier entrance to a most eccentric house which is now an hotel.
BLACKIE (1863); ROWAN (1979);
IAA Photograph B/1481/4A

**23. BELLAGHY CASTLE, Bellaghy** c1800; *demolished*

*P. Rankin*

In 1791 the Rev Joseph Sandys, brother of Francis the architect, prepared bills for work here upon the property's acquisition by Frederick Hervey, Bishop of Derry and Earl of Bristol. Sandys was supervisor and clerk of works at Downhill (qv) and the repairs and remodelling at Bellaghy could have included the building of this porter's lodge, it looks antique enough. Now no longer, it was almost square on plan, two roomed with a pyramidal roof rising to a slender chimney stack. Single storey, the sole opening on the front elevation was a central door with little narrow sidelights. Windows on opposing side walls, one peering through as a wing wall to the gates, all of which were harled with many coats of whitewash to give a nice vernacular feel. The double carriage gates hung on two tall square pillars harled with sandstone ball finials, flanking which were wicket openings.

**24. BELLARENA, Limavady (3)**

"... to mark the beauties and improvements of Bellarena, you must enter it by the grand gate." Thus wrote Atkinson in 1833 when he would have passed between a pair of lodges perhaps built by Marcus McCausland in 1797 when he undertook improvements to the house. These have since been replaced by the present main entrance.

**Main Entrance** c1920;
architects possibly Young and MacKenzie

Grand in its own right, a very extensive gate sweep on the Magilligan road. The carriage gates are hung on two tall square pillars surmounted by sandstone rusticated ball finials. Railed screen walls lead to wicket gates with similar pillars simply capped. Widespread quadrant walls beyond. Overseeing all this an early 20th century bungalow lodge, like the rest in squared coursed quarry-faced basalt. Single storey, three bay under a hipped roof, the double leaf front door flanked by canted bay windows. Built for Sir Frederick Gage, 3rd Baronet.

**Plantation Lodge** c1835

A pleasant building in mellow orange brick laid in Flemish bond, below a hipped roof. Almost square on plan the roof projects on an eaves extended to be supported on some haphazard rustic posts to form a verandah. Three bay front by two bay side elevations, the windows Georgian style square-paned sashes. Now marooned, it was formerly at the entrance to a portion of the estate opposite. Built by Conolly Gage son of the aforementioned Marcus who had changed his name from McCausland.

**Rear Entrance** c1860

Built by Sir Frederick Heygate after he married the heiress of the Gage estates in 1851, this pretty one and a half storey two up two down gabled lodge is faced in hexagonal black basalt stone with distinctive white mortar joints. The two bay front elevation has a dinky gabled porch and a lattice-paned casement window.

ATKINSON (1833); P.R.O.N.I., D.2194; YOUNG (1909); NORTH DERRY; U.A.H.S. (1975)

**25. BELLEVUE, Londonderry East**
pre 1858; *demolished*

A lodge noted by Griffith in his valuation to a house occupied by a John Henderson.
GRIFFITH

**26. BELLEVUE, Londonderry West**
pre 1831; *demolished*

The lodge to a park owned in 1835 by Hans Riddall.

**27. BELMONT, Londonderry West (3)**; *all demolished*

Two pre 1904 lodges to the rear and one to the Buncrana Road have gone, built by James Thompson Macky whose father William had bought the demesne and replaced a plain lodge with a "... large two-storey house of splendid proportions". The previous owner of the plain lodge, William Millar, had provided earlier pre 1830 porter's accommodation on the Muff Road, but all that survive here are the remnants of a later set of entrance gates in the shape of two big square pillars in V-jointed ashlar, topped with ball finials.

ATKINSON (1833); CITY OF DERRY; U.A.H.S. (1970)

**28. BOOM HALL, Londonderry West**
pre 1830; *demolished*

A lodge built for the Alexander family of Caledon, Co Tyrone (qv). Their fine mansion now lies a forlorn shell overlooking Lough Foyle.

**29. BOVAGH, Aghadowey** pre 1849; *demolished*

A land agent's house of the Beresfords, Marquesses of Waterford whose property of Bovaugh Castle was nearby. The lodge was built for Robert Hazlett.

**30. BROOK HALL, Coleraine** c1840; *demolished*

A lodge for the Boyce family probably of an age with the "good family residence" built in 1827.
OSM

**31. BROOK HALL, Londonderry West (2)**
**South Lodge** c1820

A fine single storey Classical lodge octagonal on plan, two-roomed under an umbrello roof and fronted by a tetrastyle Doric portico. Stuccoed, the front door moved to a later extension, each face has a squared-pane Georgian style sash window framed by pilastered and entablatured recesses. There is an elegant complementary and contemporary gate sweep with concave quadrant walls framing four square ashlar piers, each with a fluted frieze and corniced capping. Outside the gates is a local landmark, the anchors from the "Sunbeam", a mid-Victorian ocean-going yacht belonging to Lord Brassey. All built for Sir George Fitzgerald Hill, MP and Governor of Trinidad.

**North Lodge;** pre 1830; *demolished*

Nondescript.

**32. BROOKHILL, Drumahoe**
**South Entrance** c1800

Originally a tiny single storey lodge below a pyramidal roof with central chimney. Two bay windows to the road in harled walls. Now extended with gabled return. The fine gate screen is later, c1870. Main carriage pillars diagonally placed in quarry-faced masonry with fluted frieze and pear shaped finials. Balustrated convex quadrants.

**North Entrance**

No lodge but with a gate screen much as above with fine surviving wooden gate, vase finials to main pillars and balls to outer piers.

A seat of the Brooke family.

**33. BROOK PARK, Londonderry West**
(see GWYN'S INSTITUTE)

**34. CAMPSEY, Eglinton** pre 1904; *demolished*

A lodge for John Quinn.

**35. CASINO, Londonderry West** pre 1831; *demolished*

In 1837 the residence of Ross T Smyth, miller, which was built by the Earl Bishop as perhaps was the lodge. Both have gone.
OSM

**36. CASTLEROE, Coleraine** c1835; *demolished*

*Mrs J. Cunningham*

A quaint little lodge which, along with the 1760 "well-built 2 storey house", has been demolished as part of some commercial initiative. Single storey two roomed and octagonal on plan with a steep umbrello roof and central chimney. To each stuccoed wall face, a margined square-paned sash window, the front door had a spoked semicircular fanlight over. Ogee railed sweep to two square carriage pillars with ball finials. Built for Colonel John Cairnes.
OSM

**37. CAW, Londonderry East** pre 1849; *demolished*

A lodge probably built for Mr A Harvey.

**38. CAW COTTAGE, Londonderry East**
pre 1849; *demolished*

The lodge to a property later re-named Stradreagh. Probably for James Murray.

**39. CITY CEMETERY, Londonderry West**
c1880

In contrast to the dainty little mortuary chapel at the other side of the entrance gates, is a cumbersome design unsympathetic in scale. One and a half storey semi-detached on an irregular plan. In grey slate, dressed with sandstone quoins and hood mouldings to a combination of single, bi-and tripartite window openings. Plain bargeboards, the chimney stacks in red and yellow polychromatic brickwork.

**40. CLOVERHILL, Maghera (2)**
both pre 1858; *both demolished*

A house originally belonging to a Captain Forbes was rebuilt in 1806 by Anthony Forrester whose son Robert erected the two lodges, neither of which has survived.
OSM

**41. COLERAINE RECTORY, Coleraine**
pre 1904; *demolished*

A lodge which postdated the 1828 glebe house.
LEWIS (1837)

**42. COMBER, Claudy** (see CUMBER)

**43. COOLKEIRAGH, Londonderry East**
pre 1853; *demolished*

The Young family was resident here from the early 17th century. Ancestors of the Youngs of Bailieborough, Co Cavan (qv) and Lough Eske, Co Donegal (qv). It was Major Richard Young who was responsible for the lodge.

**44. CREEVAGH, Londonderry West** c1860

A plain lodge formerly a standard single storey two roomed affair with a hipped roof. Since unhappily enlarged by an additional bay, and the window openings widened in roughcast walls. The door is set into a large recess. To a much older house belonging to the Babington family, one of whom was the engineer Hume who was at one time partner of the architect Thomas Turner. It is hardly likely that the latter was responsible for the alterations. Simple whitewashed square gate piers.

**45. CROMORE, Portstewart (2)**
**Early Entrance** pre 1830; *demolished*

What looks from the first Ordnance Survey map to have been a little Georgian round pill-box lodge to the original south-west main entrance.

**Main Entrance** c1857;
architects probably Lanyon and Lynn

It was to the eastern perimeter of the Cromie estate that a new avenue was formed in 1856 giving access to the railway station opened that year. At this new entrance Mr John Cromie built a lodge to the "Lanyonate" formula in a honey-coloured sandstone. There were similar buildings at Lismara and Gardenvale both in Co Antrim (qqv). Single storey below a shallow hipped roof, it is dominated by a gabled "porte-cochère" that projects each side on a segmental arch below which is a turned timber balustrade. To the front, two semicircular arches with plain archivolts spring off square pillars, the central one rather awkwardly placed on an axis with the panelled front door. Flanking the "porte-cochère" are very narrow round-headed sash lights repeated in groups of three to the side elevations. Rising centrally from the ridge an outsize chimney stack with its own little gabled capping, sprouting all manner of devices to improve draw. There is an appropriate impressive Italianate style gate sweep in matching ashlar. Simple intermediate and outer piers frame ornate railings making liberal use of fleur-de-lys tops, repeated on the carriage gates. The large inner pillars are built up of big blocks with raised and fielded panels below friezes and moulded cappings. There are nice sculpted scrolled volutes to the outer piers and gate stops.

**46. CUMBER, Claudy** pre 1905; *demolished*
A demesne previously of the Ross family and known as Beaufort Lodge, it was later acquired by the Brownes one of whom, George, built the lodge.

**47. DAISYHILL, Limavady** (see ROEPARK)

**48. DERRYNOYD LODGE, Draperstown (2)** both pre 1854; *both demolished*
The absence of both porter's lodges is the inevitable result of the estate being taken over by the Forestry Service. Erected for Judge Torrens.

**49. DOWNHILL, Castlerock (3)**
Frederick Augustus Hervey was an Englishman who took holy orders in 1754 (being a younger son of the aristocracy) and he was to become the richest and most eccentric character ever to set foot in Ireland in the 18th century. After being chaplain to George III in 1763 he travelled Europe for two years before being given the Bishopric of Derry through the influence of his elder brother the 3rd Earl of Bristol. The Earldom he inherited upon his brother's death in 1779. After 1785 he was hardly ever in Ireland as he pursued a succession of jaunts about the Continent. He completed seven or eight visits to Italy alone. Derry was the richest see in Ireland, eventually bringing in about £10,000 per annum to which Hervey could add an equally large personal income. The Earl Bishop began to show a greater interest in the arts than in his Diocese and amongst other pursuits he developed a compulsive and excessive urge to build. With an income such as his he was able to indulge himself to the full. The site he chose for his first project was that exposed plateau at Castlerock, fully at the mercy of the Atlantic gales as it is to this day. He never seemed fully to realise the value of pre-planting the demesne for shelter, so obsessed and impatient was he to indulge his hobby. Such were his whims and inconsistencies and cavalier approach to architects that it is not clear who was directly responsible, if any one designer was, for many of his building ventures in the north of Ireland. The names of Brettingham, Wyatt and Soane keep cropping up. Having commenced Downhill in 1772 he went about covering the demesne with architectural adornments or follies. Among these are the Mausoleum erected in 1779, the Mussenden Temple in 1781 and two sophisticated entrance gates, which are more directly influenced by the Grand Tour than any others in the Province.

**The Lion Gate** c1780; architect possibly James Wyatt
The earlier of the two entrances formerly called, less misleadingly, the West Gate for these are Hervey ounces or leopards aloft these two grand

W.A. Green (U.F.T.M.)
*Downhill, The Lion Gate*

piers not lions. Each pier in sandstone ashlar is in the form of an aedicule with, on a plinth, a pair of part-engaged Roman Doric columns which frame a rounded niche having a garland plaque over. The entablature has aegricane interspersed with more garlands and paterae. Below hang Doric guttae. A cornice with mutules carries a plinth or base for the beast whose leading foreleg grasps a ball. These ounces were carved in Cork in a darker smoother stone, and one bill dated 3rd May 1780 is for £3.8s.3d (three Irish guineas), "... to pay Mr Foy when his Lordship's Leopards are block'd fit for carriage". In contrast the rear of the pillars are relatively plain with alternating bands of vermiculated rustication. Intriguingly there are identical gate piers to the Villa Chiericati, Vancimuglio, Vicenza which dates from 1557 and is attributed to Andrea Palladio. Further investigation may prove revealing. Peter Rankin, however, observes that the similarities between the Lion Gate and the wings of Wyatt's Radcliffe Observatory in Oxford are quite marked, in particular the niches with plaques over. Extensive concave curtain walls linked distant porters' lodges or cubed pavilions in somewhat less sophisticated stuccoed rubble stone. Single storey and gabled to the road they had small window openings in semicircular- arched recesses, one of which overlooked the gates. These curtain walls must have preceded the lodges by a considerable time for about May 1783 Michael Shanahan, the supervising architect, suggested that a small door on either side of the piers would be a convenience. The lodges were probably erected in 1791, for on 25th July of that year a payment of £3.8s.3d was made "... to John hefernan [John Hiffernan, plasterer] for three weeks subsistance for the porters lodges". There was loft bedspace lit by semicircular-headed windows on the rear elevations, the gables of which had fluted stone chimney stacks. It is both amusing and an informative insight into life at Downhill to record the experience of the Rev Dr Daniel A Beaufort when he paid a visit here in 1787. Amazed and somewhat disconcerted to be confronted by a porter dressed in tartan plaid who initially refused him admission, he still observed "Bishop's gate, Chinese wooden one between two piers of two columns and a niche each". Eventually being admitted, he discovered the Bishop confined to bed with an "attack in his bowels". Nevertheless he was provided with "a

P. Rankin

small plain dinner" including some excellent wines - burgundy, port, claret, madeira and champagne!

**The Bishop Gate** c1783; architect perhaps James Wyatt
The main entrance into the demesne from the road was known to the Bishop as the Coleraine or Coleraine Battalion Gate after the volunteer battalion of that name in the town nearby. The grand carriage archway is flanked by a pair of engaged Roman Doric columns that carry a mutuled pediment the tympanum of which has the Hervey crest, badly in need of restoration. The frieze below is sculpted alternately with bishops' mitres and bucrania, their horns hung with husks. This frames the semicircular-headed archway, its spandrels containing paterae with a sculpted archivolt of fluting punctuated by more paterae. The arch springs from a similarly treated impost with its dentil course carried beyond as a band through the wing walls. These wings are in channelled rusticated ashlar, one with a little niche now occupied by a statue of Diana, the other having a wicket doorway. Framing each wing are small pilasters with recessed panels, the same as those carrying the main archway imposts. Over the fluted band is a parapet sculpted with festoons and more paterae inserts. Again, as Peter Rankin points out, there are similarities with James Wyatt's work. In this case the pediment, spandrels and archway are similar to those to the pavilions of Heaton Hall, Lancashire. To attribute both gateways to Wyatt is logical, knowing that he and the Bishop had associated over designs for the house. The

*Downhill, The Bishop Gate*

Ordnance Survey Memoir, albeit sixty odd years later, is quite specific, "The plan [of Downhill] was first laid by Mr James Wyatt of London and built under the superintendence of Michael Shanahan ...". Be that as it may the latter in July 1784 received two payments, one on the 7th for the Coleraine Battalion Gate of £44.19s.5 d, and the other on the 8th for his poundage on the Coleraine arch of £7.4s.0d. The freestone was worked by James McBlain who was to exchange his role as mason for that of architect.

**Bishop Gate Lodge** c1785; architect James McBlain

Although not conceived as part of the original composition, it cannot have been constructed long after the archway for in July 1784 the Italian Placido Columbani, who was head stuccadore working on the house, wrote to say that "the Stone, Lime and sand I have seen at the Coleraine Gate - is sufficient to build the lodge to the height, pointed out by Mr James McBlain". This charming Gothick gate lodge is for its time commodious. Although at a glance appearing as the standard three bay affair forward of, and at right angles to, the gateway it in fact extends a further two bays behind. Single storey and also in sandstone ashlar, the windows are round-headed with rectangular panes framed by reticulated dressings. Up six steps the lancet-headed doorway is flanked by cluster columns, the moulding carried around the arch. This feature is repeated on a larger scale as quoins supporting a corniced parapet that partly hides the hipped roof, at each corner of which is a spiked pinnacle, much as used at the entrance to Hillsborough Parish Church, Co Down (qv) where McBlain also worked, in 1773. The Earl Bishop's restless enthusiasm was then directed towards his latest passion, a new palace at Ballyscullion in the same county (qv) commenced in 1787.

**Black Glen Lodge** c1860

Built by Sir Henry Hervey Bruce who hardly inherited the architectural taste of his ancestor, it is a plain one and a half storey lodge in black rubble basalt with a projecting lean-to entrance porch. Lozenge shaped gate piers with spear-topped cast iron gates.

BEAUFORT (1787); NORTH DERRY; U.A.H.S. (1975); RANKIN (1972); RANKIN (1971); MALINS (1976); ROWAN (1979); REEVES-SMYTH (1992) GREEN PHOTOGRAPH (U.F.T.M.) Ref W.A.G. 2222

## 50. DRENAGH, Limavady (2)

In 1729 the property along with the estate then known as Daisy Hill (see Roe Park), was passed upon the death of William Conolly, Speaker of the Irish House of Commons, to his agent and friend Colonel Robert McCausland. It was Robert's grandson who felt that Fruit Hill, as Drenagh was formerly called, was worthy of grander accommodation and he engaged the architect John Hargrave to prepare plans for a mansion house in about 1825. However, both client and architect were to die before these bore fruit and Hargrave's hand is to be seen solely in the first gate lodge to be built on the demesne.

**Coleraine Road Gate** (Logan's Lodge) 1830; architect John Hargrave

"The lodge at Fruithill is creditable to the taste of the proprietor ... a handsome new entrance was built by Mr McCausland on the Coleraine Road in 1830, and from it the avenue now winds gracefully to the house. The first entrance, which yet constitutes the approach to the house from the north, is also beautiful." This delightful Tudor Gothic style lodge referred to in the Ordnance Survey Memoirs of 1835 is single storey on a T plan formed by a living-room projecting towards the avenue. This is canted, in a manner typical of Hargrave's work, under a half-umbrello advanced from the hipped roof. The walls are in a pleasant honey-coloured punched ashlar, with plain raised banded surrounds to the delightful bipartite pointed windows with diamond glazing pattern. Internally these openings have panelled shutters and architraves to floor level. Sometime later the lodge was extended by an additional room in similar style but stuccoed to match. This can perhaps be explained and dated by another extract from the Ordnance Survey Memoirs of 1835: "Sarah McAfee, a Presbyterian teacher. This is a free school supported by Mrs McCausland of Fruithill. Six girls are taught plain and fancy needlework. The Misses McCausland teach the children at this school reading and writing; there are 5 Presbyterians and one Roman Catholic. This school opened in 1832; the Mistress is the gatekeeper's wife, who is paid 10 pounds per annum by Mrs McCausland for opening the gate and teaching the school. There is no school held on Saturday except for one girl who comes to clean up the house, which must be done by each girl in their turn". There are contrasting Classical ashlar square pillars with recessed panels, tall fluted friezes and corniced cappings. Spear-topped iron railings and gates.

**The Main Entrance** c1840; architect Charles Lanyon

After John Hargrave's premature death by drowning in 1833, Marcus Conolly McCausland turned to the up-and-coming young architect Charles Lanyon from Belfast to design him a chaste and crisply detailed Neo-Classical mansion. Lanyon's gate lodge to be built off the road to the North coast is equally refined, "Almost as if the Big House had come down to the front gate and had a pup." (Sydney Smith). In lovely golden-coloured ashlar it is single storey three bays by two, each window a twelve-paned sash. The front door is panelled below a semicircular-spoked fanlight. Sheltering this a tetrastyle Ionic portico, the capitals identical to those on the big house with their bands of anthemion and palmette motifs, taken straight out of Stuart and Revett's *The Antiquities of Athens*. The pediment entablature is carried around as a parapet to the hipped roof. Alistair Rowan says of the house that Lanyon was never to be so chaste again, or so careful - so too the lodge. The entrance sweep is equally distinguished, with its outer railing extended from two unusual wicket gates framed by square piers and entablatured arches over. This is an idea also to be found at Cranaghan, Co Cavan

(qv) and Knappagh, Co Armagh (qv), two earlier examples. The gates have lovely rows of ornate iron anthemions and flowers. Both lodges in caring hands.
STUART (1830); OSM; NORTH DERRY; U.A.H.S. (1975); ROWAN (1979)

**51. DROMORE, Macosquin** pre 1848; *demolished*
The lodge to a property in 1837 of James Gamble.

**52. DRUMANEE PARSONAGE, Bellaghy** pre 1830; *demolished*

**53. DUNCREGGAN, Londonderry West** pre 1858; *demolished*
The house for William Tillie, a wealthy businessman, has been incorporated in the Londonderry High School complex.
CITY OF DERRY; U.A.H.S. (1970)

**54. DUNDERG, Macosquin**
(see GREENFIELD)

**55. DUNNFIELD VILLA, Londonderry East** c1870
Right on the Strabane Road outside the gates to a seat in 1880 of Robert Macrory is a lodge which supplanted a predecessor of c1850 that seems to have served both Dunnfield House and Warren Hill. One and a half storey with an extended three bay front elevation. A front door with label moulding and little pendant dripstones is flanked by pairs of semicircular-headed windows under linked keystoned hood mouldings - a sort of Tudor Italianate mixture. Stuccoed with quoins, the single storey rear return in similar style runs alongside the public footway. Below flimsy bargeboards are attic windows treated as those below.

**56. THE ELMS, Londonderry West** c1865
Mildly Italianate in style, a single storey rectangular building under a hipped roof. The short elevation to the avenue is three bay, the entrance door to the right. All in stuccoed rustication, the horizontal channelling carried down to resemble voussoirs of segmentally-headed openings. Modillion brackets support the eaves. The chimney stack with a basic frieze, corbelled and capped. Much of a style with the house, in 1870 the property of Sir Edward Ward Reid.

**57. ENAGH LODGE, Londonderry East** c1855
A lodge for William D Smyth now derelict. Typical single storey, three bay cottage below a wide-eaved hipped roof. Large window openings in rubble walls.

**58. ENGLISHTOWN, Macosquin** pre 1831; *ruinous*
"A good slated dwellinghouse, 2-storeys high" built by James Hamill in 1810. The lodge opposite the gates either coeval with the house or added in the late 1820s when the new proprietor John Acheson Smyth of Ardmore (qv) made improvements.
OSM

**59. FAIRVIEW, Castledawson** c1845
A nicely proportioned lodge built for Mr James Henry. Single storey three bay, the central one a gabled breakfront from the hipped roof. Central octagonal stone chimney stack. Derelict.

**60. FAIRVIEW, Portglenone** pre 1850; *demolished*

**61. THE FARM, Londonderry West** c1840; *demolished*
For many years the residence of Sir Robert Alexander Ferguson long-standing MP for the city. His lodge, square Georgian house with noble Grecian portico, "and adjacent Pleasure ground, tout ensemble of the home view" have all been overrun by city sprawl.
ATKINSON (1833)

**62. FORT WILLIAM, Tobermore** pre 1832; *demolished*
The lodge probably built for John Stevenson.

**63. FOYLE COLLEGE, Londonderry West** pre 1830; *demolished*
The college building of 1814 in Classical style, its design by John Bowden of Dublin. The lodge may have been contemporary.

**64. FOYLE HILL, Londonderry West** pre 1831; *demolished*
The residence of the Scott family. It subsequently became a hospital.

**65. FOYLE PARK, Eglinton** pre 1855; *demolished*
A lodge for Mr George Ross.

**66. FOYLE VIEW, Londonderry East** 1875
A house on the site in 1830 called Salem had by 1853 been re-named Foyle View, becoming Seymour House this century before finally being demolished. A sturdy and spacious lodge of one and a half storey, rendered with hipped gables on an L plan. Big curved console brackets in pairs spring out of a stringcourse that forms a frieze below the eaves and which is returned to support large bargeboard toes. Two friezed chimney stacks, the ground floor windows have moulded surrounds. Extended in matching style and immaculately maintained. Replacing a pre 1853 lodge on the same site, it was built by John Cooke.

**67. FRUITHILL, Limavady**
(see DRENAGH)

**68. GARVAGH, Garvagh** pre 1832; *demolished*
Another park to fall foul of the Forestry Service with a fine Neo-Classical house and lodge both swept away. Once the property of the Canning family, Lords Garvagh, whose most famous son was George, British Prime Minister in 1827.

**69. GLENALLA, Claudy** c1820

An interesting solution to the problem of separating the "quality" from tradesmen visitors to a demesne with minimal road frontage. At the end of an avenue from the road is a single storey two roomed lodge facing the visitor separating two carriage entrances. Gable-on with a bow front, flanked by two simple pairs of entrance gates, one to the house the other leading to the outbuildings. The windows are peculiar in having only vertical glazing bars. This may be a modest version of a design from Edward Gyfford's *Designs for Small Picturesque Cottages*, a pattern book published in 1807. Built by the Rev Francis Gouldsbury, incumbent in 1824 when the house, which dates from 1772, was Upper Cumber Rectory or Alla Glebe.
LESLIE (1940); GYFFORD (1807)

**70. GLENDERMOTT RECTORY, Londonderry East** pre 1858; *demolished*
Built for an earlier glebe-house of 1824.
LEWIS (1837)

**71. GLENGALLIAGH HALL, Londonderry West** c1890
The house as it originally stood is of 1847 but was re-clothed in "stockbroker Tudor" manner and a gate lodge added in harmony. A single storey building on a T plan with tall gables of ornamental black and white half-timbered effect with simple hipknobs. In roughcast walls some of the windows are paired sashes, the upper halves squared pane. Behind the square gate piers is a small porch outshoot with its own decorative gable. The chimney strangely flimsy of two stacks set diagonally on a pitched base. Built by the Brown family.
ROWAN (1979)

**72. GORTNAMOYAGH, Garvagh** pre 1849
A modest lodge opposite the gates.

**73. GOVERNMENT, Londonderry West** pre 1904; *demolished*
An unprepossessing porter's lodge to a mid-Victorian Italianate villa built by the Green family.

**74. GRANGE, Magherafelt** pre 1905; *demolished*

**75. GRANSHA LODGE, Londonderry East** c1840; *demolished*
Porter's accommodation to a house occupied in 1837 by Samuel McClintock. The estate now forms the Gransha hospital.

**76. GREENFIELD, Macosquin** c1833
"The avenue is extensive and well planted, with a neat gate and lodge at the entrance." To a property owned in 1835 by Mr Stephen Bennett. Later than the 1785 residence or improvements carried out in 1820.
OSM

**77. GROCER'S HALL, Eglinton** pre 1830; *demolished*

**78. GWYN'S INSTITUTE, Londonderry West** 1840; architect Thomas Jackson

J. Shaw

The Institute was formed to help orphans and is in a Neo-Palladian style by the Belfast architect Thomas Jackson. In a sandstone ashlar the single storey lodge is on a T plan with a central back return. The building has canted end elevations under half-umbrellos, some of the "openings" blind. The front facade to the avenue three bay with a Roman Doric portico of paired columns supporting a pediment with timber bargeboards. In the centre of the ridge a row of three octagonal stone pots. It is now run down, its sash windows lacking their Georgian glazing bars, exposed to vandals in what is now the access to a public park known as Brooke Park.
CITY OF DERRY; U.A.H.S (1970); ROWAN (1979)

**79. HEATHFIELD, Garvagh**

Postcard view

There was never a lodge here but it is worthy of note since early this century it had the most remarkable topiary work at the gate. It proclaimed the name of the park, a miniature of the house and the date 1872. Formed by a David Smith, it is now no more.

**80. HERMITAGE, Garvagh** pre 1849; *demolished*
A dower house of the Canning family of Garvagh (qv) with its lodge opposite the gates.

**81. HERVEY HILL, Kilrea** c1853; *demolished*
The glebe house built by Rev Robert Torrens in 1774. Along with other improvements a lodge was added by Rev William M Napper.
OSM

**82. HOLY TRINITY RECTORY, Claudy** (see KILLALOO RECTORY)

**83. INISHRUSH, Portglenone** pre 1832; *demolished*
The house replaced an earlier one in 1825, built by Henry Ellis. It was either he, or his son Hercules, who added the lodge not long afterwards.
OSM

**84. JACKSON HALL, Coleraine** pre 1904; *demolished*
For long the seat of the Jacksons, it fell into decline after passing from their hands. The house seems to have become known as the Manor House upon being acquired by a Capt. Edmond Stronge who also built a lodge. Both house and lodge have gone.

**85. KILCATTEN LODGE, Claudy** c1820

Both house and gatekeeper's lodge were built by Alexander Ogilby, of the same family as the Ogilbys of Ardnargle and Pellipar (qqv). Here is the grotto or hermitage as gate lodge, an extraordinary progeny of the Picturesque movement. On a precise square plan, of one room 11' 0" x 11' 0" (3.3m x 3.3m), it is built of big limestone boulders. The front elevation two bay under a pyramidal slate roof, the chimney stack is on the side elevation to the road, extended by the addition, about 1860, of a totally incongruous, pretty, tall decorative cream terracotta pot, perhaps from Florence Court, Co Fermanagh. Very quaint for all but the gate keeper. Now derelict. There are ordinary square gate piers with ball finials.

**86. KILLALOO RECTORY, Claudy** pre 1849; *demolished*
The lodge built opposite the gates probably for the Rev John Hayden. Now called Holy Trinity Rectory.

**87. KILLEAGUE, Macosquin** pre 1848
To a house of 1784 built by Alderman Robert Alexander. A nondescript lodge possibly built for a family called Sayer.
OSM

**88. KILREA MANOR, Kilrea (2);** *both demolished*
Two lodges, one pre 1853 the other built before 1905, were for George Bicknell, Esq.

**89. LAKE, Ballyronan** pre 1830; *demolished*
This lodge may have formed part of the improvements carried out to the property in 1812 by the Gaussen family.
OSM

**90. LAKEVIEW, Castledawson** pre 1850; *demolished*
Hugh Crawford built the lodge here.

**91. LANDMORE, Kilrea** c1810
Now deserted, this once charming building was brick- faced like the house, but it is now pebble-dashed with some disfiguring 20th century steel windows. Single storey, its two rooms are in an irregular hexagonal plan under an umbrello type roof with central chimney stack. Erected either by Alexander Orr, the linen mill owner who built the house c1788, or by his son George who assumed his mother's maiden name of Dunbar.
MULLIN (1972); OSM

**92. LARCHMOUNT, Drumahoe** pre 1831
A nondescript affair perhaps built by Mr Carey McClelland who was resident in 1837.

**93. LARGANTOGHER, Maghera (2)**
**North Entrance** pre 1854; *demolished*
The earlier of the lodges was located opposite the gates.
**South Entrance** c1860; architects possibly Lanyon, Lynn and Lanyon; *ruinous*
James Johnston Clarke founded a demesne here from about 1845 onwards. Dr Paul Larmour has established that the architectural practice of Lanyon and Lynn was involved in designs for Mr Clarke in the 1860s but whether this ever bore fruit is not known as all that remains is the shell of this porter's lodge overlooking the now muddy, overgrown avenue. A sizeable gabled lodge on a T plan, the living room projecting from the main body of the building. Attic bed spaces were lit by tiny round-headed, hood-moulded slits with dressed stone surrounds. The walls random rubble, may have previously been stuccoed with cut stone skewtables. Large stone quoins survive, as does the moulded surround to the recessed elliptical arch about the front door, but that to the living room recess has been removed.

**94. LARGY TOWNLAND, Limavady** pre 1858; *demolished*
A lodge identified by Griffith in his valuation. Unlocated, presumed gone. To a house and offices of S Maxwell Alexander of Ballyclose.
GRIFFITH

**95. LAUREL HILL, Coleraine** c1850
An early villa designed in 1840 by architect Charles Lanyon and completed three years later for Henry Kyle, to replace an earlier house. The lodge does not seem to have formed part of Lanyon's commission having none of the Italianate features up the hill, being in a hotchpotch of styles perhaps due to some later meddling in the Tudor Picturesque. Standard plan single storey three bay with a hipped roof, an elegant entablatured distyle Greek Doric portico was flanked by Tudor label-moulded windows in channelled rustication. A further indignity was suffered with the insertion of an oriel window to the road elevation. All this is now of little consequence it having been transformed remarkably into a modern bungalow with no sign of the nice fluted columns.
COLERAINE AND PORTSTEWART; UAHS (1972)

**96. LEARMOUNT CASTLE, Feeny (2)**
On the death of Sir William Montgomery the estate was inherited by the Beresford family who let it to the McCauslands of Drenagh (qv). It was not until 1830 that Henry Barre Beresford came to live here and set about building a new "castle", placing a Tudor Gothick villa against the existing stronghold. This is very much as the architect J B Keane had also contrived at Castle Irvine, Co Fermanagh (qv) and Camlin Castle,

Co Donegal (qv). The architect's brief seems also to have included the provision of a gate lodge.

**West Lodge** c1830; architect probably J B Keane; *demolished*

(Mrs P. McElhinney)

The lodge, of which nothing survives, was a sturdy affair, spacious for its time and robustly detailed. Single storey under a hipped roof, the three bay front was dominated by a gabled breakfront with elementary foiled bargeboards above the Beresford coat-of-arms on a sculpted stone plaque. Below this projected a canted bay window to overlook the gate. Otherwise the openings, including the door on the opposing facade from the road, had debased drip-shelves over. All windows had square paned sashes in harled walls below closely-spaced eaves brackets of ample proportions. The chimney stack rose off the rear elevation. All that remains at this main entrance are the remnants of a gate screen of central iron posts, chamfered with decorative rope pattern and crowned by little pineapple finials. Beyond the wicket gates are ogee sweeps with fleur-de-lys tops to railings, terminating in outer stone piers with recessed panels. The neatly gravelled forecourt and avenue now replaced by a dirt track.

**East, or Park, Lodge** c1845; architect probably William Murray; *demolished*

Built by John Barre Beresford after his succession as eldest son in 1837, the sole record of its appearance is from an old photograph viewing the rear and side elevations. It seems to have been a standard symmetrical three bay lodge, single storey and gabled. The walls were of squared coursed quarry-faced rubble having dressed stone quoins and window surrounds with label mouldings in Tudor fashion. Windows were mullioned and transomed with casement lights. There was probably a gabled projecting hall with ornamental bargeboards to match those on the main gables, which were in the form of "continuous brackets", just like those at The Pavilion, Co Armagh (qv) and Castle Leslie, Co Monaghan (qv). The estates had the misfortune to fall into the hands of the Forestry Service with the inevitable consequences for the gate lodges.
ROWAN (1979)

**97. LISARDAHLA, Drumahoe** pre 1905; *demolished*

A lodge of few pretensions now has a modern bungalow on the site. The original was built by Sir Edward Ward Reid after moving here from The Elms (qv) in the 1870s.

**98. LISSAN, Cookstown** (see Co Tyrone)

**99. LISSAN RECTORY, Cookstown** pre 1832; *demolished*

A unique glebe house built in 1807 for Rev John Molesworth Staples to designs by John Nash in his Italianate villa style. It is frustrating to find the lodge gone as it may have been contemporary with the rectory, though no records survive to suggest it was part of the architect's commission.

**100. THE LODGE, Castledawson** (see MOYOLA)

**101. THE LODGE, Claudy** pre 1831

A linear vernacular Irish cottage but only of three bay, the doorway off centre, within a diminutive shallow gabled porch. Whitewashed rubble walling houses little squared sash windows, the one on the gable eyeing the gate. Gabled and slated it may have inherited the duties of a gate lodge later than 1831, before which no avenue existed. The only other such cottage lodge remaining is at Dresternan Castle, Co Fermanagh (qv).

**102. THE LODGE, Limavady** c1780; *demolished*

Jack Stevenson

A property which has gone through a succession of owners since its founding as New Hall by the Phillips family. Local tradition has it that the gatehouse is the one which escaped destruction by King James I on his return from the Siege of Derry and was originally built as a guard-house for the castle occupied by Sir Thomas Phillips when he was Governor of Limavady. It is more likely that it owed its ultimate appearance to a rebuild by Thomas Smith, agent of the Conynghams, to whom the property was leased c1782. A two storey two up two down structure on a perfectly square plan. Rubble walls and a pyramidal roof with central chimney stack. Aptly known as "the pepperpot". Alongside a wicket gate and two grand ashlar carriage pillars with corniced cappings.
ROWAN (1979); MULLIN (1983)

**103. LORETTO CONVENT, Coleraine** (see TIEV TARA)

**104. LUNATIC ASYLUM, Londonderry** c1828; architects Francis Johnston and William Murray; *demolished*

This was one of nine such institutions to be built on a standard plan in the country. Presumably the lodge was to the same pattern as those at Armagh and Belfast (qqv), only the former having survived. This was single storey three bay symmetrical in stone under a hipped roof. The lodge was certainly the shortest-lived of the three in Ulster having disappeared before the 1853 Ordnance Survey.
ARMAGH; UAHS (1992)

**105. MANOR HOUSE, Coleraine** (see JACKSON HALL)

**106. MAYBROOK, Londonderry West** pre 1904; *demolished*

**107. MILBURN, Coleraine** c1840; *demolished*

For long the seat of the Cary family from whom it passed in the 19th century. It was probably built by Andrew Orr. A square single storey building, three bay in facing brick with little square-paned windows. The pyramidal roof had a very high eaves line.

**108. MILTON LODGE, Londonderry West** pre 1830; *demolished*

The lodge to this pleasant mid-Georgian villa overlooking the Foyle has gone. Probably erected by Robert Bateson, ancestor of the Lords Deramore of Belvoir Park, Co Down (qv).

**109. MONEYCARRIE, Aghadowey** pre 1904; *demolished*

A lodge probably built for a Samuel Smith.

**110. MOUNT SANDEL, Coleraine** pre 1904; *demolished*

The property in 1870 of R K Knox.

**111. MOYOLA, Castledawson (3)**

At the entrances to beautiful parkland none of the lodges have the antiquity of the 1768 house once known as The Lodge, built by Arthur Dawson.

**Castledawson Lodge** c1840

The plainest of the three lodges and the earliest at a gate leading to a three mile avenue to the house. Notable only for a pair of diagonally-set chimney stacks. Built by the Hon George Robert Dawson, brother-in-law of Sir Robert Peel.

**Hillhead Entrance** c1860; architect not known

*Moyola, Hillhead Entrance*

*Postcard view (B. Watson)*

*Drumlamph Entrance*

An irregular lodge on an L plan, single storey gabled with simple serrated bargeboards. The avenue gable has a rectangular bay window alongside which advances a small gabled hall. Now rendered it has stone quoins. The windows have chamfered stone dressings, their ornamental glazing bars now removed. On a rectangular base rest two square stone chimney stacks. The extensive gate screen of fine cast iron work has two wicket gates flanking the central carriage opening. The octagonal stone gate piers have recessed panels, the central two crowned by the Dawson family bearings in the form of an etoile crest over a ring with the motto "TOUJOURS PROPICE" carried, very much as at Roxborough, Co Tyrone (qv), by four reptilian supports. The lodge lies vacant, the avenue disused and the entrance gates bound by barbed wire.

**Drumlamph Entrance** c1855; architect not known

Here is a Picturesque treasure, one and a half storey on an L plan with a single storey rear return. In Flemish bond facing brickwork with stone quoins and window dressings. The ground floor windows in single or bipartite form are label-moulded with lovely Gothick traceried glazing patterns. The very steeply-pitched gable ends have narrow lancet windows with hood mouldings to light the attic bedrooms. The carved timber foil and wave bargeboards with knobbly hipknobs and "steering wheel" toes. The roof has big scalloped slates with fancy crested ridges, penetrated by a pair of octagonal brick chimney stacks. A beautiful ornamental cottage now rendered over, its hipknobs removed and the rear return extended with a flat roof. The early 20th century postcard view shows a widespread picket fence screen between intermediate stone posts and central main octagonal gate piers much as at the Hillhead gate, but with great oversized cappings. These have now been removed to make way for more cast iron Dawson crest finials. Both Hillhead and Drumlamph entrances were for Colonel Robert Peel Dawson through whose marriage in 1872 the estates came into the possession of the Chichesters.
LEWIS (1837)

**112. MUFF GLEBE, Cookstown**
(see LISSAN RECTORY)

**113. MULLENAN, Carrigans (2)**
Carrigans Road Entrance pre 1853; *demolished*

The previous main entrance at which only modest square gate pillars remain.

**Shore Road Entrance** c1880

On a beautiful rhododendron approach is a faintly Classical late Victorian lodge of standard form. Three bay, the central one has a projecting corniced flat roof hall below a hipped roof with high eaves supported on carved modillion brackets. The windows are sashes divided into four panes. Skylights to attic rooms. A chamfered white fireclay brick chimney stack has two cream octagonal ornamental pots. The gate sweep looks older. Concave quadrants with moulded stone cappings frame four stuccoed square piers having ashlar plinths, plain friezes and corniced cappings. Good iron gates. For long the property of the Harveys, this avenue is no longer in use.

**114. NEW HALL, Limavady**
(see THE LODGE)

**115. THE OAKS, Drumahoe** c1855; *demolished*

The lodge has gone but some pretty ironwork survives for Mr Acheson Lyle. Central ornate posts have round tops enclosing pretty anthemion motifs. Concave quadrants of hooped railings terminates in square ashlar piers with raised and fielded panels. It all looks too early for the 1867 improvement works here by the architect John McCurdy.

**116. OAKS LODGE** pre 1849; *demolished*

A lodge for Mr Hugh Lyle had gone by 1905.

**117. THE PALACE, Londonderry West**
(see CASINO)

**118. PELLIPAR, Dungiven (6)**

This place was once called Mattsmount belonging to the Fanning family from whom it was acquired c1800 by the Ogilbys. The estate had at one stage six pre 1832 lodged entrances. Only two of these remain, both on the eastern boundary.

**North-East Entrance** c1820; architect not known

Robert Ogilby added to the house "... two additional wings and the whole is at present fitting up in a superior style, the approach, too, has been most tastefully improved, and two elegant lodges erected at its entrance". These are on an axis of the approach from Limavady, located to give maximum impact. A pair of solid twin Neo-Classical lodges confront each other across the avenue and form part of the gate screen. Single storey on standard two roomed plans with hipped roofs each having a breakfront hall below a pedimented gable. In sandstone ashlar the openings all semicircular, framed by similar recesses even repeated on the rear elevation in the form of a blind arcade. All are united at the spring line by a stringcourse right around. The windows are Georgian square-paned sashes. The chimney stacks stuccoed brick. Two big square stone gate pillars with corniced cappings are linked to the lodges by dwarf walls with iron railings to match the carriage gates. The elegant lodges now inexcusably allowed to fall into decay.

**South-East Entrance** c1830; *ruinous*

A single storey asymmetrical three bay lodge below a hipped roof. Originally constructed in rubble stone since partly rebuilt in brick. Later cast iron gate screen comprising good octagonal carriage piers with finialled tops framed by railed convex quadrants.
MacCLOSKEY (1821)

**119. PENNYBURN, Londonderry West** pre 1848; *demolished*

A lodge built by the Bond family which succumbed to urban advance.

**120. PREHEN, Londonderry East** pre 1831

Now lacking any architectural pretensions this is a simple single storey two bay lodge with a pyramidal roof. Roughcast, extended and modernised. Built by the Knoxes of Rathmullan, Co Donegal (qv) who came by the property from the Tomkins family. The first Ordnance Survey suggests this lodge may be the survivor of a pair.

*R. Hamilton*

*Pellipar, North-East Entrance*

**121. RICHMOND, Londonderry West (2)**
**Strand Road Gate** c1840
To the first house on the site the Watt family built this lodge. A two roomed cube with a high eaves line to the pyramidal roof which rises to a slender diagonally-set chimney stack broaching off a square base. In whitewashed walls a three bay front elevation, the front door having a projecting banded surround with semicircular head. To the side overlooking the gates is a lancet window with complicated octagonal Y-traceried glazing pattern, exactly the same as one at Glencree, Co Tyrone (qv). An amazing survival so close to the city centre, and still occupied. The MacFarland family came by the property at the turn of the century and changed its name to Aberfoyle, a name acquired from the house next door which became Talbot House (qv). They erected big sturdy cast iron ornamental carriage gates, working their monogram into each leaf. These are hung with the top hinges grasped by great iron fists.
**Northland Road Entrance** c1870

A good piece of townscape built after 1870 when Robert Corscadden bought the demesne. Entry to the park and carriage yard via two tall pedimented ashlar archways at right angles to each other, one parallel with, and forming a screen to, the public footway. The semicircular keystoned arches spring from cornice courses, one of which runs through the wing wall to meet the gatehouse, punctuated by a flat-arched wicket gate en route. Like the wall in uncoursed squared masonry, the generous two storey porter's accommodation forms a big cube below a hipped roof. Faintly Italianate in style, the front elevation alongside the footpath has a first floor pair of semicircular-headed sash windows with dressed stone surround over a transomed and mullioned timber oriel supported on four brackets. A tall corbelled four-flue chimney stack in red brick rising off a side wall has been removed.

**122. RIVER VIEW, Londonderry West**
pre 1858; *demolished*
A lodge noted by Griffith in his valuation to a property of William F Bigger, merchant.
GRIFFITH

**123. ROE PARK, Limavady (5)**
Marcus McCausland bought the property in 1743 from Capt Richard Babington and changed its name from Mullagh to Daisy Hill.
**Deer Park Lodge** c1800; *demolished*
It was Dominick McCausland, coming to the property in 1782, who built this the earliest of four surviving lodges. A charming two storey two up two down Georgian Gothick cube. Three bay front elevation its openings with lancet heads, the glazing Y-tracery. Above the front door a central oculus window. There was a slated pyramidal roof, the chimney stack rising off the rear wall. Like the simple big square gate pillars, harled and whitewashed. The Victorians

R. Hamilton

unfortunately added an inappropriate gabled single storey hall with perforated wavy bargeboards.
**Roe Bridge Lodge** c1830
Built by Sir Francis Workman McNaghten of Bushmills House, Co Antrim (qv) who purchased the estate in 1826 from John Cromie of Cromore (qv) and renamed the house Roe Park. On the banks of a reach of the Roe river off the Londonderry Road, a rather typical late Georgian lodge. Single storey three bay symmetrical under an over-sized hipped roof. In sandstone ashlar the elevation to the road is canted. At the time of writing undergoing improvement which has seen the removal of an ugly Victorian hall but a re-roofing in unsympathetic synthetic slates. Two other lodges are insignificant and a fifth has been demolished.
NORTH DERRY; UAHS (1975);
MULLIN (1983)

**124. ROSEBROOK, Dungiven** c1845;
*demolished*
A lodge built for James Douglas.

**125. SALEM, Londonderry East**
(see FOYLE VIEW)

**126. ST COLUMB'S, Londonderry East**
pre 1830; *demolished*
A lodge for the Wray family.

**127. ST EUGENE'S R C CATHEDRAL, Londonderry West** 1904;
architect E J Toye

In the shadow of the great mass of J J McCarthy's cathedral completed in 1873 is a gate lodge. Like its Armagh and Monaghan (qqv) counterparts it was designed by another architect after McCarthy's death. Edward J Toye was a local man who, in addition to completing the spire to the cathedral, planned a sturdy High Victorian Picturesque style gate lodge of generous accommodation. One and a half storey on an L plan, it has large bargeboards curved to form trefoil motifs in the spandrels. The toes and eaves are supported on a distinctive curved bracket feature springing from a course of moulded stone. Faced in coursed slate with window dressings, quoins and chimney stacks in ashlar. The road gable has a single storey flat-roofed bay and that to the avenue a bipartite window having, like the other openings, a quarry-faced stone relieving arch over. Alongside this avenue gable advances a little gabled porch carried on a turned wooden post which shelters a double-leafed panelled front door in the internal angle. The ridge has perforated sawtooth red earthenware cresting.
ROWAN (1979)

**128. SEAVIEW, Londonderry East**
(see BAYVIEW)

**129. SOMERSET, Coleraine (3)**
On a stretch of the River Bann another fine estate "highly embellished by extensive plantations" with "Many walks ... also tastefully laid out", being overrun by the expanding town. None of the lodges were early enough to have been by the architect John Nash who is known to have been approached by John Richardson for designs which seem to have gone unexecuted. Indeed the house founded in 1732 and enlarged in 1822 remains modest and now derelict.
**"Coleraine Lodge"** pre 1849; *demolished*
**"Boat Lodge"** pre 1849; *demolished*
**"Macosquin Lodge"** pre 1904; *demolished*
OSM

**130. SPRINGHILL, Moneymore (2)**
Now a National Trust property this was the fine old house and demesne of the Lenox-Conyngham family. The house is thought to date from about 1680, but it was not until a century later that the main entrance was deemed to require supervision.
**Old Main Entrance** c1790

George Lenox-Conyngham succeeded to the property in 1788 and not long afterwards built a pair of Georgian Gothick porters' lodges whose gables faced each other across the avenue entrance. One of these has survived in the shape of a simple rectangular two roomed structure with steeply-pitched gables in the leading one of which is a wide door opening with a pointed head, like the windows to the side elevations. Above the door a minuscule lancet opening to light a bed loft. The walls are harled and whitewashed and a central single-flued chimney stack is set diagonally on the ridge. The nice old rubble entrance piers reflect the lodge with their pointed tops.
**Town Lodge** c1845

George's son William, at a new avenue approach, built a single storey Tudor Picturesque style lodge on an L plan. Ornamental gables have serrated bargeboards and a little gabled hall advances alongside the projection to the avenue. The harled walls have stone quoins and label mouldings to square paned windows. There is a pair of diagonally positioned brick chimney stacks straddling the ridge of a shallow-pitched roof. Sometime later the building was extended with a sympathetic new gabled wing.

**131. STRADREAGH, Londonderry East**
(see CAW COTTAGE)

**132. STRAIDARRAN LODGE, Feeny**
pre 1858; *demolished*
A picturesque park of the Hunter family.
GRIFFITH

**133. STRAW, Dungiven** pre 1905; *demolished*
A lodge opposite the gates built for John Semple.

**134. STREEVE, Limavady** 1833; *ruinous*
In 1833 Marcus Gage Esq "... built an entrance lodge and made a new avenue which winds round the base of a hill to the house". The lodge survives to this day albeit little more than a shell. Situated opposite the gate it is a tiny two roomed structure with an overall internal dimension of 19' 0" x 12' 0" (5.7m x 3.6m). Under a hipped roof the symmetrical three bay front elevation is in facing brick, just like the pleasant old house which was occupied by the Hemphill and Thornton families, leased by the Conollys. It passed to Marcus Gage at the turn of the 19th century and the demesne was subsequently absorbed into the neighbouring estate of Drenagh (qv) by the McCauslands.
OSM; MULLIN (1983)

**135. TALBOT, Londonderry West**
(see ABERFOYLE)

**136. TAMNAMONEY, Macosquin** pre 1849; *demolished*
A lodge built for the Irwin family in the 1840s to a house of c1758.
OSM

**137. THORNHILL, Londonderry West (2)**
Andrew Alexander Watt had in 1873 married Hester, the only sister of Hume Babington of Creevagh (qv) who was in partnership with the architect Thomas Turner. He could therefore look no further than the firm to prepare designs for a new mansion and lodge, the former to replace an earlier house on the property.

**Londonderry Lodge** c1885;
architects Turner and Babington

The big house of 1882-5 and the lodge, in similar Scots Baronial manner, show Turner to have been much more at home in the handling of Picturesque outline of smaller buildings. Alternatively Babington may have felt bound to prepare the plans of the house for his brother-in-law and this dreary pile reflects the engineering side of the practice. In squared uncoursed quarry-faced buff sandstone, there is dressed

*Willsborough, West Lodge*

ashlar to quoins, window dressings and the chamfered and friezed chimney stack. Single storey on a T plan a steeply-pitched gable to the road is crowstepped with two typical Turner features, a ball finial and an oculus opening, just as at Stormont Castle, Co Down (qv). The front door has a shouldered head. To the avenue projects the living room with a canted end below a semi-octahedral roof crowned by an elaborate metal finial. Not helped by a surround of bland bitmac. The extensive gate sweep is in the form of a balustrade with square main and intermediate piers having moulded steeply sloped caps to more ball finials. Replacing an earlier lodge of pre 1858 probably for William Leatham, miller.

**Muff Lodge** pre 1858; *demolished*
ROWAN (1979)

**138. TIEVTARA, Coleraine** c1877; architects Young and MacKenzie
A big late Victorian exercise in the Picturesque on an L plan. Part one and a half storey, part single storey. To the avenue gable a bargeboard supported by carved purlin ends, the ground floor window bipartite in an ornamental surround. To the road a tall hipped gable part of the roof of which is taken down in a catslide over a canted bay window. On the internal angle another catslide to form a canopy over the front door supported by a single post. The windows margined with rectangular panes in stuccoed walls. The roof has exposed rafter ends to the eaves and a massive friezed and capped stone chimney stack penetrates the ridge. The gate piers resemble the chimney and widely-spaced ornamental cast iron railings have fleur-de-lys tops. The house, like the lodge built for Hugh Anderson, wine and spirit merchant, is now Loretto Convent.
COLERAINE & PORTSTEWART;
UAHS (1972)

**139. TROY, Londonderry West** c1897
In contrast to the large over-ornate house of the same age is a relatively modest lodge of standard form. Three bay symmetrical with a hipped roof and high eaves. In black stone, the window dressings, quoins and corbelled chimney stack in raw red brick left over from the big house.

**140. UPPER CUMBER RECTORY, Claudy**
(see GLENALLA)

**141. UPPERLANDS, Maghera**
(see AMPERTAINE)

**142. WALWORTH, Ballykelly** pre 1849; *demolished*
A lodge to the house occupied by Rev G V Sampson in 1837.

**143. WARREN HILL, Londonderry East**
(see DUNNFIELD VILLA)

**144. WIGMORE, Aghadowey**
(see BALLYDEVITT)

**145. WILLSBOROUGH, Eglinton (2)**
**East Lodge** pre 1830; *demolished*
**West Lodge** c1845
A delightful little Picturesque gabled cottage. Single storey on an L plan, it has ornamental foil and wave bargeboards and hipknobs the same as Banagher Manse. There is a diminutive projecting hall with its own fancy bargeboards. In each main gable the Scott family bearings in the form of a shield with a mullet between two crescents, an escallop shell crest over, and the motto "PERGE" below. The lodge may formerly have been in stone or brick facings with label mouldings to the windows, but it has all been rendered over and painted primrose, bargeboards and all. The windows modernised.
Built by Major Thomas Scott.

# COUNTY MONAGHAN

**1. AGHAFIN, Rosslea** c1835

I.O.G. Perrott

A charming little lodge opposite the gates apparently single storey, three bay symmetrical but in fact having a lower ground floor below road level. Under a shallow pitched wide-eaved hipped roof are nice rustic whitewashed harled walls. The panelled front door is flanked by tiny windows with lower heads to Picturesque cast iron, centre pivot, lattice glazed lights. The building remains occupied, its pretty rustic front elevation sensitively preserved. A property in the early 19th century of the Philips family.

**2. AGHERLANE, Ballybay** pre 1835; *demolished*

A lodge to the Lucas family demesne.

**3. AGHNAMALLAGH, Smithborough (2)**

**Rear Entrance** c1820

A two roomed single storey three bay symmetrical cottage with wide windows in harled brick walls. Steeply- pitched roof. Derelict.

**Front Entrance** c1840

Contemporary with the present Regency style house is this lodge of the Mayne family, opposite a good cast iron gate screen with a pair of flanking wickets and octagonal posts crowned with small urns. The gatekeeper's accommodation is typical single storey under a hipped roof with scrolled carved brackets arranged in pairs to the eaves. The three bay front elevation not quite symmetrical.

**4. ANKETELL GROVE, Emyvale** c1855

Visible from the road a highly individual house of the Anketell family. The main avenue on an axis with the front door. At the base of this avenue a relatively modest lodge. In uncoursed squared ashlar, on a standard plan the eaves is high to accommodate two attic bedrooms in the hipped roof, lit by skylights. Three bay, the centre one a gabled breakfront hall, which displays the family monogram on a shield. Over the shield the rough outline of a coronet left unsculpted, expectations obviously not having been realised. Openings in simple dressed stone with lugged heads. Two simple octagonal gate posts survive. The lodge lies empty, chimney stack and windows recently replaced inharmoniously. Built by Matthew John Anketell upon his father's death in 1851.
BENCE-JONES (1988)

**5. ANNAGHMAKERRIG, Newbliss**

A Georgian gentleman's villa called Leysborough by a pretty lough of the same name, was transformed into a shaped gable Tudorbethan style house. At least one lodge appears to date from the time of these building operations by the Moorhead family who had purchased the property in 1802.

**White Gates Lodge** c1845;
architect perhaps J B Keane

A pretty one and a half storey two up two down, gabled lodge in the Tudor Picturesque manner. In uncoursed squared basalt its three bay front dressed in red brick the windows having label mouldings over. A variety of glazing patterns, to the front elevation flamboyant curved cast iron identical to the Cottage Orné lodge at Castle Leslie (qv) and Annaghroe, Co Tyrone (qv). Below the square-paned attic gable window a canted bay with a half umbrello roof. A rather uninspired modern sun-lounge spoils the effect.

**Lynch's Lodge** pre 1857

Originally a one and a half storey lodge now altered and extended into something utterly shapeless. In 1859 Sir William James Tyrone Power married Sarah, the Moorhead heiress and upon the death of his father-in-law he made many late Victorian improvements on the estate. To designs of the young Dublin architectural practice of George Henderson and Albert Edward Murray he altered and extended the house, built outbuildings, ornamental estate workers' cottages and added a new porter's lodge by the lakeside entrance.

**Lake Lodge** c1875;
architects Henderson and Murray

In contrast to the brick-dressed blackstone cottages the lodge, replacing a pre 1835 predecessor on the site, is distinctive in red brick facings with sandstone dressings, quoins and a cill course which embraces the building. In a highly innovative Gothic Revival style, it is one and a half storey, three bay with tall eaves to a hipped gable roof carried down beyond the central projecting hall in a catslide to be carried on brackets. Flanking this are tall slit windows with pointed heads, repeated on the roadside gable. To the opposing facade a canted bay window with pretty hexagonal latticed panes to pivoting openers. In the gable over an oculus light. Squat chimney on the ridge which has earthenware sawtooth cresting stopped by cast iron finials. The square stone pillars with faintly oriental concave pointed cappings look to date from an earlier building phase on this beautiful demesne best known for its connections with Tyrone Power and Sir Tyrone Guthrie, now a workplace for artists, named after the latter.
P.R.O.N.I. D3585/D/11

**6. AVALREAGH, Castleshane** pre 1858

An unremarkable lodge.

**7. BALLYBAY, Ballybay (4)**

A house of the Leslie family burnt down in the 1920s, is survived by one gate lodge near the town, the other three, all pre 1858 having been demolished.

**Town Lodge** c1835;
architect possibly J B Keane

Presumably designed not long after the house of 1830, Charles Albert Leslie continued to improve the estate until his death in 1838.
A lodge to standard plan under a hipped roof with widespread eaves carried on carved paired brackets. Ashlar walls now rendered with projecting stone quoins. The avenue elevation is symmetrical three bay with bracketed window cills, whilst that to the road has a tripartite "Wyatt" window. Good large piers with four pedimented cappings and ogee railed sweeps. The whole estate is in a dilapidated state having been sold in lots in 1926.
BENCE-JONES (1988); LIVINGSTONE (1980)

**8. BALLYBAY RECTORY, Ballybay** pre 1858; *demolished*

The park also known as Lakeview had a long-serving incumbent, Rev Hercules Langrishe who probably built the lodge.

**9. BALLYLECK, Monaghan**
(see ROSSMORE CASTLE)

**10. BALLYMACKNEY, Carrickmacross** pre 1859

An unremarkable standard, three bay building perhaps erected by Mr Samuel Wainwright. The property was previously that of the Marquis of Bath's agent.

**11. BALLYNAHONE, Emyvale** pre 1835

Secreted up a humble approach from the public road is this tiny deserted overgrown gate lodge. Single storey gabled and constructed in rubble stone its leading elevation three bay not quite symmetrical with minute sash windows. In 1858 a property of John Pringle. Abandoned.
GRIFFITH

**12. BALLYNURE, Clones** pre 1858; *demolished*

A lodge for the Forster family.

**13. BATH ESTATE, Carrickmacross** c1835

The estates of the Marquesses of Bath which never had a major residence for the proprietor but was endowed with many architecturally sophisticated buildings including Tudor Picturesque workers' cottages of which this is an unusually substantial example. A one and a half storey gatehouse, its three bay symmetrical ground floor main elevation has a gabled canopy to the front door. Its mildly decorative bargeboards repeated in those of two gablets over which break the eaves line of the hipped roof. All immaculately restored and maintained, it is built in random coursed rubble with dressed masonry quoins. An oriel window on the side facade surveys a later pair of carriage gates hung on the most ornamental of hollow cast iron piers.

**14. BEECH HILL, Monaghan** pre 1858; *demolished*
Of this lodge for the Murray family there is no sign.

**15. BESSMOUNT PARK, Monaghan (2)** both c1850
For long the demesne of the Montgomerys. The fantastic house of the Hatchell family contrasting with two rather disappointingly mundane mid-Victorian lodges, one opposite the main avenue entrance.

**16. BLAYNEY CASTLE, Castleblayney (4)**
Originally the estates of the Lords Blayney, one lodge of that era remains.

**Dundalk Road Entrance** c1835
Probably built by Cadwallader, 12th and last Earl, upon his succession in 1832. A standard plan, single storey, three bay building under a hipped roof which is supported to the front external corners by posts set into recesses. This has a picturesque effect in forming a projecting front door on the main elevation which faces the road. In 1853 Cadwallader sold the estates to Henry Thomas Hope of Deepdene, Surrey whose father, Thomas, was a great exponent of Neo-Classicism and would have approved of his son's improvements which include the next lodge to be built on the estate.

**West Street Lodge** c1860; architect not known

"The approach to the house is by a neat gate from the end of West Street." The 1835 OS Memoir hardly applies today for here stands a remarkable composition making a Neo-Classical statement. Two huge square stone pillars of V-jointed blocks below top heavy corniced cappings are crowned with globe shaped lanterns and carry highly ornate cast iron gates. On either side linked by railings facing each other across the street are two big Classical houses. Two storey, the upper floors in mellow brick with dressed stone entablature and quoins, and moulded window architraves to three window openings. The ground floor is stone rusticated in V-jointing like the pillars and carried around into the voussoirs of three semicircular- headed windows with bracketed cills, grouped as an arcade. The rustication is carried through single storey projecting porches as are plinth and entablature, to the pillars, thus uniting the composition. Quite what the alternative function of this accommodation was, beyond housing a porter, is not clear. The estates through marriage in 1861 descended to the 6th Duke of Newcastle, Henry Pelham Alexander Pelham-Clinton who instigated further improvements on the beautifully wooded and watered park, which included many estate workers' houses and a further porter's lodge.

**Church Street Lodge** 1877; architect not known
At the end of a terrace of one and a half storey mid-Victorian Picturesque workers' cottages, a substantial two storey gatekeeper's house. In robust style, built of uncoursed squared quarry-faced basalt, contrasting dressed stone to quoins, toothed window dressings and roll-moulded

heads to openings, much as at the later Virginia Park lodge (qv) in Co Cavan. The two ground floor windows on to the street flank a projection, which houses the datestone, and widens on corbels to carry a first floor bay with bipartite windows. Over this a gable that has bargeboards with ornamental fretted overlay fillets, perforated trefoil toes, and a spiky hipknob. These features are repeated on the side elevation gable but with the addition of a collar and post feature. Below this a plaque with roll- moulded frame which houses a cryptic monogram that could be deciphered as an 'H' for Hope and perhaps a stylised 'N' for Newcastle. Behind the gate screen on the side elevation a segmental arch to the porch has the front door within the recess. Two big chimney stacks in ashlar on plinths with friezes and cornices pass through an earthenware crested ridge. Alongside, and parallel with, the street facade a pair of large stone entry pillars of channelled blocks each surmounted by a cornice and blocked capping which carried a finial of which only the stem remains intact.

**Connabury Lodge** pre 1835; *demolished*
Rendered redundant by the coming of the railway which followed the line of the avenue at that point. The Dukes of Newcastle finally deserted their Irish seat in 1916 after which the house became a convent. The demesne once comprising 2500 acres surrounding Mucknoo Lough is now a public park.
O.S.M.; DEBRETT (1920)

**17. BRANDRUM, Monaghan** pre 1835; *demolished*
The lodge built for the Cole family.

**18. CALLENBERG, Louth** pre 1859
Derelict and unremarkable.

**19. CAMLA VALE, Monaghan** c1830

The lodge, like the now demolished house, in elegant Classical style, would appear to have been erected upon Lieut-Colonel Henry Westenra buying the property from the Montgomery family. He was a younger brother of Lord Rossmore whose estates adjoined (qv). A large three bay single storey structure in pleasant coursed squared rubble, the square paned windows set into recesses formed by wide panels. In striking contrast the pure white painted distyle Doric pedimented portico shelters the double leaf panelled front door, flanked by narrow sidelights. Two stone chimney stacks crown a shallow hipped roof carried on moulded brackets, the eaves of which has recently applied ogee guttering. Now returned to domestic use but the RIC arms in the tympanum testify to another function.

**20. CAPRAGH LODGE, Carrickmacross** pre 1859; *ruinous*
A lodge built for James Reid.

**21. CARNAVEAGH, Ballybay** pre 1858; *demolished*

**22. CARRICKMACROSS DISTILLERY, Carrickmacross** pre 1835; *demolished*
To the maltings of Messrs Gartlan & Sons of whom Thomas McEvoy Gartlan of Monalty (qv) was one. By 1837 producing 200,000 gallons of spirit annually. The buildings were of 1823 foundation, from which time the lodge may have dated.
LEWIS (1837)

**23. CASSAUGH MOUNE, Aughnacloy** pre 1835; *demolished*
The lodge to the demesne of Mr Wardlow Johnston. Probably built when he acquired the property from the Anketells when it was known as Ivy Hill.

**24. CASTLE LESLIE OR GLASLOUGH CASTLE, Glaslough (6)**
In 1800 Colonel Charles Powell Leslie succeeded to the estate of upwards of 1000 acres adjoining Glaslough village and encompassing a lake of the same name. He inherited a "mansion of considerable grandeur" but not a gate lodge of any description. This he and his sons, within the space of three quarters of a century, proceeded spectacularly to put to rights with the most important and varied series of porters' lodge buildings in the Province if not in Ireland, all to a magnificent wooded backdrop.

**The Gothick Entrance** c1812; architect John Nash

Being a neighbour and contemporary of Du Pre Alexander, 2nd Lord Caledon, Colonel Leslie must have been impressed and envious of continuing improvements there under the guidance of John Nash the eminent English Regency architect, and in particular of the pair of Classical lodges. Doubtless Leslie met Nash on a round of house visiting parties. No commission was too humble for the architect to put his hand to and the outcome was this Gothic Revival lodge and gatescreen much in the manner of his work at Longner Hall, Shropshire. In good ashlar masonry the gates flanked by convex wall quadrants, the central carriageway arch four centred and hood-moulded below a crenellated parapet between octagonal turrets. The convex section finials are just like medieval jesters' hats and similar to those on the porte-cochère at Killymoon Castle, Co Tyrone (qv). On each side two small pedestrian wicket gates with flat arches and label mouldings, similarly castellated over with outer smaller octagonal turrets. The wrought iron gates are suitably flamboyant, echoing the lodge behind. This would be little more than a basic two roomed single storey lodge were it not for its remarkable disguise, the leading gable being a facade containing an Early English Gothic pointed church window with decorated tracery. Above this is a castellated gable framed by more octagonal turrets, this time with concave section finials by way of variety. A delightful and amusing folly in ashlar. Colonel Leslie's son of the same name was to continue the lodge building programme with a further three designs, two of which were executed.

**The Cottage Orné Entrance** c1840; architect not known

A substantial single storey lodge in the form of a beautiful fairy tale cottage. Double fronted with canted projections, on each side of the front door, over which half umbrello roofs extend to form a continuous verandah supported on slender iron pillars, the eaves decorated by hanging honeysuckle ornament. The double leaf front door and windows have pretty curvilinear patterned cast iron glazing bars under segmental heads all identical to those at Annaghroe, Co Tyrone (qv) nearby and similar to Tullyvin and Stradone (qqv) in County Cavan. The walls are whitewashed stucco. From what may have been a thatched roof, now slated, rise two pairs of octagonal chimney stacks. The stone gate piers are chamfered with recessed panels to each face between moulded plinths and cornices with domed cappings, the same as at Castleshane (qv) in the same county. Good cast iron gates in a wide screen.

**The Tudor Picturesque Entrance** c1845; architect probably William Murray

A one and half storey building originally a land agent's house and a dairy. Situated at the northernmost demesne entrance on which it turns its back. Spacious accommodation on an E plan formed by two advancing wings which flank the central single storey projecting hall. The hall has a skewtable gable with kneelers in contrast to the ornamental bargeboards elsewhere. Comprised of two "continuous brackets" scrolled to clasp a central carved shield. This is repeated on a smaller scale to the gablets. This bargeboard design is to be found also at Learmount Castle, Co Londonderry (qv) and The Pavilion, Co Armagh (qv). One wing is in brick facings suggesting it to be a later extension to the original in squared coursed rubble, the windows having toothed ashlar dressings. Unfortunately few of the former transomed and mullioned lattice lights remain intact, and there is a silly DIY fanlighted front door. Not all the octagonal stone chimney pots survive. About 1847 the demesne wall was built to provide much needed famine relief.

**The Castellated Romantic Entrance** 1854; architect Alfred G Jones; *unexecuted*

Retained amongst family records is a drawing for a vast entrance complex on the scale of that at Markree Castle, Co Sligo, from which the architect may have gained inspiration and which was published in Francis Goodwin's *Rural Residences* of 1835. A central group of elements gives an irregular outline. The porte-cochère carriage entrance was to have been below

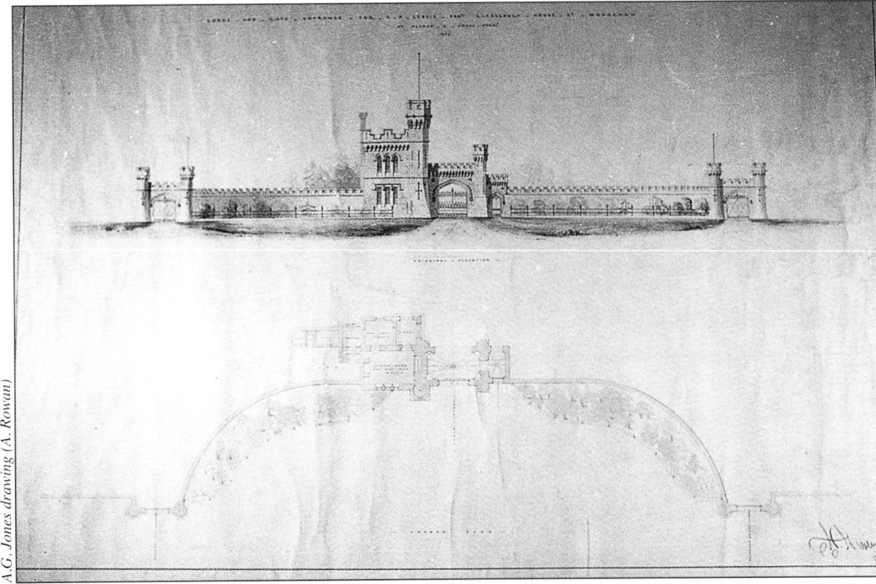
*A.G. Jones drawing (A. Rowan)*

hood- moulded four-centred Tudor arches, machicolated and crenellated aloft, a groin vaulted ceiling within. To its right separated by a battered octagonal turret a smaller wicket gate porch, and on its left a grand flagstaff tower 45' 0" (13.5m) high housing a spiral staircase, lit by loopholes. The porter's accommodation of generous proportions on two levels. On the ground floor, pantry, scullery, bedroom, entrance porch and large living room 18' 0" x 13' 0" (5.5m x 4.0m) over which, a grand bedroom of the same dimensions. Lit by tripartite windows at both levels, the lower flat arched with label mouldings, the upper lancets hood moulded. The whole suitably machicolated with stepped battlements, Irish style. Great sweeping concave castellated walls form a forecourt, landscaped by Ninian Niven who has countersigned the drawing. Niven was a landscape architect and disciple of J C Loudon, who had come to Ireland and worked on the Leslie estate as early as 1843. The wall sweeps terminate in secondary gates flanked by round turrets. Quite where this complex, which would have extended to 100 yards (90m), was to have been located is not known. It may have been for financial reasons that it remained a Romantic dream. Charles Powell Leslie died in 1871 to be succeeded by his younger brother John who seven years later became the first Baronet. He had planned extensive rebuilding on the estate and wasted no time in engaging the Belfast architectural practice of Lanyon, Lynn and Lanyon. Partner in charge was William Henry Lynn whose first commission was for a memorial in the village to John's elder brother. Drawings for the grand new mansion house testify to John Leslie being the most demanding of clients, not to say indecisive. Having discarded designs in French Renaissance, High Jacobean and Scots Baronial, as well as for extensions to the existing house, eventually a sort of Italianate-Scots Baronial hybrid was settled upon. By this time however (1872) Lynn had resigned from the practice, a decision probably influenced by the frustration of having to work on such a tight rein. Building operations eventually commenced in 1874 reaching completion five years later, during which time Sir John Leslie had also had time to consider further gate lodges for the estates and his ideas can be seen in the form of sketches by him, and retained in family papers.

**The Scots Baronial Entrance** c1875; architects: Lanyon and Lanyon

Situated at the head of Glaslough's main street a semidetached pair of estate houses, double crowstepped gables to the fore. One and a half storey, each two up two down, symmetrical

about a dressed stone chimney stack. The composition is flanked by single storey projecting hallways with little crowstepped gables of their own. In squared coursed quarry-faced stone, only one pretty arcaded Y-traceried sash window survives. To the left are the entrance gates with rusticated ball finials to the piers, beyond which the avenue leads to the dower house in matching style.

**The Jacobean Entrance** c1878; architects Lanyon and Lanyon

Here again, as in the village entrance, are clear signs of John Lanyon's mastery of the small Romantic composition. A large lodge with high ceilings on a complex plan, shaped gables predominating. Dressed stone to skewtable gables, transomed and mullioned windows, quoins and tall channelled chimney stacks. Otherwise all faced in squared, coursed, quarry-faced stone. One chimney breast rises up the roadside gable to display the Leslie coat-of-arms,

repeated on the avenue gable, alongside which projects a smaller hallway gable that sports the monogram of John Leslie and the motto "GRIP FAST". The steeply pitched roofs have earthenware sawtooth cresting and the distinctive carved apex finials repeated from the house are also to be found on the lodge to Kintullagh, Co Antrim (qv) by the same architects. The gate screen is huge with ogee curved railings leading to two wicket gates and main carriage entrance hung on tall square stone pillars with fluted friezes and steep concave pyramidal cappings supporting rusticated ball finials. The terminating pillars are banded, the gates and matching railings highly decorative cast iron.
DIXON (1972); ALISTAIR ROWAN PHOTOGRAPH Ref 73 0961 34

**25. CASTLESHANE, Monaghan (3)**
The Rt Hon Edward Lucas erected a large square, gabled and chimneyed Elizabethan style pile completed in 1836 and with it a complementary entrance on the main road.

**Main Entrance** c1835;
architect not known

"... a handsome entrance lodge in the later English style of architecture, and forming an interesting object as seen from the new line of road winding through the valley". Thus wrote Samuel Lewis in 1837, a rare occasion indeed for him to be moved to record an estate entrance. This was clearly a novelty for its time, a Picturesque Tudor one and a half storey building on an L plan with a lower porch in the internal angle. Although much "improved" and extended, many of its Picturesque features having been discarded, two gables retain their decorative foiled bargeboards. The elevation to the avenue has a single storey canted bay window which must, like the others, have had lattice panes in chamfered openings. The pretty double gabled porch has Tudor arches like the entrance doorway. The building perhaps formerly in facing brick with stone dressings, is rendered, the dominant Tudor Revival chimney stacks taken away. The entrance pillars are identical to those at the Castle Leslie Cottage Orné entrance (qv), which suggests a common designer, although unknown, well versed in the Picturesque. Chamfered stone, recessed panels to faces between moulded plinth and cornice, with domed cappings. Good cast iron railings and gates also survive the improver intact.

**Rear Entrance** pre 1835; *demolished*

**Monaghan Entrance** c1820/c1835

Once the entrance to the previous "... ancient mansion in a highly embellished demesne ...". Originally a two bay, two roomed single storey lodge with simple paired timber sash windows, gable entrance and central chimney. Sometime later extended by two bays with wide lattice paned windows. Harled and whitewashed now under a corrugated iron roof, it faces the road without a semblance of entrance gates. The big house was burned down in 1920.
LEWIS (1837); BENCE-JONES (1988); BURKE (1855)

**26. CLONCALLICK, Clones** c1850
Mean two roomed, single storey accommodation. Unprepossessing below a hipped roof, the short elevation to the avenue contains only the door opening. Constructed in rubble stone with red brick dressings. Situated outside the gates.

**27. COOLDERRY, Kingscourt** pre 1835; *ruinous*
A lodge to the now demolished house of the Brownlows.

**28. COOLSHANNAGH GLEBE, Monaghan** pre 1835; *demolished*

**29. CORFAD, Rockcorry** pre 1835
A commonplace building probably for Mr James McCullagh. Now derelict.

**30. CORNACASSA, Monaghan** c1820

This fine demesne has been broken up and its dignified early 19th century residence of Dacre Hamilton demolished. Probably contemporary with the big house, this splendid little gate lodge's original role is no longer clear as it has been engulfed by 20th century housing and has lost its entrance avenue and gate sweep opposite, swept away by road widening. Essentially a standard single storey symmetrical three bay composition below a hipped roof, raised out of the ordinary by its unusually wide windows. Each opening contains a sophisticated tripartite light, its sash boxes faced with recessed panel miniature Classical pilasters carrying a carved entablature. There are elegant carved scrolled brackets to the eaves. The internal hall is semicircular on plan with curved sheeted doors to each room. Now roughcast on a stone plinth, it has been sympathetically extended by a bay with the original side window incorporated. A new plastic "Georgian" front door is not entirely inappropriate.
YOUNG (1909); BENCE-JONES (1988)

**31. CORTOLVIN HILLS, Monaghan**
(see ROSSMORE CASTLE)

**32. CREEVE, Ballybay (2)** both pre 1835; *both demolished*
Two lodges for the Cunningham family.

**33. CREMORNE, Ballybay** pre 1858; *demolished*
The lodge built for Mr John Jackson.

**34. DARTREY (formerly DAWSON'S GROVE) Cootehill (8)**
A once proud and beautiful estate extending from near Cootehill to Rockcorry, planted and embellished with fine architecture and lakes. Now tragically suffering from all manner of indignities, vandalism (official and otherwise), deforestation and afforestation. Richard Dawson purchased the lands granted to Cromwellian soldiers and it was his great grandson Thomas, created Baron Dartrey in 1770 and Baron Cremorne in 1797, who built the grand Georgian house, Dawson's Grove, about 1760 and erected the fine mausoleum ten years later to designs by James Wyatt. He continued, before his death in 1813, along with his nephew Richard Thomas to furnish the estates to include, "... several exceedingly neat and ornamental farm houses. They are all built of brick, two stories [sic] high". Eight years after this comment by Sir Charles Coote in 1801, Thomas Bell, architect and artist of Dublin notes "Dawson Grove on the opposite side of the river seems to vie in natural beauties with Bellamont Forest though during the minority of the present owner they have been too much neglected. The Mansion House is an elegant structure. There has been much taste displayed in the erection of lodges and gatehouses throughout the Grove". Some of these survive to this day in varying degrees of dilapidation.

**Cootehill Entrance** c1805; *ruinous*

Lord Cremorne was obviously as taken with the novel new decorative material of Coade stone as landowners throughout the British Isles. Items of Coade were in position on the estate by 1811 and crowning the pyramidal roof of this lodge is a fine funerary urn in the material. It is hung with swags, to a design by Sir William Chambers, and once acted as an elaborate chimney pot. Opposite the entrance gates and on an eminence approached by a flight of steps, the lodge is single storey on a cruciform plan formed by recesses at each corner, the roof carried on four Tuscan columns. The walls in brick, the main facade overlooking the gates once had a Wyatt window. In the right hand recess was the doorway with a Coade keystone over, decorated by the mask of a jolly bearded and bald chap. Framed by tall concave wall sweeps in maroon brick, four tall ashlar pillars once carried central carriage gates and two flanking wicket entrances. Now damaged, the two central pillars taken away.

**Church Lodge** c1800; *demolished*
Facing the gates at a distance within, a single storey four bay lodge under a hipped roof. In brick with segmental heads, the casement windows latticed paned. Recently removed to make way for a modern bungalow. Two very fine tall and slender gate pillars in ashlar survive. Of about 1790 their friezes have eight- petalled flower ornaments to two faces, and swags to the others. Above, the moulded cornices now minus their finials. Nice simple contemporary wrought iron gates. The entrance to Kilcrow Church.

**North Lodge** c1805
A pretty brick lodge under a shallow pyramidal roof rising to a central stack. Another of the lodges noted by Bell on his *Rambles Northwards*, single storey, three bay again with wide Wyatt window openings, sometime after having the Georgian panes replaced with a more fashionable decorative cast iron lattice type. To complement this is a wooden trellis ornament hung from the extended eaves. The front door, formerly central, bricked up and moved to a new lean-to structure at one end.

**Inner Lough Lodge** c1830
A pleasant single storey three bay lodge with a hipped roof, hides behind what remains of the tall estate wall. In mellow brick, the narrow entrance doorway has a segmental head, between two rectangular Wyatt window openings, the mullions with console brackets. The Georgian squared-pane sashes survive. Dawson's Grove was uninhabited for some years, and the neglect noted by Bell suggests that Richard Dawson had overspent. By 1846 though another Richard Dawson, 3rd Baron Cremorne, later to be the 1st Earl of Dartrey, with the family fortunes clearly replenished planned the replacement of the out-dated Georgian mansion with something in new fangled mode. His father had not long before bought the neighbouring demesne of Fairfield Park from T C Stewart Corry to extend the estates. Richard chose as his architect that prolific domestic designer William Burn, a Scot who was happiest working in the Tudor Revival style, and here he was afforded full rein not only

W. Burn perspective (R.I.B.A.)

*Dartrey, The Tudor Revival Lodges*

with the vast mansion but in two very ornamental entrance gates, neither of which was executed.

**The Tudor Revival Lodges (2)** 1846;
architect William Burn; *unexecuted*
Whether these were alternative designs for a single main entrance or for two separate gates is not known but both were in lavish Jacobean Revival style to complement the house. Both featured a single storey lodge with a distant pavilion, united by elaborate entrance gates, one with a triumphal archway preceded by a lion and unicorn rampant, the other with elegant Renaissance Baroque niched central pillars. The lodges were to be a riot of every conceivable device, shaped and Dutch gables, strapwork, balustraded parapets, coats of arms, mullioned windows with hexagonal-paned lights, "morgenstern" finials as at Clandeboye, Co Down (qv), tall octagonal chimney pots, fish-scale slates and much else besides. Here was Burn at his most flamboyant. In the event a fire at the house during construction, which necessitated considerable rebuilding focused the client's attention on his finances and he settled for two relatively modest ornamental bargeboard designs instead.

**Main Entrance** c1847;
architect probably William Burn
A two up two down, one and a half storey structure, three bay symmetrical. The centre bay a breakfront porch with very steeply-pitched roof, Tudor archway and blank shield over. All in ashlar stone, unlike the rest of the lodge, which is in Flemish bond facing brickwork. Timber transomed and mullioned windows with

*Dartrey, Main Entrance*

their cast iron lattice panes now removed. The wooden bargeboard carved into prickly wave patterns with hipknobs and quatrefoil toe ends. Two little brick chimney stacks sit diagonally, alongside one another, broaching off square bases. Later extensive back return in matching style. Gate screen missing.

**Rockcorry Entrance** c1847;
architect probably William Burn
The furthest north of the lodges, located at the other side of the entrance from a lodge (pre 1835) to Fairfield Park which it replaced. The original gatesweep of about 1820 survives, tall concave quadrant stone walls connect to Classical rusticated ashlar pillars with corniced

*Dartrey, The Tudor Revival Lodges*

W. Burn perspective (R.I.B.A.)

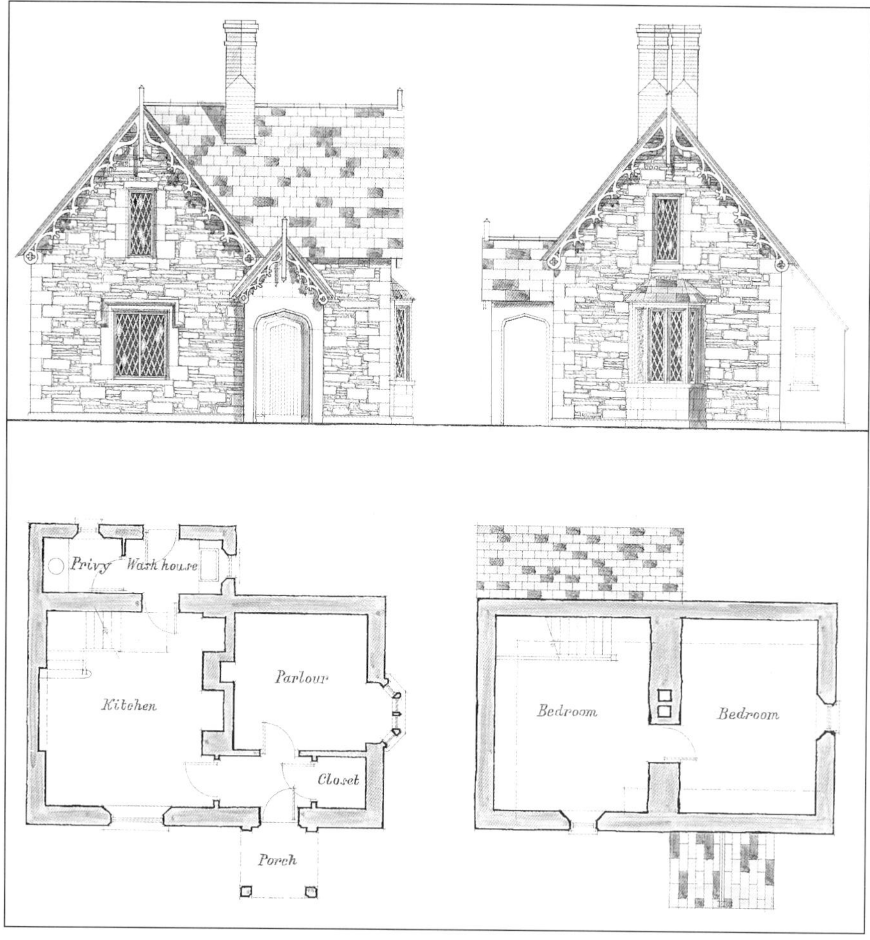

*Dartrey, Rockcorry Entrance*

and blocked cappings. The porter's lodge very much as the main entrance, in Picturesque Tudor bargeboard style, but irregular in appearance with the left hand bay gabled and a projecting ashlar porch slightly offset, with Tudor arches. Here the material is dark grey uncoursed slate rubble with ashlar quoins. To the far gable a single storey canted bay window, views the park rather than the entrance. Chimneys as at the main entrance but at right angles to the ridge. Bargeboards in startling red paint. This pretty little building lies deserted demanding an unobtrusive extension to the rear and reoccupation. The mansion was demolished in 1948, the stable blocks are disintegrating, the mausoleum and its sculpture vandalised, much of the wall removed, the lovely demesne raped, and the Earldom extinct.
COOTE (1801); O'LOINGSIGH (1965); O.S.M.; DEBRETT (1920); RIBA DRAWINGS COLLECTION (AF3 VOL 2: 19 & 20); I.A.A.; KELLY (1990)

**35. DAWSON'S GROVE, Cootehill**
(see DARTREY)

**36. DONAGHMOYNE, Carrickmacross**
c1900
An unusual lodge which had a predecessor on the same site. Bulky one and a half storey with clipped gables, three bay but not quite symmetrical. Casement windows, square paned to the top half only, tripartite with stone label moulding curved in the centre to form a sort of Venetian feature. The walls harled, there was a late Victorian carved gabled timber porch, part glazed. The roof slates reducing towards the ridge with apologetic chimney stacks to each gable. Probably built for a Mr Richard Bolton.

**37. DRUMARD, Clones** pre 1834;
*demolished*
The lodge built by a William Cochrane on a site surrounded by Co Fermanagh.

*Donaghmoyne*

**38. DRUMBREAN COTTAGE, Newbliss**
pre 1835; *demolished*
The lodge to the house occupied by T Phillips in 1837.

**39. DRUMFALDRA, Ballybay** c1835
A standard two roomed single storey lodge with a hipped roof. The main two bay elevation to the road has square-paned sash tripartite "Wyatt" windows in whitewashed walls with toothed stone quoins.Crude square carriage piers alongside. Probably built for Mr John Cunningham.

**40. DRUMREASKE, Monaghan**
pre 1835/c1840/c1870

A lodge perhaps of three periods opposite the gates. Initially a simple symmetrical three bay single storey gabled lodge, sometime around 1840 extended to form a Tudor Revival cottage composition, in keeping with the house for Mr Henry Mitchell. To the right was added a one and a half storey structure with gable to the road, a wide gabled single storey hall projecting alongside to unite and form a Picturesque outline. The bargeboards pretty carved foil affairs with corkscrew pendants to the toes. In harled walls, the windows square paned under label mouldings, as in the wide door opening with double leaves and side lights. In about 1870 the property was acquired by William Francis de Vismes Kane who made his mark with the insertion of his coat of arms in a shield above the doorway, "three salmon fishes rising as if to breathe". Two tall chimney stacks, dentilled, corbelled and diagonally set were built in red brick, along with a rather paltry and inept bay window. Very quaint but in need of upkeep.
BURKE (1904)

**41. DUNGILLICK, Emyvale** pre 1835;
*ruinous*
A minute three bay two roomed lodge opposite the gates for Roger Anketell.

**42. DUNRAYMOND, Rockcorry** pre 1835;
*demolished.*

**43. FAIRFIELD PARK, Rockcorry**
(see DARTREY)

**44. FARMOYLE, Cootehill** pre 1835;
*demolished*
In 1837 the property of Lieut-Col Kerr. Previously called Mountain Lodge.

**45. FOREST VIEW, Cootehill** pre 1834;
*demolished*

**46. FORT JOHNSTON, Emyvale** pre 1834;
*demolished*
A lodge opposite the gates, for the Johnston family.

**47. FORT SINGLETON, Emyvale (2)**
both pre 1835; *both demolished*
Both lodges built for the Singletons.

**48. FREAMEMOUNT, Cootehill** pre 1858; *demolished*
A gate lodge built for a Mr Mayne was a standard plan, single storey, three bay harled building below a hipped roof.

**49. GALLANAGH, Monaghan** pre 1858; *demolished*
Only cast iron gate posts remain of c1880. Off-the-shelf castings much as those at Ballyedmond, Co Down (qv) and Trewmount, Co Tyrone (qv). The cappings in the form of little pyramidal roofs with their own dormers. A property in 1858 of William Watson.

**50. GLASLOUGH CASTLE, Glaslough**
(see CASTLE LESLIE)

**51. GLENBURN COTTAGE, Rockcorry**
pre 1858
The lodge formerly on the site was erected by T C Stewart Corry after selling neighbouring Fairfield Park (qv). Sometime around 1870 it was reworked or rebuilt by Mr Allan Murray, in red brick. Mildly Picturesque.

**52. GLINCH, Newbliss (2)**
Two lodges built by the Thompson family, neither of which has the look of Sir Richard Morrison's work unlike the elegant villa.

**West Lodge** c1830
Opposite the entrance on the Clones Road the ubiquitous single storey, three bay, two roomed lodge under a hipped roof, typical late Georgian format. Plain and abandoned.

**East Lodge** c1840/c1880
The original tiny standard lodge with a hipped roof remains as an adjunct to the later one which fronts it. Gabled three bay symmetrical, the front door in a gabled breakfront with a "mouth-organ" fanlight. The flanking windows transomed and mullioned, their timber lights with rectangular panes. Brick dressed rubble walls. In an advanced stage of decay.

**53. GOLAGH, Scotshouse (2)**
An important villa, striking with its central attic lantern built in 1742 by the Wright family, sadly burnt down in 1920 and subsequently demolished. "The principal approach is by a straight avenue of oak and elm", or so it was in 1855 but now lost without trace. This avenue led from a lodge built for James Woodwright who as plain James Wood had married Elizabeth Isabella Wright.

**Front Entrance** c1820
Opposite what appears at first sight as a traditional single storey symmetrical three bay harled lodge below its hipped roof, is in fact a two storey building its basement hidden below road level with its own three bay rear facade. Closer inspection also reveals a recessed centre bay to the main front containing a sophisticated Classical wooden doorcase of recessed panel pilasters and little entablature. Given a further sense of moment by an approach of two wide stone steps. Flanked by segmentally-headed windows with paired sashes. Deserted.

**Side Entrance** pre 1835
A building noted on the first O.S. Map as a "Schoolhouse", it would also have had the dual function of monitoring the toing and froing opposite. Looking just like a lodge with its three bay symmetrical front, single storey below a gabled roof. Plain but occupied.
BURKE (1855)

**54. GORT GRANARD, Newbliss** pre 1835; *demolished*
A lodge built for Major T C Graham.

**55. HILTON PARK, Clones (2)**
A grand mansion and estates of the Madden family one of whom, Samuel, had restored the house after a fire in 1804, his son Colonel John adding two lodges not long after his succession in 1814.

**Town Lodge** c1825
Simple single storey, two roomed building. Roof with hipped gables.

**Main Entrance** c1825
A one and a half storey, two up two down harled version of the above. Located on an elevated site within the estate a fair distance from the gates upon which it keeps a wary cyclopic eye in the form of a lunette window below the leading hipped gable. Below it the front door sheltered under a pretty Regency style canopy supported on decorative cast iron trellis work. Like the hood moulding to the lunette this may have been added when the mansion was refaced and new entrance gates provided in 1872 by the Colonel's son, also John. Convex wall sweeps frame four square cast iron posts which carry central double carriage gates and flanking wickets. The outer posts topped by spiked ball finials, the inner ones having splendid Madden falcons, wings flapping, rising from coronets.
YOUNG (1909); BENCE-JONES (1988)

**56. INISHDEVLIN, Emyvale** pre 1834; *demolished*

**57. IVY HILL, Aughnacloy**
(see CASSAUGH MOUNE)

**58. KILLEEVAN GLEBE, Newbliss** c1845
A one and a half storey, two up two down lodge, three bay symmetrical. A hipped gable roof and "high-brow" eaves the only notable features, the windows now bland modern casements in rough cast walls. Located opposite the rectory gates to enable it to preside over those to the church as well. Built by the Rev John Wright.
LESLIE (1929)

**59. KILLYCOONAGH, Clones** c1850
A two storey gabled lodge in blackstone, with red brick as window dressings, semicircular-headed doorway arch and eaves course. Commodious but derelict. The property in 1858 of William Forster.

**60. KILLYMARAN GLEBE, Monaghan**
pre 1858; *demolished*
Probably built for Rev Robert Wynne.

**61. LAKEVIEW, Ballybay**
(see BALLYBAY GLEBE)

**62. LISANISK, Carrickmacross** pre 1859; *demolished*
A lodge built for Adam Gibson.

**63. LISCARNEY, Monaghan** pre 1858
A dull building with mildly decorative bargeboards, and late Victorian chimneys. Probably for Major James Ross.

**64. LISNAROE, Clones** c1840
A most attractive one and a half storey, two up two down Picturesque cottage in the "Nash" manner. Three bay below a hipped roof its eaves, with rafter toes exposed, interrupted by two little window gablets to the front elevation. Matching these over the central front door a gabled canopy carried on timber brackets. In roughcast walls the effect spoiled by modern casement windows and a yellow brick Edwardian chimney stack. Built for Mr Nicholas Ellis.

**65. LONGFIELD, Carrickmacross (2)**
both pre 1859
Both undistinguished lodges of a late Georgian type for Thomas Johnston.

**66. LOUGH BAWN, Shercock** c1820
For William Barton Tenison. Originally a square plan, two roomed structure below an almost pyramidal roof with oversailing eaves. The banded ashlar chimney stack a remnant of what may have been something more sophisticated than it now appears. The walls roughcast after unseemly modernisation which also saw the insertion of enlarged window openings to its two bay elevations and the addition of a nasty flat-roofed hall to one side. "Irish pilasters" or channelled quoin stones.

**67. LOUGH FEA CASTLE, Carrickmacross (8)**
The lands by Carrickmacross came into the Shirley family upon the marriage of Sir Henry to the daughter of Elizabeth I's favourite, the 2nd Earl of Essex. However they lived almost entirely at their Warwickshire seat and there was little more than "a neat autumnal residence" here until Evelyn John Shirley employed the English architect Thomas Rickman, who designed for him a very large and unusual Tudor Gothick house by the lake. Thus commenced a programme of building that more than made up for the inertia of the previous centuries. From 1825 onwards the estate was a hive of activity, the huge mansion reaching completion twenty years later with the addition of a great Baronial hall. The architect responsible for the series of porters' lodges cannot have been Rickman who had died in 1841 and they would seem to be the work of George Sudden of Dublin who is recorded as having worked at Lough Fea between 1846 and 1848. Although Evelyn P Shirley had succeeded his father to the family estates in 1856 and commissioned Pritchard and Seddon to rebuild their main seat at Ettington Park there is nothing in their Irish lodges to relate to the architectural excesses there. By 1876 E. P Shirley was the biggest landlord in Co Monaghan with 26,386 acres, some of which in the form of woodland were separated by a public road.

**"Dublin Gate" Lodge** c1850
Thus called on the 1835 Ordnance Survey Map, the square ashlar gate piers, corniced with big ball finials, must predate the lodge by at least a quarter of a century. Constructed in rugged coursed rubble the lodge is particularly notable for its great boulder dressings to openings. Otherwise standard in plan. There is a flimsy flat-roofed lattice porch of late Victorian vintage.

**Drumcondra Road Entrance** c1850
Opposite the other woodland gate a plain two storey lodge with some of the same characteristics as the above. The gate lodges to the demesne proper show much greater architectural sophistication, all in Tudor Revival style.

**Lake Avenue Lodge** 1842;
architect probably George Sudden

To the northern extremity of the property on the demesne, conspicuously situated at a road junction is a cute little three roomed informal building, single storey but with bedspace to one loft. All skewtable gables, kneelers and roll-mould apex stones in dressed stone like the quoins and mullioned windows. The latter in a variety of single, bi-and tripartite openings some with label mouldings over lattice-paned lights. The little projecting hall has a datestone shield in its gable, the doorway outside the gate screen. All in squared coursed rubble, a pair of square chimney stacks above, the whole inconspicuously extended. The low entrance screen has octagonal stone posts with moulded capping.

**Sforza Lodge** c1845; architect probably George Sudden

So called apparently because it was inhabited by May Shirley, daughter of Lord Ferrers and widow of the Italian Duke of Sforza-Cesarini. Having all the architectural detailing of Lake Avenue Lodge but with a shallower roof pitch and on a more regular single storey T plan. The projecting gable sports the Sforza crest, a citrus fruit below a coronet. Now lacking its former fancy windows it is inconspicuous behind a high wall. Flanking the narrow opening two plain square ashlar gate pillars with ball finials.

**Middle Lodge** c1845; architect probably George Sudden

Unlike the rather drab grey stone of the other lodges this has a nice mellow blotchy pink stone quarried on the estate and perhaps left over from the building of the mansion. It differs also in having bargeboard gables to low pitched roofs. Single storey on an L plan, the leading gable has a tiny canted bay window with lattice-paned lights under a half-umbrello roof. The other windows mullioned in dressed stone. Ashlar quoins.

**Home Lodge** 1862; architect possibly George Sudden

By far the most pretentious composition, on a simple plan, two up two down, one and a half storey. Dressed up to look irregular and Picturesque, by the trick of adding an asymmetrically positioned porch to the front elevation, a single storey canted bay to the avenue gable and an octagonal stair tower expressed to the rear, broaching off a square base and terminating in a finialed octahedral roof. The spiral staircase is lit by arrowslit windows. Dressed stone to skewtable gables, big kneelers and window surrounds which frame wooden

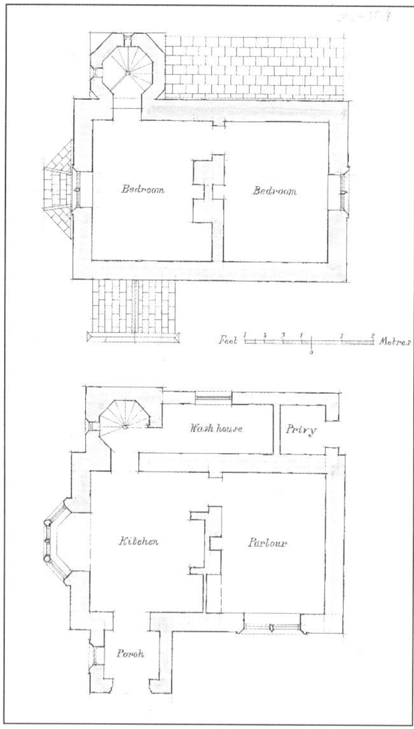


lattice-paned casements. Ashlar chimney and quoins to coursed squared masonry walls. To the rear a lean-to structure provides an additional room and outside toilet. Decorative cast iron cresting to main ridge and that of the porch which has the datestone above the arch. The gate screen is the same as the Lake Avenue entrance.

**Rookety Cottage** pre 1859; *ruinous*

Defies description as it lies choked in vegetation. Nearest Carrickmacross on an eminence opposite the gates.

**Bracken Lodge** c1859; architect possibly George Sudden

At the rear of the demesne the most generous accommodation provided by a lodge which functioned also as the land steward's house. Mainly two storey on an H plan, two skewtabled gables address the road, between them a one and a half storey link with gablets and two big chimneys. Behind the gate screen a single storey hall projects in similar manner. As elsewhere in coursed squared drab grey stone with ashlar quoins, dressed stone to chamfered, mullioned windows with label mouldings. Nice little front cottage garden surrounded by a low spear-topped railing, repeated on a grander scale to the gate screen alongside, which has familiar octagonal stone posts with moulded cappings.

SHIRLEY (1879); McCOLLUM (1856); P.R.O.N.I. D.3531/C/3/4

**68. LOUGHOONY or LOUGHOONAGH, Smithborough (2)**

**Side Entrance** pre 1835; *ruinous*

Across the road from the gates the remains of a lodge masquerading as single storey but with a basement below road level.

**Main Entrance** pre 1835; *demolished*

Also opposite the gates a lodge built by Andrew Murray which was recently taken down to make way for Clones to Monaghan road improvements. Formerly a typical single storey three bay cottage below a hipped roof. Late Georgian it was extended by an additional room and suffered the indignities of modern window enlargement.

**69. MADDENSTOWN, Clones**
(see HILTON PARK)

**70. MINORE, Cootehill** pre 1858; *demolished*

A lodge for Captain Cottnam.

**71. MONALTY, Carrickmacross** pre 1859

Opposite the gates a standard plan lodge, single storey with hipped roof and tiny windows, three bay. The seat in 1876 of T McEvoy Gartlan of the Carrickmacross distillery (qv).

**72. MOUNTAIN LODGE, Cootehill**
(see Farmoyle)

**73. MOUNT CARMEL, Rockcorry** pre 1858

A nondescript lodge for the Williamson family.

**74. MOY, Castleblayney** c1830; *ruinous*

Standard single storey three bay symmetrical with a gabled breakfront hall. Constructed in stone rubble with red brick dressings to square windows, harled. To the hipped roof a projecting eaves having paired carved bracket decoration. On the road elevation a single window framed in a segmentally-headed recess. The property in 1858 of Mary Harrison leased from the Hopes of Blayney Castle (qv).

**75. MULLAGHMORE GLEBE, Aughnacloy** pre 1835

The omnipresent single storey, two roomed, three bay, hipped roof gate lodge.

**76. MULLANARY GLEBE, Rockcorry** pre 1858; *demolished*

**77. NEWBLISS, Newbliss (3)**

A graceful Greek Revival house built by Alexander Ker in 1814 to replace a previous one. The two earlier lodges both pre 1835 may date from this time, one gone and the other ruinous.

**Main Entrance** c1860

The Murrays of Beech Hill, Monaghan (qv) married into the Ker female line and Andre Allen Murray-Ker thus came by the property and built this entrance. Once Picturesque it has now acquired mundane modern plate glass casement windows, probably losing in the process fanciful lattice panes, label mouldings and decorative bargeboards. Single storey stuccoed with low-pitched gable roofs, a hallway projects in similar fashion. The only architectural detailing of any note to survive the radical alterations are stone quoins and carved purlin brackets. The extensive gate screen is intact, the avenue beyond disused and stopped by a ramshackle garage. Six square stone piers with recessed panels and layered pyramidal caps terminate the convex quadrant sweeps and carry ornamental cast iron wicket and carriage gates. All with spear tops to match the railings.

BURKE (1904)

**78. NEWPARK, Cootehill** pre 1834; *demolished*

A gate lodge for another demesne of Dacre Hamilton of Cornacassa (qv).

**79. RAHANS, Carrickmacross** pre 1859

A featureless building, probably built for J Reid, Esq.

**80. ROCKSAVAGE, Louth** pre 1835; *ruinous*

Within the neglected park of the Kenny family by a bridge over a pretty rivulet the remains of a tiny rubble stone gabled single storey lodge. The big house still vacant just as Griffith noted it in 1858.

GRIFFITH

**81. ROSSMORE CASTLE, Monaghan (5)**

It is said that Warner William Westenra, the 2nd Lord Rossmore vied with E J Shirley of Lough Fea (qv) as to which great landowner could carry out the grandest of building. If this competition carried through to gate lodges, Shirley won hands down. Serious building work on the castle was to designs of 1824 by William Vitruvius Morrison but there was only one lodge of around this date within the demesne at the Ballyleck gate and this has not survived. In 1858 William Henry Lynn was the architect for Scottish Baronial style additions to the castle for Henry Robert Westenra, 3rd Baronet. The massive gates and pretty Tudor Revival lodge may also date from this period. Three further lodges were added by the 4th and 5th Lords Rossmore.

**Ballyleck Gate** c1855; architect perhaps W H Lynn

A good Tudor Revival cottage across the road from, and in contrast to, the Classical style gate screen from which it seems to turn away in awe. It probably also served as lodge to the Ballyleck demesne acquired from John Burnett by the Westenra family. One and a half storey three bay two up two down gabled, as is the projecting hall which displays the family crest (a lion rampant proper) on a plaque over the Tudor-arched doorway. In squared coursed rubble the openings are in dressed stone, the main ground floor windows mullioned tripartite with pretty latticed diamond panes. Big plain central chimney stack. There are neat chamfered stone gate posts with cusp-headed recesses and four-pediment cappings. Across the road two grand rusticated masonry block pillars with moulded plinths and cornices below stepped block cappings. Flanking wing walls in uncoursed squared rubble have wicket gates framed by square ashlar columns supporting pediments. The gates later curvilinear and too fussy. Beyond these gates was an earlier pre 1835 lodge now gone.

**Newbliss Lodge** c1860

In attractive straw-coloured brick, a single storey, three bay, symmetrical building with spiky waved bargeboards terminating in good carved finialed hipknobs to a steeply pitched roof. The main windows paired sashes, dressed in ashlar as are the quoins. Projecting front hall and rear return to match. A Picturesque design which looks older.

**Monaghan Lodge** c1880

Formerly in polychromatic red and cream brick now obvious only from the chimney stack, the whole now rendered over thus reducing the Picturesque effect. Like the previous lodge, single storey, gabled with similar front porch and rear wing. Again, carved spiky wave bargeboards survive in good condition, but the sharp finialed hipknobs removed. Semicircular head to the front door fanlight and on the side elevation a round relieving brick arch above a flat-arched window with tripartite sashed lights each with its own round head. Stone quoins. Contemporary cast iron gate posts, off-the-shelf, as at Ballyedmond, Co Down, (qv) Trewmount, Co Tyrone (qv) and nearby Gallanagh (qv) with their little dormered roofs. Fleur-de-lys topped railings and gates.

**Cootehill Gate** c1880

The most splendid of late Victorian cast iron gate screens is banished to the southermost extreme of the estate. Four perforated central square pillars rise from solid plinths, with intertwined foliage to culminate in four-pediment cappings. The double carriage gate and wicket entrances a further extravaganza of curvilinear design. The extensive railed sweeps beyond are comparatively plain. All contemporary with the lodge which lurks behind, paling in comparison. Square under a pyramidal roof, from which a hipped roof hall projects awkwardly. Walls in facing brick.

BENCE-JONES (1988); McPARLAND (1989)

**82. ST. MACARTAN'S R.C. CATHEDRAL, Monaghan** 1884; architect William Hague

A masterpiece of J.J. McCarthy, the cathedral stands impressively at the summit of a series of terraces. Building commenced in 1861 in the Early English Gothic style, but the architect died in 1882 before its completion and as at St Patrick's, Armagh (qv) a replacement architect had to be commissioned. In this case it was William Hague who, although based in Dublin, was a Cavan man. He it was that designed the spire and gate lodge. Turning its back on the entrance and instead deferentially facing the Cathedral, it is a chunky little composition in the High Victorian Gothick manner constructed in squared coursed limestone with ashlar quoins and dressings. Single storey on an irregular plan, almost cruciform, the gables with skewtables, carved kneelers and curly metal finials to all four trefoil apex stones. Some window openings are shouldered with roll-moulded heads. The gable to the pedestrian approach has a canted bay over which, within a cusped trefoil, is a decorative panel sculpted in bas-relief, a Bishop's hat and hanging tassels framing Bishop Donnelly's coat-of-arms and the motto "PRO DEO ET PATRIA". Above the return gable window another overpanel in the form of a Gothic Serliana carved again in bas-relief, two pointed arches contain St Macartan and St Dympna, crowned by a blank shield. Both panels hood-moulded as is the trefoiled front door fanlight. The dripstones all have remained unsculpted. Moulded eaves course, battered and chamfered chimney stack and perforated ridge crestings. The gates appropriately High Victorian and extensive.

GALLOWAY (1992)

**83. ST MACARTAN'S SEMINARY, Monaghan** c1845; architect probably Thomas J Duff

In contrast to Duff's austere Classical college block of 1840 is this jolly Picturesque lodge elevated from the gate screen. Single storey symmetrical three bay constructed in blotchy brick dressed with stone to quoins and narrow chamfered window opening. Steep gables ornamented with carved timber wavy bargeboards. Advancing gabled hall in similar fashion. Hefty stone chimney on a brick base. Not unlike Rossmore Castle's Newbliss lodge (qv). Ogee quadrants frame the carriage opening with its later cast iron gates and overthrow.

MONAGHAN; U.A.H.S. (1970)

**84. SCARVY, Clones** c1840

A nicely proportioned building with low lines built for Major Campbell Graham. Single storey, three bay under a shallow-pitched hipped roof with central chimney. The two large rooms are accessed from a semicircular- recessed open porch which extends below a pedimented portico supported on two pairs of slender cast iron

*St. Macartan's R.C. Cathedral*

columns. On each side pretty mullioned sash windows with octagonal pattern glazing bars. Now undergoing rehabilitation which has exposed nice dark grey rubble walls with red brick window dressings. Pilaster quoins to imitate those on the elegant gentleman's villa beyond. Fine square stone outer piers with panelled friezes flank railed sweeps leading to ornate inner cast iron posts with ball finials.

**85. SHANTONAGH, Shercock** pre 1859; *demolished*
A lodge for Thomas Rothwell whose father had acquired the demesne through marriage into the Corry family.

**86. SHIRLEY, Carrickmacross** c1780
In a busy town rich in architectural interest secreted down Evelyn Street a once grand entrance in the Palladian manner. To a former property of the Shirley family of Lough Fea Castle (qv) long occupied by their agents. Flanking the wide gate screen a pair of commodious dwellings, two storey gabled to the approach each once crowned by a central ashlar chimney stack. Both elevations given relief by full height semicircular- headed recesses originally containing first floor squared sash windows. Constructed in rubble stone harled and framed by V-jointed masonry toothed quoins. The tall square carriage pillars are in refined V-jointed rusticated stone linked to the dwellings by walls containing wooden panelled wicket doors. Although many of the original details are spoiled by modernisation or neglect it remains an important and impressive feature.

**87. TARTATE GLEBE, Clones** pre 1835; *demolished*

**88. THORNFORD, Castleblayney** pre 1859; *demolished*
A lodge for Hamilton McMath Esq.

**89. THORNHILL, Smithborough (2)**
**Monaghan Lodge** pre 1835; *demolished*
**Smithborough Lodge** c1830
A small standard lodge opposite the gates hidden in undergrowth. Constructed in brick, single storey three bay symmetrical below the hipped roof, its eaves decorated with paired scrolled brackets. Stone chimney. To a house built c1820, the seat in 1824 and 1837 of John Johnson.

**90. TONNAGH, or TANNAGH, Cootehill** pre 1858; *demolished*
A lodge built for Captain C Dawson.

**91. VICARSDALE GLEBE, Carrickmacross** pre 1859; *demolished*
The big Tudor Revival villa rectory to Donaghmoyne Parish is ruinous and its lodge, built for Rev James Francis McCormick, gone without trace.
LESLIE (1929)

*Shirley*

# COUNTY TYRONE

**1. AGHENIS, Caledon** pre 1834; *demolished*
Opposite the gates to a demesne once belonging to the Lowrys, later Earls of Belmore, Castlecoole, Co Fermanagh (qv).

**2. AGHNAHOE, Ballygawley (2)**
Two lodges in even worse condition than the now dilapidated long low Georgian farmhouse belonging to the Crossle family for whom they were originally built.

**Outer Lodge** c1850; architect not known

A single storey Neo-Classical style lodge identical to that at Killymeal, Dungannon (qv). Symmetrical three bay below a hipped roof with big eaves brackets which continue, paired, into the gable of the front door breakfront hall. The door panelled below a segmentally- headed fanlight, the window openings similarly treated with moulded surrounds in stuccoed walls with quoins. A heavily corniced tall chimney stack rises off a plinth on the ridge. Deserted and in the early stages of decay. Good ogee railed sweeps with flanking wicket gates to the carriage entrance. Octagonal ashlar piers.

**Inner Lodge** c1845
Modest, very much a gabled version of the above, reduced to the bare bones without any of the architectural ornamentation. In a simple fabric of rubble stone and brick. Derelict. Both probably built by James Crossle who succeeded to the property in 1855 upon the death of his father Capt Henry Crossle. The family for long managers of the Verner estates in Counties Armagh and Monaghan and of neighbouring Inishmagh (qv).
CROSLEIGH (1904)

**3. ALTINAGHRES CASTLE, Donemana** c1870; architect not known

[Fig. 88. Entrance lodge to Blaise Castle.]

J.C. Loudon (1840)

Staring out through windowless openings at a bare park, a short-lived whim of C William L Ogilby of the Pellipar (qv) and Ardnargle (qv) properties of the same Co Londonderry family. To the great gaunt castellated pile is a gatehouse and archway contemporary with it and in a similarly dilapidated condition. An impressive composition taken straight from a design by Humphry Repton at Blaise Castle, Somerset, built in 1801 and illustrated in J C Loudon's 1840 edited reprint of the great landscape architect's original *Landscape Gardening* of 1803. In a Picturesque Tudor castellated style not far removed from that at Killymoon Castle (qv). The lodge a one up one down cube with embattled parapet having small turrets to each corner, one functioning as the chimney stack. Chamfered dressed stone label moulded mullioned windows with squared sash windows, the upper bipartite, the lower tripartite. Alongside is the grand carriage opening with a four centred Tudor archway springing from vermiculated impost blocks, below a mock machicolated and battlemented parapet which unites two flanking square towers. One of these purely ornamental with arrowloops, the other against the gatehouse containing the entrance hall with closet over. The lodge doorway has a pointed arched head over which is a blank shield. All in a mixture of uncoursed random rubble and oblong-shaped coursed masonry with smooth dressing. A once impressive building now derelict having suffered the indignities of modern metal windows and removal of its parapet to accommodate a corrugated iron roof.
LOUDON (1840); ROWAN (1979)

**4. ANNAGHROE, Caledon** c1830; *demolished*

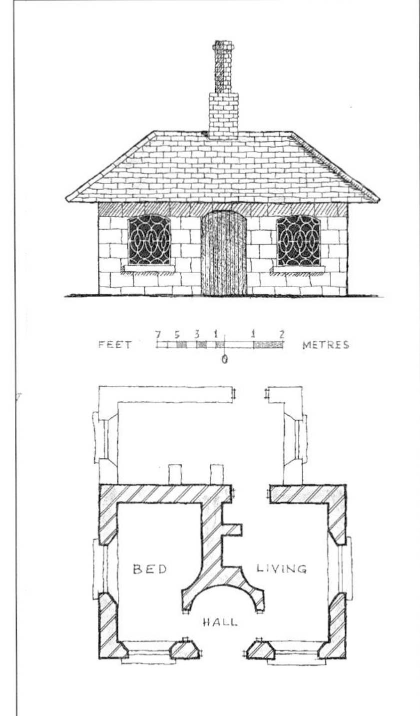


Probably contemporary with the now deserted house, a jolly little building of standard plan under a jaunty oversized hipped roof with a precarious brick chimney. Single storey three bay front with segmental headed openings in harled walls. Beautiful curvilinear pattern cast-iron glazing the same as at Castle Leslie (qv) and Annaghmakerrig (qv) both in Co Monaghan. Semicircular internal hallway. Once a property of the Leslies of nearby Castle Leslie.

**5. ANNAGINNY or ANNAGUINEA LODGE, Newmills (2)**

To a mid-Georgian house of the Young family a late Victorian half-timbered face-lift by Col R J Howard. Each of the lodges seem to relate to those building periods.

**East Lodge** pre 1833

Nondescript.

**West Lodge** pre 1906; *demolished*

**6. ARDBOE GLEBE, Stewartstown**
pre 1833

A nondescript building probably for Rev Dr Francis Hall.

**7. ARTREA RECTORY, Cookstown**
c1845

A seemly single storey three bay lodge below a hipped roof from which projects a pedimented porch supported on Doric pilasters, imitating the big house. Panelled front door. A pair of octagonal chimney pots crowns the ridge. Concave quadrants lead to two square stone gate piers with ornamental fluting and corniced cappings. Built by the Rev J Kennedy Bailey.

**8. ASHFIELD PARK, Clogher (3)**
all pre 1852; *all demolished*

To a mid-Victorian Italianate villa three contemporary lodges all of which have now gone. Record survives of one. Referred to locally as the "Noggin lodge" this was a distinctive single storey building in random masonry on an ovoid plan with a conical thatched roof, not unlike those at Ballymenoch, Co Down (qv). There was a small breakfront to the front door below a corbel course eaves. Last occupied in the 1930s it has sadly disappeared. As eccentric as its builder George C Breckenridge who immortalised himself in an aggressive monument on a hillside nearby.
JACK JOHNSTON PHOTOGRAPH

**9. ATHENRY, Carrickmore**
(see TERMON RECTORY)

**10. AUGHER CASTLE or SPUR ROYAL, Augher**

An exquisite lakeside picture of Sir Thomas Ridgeway's keep of c1613, given its present appearance in 1832 by the splendidly named Sir James M Richardson Bunbury Bart, to designs of the Sligo architect William Warren. At the time of these pretty additions when the property was called Castle Hill there would appear, from the contemporary Ordnance Survey Map, to have been a pair of little circular sentry box lodges at the main entrance. In any case these were superseded by a lodgeless gate sweep of about 1855. In the form of castle chess pieces are six octagonal stone crenellated pillars flanking ogee sweeps, wicket and carriage gates in very decorative Great Exhibition ironwork.

**Side Lodge** c1840

A rather modest building, single storey below a hipped roof. Two bay to the avenue its sash windows Georgian squared, a doorway to the leading gable. Replaced another pair of circular lodges
ATKINSON (1833); O.S.M.; YOUNG (1909)

**11. AUGHNACLOY RECTORY, Aughnacloy** pre 1850; *demolished*

The lodge opposite the gates to a house previously called Bellmont and Archdeaconry, probably built for the Rev John Abraham Russell.

**12. AUGHNACLOY ALMSHOUSES, Aughnacloy** c1854;
architect Sandham Symes

These almshouses were built between 1850 and 1854 with an endowment of £10,000 from the

estate of Dr Alexander Jackson of Dublin, a sum which extended to the erection of a gate lodge in similar manner. In the same Tudor cottage style a lodge on an informal L plan. The main two storey block, gabled to the avenue, has a single storey outshoot the roof of which catslides to form a canopy to the front door, supported on wooden brackets. The squared pane windows top hung in walls of squared uncoursed stone. A splendidly Picturesque pair of chimney stacks, vertically channelled. The fancy bargeboards to match the main building missing.
ROWAN (1979)

**13. BALLYGAWLEY PARK, Ballygawley (2)**

An imposing mansion, impressively located, built between 1825 and 1833 to designs of John Hargrave of Cork for Sir Hugh Stewart, 2nd Baronet. Neither of the gate lodges are early enough to form part of that period of building.

**Omagh Lodge** c1850; *demolished*

Only the commanding stone pillars and ironwork survive. From a moulded base rises a recessed panel shaft topped by wide cornice and rounded capping each face of which has a beautiful anthemion moulding. Luxurious ironwork to railing and gates with repeating laurel wreath motif.

**Ballygawley Lodge** c1850

(*I.A.A.*)

Behind a modest but more extensive entrance screen, a Classical lodge. Single storey, three bay symmetrical and boxy with an entablatured parapet to its hipped roof. In ashlar the wide openings surrounded by moulded architraves, the windows bipartite with margined glazing bars. There was a double-leafed, panelled front door, the central chimney stack also suitably panelled. Now vandalised, it completes a sorry scene of dereliction with the shell of the big house on the hill behind burnt down in the 1920s.
I.A.A. PHOTOGRAPH Ref: B/1469/25

**14. BARNHILL, Stewartstown** pre 1833; *ruinous*

A lodge to the respectable Palladian style villa of a Rev Dr Hill.

**15. BARONAGH, Fintona** pre 1833; *demolished*

A lodge house and corn mill belonging to John Buchanan as identified by Griffith in his valuation of 1860. Located opposite the entrance.
GRIFFITH

**16. BARONSCOURT, Newtownstewart (8)**

That these estates should boast such a history of lodge building is wholly appropriate for the greatest landowner in County Tyrone. That this is recorded from early Georgian times is thanks to the splendid surviving family papers of the Hamiltons, Earls and later Dukes of Abercorn. These give a fascinating insight into the importance placed upon the duties of, and the problems caused by, the gatekeeper. They are mainly in the form of letters between the land agents of the day and successive Earls residing in their Scottish or English seat. As early as 6th October 1750 the demesne wall was under construction and by 16th February 1755 John Colhoun reports that "The two lodges at Baronscourt are nearly finished" and two months later "Old McConomy plastered the 2 new Baronscourt Cottages, and puts on slates". By 6th May that year they "... are plastered and look very well: they were done by old McConomy who was employed by Doyle without my father's knowledge ...".Not all occupants of the lodges came up to expectation. On 27th November 1779 the bachelor and teetotal 8th Earl "who never drank anything but water" was not amused to find. "... Arthur, I understand, has taken up the selling of spirituous liquors. In short, for this and other reasons, he must be discharged. The time when I submit entirely to you. A decent person will be wanted to take care of the gate. And as Hudson will have the principal care of the park, it is best it should be a person of his recommendation and under his control." By 7th December 1783 the problem had been remedied for the 9th Earl wrote to his agent "Be pleased to allow Semple the gatekeeper a livery ... same as the park keeper". That the office of gatekeeper, in many cases, became a highly respected institution is clear from references to the likes of "James Carron's gate", "Foster's Gate" and of course "Semple's Lodge". In September 1781 the architect George Stewart's new house for the 8th Earl was nearing completion and he presented his accounts along with drawings for lodges with "temple-fronts". Two years later from James Hamilton, Strabane to the Earl: "... I will also send a sketch of the lodge, and the entrance at the lake". That these were not executed is likely and certainly nothing of the 18th century lodge building survives today although one at the southernmost end of the demesne was taken down within living memory.

**"Moore's Gate" lodge** c1780; *demolished*

Described as an "inkpot" by those who can remember it. From its appearance on early OS maps it was round on plan. It was probably two roomed, single storey with a central chimney stack to a thatched roof. In 1791-92 the 1st Marquess of Abercorn employed the eminent English architect John Soane to remodel the house and it has been traditionally assumed that he was also responsible for the ornamental "Rock Cottage" lodge. However there is no documentary evidence for this either in surviving estate records or in the Soane Museum in London. That he had an influence is to be seen in designs by Richard Morrison almost half a century later. It is neither easy to make attributions for the lodges built in the Regency and early Victorian period, nor is it easy to identify the sequence of their erection. What is clear is that the lodges of almost a century before had become outmoded and that a series of pretty Picturesque English cottages were built between 1831 and 1838 to replace them. In this period of building activity at Baronscourt first William Farrell produced unaccepted designs for alterations to the house and instead William Vitruvius Morrison's proposals were executed. Whilst records survive for this work, only the source for two of these lodges is obvious, both being designs from Peter Frederick Robinson's

P.F. Robinson (1833)

Baronscourt, "Rock Cottage"

*Designs for Lodges and Park Entrances* published in 1833. It is likely that Robinson was recommended by Sir John Soane to the 2nd Marquess, James Hamilton, for not only had Soane ceased to practice by then but the two architects are known to have been close, Robinson having proposed the older man for Presidency of the Institute of British Architects. There is also a truncated version of the parsonage illustrated in Robinson's *Designs for Village Architecture* (1830) on the perimeter of the demesne.

**"Rock Cottage"** c1832;
architect P F Robinson

At the Largybeg gate this lovely building is a variation of Design No 2 in Robinson's pattern book. Although the internal layout differs, the illustrated front elevation and perspective are proof of its provenance. Here is the duality of the two big ornamental gables flanking a three bay recess containing the central sheeted entrance doorway and two pretty wooden lattice paned windows. In reality the label-moulded windows and smooth walls are replaced by mullioned lights and the most unique construction of rock boulders which give it its name. Dominating the design are the two exaggerated brick chimney stacks set diagonally on great square bases. The spiked wavy carved bargeboard design is also to be found on Milltown Lodge (qv) designed by W V Morrison, suggesting alternatively that the latter may have been executant architect. A remarkable and durable composition nicely framed between two big Irish yews.

**Newtownstewart Gate** c1835;
architect P F Robinson

An adaptation of Design No 4 from Robinson's *Designs for Lodges and Park Entrances* this is a one and a half storey variant on an irregular plan. From the front elevation a canted living room bay projects asymmetrically with pretty lattice lights below a half umbrello roof. Alongside a full height gabled breakfront containing the front door with a little label moulded square window over. Originally faced in nice rustic rubble stone with brick dressings this was rendered over when the lodge was extended and the decorative bargeboards were also lost. Thankfully the trio

P.F. Robinson (1833)

Baronscourt, Newtownstewart Gate

of big diagonally-set brick Picturesque chimneys which rise off the rear wall have survived these unfortunate alterations. To one side is the gatescreen, a rather incongruous range of classical pillars with ball finials to the outer ones and urns to the inner carriage pillars. Good cast ironwork between. That P F Robinson was active in Ireland at this time is shown by his work at Seaforde, Co Down (qv) and he would seem to be the sole English architect to have subscribed to Lewis' *Topographical Dictionary of Ireland*. He may also have been responsible for the third Picturesque cottage.

**Church Lodge or "Devine's Gate"**
c1835; architect possibly P F Robinson;
*demolished*

In the same Picturesque cottage manner as before but without a known source. This was a regular single storey three bay building, the front elevation had a central breakfront porch in brick with hood-moulded elliptical archway and round arched lights to the side. Foiled bargeboards decorated the gables and there were the distinctive brick diagonally-set chimney stacks to each gable. Before its demolition it had odd front windows, one square-paned, the other with lattice glazing, all in rubble walls. Built to replace an earlier pair of pre-1833. William Vitruvius Morrison did not quite live long enough to see the execution of his designs to remodel the big house and it was to his father Richard that the 2nd Marquess turned for yet more ideas for estate entrances after 1838. Three designs survive. If they are three alternative drawings for a single location, and this is not clear, they display either a gradual dilution of ideas or indicate increasing ostentation

B.N.L.

Baronscourt, Church Lodge

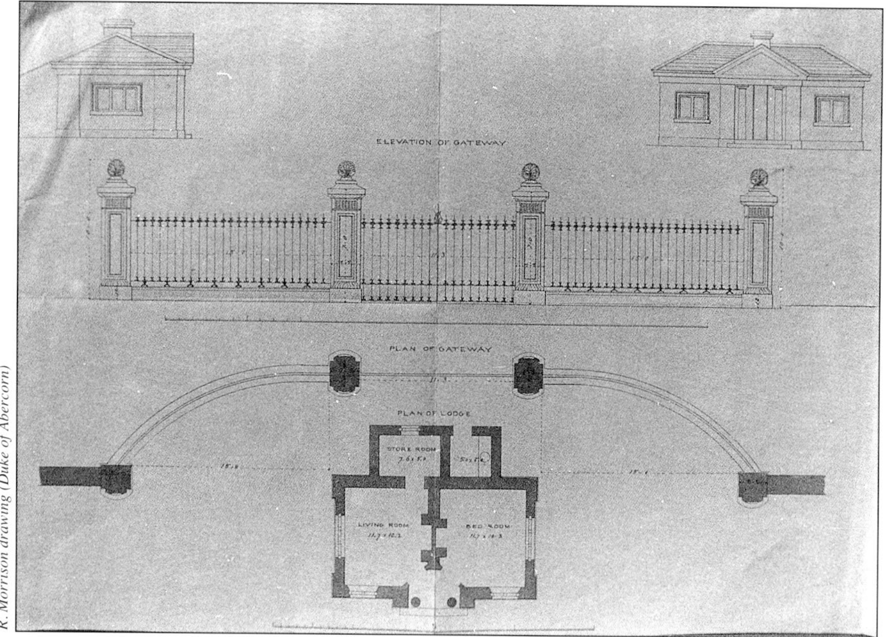


R. Morrison drawing (Duke of Abercorn)

*Doric Lodge and Gates*

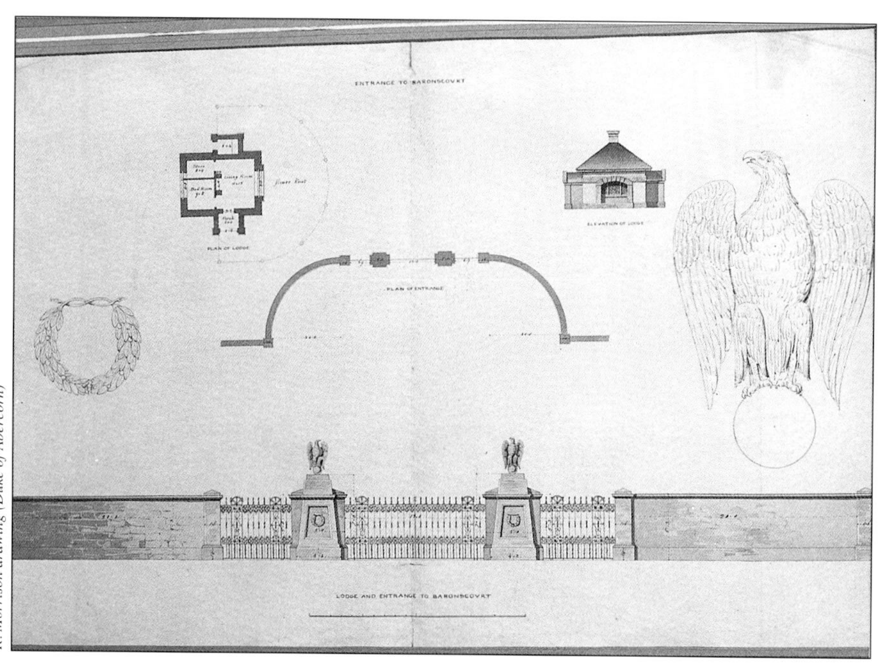


R. Morrison drawing (Duke of Abercorn)

*Greek Rustic Cottage and Gates*

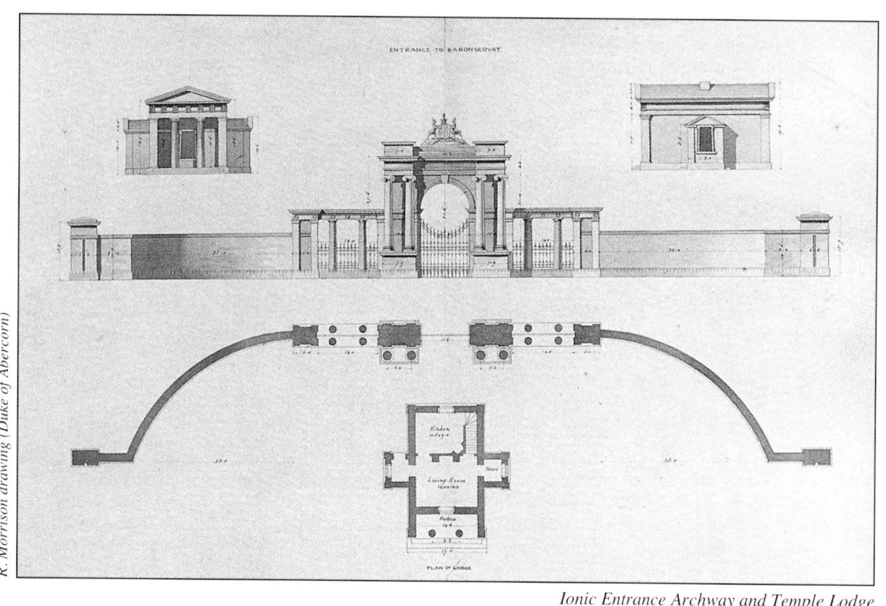


R. Morrison drawing (Duke of Abercorn)

*Ionic Entrance Archway and Temple Lodge*

depending upon the sequence of their presentation to the client. Be that as it may, the architect was to be frustrated for not one was carried out and the mansion house was destined never to receive the dramatic overture it warrants.

**Doric Lodge and Gates** c1838; architect Richard Morrison; *unexecuted*

The least pretentious of the three proposals shows a standard single storey two roomed lodge with small back return accommodation to house a store and privy. The symmetrical three bay front under a hipped roof has a pedimented breakfront to an open porch with two Doric columns in antis. On each side windows bipartite within moulded surrounds. The simple iron gatescreen would have been framed by four square stone pillars with fluted friezes, panelled shafts and anthemion finials.

**Greek Rustic Cottage and Gates** c1838; architect Richard Morrison; *unexecuted*

Here Morrison reverts to his favourite gable-on approach, in this instance copied from John Soane's design in *Sketches in Architecture* of 1793. Under a bracketed hipped roof the front elevation is dominated by a single window, tripartite with lattice glazing, all below a wide heavily vermiculated and voussoired segmental arch. This stone treatment is repeated on side panels to the window, a high level stringcourse and deep plinth. The side elevations show balancing gabled projections, one the entrance porch, the other the privy. This single storey lodge was to be set in a knot garden. This design is basically the same as that built to Morrison's plans many years earlier at the Thomastown entrance at Castlecoole, Co Fermanagh (qv). The entrance gates are taken from J B Papworth's *Rural Residences* of 1818, the gate pillars in the form of Greek stellae, an idea which Morrison repeatedly used throughout the country and was once to be seen at Langford Lodge, Co Antrim (qv). Here he adds his personal laurel wreath motif within the panels of tapering breakfront pillars. Central carriage gates and their flanking wickets were to be carried on secondary piers as recommended by Papworth. Crowning the pillars were to have been big proud eagles clasping ball finials. Framing this concave wall quadrants were proposed. The architect had already seen this design executed c1829 at Kilruddery, Co Wicklow, lodge and gates identical, eagles and all.

**Ionic Entrance Archway and Temple Lodge** c1838; architect: Richard Morrison; *unexecuted*

The most grandiose scheme of the trio, almost a replica of that which failed to be built at Castlecoole, Co Fermanagh (qv) A 21ft 6in (6.5m) high semicircular-headed triumphal arch carries a deep entablature crowned by a great sculpted coat-of-arms. Flanking the archway are two pairs of free-standing Ionic columns on tall plinths. The main arch imposts are continued over Doric colonnade wings their ironwork stopped by aedicules having the inevitable laurel wreath signature over. Beyond are shown extensive concave wall sweeps terminating in square pillars, the whole composition extending to a 166ft (50m) frontage. A truncated version of this design was erected at Oak Park, Co Carlow (c1833). The lodge was to have been a little Doric temple exactly as intended for Castlecoole although here to accommodate a bedspace in an attic storey. The gabled roof is shown stopped in the pedimented front elevation with Doric columns in antis and triglyphed entablature. Recessed behind the portico a single tapered window with lugged moulded surround. To opposing side elevations balancing pedimented projections, pilasters to all corners and raised on a plinth. A shame that this fine composition remains unrealised, the demesne lacking as it does the appropriate introduction to an important house.

**Golf Club Entrance** c1850

A two storey mid-Victorian Tudor style lodge with hood mouldings.

**Johnston's Gate** c1840

A plain lodge were it not for its excess of applied half-timbered work of about 1890. It is likely that this disguises an earlier fabric probably from the same date as the other Picturesque lodges. One and a half storey, three bay gabled with a projecting porch asymmetrically placed. There is a canted bay window to the road. Windows modern square-paned.

**Lower Deerpark Lodge** pre 1833

A nondescript gabled building blocked up and deserted.

**Upper Deerpark Lodge** pre 1833

Small single storey lodge with a pyramidal roof and two bay front. The windows lattice-paned. Abandoned.

McPARLAND (1989); P.R.O.N.I. T.2541; ROWAN (1979); SOANE (1793); PAPWORTH (1818); ROBINSON (1833); GEBBIE (1972)

**17. THE BAWN, Aughnacloy (2)**
**Front Entrance** c1825

Within a stone's throw of George Moore's 1800 house is a Georgian Gothick lodge. Unusually one and a half storey, bedroom space being secreted away within a hipped roof, the only clue to which is an abnormally "high-brow" eaves line the same as at The Argory, Co Armagh (qv). Otherwise a standard plan three-bay stuccoed building. The window cills rest on a tall plinth, the bipartite lights each with lancet heads in a flat-arched opening. Decorating the wall at eaves level a band of pointed motifs in reverse.

**Rear Entrance** c1850; *ruinous*

A simple two roomed single storey cottage, its three bay front, below a hipped roof featuring a gable over the central front door. Brick quoins and dressings to stuccoed walls. There is a novel little rotating wicket gate. All built for Captain Edward Moore.

**18. BELLMONT, Aughnacloy**
(see Aughnacloy Rectory)

**19. BELLMOUNT, Stewartstown** pre 1833; *demolished*

A lodge built by the Bell family probably contemporary with the c1830 house.

**20. BELTRIM CASTLE, Gortin (4)**

The house realised its long low plain appearance in alterations of c1820 when three of the lodges

*Mrs A Metfford*

may have been added to the Hamilton estate. Of these, one of which was opposite the gates, there is a single survivor.

**North Lodge** pre 1833

Plain and derelict.

**South Lodge** c1850; *demolished*

An interesting lodge distinctive for its glazing pattern of little rectangular panes, reminiscent of the Arts- and-Crafts era. Single storey three bay below a gabled roof from which projects a gabled hall the entrance to which has a round headed arch in chamfered dressed stone. This treatment is repeated to window openings in harled walls. To the leading gable an unusual canted bay window below a half-umbrello roof. Built for Arthur W Cole Hamilton.

**21. BENBURB MANOR, Benburb (3)**

A big house as gaunt and austere as one would expect of the aged W H Lynn, in the manner of his Riddell Hall and Campbell College (qqv) both in Belfast.

**Early Entrance** pre 1833; *demolished*

This served an old cottage style dwelling occupied by Thomas Ayre for many years within the bawn walls of the previous castle of the Wingfields. Sir James Bruce took up residence in his new manorial home in 1886 and added a gate lodge.

**East Lodge** c1887; architect W H Lynn

Although in the same red brick with its sandstone stringcourses this is altogether gayer. A tall one and a half storey, three bay gabled lodge. Two up two down under a steeply pitched roof as is that to the projecting porch. This extends to form part of the gatescreen, one of its archways with moulded sandstone surround forms a pedestrian gate opening. Simple late Victorian sash windows, the bargeboards have a mildly decorative sawtooth overlay. Typical plinthed, friezed and capped Lynn chimney stack. There are good sculpted sandstone pillars.

**West Lodge** c1890; architect not known

In squared uncoursed masonry an unusual one and a half storey lodge looking too innovative to have been by the aged Lynn. From the main body of the building with its hipped gables ornamented by foiled and lobed bargeboards and novel Gothick Art Nouveau attic window is a single storey living room projecting towards the footpath with a steeply-pitched hipped roof. Alongside diagonally-set gate pillars with crude cappings. The Manor house now a priory.

ROWAN (1979)

**22. BERNAGH, Dungannon** pre 1854; *demolished*

A house that in the first half of the 19th century was another property of the Knox family of Northland (qv).

**23. BLESSINGBOURNE COTTAGE, Fivemiletown** c1845

*A. Rowan*

A cute little ornamental Tudor style lodge to the previous cottage residence of 1810 which has since been labelled Blessingbourne Manor by the Montgomerys upon its transformation into the present big late Victorian mansion by the architect F P Cockerell in 1874. Probably built by Hugh Ralph Severin Montgomery upon his succession to the property in 1838, it is apparently a single storey structure but has bedspace compressed into its gabled roof. Its wavy bargeboards are carried down and around as a fascia to the front eaves which projects beyond the front elevation to form a verandah supported on four octagonal wooden posts, with brackets, which rest on stone stools. Behind the verandah is a pretty three bay facade of stucco framed by quarry-faced stone quoins. On each side of the front door the window openings, chamfered with label mouldings, once had delightful paired latticed lights each with pretty Tudor cusped heads. Sadly these windows were replaced by "leaded" lights and synthetic slates were also substituted for natural ones in an otherwise excellent rehabilitation. Nevertheless cosy and well tended.

ALISTAIR ROWAN PHOTOGRAPH REF: B146828; ROWAN (1979)

**24. BLOOMHILL, Ballygawley** pre 1854; demolished

A lodge for the Simpson family.

**25. BLOOMHILL, New Mills** c1870; architect not known

*S. Leighton*

Variously described disparagingly as ugly and grotesque. Outrageous perhaps but also a delicious conceit in a High Victorian Picturesque Gothick style the likes of which is unequalled in the Province. Probably built for James Scott when he refaced a 1783 house as a stuccoed Classical house which looks as if it has escaped from the suburbs. In squared uncoursed smooth

sandstone laid to a regular pattern the lodge is raised on a high plinth, single storey on an L plan, the front elevation three bay symmetrical, dominated by a projecting porch. Like the main gables this is half hipped with huge curved timber bargeboards above the front archway, the pointed panel of which has a roundel in its tympanum for relief. The porch side arches are similarly pointed, one with a little stepped and balustraded approach. Flanking this the two windows are set in chamfered openings to breakfronts under their own carved mock gables with foiled bargeboards. On opposing side elevations are matching rectangular bay windows with flat entablatured roofs, the openings having paired lights each with pretty lancet heads and quatrefoils in the spandrels. The carved curved main bargeboards lead the eye to jagged cresting to ridges and a roof with bands of diagonally set slates. The little panelled chimney is relatively modest. There is a later addition to the rear with hipped gables to match. The gate sweep is appropriately eccentric with sharp ironwork and Victorian Gothick pillars with steep gableted cappings and quatrefoil ornaments. A remarkable curiosity, highly desirable, listed, and yet apparently unwanted and derelict.
DUNGANNON AND COOKSTOWN;
U.A.H.S. (1971); ROWAN (1979); O.S.M

**26. CALEDON, Caledon (5)**
The Alexander family acquired the property from the 8th Earl of Cork and Orrery in 1778 and one year later James was to engage the English architect Thomas Cooley to design his new house. The earliest gate lodge to the demesne is located behind the main street and may date from not long after completion of the house.

**Doric Lodge** c1780;
architect possibly Thomas Cooley

A very distinguished building which for about fifty years performed the joint function of gatekeeper's accommodation and school (until superseded by the Picturesque lodge outside the gates). Single storey, with three large rooms on a T plan. Projecting from the hipped roof main body is a single room fronted by the full width pedimented tetrastyle portico with fundamental Doric columns. In fine ashlar, as are the quoins which ornament mellow facing brick walls, the windows squared sash. Criminally permitted to fall into the most pitifully dilapidated state, the fine three- flued chimney having collapsed. The gatescreen is contemporary with tall stone quadrant walls and fine square masonry pillars of V-jointed blocks with fluted friezes and wide corniced cappings. In the library of the big house is a veritable treasure-trove of informative architectural drawings - but sadly these are inaccessible. Most of these reveal much about the commissions of the great Regency architect John Nash, both here and elsewhere. Nash had been briefed by Du Pre Alexander, the 2nd Earl of Caledon upon his inheriting the property in 1802. The architect in remodelling the house was to visit Caledon at least twice and there is evidence that he produced gateway designs both for the estate and other locations. That there was much agonising over an appropriate design for the new main entrance is clear from the abundance of sketches produced. These include a drawing for a single Classical cube lodge very much in the fashion of the Pavilion Notebook type much employed by George Stanley Repton who was one of Nash's assistants at this time. Although an abortive design, a variant was used by the 2nd Earl's maternal grandfather on his estate at Crawfordsburn Co Down (qv). The eventual preferred solution is in the manner of Nash's contemporary work on Park Crescent and Regent's Park, London.

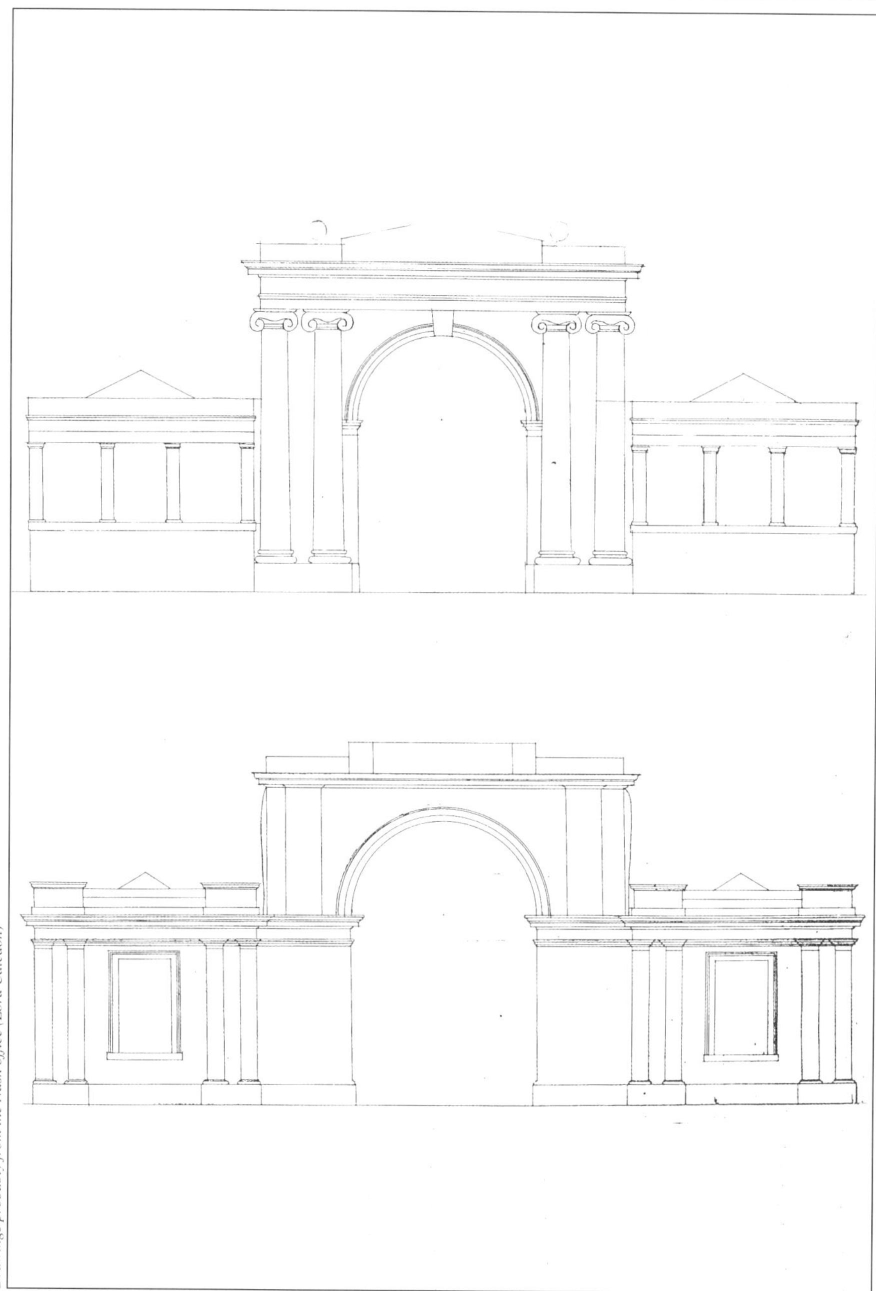

*Drawings probably from the Nash office (Lord Caledon)*

*Caledon, unexecuted designs*

*J. Nash drawing (Lord Caledon)*

*Caledon, unexecuted design*

**The Twin Lodges** 1812;
architect John Nash

A pair of trim Regency lodges in a pristine stuccoed state now no longer subjected to heavy

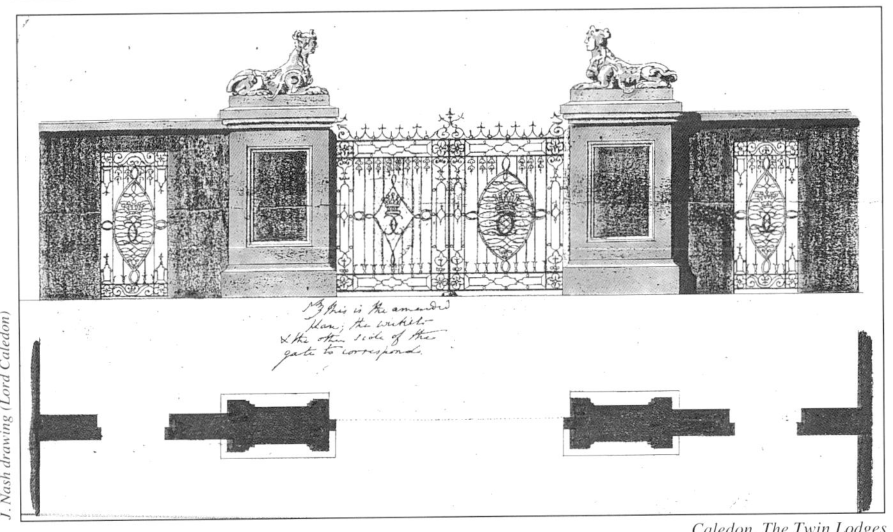


J. Nash drawing (Lord Caledon)

*Caledon, The Twin Lodges*

traffic trundling past the gates since a recent road realignment has provided them with a grand forecourt approach. Each two roomed, their gabled fronts forming part of the gatescreen whilst their two bay elevations face one another across the avenue behind. Both have semicircular porch recesses fronted by a pair of Doric columns. The road elevations contain wide tripartite Wyatt-type windows. Above, full width pediments their tympanums embellished with Coade stone coats-of-arms incorporating lions, mermaids admiring themselves in looking glasses and the motto PER MARE, PER TERRA which certainly explains the method of carriage of these pieces from England. William Croggon's letter book notes from the Lambeth works record "3.8. 13 For Newry 4 cases 2 sphinx and 2 arms for Earl of Caledon". The sphinxes rest atop two wide carriage pillars with recessed panels and cornices. Uniting these with the lodges, screen walls which contain wicket gate openings. All the highly ornamental ironwork gates contain the Caledon crest for which drawings survive in Nash's hand, with his flap technique for alternative proposals. At the base of the main piers stone pyramidal buffers which repeat the Egyptian theme created by the sphinxes. That there were even more grandiose schemes afoot for estate entrance gates is seen from proposals for more pairs of lodges linked by tall archways. These are on watermarked paper of the 1820s and one at least is a forerunner of the architect's work at Cumberland Terrace and Marble Arch in London. Nash's contribution to the estate ceased at this point, lucrative as it was, it had by-products in designs not only for the Crawford family but also for the neighbouring landowners at Tynan Abbey, Co Armagh (qv) and Castle Leslie, Co Monaghan (qv). That he had been found an extravagant commodity is obvious from John Pringle (Caledon's agent) "... we are certainly at his mercy as to ornaments". In any case the great Regency architect was fully committed at home and the 2nd Earl was to look no further than the Newry architect Thomas J Duff for Classical additions to the house, and probably a host of estate workers cottages peppered about the estate which included three further gate lodges, all in the fashionable new Picturesque English cottage style.

**Glaslough Gate** c1833;
architect probably T J Duff

Opposite a wide entrance gatescreen with big square stone corniced piers, a group of three one and a half storey cottages gathered together as one symmetrical composition. Forming an H on plan, the two outer buildings project as gabled wings to flank a central three bay cottage facing the gates. This has an advancing gabled porch

with elliptical archway with chamfered, transomed and mullioned windows both sides, now minus their lattice glazing. Above them corresponding gabled dormers with simple hipknobs. Each of the wings sport ground floor oriel windows, the attic windows over label-moulded. The gables rise to stone onion finials. The side lodges have big recessed Tudor style entrance surrounds. Rising from the party walls are two massive pairs of Picturesque chimneys diagonally set. All in squared coursed masonry.

**School Gate** c1833;
architect probably T J Duff

To supplant the gatekeeping function of the Doric school lodge within the gates, something less regular and rustic in rubble stone with brick dressings. A one and a half storey building with a simple three down, two up plan given an informal outline by the two left hand bays incorporated into a gabled breakfront rising to a rickety timber hipknob. Simple casement windows now lacking their Picturesque panes. Here again is a massive brick chimney stack carrying a pair of diagonally set pots. Derelict.

**Tynan Gate** c1833;
architect probably T J Duff

Abandoned and in the final stages of decay another pretty ornamental cottage. One and a half storey, three bay symmetrical, gabled and built in rubble stone. The windows, as before without the former fancy glazing, on either side of a gabled breakfront hallway. The bargeboards fretted to form foils with decorative toes. The roof ridge with the obligatory pair of brick diagonal stacks with iron cresting on each side badly eroded.
ROWAN (1979); DIXON (1972); P.R.O.N.I. D2431-2433 and T.3020

**27. CARRICKLEE, Strabane** c1891;
architect probably W J Unsworth

For long a property of the McCauslands. John Herdman of the wealthy Sion Mills family built a new house here in 1891, in the Elizabethan Revival manner. At the entrance he added a gatehouse, or rather gatehouses for there are two cottages dressed up as one, in the "Stockbroker Tudor" style. One and a half storey symmetrical three bay the centre bay highlighted by a canted oriel which "carries" a bracketed projecting black and white work gablet over. The ground floor windows are wide, transomed and mullioned in rendered walls with red brick quoins. Canopied porches shelter the two gable entrances. Two dominant brick chimney stacks rise from an earthenware tiled roof, in the best Arts and Crafts fashion. In a gable an ornamental terracotta plaque with the monograph J H surrounded by an egg and dart motif. William F Unsworth carried out much more of this style of work at Sion House (qv) with its model village and attribution can be made on the strength of this.

**28. CASTLEDERG RECTORY, Castlederg**
pre 1855; *demolished*

Also known as Mount Bernard, the house dating from 1793. The lodge perhaps added for the Rev Archibald H Hamilton.
O.S.M.

**29. CASTLEMOYLE, Newtownstewart**
(see MOYLE)

**30. CASTLETOWN, Strabane** pre 1832;
*demolished*

A lodge opposite the gates probably built for a Major Semple.

**31. CECIL MANOR, Clogher (4)**

A property once of the Cairnes family known as Saville Lodge, it was purchased in 1811 by the Rev Francis Gervais who eighteen years later built a handsome classical mansion house probably to plans by the architect William Farrell. This has been survived by lodges in varying stages of dilapidation none of which had any great architectural pretensions.

**North-East Lodge** c1840

Opposite the entrance a single storey gabled four bay cottage, plain other than for the row of three little canted oriels each with a pretty fretwork timber parapet. Harled walls.

**South-East Lodge** c1860

Now a garden building in the back garden of a bungalow a tiny one and a half storey three bay gabled cottage with harled walls. There are still nice chinoiserie iron gates.

**South-West Lodge** c1850

The most ornate of the four lodges. A generous one and a half storey three bay gabled building now without any of its previous Picturesque features. Rough cast, its front elevation disfigured by a lean-to extension and modern windows.

**North-West Lodge** c1840

An unusual one and a half storey lodge on an L plan with hipped gables and harled walls. Derelict. The Rev Gervais found when he acquired the property that it was in "a wretched state" a condition to which much, including the gate lodges, has reverted.

LAWLOR (1906); O.S.M.

**32. CLANABOGAN, Omagh (2)**

Two pre 1853 lodges built by Samuel Galbraith as part of an ambitious redevelopment of the estate which included a new family church with its own rectory. Neither lodge today appears in its original state. One "improved" the other replaced.

ROWAN (1979)

**33. CLOGHER DEANERY, Clogher** c1830; *demolished*

The lodge was two storey with diamond paned windows. Probably built for "the Honourable and Very Rev Robert William Henry Maude who has much improved this pleasant and retired residence by opening up a new avenue ..."

O.S.M.

**34. CLOGHER PALACE, Clogher (2)**

The elegant episcopal palace essentially assumed its present appearance in works for Bishop Lord Robert Tottenham to designs by the Sligo architect William Warren 1819-20. The main entrance is contemporary.

**Town Gate** c1820;
architect probably William Warren

A seemly Classical lodge with stuccoed walls dressed in sandstone masonry. Single storey, gabled, the front elevation is dominated by a tetrastyle Doric portico with a mutuled pediment. Recessed behind this, before improvement, the three bays were in the form of a central niche flanked by a panelled entrance door and a spoke-headed Georgian window carried down to floor level with an underpanel. All three bays have semicircular heads. Beyond the portico blind walls framed by pairs of Doric pilasters with an entablature over. The doorway has since been relocated in sensitive alterations to this very fine little building. To the main street an impressive stone gate with very tall square pillars having recessed panels, fluted friezes, cornices and blocking caps. Separate wicket openings. Modern ecclesiastical gates.

**Side Entrance** c1890

When the palace became a private residence Thomas S Porter added another lodge. Two storey, gabled in quarry-faced stone with brick dressings. One gable carries Porter's monogram. The house was later to became a convent of the Sisters of St Louis.

LEWIS (1837); ATKINSON (1833); O.S.M.; SLATER (1846); YOUNG (1909)

**35. CLONFEACLE RECTORY, Benburb**
pre 1851; *demolished*

The glebe house of 1751 and the lodge probably built for Rev Henry Griffin.

**36. CLONOE RECTORY, Coalisland**
pre 1833; *demolished*

To a rectory built in 1810, a lodge built for the Rev John Anketell.

**37. COOLNAFRANKY, Cookstown (2)**

An estate previously known as Loymount acquired by John B Gunning Moore c1868.

**Molesworth Street Gate** c1870;
architect possibly John Lanyon

A single storey three bay symmetrical building of confused styles. In squared uncoursed quarry-faced stone with smooth dressings. Skewtable gables with Classical semicircular-pedimented kneelers and rusticated ball finials to apexes. A similarly treated projecting hall has a Tudor hood-moulded semicircular headed fanlight to the doorway. Single stone octagonal chimney pot and perforated earthenware crestings to ridges. Gates missing.

**Loy Street Gate** c1870; *demolished*

The house now part of a school complex.

**38. CORCREEVY, Fivemiletown (2)**

The pleasant Georgian villa built in 1810 by Matthew James Burnside is now a shell, burnt in the 1920s. To a 134 acre demesne were later added two gate lodges.

**West Lodge** c1840; *ruinous*

Replacing an earlier lodge to the opposite side of the avenue (doubtless of an age with the house) was a delightful Picturesque cottage. Single storey below a steeply-pitched thatched hipped roof, its walls were harled and whitewashed. Rectangular two roomed on plan. To one corner a recessed porch, the roof projecting, supported on a post, to cover it and the little hall alongside. A little slit window with lattice panes from the living room surveys this rustic sitting out area. To the avenue elevation two bipartite windows with pretty elongated hexagonal cast iron patterned casements. Piercing the thatch a pair of octagonal chimneys. Sadly this once idyllic scene has become an overgrown ruin. Octagonal stone gate posts with contemporary ornate iron gates remain.

**East Lodge** c1840; *demolished*

ATKINSON (1833); O.S.M.

**39. CORICK, Clogher (3)**

The Rev John Benjamin Story junior had Lanyon, Lynn and Lanyon design him modest Italianate additions to the existing house in 1863. It is to be regretted that the architects had clearly no hand in a most unnoteworthy trio of gate lodges all of which predate the house. One of these pre 1854 buildings to the east opposite the gates. The West lodge is a tiny one and a half storey building with skewtables and its back to the road.

DIXON (1972); ROWAN (1979)

**40. CRANEBROOK, Coalisland (2)**
both pre 1853; *both demolished*

Two lodges for Mr John Cranston.

**41. CREEVANAGH or CREVENAGH,**
Omagh c1845

In pristine condition a single storey stuccoed lodge below a hipped roof with big crude paired brackets to the eaves. Its sheeted front door and sash windows of the three bay front gathered under an all-embracing label moulding. Built for Daniel Auchinleck of a family whose most famous son was to be Field Marshall Sir Claude John Eyre Auchinleck.

**42. CRILLY, Aughnacloy** pre 1833;
*demolished*

To a nice big gentleman farmer's house of the Pettigrew family.

**43. CROSH, Newtownstewart** pre 1854;
*demolished*

A house of 1835 to which the lodge may have been contemporary. Built by Crawford Colhoun or his successor Alexander William Colhoun.

O.S.M.

**44. DAISY HILL Clogher (2)**

**East Lodge** c1840

Standard single storey lodge three bay below a hipped roof.

**West Lodge** pre 1852

One and a half storey building altered out of all recognition. Both for a Captain Andrew Miller.

**45. DERRYBARD, Fintona** c1850

120 acres over which Atkinson in 1833 waxed lyrical "... the picturesque pleasures of this little panoramic scene, which presses with indescribable vigour and activity upon the organ of enjoyment, even in a first embrace ... the most perfectly finished feature of retired beauty, of which this section of Tyrone can boast ...". Today the fine big Classical villa, built in 1832 by the Rev Dr George Vesey, lies a pathetic shell. That the improvements to the idyll continued after Atkinson's visit is proved by a surviving gate lodge. In the fashion of the time is a one and a half storey three bay gabled Tudor Picturesque building. In nice mellow stone with smooth quoins, the gables ornate with serrated bargeboards. A similarly treated breakfront gabled hall, with semicircular-headed doorway, is asymmetrically positioned. Banded window surrounds frame modern lights. Built by Samuel Vesey upon succeeding his father in 1845. Much extended. Probably contemporary with the house is an excellent Gothick gate sweep with four big quatrefoil section cluster-column pillars. In

dressed stone only one ball finial remains. Arrowhead topped railings and gates, the quatrefoil motif is repeated in a continuous band. There are identical pillars at Elm Park, Co Armagh (qv).
ATKINSON (1833); O.S.M.

**46. DERRYGALLY, Moy** pre 1833; *demolished*

**47. DERRYLORAN GLEBE, Cookstown** pre 1854; *demolished*
The lodge opposite the gates built for Rev Arthur Molony. To a big square rectory of 1820.

**48. DONAGHENRY GLEBE, Stewartstown** pre 1833; *demolished*
Perhaps contemporary with the rectory of 1811 and built for Rev Francis L Gore.
Described in 1971 as "a pleasant 3 bay gate lodge, Georgian glazed with side panels to door, now abandoned".
DUNGANNON AND COOKSTOWN; U.A.H.S. (1971)

**49. DONAGHMORE, Donaghmore** (see MULLAGRUEN)

**50. DROMORE RECTORY, Dromore (2)** both pre 1853; *both demolished*
The lodges may have been built along with the rectory which was commenced in 1832 by the Rev Henry Lucas St George who remained the incumbent until his death in 1872.
O.S.M.; LESLIE (1929)

**51. DRUMCAIRNE, Stewartstown (2)**
An early 19th century seat of the Caulfield family Earls of Charlemont. In contrast to the Classical style house were two Picturesque lodges which postdate it.
**South Lodge** c1840; *demolished*

*Postcard view (P. Leonard)*

A picture postcard scene of a delightful Hansel and Gretel English Picturesque cottage totally ivy-clad below a very steeply-pitched thatch from the centre of which rose a pair of diagonally-set brick chimneys. The gables had delicately fretted foiled timber bargeboards with quatrefoil toes and carved hipknobs. In the same manner a projecting porch supported on a pair of wooden posts. Visible on the gable elevation a canted lattice-paned bay window. Three bay and probably one and a half storey it rested in neatly manicured lawns, flowerbeds and gravel paths.
**North Lodge** c1860; *demolished*
Another postcard view shows a lodge much as the above but later in date with slightly cruder bargeboards to a lower pitched roof, slated and

*Postcard view (P. Leonard)*

crested. The outside of the lodge again shrouded in ivy creeper. A similar church-type porch beside which sits the bearded gatekeeper.

**52. DRUM MANOR, Cookstown (2)**
Captain Stewart Richardson built a house here in 1829 which had two pre 1854 gate lodges, predecessors of those to be found today at the same entrances. Many alterations were made over the years before the architect William Hastings completed it in the 1870s. Prior to this the property had passed to various owners through the female line before in 1866 Henry James Stuart, 5th Earl of Castlestuart married Augusta Le Visconte only surviving child of Major William Stewart Richardson-Brady of Oaklands, as the seat was then known. She had assumed by Royal Licence the name and arms of Richardson and Brady whilst he took the surnames Richardson and Stuart, which perhaps goes a long way to explain the elaborate coats-of-arms at both new entrances.
**Wellbrook Gate** c1876;
architect William Hastings

To the big Tudor Gothick castellated mansion the architect added the gate lodges in suitably complementary style. This is a pert little design, one and a half storey, three bay and gabled. Built in square coursed stone with a high bracketed eaves, skewtables with kneelers and label-moulded chamfered window openings. Almost central, projects a buttressed hallway with a hood-moulded four-centred Tudor arched doorway. Below a cast iron finial on the leading gable the elaborately carved coat-of-arms flanked by two attic windows and gathered under a stepped label moulding. Two big stone chimney stacks with tops corbelled as the eaves. The whole now expanded into a commodious modern dwelling in sympathetic style. To this a relatively modest gatescreen with railed convex quadrants and square stone corniced pillars.
**Cookstown Gate** 1876;
architect: William Hastings
The lodge much as the above but lacking some of the finer detailing and substituting octagonal chimney pots. On an axis with the Cookstown road approach for maximum impact, an impressive entrance archway. In squared coursed stone the carriage archway segmental pointed and hood moulded below a stepped gable which contains the coat-of-arms and the mottoes VIRTUTI PARET ROBUR/FORWARD. Extending to each side tall embattled and buttressed walls pierced by embrasured loops. An octagonal castellated bartizan to one side only lends an irregular outline. Further framing this convex quadrant walls with more arrow loops. Now lacking its original gates but recently meticulously repaired.
P.R.O.N.I. Photograph Ref D1618/18/11; DEBRETT (1920); ROWAN (1979)

**53. DRUMGLASS, Dungannon** (see DUNGANNON HOUSE)

**54. DRUMNAKILLY, Omagh** pre 1854; *demolished*
Probably built for Alexander Sanderson McCausland.

**55. DULLERTON, Donemana (2)**
In the 1890s the Bond family acquired the neighbouring Glenview House (qv) moving from the old house to build a remarkable new timber-framed Elizabethan Revival house on the site of the McRae residence, giving it the same name.
**South Lodge** c1890
A plain two storey gabled house, three bay notable only for huge timber curved brackets arranged in pairs under the eaves. Now abandoned it was built at the entrance to the previous house which became Dullerton Farm House, now demolished.
**North Lodge** 1898; architect not known
A striking sight with the backdrop of Gortmonly Hill is this "Stockbroker Tudor" escapee from the suburbs. A two storey gatehouse on an L plan

*(P.R.O.N.I.)*

*Drum Manor, Cookstown Gate*

with generous proportions. Its ground floor built in orange brick with, to the avenue, a canted bay over which projects a half timbered gable on big brackets. The road elevation has a triple window below a jettied first floor also in "black-and-white" work which contains a canted oriel window under which is the datestone. The Rosemary- tiled crested roof plunges down in a catslide to form a porch to the front door. This is rich in excellent joinery work, supported by turned posts with a balustrade where you would expect but also one forming a frieze over. There is a tall brick corbelled chimney stack. The lodge nicely set off by a terrace with an ornamental fretwork railing. A lodge very much akin to that at Conway Co Antrim (qv).

**56. DUNGANNON, Dungannon** pre 1907 *demolished*

Previously the rectory before coming into the hands of Thomas S Irwin who built the lodge c1870 and who changed its name to Drumglass. The lodge now gone, the house forming part of a hospital complex.

**57. DUNGANNON PARK, Dungannon** (see NORTHLAND)

**58. DUNMORE, Omagh** pre 1907; *demolished*

**59. DUNMOYLE LODGE, Sixmilecross (3)**

Not one of the three lodges remains to a once prosperous but now forgotten demesne. The big Neo-Classical house, extensive outbuildings and lodges survived only by the Mann family church which is itself now pathetically abandoned.

**West Lodge** pre 1854; *demolished*
**East Lodge** pre 1907; *demolished*
**North Lodge** 1846; architects Weightman and Hadfield; *demolished*

The estate also became associated with the Jeffcock family and in the Public Record Office of Northern Ireland there is a drawing of a gate lodge for William Jeffcock dated 19th October 1846. All that remains on the site of this pretty building is part of a dressed stone plinth. Designed by the Sheffield firm of Weightman and Hadfield. John Grey Weightman was a pupil of P F Robinson, one of the pioneers of the Picturesque movement, and this design clearly shows the master's influence. Single storey Tudor Revival of irregular outline but with only two main rooms. Tall skewtable gables with a variety of finials on apexes and big moulded kneelers, all in dressed stone as were plinth, quoins and surrounds to single and mullioned tripartite leaded windows. A breakfront hall eccentrically located on the front elevation has a similarly treated gable over a Tudor arched sheeted timber front door with big decorative iron strap hinges and knocker. Behind the main body of the lodge with its living room and bedroom was a flat-roofed structure which housed pantry, closet and scullery. The whole composition was surmounted by a coupled chimney stack. Latterly the seat of Sir John Ross, last Lord Chancellor of Ireland.
COLVIN (1978); P.R.O.N.I. D957

**60. ECCLESVILLE, Fintona (2)**

A property that by 1668 had passed to the Eccles family, the manor house built in 1703 was enlarged in 1795 and further extended in 1825 by John Dixon Eccles. It was not until a quarter of a century later that the estates acquired a gate lodge.

**Main Entrance** c1850; architect not known; *demolished*

H.M.B.B.

Picturesque Gothic style lodge. Simple one and a half storey, symmetrical three bay, two up two down gabled building. The walls stuccoed with quoins had lancet openings with Y-tracery. Serrated bargeboards with pendants at the toes on little delicate hipknobs. Looking as if it may have been by the same architect as that at

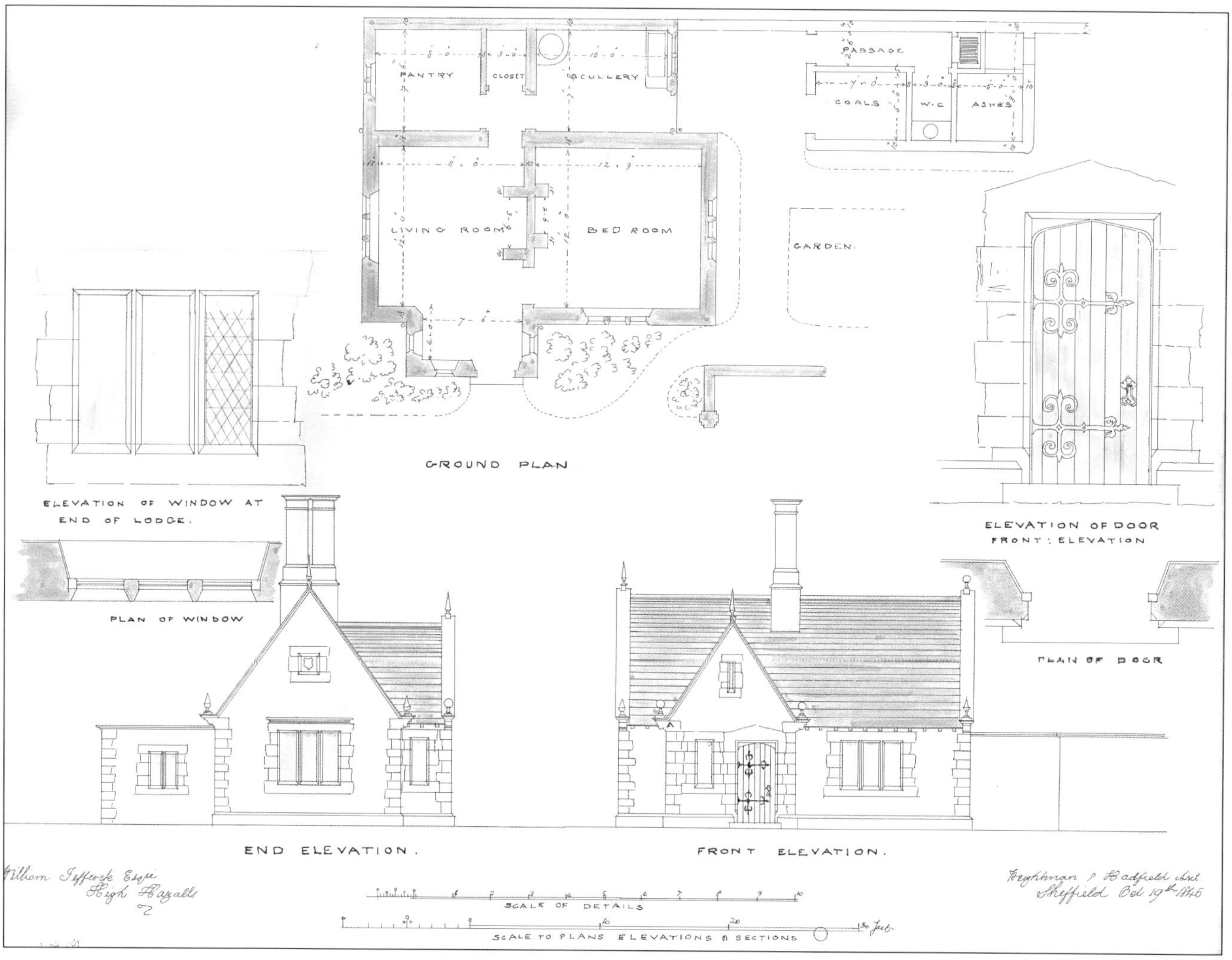

PANTRY CLOSET SCULLERY PASSAGE COALS W.C ASHES LIVING ROOM BED ROOM GARDEN GROUND PLAN ELEVATION OF WINDOW AT END OF LODGE. PLAN OF WINDOW ELEVATION OF DOOR FRONT: ELEVATION PLAN OF DOOR END ELEVATION. FRONT ELEVATION. SCALE OF DETAILS SCALE TO PLANS ELEVATIONS & SECTIONS

William Jeffcock Esq. High Hazells

Weightman & Hadfield Arct. Sheffield Oct 19th 1846

Weightman & Hadfield drawing (P.R.O.N.I.)

*Dunmoyle, North Lodge*

Derrybard (qv). Impressive railed ogee sweeps to big square Classical piers with semicircular headed cappings to four faces.

**Rear Lodge** pre 1906; *demolished*
Gone, as has the big house.
ATKINSON (1833); O.S.M.; H.M.B.B. Photograph

**61. ELAGH, Coagh** pre 1853; *demolished*
Occupant in 1846 Rev J C Gauson.

**62. ELM LODGE, Dungannon** c1855
Standard single storey three bay lodge below a hipped roof. Projecting from the front a hallway with a hipped roof of its own. Classical channelled pilaster quoins and Picturesque lattice-paned windows and fanlight. Stuccoed walls. Good late Georgian square gate pillars in V-jointed rusticated blocks with friezes and pyramidal cappings.

**63. ERGANAGH RECTORY, Omagh** pre 1854; *demolished*
Built by the Rev H H Harte to an early glebe house of 1836.
ROWAN (1979)

**64. FACCARY LODGE, Mountfield (2)**
**South Lodge** pre 1833; *demolished*
This may have been contemporary with the house of c1826. "The late Sir W McMahon built a very handsome house, surrounded by extensive plantations and also laid out a new town at Mountfield."

**North Lodge** pre 1854; *demolished*
A lodge built for Robert McMahon.
LEWIS (1837); O.S.M.

**65. FARDROSS, Clogher** c1840
The ancient seat of Ambus Upton Gledstanes in 1837 when it was a small house very plain in appearance and unoccupied. Robert Hornidge acquired the dilapidated property not long after and instigated a revival in its fortunes, repairing the house and adding a gate lodge. Opposite the gate on an L plan a Picturesque English cottage style structure. One and a half storey with carved ornamental bargeboards. In the internal angle a hipped roof porch on a timber post support. Sash windows in harled walls. Dominating the steeply-pitched roof a pair of octagonal brick chimney stacks on a stone base. Now unrecognisable in modern attire.
JACK JOHNSTON Photograph; O.S.M.; LEWIS (1837)

**66. FAVOUR ROYAL, Aughnacloy (2)**
A portion of the 740 acres of land granted along with that of Spur Royal (see Augher Castle) by James I to Sir Thomas Ridgeway in 1613. It eventually passed via a daughter of Sir James Erskine to the Moutrays. The "spacious and handsome mansion" was destroyed by accidental fire in 1823. It was replaced by the present Tudor style structure for Captain John Corry Moutray to designs from John Hargrave of Cork. To complement this "interesting and beautiful object" the architect designed at least one gate lodge.

**Side Entrance** pre 1834; *demolished*
**Main Entrance** c1825; architect J Hargrave

In appropriate Tudor style opposite the gates a seemly little building, three bay one and a half storey gabled. Constructed in sandstone rubble with dressed surrounds and label mouldings to wide openings. The original windows each a pair of squared casements. The eaves of a shallow-pitched roof emphasised by a row of distinctive brackets. Admirably restored from a shell in 1991. The gates opposite hung on big square stone pillars, corniced with ogee cappings less their finials. Concave wall quadrants beyond.
LEWIS (1837)

**67. GALLANY, Strabane (2)**
To a plain mid-Georgian house, originally of the Smyth family, two porters' lodges.

**East Lodge** pre 1832; *demolished*
Cruciform on plan. Built for a John Smyth.

**West Lodge** pre 1907
Unremarkable building probably for a T H Hamilton.

**68. GARVEY, Aughnacloy** pre 1834; *demolished*
A lodge to the big gaunt, short-lived mansion c1800 for Nathaniel Montgomery Moore by the architect Francis Johnston. The expense on the building was such that the client had to flee to France to escape his debtors in 1815. The shell of the house remains.

**69. GLENCREE, Omagh** c1855

To a gentleman's residence of c1840 pre-dating its gate lodge. A pretty whitewashed harled Gothick cottage. Single storey three bay front elevation but on a basement forming a two storey facade to the rear. Under a hipped roof there are two lancet head windows with composite cast iron pattern of octagons, diamonds and Y-tracery, exactly as on the Strand Road lodge to Richmond, Co Londonderry. Plain lean-to hall breakfront.

**70. GLENVIEW, Donemana** pre 1853; *demolished*
The occupant in 1837 R McRae who nine years later appears at Grange (qv). This may have been when the property was added to the neighbouring Dullerton estate by the Bonds.

**71. GORTALOWRY TOWNLAND, Cookstown** pre 1833; *demolished*
A property of Godfrey O Lyle, leased to John Lind in 1860 when lodge, house, corn and flax mills were identified in the Griffith valuation.
GRIFFITH

**72. GORTMERRON, Moy** pre 1854; *demolished*
The lodge to a late Georgian Palladian style house of John Wilcocks. The property had been acquired by a Mr R Evans by 1837 soon after which he built the lodge.

**73. GORTMORE, Fivemiletown** pre 1907
Nondescript.

**74. GRANGE, Artigarvan** c1830
A standard lodge, three bay single storey below a hipped roof with no eaves projection. Harled walls. Abandoned. Probably built for a T Hutton.

**75. GRANGEFOYLE, Artigarvan** pre 1832; *demolished*
The lodge is survived by a delicate cast iron gate sweep.

**76. GREENFIELD, Strabane** pre 1854
A lodge built for Rev Edward Atkinson.

**77. GREENMOUNT LODGE, Seskinore (2)** both pre 1834; *both demolished*
A residence described in 1834 as a snug modern building of moderate dimensions of Mr John Galbraith. Both lodges contemporary with the house, one of which was opposite its gates.
O.S.M.

**78. GREENVALE, Cookstown** c1840; architect possibly William Farrell

The 18th century home of the Adair family who owned the adjacent flax-spinning mills. Although there is no documentary evidence it seems safe to attribute this design to Farrell it being a very close copy of the Classical lodge at Ely Lodge, Co Fermanagh (qv). It differs in not being as well proportioned and carrying its chimney stack on the ridge. Single storey three bay, the central one of which is marked by a projecting semicircular portico with half conical roof carried on two Tuscan columns. Equivalent pilasters to all corners and a frieze below the eaves. Reflecting the portico is a semicircular recessed porch. Georgian style squared sash windows in stuccoed walls.
LEWIS (1837); ROWAN (1979)

**79. HAZEL HILL, Carrickmore** (see TERMON RECTORY)

**80. HOLLY HILL, Artigarvan** pre 1833; *demolished*
The lodge probably built for James Sinclair whose family was established here since the late 17th century.

**81. INISHMAGH, Ballygawley** c1790
A delightful little antique lodge off the beaten track. Single storey below a bellied hipped roof. One by two bay front elevation harled walls. Seat of the Verner family.

**82. KILDRESS RECTORY, Cookstown** pre 1854; *demolished*
To the glebe house of 1791, a lodge built by Rev Richard Stewart.
ROWAN (1979)

**83. KILLESHIL RECTORY, Ballygawley** pre 1834; *ruinous*
The gate lodge may have been contemporary with the house of 1817. The occupant in 1837 Rev Arthur Young.
LEWIS (1837)

**84. KILLYBRICK, Augher** c1820
Another seat of the Moutrays of Favour Royal (qv) nearby. The lodge across the road from the gates was formerly a tiny and modest three bay affair, single storey and square on plan. Constructed in rubble stone it was more than doubled in size later in the century, its original entrance door sealed up and access moved to the elongated side elevation. Georgian square sash windows. It has recently suffered pub-interior designer improvements, all cake icing render and half doors.

**85. KILLYFADDY, Clogher (3)**
For long the property of the Cairnes family it was bought in the late 18th century by Major-General Edward Maxwell of Finnebrogue, Co Down (qv) of which family Robert Waring Maxwell built the fine big Neo-Classical house probably to designs of William Farrell. Two of the gate lodges also date from the early 19th century.

**North Lodge** pre 1834; *demolished*

**West Lodge** c1830
In squared coursed masonry a standard plan one and a half storey three bay building. Its skewtables are returned to form open pediments to the gables. Derelict.

**South Lodge** pre 1854; *demolished*
ROWAN (1979); LAWLOR (1906)

**86. KILLYMAN RECTORY, Dungannon** c1840
To a rectory founded in 1748 a typical late Georgian style lodge. Below a hipped roof an originally two roomed single storey three bay symmetrical structure with windows contained in segmentally-headed recesses flanking a projecting gabled hall. Now extended to left and right, spic-and-span in a new pebble-dashed livery and inappropriate windows. Built for the Rev Mortimer O'Sullivan.

**87. KILLYMEAL, Dungannon (2)**
For long a seat of the Sheil family it came to Courtney Newton in about 1860 who added a mid-Victorian gate lodge to add to that at the earlier entrance.

**Rear Lodge** c1840; *demolished*
A late Georgian style lodge, ruinous in 1971 now gone. There were once also four piers to the gate sweep, in channelled blocks with concave pyramidal cappings.

**Front Lodge** c1860

The substantial highly ornamental cast iron railings and gate piers evident in 1971 no longer extant. Surviving is a fine Classical style lodge, differing only from that at Aghnahoe (qv) in substituting for the fanlight above the front door a panel containing the Newton coat-of-arms complete with Martlett crest and the motto FAVEAT FORTUNA. Single storey three bay with a hipped roof from which projects the gabled hall highlighted by modillion brackets continued around from the eaves. Stuccoed with quoins, all openings are architraved with segmentally-arched heads. There is a dominant chimney stack with plinth, frieze and cornice.
DUNGANNON AND COOKSTOWN; U.A.H.S. (1971); BURKE (1904)

**88. KILLYMOON CASTLE, Cookstown (5)**
The great Regency architect John Nash's first commission in Ireland resulted in this brilliant little Picturesque castle in a sort of Norman Revival style, in a beautiful setting on the banks of the meandering Ballinderry river. It was built to replace and incorporate part of the earlier house on the site following a fire in about 1800 which all but destroyed it. This former early 18th century residence was built by James Stewart and the remnants of its gate lodge can still be traced.

**Early Entrance** c1750

At the southern extremity of Cookstown's broad main street a straight avenue, along which survive simple square stone pillars, led east to the house. Beside the pillars, built into what is now a corrugated roofed roughcast shed, a sophisticated early Georgian doorcase, effectively presented like a museum exhibit. In Palladian style the door was flanked by a pair of narrow sidelights all in V-jointed rusticated dressed stone the flat arches of which are marked by tall keystone blocks. From 1801 onwards this avenue was down-graded to be the farmyard access when Colonel William Stewart was rebuilding the house and embellishing the demesne with other buildings. These included a temple, ornamental cottage and a new gatehouse entrance to a relocated and tortuous Romantic approach.

**Tudor Gatehouse** c1803;
architect John Nash; *demolished*

A composition which shows much of the influence of his erstwhile partner, the landscape architect Humphry Repton who had departed the practice in 1802. Here is a more rustic version of Repton's entrance to Blaise Castle near Bristol. The avenue passed beneath a pair of Tudor carriage archways in dressed stone each of which contained double gates of wood and iron. These formed a roofed enclosure united to the porter's accommodation alongside by a small castellated hallway. In the form of a cube, probably one up one down, the lodge was constructed in random rubble, the ground floor window tripartite with squared panes below a minimal label moulding. Above it the first floor opening narrower and bipartite. Crowning it all a crenellated parapet with a chimney stack sprouting from one corner. This charming scene is no more and the avenue now leads instead to a golf club. An absentee landlord even when the castle was being built Colonel Stewart left his wife to cater and correspond with the architect over such matters as cottage bargeboard designs and drawing room curtains. Her husband was involved with the Prince Regent's racy set and he is said to have lost Killymoon in a night's gambling but that the following day the Prince told him to "keep his Irish cabin". Sadly gatehouse, temple and cottage have all gone.

**South Lodge** c1840
A modest standard plan three bay single storey lodge with hipped gable roof.

**Grange Gate** pre 1833; *demolished*

**Cloghog Gate** pre 1833; *demolished*
SUMMERSON (1980); ROWAN (1979); DAVIS (1973)

**89. KILMORE LODGE, Drumquin** pre 1853; *demolished*
A lodge built for the Mansfield family.

**90. KILSKEERY GLEBE, Trillick** c1800
Built by the immensely prosperous and long-lived incumbent John Grey Porter of Belleisle, Co Fermanagh (qv). The 1774 rectory has been demolished, the lodge derelict. An irregular front elevation with doorway to one side. Otherwise a typical Georgian structure, squared sash windows in whitewashed harled rubble walls. Single storey below a slated hipped roof with central chimney stack.
O.S.M.

**91. LIME PARK, Caledon** c1830; *demolished*
Opposite the gates was a pretty little standard lodge. Single storey three bay below a hipped roof, its lattice paned windows flanked a flat roofed portico supported by two cast iron columns. The 1836 resident was the Hon A Stewart.

**92. LISANELLY, Omagh** pre 1833
This nondescript lodge was probably built for one Alexander Campbell who could be one of the unfortunates mentioned in the 1834 O.S. Memoirs. "The house is large but in bad repair and everything is falling into decay . The former proprietor was killed in this house by lightning, the last destroyed himself by whiskey."
O.S.M.

**93. LISDHU, Coalisland (3)**

**North Lodge** pre 1833; *demolished*
Possibly to the original 1782 house for William Pike.

**Middle Lodge** c1840
This stone building with brick dressings seems to have had a pre 1833 predecessor at the same entrance. Plain, single storey and built by the Hon Andrew Stuart.

**South Lodge** c1850/1880
A fascinating structure the building sequence of

which is difficult to disentangle but all adding up to a one and a half storey structure with a single storey extension at right angle to form an L plan. The early lodge with its gable to the road is a quaint and naive multi-gabled Picturesque composition. Three bay two up two down, built in coursed basalt rubble with brick dressings. A mock gable above the original central front door is flanked by two gablets to the attic bedrooms. To this accommodation with very restricted headroom was added about thirty years later the single storey addition with a matching ridge line. Contrasting in squared uncoursed quarry-faced Dungannon stone it also has a contrary clipped gable. The new front door in a little breakfront under a very shallow pediment which contains the datestone. All making for a charming composition, amusing were it not in the final stages of decay. The later extension by Armitage Lennox Nicholson.
DUNGANNON AND COOKSTOWN; U.A.H.S. (1971); O.S.M.

**94. LISNACLOON, Castlederg** pre 1853
A nondescript building built for James Anderson land agent to Sir Robert Ferguson of The Farm, Co Londonderry (qv).
O.S.M.

**95. LISNAMALLARD, Omagh** pre 1854
A forgettable lodge built for the Orr family.

**96. LISSAN, Cookstown (2)**
**Cookstown Entrance** c1830
For Sir Thomas Staples a standard plan single storey two roomed lodge with a wide-eaved hipped roof which has a pair of diagonally-set Picturesque chimneys. Sometime later it had applied to front and side windows little oriel bays. Now derelict.
**Castor's Gate** pre 1833; *demolished*

**97. LISSENDERRY, Aughnacloy**
pre 1834/c1850

Opposite the fine railed entrance gate sweep with round stone piers, a tiny lodge which had its origins from the occupancy of G Pettigrew in the big house. It was either completely refaced or rebuilt in the Picturesque manner when the Waller family purchased the property also changing its name from Storm Hill. This is a perky little three bay single storey building with fretted foil bargeboards to main gables and that of the tiny projecting hall. This decoration is carried on as fascias with ornamental pendants at the junctions. Label moulded windows in stuccoed walls. In the leading gable a blank shield. Unoccupied but well tended as a pretty folly.

**98. LOUGHMACRORY LODGE, Carrickmore (2)**
By a lake of that name in a remote elevated spot a Regency shooting lodge in 1837 of Sir Hugh Stewart of Ballygawley Park (qv).
**South Entrance** pre 1854; *demolished*
**North Entrance** pre 1854
Plain and improved.

**99. LOUGHRY, Cookstown (2)**
The estates granted in 1604 by James I to his chief harbinger Sir Robert Lindesay. This tranquil and well-wooded property saw visits by Dean Swift who is said to have written part of *Gulliver's Travels* here.
**Western Lodge** c1845
Mildly Classical, plain single storey below a hipped roof with bracketed eaves. Four bay having square-paned windows in stuccoed walls with rusticated quoins. Two masonry gate pillars survive surmounted by a Lindesay swan and Sandys griffin eyeing each other across the entrance.
**Eastern Lodge** c1860; *demolished*
A faintly Picturesque version of the above. It was four bay single storey stuccoed below a wide eaved low pitched roof. The windows were transomed and mullioned with lattice panes under label mouldings. To the ridge was a pair of tall octagonal chimney stacks. To Chinese lantern type cast iron gate piers again the swan and griffin confront one another to celebrate the marriage of Frederick Lindesay to Agnes Cornish Bayntum Sandys in 1823.
DUNGANNON AND COOKSTOWN; U.A.H.S. (1971); BURKE (1904)

**100. LOYMOUNT, Cookstown**
(see COOLNAFRANKY)

**101. MARTRAY, Ballygawley (2)**
A mildly Tudor style villa of the Stewart family of nearby Ballygawley Hall (qv) beautifully situated overlooking a lake of the same name. Probably dating from c1830 to designs by John Hargrave who may have planned the two pretty Picturesque lodges before his death in 1833.
**West Lodge** c1835;
architect possibly John Hargrave

In nice mellow brick, a Picturesque one and a half storey two up two down symmetrical three bay lodge. The steep main gables and that to the little projecting hall decorated with simple foiled bargeboards now less their hipknobs. The front door has a lancet head. Parallel to the ridge is a pair of octagonal brick chimney stacks much as at Rockhill, Co Donegal (qv) where Hargrave was also employed. Boarded up and abandoned. The broad entrance gate sweep with ogee quadrants having fleur-de-lys topped railings. The big square dressed stone pillars have recessed and fielded panels and four-sided semicircular pedimented cappings as at Ballygawley Hall.
**East Lodge** c1835;
architect possibly John Hargrave
A less formal version of the above in the same pretty brick facings. Again one and a half storey gabled the hall projection asymmetrically placed, a covered rustic sitting-out recess alongside, the roof over carried by a chamfered timber post. Here, by way of variety, the bargeboards are serrated and the octagonal brick chimney stacks set at right angles to the ridge. Tiny squared cast iron windows, the front door surround incorporated two narrow sidelights, all below a semicircular fanlight. This desirable building now lies mysteriously deserted in a quiet

backwater because a realignment of the Dungannon/Ballygawley Road has left it secluded and severed from the main avenue. The gatescreen is much as before but the pillars with pyramidal cappings and the ironwork having fine quatrefoil motif and topped by palmette finials. Both lodges built by Mervyn Stewart after acquiring the property from Hamilton Gorges.

**102. MILLTOWN, Dungannon** c1855

A minute three bay single storey lodge hipped roof and projecting eaves. The walls roughcast have plain banded quoins. Little panelled chimney stack to complement the front door. Almost dwarfing the lodge big circular stone gate pillars with concave conical caps. Modern ironwork. The lodge post-dates the house of the Falls family of the local distillery.
ROWAN (1979)

**103. MILLTOWN LODGE, Strabane** c1836;
architect W V Morrison

When William Vitruvius Morrison was working at Baronscourt (qv) he designed a villa and gate lodge, both in his multi-gabled Picturesque mode, for the Abercorn agent Major John Humphreys. The lodge was built for the princely sum of £120 in random rubble with red brick dressings. One and a half storey three bay but not irregular like the house, it has abnormally high coved eaves and carved spiky waved bargeboards crowned by sturdy hipknobs with ball finials and fancy pendants. From the front elevation projects a brick porch with Tudor arched opening and triangulated and cusped

wooden bargeboards over. To each side elevation pretty Venetian-arched openings with simple Gothick tracery in chamfered reveals. To the road facade a single storey canted bay window with semicircular-headed lights. All the details on this lodge are also to be found on similar lodges at Drumboe Castle and Ballymacool (qqv) both in Co Donegal. Major Humphreys is best known as the father of Mrs C F Alexander the hymn writer, creator of "All things bright and beautiful". The house now incorporated into Strabane Grammar School.
P.R.O.N.I. D623; McPARLAND (1979)

**104. MOUNT BERNARD, Castlederg**
(see CASTLEDERG RECTORY)

**105. MOUNT PLEASANT, Omagh**
pre 1833; *demolished*
In 1833 "The new creation of the Rev Mr Crigan, ... converted by him from a wild boggy moor into its present well-merited character of a handsome Irish villa". The contemporary lodge has gone, to be replaced by a modern bungalow.
ATKINSON (1833); O.S.M.

**106. MOUNTJOY FOREST, Omagh (2)**
An estate with a convoluted history. Sir William Stewart bought the property here at Rash in 1631, his grandson becoming Lord Mountjoy in 1688. By 1782 the property had passed to Luke Gardiner, a rich Dublin banker who became Viscount Mountjoy in his own right. It was he who was mainly responsible for giving the estate its present appearance, planting upwards of 200,000 trees in a programme of afforestation that was to be continued by his son Charles John who became Earl of Blessington in 1816. At this time the demesne was " 7-8 miles in circumference, and enclosed in an 8ft high stone wall for much of its length". He also gave the house, then called "The Cottage" its present castellated Tudor character. Although he is known to have consulted Charles James Mathews, a pupil of Augustus Charles Pugin, and the architect Benjamin Dean Wyatt in the 1820s there is nothing identifiable as being their work. The Earl is best known for his lavish theatrical entertainments here, his beautiful and wayward wife and the squandering of his inheritance before his death in 1829. A visitor in 1854 refers to an auction six years previous: "... the once magnificent demesne ... affords nothing of the attention of the tourist, being quite broken up, and sold to different proprietors". What with the uncoordinated building on the estate and spending on other priorities it is little wonder that there are no gate lodges of any significance.

**North Lodge** pre 1833
Within the estate an old building with vestiges of its Georgian origin mostly lost in modern improvements.

**South Lodge** pre 1833; *demolished*
COLVIN (1978); DOYLE (1854); ROGERS (1988); SADLEIR (1933)

**107. MOYLE or CASTLEMOYLE, Newtownstewart** c1855
A four bay single storey building with squared Georgian style sash windows. Rendered with quoins below a hipped roof. Good rusticated square stone gate pillars with ball finials on extended pedestals on moulded corniced caps. For long the residence of Rev R H Nash.

**108. MULLAGHMORE, Seskinore** c1840
A portion of the estates of the Perry family of Seskinore Lodge, this lodge may have been built by the McClintocks when the property passed to them through marriage to the Perrys. A quaint little creation in the Picturesque manner, the main body single storey two bay with ornamental foil and wave bargeboards. Constructed of rubble with dressed stone quoins, the windows bipartite each light being semicircular-headed to sashes. By accident or design the building derives much of its character from the gabled hall which projects from the leading elevation and has a little gablet over the front door. This is probably a more recent addition. Abandoned.
ATKINSON (1833)

**109. MULLAGRUEN, Donaghmore (2)**
An original thatched glebe house of 1683, for the famous Rev G Walker whilst rector of this parish, was superseded by an intermediate dwelling of 1707. It is now fronted by the present Ionic villa of c1830, built by Alexander MacKenzie brewer and patriot, to which there is a contemporary gate lodge.

**Front Entrance** c1830

Sandwiched between the public road, to which it displays a two storey facade, and the higher avenue approach where it appears as a single storey three bay lodge is a delightfully naive Classical composition. Carrying an entablatured parapet, which disguised the hipped roof, two square outer columns flank two engaged round inner ones all with their squashed Ionic capitals. The panelled front door is flanked by rectangular-paned cast iron windows with intricate intertwined glazing bars to the heads. To complete the picture extending from each side of the lodge concave railed quadrants which terminate in V-jointed rusticated stone pillars with recessed panel friezes surmounted by concave pyramidal cappings. At their bases octagonal stone buffers. A back door at basement level gives access to the road. The lodge is now in a tragically dilapidated state, the corniced chimney stack having collapsed and the railings overgrown.

**Side Entrance** pre 1854; *demolished*
A nondescript building. The house, alternatively called Donaghmore House, became the property of the Lyle family, and is now a school.
DUNGANNON AND COOKSTOWN; U.A.H.S. (1971); ROWAN (1979)

**110. MULLANTAINE, Stewartstown (2)**
**East Lodge** pre 1906; *demolished*
**West Lodge** c1855
Opposite the gates a one and a half storey three bay symmetrical lodge of confused styles. To the hipped gable roof a pair of diagonally-set Picturesque chimney stacks. Bipartite casement windows flank a projecting pedimented distyle portico of Tuscan order. High in the gables tiny attic windows. The 1820 house of Mr Lynd predates the two lodges built for the Kennedy family.
YOUNG (1909)

**111. MULLNAGORE LODGE, Donaghmore**
pre 1854; *demolished*
Originally a glebe house, the rector in 1846 Rev Thomas Carpendale.

**112. NORTHLAND, Dungannon (4)**
Thomas Knox purchased these once grand and extensive estates known as the manor of Dungannon from Lord Donegall in 1692. The family of Knox was raised to the Viscountcy of Northland and built a house here in 1785. Further titled as Earls of Ranfurly it was the 2nd Earl on his succession in 1840 who set about extensive improvements which included enlarging the mansion house into a vast irregular Classical pile in the Ionic order complemented by a matching gate lodge.

**Town Lodge** c1845;
architect perhaps Thomas Smith
In high quality sandstone ashlar of a sort of columnar excess, Ionic like the house but symmetrical. Single storey, a one bay pedimented projection to the road is flanked by recesses each fronted by two Ionic columns. These columns carry through identical side elevations as peristyle loggias. The whole T plan and recesses contained under an embracing entablature the cornice of which carries through front and back pediments. On each of the opposing side facades are matching panelled doors with architraved surrounds as have all the square Georgian sash windows. The rear elevation is also a conscious design with the central pedimented window flanked by two blank bays. A panelled corniced chimney stack sits on the ridge of a pitched roof which spans between front and back pediments flanked by two flat roofs. It is pleasing to report that the shocking dilapidation noted by the U.A.H.S. in 1971 has been reversed and the lodge is now in pristine condition. Much loved of photographers at the turn of this century was the extensive and pretentious entrance screen. The lodge was located behind the relatively plain central railing but this was flanked by matching exuberant carriage entrances and framing pairs

W.A. Green (U.F.T.M.)

*Northland, Town Lodge*

of pedestrian gates with their intermediate hollow "Chinese lantern" cast iron pillars, all four crowned by gas lantern lights. Beyond this again are four big stone square pillars with recessed panels banded by carved egg and dart moulding. Their corniced cappings once proudly supported cast iron Knox falcons. Wider still tall screen walls terminate in massive pillars in rusticated masonry. This flamboyant screen looks to post-date the lodge by about ten years perhaps in response to the Earl of Charlemont's efforts at Roxborough (qv). The whole scene now sadly bare compared with the well- wooded early 20th century photograph, the original ironwork replaced by something much plainer, to the backdrop of a nasty modern school classroom block. The architect is not known but Thomas Smith of Hertford (1799-1875) was employed by Lord Ranfurly about this time. The big house is now demolished and the proud demesne broken up. Broken up it always was to some extent as noted in the Ordnance Survey Memoirs of 1834 "... a beautiful demesne divided into 2 parts by the high road from Dungannon to Armagh, under which it is joined by a tunnel lately constructed". To this portion of the estates known as Dungannon Farm there were three further and later gate lodges.

**Tunnel Lodge** c1870

A substantial building, one and a half storey symmetrical three bay Picturesque style lodge. On either side of a breakfront gabled hallway extend pents supported on posts. Corresponding with the two ground floor windows to the front elevation are two gablets over. All gables are decorated with diamond pattern sawtooth carved bargeboards with fancy hipknobs. Once guarding the tunnel below the road it is now a beautifully secluded private residence in a pretty garden.

**Quarry Lodge** pre 1906; *demolished*

Survived by two large square channelled rusticated block pillars.

**Moygashel Lodge** pre 1906; *demolished*

LAWRENCE PHOTOGRAPH COLLECTION (N.L.I.) Refs 2166(C), 9103(R); GREEN PHOTOGRAPH COLLECTION (UFTM) Ref WAG 1777; YOUNG (1909); DUNGANNON AND COOKSTOWN, U.A.H.S. (1971); COLVIN (1978)

**113. OAKLANDS, Cookstown**
(see DRUM MANOR)

**114. OAKLANDS, Omagh (2)**
both pre 1854; *both demolished*

**115. OMAGH CEMETERY, Omagh** c1890;
architect not known

A solid commodious superintendent's lodge in squared uncoursed quarry-faced stone with smooth dressings and quoins. Single storey with a hipped roof from which projects a central breakfront to the three bay front. Skewtabled with a shamrock finial the gable contains a quatrefoil relief over a blank panel below which is the shouldered head front door flanked by a pair of chamfered window openings. Set back to each side is a long mullioned tripartite window. Two friezed stone chimney stacks and perforated terracotta crestings to the roof. The chimney stacks are identical to those on the lodge to St Patrick's Cathedral, Armagh (qv) by Ashlin and Coleman. Carrying flamboyant multi-curled cast iron gates a pair of Tudor Gothick pillars. Each in dressed stone, nicely sculpted, broaches from a square base to octagonal shafts decorated on alternate faces with trefoil motifs. It rises through an octahedral capping with foiled and cusped lucarnes to culminate in finely carved poppy finials.

**116. OMAGH LUNATIC ASYLUM, Omagh**
c1854; architect probably William Farrell

A huge institution built in 1847-53 to designs by the Dublin architect William Farrell. Rather more lighthearted but in matching Tudor Revival manner is the gate lodge in similar squared uncoursed quarry-faced stone with tall kneelers to skewtabled gables. Over the dressed stone chamfered window openings are relieving arches. A miniature dressed stone hallway projects from the internal angle. Unfortunately the original little squared timber windows and the tall exaggerated three flue chimney stack with vertical channels have all gone, as has the gate sweep survived by a couple of squat stone pillars with corniced cappings.

ROWAN (1979)

**117. PARKANAUR, Castlecaulfield (2)**

A charming rambling Tudor Revival mansion which evolved over a number of years. From the time when John Henry Burgess purchased the land in the 1770s and built a small cottage called Edenfield 1802-04, it was added to continually by him in 1820 and subsequently from 1839 to 1854 by his son John Ynyr. Most of this later work was to designs by the Newry architect Thomas J Duff. In immaculately tended grounds, wooded by the planting of 40,000 trees by John Henry are two avenues leading from two gate lodges added in the mid 1840s.

**Main Entrance** c1845;
architect P F Robinson/T J Duff

In complementary style with the house here, as at Baronscourt (qv), is an idea of P F Robinson's illustrated in his *Designs for Lodges and Park Entrances* (1833), in this case Design No 1. But unlike those for the Abercorns, it seems improbable that Robinson was directly involved, for Duff is known to have been a collector of architectural pattern books and it is likely that he was responsible for this adaptation, probably not long prior to his death in 1848. What was built was remarkably faithful to the original, right down to the creeper-embowered arboreal porch. Differing marginally in layout and position of the gable bay window to suit its orientation on site. It sadly has lost its Picturesque porch, to be replaced by an incorrect hall with bargeboards which are in conflict with the skewtable gables with kneelers elsewhere. One and a half storey, two up two down regular plan given its informal appearance by placing of single storey rectangular bay windows, the porch, gablet and big tall octagonal chimney stacks. To complete the Cotswold manor house idiom the windows mullioned as bi- and tripartite openings to pretty lattice-paned cast iron lights which cleverly contained large diamond shaped pivot openers. These delightful features were lost in a piece of

*P.F. Robinson (1833)*

*Parkanaur, Main Entrance*

(R. Loe)
Parkanaur, Main Entrance

reckless restoration, since redeemed to some extent by the installation of "leaded" lights. All constructed in fine grey ashlar, this design was also "erected as a gate lodge in Scotland, in South Wales [Singleton, Swansea], and in Sussex". There is an extensive and grandiose entrance gatescreen with tall octagonal stone pillars, with octahedral cappings, which support sturdy cast iron railings in convex quadrants with matching carriage and wicket gates.

**Side Entrance** c1845

An identical form to the above but with bargeboard gables and in a honey-coloured sandstone. It has become steadily more mundane with successive "improvements". There is a canted single storey bay window to the road.
ROBINSON (1833); ROWAN (1979); DUNGANNON AND COOKSTOWN; U.A.H.S. (1971)

**118. POMEROY, Pomeroy (2)**

**East Lodge** pre 1833; *demolished*

A lodge on the Stewartstown approach.

**West Lodge** pre 1833/c1860

Opposite the gates still recognisable as a Picturesque gabled affair with ornamental bargeboards and untoothed quoins. This may be a replacement c1860 for an earlier building on the site. The 1780 house built by Rev James Lowry has also been swept away by the Forestry Service. Both original lodges for Robert William Lowry.
DUNGANNON AND COOKSTOWN; U.A.H.S. (1971)

**119. RASH, Omagh**
(see MOUNTJOY FOREST)

**120. RED HOUSE, Omagh** c1910

Of an age with the fine Arts-and-Crafts house is a lodge in the same manner. In appropriate red brick its gable is presented to the avenue with diagonal black and white work. The elliptically-arched recessed porch has now been enclosed. Squared panes to upper sliding sashes. Like the neighbouring property of Carricklee (qv) probably built by the Herdmans.

**121. RELAGH or RALEIGH LODGE, Dromore** pre 1833; *demolished*

Opposite the gates the lodge built by James Hamilton Story like the house of 1814, now gone. The "small neat double cottage" of the 1830s built by Samuel Story was by 1855 being rejected in favour of the family's new residence of Errington nearby.
BURKE (1855); O.S.M.

**122. RHONE HILL, Moy (2)**

An antique house (c1724) of the Greer family.

**South Lodge** pre 1833; *demolished*

This lodge seemingly gone by the turn of this century is survived by fine rusticated Georgian gate piers.

**North Lodge** pre 1833; *demolished*

An entrance to both house and beetling mill.

**123. ROCKDALE, Cookstown** c1855

Even in its present derelict state the lodge still contrives to look appealing. Simple three bay symmetrical and single storey. Supported on big timber eaves brackets is the hipped roof from which projects a gabled porch. This has a segmentally-headed doorway with fanlight in harled walls with V-jointed quoins. Tall central chimney stack, this looks like a simpler version of the lodges at Killymeal (qv) and Aghnahoe (qv) both in the same county. Extensive concave railed quadrants with fleur-de-lys tops. Square stone gate pillars with recessed panel relief. There is another lodgeless gatesweep of rusticated gate piers with concave pyramidal cappings. Built by James Corry Lowry, a younger branch of the Pomeroy (qv) family.
DUNGANNON AND COOKSTOWN; U.A.H.S. (1971)

**124. ROSCAVEY, Beragh (2)**

both pre 1854; *both demolished*

There must have been something of a renaissance here for despite a report in 1834 of "... the house fast falling into ruin and the whole place very much neglected", a seat of the Galbraiths has survived and two short-lived porters' lodges were provided not long afterwards.
O.S.M.

**125. ROUGHAN, Newmills** pre 1854

A lodge contemporary with the house, in 1846 occupied by Mrs Jane King, now modernised.

**126. ROXBOROUGH CASTLE, Moy (4)**

An old mansion was built here in 1774, by the Hon Capt Francis Caulfield MP younger brother of the "Volunteer" 1st Earl of Charlemont, to which there was a lodged entrance to the north.

**Clonbeg Gate** c1800

A small three bay brick lodge on a standard plan under a clipped eaves hipped roof. Derelict, it survives as an adjunct to its successor. By 1846 the 2nd Earl of Charlemont had erected on the site an austere Classical house "... in the severest and simplest style of Italian Villa work". His architect was William Murray who also produced many schemes for gate lodges all based on a cruciform plan three of which were executed with the same Classical theme. Of the numerous drawings dating between August 1842 and October 1843 it is difficult to positively relate a specific design to those executed, there having been some on-site adaptation. Common to all three buildings are two main rooms, the cruciform layout being achieved by hall and porch arrangement to the front and small bedroom and closet to the rear.

**North Lodge** c1845;
architect William Murray

P. Rankin

Fronting the earlier Clonbeg lodge an upright three bay symmetrical building with entablature parapet hiding a hipped roof. The front elevation has a projecting hall of three bays in its own right, four engaged square columns frame the doorway flanked by two narrow sidelights. The two main outer bays contain margined glazed windows with architraved surrounds. Two bay deep the whole in fine ashlar as is the corniced chimney stack. In an advanced stage of decay.

**Side Entrance** c1845;
architect William Murray

A variation on the above but with the advanced central feature pedimented over two semicircular-headed narrow lights flanking a central niche. The entrance door to the side of the projection has, like the side windows, a Classical hood carried on console brackets. Under the main hipped roof the windows margined as are those on the correct and sympathetic extension. All in squared uncoursed masonry. There are dome-capped stone pillars to tall convex wall quadrants at the road.

**Moy Entrance** c1845;
architect William Murray; *demolished*

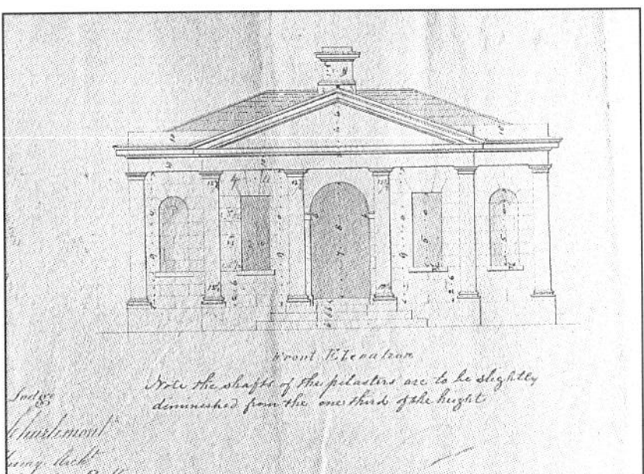

*W. Murray drawing (I.A.A.)*

The third in the series of Neo-Classical lodges and as befitted the main entrance, the grandest. Ironically it is the only one not to have survived, disgracefully having been replaced by a modern bungalow. Single storey on a cruciform plan formed by the rear projection which housed the staircase to a basement, and to the fore by a wide pedimented tetrastyle Tuscan portico. Two bays deep below an otherwise hipped roof. From what can be detected from old photographs the windows were square-paned sashes in ashlar walls. What survives of this entrance complex is truly impressive. Probably post-dating the lodge by about ten years is an extensive gatescreen in the "Great Exhibition" manner with lavish ironwork. Flanked by two grand square stone pillars with panelled shafts topped by shallow pedimented four sided cappings are ogee sweeps of tall railings leading to four "Chinese lantern" type cast iron piers. Each of these is rich in scrolled ornamentation below a frieze of flowers with cappings similar to the pillars. Crowning the two inner piers are coronets with serpent support, as at Moyola, Co Londonderry, whilst the outer ones are surmounted by angry Charlemont dragon crests. These piers flank secondary concave quadrants which contain wicket gates. Railings and gates plentiful with anthemion decoration flowers and kindred other tricks of the ironsmith who in this case may have been Richard Turner of Kew Gardens and Belfast Palm House fame and who is known to have been employed here by the Charlemonts. In 1863 to designs of William J Barre, Murray's house was transformed into a vast French Classical chateau for James Molyneux Caulfield, the 3rd and last Earl of Charlemont. From his death in 1892 the fortunes of house and estate went into steady decline until both were sold off and dismantled in 1920, presenting a sorry sight today.
SLATER (1846); DUNLOP (1868); MURRAY DRAWING COLLECTION (I.A.A.); Ref 76/1107-1111

**127. SAVILLE LODGE, Clogher**
(see CECIL MANOR)

**128. SESKINORE LODGE, Seskinore (5)**
The small house here in 1834 of the Perrys passed by marriage to the McClintock family of whom Colonel George Perry McClintock built a new residence in 1862 probably to designs of Sir Charles Lanyon. Of the numerous gate lodges to the estate, one pre 1833 the others built before 1854, not one has survived the Forestry Service axe. One entrance became known locally as the Lion's Lodge for the McClintock crest which surmounted the gate piers. By all accounts its lodge was of standard format in brick below a hipped roof with central chimney stack.
ROWAN (1979); YOUNG (1909)

**129. SION, Sion Mills** c1884;
architect W F Unsworth

*Trustees of Stokesay Castle*

*Stokesay Castle, Gatehouse*

From the modest beginnings of purchasing an unfinished flour mill from the Marquess of Abercorn, the Herdman brothers and Andrew Mulholland built up a huge flax-spinning industry, surrounded by a "model" village.
In 1884 the core of the original 1842 house blossomed into a big half timbered Elizabethan Revival mansion for Emmerson Tennent Herdman to a design by his brother-in-law, the English architect William F Unsworth of Petersfield who also provided a "medieval" gatehouse on the main Strabane-Omagh Road. Now in a pitiful condition despite its listed status is this eccentric piece of architecture in the Ulster landscape. This is a facsimile of the c1570 gatehouse to Stokesay Castle in Shropshire and in greatly inferior state than the original. In a surplus of black-and-white half-timbered work this is a tall two and a half storey gabled structure providing generous accommodation. The ground floor is raised on a stone plinth to give sufficient headroom for carriages to pass below the central archway which is spanned by the jettied upper floors. Fine double timber gates with turned balusters to the upper halves. High above gablets back and front. Ornamented by ogee and diamond bracing struts authentic angle posts and brackets with plaster nogging, the composition is basically symmetrical apart from the informally located mullioned windows with their square leaded lights. The big vertically-ribbed red brick chimney, just like that at Stokesay, is now missing and the earthenware tiled roof damaged.
B.N. (1884); ROWAN (1979)

**130. SPUR ROYAL, Augher**
(see AUGHER CASTLE)

**131. STANGMORE LODGE, Dungannon**
pre 1906
To a gentleman farmer's house a plain lodge.

**132. STORMHILL, Aughnacloy**
(see LISSENDERRY)

**133. STRABANE TECHNICAL COLLEGE, Strabane** 1937; architect James S Lawson

Stretching along the Londonderry road the college building is a remarkably gauche essay in a sort of delayed Edwardian Classical Revival manner. Fronting this in close proximity a porter's lodge in stylistic harmony. Single storey on a square plan in brown rustic brick with contrasting stark white lintels, quoins and a deep surrounding parapet. The front elevation suitably symmetrical, four bay with a two bay frontispiece breakfront like the main block dominated by a big square gable contained by two little pedestalled ball finials. Central to this, carrying nothing, a base corbelled out in "silver screen" style imitating the college. Rather more pleasing is the irregular side elevation of two bays, the right hand one having a pedimented doorcase, repeating that of the main building. The left hand bay a window, over which the parapet expands to become an eccentrically positioned gable. The windows retain their little squared panes. Two square gate pillars with ball finialed capping in matching materials.

**134. STUART HALL, Stewartstown**
pre 1853; *demolished*
Only the magnificent gatescreen survives. Both lodge and the big house of the Earls of Castlestuart have gone, the latter following a terrorist bomb attack. Wide outer railed sweeps with slight concave curves terminate in grand square pillars built of V-jointed rusticated stone. Similar inner pillars flank the main carriage gates and two outer pedestrian openings. The ironwork looks c1850 and was probably erected when Robert Stuart the 2nd Earl was Victorianising the plain old Georgian block with unlovely castellated additions.

**135. TERMON RECTORY, Carrickmore (2)**
both pre 1833
Originally built as a big Church of Ireland rectory by the Rev Charles Cobbe Beresford in 1815, its size must have made it a burden for future incumbents for it fell into lay hands. The two gate lodges, both very plain and modernised, may be contemporary with the house or have been added when the property was acquired by the Stewarts of Ballygawley Hall and Loughmacrory Lodge (qqv) and they altered the name to Athenry. For a while it was known as Hazel Hill before finally being called Termon House by the Alexander family.
YOUNG (1909); ROWAN (1979)

**136. THORNHILL, Artigarvan** pre 1832
A distinctly unremarkable lodge for the Edie family.

**137. TREWMOUNT, Moy** c1870;
architect Thomas Jackson

A charming little park and Georgian villa previously more suitably known as Trew Cottage. About 1870 James G Richardson made alterations to the house, rechristened the property and built a gate lodge. Indiscreet in this rural spot is the architect's intractable and unmistakable stuccoed Neo-Classical style. A single storey standard plan lodge below a hipped roof. Three bay by two, each opening in a segmentally headed recess is flanked by pairs of Tuscan pilasters raised on plinths. The windows with matching arches have moulded bands, the cills bracketed. In spandrels below the paired bracketed eaves are decorative roundels. Crowning the hipped roof a plinthed and corniced chimney stack. The composition a cross between Jackson's two lodges at Barn Cottage (qv) and Sea Park (qv) both near Carrickfergus, Co Antrim. Concave railed quadrants with matching gates hung on off the shelf cast iron piers the same as at Beech Hill, Co Monaghan (qv) and Ballyedmond, Co Down (qv). These have arabesque decorated shafts, surmounted by little pyramidal roofs with finials, imitation tiles and miniature cusped ogee lucarnes. On the friezes, the name of the property.

**138. TULLYDOEY, Benburb (3)**
A residence of the Jackson family who built two remarkable gate lodges.
**South Lodge** 1793; architect not known

For the Province a lodge unique in its precocity being of a date when the newfangled Picturesque cottage style was still a novelty in England. That it should have bridged this quarter century time lag suggests that it may have been designed by a cross channel architect. A cute one and a half storey steeply gabled structure of unusual layout. Two attic bedrooms are approached by a winding staircase from the single large living room below. Opening from this a single storey kitchen return to the rear, whilst to the front is a little gabled hall projection giving an irregular appearance. To accentuate this, mounted on the front elevation for maximum Picturesque effect, is the two flue chimney stack in the form of large octagonal pots rising out of a gablet with ornamental bargeboards. This houses a stone with the date and the monogram "T.J.". Windows transomed and mullioned with fancy latticed paned lights below label mouldings. The sheeted front door has a Tudor archway. Walls harled with stone quoins. The bargeboards are foiled, looking too robust to be original. On the gable furthest from the gates a rectangular single storey bay window. Crude stone gate pillars, their block cappings semicircular-headed to each face. The lodge unoccupied but well maintained as an eyecatcher.

**North Lodge** 1843; architect not known

Another highly individual design in the English Picturesque cottage manner. Located outside the gates, one and a half storey with its gable facing the approach. This gable has the most unusually intricate carving to its bargeboards inscribed with the message LET US WATCH AND BE SOBER; WELCOME AND GOD SPEED, JOHN LAWSON 1844. Below is a window with the date 1843 on the head. This timber-framed attic gable is cantilevered out on big curved beams to form nice recessed rustic sitting-out areas beneath, one of which contains the front door. The walls, now rendered, contained a mixture of single, bi- and tripartite lattice-paned lights. On each of the side elevations is a canted oriel window. Stone quoins. There is a most disappointing replacement brick chimney stack to this otherwise delightful composition. Probably built for J Eyre Jackson. Griffith in his 1860 valuation mentions a third lodge, not located, probably demolished.
ROWAN (1979); GRIFFITH

**139. TULLYNISKAN GLEBE, Coalisland (2)** both pre 1853;
*both demolished*
Probably built for the Rev Robert Kingsmore.

**140. TULLYNURE LODGE, Donaghmore**
pre 1854; *demolished*
The lodge postdated a Georgian farmhouse. The 1846 occupant Rev Michael Kearney.

**141. URNEY, Clady** pre 1832
At an oblique angle to the road a derelict single storey two roomed lodge, unremarkable but for its arrowhead projection beyond the gates alongside. The only architectural pretension allowed is to the public road where the two windows are framed in semicircular-headed recesses just like one half of John Soane's pair at Tendring Hall in Suffolk. In 1824 the glebe house of Rev James Jones.
SOANE (1788)

**142. URNEY PARK, Clady** pre 1832; *ruinous*
A plain single storey lodge on an L plan fronting the road with the gates. Built for Sir James Galbraith.

**143. WELLBROOK, Cookstown (2)**
**South Lodge** pre 1854; *demolished*
**North Lodge** pre 1854
A plain lodge opposite the gates survives. Both built for the Gunning family who succeeded the Faulkners of the adjacent Beetling Mill.

# GLOSSARY

# A GOTHICK COTTAGE ORNÉ LODGE

1. Pent
2. Cluster column
3. Pinnacle
4. Crockets
5. Finial
6. Eyebrow eaves
7. Diocletian window
8. Lancet head
9. Y-tracery
10. Harling
11. Hexagonal
12. Ogee arch
13. Arrowloop or loophole (mock)
14. Trefoil window
15. Half hipped gable
16. Broach
17. Diagonally set chimney stack

# A NEO-CLASSICAL LODGE

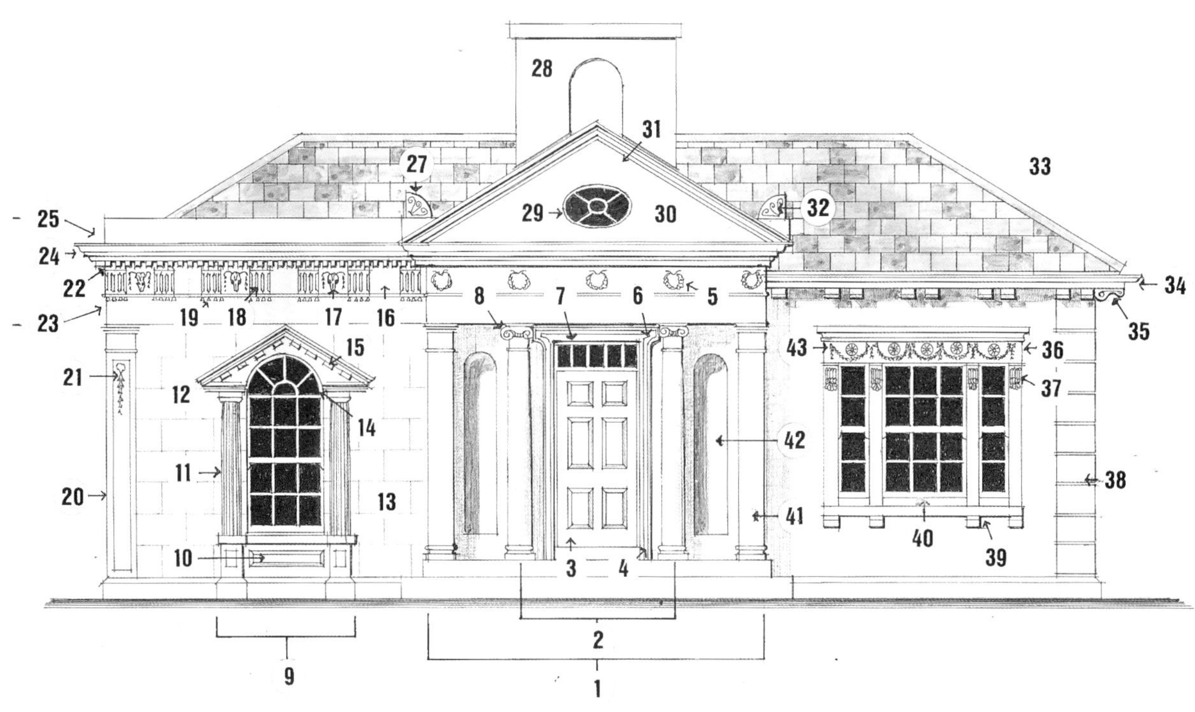

1. Portico
2. Columns In Antis
3. Panelled door
4. Architrave surround
5. Laurel wreath or garland
6. Lugged head
7. "Mouthorgan" fanlight
8. Ionic capital
9. Aedicule
10. Underpanel
11. Doric column (fluted)
12. Open pediment
13. Ashlar (masonary) or stucco (applied)
14. Spoked head
15. Mutules
16. Metope
17. Bucrania (oxhead) or Aegricane (ram's head)
18. Triglyph
19. Guttae
20. Pilaster
21. Margent
22. Dentil course
23. Frieze
24. Cornice
25. Blocking course
26. Entablature
27. Acroterion
28. "Vanburgh" or bridged chimney stack
29. Oeils-de-boeuf or ox-eye opening
30. Tympanum
31. Pediment
32. Anthemion motif
33. Hipped roof
34. Eaves
35. Modillion bracket
36. Flat entablature
37. Crossette
38. "Irish pilaster" (quoins)
39. Bracketed cill
40. "Wyatt" or tripartite window
41. Antae
42. Niche
43. Patera and festoon (or swag) ornament

# A TUDORBETHAN LODGE

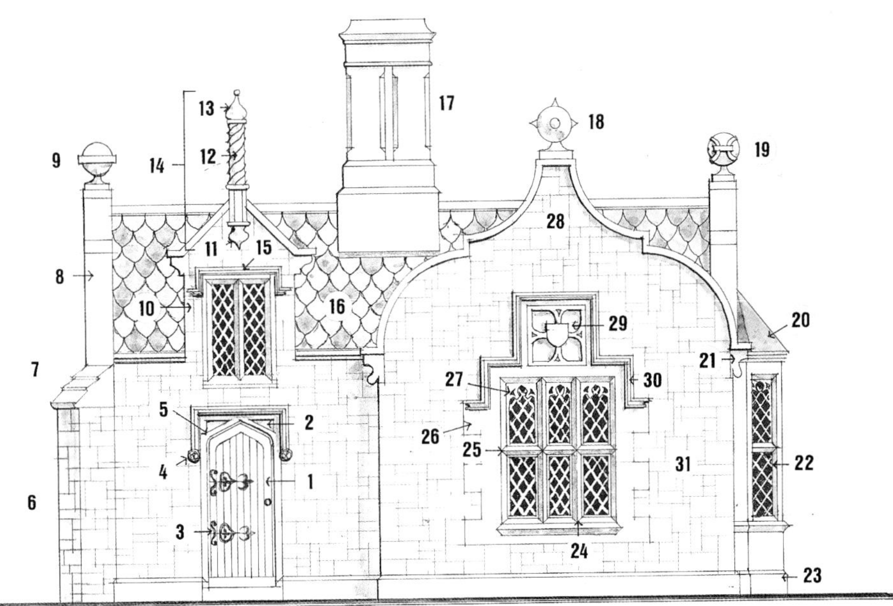

1. Sheeted door
2. Spandrel
3. Strap hinges
4. Drip stone
5. Tudor arch
6. Buttress
7. Weathering
8. Skewtable
9. Rusticated ball finial
10. Gablet
11. Pendant
12. "Barley twist" shaft
13. Finial
14. Hipknob
15. Label moulding
16. Fishscale slates
17. Coupled chimney stack
18. "Morgenstern" ball finial
19. Strapped ball finial
20. Half umbrello roof
21. Kneeler
22. Latticed glazing
23. Plinth
24. Mullion
25. Transom
26. Dressing
27. Cuspidated head
28. Shaped or curvilinear gable
29. Foiled quarter with blank shield
30. Stepped label moulding
31. Squared, uncoursed masonry

# A PICTURESQUE ENGLISH COTTAGE LODGE

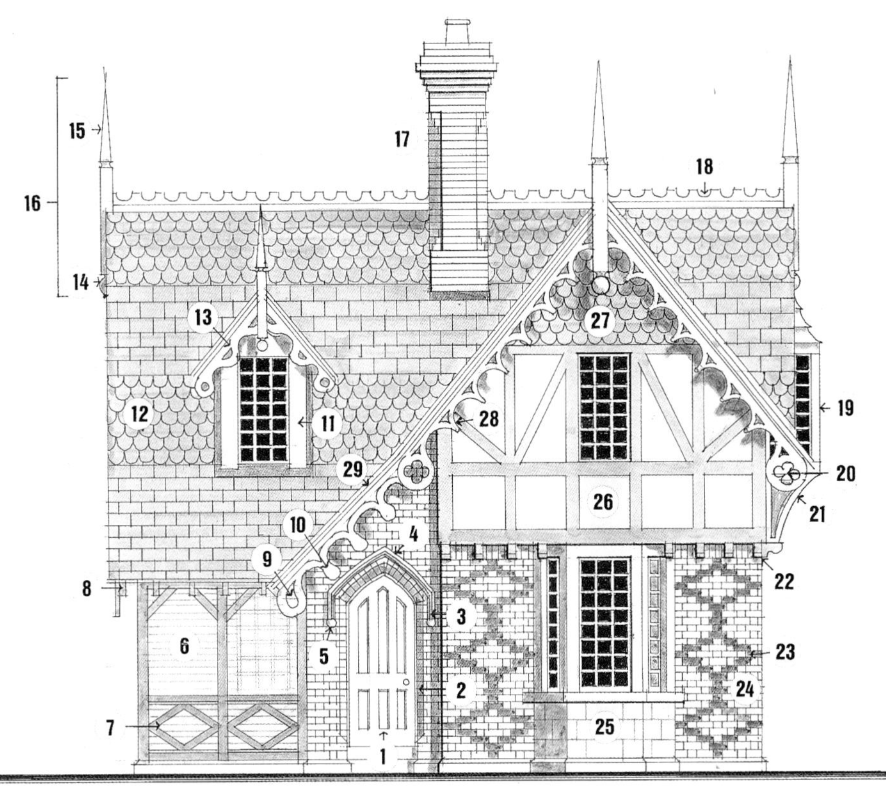

1. Panelled door
2. Chamfer
3. Hood moulding
4. Segmentally pointed arch
5. Dripstone
6. Verandah
7. Lozenge pattern balustrade
8. Exposed rafter ends
9. Mouchette motif
10. Lobed bargeboard
11. Dormer window
12. Scalloped slates
13. Waved bargeboard
14. Pendant
15. Finial
16. Hipknob
17. Modelled chimney stack
18. Cresting (serrated)
19. Oriel window
20. Quatrefoil motif
21. Corbel
22. Jettying
23. Diaper work
24. Flemish bond brickwork
25. Canted bay window
26. Black and white work or half timbering
27. Tile hanging
28. Foiled bargeboard
29. Catslide roof

# AN ITALIANATE LODGE

1. "Porte cochère"
2. Raised and fielded panelled door
3. Fanlight
4. Cartouche
5. Acone (scrolled keystone)
6. Archivolt
7. Balustrade (fretted)
8. Channelled rustication
9. Plinth
10. Oculus
11. String course
12. Balconette (balustrade)
13. Belvedere tower
14. Exposed rafter ends
15. Pyramidal roof
16. Plinth
17. Bracketed cornice
18. Blocked capping
19. Recessed panel
20. Gabled roof
21. Fascia
22. Quoins
23. Raised
24. Diamond pointed
25. Vermiculated or reticulated
26. Venetian window
27. Margined glazing
28. Purlin ends
29. Impost
30. Pier

# A CASTELLATED SCOTS BARONIAL LODGE

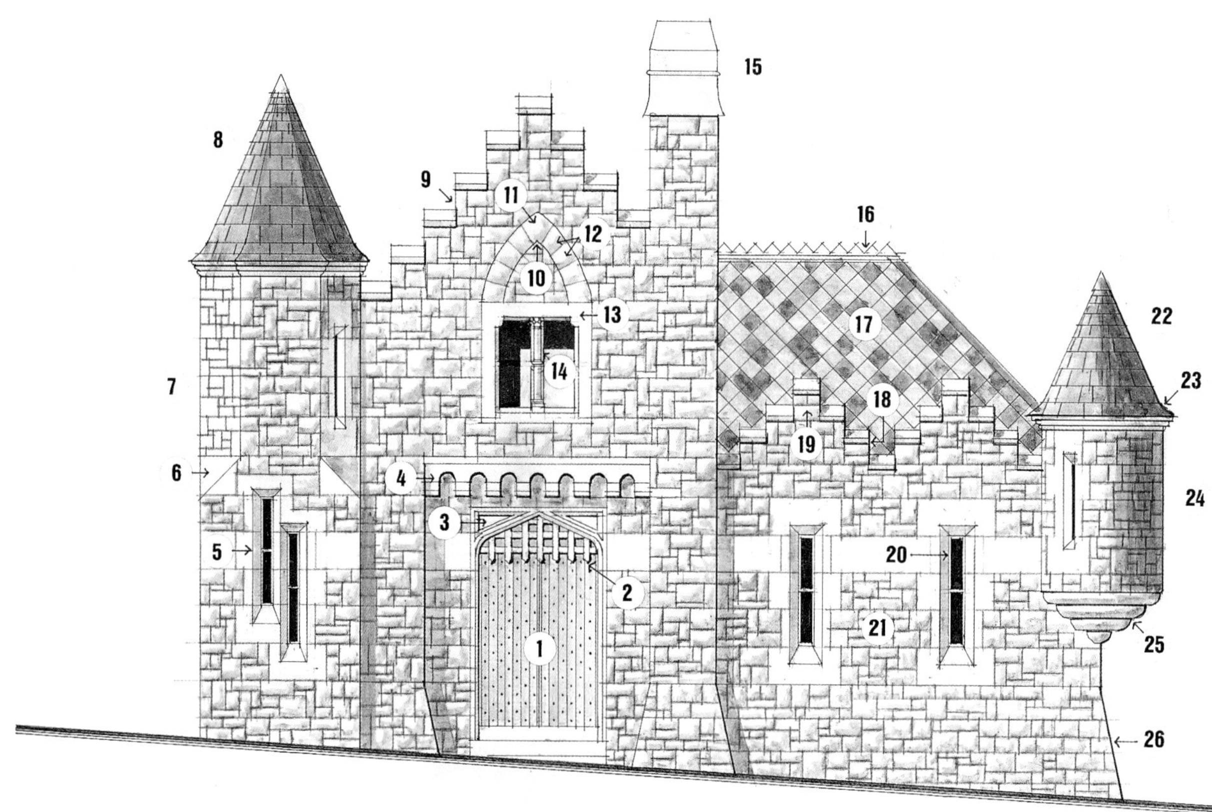


1. Studded doors
2. "Portcullis"
3. Spandrel
4. "Machicolation"
5. Batement window
6. Broach
7. Turret
8. Octyhedral roof
9. Crowstepped gable
10. Relieving arch
11. Keystone
12. Voussoirs
13. Shouldered arch
14. Colonette (banded)
15. Chimney capping
16. Cresting (sawtooth)
17. Lattice pattern slating
18. Allure or Ramparts
19. Crenellations (Irish)
20. Chamfered slit opening
21. Squared course masonry (quarry-faced)
22. Conical roof
23. Bellcast
24. Bartizan
25. Corbel
26. Batter

# BIBLIOGRAPHY


Adam, Robert. *Classical Architecture, a Complete Handbook*. London; Viking, 1990

Adam, Robert and James. *The Works in Architecture*. vol. I. London; The authors, 1778

Adams, Jack. *Ballymena, My Own Native Town*. Ballymena; Adams Enterprises, 1989

Adams, Jack. *Ballymena, The Middle Town*. Ballymena; Adams Enterprises, 1985

A. J. The Greenmount Agricultural College. *The Architect's Journal*, vol. 62, no. 161, 11th November 1925. pp. 719-725

Allibone, Jill. *Anthony Salvin: Pioneer of Gothic Revival Architecture*. Cambridge; Lutterworth Press, 1988

Allison, R S. *The Seeds of Time*. Belfast; Brough, Cox and Dunn, 1972

Atkinson, A. *Ireland Exhibited to England*. 2v, vol. I: *Co Down;* vol.II: *Co Antrim*. London; Baldwin, Cradock & Joy, 1823

Atkinson, *A. Ireland in the Nineteenth Century*. London; Hamilton, Adams & Co, 1833

Bardon, Jonathan. *Belfast, an Illustrated History*. Belfast; Blackstaff Press, 1982

Barrow, John. *A Tour Round Ireland in the Autumn of 1835*. London; J Murray, 1836

Barry, Canon John. *Hillsborough: A Parish in the Ulster Plantation*. Belfast; William Mullan, 1962

Bassett, George H. *The Book of Antrim, A Guide and Directory*. Dublin; Sealy, Bryers & Walker, 1888

Bassett, George H. *The Book of Armagh, A Guide and Directory*. Dublin; Sealy, Bryers & Walker, 1888

Bassett, George H. *The Book of Down, A Guide and Directory*. Dublin; Sealy, Bryers & Walker, 1886

Beaufort, Rev Dr Daniel Augustus. *Journal of a Tour Through Part of Ireland 1787*. Manuscript in Library of Trinity College, Dublin.

Bell, Fergus Hanna. *Newry, Warrenpoint and Rostrevor, Early Photographs from the Lawrence Collection 1865-1880*. Belfast; Friar's Bush Press, 1989.

Bence-Jones, Mark. The Building Dreams of a Viceroy, - I, II. *Country Life*, vol. CXLVIII, no. 3832, 1st October 1970. pp.816-819; and no. 3833, 8th October 1970. pp.900-904

Bence-Jones, Mark. *A Guide to Irish Country Houses*. London; Constable, 1988

Benn, George. *A History of the Town of Belfast from the Earliest Times to the Close of the 18th Century*. Belfast; Marcus Ward, 1877

Benn, George. *A History of the Town of Belfast from 1799 til 1810*. Belfast; Marcus Ward, 1880

Biggar, Francis Joseph. The Franciscan Friary at Carrig-fergus. *Ulster Journal of Archaeology*, vol. XV., no. 2, May 1909. pp.49-60

Bingham, Madeleine. *Peers and Plebs: Two Families in a Changing World*. London; Allen & Unwin, 1975

Binns, Jonathan. *Miseries and Beauties of Ireland*. 2v. London; Longman, Orme, Brown & Co, 1837

Birch, John. *Picturesque Lodges*. Edinburgh & London; W Blackwood & Sons, 1879

Black, Eileen. Ballydrain House. *Lisburn Historical Society Journal*, vol. 5, 1984. pp.17-28

Blackie & Son. *Villa and Cottage Architecture*. Edinburgh; Blackie & Son, 1863

Blore, Edward. Account Books. Cambridge University Library, Add MS 3956, f40

B.N. Sion House, Strabane. *Building News*, vol. 48, no. 1542, 25th July 1884. p.128

Bradshaw, Thomas. *Directory of Newry*. Newry; Alexander Wilkinson, 1819

Brett, C.E.B.. *Buildings of Belfast 1700-1914*. London; Weidenfeld & Nicolson, 1967

Burke, Sir Bernard. *The Landed Gentry of Ireland*. London; Harrison & Sons, 1904

Burke, Sir Bernard. *Peerage, Baronetage & Knightage*. London; Burke Publishing Co Ltd, 1921

Burke, Sir Bernard. *A Visitation of Seats*. 4v vol. 1: London; Colburn & Co, 1852. vol.2: London; Hurst & Blackett, 1853. vols. 3 & 4: London; Hurst & Blackett, 1855

Camblin, Gilbert. *The Town in Ulster*. Belfast; William Mullan, 1951

Campbell, M. P. Gilford and its Mills. *Banbridge & District Historical Society Journal*, vol.2 1990. pp.13-19

Carleton, S Trevor. Malone, Belfast: The Early History of a Suburb. *Ulster Journal of Archaeology*, vol. XLI, 1978. pp.94-101

Clarke, Kenneth. *The Gothic Revival*. London; Penguin, 1962

Colvin, Christina (Editor). *Maria Edgeworth, Letters from England 1813-1844*. London; Clarendon Press, 1971

Colvin, Howard. *A Biographical Dictionary of British Architects 1600-1840*. London; John Murray, 1978

Connop, J H. *Bird's Eye View of Belfast 1863*. Original in Linenhall Library, Belfast

Connop, J H. *View of Sydenham, Belmont and Glenmachan 1864*. Original in Harbour Commissioner's Office, Belfast

Cooper, H.F.T. *Photographs in the Cooper Collection c1900-1950*. Public Record Office of Northern Ireland

Coote, Sir Charles. *Statistical Survey of the County of Armagh*. Dublin; Graisberry & Campbell, 1804

Coote, Sir Charles. *Statistical Survey of the County of Cavan*. Dublin; Graisberry & Campbell, 1802

Coote, Sir Charles. *Statistical Survey of the County of Monaghan*. Dublin; Graisberry & Campbell, 1801

Corbett, Eugene T. *The Architecture of Henry Hobart and Samuel Heron*. DAAS Dissertation Belfast; Q.U.B., 1990

Craig, Maurice. *The Architecture of Ireland*. London; Batsford, 1989

Craig, Maurice. The Knight of Glin. *Ireland Observed*. Cork; Mercier Press, 1970

Crawford, Joseph. *Lisbellaw, The Hard Rocks*. Lisbellaw Community History Project, 1992

Crookshank, Anne and others. *Irish Houses and Landscapes*. Catalogue of an exhibition in the Ulster Museum. Belfast, 1963

Crosleigh, Charles. *Crossle Family*. London; De La More Press, 1904

Crowe, W Haughton. *Village in Seven Hills: The Story and Stories of Rostrevor*. Dundalk; Dundalgan Press, 1973

Curl, James Stevens. *Encyclopaedia of Architectural Terms*. London; Donhead, 1993

Curl, James Stevens. *The Fishmongers' Company*. Belfast; U.A.H.S., 1981

Curl, James Stevens. *The Life and Works of Henry Roberts, Architect 1803-1876*. Chichester; Phillimore, 1983

Davis, Terence. *John Nash, the Prince Regent's Architect*. Newton Abbot; David & Charles, 1973

D.B. Montalto House. *Dublin Builder*, vol III, no 39, 1st August 1861. pp. 559-561

Deane, C Douglas. *Save this Sanctuary*. Belfast; The Newsletter, 15th January 1977

Dearn, T.D.W. *Designs for Lodges and Entrances*. 1st ed., London; J Taylor, 1811; 2nd ed., London; J Taylor, 1823

Dearn, T.D.W. *Sketches in Architecture*. London; J Taylor, 1807

Debrett. *Peerage and Titles of Courtesy*. London; Dean & Son, 1920

Deery, Hugh. Rambles in Drumholm. *Journal of the Co Donegal Historical Society*, vol I, no. 2, December 1948. pp.98-106

Delany, Mrs Mary. *The Autobiography and Correspondence of Mary Granville*. ed. by Lady Llanover. 6v.London; Richard Bentley, 1861-62

Department of Finance (NI). *Ancient Monuments in State Care*. Belfast; H.M.S.O., 1963

Department of Finance (NI). *Ancient Monuments not in State Care*. Belfast; H.M.S.O., 1962

Department of Finance (NI). *Archaeological Survey of County Down*. Belfast; H.M.S.O., 1966

*Directories of Belfast and the Province of Ulster for 1852, 1854, 1856, 1858-9, 1861-2, 1863-4*. Belfast; Henderson

*Directories of Belfast and the Province of Ulster for 1856, 1868, 1870, 1877, 1880, 1884, 1887, 1890, 1892, 1894-1939*. Belfast; Newsletter
Dixon, Hugh. *An Introduction to Ulster Architecture*. Belfast; U.A.H.S., 1975
Dixon, Hugh. *Honouring Thomas Jackson 1807-1890*. Belfast; Belfast Natural History & Philosophical Society, 1978
Dixon, Hugh. *Ulster Architecture 1800-1900*. Catalogue of an exhibition of architectural drawings, Ulster Museum. Belfast; U.A.H.S., 1972
Dixon, Hugh and Heatley, Fred. *Belfast Scenery in Thirty Views*. Belfast; Linenhall Library, 1983
Dixon, Hugh and Walker, Brian M. *In Belfast Town 1864-1880*. Belfast; Friar's Bush Press, 1984
Dixon, Hugh and Walker, Brian M. *No Mean City 1880-1914*. Belfast; Friar's Bush Press, 1983
Doloughan, Andrew. Cowan Heron Hospital, a Gift to the People of Dromore. *Dromore Historical Society Journal*, vol. 1, 1991. p.59
Domville, Lady Helena Sarah. *Eighteen Designs for Glebe Houses and Rural Cottages*. London; Mitchell & Weald, c1840
Doyle, J B. *Tours in Ulster*. Dublin; Hodges and Smith, 1854
Dundas, W H. *Enniskillen, Parish and Town*. Dundalk; Dundalgan Press, 1916
Dunlop, Durham. *Life of W J Barre*. Belfast; James Magill, 1868
Edgeworth, Maria. An original letter held in The National Library of Ireland dated 21st March 1806
Elsam, Richard. *Essay on Rural Architecture*. London; E Lawrence, 1803
Fairbairn, James. *Fairbairn's Crests of the Families of Great Britain and Ireland*. London; New Orchard, 1986
Felstead, Alison and others. *Directory of British Architects 1834-1900*. London; Mansell, 1993
Ffolliott, Rosemary and De Breffney, Brian. *The Houses of Ireland*. London; Thames and Hudson, 1975
Ffolliott, Rosemary. The Charm of Irish Gate Lodges. *Irish Ancestor*, vol. III, no. 2, 1971. pp. 102-104
Fletcher, Sir Banister. *A History of Architecture on the Comparative Method*. 17th ed. London; Athlone Press, 1961
Fraser, James. *Guide through Ireland, Descriptive of its Scenery, Towns, Seats, Antiquities etc*. 1836. Dublin, 1838
Gailey, Alan. *Rural Houses of the North of Ireland*. Edinburgh; John Donald, 1984
Galloway, Peter. *The Cathedrals of Ireland*. Belfast; Institute of Irish Studies, QUB, 1992
Gandy, Joseph M. *Designs for Cottages, Cottage Farms and other Rural Buildings*. London; John Harding, 1805
Gandy, Joseph M. *The Rural Architect*. London; John Harding, 1805
Gebbie, Canon John B. *An Introduction to the Abercorn Papers as Relating to Ireland 1736-1816*. Omagh; Strule Press, 1972
*The Georgian Society Records of 18th Century Domestic Architecture and Decoration in Dublin*. vol. V. Dublin; Ponsonby and Gibbs, 1913
Gibbs, James. *A Book of Architecture*. London, 1728
Girouard, Mark. Castleward, Co Down - I, II. *Country Life*, vol. CXXX, no. 3377, 23 November 1961. pp.1260-63; no. 3378, 30 November 1961. pp.1320-23
Girouard, Mark. *The Victorian Country House*. London; Yale University Press, 1979
Goodwin, Francis. *Rural Architecture*. 3rd ed. 2v. London; Henry G Bohn, 1850
Gould, Michael H. *The Workhouses of Ulster*. Belfast; U.A.H.S., 1983
Green, E R R. *The Industrial Archaeology of County Down*. Belfast; H.M.S.O., 1963
Green, E R R and Jope F M. Patron and Architect: An Example of Relations in the Late 18th Century. *Ulster Journal of Archaeology*, vols. XXIV & XXV, 1961-2. pp.145-51
Green, W.A. *Photographs in the Green Collection 1910-1939*. Ulster Folk and Transport Museum (U.F.T.M.)
Griffith, Richard, Bart. *General Valuation of Rateable Property in Ireland*. Antrim 1861, Armagh 1864, Belfast 1860, Cavan 1856, Donegal 1858, Down 1863, Fermanagh 1862, Londonderry 1858, Monaghan 1858, Tyrone 1860. London; Alex Thom
Guinness, Desmond and Ryan, William. *Irish Houses and Castles*. London; Thames & Hudson, 1971
Gyfford, Edward. *Designs for Small Picturesque Cottages*. London; J Taylor, 1807
Hamilton, John. *60 Years Experience as an Irish Landlord*. London; Digby & Long, 1894
Harris, Walter. *Topographical and Chorographical Survey of County Down*. Dublin & London; Thomas Boreman, 1740
Harris, Walter and Smith Charles. *Ancient and Present State of the County of Down*. Dublin; Edward Exshaw, 1744
Hart, Henry Travers. *The Family History of Hart of Donegal*. London; Mitchell, Hughes & Clarke, 1907
*Heraldry, The Manual of*. London; Virtue & Co
Hoare, Sir Richard Colt. *Journal of a Tour in Ireland in 1806*. London; W Miller, 1807
Hogg, A R. *Photographs in the Hogg Collection 1884-1938*. Ulster Museum (U.M.)
Howley, James. *The Follies and Garden Buildings of Ireland*. London; Yale University Press, 1993
Hunt, T F. *Architettura Campestre*. London; Longman & Co, 1827
Hunt, T F. *Exemplars of Tudor Architecture*. London, Longman & Co, 1830
Hunt, T F. *Half-a-dozen Hints*. London; Longman, Hurst, Rees, Orme, Brown & Green, 1825
I.B. Antrim Castle Gatehouse. *The Irish Builder*, vol. XXVII, no. 619, 1st October 1885. p.271
I.B. Gretton Villas. *The Irish Builder*, vol. XIX, no. 415, 1st April 1877. p.101
I.B. Gretton Villas. *The Irish Builder*, vol. XXII, no. 498, 15th September 1880. p.260
An Irish Gentleman. *The Scientific Tour Through Ireland*. London; John Booth, 1818
Jackson - Stops, Gervase. The Argory, Co Tyrone - I, II. *Country Life*, vol. CLXXIII, no. 4480, 30th June 1983. pp.1768-71; vol. CLXXIV, no. 4481, 7th July 1983. pp.20-24
Jackson - Stops, Gervase. Crom Castle, Co Fermanagh - I, II. *Country Life*, vol. CLXXXII, no. 21, 26th May 1988. pp.182-185; no. 22, 2nd June 1988. pp.144-147
Johnston, Francis. A Letter From Francis Johnston to J. N. Brewer 29th February 1820. *Irish Georgian Society Bulletin*, vol. VI, no. 1, Jan-Mar 1963. pp.1-5.
Jones, Barbara. Follies and Grottoes. 2nd ed. London; Constable, 1974
Jope, E M. Moyry, Charlemont, Castleraw and Richhill: Fortification to Architecture in the North of Ireland 1570-1700. *Ulster Journal of Archaeology*, vol.XXIII, 1960. pp.97-125
Kelly, Alison. *Mrs Coade's Stone*. Upton-on-Severn; Self Publishing Association, 1990
Killanin, Lord and Duignan, Michael V. *Shell Guide to Ireland*. 2nd ed. London; Ebury Press, 1967
King, Sir Charles (Editor). *Upper Lough Erne in 1739*, by William Henry. London; William Magee, 1892
Langley, Batty. *The City and Country Builder's and Workman's Treasury of Designs*. London; Thomas Langley, 1740
Larmour, Paul. *Belfast, An Illustrated Architectural Guide*. Belfast; Friar's Bush Press, 1987
Lawlor, H C. *History of the Cairnes Family*. London; Elliot Stock, 1906
Lawrence, W M. *Photographs in the Lawrence Collection, 1864-1914*. National Library of Ireland
Leask, Harold, G. *Irish Castles*. Dundalk; Dunalgan Press, 1964

Leigh, M A. *New Pocket Road-Book of Ireland*. London; Leigh, 1832
Leslie, Rev James B. *Clogher Clergy and its Parishes*. Enniskillen; Fermanagh Times, 1929
Leslie, Rev James B. *Derry Clergy and Parishes*. Enniskillen; Fermanagh Times, 1937
Leslie, Rev James B. *Raphoe Clergy and Parishes*. Enniskillen; Fermanagh Times, 1940
Leslie, Rev James B and Swanzy, Rev Henry B. *Biographical Succession Lists of the Diocese of Down*. Enniskillen; Fermanagh Times, 1936
Lewis, Samuel. *Topographical Dictionary of Ireland*. 3v. London; S Lewis, 1837
Livingstone, Rev P. *The Monaghan Story: A Documented History of the County Monaghan from the Earliest Times to 1976*. Enniskillen; Clogher Historical Society, 1980
Loeber, Rolf. *A Biographical Dictionary of Architects in Ireland 1600-1720*. London; John Murray, 1981
Loudon, J C. *Designs for Ornamental Cottages, as a Supplement to An Encyclopaedia of Cottage, Farm and Villa Architecture and Furniture*. edited by Mrs Jane Loudon. 2nd ed. London; Loudon, 1846
Loudon, J C. *An Encyclopaedia of Cottage, Farm and Villa Architecture and Furniture*. London; Longman, Rees, Orme, Brown, Green & Longman, 1833
Loudon, J C. *An Encyclopaedia of Gardening*. New ed. London; Longman, Hurst, Rees, Orme & Brown, 1833
Loudon, J C. *The Landscape Gardening and Landscape Architecture of the Late Humphry Repton, Esq*. London; Loudon, 1840
Loudon, J C. *The Suburban Gardener and Villa Companion*. London; Loudon, 1838
Luckombe, Robert. *A Tour Through Ireland in 1779*. London; Lowndes, 1780
Lugar, Robert. *Architectural Sketches for Cottages, Rural Dwellings and Villas*. London; J Taylor, 1805
Lyle, Sutherland. *Dream Cottages*. London; Hale, 1988
Lyons, Maria Cecelia. *Illustrated Incumbered Estates, Ireland 1850-1905*. Whitegate; Ballinakella Press, 1993
McCarthy, Michael. *The Origins of the Gothic Revival*. London; Yale University Press, 1987
MacCloskey, John. *Statistical Reports of Six Derry Parishes*. Ballinascreen Historical Society, 1821
McCollum, R. *Sketches of the Highlands of Cavan and of Shirley Castle*. Belfast; J Reid, 1856
McCullough, Niall and Mulvin, Valerie. *A Lost Tradition*. London; Gandon Editions, 1987
McCutcheon, W A. *The Industrial Archaeology of Northern Ireland*. Belfast; H.M.S.O., 1980
McErlean, Thomas. *Castlecoole*. 2v. Unpublished. National Trust, Committee for Northern Ireland, 1984
McErlean, Thomas and Reeves-Smyth, T J C. *Castleward*. 2v. Unpublished. National Trust, Committee for Northern Ireland, 1990
McMillan, Rosemary. Henry Hobart, Dromore Architect 1858-1938. *Dromore Historical Society Journal*, vol. 1, 1991. pp.5 & 6
McNaghten, Angus I. *Chiefs of the Clan of MacNaghten and Their Descendants*. Windsor; Oxley & Son, 1951
McParlan, James. *Survey of the County of Donegal*. Dublin; Graisberry & Campbell, 1802
McParland, Edward and others. *The Architecture of Richard Morrison and William Vitruvius Morrison*. Dublin; I.A.A., 1989
McTear, Thomas. Personal Recollections of the Beginning of the Century, Notes of 1820s. *Ulster Journal of Archaeology*, vol. V, no. 1, October 1898. pp.67-80. no. 3, May 1899. pp.162-174
Magill, Paul. *Garron Tower*. Belfast; Ulster Tatler Publications, 1990
Maguire, W A. *Heydays*. Belfast; Friar's Bush Press, 1986
Maguire, W A. Ormeau House. *Ulster Journal of Archaeology*, vol. XLII, 1979. pp.66-71
Malins, Edward and Bowe, Patrick. *Irish Gardens and Demesnes from 1830*. London; Barrie & Jenkins, 1980
Malins, Edward and The Knight of Glin. *Lost Demesnes 1660-1845*. London, Barrie & Jenkins, 1976
Malton, James. *British Cottage Architecture*. London; for Hookham & Carpenter, 1798
Mansbridge, Michael. *John Nash, A Complete Catalogue*. London; Phaidon, 1991
Maps consulted:-
Lendrick, J. *A Map of the County of Antrim*. London, 1780
O'Hagan, James. *Map of Coleraine*. 1845

| Ordnance Survey | 1st | 2nd | 3rd |
|---|---|---|---|
| Co Antrim | 1829-33 | 1855-58 | 1900-06 |
| Co Armagh | 1834-35 | 1859-60 | 1905-07 |
| Co Cavan | 1835-36 | 1876-81 | |
| Co Donegal | 1833-36 | 1847-52 | 1900-06 |
| Co Down | 1833-34 | 1858-60 | 1899-1903 |
| Co Fermanagh | 1834 | 1855-57 | 1905-07 |
| Co Londonderry | 1830-33 | 1848-54 | 1904-05 |
| Co Monaghan | 1833-35 | 1857-59 | |
| Co Tyrone | 1832-34 | 1850-55 | 1904-07 |

Marshall, J J. *History of Charlemont and Mountjoy Forts*. Dungannon; Tyrone Printing Company, 1921
Marshall, J J. *History of Dungannon*. Dungannon; Tyrone Printing Company, 1929
Marshall, J J. *History of the Parish of Tynan*. Dungannon; Tyrone Printing Company, 1932
Mason, William Shaw. *Statistical Account or Parochial Survey of Ireland*. 3v. Dublin, London & Edinburgh; John Cunningham & Others, 1814, 1816, 1819
Maxwell, Constantia. *Town and Country in Ireland under the Georges*. Dundalk; Dundalgan Press, 1949
Merrick, A C M. *Buildings of Holywood*. Holywood Advertiser, 1986
Miller, John. *The Country Gentleman's Architect*. London; J Taylor, 1787
Montgomery, Lt.-Col, George S. *Family History of the Montgomerys of Ballyleck, Monaghan*. Belfast, 1887
Morris, Rev F O. *Views of Country Seats in Great Britain and Ireland*. 6v. London; William McKenzie, 1880
Mowl, Timothy. The Evolution of the Park Gate Lodge as a Building Type. *Architectural History*, vol. 27, 1984. pp.467-480
Mowl, Timothy and Earnshaw, Brian. *Trumpet at a Distant Gate*. London; Waterstone, 1984
Mullin, Rev T H. *Aghadowey*. Belfast; Century Services, 1972
Mullin, Rev T H. *Limavady and the Roe Valley*. Limavady District Council, 1983
National Trust, Committee for Northern Ireland. *Guide Books to Properties*. Belfast; 1962-89
Neale, J P. *Views of the Seats of Noblemen and Gentlemen in the United Kingdom*. 1st series. 6v. London; W H Reid, 1818-23. 2nd series. 5v. London; Sherwood, Jones & Co, 1824-29
O'Hanlon, Rev John. *Lives of the Irish Saints*. vol. III. Dublin; James Duffy & Sons, 1875
O'Loingsigh, Seamus. An Excursion to County Cavan 1809. *Breifne Historical Journal*, vol II. no 8. 1965. pp.495-504

Oram, Richard. The Buildings of Portaferry. *Journal of the Upper Ards Historical Society*, no. 16, 1992. pp.24-28

Ordnance Survey Memoirs of Ireland 1830-39. Entire transcriptions held in the Public Record Office of Northern Ireland and The Queen's University of Belfast Library

Papworth, John B. *Rural Residences*. London; Ackermann, 1818

Parker, Charles. *Villa Rustica*. London; J Carpenter & Son, 1832

Parker, J Henry. *Classic Dictionary of Architecture*. 4th ed. London; New Orchard, 1986

Patterson, T G F. *Harvest Home*. Dundalk; Dundalgan Press, 1975

Pigot, J. *Directory of Ireland*. London; Pigot & Co, 1824

Pilson, James Adair. *History of the Rise and Progress of Belfast and Annals of County Antrim*. Belfast; Hodgson, 1846

Pilson, James Adair. *Historical and Topographical Illustrations of the County of Down*. Newtownards Chronicle & Co Down Observer, 1910

Plaw, John. *Sketches for Country Houses, Villas and Rural Dwellings*. London; J Taylor, 1800

Playfair, William. *British Family Antiquity*. vol. 9: *Baronetage of Ireland*. London; T Reynolds & W Playfair, 1811

Pocock, W F. *Architectural Designs for Rustic Cottages*. London; J Taylor, 1807

*Post Chaise Companion*. Dublin; R Lewis, 1786

P.R.O.N.I. Deposits in The Public Record Office of Northern Ireland (Individually identified under gazetteer entries)

Pugin, Augustus Charles. *Ornamental Timber Gables from Existing Examples in England and France*. London; Henry G Bohn, 1831

Rankin, Peter. Downhill, Co Londonderry - I, II. *Country Life*, vol. CL, no. 3865, 8th July 1971. pp.94-7. no. 3866, 15th July 1971. pp.154-7

Rankin, Peter. *Irish Building Ventures of the Earl Bishop of Derry*. Belfast; U.A.H.S., 1972

Reeves-Smyth, T J C. *Crom Castle*. 2v. Unpublished. National Trust, Committee for Northern Ireland, 1989

Reeves-Smyth, T J C. *Downhill*. 2v. Unpublished. National Trust, Committee for Northern Ireland, 1992

Reeves-Smyth, T J C. *Florencecourt*. 3v. Unpublished. National Trust, Committee for Northern Ireland, 1990

Roberts, Henry. *The Dwellings of the Laboring Classes*. London; Society for Improving the Conditions of the Laboring Classes, 1850

Robinson, P F. *Designs for Lodges and Park Entrances*. London; Priestley & Weale, 1833

Robinson, P F. *Rural Architecture or a Series of Designs for Rural Cottages*. London; Henry G Bohn, 1823

Roebuck, Peter. *Macartney of Lisanoure 1737-1806*. Belfast; Ulster Historical Foundation, 1983

Rogers, Mary. *Prospect of Erne*. Belfast; Fermanagh Field Club, 1967

Rogers, Mary. *Prospect of Tyrone*. Enniskillen; Watergate Press, 1988

Rowan, Alistair. Ballywalter Park, Co Down - I, II. *Country Life*, vol. CXLI, no. 3652, 2nd March 1967. pp.456-60. no. 3653, 9th March 1967. pp.516-20

Rowan, Alistair. Killyleagh Castle, Co Down - I, II. *Country Life*, vol. CXLVII, no. 3811, 19th March 1970. pp.690-93, no. 3812, 26th March 1970. pp.774-7

Rowan, Alistair. *North-West Ulster: The Counties of Londonderry, Donegal, Fermanagh & Tyrone. (The Buildings of Ireland)*. Harmondsworth; Penguin, 1979

Ruvigny, Marquis de. *The Nobilities of Europe*. London; Melville & Co, 1909

Sadleir, Michael. *Blessington D'Orsay, A Masquerade*. London; Constable, 1933

Sampson, G V. *Statistical Survey of the County of Londonderry*. Dublin; Royal Dublin Society, 1802

Saunderson, Henry. *The Saundersons of Castle Saunderson*. London & Frome; Butler & Tanner, 1936

Savage, Armstrong. *The Savage Family in Ulster*. London; Chiswick Press, 1906

Seaver, George. *History of the Seaver Family*. Dundalk; Dundalgan Press, 1950

Seward, W W. *Topographia Hibernia*. Dublin; Seward, 1795

Shirley E P. *History of the County of Monaghan*. London; Pickering & Co, 1879

Slater, Isaac. *National Commercial Directories of Ireland*. Manchester; Slater 1846, 1856, 1870

Soane, John. *Plans, Elevations and Sections of Buildings*. London; J Taylor, 1788

Soane, John. *Sketches in Architecture. Containing Plans and Elevations of Cottages, Villas and other Useful Buildings with Characteristic Scenery*. London; J Taylor, 1793

Stevenson, J. *Two Centuries of Life in County Down 1600-1800*. Belfast; McCaw, Stevenson & Orr, 1920

Stroud, Dorothy. *Humphry Repton*. London; Country Life, 1962

Stuart, James. *Historical Memoirs of the City of Armagh*. Newry; Alex Wilkinson for Longman, 1819

Stuart, James and Revett, Nicholas. *Antiquities of Athens*. 2nd ed. London; Tilt & Bogue, 1841

Summerson, John. *The Life and Works of John Nash, Architect*. London; Allen & Unwin, 1980

Swanston, William. Maps of Carrickfergus. *Ulster Journal of Archaeology*, vol. II, no. 1, October 1895. pp.2-3

Taylor, Arthur Creagh. *Designs for Agricultural Buildings Suited to Irish Estates*. Dublin; Grant & Bolton, 1841

Taylor, George and Skinner, Jeremy. *Maps of the Roads of Ireland*. Dublin; 1778

Temple, Nigel. *George Repton's Pavilion Notebook - A Catalogue Raisonné*. Aldershot; Scholar Press, 1993

Temple, Nigel. *John Nash and the Village Picturesque*. Gloucester; Alan Sutton, 1979

Tonna, Mrs Charlotte Elizabeth. *Letters from Ireland in 1837*. London; Seeley & Burnside, 1838

Trench, Charlotte Violet. *The Wrays of Donegal*. Oxford; University Press, 1945

Trimble, W Copeland. *The History of Enniskillen*. 3v. Enniskillen; W Trimble, 1919-21

Tyner, George. *The Traveller's Guide through Ireland*. Dublin; P Byrne, 1794

U.A.H.S. Ulster Architectural Heritage Society. *Historic Buildings, Groups of Buildings and Areas of Architectural Importance*. (Lists individually identified under gazetteer entries.) Belfast; U.A.H.S., 1968-1993

Walker, Brian M. *Faces of Ireland 1875-1925*. Belfast; Appletree Press, 1980

Ward and Lock. *Picturesque and Descriptive Guide to the Donegal Highlands*. Belfast; Ward & Lock, 1894

Waterhouse, Prudence and Cunningham, Colin. *Alfred Waterhouse*. Oxford; Clarendon Press, 1992

Welch R.J. *Photographs in the Welch Collection c1880-c1932*.Ulster Museum (U.M.)

Wilson, Anthony M. (Editor). *A History of Cabin Hill 1785-1979*. Belfast; The Northern Whig, 1979

Young, Amy Isabel. *300 Years in Innishowen*. Belfast; McCaw, Stevenson & Orr Ltd, 1929

Young, Arthur. *A Tour in Ireland in the Years 1776, 1777 & 1778*. ed. by A W Hutton. 2v. London; T Cadell & J Dodsley, 1892

Young, Robert Magill. *Belfast and the Province of Ulster in the 20th Century*. Brighton; Pike, 1909

# INDEX

## of Architects, Artists, Craftsmen, Engineers, Landscape Architects and Manufacturers

*Letters and numbers in italics refer to counties and entries.*

# INDEX
## of Patrons, Proprietors and Others

*Letters and numbers in italics refer to counties and entries.*

## C.

## D.



## E.



## F.

## G.



## H.



## I.



## J.

## K.



## L.



## M.

## N.



## O.



## P.

## Q.



## R.



## S.